Eroticism and Love in the Middle Ages

SIXTH EDITION

Edited by

Dr. Albrecht Classen

University Distinuished Professor

University of Arizona

CENGAGE
Learning™

**Eroticism and Love in The Middle Ages,
Sixth Edition**

Dr. Albrecht Classen

Executive Editors:
Michele Baird

Maureen Staudt

Michael Stranz

Project Development Manager:
Linda deStefano

Senior Marketing Coordinators:
Sara Mercurio

Lindsay Shapiro

Senior Production / Manufacturing Manager:
Donna M. Brown

PreMedia Services Supervisor:
Rebecca A. Walker

Rights & Permissions Specialist:
Kalina Hintz

Cover Image:
Getty Images*

* Unless otherwise noted, all cover images used
by Custom Solutions, a part of Cengage
Learning, have been supplied courtesy of Getty
Images with the exception of the Earthview
cover image, which has been supplied by the
National Aeronautics and Space Administration
(NASA).

For product information and technology assistance, contact us at
Cengage Learning Customer & Sales Support, 1-800-354-9706
For permission to use material from this text or product,
submit all requests online at **cengage.com/permissions**
Further permissions questions can be emailed to
permissionrequest@cengage.com

ISBN-13: 978-1-4266-4831-1

ISBN-10: 1-4266-4831-6

Cengage Learning
5191 Natorp Boulevard
Mason, Ohio 45040
USA

Cengage Learning is a leading provider of customized learning solutions with
office locations around the globe, including Singapore, the United Kingdom,
Australia, Mexico, Brazil, and Japan. Locate your local office at:
international.cengage.com/region

Cengage Learning products are represented in Canada by Nelson Education, Ltd.

For your lifelong learning solutions, visit **custom.cengage.com**

Visit our corporate website at **cengage.com**

Printed in the United States of America

Eroticism and Love In the Middle Ages

Edited by

Dr. Albrecht Classen
University Distinguished Professor

University of Arizona

SIXTH EDITION

Rough Dateline for the Middle Ages
(by Albrecht Classen)

Ca. 750	B.C.E. Foundation of Rome
Ca. 3rd-5th c.	C.E. Age of Migration
313	Edict of Milan: Toleration of Christians
324-337	Emperor Constantine
476	Romulus Augustulus (last Roman Emperor) forced to abdicate by Odoacer
772-814	Charlemagne rules the Carolingian Empire; beginning of the Middle Ages
8th-10th c.	Christianization of Europe
8th-10th c.	Attacks by Arabs and Vikings
9th and 10th c.	Establishment of England, France, and Germany, along with smaller states on the Iberian Peninsula
10th c.	Development of the Empire of Kiev
1066	William the Conqueror defeats the English King Harold, controls all of England
8th-12th c.	Romanesque art and architecture
8th-9th c.	Carolingian Renaissance
9th c.	*Beowulf*
ca. 1071-ca. 1141	Judah Halevi, *Book of the Kuzari*
1096-1099	First Crusade
1291	Last Christian fortress, Acre, falls against the Muslims
10th and 11th c.	Scandinavian countries, Poland, and other kingdoms in the east form
1179-1241	Snorri Sturluson, *Edda*
12th -14th c.	Beginning of the colonization of central and eastern Europe from the west
12th-15th c.	Gothic art and architecture
12th c.	Twelfth-Century Renaissance
12th-13th c.	High point of courtly literature: Chrétien de Troyes, *troubadour* poets, Marie de France, Hartmann von Aue, Walther von der Vogelweide, Wolfram von Eschenbach (ca. 1205), Gottfried von Strassburg (ca. 1210), German *minnesinger*, and Italian poets of the *stil dolce nuovo*
ca. 1220-1240	Guillaume de Lorris, *Roman de la rose*
ca. 1235/40-1305	Jean de Meun, continuator of the *Roman de la rose*
1265-1321	Dante Alighieri, *Divina Commedia*
13th c.	Attack by Mongols (death of Dschinghis Khan in 1241)
12th-15th c.	Evolution of the trade organization *Hanse*
1304-1374	Francesco Petrarca
1313-1375	Giovanni Boccaccio
11th-15th c.	Reconquista on the Iberian Peninsula (last Arabic fortress, Granada, falls in 1492)
1339-1453	Hundred Years War between England and France
1347-1351	Black Death
ca. 1343-1400	Geoffrey Chaucer, *Canterbury Tales*
14th-15th c.	Rise of national states in Europe (Switzerland, Bohemia, England, France, Spain, Denmark, Lithuania, Poland, Russia, etc.)
ca. 1364-1430	Christine de Pizan, feminist writer, prolific author
14th-15th c.	Growth of cities all over Europe
14th-15th c.	Italian Renaissance, which then spreads to other parts of Europe
1453	Mohammed II conquers Constantinople — the end of the Eastern Roman Empire
ca. 1450	Johannes Gutenberg invents the moveable type/printing press
1492	Christopher Columbus discovers America

CONTENTS

ACKNOWLEDGMENTS

The selections in Section 1 are reprinted from *The Love Songs of the Carmina Burana* by E. D. Blodgett and Roy Arthur Swanson. Copyright © 1987 E. D. Blodgerr and Roy Arthur Swanson.

The selections in Section 2 are reprinted from *Lyrics of the Middle Ages* by James J. Wilhelm. Copyright © 1990 Garland Publishing.

The selections in Section 4 are reprinted from *Lyrics of the Troubadours and Trouvères* by Frederick Golden. Copyright © 1973 Doubleday Anchor Books.

"The Letters of Abelard and Heloise" by Guy Chapman is Copyright © 1925 Guy Chapman.

The selections in Section 5 are reprinted from *The Women Troubadours* by Meg Bogin. Copyright © 1976 Paddington Press, Ltd.

"The Unfortunate Lord Henry" is reprinted from *German Medieval Tales* by Francis G. Gentry. Copyright © 1983 Continuum Publishing Co. Used by permission.

The selections in Section 6 and 8 are reprinted from *Medieval German Lyric Verse* by J. W. Thomas. Copyright © 1968 University of North Carolina Press, and The Best Novellas of Medieval Germany by J. W. Thomas. Copyright © 1984 Camden House.

The selections in Section 7 are reprinted from *German and Italian Lyrics of the Middle Ages* by Frederick Golden. Copyright © 1973 Doubleday & Co.

"Blissfully He Lay" is reprinted from *Medieval German Lyric Verse* by J. W. Thomas. Copyright © 1968 The University of North Carolina Press. Used by permission.

The selections in Section 9 are reprinted from *Titurel and the Songs* by Marion E. Gibbs and Sidney M. Johnson. Copyright © 1988 Garland Publishing.

Excerpts from *The Lais of Marie de France* by G. S. Burgess and K. Busby. Copyright © 1986 G. S. Burgess and K. Busby. Reprinted with the permission of Penguin Books Ltd.

The selections in Section 11 are reprinted from *The French Fabliaux B.N. M.S. 837.* edited and translated by Raymond Eichmann and John DuVal. Volume II. Copyright © 1985 Garland Publishing.

Excerpts from *The Best Novellas of Medieval Germany* by Moriz von Craun are Copyright © 1984 Camden House. Used by permission.

The selections in Section 12 are reprinted from *Medieval Romances* by R. Sherman Loomis and L. Hibbard Loomis. Copyright © 1957 The Modern Library.

The selections in Section 13 are reprinted from *The Writings of Medieval Women* by Marcelle Thiebaux. Copyright © 1994 Marcelle Thiebaux.

The selections in Section 15 are reprinted from *Allegorica*. Copyright © 1983 University of Texas at Arlington.

Excerpts from *Mechthild von Magdeburg—Flowing Light of the Divinity* by Christiane Mesch Galvani & Susan Clark are Copyright © 1991 Christiane Mesch Galvani & Susan Clark. Reprinted with the permission of Garland Publishing.

Excerpts from *The Romance of the Rose* by Guillaume de Lorris & Jean de Meun, translated by Harry W. Robbins, Translation Copyright © 1962 by Florence L. Robbins, Introduction by Charles W. Dunn Copyright © 1962 E. P. Dutton. Used by permission of Dutton Signet, a division of Penguin Books USA Inc.

PREFACE

Several years ago I was given the opportunity to develop a new course in the General Education program at the University of Arizona that was supposed to be attractive and scholarly at the same time. When I conceived of the title "Eroticism and Love in the Middle Ages," I was very uncertain as to what to expect both from my future students and myself in this course. The ideal was to bring to life the Middle Ages through a selection of meaningful texts in English translation. In my mind it was certainly important to emphasize philology as the basis of any medieval literature course; on the other hand such a course was intended to open a window toward an era long gone, yet still offering fascinating ideas about one of the most vexing aspects of life: love. Very soon my students realized that the literature we covered in this course did not really aim for eroticism in its physical sense, but rather dealt with fundamental philosophical issues of human life, though within a very specific historical and cultural framework. Of course, love poetry always implies a wide range of meanings, but love in its sexual, erotic connotations was certainly not the prime theme of this literature in the Middle Ages. As it becomes clear after reading Andreas Capellanus' *Art of Courtly Love* and Gottfried von Strassburg's *Tristan,* for instance, medieval love discourse utilizes the theme of love as a springboard to reach a higher level of philosophical insight. Basically, medieval love literature deals with the question of what life and death mean, how the individual must cope with both, how to reach for happiness, how to overcome pain, how to win the favor and love of others, how to stay away from evil people, and how to gain a noble character. The latter in itself carries a host of other meanings, the least of which might be eloquence, intelligence, generosity, trustworthiness, love, truthfulness, etc. Once these values have been extracted from medieval love literature, it might become clear to the reader that the Middle Ages are not simply an historical time period far removed from ours, but rather represent another historical age in which individual poets were struggling to gain a deeper understanding of the essence of life, best expressed by erotic love tales and songs, and most poignantly formulated through images of courtly love. Juan Ruiz, for example, discusses the basic problems with human language in his *Libro de buen amor,* and also demonstrates the wide range of possible literary genres as means to examine any or many of these problems. Wolfram von Eschenbach, on the other hand, confronts his readers with death as the consequence of a failed reading process involving narratives about love. Raimbaut de Vaqueiras exemplifies the intricacies of human language and its many variants in one of his *troubadour* songs. And Walther von der Vogelweide argues in his *minnesongs* that the courtly love poet occupies the center position of society. It seems as if the various medieval voices assembled here maintain that only he or she who can talk about love in the true sense of the word knows something about the essence of life and has entered the world of adulthood.

The following anthology is not an exhaustive selection of medieval literature in English translation, but some of the best texts treating courtly love can be found here. Some of them could only be included in abbreviated form because of their length. Others, such as Andreas Capellanus' *Art of Courtly Love*, Gottfried von Strassburg's *Tristan*, Juan Ruiz's *Libro de Buen Amor*, and Chaucer's *Troilus and Criseyde* had to be left out for that reason because it would not make sense to take only several chapters or a certain number of lines as representative pieces.

Each of these texts must be read in their entirety, and there are good affordable paper back editions available to include them in any college reading list. Especially such classical and well-known authors as Chrétien de Troyes, Wolfram von Eschenbach *(Parzival)*, Dante Alighieri, and Geoffrey Chaucer were excluded because their work is touched upon in so many other courses in French, Italian, German, and English departments. This anthology aims, by contrast, to familiarize the reader with the plethora of equally important, though much less known medieval texts treating the theme of courtly love, originally expressed in medieval Latin, Old French, Occitan, Middle High German, medieval Italian, and medieval Castilian.

The strength of this anthology will hopefully be, among other aspects, its interdisciplinary approach. The Middle Ages did not know the same national and cultural boundaries as the modern world, although the differences between French and German culture and language, for instance, were very obvious even then. Nevertheless many poets translated the works of their contemporaries or copied the melodies of their songs (contrafacta). Latin was, at any rate, the common language of all intellectuals, but in a world characterized by orality people possessed much better mnemonic capacities and seem to have understood more languages than people in our modern world. For a medievalist it would therefore not make sense to read Marie de France without knowing Hartmann von Aue. To create a reading list focusing only on Middle High German literature radically fragments the literary map of medieval Europe and deprives us of a full understanding of medieval literary culture. When we read poems by the *troubadours*, we must also include the songs by the *Minnesänger* and the works of the Italian poets from the school of the *dolce stil nuovo*. The *Carmina Burana* need to be studied in light of German *Minnesänger*, and *trobairitz* poetry should be studied in light of medieval mystical literature, such as by Mechthild von Magdeburg. Some texts, such as *Apollonius King of Tyre*, were translated into most European languages and thus disseminated the same values and ideals among the aristocratic courts.

In the fourteenth and fifteenth centuries the entire outlook of the medieval world began to change, and these changes are reflected, for example, in the texts by Oswald von Wolkenstein and Poggio Bracciolini. Nevertheless, even these two authors, as diverse as they were in their education, social status, and literary interests, need to be studied in tandem as different voices of the same choir, glorifying the idea of love and eroticism as fundamental aspects of human life. Oswald, however, still represents the Late Middle Ages, whereas Poggio already belonged to the group of Florentine humanists and Renaissance writers.

As the editor I can only hope that the readers will enjoy this anthology and gain a meaningful overview of medieval literature and culture. Perhaps, I might add, the study of these texts will also contribute to the education and intellectual maturity of those fascinated by these narratives and poems.

Without the help of many people this textbook would not have been possible. First, I would like to thank David Bouvier from American Heritage Custom Publishing for his interest in this project and his untiring work to see the original manuscript and the subsequent editions through the publication process. I am very grateful for Jan Gilboy's work on the fourth edition and I would like to express my gratitude to Linda deStefano for her help with the fifth edition. I also need to thank the large number of students who took this class over the last ten years at the University of Arizona and thus made it possible, through their enthusiasm for the topic and their sheer numbers, that the basic step could be taken from using simple photocopies as the class reading materials to using a solid textbook. My students encouraged me every semester anew to continue with my teaching efforts and also to improve this anthology. I am also very grateful to my former head and colleague, Professor Renate Schulz, who supported me in developing and offering this course for the first time in Fall of 1989 and ever since then; and so to Professor Thomas Kovach, past head, and Professor Mary Wildner-Bassett, current head, of the Department of German Studies, for their unceasing effort in promoting this course. In the fifth edition, new text sections and selections are incorporated, and new introductory notes and bibliographies are included. For the sixth edition I have updated most of the bibliographies, eliminated mistakes, and added a historical timeline for the Middle Ages.

This sixth edition is an amazing tribute to the everlasting fascination with the medieval world for us today, particularly with regard to eroticism and love. Those who expect crude sex here will be disappointed; those, however, who can read between the lines and grasp the spiritual meaning even of most earthly expressions of love will be rewarded.

I would like to dedicate this book to all lovers of this world! Read the tales of love and pain as experienced at the medieval courts and think about your own life!

Albrecht Classen
Tucson, Arizona, November 2008

SECTION 1

THE STORY OF APOLLONIUS KING OF TYRE

Introduction by Albrecht Classen

The *Historia Apollonii*, as this popular tale was known throughout the Middle Ages and into the Renaissance, is an important example of how strong and long-lasting the literary tradition was in certain cases. The earliest versions of this tale circulated as early as in the fifth century A.D., and it was printed as late as in the seventeenth century. The English critic Ben Jonson ridiculed and discredited the *Historia* as a "mouldy tale," but it enjoyed, nevertheless, a considerable reputation among the wider readership all over Europe. The text has been copied in at least one hundred and fourteen Latin manuscripts, written between the ninth and the seventeenth centuries. Vernacular versions were written and printed in almost all European languages. In the sixteenth century both Shakespeare and Juan de Timoneda composed their own versions of the *Historia Apollonii* and thus elevated the story to its perhaps highest literary level. Although the following centuries appear to have lost some interest in this tale, many more prints appeared throughout the following hundred years. The narrative motif exerted a considerable influence upon other texts throughout the Middle Ages and the Renaissance, such as the French *Floire et Blancheflor,* the Occitan *Daurel et Beton,* the French *chanson de geste Jourdain de Blaye*, the Middle High German, *Orendel,* the Latin *Life of Mary Magdalene,* the Old Norse epic *Thidreks Saga af Bern,* Chaucer's *Man of Law's Tale* (Middle English), Barnabe Riche's *Apollonius and Silla,* and, of course, on Shakespeare's *The Comedy of Errors.*

Although the number of manuscripts, and thus of various versions of this tale goes into the hundreds, Apollonius was not radically changed throughout time. The translation in our anthology relies both on eleventh and fourteenth-century manuscripts with a Latin text. No clear answer can be given why this narrative met with such popularity, but the incest motif, the emphasis on fortune, and the offering of consolation in face of suffering maintained their timeless appeal. Apollonius contains many archetypal themes, be it good and bad fathers, the wicked foster-mother, search for personal identity, separation and reunion of a family, travels, accidents, rape, incest, despair and happiness. The tale could be considered either as a Christian *exemplum* or as a chivalric romance. It could serve as a fairy tale or for moral exhortation, and hence invited endless interpretations by readers from all social classes, highly diverse cultural and religious backgrounds, and many different historical periods.

BIBLIOGRAPHY

Archer Taylor, "Riddles Dealing with Family Relationships," *Journal of American Folklore* 51 (1938): 25–37.

A. D. Deyermond, *Apollonius of Tyre: Two 15th Century Spanish Prose Romances.* Exeter Hispanic Texts, 6 (Exeter: University of Exeter Press, 1973).

Elizabeth Archibald, *Apollonius of Tyre. Medieval and Renaissance Themes and Variations. Including the Text of the Historia Apollonii Regis Tyri with an English Translation* (Cambridge: D. S. Brewer, 1991).

Margaret Anne Doody, *The True Story of the Novel* (New Brunswick, N.J.: Rutgers University Press, 1996).

Albrecht Classen, "Reading and Deciphering in *Apollonius of Tyre* and the *Historia von den sieben weisen Meistern:* Medieval Epistemology within a Literary Context," *Studi Medievali* 49 (2008): 161–88.

TEXT

1. In the city of Antioch there was a king called Antiochus, from whom the city itself took the name Antioch. He had one daughter, a most beautiful girl; nature's only mistake was to have made her mortal. When she became old enough to marry and was becoming increasingly beautiful and attractive, many men sought her in marriage, and came hurrying with promises of large marriage gifts. While her father was considering to whom best to give his daughter in marriage, driven by immoral passion and inflamed by lust he fell in love with his own daughter, and he began to love her in a way unsuitable for a father. He struggled with madness, he fought against passion, but he was defeated by love; he lost his sense of moral responsibility, forgot that he was a father, and took on the role of husband.

Since he could not endure the wound in his breast, one day when he was awake at dawn he rushed into his daughter's room and ordered the servants to withdraw, as if he intended to have a private conversation with her. Spurred on by the frenzy of his lust, he took his daughter's virginity by force, in spite of her lengthy resistance. When the wicked deed was done he left the bedroom. But the girl stood astonished at the immorality of her wicked father. She tried to hide the flow of blood: but drops of blood fell onto the floor.

2. Suddenly her nurse came into the bedroom. When she saw the girl blushing scarlet, her face wet with tears and the floor spattered with blood, she asked: 'What is the meaning of this distress?' The girl said: 'Dear nurse, just now in this bedroom two noble reputations have perished.' Not understanding, the nurse said: 'Lady, why do you say this?' The girl said: 'You see a girl who has been brutally and wickedly raped before her lawful wedding day.' The nurse was horrified by what she heard and saw, and she said: 'Who was so bold as to violate the bed of the virgin princess? The girl said: 'Disregard for morality caused this crime.' The nurse said: 'Then why do you not tell your father?' The girl said: 'And where is my father? Dear nurse,' she went on, 'if you understand what has happened: for me the name of father has ceased to exist. So rather than reveal my parent's crime, I prefer the solution of death. I shudder at the thought that this disgrace may become known to the people.' When the nurse saw that the girl sought a solution in death, she managed with difficulty to persuade her through cajoling words and arguments to give up the horrible idea of killing herself; and she encouraged the reluctant girl to satisfy her father's desire.

3. He presented himself deceitfully to his citizens as a devoted parent, but inside his own walls he delighted in being his daughter's husband. And so that he could enjoy this immoral relationship for ever, he posed riddles to get rid of her suitors. He said: 'Whichever of you finds the solution to the riddle I have set, he shall have my daughter in marriage. But whoever does not find it shall lose his head.' And if anyone happened to find the solution to the riddle through intelligence and learning, he was beheaded as if he had not answered at all, and his head was hung on the top of the gate. And yet kings and princes from far and wide hurried there in great numbers, scorning death because of the girl's incredible beauty.

4. While King Antiochus was engaged in these cruel practices, a very rich young man, a Tyrian by birth named Apollonius, arrived by ship at Antioch. He entered the presence of the king and greeted him: 'Hail, my lord King Antiochus' and 'As you are a devoted father, I have come in haste to carry out your wishes. As a son-in-law of royal birth, I ask for your daughter's hand in marriage.' When the king heard what he did not want to hear, he looked angrily at the young man and said to him: 'Young man, do you know the terms for the marriage? Apollonius replied: 'I do, and I saw them on the top of the gate.' 'Then listen to the riddle: "I am borne on crime; I eat my mother's flesh; I seek my brother, my mother's husband, my wife's son; I do not find him."' When he had heard the riddle the young man withdrew a little from the king. He thought about it intelligently, and with God's help he found the answer to the riddle. Going in to the king again, he said: 'Lord King, you have set me a riddle: so listen to the answer. When you said "I am borne on crime," you did not lie: look at yourself. Nor did you lie when you said "I eat my mother's flesh": look at your daughter.'

5. When the king saw that the young man had found the answer to the riddle, he spoke to him as follows: 'You are wrong, young man, there is no truth

in what you say. Indeed you deserve to be beheaded, but you have thirty days' grace: think it over again. And when you have come back and have found the answer to my riddle, you shall have my daughter in marriage.' The young man was disturbed. He had his ship ready, and embarked for Tyre, his home.

When the young man had departed, King Antiochus summoned his steward, a most loyal man named Taliarchus, and said to him: 'Taliarchus, most loyal accomplice in my secrets, you must know that Apollonius of Tyre has found the answer to my riddle. So take ship at once and pursue the young man, and when you come to Tyre, his home, seek out some enemy of his, who would kill him with a sword or with poison. When you return you shall have your freedom.' When Taliarchus heard this, he provided himself with money and also poison, boarded a ship, and made for the country of the innocent man.

The innocent Apollonius arrived in his homeland first, however, and went into his palace. He opened his bookchest, and examined all the riddles of the author and the debates of almost all the philosophers and also of all the Chaldaeans. Since he found nothing except what he had already thought out, he said to himself: 'What are you doing, Apollonius? You have solved the king's riddle. You have not obtained his daughter. You have been put off only to be killed.' So he ordered his ships to be loaded with grain. He himself, accompanied by a few very loyal servants, boarded his ship in secret, taking with him a large amount of gold and silver and a great deal of clothing. And at the third hour of the night, when it was very quiet, he entrusted himself to the open sea.

7. Next day in the city his people looked for him in order to pay their respects, but did not find him. They were alarmed, and the sound of great lamentation was heard throughout the entire city. So great was his people's love for him that for a long time the barbers were deprived of clients, the shows were cancelled and the baths were closed. While this was happening at Tyre there arrived Taliarchus, the man who had been sent by King Antiochus to kill the young man. When he saw everything closed, he asked a boy: 'If you can, tell me why this city is in mourning.' The boy replied: 'What a shameless man! He knows perfectly well and yet he asks! Who does not know that this city is in mourning for this reason, because the prince of this country, Apollonius, came back from Antioch and then suddenly disappeared.'

When Taliarchus the king's steward heard this, he was delighted and returned to his ship, and after sailing for two days arrived at Antioch. He entered the presence of the king and said: 'Lord king, rejoice and be glad, for that young Apollonius of Tyre has suddenly disappeared, fearing your royal power.' The king said: 'He can run away, but he cannot escape.' Immediately he announced the following edict: 'Whoever delivers to me alive Apollonius of Tyre, who is guilty of treason against my crown, shall receive one hundred talents of gold; whoever brings me his head shall receive two hundred. When this edict was proclaimed, not only Apollonius' enemies but also his friends were influenced by greed and hurried to track him down. They looked for him on land, in the mountains, in the forests, in every possible hiding-place; but they did not find him.

8. Then the king ordered the ships for his fleet to be made ready in order to pursue the young man; but the men responsible for preparing the ships for the fleet were dilatory. Apollonius arrived at the city of Tarsus. As he was walking on the beach, he was seen by Hellenicus, a fellow-citizen of his, who had arrived at that very moment. Hellenicus approached him and said, 'Greetings, King Apollonius!' Apollonius reacted to this greeting as great men are inclined to do: he ignored the lowborn man. Then the indignant old man greeted him again and said: 'Greetings, I say, Apollonius. Return my greeting, and do not despise my poverty, for it is distinguished by an honest character. If you know, you must be careful; if you do not know, you must be warned. Listen to what perhaps you do not know, that you have been outlawed.' Apollonius said to him: 'And who had the power to proscribe me, the ruler of my country?' Hellenicus said: 'King Antiochus.' Apollonius said: 'What was the reason?' Hellenicus said: 'Because you wanted to marry his daughter.' Apollonius asked: 'For what price has he proscribed me? Hellenicus answered: 'Whoever brings you in alive will get one hundred talents of gold; but whoever cuts off your head will get two hundred. So I give you warning: take refuge in flight.'

When Hellenicus had said this, he went away. Then Apollonius had the old man called back, and said to him: 'You have done very well to inform me. In return, imagine that you have cut my head off my shoulders and brought joy to the king.' And he ordered one hundred talents of gold to be given to him, and said: 'Very poor as you are, you set a most excellent example. Take it, for you deserve it. And imagine, as I said just now, that you have cut off my head from my shoulders and brought joy to the king. You see, you have one hundred talents of gold, and your hands are not stained by the blood of an innocent man.' Hellenicus replied: 'Far be it from me, lord, to accept a reward for this affair. Among good men, friendship is not acquired for a price.' He said goodbye and went away.

9. After this, as Apollonius was walking on the beach in the same place he met another man called Stranguillio. Apollonius said to him: 'Greetings, my dearest Stranguillio.' He replied: 'Greetings, lord Apollonius. Why are you pacing up and down here in agitation?' Apollonius said: 'You are looking at a man who has been outlawed.' Stranguillio asked: 'Who has outlawed you?' Apollonius replied: 'King Antiochus.' Stranguillio asked: 'On what grounds?' Apollonius said: 'Because I wanted to marry his daughter, or, to put it more accurately, his wife. So if possible, I should like to hide in your city.'

Stranguillio said: 'Lord Apollonius, our city is poor and cannot support a man of your standing. Besides, we are suffering a severe famine and desperate lack of grain, and there is no hope of survival for our people; instead we face the prospect of a most agonising death.' But Apollonius said to Stranguillio: 'Well, give thanks to God, that He has brought me to your land as a fugitive. I will give

your city a hundred thousand measures of grain if you will conceal my flight.'
When Stranguillio heard this, he threw himself at Apollonius' feet, saying: 'My
lord King Apollonius, if you help the starving city, not only will the people
conceal your flight but if necessary they will also fight for your safety.'

10. When he had said this they proceeded into the city. Apollonius mounted
the platform in the forum and addressed all the citizens and leaders of the city:
'Citizens of Tarsus, distressed and oppressed by lack of grain, I, Apollonius of
Tyre, will bring you relief. For I believe that in your gratitude for this favour you
will conceal my flight. For you must know that I am banished by the decree of
King Antiochus. But it is your good fortune that has brought me here to you. So I
will supply you with one hundred thousand measures of grain at the same price
that I paid for it in my own land, that is eight bronze pieces a measure.' Then the
citizens of Tarsus, who had been paying one gold piece a measure, were
delighted; they thanked him with cheers, and eagerly received the grain. But in
order not to appear to have abandoned his royal dignity and to have taken on the
role of a merchant rather than a benefactor, Apollonius gave back the price which
he had received for the benefit of the city. But the citizens, loaded with so many
kindnesses, decided to erect a bronze statue to him, and they placed it in the
forum. Apollonius was standing in a chariot: in his right hand he held ears of
grain, and his left foot rested on a bushel. On the base they put the following
inscription: THE CITY OF TARSUS GAVE THIS GIFT TO APOLLONIUS BECAUSE HE
RELIEVED THEIR FAMINE AND HUNGER.

11. After a few months or days, at the encouragement of Stranguillio and
Dionysias his wife, and urged on by Fortune, Apollonius, decided to sail to
Pentapolis in Cyrene in order to hide there. So he was escorted with great honour
to his ship, said farewell to the people, and went on board. Within two hours of
sailing the sea, which had seemed trustworthy, changed.

> Stability turned into instability . . .
> A storm arose and illuminated the sky with a red glow.
> Aeolus with rainy blast attacks [Neptune's] fields,
> Which are agitated by storms.
> The South Wind is enveloped in pitch-black darkness,
> And slashes every side of the ocean . . .
> The South Wind roars.
> The North Wind blows from one side, and now
> There is not enough ocean for the East Wind,
> And the sand engulfs the wild sea.
> . . . everything is mixed up with the ocean which is
> Summoned back from the heavens. The sea strikes the stars, the sky.
> The storm gathers itself together, and at the same time
> There are clouds, hail, snow showers, winds, waves, lightning flashes, rain.
> Flame flies on the wind, and the sea bellows in its turmoil.

On one side the South Wind threatens, on another the North Wind, on another the fierce South-West Wind.
Neptune himself scatters the sands with his trident.
Triton plays his dreadful horn in the waves.

12. Then each sailor grabbed a plank for himself, and death was imminent. In the darkness of that storm all perished, except Apollonius, who was cast up on the shore of Pentapolis, thanks to a single plank. As he stood soaked on the shore and looked at the peaceful sea, he said: 'O Neptune, ruler of the ocean, deceiver of innocent men, have you preserved me, destitute and impoverished, just so that the most cruel King Antiochus can persecute me with greater ease? So where shall I go? Which direction shall I take? Who will provide the necessities of life for a stranger?'

While he was complaining to himself, he suddenly noticed an elderly man wearing a dirty cloak. Apollonius threw himself at his feet and said, weeping: 'Have pity on me, whoever you are! Help a destitute, shipwrecked man, who is not of lowly birth. So that you know on whom you are taking pity, I am Apollonius of Tyre, prince of my country. Listen to the tragedy of the misfortunes of the man who has fallen at your knees and is begging for help to stay alive. Help me to survive.' When he saw the handsome appearance of the young man, the fisherman was touched by pity. He raised him up, led him by the hand into the shelter of the walls of his own house, and served him the best food that he could. And to satisfy his sense of companion more fully he took off his cloak, cut it into equal halves, and gave one to the Young man, saying: 'Take what I have, and go into the city. Perhaps you will find someone who will take pity on you. And if you do not find anyone, come back here, and You shall work and fish with me: however poor I may be, there will be enough for us. But I give you this warning: if ever through God's favour you are restored to your birthright, be sure to remember my suffering and my poverty.' Apollonius said to him: 'If I do not remember you, may I be shipwrecked again, and not find anyone like you!'

13. With these words he set out on the road which had been pointed out to him, and entered the city gate. While he was pondering where to find the means to survive, he saw running along the street a boy smeared with oil, with a towel wrapped round his waist, carrying equipment for a young man's gymnasium exercise. He was shouting in a very loud voice: 'Listen, citizens, listen, foreigners, freemen and slaves: the gymnasium is open!' When Apollonius heard this he took off his cloak and went into the bath, and made use of the liquid of Pallas [oil]. As he watched each man exercising he looked for someone of his own standard, but found no one.

Then Archistrates, the king of that city, suddenly came into the gymnasium with a great crowd of attendants. When he was playing a game with his men, by God's favour Apollonius got close to the king's crowd. He caught the ball as the king was playing and returned it with accuracy and speed; when it came back he hit it back again even faster, and never let it fall. Then since King Archistrates had noticed the young man's speed and did not know who he was, and since he had no equal at the ballgame, he looked at his servants and said: 'Draw back, servants. For I believe that this young man is a match for me.' When the servants had drawn back, Apollonius returned the ball with well-judged speed and a skilful hand so that it seemed quite miraculous to the king and everyone else, and even the boys who were present. When Apollonius saw that the citizens were applauding him, he boldly approached the king. Then he rubbed him with wax ointment so expertly and gently that the old man was rejuvenated. Again in the bath he massaged him very agreeably, and helped him out courteously. Then he went away.

14. When the king saw that the young man had gone, he turned to his friends and said: 'I swear to you, my friends, by our general welfare, I have never had a better bath than today, thanks to one young man whom I do not know.' He looked at one of his servants and said: 'See who that young man is who gave me such excellent service.' So the servant followed the young man, and when he saw that he was wrapped in a dirty old cloak, he came back to the king and said: 'Good king, best of kings, the young man has been shipwrecked.' The king said:

'And how do you know?' The servant replied: 'Because his clothes make it clear, although he said nothing.' The king said: 'Go quickly and say to him "The king invites you to dinner."' When the servant told him, Apollonius accepted and followed him to the king's palace. The servant went in first and said to the king: 'the shipwrecked man is here, but he is embarrassed to come in because of his shabby clothes.' At once the king ordered that he should be dressed in suitable clothes, and should come in to dinner.

When Apollonius entered the dining room, the king said to him: 'Recline, young man, and feast. For the lord will give you what will make you forget the losses of the shipwreck.' At once Apollonius was given a place, and he reclined opposite the king. The hors d'oeuvre was served, and then the royal banquet. Everyone was feasting; Apollonius alone did not eat, but looking at the gold, the silver, the table and the servants, he wept for grief as he observed it all. One of the elders reclining next to the king saw how the young man looked at every single thing carefully. Turning to the king he said: 'Do you see, noble king? Look, the man to whom you are showing the kindness of your heart is envious of your possessions and your good fortune.' But the king said to him: 'Friend, you are wrong to be suspicious. This young man does not envy my possessions or my good fortune, but in my opinion he is showing that he has lost much more.' And turning cheerfully to the young man he said: 'Young man, join in our feast; be happy, enjoy yourself, and hope for better things from God!'

15. While the king was encouraging the young man, suddenly in came his daughter, already a grown-up girl, beautiful and glittering with gold. She kissed her father, and then all his friends as they reclined. As she was kissing them she came to the shipwrecked man. She went back to her father and said: 'Good king and best of fathers, who is the young stranger who is reclining opposite you in

the place of honour, and who is grieving and looking unhappy for some unknown reason?' The king said to her: 'This young man has been shipwrecked. He gave me excellent service in the gymnasium, and so I invited him to dinner. I do not know who he may be or where he comes from. But ask him, if you like; for it is fitting that you should know everything, my most wise daughter. Perhaps when you have found out you will feel sorry for him.'

So with her father's encouragement the girl asked Apollonius questions, speaking very modestly. She approached him and said: 'Although your silence is rather melancholy, yet your manner reveal your noble birth. If it is not too painful, tell me your name and your misfortunes.' Apollonius replied: 'If you want to know my name, I am called Apollonius; if you ask about my fortune, I lost it in the sea.' The girl said: 'Explain to me more clearly, so that I can understand.'

16. Then Apollonius recounted all his misfortunes, and when he had finished talking he began to weep. When the king saw him weeping, he looked at his daughter and said: 'Sweet child, you have done wrong; when you wanted to know the name and misfortunes of this young man, you renewed his old sorrows. Therefore it is only just, my sweet and clever daughter, that, like a queen, you should show generosity to the man from whom you have learned the truth.' The girl looked at Apollonius and said: 'Now you are one of us, young man; put aside your grief, and since my kind father has given me permission, I will make you rich.' Apollonius sighed and thanked her.

The king was delighted to see his daughter being so kind, and said to her: 'Dear child, bless you. Send for your lyre, take away the young man's tears, and cheer him up for the feast.' The girl sent for her lyre. When she received it, she mingled the sound of the strings with her very sweet voice, tune with song. All the feasters began to marvel, and said: 'Nothing could be better, nothing could be sweeter than this which we have heard.' Apollonius alone among them said nothing. The king said to him: 'Apollonius, your behaviour is disgraceful. Everyone is praising my daughter's musical skill: why do you alone criticize her by your silence?' Apollonius replied: 'My lord king, with your permission I will say what I think: your daughter has stumbled on the art of music, but she has not learned it. Now have the lyre given to me, and you will find out at once what you did not know before.' The king exclaimed: 'Apollonius, I realize that you are richly gifted in every way.'

Apollonius put on the costume and crowned his head with a garland; he took the lyre and entered the banquet hall. He stood in such a way that the feasters thought him not Apollonius but Apollo. When there was silence, he took the plectrum and devoted his mind to his art.' In the song his voice blended harmoniously with the strings. The banqueters and the king began to call out in praise and said: 'Nothing could be better, nothing could be sweeter!' After this Apollonius put down the lyre, came in dressed in comic costume, and acted out a mime show with remarkable hand movements and leaps. Then he put on tragic costume, and delighted them no less admirably, so that all the king's friends declared that they had never heard or seen anything like this either.

17. Meanwhile, when the princess saw that the young man was full of every kind of talent and learning, she was wounded by a fiercely burning passion,*and fell very deeply in love. When the feast was over the girl said to her father: 'A little earlier you gave me permission, best of kings and fathers, to give Apollonius whatever I wanted—of yours, that is.' He replied: 'I did give permission; I do give permission; I wish it.' With her father's permission for what she herself wanted to give, she looked at Apollonius and said: 'Master Apollonius, through the generosity of my father receive two hundred talents, forty pounds of silver, twenty servants and most lavish clothing.' Then looking at the servants whom she had given to him, she said: 'Bring everything that I have promised, and display it in the dining room in front of all who are present.' Everyone praised the generosity of the girl. And when the banquet was over they all got up, said goodbye to the king and the princess, and left.

Apollonius too said: 'Noble king who takes pity on the wretched, and you, princess who loves learning, goodbye.' After this speech he looked at the servants whom the girl had given to him and said: 'Servants, pick up these things which the princess has given me, the gold, the silver and the clothes, and let us go and look for lodgings.' But the girl, fearing that it would be torture not to see her beloved, looked at her father and said: 'Good king, best of fathers, is it your wish that Apollonius, who has been made rich by us today, should leave, and that your gifts may be stolen from him by wicked men?' The king replied: 'You are right, lady; so order that he be given a suitable room to rest in.' Apollonius was given lodgings for the night; he was well received and lay down to rest, thanking God Who had not denied him a king to be his consolation.

18. But 'the princess, who had long since been wounded by love's care, fixed in her heart the appearance and conversation' of Apollonius; the memory of his singing made her believe 'that he was descended from the gods.' Her eyes got no sleep, 'her limbs got no rest because of her love.' She lay awake, and at the crack of dawn rushed into her father's bedroom. When he saw his daughter he said: 'Sweet daughter, why are you awake so unusually early?' The girl said: 'Yesterday's display of learning kept me awake. I beg you, father, send me to our guest Apollonius to have lessons.' The king was delighted; he sent for the young man and said to him: 'Apollonius, my daughter has formed a desire to be taught the happiness of your learning by you. This is my request, and I swear to you by my royal power that if you will comply with my child's wish, I will restore to you on land whatever the hostile sea took away from you.' After this conversation Apollonius began to teach the girl, just as he himself had been taught.

After a little time, when the girl could not bear the wound of love in any way, she became very ill: her feeble limbs gave way and she lay helpless in bed. When the king saw that a sudden illness had attacked his daughter, he was worried and sent for doctors. When the doctors came, they took her pulse and examined each part of her body, but they did not discover any reason at all for the illness.

19. A few days later, the king took Apollonius by the hand, went to the forum and walked there with him. Three scholarly and very aristocratic young men who had long been seeking his daughter's hand in marriage all greeted him in unison. On seeing them the king smiled and said to them: 'Why have you all greeted me in unison?' One of them said: 'We seek your daughter's hand in marriage, and you keep tormenting us by putting us off so often; that is why we have all come together today. Choose which of us you want as a son-in-law.' The king said: 'This is not a good time to disturb me. For my daughter is devoting herself to study, and because of her love of learning she is lying ill. But so that I do not seem to be putting you off further, write your names on a tablet, and the amount of your marriage gifts. I will send the tablet to my daughter, and she may choose for herself whom she wants as a husband.' So the three young men wrote down their names and the amount of their marriage gifts. The king took the tablet, sealed it with his ring, and gave it to Apollonius, saying: 'Take this note, master, if you do not mind, and deliver it to your pupil. You are needed in this situation.'

20. Apollonius took the tablet, went to the palace, entered the bedroom, and delivered it. The girl recognized her father's seal. She said to her beloved: 'What is the matter, master, that you enter my bedroom alone like this?' Apollonius replied: 'Lady, you are not yet a grown woman, and you are offended! Take this note from your father instead, and read the names of your three suitors.' She unsealed the tablet and read it, but when she had read it through she did not see the name that she wanted and loved. She looked at Apollonius and said: 'Master Apollonius, are you not sorry that I am going to be married?' Apollonius said: 'No, I am delighted that now that I have taught you and revealed a wealth of learning, by God's favour you will also marry your heart's desire.' The girl said: 'Master, if you loved me, you would certainly be sorry for your teaching.' She wrote a note, and when she had sealed the tablet with her ring she handed it to the young man. Apollonius carried it to the forum and delivered it to the king. The king took the tablet, broke the seal and opened it. His daughter had written as follows: 'Good king and best of fathers, since you graciously and indulgently give me permission, I will speak out: I want to marry the man who was cheated of his inheritance through shipwreck. And if you are surprised, father, that such a modest girl has written so immodestly, I have sent my message by wax, which has no sense of shame.'

21. When he had read the note, the king did not know whom she meant by the shipwrecked man. Looking at the three youths who had written their names and specified their marriage gifts in the note, he said to them: 'Which of you has been shipwrecked?' One of them whose name was Ardalio said: 'I have.' One of the others said: 'Be quiet, may a plague take you, and may you not be saved! I know you, you are the same age as I am, you were educated with me, and you

have never been outside the city gate. So where were you shipwrecked?' Since the king could not discover which of them had been shipwrecked, he looked at Apollonius and said: 'Master Apollonius, take the tablet and read it. Perhaps you who were on the spot will understand what I have not discovered.' Apollonius took the tablet and read it, and when he realized that the princess loved him, he blushed. The king took him by the hand, drew him a little away from the young men and said: 'What is it, Master Apollonius? Have you found the shipwrecked man?' Apollonius replied: 'Good king, with your permission, I have.' When he said this, the king saw his face blushing scarlet, and understood the remark. He said with delight 'What my daughter wants is my wish too. For in a matter of this kind, nothing can be done without God.' Looking at the three young men, he said: 'I have already told you that it was not a good time to disturb me. Go away, and when the time comes I will send for you.' So he dismissed them from his presence.

22. So the king took the hand of the man who was now his son-in-law, not his guest, and went into the palace. But he left Apollonius and went in alone to his daughter, and said: 'Sweet child, whom have you chosen as your husband?' The girl threw herself at her father's feet and said 'Dearest father, since you want to hear your child's desire: the man I want for my husband, the man I love, is the man who was cheated of his inheritance and shipwrecked, my teacher Apollonius. If you will not give me to him, you will immediately lose your daughter!' The king could not bear his daughter's tears; he lifted her up and said: 'Sweet child, do not worry about anything. The man you want is the very man I have wanted you to marry from the moment I saw him. I certainly give you my permission, for I too became a father as a result of being in love!'

He went out, looked at Apollonius, and said: 'Master Apollonius, when I questioned my daughter closely about her inclinations concerning marriage, she burst into tears and among many other things which she told me, she made this appeal to me: "You swore to my teacher Apollonius that if he complied with my wishes in his teaching, you would give him whatever the raging sea had taken away. Now that he has dutifully obeyed, and has carried out your orders and my wish in his teaching, he does not seek silver, gold, clothes, servants or possessions, but only the kingdom which he thought he had lost. So according to your oath, give it to him through marriage to me!" So, Master Apollonius, I beg you, do not be scornful of marriage with my daughter!' Apollonius replied: 'Let God's will be done; if it is your wish, let it be fulfilled.' The king said: 'I will fix the wedding day without delay.'

23. The next day he summoned his friends and sent for the rulers of neighbouring cities, great men and nobles. When they had gathered together the king said to them: 'Friends, do you know why I have assembled you together?' They answered: 'We do not.' The king said: 'Let me tell you that my daughter wishes to marry Apollonius of Tyre. I urge you all to rejoice that my very wise daughter

is marrying a very clever man.' In this speech he announced the wedding day without delay and told them when they should assemble.

In short, the day of the wedding arrived, and they all assembled joyfully and eagerly. The king and his daughter were delighted, and so was Apollonius of Tyre, who deserved to get such a wife. The wedding was celebrated in the royal manner with appropriate grandeur. Them was great rejoicing throughout the city: citizens, foreigners and guests revelled. Great joy was expressed with lutes and lyres and songs and organs melodiously accompanying voices. When the joyful feasting came to an end, great passion grew between the husband and wife, remarkable affection, unparalleled fondness, unheard-of happiness, encompassed by an unending love.

24. Some days and months later, when it was already the sixth month and the girl's stomach was swelling, her husband king Apollonius came to her. When he was walking beside his dear girl on the sea shore, he saw a most beautiful ship; as they were both admiring it together, Apollonius recognized that it was from his own country. He turned to the helmsman and said: 'Tell me, please, where do you come from?' The helmsman said: 'From Tyre.' Apollonius said: 'You have named my own country.' The helmsman said: 'So you are a Tyrian?' Apollonius said: 'As you say, so I am.' The helmsman said: 'Be kind enough to tell me the truth: did you know a prince of that country called Apollonius?' Apollonius said: 'I know him as well as I know myself.' The helmsman did not understand this remark, and said: 'Then I have a request: if you see him anywhere, tell him to rejoice and be glad, because the most cruel King Antiochus has been struck by God's thunderbolt as he was lying in bed with his own daughter. But his wealth and his kingdom are being kept for King Apollonius.'

When Apollonius heard this, he turned to his wife, full of delight, and said: 'Lady, now you have had confirmation of what you took on trust when I was shipwrecked. I ask your permission, dearest wife, to go and take possession of the kingdom being kept for me.' But when his wife heard that he wanted to set off, she burst into tears and said 'Dear husband, if you had been on a long journey somewhere, you would certainly have had to hurry back to my confinement. But now, when you are here, are you planning to abandon me? Let us sail together: wherever you are, on land or sea, let us live or die together.'

After this speech the girl went to her father and said to him: 'Dear father, rejoice and be glad, for the most cruel King Antiochus has been struck down by God as he was lying in bed with his own daughter; his wealth and crown are being kept for my husband. So please give me your willing permission to set sail with my husband. To encourage you to let me go more willingly, you are sending away one daughter, but think, you will get two back!'

25. When the king heard all this, he was delighted and rejoiced. At once he ordered ships to be drawn up on shore and filled with all Apollonius's property. Because of his daughter's confinement he also ordered Lycoris, her nurse, and a very experienced midwife to sail with them. After a farewell banquet he escorted

them to the shore, kissed his daughter and son-in-law, and wished them a fair wind. Then the king returned to the palace. But Apollonius embarked with many servants, and with a great quantity of equipment and money, and they set sail on a steady course with a following wind.

For several days and nights they were detained on the wicked sea by various strong winds. In the ninth month, at Lucina's urging, the girl gave birth to a girl. But the afterbirth went back again, her blood congealed, her breathing was blocked, and suddenly she died. She was not dead, but she seemed to be. When the servants saw this, and shouted and wailed loudly, Apollonius came running and saw his wife lying lifeless; he ripped the clothes from his breast with his nails, tore out the first growth of his youthful beard, and in a flood of tears threw himself on her slight body. He began to cry most bitterly, and said: 'Dear wife, beloved only daughter of a king, what has happened to you? How shall I answer for you to your father? What shall I say about you to the man who took me in, poor and needy, when I was shipwrecked?'

As he lamented in these and similar terms and wept profusely, the helmsman came in and said: 'Lord, your behaviour is quite proper, but the ship cannot bear a corpse. So give orders for the body to be thrown into the sea, so that we can escape the turbulent waves.' Apollonius was upset by this speech, and said to him: 'What are you saying, worst of men? Do you want me to throw into the sea the body of the woman who took me in, poor and needy, after my shipwreck?' There were some carpenters among the servants; he sent for them and ordered them to cut and join planks, and to stop up the cracks and holes with pitch; he told them to make a very spacious coffin, and to seal the joints with lead leaf. When the coffin was ready he adorned the girl in royal finery, laid her in it, and put twenty thousand gold sesterces at her head. He kissed the corpse for the last time, and showered it with tears. Then he ordered the baby to be taken and nursed with great care, so that he might have some consolation among his troubles, and might show the king his granddaughter instead of his daughter. Weeping very bitterly, he ordered the coffin to be thrown into the sea.

26. After two days the waves cast the coffin ashore: it arrived on the coast of Ephesus, not far from the estate of a doctor. This man was walking on the shore that day with his pupils and saw the coffin lying where the waves had flowed away. He said to his servants: 'Pick up that box with the greatest care and carry it to my house.' When the servants had done this, the doctor eagerly opened it, and saw a very beautiful girl lying there adorned with royal jewels, apparently dead. 'Think how many tears this girl bequeathed to her relations!' he said. Suddenly he saw the money which had been put at her head, and the tablet underneath it; he said: 'Let us find out the desires or injunctions of Grief.' When he broke the seal he found the following message: 'Whoever finds this coffin, which contains twenty thousand gold sesterces, I beg him to keep ten thousand, but to spend ten thousand on a funeral. For this corpse has left behind many tears and most bitter

grief. But if he does not act according to this grief-stricken request, may he die as the last of his line, and may there be no one to give him burial.'

When he had read the tablet, the doctor said to his servants: 'Let us treat the corpse as the mourner asks. Indeed, as I hope to live, I have sworn that I will spend more on this funeral than Grief demands. After this speech he ordered a pyre to be prepared at once. But while they were carefully and diligently building the pyre, there arrived a student of the doctor, a young man in appearance, but an old man in wisdom. When he saw that the corpse of a beautiful girl was going to be put on the pyre. he looked at his master and said: 'Where has this strange, unknown corpse come from?' The master replied: 'I am glad that you have come; this is a time when you are needed. Take a flask of ointment and pour it over the body of the dead girl, in the last rite.'

The young man took the flask of ointment, went to the girl's couch, and drew her clothes back from her breast. He poured on ointment and suspiciously examined all her limbs again with his hand, and felt the stillness and numbness deep in her bosom. The young man was amazed, for he realized that the girl was lying in a coma. He checked her veins for signs of a pulse, and examined her nostrils for breathing, and tried her lips with his own. He felt the delicate breath of life on the point of struggling with false death, and he said: 'Put little torches underneath at all four sides.' When they had done this, the girl began to draw back her hands which were dangling immobile under the bed; as a result of the rubbing with ointment her blood, which had coagulated, became liquid.

27. When the young man saw this he ran to his master and said: 'Master, the girl whom you believe dead is alive! And so that you may believe me more readily, I will unblock her obstructed breathing.' Taking equipment with him, he brought the girl into his own room and put her on the bed. He opened her coverings, warmed the oil, moistened some wool, and applied it to the girl's breast. Her blood, which had congealed because of the extreme cold, liquefied when it was warmed, and the force of life which had been blocked began to penetrate her marrow. When her veins were cleared the girl opened her eyes and recovered the power to breathe, which she had lost; in a soft and quavering voice she said 'I implore you, doctor, not to touch me except as is proper, for I am the wife of a king and the daughter of a king.'

When the young man saw that through his skill he had noticed what his teacher had missed, he was overjoyed. He went to his teacher and said: 'Come, master, look at your pupil's demonstration.' The teacher came into the bedroom, and when he saw that the girl whom he had believed to be dead was now alive, he said to his pupil: 'I commend your skill, I praise your knowledge, I admire your attentiveness. But listen, my pupil, I do not want you to lose the benefit of your skill. Take the reward; for this girl brought money with her.' So he gave him the ten thousand gold sesterces. Then he ordered that the girl be restored to health with nourishing foods and warm compresses. After a few days, when he learned that she was of royal birth, he summoned his friends and adopted her as his daughter. She made a tearful plea that no man should touch her. He took heed, and supported her and established her among the priestesses of Diana, where all the virgins preserved their chastity inviolate.

28. Meanwhile Apollonius had sailed on, in deep mourning. Steered by God, he arrived at Tarsus, where he disembarked and made for the house of Stranguillio and Dionysias. After greeting them he sadly recounted all his misfortunes, and said: 'However many tears I have shed for the loss of my wife, I shall receive equal consolation from the survival of my daughter. Because of my wife's death, I do not want to accept the kingdom being held for me, nor to return to my father-in-law, whose daughter I have lost at sea; instead I shall become a merchant. So, most worthy hosts, I entrust my daughter to you, to be raised with your daughter. Bring her up honestly and simply, and name her Tarsia after your country. Together with her, I also hand over to you my wife's nurse Lycoris: I want her to rear my daughter and look after her.'

After this speech he handed over the baby, and gave them gold, silver and money, as well as very valuable clothes. He swore a great oath not to cut his beard or hair or nails until he had given away his daughter in marriage. They were amazed that he had sworn such a solemn oath, and promised most faithfully to bring up the girl. When Apollonius had handed over his daughter he boarded his ship, made for the open sea, and arrived in the unknown and far-off parts of Egypt.

29. When Tarsia was five, she was put to study the liberal arts, and their daughter was taught with her. They were taught to use their intelligence, and the arts of listening, discussion and decent behaviour. When Tarsia was fourteen, she came back from school to find that her nurse had suddenly been taken ill. She sat down next to her and asked about the nature of her illness. But her nurse raised herself up and said to her: 'Listen to the last words of an old woman who is dying, Lady Tarsia. Listen, and remember them in your heart. I have a question for you: who do you think your father and mother are, and what is your country?' The girl said: 'My country is Tarsus, my father is Stranguillio, my mother is Dionysias.' But the nurse sighed and said: 'Lady Tarsia, listen to your ancestry and family origins, so that you know what you must do after my death. Your father's name is Apollonius; your mother was the daughter of King Archistrates; Tyre is your native land. When your mother gave birth, the afterbirth went back straightaway and her breathing was obstructed; she came to the end of her allotted span.

'Your father had a coffin made; he committed her to the sea with royal finery and twenty thousand gold sesterces, so that wherever she was carried, she would be her own witness. Your father was in mourning, you were put in a cradle, and because of the turbulent winds the ships arrived at this city. So your father entrusted you to these friends, Stranguillio and Dionysias, together with some splendid clothes. He also took a vow not to cut his nails or his hair until he gave you in marriage. Now after my death, if your hosts, whom you call parents, should happen to do you any harm, go up to the forum and you will find the statue of your father Apollonius. Cling to the statue and cry out: "I am the daughter of the man whose statue this is!" Then the citizens, remembering the benefactions of your father Apollonius, will certainly rescue you.'

30. Tarsia said to her: 'Dear nurse, God is my witness that if by chance any such thing had happened to me before you revealed this to me, I should have been absolutely ignorant of my ancestry and birth.' As they were having this conversation together, the nurse breathed her last in the girl's lap. Tarsia organised the burial of her nurse, and mourned her for a year. When she took off her mourning, she dressed in suitably splendid clothes again, and went to school, and returned to her study of the liberal arts. But she never touched food until she had gone into the tomb with a flask of wine and garlands, and she called on the spirits of her parents there.

31. While this was happening, Dionysias was walking about in the streets on a holiday with her daughter, whose name was Philomusia, and with young Tarsia. When they saw Tarsia's beauty and finery, all the citizens and officials thought her a marvel, and kept saying: Tarsia's father is a lucky man; but that girl at her side is very ugly and a disgrace.' When Dionysias heard Tarsia praised and her own daughter criticized, she became furiously angry. She sat down alone and began thinking as follows: 'It is fourteen years since her father Apollonius set out from here, and he has never come back to collect his daughter, or sent us a letter. I think it is because he has died, or perished at sea. Her nurse is dead. No one stands in my way. My plan cannot be accomplished unless I do away with her, by the sword or by poison; and I shall adorn my daughter in her finery.'

While she was pondering this, she was told that an overseer called Theophilus had arrived. She summoned him and said: 'If you want your freedom and a reward, do away with Tarsia.' The overseer said: 'What has the innocent girl done wrong?' 'Are you disobeying me already?' said the wicked woman. 'Just do what I tell you. If you do not, you may feel the wrath of your master and mistress.' The overseer said: 'How can it be done?' The wicked woman said: 'It is her habit, as soon as she comes from school and before she eats anything, to go to her nurse's tomb. You must hide there with a dagger: when she arrives, kill her and throw her body into the sea. When you come and tell me that the deed is done, you will receive your freedom and a reward.'

The overseer took a dagger and hid it at his side. Looking up to heaven he said: 'God, have I not earned my freedom without spilling the blood of an innocent girl?' With these words he went, sighing and weeping, to the tomb of Tarsia's nurse, and hid there. When Tarsia came back from school, in the usual way she poured a flask of wine, went into the tomb, and hung up wreaths. As she was calling on the shades of her parents, the overseer attacked her, seized her from behind by the hair, and threw her to the ground. As he was going to strike her, the girl said to him: 'Theophilus, what have I done wrong, that an innocent girl should die at your hand?' He said to her: 'You have done nothing wrong, but your father Apollonius was at fault to leave you in the care of Stranguillio and Dionysias with lots of money and royal robes.' On hearing this the girl burst into tears and entreated him: 'If there is no hole of life or solace for me, let me pray to God.' The overseer replied: 'Do pray. For God Himself knows that I do not commit this crime willingly.'

32. While the girl was praying to the Lord, some pirates suddenly arrived. Seeing a man with a weapon in his hand, about to strike, they called out: 'Spare her, you thug, spare her, don't kill her! This girl is booty for us, not your victim.' When the overseer heard this shout he let Tarsia go, and ran away and hid behind the tomb. The pirates put in to the shore, took the girl, and sailed off, making for the open sea. After waiting a while, the overseer came back: when he saw that the girl had been snatched from death, he thanked God that he had not committed a crime. He went back to his mistress and said: 'What you ordered has been done. Fulfil your promise to me.' The wicked woman replied: 'You have committed a murder: do you expect freedom on top of that? Go back to the farm and get on with your work, or you will feel the wrath of your master and mistress.' When the overseer heard that he raised his eyes to heaven and said: 'You know, God, that I have not committed a crime. Be the judge between us.' And he went off to his farm.

Then Dionysias turned over in her mind how she could conceal the crime which she had planned. She went in to her husband Stranguillio and said: 'Dear husband, save your wife, and save our daughter. Insults drove me into a mad rage, and I suddenly thought to myself: "Indeed, more than fourteen years have passed since Tarsia was left in our care by her father, and he has never sent us any letter of greeting. Perhaps he has died of grief, or he must have perished in the stormy seas. Tarsia's nurse has died. No one stands in my way. I will get rid of Tarsia and adorn our daughter with her finery." Let me tell you that this has actually happened. But now, because of the curiosity of the citizens, put on mourning clothes for the time being, as I am doing, and let us announce with feigned tears that Tarsia has died from a sudden stomach pain. Let us build an enormous tomb on the outskirts of the town, where we can say that she is buried.'

When Stranguillio heard this he was amazed and began to tremble, and he answered thus: 'Yes, give me mourning clothes, so that I can mourn for myself, whose lot it is to have such a wicked wife. Alas! Oh, the grief!' he said. 'What shall I do, how shall I deal with her father? When I first took him in, when he delivered this city from death and from the threat of famine, it was at my encouragement that he left the city. Because of this city he was shipwrecked, faced death, lost all his possessions, endured the fate of poverty. But when God restored him to better fortune, as he was a moral man, he did not think of doing evil for good, nor kept the idea in mind, but let it all be forgotten; furthermore, he remembered us kindly in his prosperity, singling out our loyalty, rewarding us, thinking us responsible people. He handed over his daughter to us to rear, and treated us with such honesty and affection that he named his daughter after our city. Alas, I have been blind. Let me mourn for myself and for the innocent girl, for I am yoked to a most evil and poisonous snake, a wicked wife!' Raising his eyes to heaven he said: 'God, you know that I am innocent of Tarsia's blood. Seek her out, and take vengeance for her on Dionysias.' Looking at his wife he said: 'Enemy of God, how will you be able to hide this abominable crime?'

But Dionysias dressed herself and her daughter in mourning and wept feigned tears. She summoned the citizens and addressed them: 'Dearest citizens, we have summoned you because we have lost the hope of our eyes, the object of our labours, the goal of our lives: I mean that Tarsia, whom you know well, has died, leaving us torment and bitter tears. We have had her suitably buried.' Then the citizens went to the tomb which Dionysias had had made. Because of the kindness and benefactions of Apollonius, Tarsia's father, they had a monument raised by public subscription, and put the following inscription on it: TO THE SPIRITS OF THE DEAD: THE CITIZENS OF TARSUS ERECTED THIS MONUMENT BY SUBSCRIPTION TO THE MAIDEN TARSIA BECAUSE OF THE BENEFACTIONS OF APOL-LONIUS OF TYRE.

33. So Tarsia's abductors arrived in the city of Mytilene. She was landed among the other slaves and put up for sale in the market-place. The news reached a pimp, an extremely disreputable man. He was not interested in buying anyone, male or female, except Tarsia, and he began to bid for her. But when the prince of the city, Athenagoras, realized that the girl up for sale was of noble birth, intelligent and very beautiful, he bid ten thousand gold sesterces for her. But the pimp bid twenty thousand. Athenagoras bid thirty thousand, the pimp forty thousand, Athenagoras fifty thousand, the pimp sixty thousand, Athenagoras seventy thousand, the pimp eighty thousand, Athenagoras ninety thousand. At once the pimp put down one hundred thousand gold sesterces and said: 'If anyone often more, I will go ten thousand higher.' Athenagoras said: 'If I want to compete with this pimp, I shall have to sell several slaves to buy one girl. So I will let him buy her, and when he puts her in the brothel I will be her first client, and will deflower her for a low price, and I shall feel just as if I had bought her.'

What more need be said? The pimp bought the girl and led her into a reception room where he had a statue of Priapus made of gold, covered with precious stones and gold. He said to her: 'Worship my god, who is very powerful.' The girl asked: 'Do you come from Lampsacus?' The pimp said: 'Wretched girl, don't you know that you have entered the house of a greedy pimp?' When Tarsia heard this, she trembled all over, throwing herself at his feet she begged: 'Have pity on me, master, protect my virginity! I implore you not to prostitute my tender body under such a vile sign.' The pimp replied: 'Get up, you wretch. You do not realize that neither prayers nor tears have any effect on pimps or torturers.' He summoned the overseer in charge of the girls and said to him: 'Have a room carefully decoratedand put this sign on it: "Whoever wants to deflower Tarsia will pay half a pound of gold; but after that she will be open to the public for one gold piece.'" The overseer did as his master the pimp had told him.

34. Two days later Tarsia was taken to the brothel, preceded by a crowd and musicians. Prince Athenagoras arrived first; he covered his head and went into the brothel. When he came in, he sat down. Tarsia went over to him, fell at his feet, and said: 'Have pity on me! I implore you by your youth, do not dishonour me under such a vile sign. Restrain your shameless lust, and listen to the wretched misfortunes of a helpless woman, think of my ancestry.' When she had told him all her misfortunes, the prince was disconcerted and moved by pity. In his great astonishment he said to her: 'Get up. We all know the mishaps of fortune; we are all human. I too have a daughter who is a virgin: I can be afraid of a similar disaster in her case.' With these words he produced forty pieces of gold and put them in Tarsia's hand. 'Lady Tarsia,' he said, 'here is more than the price demanded for your virginity. Behave in the same way with all comers, until you are freed.' Tarsia wept and said: 'I am extremely grateful for your compassion.'

When Athenagoras went out he met a companion who asked him: 'Athenagoras, how did you get on with the new girl?' Athenagoras said: 'It couldn't have been better: even tears!' After this conversation Athenagoras followed him when he went inside, and lay in wait to see how things would turn out. So he went in and Athenagoras stayed outside. The girl closed the door in the usual way. The young man said to her: 'Please tell me, how much did you get from the young man who came in to you just now?' The girl said: 'He gave me forty gold pieces.' 'Damn him!' said the young man. 'For such a rich man it would not have been much to give you a whole pound of gold! To show you that I am a better man, here is a whole pound of gold.' But Athenagoras, who was standing outside, said: 'The more you give, the more you will cry!' The girl threw herself at his feet and told him her misfortunes in the same way as before. He was disconcerted and distracted from his lust. He said to her: 'Get up, lady! We are human too, and subject to misfortunes.' The girl replied: 'I am extremely grateful for your compassion.'

35. When he went outside he found Athenago, as laughing, and said to him: 'You're a great man! Did you have no one over whom to shed your tears?' They both swore not to betray her to anyone, and began to watch the others coming out. What more is there to tell? They watched from a hidden place: whoever went in handed over some gold pieces and came out crying. When this came to an end Tarsia gave the money to the pimp, and said: 'Here is the price of my virginity.' The pimp said: 'How much better it is when you are cheerful, not sad! Carry on like this, so that you bring me more money every day.' The next day she said to him again: 'Here is the price of my virginity: I collected it as before with tears and prayers, and I preserve my virginity.' When he heard this the pimp was furious that she was still a virgin. He called the overseer in charge of the girls and said to him: 'I see you are so careless that you do not know that Tarsia is a virgin.

If she brings in so much as a virgin, what will she bring as a woman? Take her to your room and deflower her.'

The overseer took her to his room at once and said to her: 'Tell me the truth, Tarsia, are you still a virgin?' The girl Tarsia said: 'For as long as God wishes, I am a virgin.' The overseer said: 'Then where did you get so much money in these two days?' The girl said: 'With my tears: I told all the men the whole story of my misfortunes, and they were upset and took pity on my virginity.' She threw herself at his feet and said: 'Have pity on me, master, help the captive daughter of a king.' When she had told him all her misfortunes, he was moved by pity, and said to her: 'That pimp is too greedy. I do not know if you will be able to stay a virgin.'

36. Tarsia replied: 'I have the benefit of the study of the liberal arts: I am fully educated. I can also play the lyre with a rhythmic beat. Have benches put up tomorrow in some crowded place, and I shall offer entertainment with my eloquent talk. Then I shall make music with a plectrum, and through this skill I shall make more money every day.' The servant did this; so great was the people's applause, so great was the citizens' love for her, that both men and women gave her a lot of money every day. Tarsia became famous for her pure virginity and her noble nature, and prince Athenagoras watched over her as if she were his own only daughter, to the extent that he gave a lot of money to the overseer and entrusted her to him.

37. While this was happening at Mytilene, Apollonius arrived at Tarsus after fourteen years and came to the house of Stranguillio and Dionysias. When Stranguillio saw him a long way off, he ran very fast to his wife, saying to her: 'You said it was certain that Apollonius had died in a shipwreck. Look, he is coming to fetch his daughter. What shall we tell the father about his daughter, to whom we were parents?' The wicked woman trembled all over when she heard this, and said: 'Be merciful! I confess it is as I said, husband. Because I love our own daughter, I killed the daughter who was not ours. Now put on mourning clothes for the time being, and let us weep false tears, and say that she died suddenly from a stomach pain. When he sees us in these clothes, he will believe it.'

Meanwhile, Apollonius came into Stranguillio's house; he pushed away the hair from his forehead, and removed the shaggy beard from his face. When he saw them in mourning dress, he asked: 'My most faithful hosts—if that name still applies to you—why do you weep profusely at my arrival? Can it be that these tears are not on your own account, but on mine?' The wicked woman replied tearfully: 'If only someone else could bring this news to your ears, not myself or my husband! For you must know that your daughter Tarsia was taken from us, and died of a sudden stomach pain.' When Apollonius heard this, he trembled all over and went pale, and stood grief-stricken for a long time. When he got his breath back, he looked at the woman and said: 'My daughter Tarsia died a few days ago. Surely her money and jewels and clothes have not gone too?'

38. When he said this, the wicked woman fetched everything and handed it over, according to the agreement. She said: 'Do believe us, if the stars at her birth had permitted it, we would have returned your daughter to you just as we are returning all this. So that you know that we are not lying, we have the testimony of the citizens on this matter. Remembering your benefactions, they have put up a monument to your daughter by subscription, which your honour can see.' Then Apollonius, believing that she was really dead, said to his servants: 'Take all these things and carry them to the ship. I am going to see my daughter's tomb.'

When he came to it he read the inscription: TO THE SPIRITS OF THE DEAD: THE CITIZENS OF TARSUS ERECTED THIS MONUMENT BY SUBSCRIPTION TO THE MAIDEN TARSIA, DAUGHTER OF KING APOLLONIUS, OUT OF RESPECT FOR HIS BENEFACTIONS. When Apollonius read the inscription, he stood stunned. He was surprised that he was unable to cry, and cursed his own eyes, saying: 'O cruel eyes, you see the inscription for my daughter, and you cannot produce tears! Alas! I think my daughter is alive.' With these words he returned to the ship and addressed his men as follows: 'Throw me in the hold of the ship, for I want to breathe my last at sea, since I have not been allowed to see light on land.' He threw himself in the hold, they weighed anchor, and he made for the open sea in order to return to Tyre.

39. He was sailing with favourable winds when the sea suddenly changed its trustworthy mood, and they were tossed about in various dangerous situations. All prayed to God, and they arrived at the city of Mitylene. The feast of Neptune was being celebrated there. When Apollonius learned this, he groaned and said: 'So everyone is celebrating a holiday except me! Let me not appear mean as well as grief-stricken. It is punishment enough for my servants that fate has sent them such an unhappy master.' He called his steward and said to him: 'Give ten gold pieces to the boys; let them go and buy whatever they want, and celebrate the feast day. But I forbid any of you to address me. If one of you does, I shall have his legs broken.'

While all Apollonius' sailors were celebrating with a better feast than the other ships, it happened that Athenagoras, the prince of the city, who loved Apollonius' daughter Tarsia, was walking on the beach and looking at the festivities on the ships. As he observed each ship in turn, he noticed that this ship was finer and more decorated than the others. He went up to it and stood admiring it. Apollonius' crew and the servants greeted him and said: 'We invite you aboard, noble prince, if you would do us the honour.' At this invitation he went aboard with five of his servants. When he saw them reclining in harmony, he took his place among the feasters and gave them ten gold pieces. Putting the money on the table, he said: 'Here, so that you haven't invited me for nothing.' They all replied: 'We thank your lordship very much.'

When Athenagoras saw them all reclining so freely without anyone senior to oversee them, he said to them: 'Who is the master of this ship, that you all recline and enjoy yourselves?' The helmsman said: 'The master of this ship is in mourning, and lies below in the hold in the dark. He is weeping for his wife and daughter.' On hearing this Athenagoras was distressed. He said to the helmsman: 'I will give you two gold pieces. Go down to him and say to him, "Athenagoras, prince of this city, asks you to come out to him from the dark into the light."' The youth replied: 'Yes, if I can get four legs with two gold pieces' and 'Could you not choose anyone suitable for the task among us except me? Ask someone else to go, for he gave orders that whoever addressed him would have his legs broken.' Athenagoras said: 'He made this rule for you but not for me, whom he does not know. I will go down to him myself. Tell me what his name is.' The servants said: 'Apollonius.'

40. But when Athenagoras heard the name he said to himself: 'Tarsia's father was also called Apollonius.' The servants showed him the way, and he went down to him. When he saw Apollonius lying in the dark with an unkempt beard and a dishevelled, dirty head, he greeted him in a low voice: 'Greetings, Apollonius.' But Apollonius thought he was being mocked by one of his crew; when he looked up with a furious expression to see a noble, well-dressed stranger, he concealed his anger in silence. Athenagoras, the prince of the city, said to him: 'I know that you are surprised to be greeted by name like this. Let me inform you that I am the prince of this city.' When Athenagoras heard no comment from him, he spoke to him again: 'I came down from the road to the shore to inspect the ships, and I noticed yours among all the rest because of its fine decoration and attractive appearance. When I came nearer, your friends and the crew invited me aboard. I came on board and took a place with pleasure. I asked about the master of the ship; they told me that you were in deep mourning, as indeed I see. But in response to the desire which brought me to you, come out of the dark to the light and feast with us for a little while. I hope that after such great grief God will give you even greater joy.'

But Apollonius, worn out by his grief, raised his head and said: 'Whoever you are, lord, go away, recline and feast with my men as if with your own. For I am overwhelmed by my misfortunes, so that not only do I have no desire to feast, but I do not want to live.' Rebuffed, Athenagoras went back from the hold to the main ship. He lay down and said: 'I have not been able to persuade your master to come into the light. So what can I do to dissuade him from his determination to die? I have an idea: boy, go to that pimp and tell him to send Tarsia to me.'

When the boy arrived at the pimp's house, the pimp listened and could not ignore him; although it was against his will, he sent her along. When Tarsia reached the ship, Athenagoras saw her and said: 'Come here to me, lady Tarsia. We have need here of your skill and learning to console the master of this ship and of all these men. He is sitting in the dark, mourning his wife and daughter: you must persuade him to listen to consoling words and rouse him to come out into the light. This is an occasion for an act of charity, through which God is made well-disposed to men. So go to him and persuade him to come out into the light. Perhaps it is God's will that we should save his life. If you succeed, I will redeem you from the pimp for thirty days, so that you can devote yourself to your vow of chastity. And over and above this I will give you ten thousand gold sesterces.' When she heard this, the girl went down resolutely into the hold to Apollonius and greeted him quietly: 'Greetings, whoever you are, and be cheerful. I am no fallen woman who has come to console you, but an innocent girl, who keeps her virginity, intact in the midst of moral shipwreck.'

41. In a musical voice she began to sing this song:

'I walk among corruption, but I am unaware of corruption,
Just as a rose among thorns is not pricked by their spines.
Pirates abducted me, striking with wicked swords.
Now I have been sold to a pimp, but I have never tarnished my honour.
If it were not for weeping and grief and tears for my lost parents,
If my father knew where I am, no woman would be better off than I.
I am of royal birth, born of an honourable line,
But I endure contempt, and am told besides to rejoice!
Restrain your tears, put an end to your sorrows and cares,
Return your eyes to heaven, raise your heart to the stars!
God the Creator and Maker of all things will help you:
He does not allow these tears to be shed in useless grief!'

At these words Apollonius raised his head and saw the girl. He groaned and said: 'Alas! How long shall I struggle against pity?' He got up and sat beside her, and said to her: 'I am very grateful for your intelligence and generosity. This is my answer to your words of encouragement, as you deserve. If ever it is given to me to be happy, I may be able to relieve you with the resources of my kingdom; and so perhaps I shall return you to your parents, since you say you are of royal birth. But now take two hundred gold pieces; rejoice as if you had led me into the light. Go away; and please, do not speak any more to me. For you have renewed my recent sorrow.'

Tarsia took the two hundred gold pieces and went away from that place. Athenagoras said to her: 'Where are you going, Tarsia? Have you failed in your work? Could we not do a good deed and help a man who is killing himself?' Tarsia answered: 'I have done all I could, but he gave me two hundred thousand gold sesterces and asked me to go away, declaring that the renewed grief and pain was torture to him'. Athenagoras said to her: 'I will give you four hundred gold pieces if you will just go down to him. Give back the two hundred which he gave you; make him come out into the light, say to him, "I am not interested in your money but in your wellbeing."'

So Tarsia went down to him and said: 'Even if you have decided to stay in this squalor, since you have kindly given me a great deal of money, let me have a talk with you here in the darkness. If you can unknot my riddles, I will go; if not, I will give you back the money that you gave me, and leave.' In order not to look as if he was taking back the money, and also because he wanted to hear the conversation of the clever girl, Apollonius said: 'Although in my troubles I am not interested in anything except weeping and grieving, still, so that I can stop being urged to cheer up, ask your questions and go. Please allow me time for my tears.'

42. Tarsia said to him:

'There is a house on earth which resounds with a clear voice.

The house itself is full of sound, but the silent inhabitant makes none.

But both move swiftly, inhabitant and house together.

Now if as you claim you are a king—for in my country it is not proper for anyone to be cleverer than the king—answer this riddle and I will go.'

Apollonius nodded and said: 'So that you know that I was not lying: the house which resounds over the earth is the sea; the silent inhabitant of this house is the fish, which moves swiftly with the house.' The girl was impressed by this clever interpretation which showed that he really was a king, and she pressed him with more difficult riddles. She said:

'The sweet friend of the bank, always close to deep water,

Singing sweetly to the Muses, dyed black,

I am the messenger of the tongue, sealed by the master's fingers.'

Apollonius said to her. The sweet friend of the god who sends her songs up to heaven is the reed, always close to the bank, because it makes its home next to the water. It is dyed black, it is the messenger of the tongue, because the voice is conveyed through it.'

Next the girl said to him:

'Long lovely daughter of the forest. I travel fast.

Crowded round by an innumerable throng of companions.

I run over many roads, yet I leave no tracks.'

Nodding again Apollonius said to her 'If only I could put aside my long grief, I would show you what you do not know. But I will answer your riddles; it amazes me that you are so clever at such a tender age. The long tree which travels, the lovely daughter of the forest, is a ship. It travels fast with a following wind, in a crowd of companions. It travels along many roads, but leaves no tracks.'

Excited by the cleverness of the riddles, the girl asked another:

'The fire goes through the whole house without harm:

The walled area is surrounded by flames on every side, but I am not burned;

The house is naked, and so is the guest who arrives there.'

Apollonius said: 'If only I could give up this mourning, I would go in through that fire unharmed. For I would go into a bath, where flames rise through pipes on every side; where the house is naked, because it has nothing in it but benches; where the guest goes in naked, without clothes.'

Next the girl said to him:

'I have a double point joined in one piece of iron.

I struggle with the wind. I fight with the deep current.

I explore the middle waters, and also bite the earth at the bottom.'

Apollonius answered her: 'It is the anchor, which holds you still as you sit in this ship. It has two points joined in one piece of iron. It struggles with the wind and with the deep current. It explores the middle waters, and bites the earth at the bottom.'

Next the girl said to him:

'I am not heavy myself, but a weight of water clings to me.

All my innards are swollen, extended in deep hollows.

The water hides inside, and does not flow out spontaneously.'

Apollonius replied: 'Although a sponge is light, when heavy with water it swells and is extended in deep hollows, and the water does not flow out spontaneously.'

43. Then the girl said to him:

'I am not adorned with tresses or with hair.

But inside me there is hair which no one sees.

Hands throw me, and by hands I am tossed back in the air.'

Apollonius said: 'I had this for a guide when I was shipwrecked at Pentapolis, so that I became the king's friend. It is a ball, which is not covered with hair, but is not devoid of hair either; for it is full of hair inside. It is thrown by hand and returned by hand.'

Then the girl said to him:

'I have no fixed shape, no foreign shape.

There is a radiance in me, flashing with bright light,

But it shows nothing except what it has seen before.'

Apollonius answered: 'There is no fixed shape in a mirror, for it changes in appearance; there is no foreign shape, because it shows what is facing it.'

Next the girl said:

'Four identical sisters run skilfully

As if racing, although they all share the same work,

And even though they are dose together, they cannot touch.'

Apollonius said to her: 'The four sisters identical in shape and behaviour are wheels, which run skilfully as if racing; and although they are close together, none of them can touch another one.'

Then the girl said to him:

'We are the ones who seek the heights, climbing to the sky,

We are of matching workmanship, one sequence links us. Whoever seeks the heights, we accompany him aloft.'

Apollonius answered: 'I beg you in God's name not to rouse me further to be cheerful, in case I seem disrespectful to my dead. The rungs of a ladder seek the heights, remaining equal in their positioning and linked in a single sequence. Whoever seeks the heights is accompanied aloft by them.'

44. After this he said: 'Here, take another hundred gold pieces and go away, so that I can weep over the memory of my dead.' But the girl was sad that such a clever man wanted to die—it was shocking. She poured the gold back into his lap, took hold of his mourning clothes, and tried to drag him into the light. But he pushed her so that she fell down. When she fell she began to bleed from the nose. The girl sat down and began to cry, and said in deep sorrow: 'Relentless heavenly power, who allows an innocent girl to be harassed from the cradle by so many disasters! For as soon as I was born at sea, amidst waves and storms, my mother died giving birth to me; the afterbirth went back into her stomach and her blood clotted; she was denied burial on land. But my father adorned her with royal finery, put her in a coffin with twenty thousand gold sesterces, and committed her to the sea. As for me, I was put in a cradle, and handed over by my father to wicked Stranguillio and his wife Dionysias, with jewels and splendid clothes. Because of these I was betrayed and nearly murdered: a disreputable servant called Theophilus was ordered to kill me, But as he was about to kill me. I begged him to let me pray to the Lord. As I was praying, some pirates appeared: they carried me off by force, and brought me to this country, and I was sold to a wicked pimp.'

45. As the girl was tearfully saying this and similar things, Apollonius rushed to embrace her and began to speak to her, weeping for joy: 'You are my daughter Tarsia, you are my one hope, you are the light of my eyes: for you, and for your mother, I have been weeping guiltily for fourteen years. Now I shall die happy, for my hope has been reborn and returned to me.' *When Apollonius heard this revealing story, he cried out tearfully in a loud voice: 'Hurry, servants, hurry, friends, and put an end to a father's anxiety.' When they heard the noise they all came running. Athenagoras, the prince of the city, ran too, and found Apollonius weeping on Tarsia's neck and saying: 'This is my daughter Tarsia, whom I have been mourning. It was for her that I started weeping and grieving again. For I am Apollonius of Tyre, who entrusted you to Stranguillio. Tell me, who was your nurse?' And she said: 'Lycoris.' Apollonius began to shout even more loudly: 'You are my daughter!' And she said: 'If you are looking for Tarsia, I am she.'*

Then Apollonius got up and changed his mourning dress for very elegant clothes, and hugged her and kissed her as he wept. When Athenagoras saw them embracing and weeping, he too wept very bitterly. He explained how the girl had once told him her whole story in sequence when she was put in the brothel, and how long it was since she had been brought by the pirates and sold. Then Athenagoras threw himself at Apollonius' feet and said: 'By the living God, who has restored you as father to your daughter, I beg you not to marry Tarsia to any other man! For I am the prince of this city, and through my help she has remained a virgin.' Apollonius said: 'How can I be hostile to such goodness and compassion? Indeed I am willing, because I made a vow not to give up my mourning until I had given my daughter in marriage. But it remains for my daughter to be revenged on the pimp whose hostility she endured.'

Apollonius said: 'Let this city be destroyed.' When prince Athenagoras heard this, he began to call out in the streets, in the forum, in the senate house, saying: 'Hurry, citizens and nobles, or the city will be destroyed.'

46. An enormous crowd gathered, and there was such an uproar among the people that absolutely no one, man or woman, remained at home. When they were all gathered together, Athenagoras said: 'Citizens of Mitylene, let me inform you that Apollonius of Tyre has arrived here—look, there are the ships of his fleet. He is pressing forward with many armed men to destroy this province because of the accursed pimp who bought his daughter Tarsia and put her in a brothel. So to save the city, the pimp must be handed over: let Apollonius take revenge on one wicked man, so that we are not all in danger.'

When the people heard this, they seized the pimp by the ears; he was led to the forum with his hands tied behind his back. There was a huge platform in the forum. When Apollonius had taken off all his filthy mourning clothes they dressed him in royal costume; after cutting his hair they put a crown on his head; and with his daughter Tarsia he mounted the platform. He took her in his arms in front of all the people, but could not speak for tears. With difficulty Athenagoras succeeded in silencing the people with his hand. When they were silent, Athenagoras said: 'Citizens of Mitylene, whom your prompt sense of urgent duty has gathered here: you see that Tarsia, whom the greedy pimp has oppressed in order to ruin us up to this very day, has been recognized by her father. Through your kindness she remained a virgin. Take revenge on the pimp, so that she can thank you even more for your good fortune.'

But they all cried out with one voice: 'Let the pimp be burned alive, and let all his wealth be awarded to the girl!' At these words the pimp was consigned to the flames. But his overseer and all the girls and all his wealth were handed over to the maiden Tarsia. She said to the overseer. 'I have given you your life, because it was through your goodwill that I remained a virgin.' And she gave him two hundred talents of gold and his freedom. Then all the girls were brought before her, and she said to them: 'Whatever you earned for the accursed pimp with your bodies, I give it back to you to keep; and indeed because you were slaves with me, you shall be free with me from now on.'

47. Then Apollonius of Tyre got up and addressed the people in these words: 'Most honourable and worthy citizens, I thank you for your kindness; it was your longlasting loyalty which created charity and offered peace and < . . . > health and produced glory for me. "It is your doing that false death and the subsequent mourning have been exposed; your doing that a virgin did not endure any battles; your doing that an only daughter has been restored to her father's embrace. For this great service, I donate to this city of yours one hundred talents of gold, for the restoration of all the walls.' After this speech he gave orders for the money to be handed over to them at once. The citizens accepted

the gold, and they cast a huge statue of him standing on the prow of a ship, with his heel on the pimp's head, and his daughter clasped in his right arm. The inscription read: IN GREAT AFFECTION AND AS A SIGN OF ETERNAL HONOUR AND REMEMBRANCE, THE ENTIRE POPULATION OF MITYLENE GAVE THIS STATUE TO APOL- LONIUS OF TYRE, FOR RESTORING OUR BUILDINGS, AND TO THE MOST CHASTE TARSIA, FOR KEEPING HER VIRGINITY IN THE FACE OF THE MOST DEMEANING MISFORTUNE. To cut a long story short, in a few days Apollonius gave his daughter in marriage to Prince Athenagoras, amidst great ceremony and popular rejoicing.

RB: 'It is your doing that renewed life has succeeded renewed wounds; . . . '

48. Then he set sail with all his men and with his son-in-law and daughter, intending to make for Tarsus and return to his own land. In a dream he saw someone who looked like an angel, who said to him: 'Apollonius, tell your helmsman to steer for Ephesus. When you arrive there, go into the temple of Diana with your daughter and son-in-law, and recount in order all the misfor- tunes which you have suffered from your youth on. After that go to Tarsus and avenge your innocent daughter.' When Apollonius woke up, he roused his daughter and son-in-law and told them his dream. They said: 'Lord, do what was ordered.' So he directed the helmsman to make for Ephesus. They arrived after a successful journey. Apollonius disembarked with his family and went to the temple of Diana, where his wife was the chief priestess. For she was very gracious in appearance, and accustomed to total devotion to chastity, so that no one was more pleasing to Diana than she. Appollonius came into the temple with his family and asked for the shrine to be opened for him, so that he could recount all his misfortunes in the presence of Diana.

The chief priestess was informed that an unknown king had arrived with his son-in-law and daughter, and with great gifts, and that he wanted to tell some story in the presence of Diana. But when she heard that a king had arrived, she put on royal clothes, adorned her head with jewels, and came dressed in purple, accompanied by a throng of female servants. She came into the temple. When Apollonius saw her, he and his daughter and son-in-law fell at her feet. Such was the splendour that radiated from her beauty that they thought she was the goddess Diana herself. Meanwhile the shrine had been opened and the gifts had been offered. In Diana's presence Apollonius began to speak, weeping profusely: 'From my youth I have borne the title of a noble king, and I have mastered all the arts which are practised by nobles and kings. I solved the riddle of wicked king Antiochus in order to marry his daughter. But he had a relationship of the most horrible kind with the girl whose father he had been appointed by nature; flouting morality, he became her husband, and plotted to kill me. While I was fleeing from him I was shipwrecked, and was taken in by Archistrates the king of Cyrene, so that I was found worthy of marrying his daughter. She wanted to come with me to take possession of my kingdom: after she bore this little daughter (whom you ordered me in a dream at an angel's bidding to bring before you, great Diana) on board ship, she died. I dressed her in splendid

clothes suitable for royalty and put her in a coffin with twenty thousand gold
sesterces, so that when she was found, she would be her own witness, so that she
would be suitably buried. As for this daughter of mine, I entrusted her to the care
of Stranguillio and Dionysias, most wicked creatures, and took myself to Egypt
for fourteen years, mourning deeply for my wife. Then I came to fetch my
daughter. They told me that she was dead. Again I was plunged into renewed
grief, and longed to die now that mother and daughter were dead, but you have
given me back life.'

49. While Apollonius was recounting this and other things of the same
sort,his wife gave a great cry and said: 'I am your wife, the daughter of King
Archistrates!' And throwing herself into his arms she began to speak: 'You are
my Apollonius of Tyre, you are the master who taught me with skilful hand, you
are the man who received me from my father Archistrates, you are the man with
whom I fell in love not out of lust, but as a guide to wisdom. Where is my
daughter?' He showed her Tarsia and said to her: 'Look, here she is!'

All Ephesus was ringing with the news that Apollonius of Tyre had recognized as his wife the woman whom they themselves had as a priestess. There
was great rejoicing throughout the city: garlands were hung in the streets,
musical instruments were set up in several places, all the citizens feasted and
celebrated together. Apollonius' wife appointed in her place the woman who
was next to her in rank, and dear to her. Amid the rejoicing and tears of all the
Ephesians, and very bitter lamenting that she was leaving them, she said
goodbye and boarded the ship with her husband and daughter and son-in-law.

50. And he established his son-in-law Athenagoras as king in his place.
Sailing on with him and his daughter and his army he came to Tarsus. At once
Apollonius gave orders that Stranguillio and Dionysias should be arrested and
brought to him as he sat on the judgement-seat in the forum. When they had
been brought, he said in front of everyone: 'Most fortunate citizens of Tarsus, has
Apollonius of Tyre shown himself ungrateful to any of you in any matter?' But
they shouted unanimously: 'We said that you were our king and the father of our
country, and we say so forever; we were willing to die for you, and we still are,
because with your help we overcame the danger of famine and death. The proof
of this is the statue of you in a chariot that we put up.'

Apollonius said to them: 'I entrusted my daughter to Stranguillio and
Dionysias his wife. They refuse to return her to me.' Stranguillio said: 'By your
royal mercy, because she has used up her allotted span.' Apollonius said: 'You
see, citizens of Tarsus, as for their wickedness, it is not enough that they have
committed a murder; on top of that they have decided to commit perjury,
invoking my royal power. Look, I will show you visible evidence, and prove it to
you with witnesses.' Apollonius brought forward his daughter before all the
people and said: 'Look, here is my daughter Tarsia!' When the evil woman,
wicked Dionysias, saw her she trembled all over. The citizens were amazed.

Tarsia ordered that Theophilus the overseer be brought into her presence. When he was brought, Tarsia said to him: 'Theophilus, if you want to be excused the torture and death which you deserve, and to earn indulgence from me, say in a clear voice who ordered you to murder me.' Theophilus said: 'My mistress Dionysias.' After this evidence, when a confession had been made and the true account had been given too the citizens rushed together, seized Stranguillio and Dionysias, took them outside the city, stoned them to death, and threw their bodies on the ground for the beasts of the earth and birds of the air, so as also to deny their corpses burial in the earth. They wanted to kill Theophilus too, but because Tarsia intervened he was not touched. For she said: 'Most worthy citizens, if he had not given me time to call on the Lord, even your good fortune would not have protected me.' Then she gave Theophilus his freedom on the spot, and a reward.

51. So Apollonius added to the public rejoicing in return for this: he restored public works, he rebuilt the public baths, the city walls, and the towers on the walls. He and all his people stayed for fifteen days during the rebuilding. But then he said goodbye to the citizens and sailed to Pentapolis in Cyrene, and arrived there safely. He went in to King Archistrates, his father-in-law. Archistrates saw his daughter with her husband, and his granddaughter Tarsia with her husband. He greeted the children of the king with honour, and received Apollonius and his own daughter with a kiss. He spent a whole year in continuous celebration with them; then when his life came to an end he died in their arms, leaving half the kingdom to Apollonius and half to his own daughter.

At the time when all this had happened, Apollonius was walking by the sea when he saw the fisherman who took him in after the shipwreck and gave him half of his cloak. He ordered his servants to seize him and bring him to the palace. When the fisherman saw that he was being taken to the palace, he thought he was going to be killed. But when he came into the palace, Apollonius of Tyre, who was sitting with his wife, ordered the fisherman to be brought to him, and said to his wife: 'Lady queen and chaste wife, this is my "best man," who helped me and showed me the way to come to you.' Looking at him Apollonius said: 'Most generous old man, I am Apollonius of Tyre, to whom you gave half your cloak.' He gave him two hundred thousand gold sesterces, servants and maids, clothes and silver to his heart's content, and made him a count for the rest of his life.

But then Hellenicus, who told Apollonius everything when Antiochus was persecuting him and would not accept anything from him, followed him and presented himself as Apollonius was walking along and said to him: 'Lord king, remember your servant Hellenicus.' Apollonius took him by the hand, raised him up and kissed him. He made him a count and gave him great wealth.

When all this had been settled, Apollonius' wife bore him a son, whom he made king in the place of his grandfather Archistrates. Apollonius himself lived with his wife for seventy-four years. He ruled Antioch and Tyre and Cyrene as his kingdom, and led a peaceful and happy life with his wife. At the end of the time we have mentioned, they died in peace and virtuous old age.

Here ends the book of Apollonius.

SECTION 2

Selections from THE LOVE SONGS OF THE CARMINA BURANA

Translated by E. D. Blodgett and Roy Arthur Swanson

Introduction by Albrecht Classen

The *Carmina Burana* are a collection of songs copied in the *Codex Buranus* or *Codex latinus Monacensis* (Clm) 4660, today in the *Bayerische Staatsbibliothek München* (Munich). The manuscript came from the Benedictine abbey Benediktbeuren near Bad Tölz/Bavaria and was transferred to Munich in 1803 when a large number of monasteries where secularized and closed. We assume that these songs were copied in this manuscript sometime in the first half of the thirteenth century (maybe around 1230), but there are no historical records to identify the scribes, or most of the authors, the previous owners of the manuscript or any other aspect of these songs. The *Carmina Burana* consist of more than 250 lyrical pieces, most of them composed in medieval Latin, but a considerable number of them also contain Middle High German phrases or are entirely composed in that language. The codex was written somewhere near the Italian language border, probably in Southern Tyrol. Recently scholars have pointed to the Augustinian convent of Neustift near Brixen as a likely location where the songs might have been copied. Linguistic evidence and the fact that Neustift enjoyed a high reputation as a center of book production ("scriptorium") confirm this thesis.

Although a considerable number of songs are of a moral-religious nature, the characteristic features of the *Carmina* are themes of love, drinking, wooing, gambling, and dancing. Despite their often very worldly, erotic nature, many of the best known poets and teachers from that time seem to have composed these songs. Among them we find Walther of Châtillon, Othloh of St. Emmeram, Marbod of Rennes, Geoffrey of Winchester, and Hugo Primas. Others are Hilarius of Orléans, the Archpoet, Philipp the Chancellor, and Peter of Blois. Most of these poets were members of the Church and taught at the universities, but nevertheless seem to have enjoyed this kind of literary entertainment.

The *Carmina Burana* became fully known not until the nineteenth century, when they were translated into many modern languages. In 1937 Carl Orff composed his own music to these *Carmina,* disregarding the extant medieval notations and creating his own, by now famous rhythms and melodies.

BIBLIOGRAPHY

David Parlett, *Selections from the Carmina Burana. A Verse Translation* (Harmondsworth: Penguin, 1986).

Carmina Burana. Ed. Benedikt Konrad Vollmann. Bibliothek des Mittelalters, 13 (Frankfurt a.M.: Deutscher Klassiker Verlag, 1987).

Peter Dronke, *Medieval Latin and the Rise of the European Love-Lyric.* 2 vols. 2nd ed. (Oxford: Oxford University Press, 1968).

Boris Ford, ed., *Medieval Literature: The European Inheritance.* Pt. 2 of Vol. I of *The New Pelican Guide to English Literature* (London: Penguin, 1983).

W. T. H. Jackson, *The Literature of the Middle Ages* (New York: Columbia University Press, 1960).

Olive Sayce, *The Medieval German Lyric 1150–1300* (Oxford: Oxford University Press, 1982).

Olive Sayce, *Plurilingualism in the Carmina Burana. A Study of the Linguisitic and Literary Influences on the Codex* (Göppingen: Kümmerle, 1992).

Tuomas M S Lehtonen: *Fortuna, Money, and the Sublunar World: Twelfth Century Ethical Poetics and the Satirical Poetry of the Carmina Burana* (Helsinki: Finnish Historical Society, 1995).

Composed ca. late 12th Century; copied ca. 1220–1250; final correction ca. 1300

IANUS ANNUM CIRCINAT

1. Janus brings the year full circle,
    spring heralds summer,
    Phoebus strikes his hoof
    as he wends into Taurus
    beyond the confines of Aries.
    Refr. Love conquers all,
    Love penetrates the hardest matter.

2. Away with everything
    sad!
    Sweet
    joys

let the schools of Venus consecrate!
  It's right to make merry
  for all who happen to serve
  in Dione's shrine.
Refr. Love conquers all,
  Love penetrates the hardest matter.

3. Once while a student of Pallas Athena
  I entered the school
of Cytherea, among a host
  of elegant girls
I saw one alone
  with the face
of Helen
and second only
  to Venus,
full of elegance
and rather shy.
Refr. Love conquers all,
Love penetrates the hardest matter.

4. Different from all
  is the one I love in my different way.
A new fire rages in me
  and burns
  unremittingly
No more noble,
  supple,
beautiful or lovable,
no less fickle,
  unpredictable,
foolish girl can be found
  or one that can be trusted less.
  Her happiness
  is my joy.
  If I were worthy of her love,
  it would be a blessing for me
Refr. Love conquers all,
  Love governs all.

5. Spare me, boy, a mere boy!
  Help me, Venus, a raw youth,
  stirring the fire,
  feeding the fire,
to keep it from dying that I might live,

to keep from being Daphne to Phoebus,
to whom I have offered myself!
Once a recruit of Pallas,
  now I yield to your law.
Refr. Love conquers all,
  Love governs all.

IAM VER ORITUR

1. Spring is coming now.
Earth bedecks herself
  with the many flowers of spring.
The harmony of the birds
arouses the heart to joy
  greeting Jove
in modulating tones.
  Among them Philomena
"Tereus" repeats
  and now recounts again
  the ancient story
of her lament.
But though she accuses fate
  of Itys's loss,
  the tuneful
  blackbird
  composes
  its songs.

2. Tragic tales
  of fated
  adversities
are told back and forth
in choral response.
And yet within these councils
our Jupiter sits
  with his Juno,
  Cupid with Dione,
behind them starry Argus,
flowery Narcissus
and lyre-bearing Orpheus,
and also horny Faunus.

3. Among these festivities
  everywhere,

swinging their sides back and forth,
lustily they throw their bodies
  joined together
now rushing apart
now rushing back
in feathery flock:

4. The watery diver,
the bountiful eagle,
the night-wandering owl
 the river-loving swan,
  the phoenix alone,
 the languid plover,
the household swallow,
the pigeon that sounds like a dove,
the crested lapwing,
  the keen goose,
  the greedy vulture,
the yellow-green parrot,
the circling kite
the chattering lark,
the stork with resonant bill.

5. Among them and their like
   equal
   are the joys.
Surely it caresses everything,
this harmonious harmony.

6. Now is the season of joyfulness.
In our time
   the flowers spring forth again
    among the green fields,
   and Phoebus increases
the glory of his things
  throughout our land.

CUPIDO MENTEM GYRAT

1.   Cupid makes the heart spin
    and shakes his spear with menace.
    The west wind blows
    its nectar, swelling the blood

2.   Within the marrow; for women
          in their tender youth it's fine,
          women who are brought up on friendliness
          and simplicity of heart.

3a.   Now I must have the kisses
          she might offer me,
        from her chosen from birth for me,
          she whom Nature beautifies.

3b.   None can please me much after her
          whom I would take,
      and because of you I despise
         even more lovable girls.

4a.   Now all perfumed
     our bed
waits; you've no idea

4b.   How much you are desired,
      but called,
dearest, you do not come.

5a.   Rejoice, royal child,
      you enjoy the best
        that life can bring! Look, the girls
          serving Venus
       have blossomed for you.

5b.   If what I wish comes true—
      that I might enjoy your kiss
      and body in the twilight
        at leisure—
     you will not find me rough.

6a.   Wherever you walk, the light
        of the morning-star precedes you,
        and the lily
   and the rose fade.

6b.   Your teeth shine as ivory
        through your lips
        as if Sirius
were shining there.
7.   If Menalus the prophet
          permitted me to speak

all about girls
   Aetna, the western mountain,
would threaten the Black Sea
   before your honor, my girl,
      would fail to be praised.

8.   So must I sing of love
   upon my rustic lyre.
   May this be the food of love:
   Venus will be the reward,

9.   When Venus calms the storm
    that tears my heart apart.
The arousal that Venus gives
is not to everyone's taste.
But she's entitled to praise from me,
so earning my flawless faith.

10.   Of all girls the stormiest,
    gaze upon me with a calm face,
   be generous to my pleas
    and answer my prayers.

AXE PHEBUS AUREO

1a.   Phoebus brightens the heavens
    with his chariot of gold
and his rays shine
    with rosy splendor.

1b.   Graceful Cybele,
    her face in bloom,
gives to Semele's son
    a flower which Phoebus Apollo smiles upon.

2a.   Aided by the grace
    of gentle airs,
the grove resounds
    with trilling voices of the birds.

2b.   Philomena repeats
    her complaint against Tereus,
and singing with the blackbird
    she harmonizes her song.

40

3a.   Now Dione's
        joyful chorus
zealously echoes   with their songs,

3b.   Now Dione
        with play and grief
eases and torments   the hearts of her train.

4a.   She draws me as well away from sleep
        and urges me on to stand the watch of love.

4b.   The golden darts of Cupid I wield,
        kindling hearts with blazing Fire.

5a.   Whatever I get
        I dread,
    and whatever I'm denied,
        I long for
    with heavy heart.

5b.   Whoever yields to me
        I'm wary of,
    Whoever does not wait on me
        I favor her
    and am in truth

6.   True, whether I die
    or am consoled by her.
    Whoever wants me, her I avoid;
    whoever runs from me, her I want;
    the more I oppose what's right,
    the more I'm drawn to what's wrong;
    the more I enjoy what's wrong to enjoy,
    the more I want what's wrong to have.

7a.   O decrees of Dione
that must be feared!
    O secret poison
that must not be taken,
    fearfully treacherous
and full of guile!

7b.   Taught to chasten
in passion's heat
       all whom she forces
to suffer love's gall,

so full she is of spite
and burning anger.

8a.   So my fear
      abounds,
  so tears
      flood my face.

8b.   So my face
      pales,
  for I'm a fool
      of love.

GRATES AGO VENERI

1a.   I give thanks to Venus
      who smiled on me
  with favorable authority
      concerning my
      girl whom she
      conferred on me
      as a welcome and desired prize.

1b.   For a long time I campaigned
      unable
  to enjoy what I had earned;
      now I feel
      blest,
      cheered
      by Dione's face.

2a.   Smile, talk,
      touch, kiss
my girl has given to enjoy.
      All that's missing
is the last
    and best
      degree of love.
This, unless I move too fast,
    is
what remains, given
    as grist
      to my lust.

2b.   I hasten to my goal.
        But with tender tears
my girl leads me on,
        yet hesitates
to slip aside the virginal
        bars
          of modesty.
I drink the sweet tears
        she sheds;
and so the drunker I get
        the more I thirst
          with lust.

3a.   The more I savor
        her kisses anointed with tears,
        the more they entice my heart
        with inward charms.
        So I am seized the more,
          and still more keenly the flame's
        force grows hot again.
        Still Coronis's grief
          in heaving sighs
        grows
            nor is it soothed
             by prayer.

3b.   Prayer on prayer I pile up
and kiss after kiss;
tears she adds to tears,
reproach upon reproach,
and now with hostile eye
        she fixes me
as one who would seek my pity now;
for now she puts up a fight,
        now she entreats;
and while I urge her on with prayers,
        she grows deaf
          to every word.

4a.   Boldly I attack with more than needed force.
She goes wild with sharp claws,
          she yanks my hair
          she does her best
            to beat me back,
          she folds herself up

and crosses
    her knees,
  to keep the gate
  of modesty from giving way.

4b.   But at last I gain the field
and victory follows my plan.
      With embraces
        I secure the bonds,
          her arms
          I bind,
        I hold her down
          with a kiss;
        thus the realm
  of Dione is unlocked.

5a.   The whole thing pleased us both
and my beloved, tamer now,
charged me less,
      giving kisses
        laced with honey,

5b.   And smiling up at me with tremulous,
  half-closed eyes,
  as one falling asleep beneath
      a troubled
        sigh.

OMITTAMUS STUDIA

1.   Let's abandon studies,
      it's sweet to play the fool
      let us take the best of life
        while we are young and innocent.
    It's best for age
      to ponder serious things,
[. . .]
Refr. Life passes swiftly
      when occupied by study,
    to play is what
      our tender youth suggests.

2.   The spring of life slips away,

our winter hastens on,
life suffers harm,
 care eats up the flesh.
 The blood dries, the heart grows dull,
  joys grow less and less,
 age now frightens us
 and all its tribe of ills.
Refr. Life passes swiftly
 when occupied by study,
 to play is what
 our tender youth suggests.

3.   "Let's act like the gods!"
 is a worthy saying,
 and now the nets of love
 hunt an innocent affair.
 Let us keep our vow!
  That is the way of the gods.
 Let's run down to the squares
  where the girls are dancing in a ring!
Refr. Life passes swiftly
 when occupied by study,
 to play is what
 our tender youth suggests.

SI LINGUIS ANGELICIS LOQUAR ET HUMANIS

1. If I should speak with the tongues of men and angels,
 it would not be enough to tell of my great prize
 by which I'm rightly raised above all who share my faith,
 as well as those who envy me, grudging men of wicked ways.

2. Celebrate in song, my tongue, the causes, then, and deeds!
 But keep my Lady's name well disguised
 so that to the people it might not be revealed
 which is a secret to the nations and remains hidden away.

3. In a flowery, pleasant grove I stood,
 thinking to myself: "What shall I do?
 I am unsure whether I sow my seed upon sand,
 loving the flower of the world: that's how desperate I am.

4. If I despair, no one truly ought to be surprised;
 for the rose is guarded by some old crone—

neither may she love nor may she be loved in return.
O Pluto, I entreat, deign to carry off the creature!"

5. While I was considering what I just said,
   desiring that he seize the hag with a thunderbolt,
   behold, looking back upon the meadow left behind,
   hear what I saw while I lingered thus.

6. I saw the blossoming flower, I saw the flower of flowers,
   I saw the rose of May more beautiful than all,
   I saw the radiant star brighter than all,
   for whom I have lived once fallen in love.

7. Thus when I saw the creature I've always loved,
   without the help of words I exulted within myself,
   and quickly leaping up I ran towards her,
   and genuflecting greeted her:

8. "Hail most beautiful, precious jewel,
   hail, grace of virgins, virgin glorious,
   hail, light of lights, hail rose of the world,
   Blancheflor and Helen, noble Venus!"

9. Thus she answered, this star of morning, saying:
   "He, Who all things earthly rules and things divine,
   scattering violets in the grass and roses on the thorn,
   may He be your grace, your fame and health."

10. To whom I said: "Sweetest, my heart affirms
    what my soul conveys: through you salvation lies.
    For I have learned from someone, as it's said,
    that he who wounds provides the better cure."

11. "Thus, the arms I bear cause such wounds—
    is this what you say? No, I say, but, complaints aside,
    the wound and the wound's cause, now reveal,
    that I might heal you afterwards with some sort of cure!"

12. "Why shall I hide my wounds which are obvious enough?
    Five summers have passed, the sixth hastens on,
    that I saw you dancing—it was a holiday—
    you who were to all a window and a mirror.

13. "And thus while I looked, I then began to be amazed
    and said: 'That's a woman worthy of devotion!
    She surpasses every virgin, she's without peer,
    her shape is perfect, her looks resplendent!'

14. "Your face was splendid, a plain delight,
as brilliant air glistening and serene.
How often I said: 'God, my God!
Would this be Helen or holy Venus?

15. "'Wonderfully golden her hair flowed down,
as a rise of snow her neck brightly shone,
her breasts were small, hinting to all
how sweet was the odor there, better than all perfume.

16. "'And in her charming face twin stars glowed,
the substance of ivory her teeth surpassed,
her limbs embrace beauty's bloom, more than I can say:
could it be she who binds as one the soul of all?'

17. "Then your dazzling shape bound me in chains;
it changed my mind my soul and heart.
To speak with you, then and there, was what my spirit hoped,
but never did it have the hope that this would ever be.

18. "So my soul is deeply wounded.
My life, as you can see, is profoundly cursed.
Who, I ask you, who could ever harm another so,
that he would hope and of his hope be cheated?

19. "Forever a dart within my breast I've carried enclosed.
Twice a thousand times since then I've sighed,
saying: 'Maker of all, how have I sinned against You?
Of all lovers I have borne heavy burdens.

20. "'Drink does not help me, nor food, nor sleep:
a remedy I cannot find against my ills.
O Christ, do not decree that so I die,
but deign to succor me, a worthy wretch.'

21. "These harms I've endured and many more in number,
and no solace shields me from my pain,
no matter how often in the gloomy nights
I am with you in fancied shapes.

22. "Rose, now that you see how wounded I am,
how much I have deeply borne, crucified for you,
say 'I am content!' Do this that I be cured,
that I be saved through you, restored to life again!

23. "If in fact you will do this, in you I shall he honored,
as the flowering cedar of Lebanon, I shall be praised,

but if, which I do not fear, I am betrayed by you,
I shall be wrecked and put in peril of life."

24. The shining rose spoke: "You have raised many things;
you have revealed to me things I know quite well,
But if things I've borne for you you've never dreamt;
the things I've borne are more than those that you have recited.

25. "But I omit a recital of them all,
wishing to get such satisfaction
as holds the promise of joy and healing
and offers a cure sweeter than honey.

26. "Tell me, then, young friend, what you have in mind!
Is it money you require by which you might be rich,
or a precious gem with which you might adorn yourself?
For if it's possible, I'll give whatever you want."

27. "That's not what I want, neither gems nor silver;
giving them to someone else would be better nurture—
giving easy resolution to impossible affairs—
and which confers upon the gloomy a bright joy."

28. "Whatever it is you want I can't divine,
yet with your prayers I want to come to terms.
Thus whatever I have, look it over carefully,
and take it if you can find what you want!"

29. What more was needed? I threw my arms around her neck,
I kissed the girl a thousand times and got a thousand more,
and over and over I said with certainty:
"Truly, truly this is what I was panting for!"

30. Who does not know what happened next?
Grief and sighs are driven far away,
the joys of paradise come over us
and all delights are furnished at once.

31. Now my embrace is joy a hundred-fold,
now for my Lady and me, what we longed for thrives,
now the lovers' prize is borne by me,
now therefore is my name raised on high.

32. Whoever loves, keep me thus ever in mind
and don't despair instantly, although you may be full of bitterness!
Surely for you some day will come
when praise for pains will finally be achieved.

33. Surely from gall grace is born,
    and only with labor are great things accomplished,
    those who desire sweet honey are often goaded on.
    May they hope for better, those who deeply suffer.

EXIIT DILUCULO

1. There was a country maid
       going forth at dawn.
   She had a flock and crook
       and fleece all new.

2. There are in the little flock
       a sheep and an ass's foal,
   a heifer and a calf,
       a billy and a nanny-goat.

3. She saw upon the grass
       a youthful scholar sit:
   "What are you doing, my lord?
       Come, and play with me."

ANNI PARTE FLORIDA, CELO PURIORE

1. When the flowers are first in bloom, and the skies are clear,
   when the earth's broad fields are painted in various hues,
   when the herald of the dawn has put the stars to flight,
   sleep departs from the eyes of Phyllis and of Flora.

2. What the girls decide to do is to take a little walk,
   for hearts that have been sorely wounded are quick to spurn sleep;
   thus with steps of equal pace, they go out to the fields
   where the place itself makes the game a joy to play.

3. Both go, each a girl and each noble besides,
   Phyllis with her hair unbound and Flora neatly combed.
   They do not seem girls so much as goddesses divine,
   and each face reflects the splendor of the morning light.

4. In race and face and dress they are of noble stock,
   both are young in spirit and in years;
   but they are a little unlike and, to a certain extent, enemies,
   for one loves a cleric deeply, the other loves a knight.

5. Nor is there any difference in how they look and speak,
   They are the same in all respects both inside and out,
   the same disposition and character they have;
   the one difference they have is how they choose to love.

6. A somewhat timely wind began to blow,
   pleasant was the place they walked with grasses green and gay,
   and in this grassy place there was a stream that rippled past,
   a stream full of life that gurgled and murmured playfully.

7. Increasing the beauty of the place and helping against the heat
   a large and spacious pine stood beside the rivulet,
   it was a charming bower, casting shade far and wide,
   the erring of the heat could never enter there.

8. The girls sat down beneath it, the grass providing seats.
   Phyllis sat beside the Stream, Flora farther on.
   And while each sat where she wished, getting control of themselves,
   Love struck them in their hearts and wounded them both.

9. Love is somewhere deep within, hidden and occult,
   and from the heart it summons forth most assured sighs;
   their cheeks grow pale, their faces change color,
   but buried deep in modesty there lies a raging storm.

10. The moment Flora sighs Phyllis discovers it,
    and Flora catches Phyllis doing the same thing;
    each pays the other in kind, balancing their sighs
    until each reveals her sickness, and bears her wounds.

11. This discussion then takes place, going on at length,
    assuredly its burden is all about love;
    love is in their souls, love is in their mouths.
    Finally Phyllis speaks, smiling at Flora.

12. "Paris," she says, "my love and famous knight!
    Where do the wars take you now and where are you stationed now?
    O the military life, there's no life like it,
    worthy alone of the joy that dwells where Venus dwells."

13. While the girl casts her mind upon her knightly friend,
    Flora laughing looks at her askance,
    and Flora speaks, laughter falling through her hostile words:
    "You love," she says, "and you could even say it: he's a beggar.

14. "But what does he do, Alcibiades? the one I love,
    a creature worthier than any living thing

whom Nature has blessed with all her gifts and grace?
O solely happy they who live the cleric's life and rule!"

15. Phyllis then accused her friend of using harsh words
and spoke to Flora her speech gone wild,
saying: "Behold the little girl pure in heart,
whose noble heart has now become Epicurus's slave!

16. "Arise, arise, wretched girl, from this foul rage!
I believe a cleric is only an Epicurean;
nor can I concede that clerics have any elegance,
their hips are heavy and full of fat.

17. "A cleric's heart is far away from Cupid's war and strife:
his only need is sleep and lots to eat and drink.
O high and noble girl, everyone knows
the oath the knight takes is far from a cleric's vow.

18. "The knight knows how to get along with bare necessities,
he does not live intent upon food and drink and sleep;
Love prevents him from falling asleep on watch,
food and drink for knights are love and youthful character.

19. "Who would ever yoke our friends beneath a common rein?
Would law or Nature allow these two to be yoked together?
Mine knows how to play at love; yours,to be a glutton;
mine knows how to give what is his; yours, to take."

20. Flora's modest face grows pale,
and she appears lovelier, as she laughs again;
and eloquence opens at last the gates of Flora's speech,
whatever she conceived with skill within her clever heart.

21. "Enough,"she says, "you've spoken, Phyllis, very freely,
your rhetoric is very sharp and shrill;
and you do not reach the goal of truth
to overcome the lily with the hemlock of your words.

22. "Of the cleric you have said that he is self-indulgent,
you say that he's the servant of his food and drink and sleep.
Thus envy usually describes the honest life.
But now look out, wait a little, as I reply to you.

23. "My friends are such, I must confess, and to such a degree
that never do they give a thought to what others own.
Honeycombs, oil, grain, and vineyards full of wine,
jewels, gold, and drinking-cups all serve him well.

24. "In such sweet plenty rests the cleric's life
    that no word can describe it in any way;
    Love flies and applauds, beating his pair of wings together,
    Love whose bounty never fails, Love who never fails.

25. "The cleric feels the darts of Venus and the blows of Love,
    yet he's never faint with hunger nor is his torment hard;
    for never is he derelict whenever joy invites,
    and the heart of his Lady is faithfully in accord with his.

26. "Gaunt with hunger, pallid too, is your chosen one,
    poor he is and barely covered in a ragged cloak,
    nor is his body strong enough, nor his sturdy chest;
    for when cause fails, then effect gives way.

27. "Poverty is filthiness, a threat to any lover.
    What will the knight be able to offer to his bride to be?
    The cleric, on the other hand, gives and gives abundantly;
    copious his riches are, and what he gives the same."

28. Phyllis snaps at Flora so: "Familiar you are
    with how they pass their lives and what pursuits are theirs,
    quite probably you've thought the matter through, and nicely too,
    but our debate will not rest so.

29. "When a time for holiday makes the world glad,
    then the cleric shows himself a wholly phoney man,
    with his head neatly tonsured, wearing a black habit,
    bearing witness of pleasure tinged with gloom.

30. "He's nothing but a simpleton or blind, then, to boot
    who does not see how splendid is the life the soldier leads.
    Yours wallows in ease as any beast.
    Mine sports his polished gear and rides a horse.

31. "Mine in arms puts to rout the mount he's matched against,
    and if it happens that he fights dismounted and alone,
    while his Ganymedes holds Bucephalus aside,
    my hero thinks ever of me, cutting heroes down.

32. "Enemies overthrown, the battle done, mine returns,
    and often with his vizor up, he gazes back at me.
    On these grounds and others too, its absolutely true,
    the soldier's life must surely be the best for me."

33. Flora observed the anger and heaving breast Phyllis has
    and fired back against her then missiles of many kinds

"In vain," she said, "you speak, your words dissolve into air,
and strive to force a camel through a needle's eye.

34. "You forsake honey for gall and truth for falsity,
when you approve the knightly life, reproving all clerics.
Say, does Love make the knight vigorous and fierce?
No, it is indeed poverty and want and need!

35. "Lovely Phyllis, O if only you would love wisely,
you would not loudly challenge truthful judgements!
Thirst and hunger, these are what subdue this knight of yours,
by which he is urged on the road to death and hell.

36. "How much misfortune he endures, wearing him down,
and heavy is the fate that dwells in every joint and limb,
his life is ever in doubt, swaying like a pendulum,
merely surviving to live upon bare necessities.

37. "You would not call it a disgrace, if you knew his life,
the black habit that he wears, his hair shorn close:
the cleric has each of these for high glory's sake,
that he might show himself greater than us all.

38. "Clearly the world lies at the cleric's feet
and in his tonsure he bears the sign of authority.
Knights stand beneath his rule, and he is generous with gifts:
greater than the servant is the one who governs.

39. "You contend the cleric always leads an easy life:
I must confess that he disdains hard and dirty work;
but when his soul ascends to care for things with diligence,
it scans the motions of the skies and seeks the core of things.

40. "Mine wears a purple robe; yours, a coat of mail.
Yours rides to battle, mine's ensconced in easy chairs;
when yours reads once again the ancient feats of kings,
mine writes and seeks and cogitates all about his girl.

41. "In what manner Dione provides, and Cupid too,
my cleric was the first to know and first to teach;
the knight became Cytherean through the cleric's work.
You stand accused by what you've said, and also how you've said it."

42. Flora now gives up the fight and also gives up speaking;
she requests that Cupid take up the case himself.
Phyllis first protests, but then concedes,
and having settled on the judge, they return through the grass.

43. Now the contest rests wholly with the god of love.
    They say the judgement that he gives is true and accurate
    because he knows how knight and cleric each lead their lives;
    and now they both prepare themselves to go and hear him speak.

44. Both girls look alike, their modesty the same,
    both their prayers are the same, their aspects equal too:
    Phyllis' dress is colored white, Flora's has two colors,
    a mule conveyed Phyllis, while Flora rode a horse.

45. The mule indeed that Phyllis rode was once a mule
    that Neptune made and nourished, and finally tamed.
    After the fury of the boar, after Adonis died,
    it was sent to Venus, a gift of solace for her love.

46. At length Venus gave it away and gave it to
    Phyllis's mother, a lovely, upright Spanish lady,
    for she had once assisted Venus in some divine service;
    and now Phyllis owns him as a happy result.

47. The mule made a perfect match for the lovely girl:
    it was handsome, easy to ride, its height exactly right,
    and such it should have been, who came from such a distance,
    whom Neptune sent long ago to Venus far away.

48. Let those who ask about the bridle and about the bit,
    which the mule ground its teeth on are trappings made of silver,
    let them know that all these things were such
    as any gift that Neptune gives, the kind that comes from gods.

49. This was Phyllis's moment, her beauty lacked nothing then,
    she came into sight richly clothed and very beautiful,
    nor was Flora any less adorned in either respect,
    for she held the reins of a splendid horse.

50. This horse, broken by the whips of Pegasus,
    possesses great beauty and great valor too.
    He is a horse of many colors splashed artfully here and there,
    for mixed against the black he has the color of a swan.

51. He was a horse of proper form and still in early life,
    he was somewhat haughty but not fierce,
    he held his neck aloft, and his mane was well brushed;
    his ears tiny, his chest broad, his head somewhat small.

52. His back lay curved and ready for the girl to take her seat,
    a back which never yet had felt any weight.

His hollow hoof, his straight bones, his large and sturdy shank
all composed a steed that was a perfect paragon of nature.

53. Placed upon the horse's back the saddle shone,
for the buckle of the girth was clasped with gold and ivory;
and when four raised corners, were placed upon the saddle,
each was graced by one precious stone bright as a star.

54. Many tales of olden days and now known no more
there were inscribed in marvelous markings;
when Mercury wed Philology witnessed by the gods—
the troths they pledged, the marriage and multitude of gifts.

55. There was no place upon the saddle plain, untouched by art;
more it contained than what the human soul might conceive.
Vulcan alone made those engravings, and when he looked,
he scarcely could believe his hands could do so much.

56. Vulcan laid aside his work on Achilles's shield
to put his breast-plate into shape with all his loving care;
he made the horseshoes for his feet, the bridle for his jaws,
then he made the reins from strands of his dear wife's hair.

57. A cloth lay upon the saddle, embroidered with purple linen,
which Minerva, laying all her other work aside,
wove from acanthus and narcissus when in flower
to make a ribboned fringe along the edge, cutting the hem.

58. The steeds of the maidens flew along at equal pace,
their faces fully of modesty, their cheeks soft and young.
Thus lilies appear in spring and roses new,
thus they rode at equal pace, these two heavenly stars.

59. To go to Love's paradise, this was their firm resolve
Sweet was the wrath that animated each girl's face;
Phyllis threw a laugh at Flora, Flora laughed at Phyllis.
A falcon perched on Phyllis's wrist; a sparrow-hawk on Flora's.

60. After a short space of time, they found the grove.
At the entrance of the wood, a stream murmured by,
there the wind was redolent of myrrh and sweet spice.
timbrels could be heard and a hundred citherns playing.

61. Whatever sound there is that human hearts can perceive,
there the girls hear them all and all at once:
the differences in pitch are all found there,
there the fourth resounds and there the fifth resounds as well.

62. The air is filled with throbs and sounds and wondrous harmony,
    of timbrel, psaltery, lyre and bagpipe,
    there the ringing glass resounds with strong and faithful voice,
    and box-wood pipe, the song coming forth from its several holes.

63. All the birds sing their several songs in full voice:
    the blackbird's song is heard, a sweet and pleasant song,
    the jackdaw and the lark are heard, and Philomena's song,
    which never ceases to complain of all the grief it has borne.

64. From the instrumental music, the voices raised in song,
    then from all the kinds of flowers that they gaze upon,
    and then from the graceful odor whose perfume pervades the air
    it can be guessed that here the couch of tender Love is spread.

65. The maidens enter Love's grove somewhat fearfully;
    the farther in the maidens go, the more they grow in love.
    Whatever songs the birds sing in their several tongues,
    their hearts are soon afire from all the kinds of sounds.

66. Any mortal remaining there soon becomes a god.
    Any tree that grows there rejoices in its fruit,
    balsam, cinnamon and myrrh smell along the paths;
    the lord himself may readily be guessed from where he lives.

67. They see a chorus of young men and damsels singing there,
    the bodies of them all splendid as stars.
    And on the spot the maidens' hearts are seized
    by such a wonderful display of novelties to see.

68. Their horses stop side by side, and they dismount, almost
    made forgetful of their purpose by the sound of singing,
    but once again the complaint of Philomena is heard
    and straightway the maidens' hearts are heated up again.

69. Near the middle of the grove there is a secret place,
    for there the service of the god is cultivated strongly:
    Fauns and Nymphs and Satyrs too, all their several clans,
    strike their cymbals, and sing harmoniously in the presence of the god.

70. They carry in their hands vine-leaves and flowered crowns;
    Bacchus instructs the Nymphs and choruses of Fauns to dance.
    The instruments and all who dance keep a perfect measure
    except the god Silenus who doesn't play but reels.

71. Almost dropping off to sleep, he bumps into an ass
    and the god's breast bursts into gales of laughter.

He cries aloud for wine, and what he wants is barely heard:
wine and old age obstruct the passage of his voice.

72. Amid all this, the Cytherean boy is finally seen:
his face is shining like the stars, his upper back bears wings,
his left hand holds his bow, and at his side are his arrows:
it can be inferred that he is powerful and noble.

73. The boy leans upon his scepter, entwined with flowers,
and the odor of nectar wafts from his tidy hair.
At his side the three Graces stand, their fingers joined,
profering the cup of Love on bended knee.

74. The maidens draw near the god, permitted to adore
the god who is invested with all the venerable marks of youth;
they pay homage to all the force of divine will.
The god looks at the girls, greeting them before they speak.

75. He asks the reason for the journey. The case is put,
and when he's heard them both, he praises the burdens they've borne.
Then he speaks to each and says: "Wait a bit,
until the judge pronounces on this unresolved case!"

76. Clearly he was divine; the maidens knew he was a god,
nor did they find it necessary to reexamine the case in detail.
They dismounted from their horses, and, tired, took their rest.
Love ordered his followers to make a clear judgement.

77. Love has judges, Love has laws that all who love must keep;
the judges the god retains are called Custom and Nature;
any judgement made in Love's court is theirs to make
since they know all that was and is to be.

78. They withdraw to try the force of justice,
and air the merits of the case according to the court
in accord with his knowledge and also his way of life,
they pronounce a cleric's love a much better love.

79. The court confirmed and gave support to what the judges said
and then declared it to be law in any future case.
Therefore little do they guard against what harm may befall them,
girls who follow a knight and claim he is a better man.

FERVET AMORE PARIS, TROIANIS IMMOLAT ARIS

1. Paris is hotly in love, makes sacrifices at the Trojan altars,
   And without his brothers' knowledge sails across the sea.

2. He excites Tyndareus's daughter, who indulges him, deserts Atreus' son,
   And readily follows Paris, letting fidelity die.

3. The ravisher ploughs the seas, and keeps the object of his affection;
   The affair is made public, and Greece prepares for war.

4. The affair rouses Diomedes's anger against the Dardanian,
   And Athena urges Achilles likewise to the attack.

5. Argos is emptied, a fleet assembles, the sea is becalmed,
   Sacrifice is offered, and a favoring breeze is given.

6. The clash of the strait is met, the anchor grasps Phrygian shore.
   Hector, rapidly armed, holds up the invasion.

7. Ilium takes to arms, Helen's Greece is in quest for Helen,
   Trickery renders access, and enemy lays enemy low.

8. Alarmed by the cloud of spears sent by the Danaan youth,
   The city of Hecuba rages, and trumpets blare and resound.

9. The soldiery roars to arms, deceit deprives Hector of life,
   The city is under siege, Troy trembles before the foe.

10. Had the Danaans lacked the advantages of craft and deity's aid,
    The wall would still be standing, lacking only a king.

11. Craft is sought, a horse is built, and Greece hides in its belly;
    Priam is hoodwinked, and the beast is brought within.

12. Sinon entreats in tears, Odysseus works at deceiving,
    Fire devours the city, contrivance breaches the barricades.

13. Gullible to intrigue, subjected to hungering fire,
    Done in by Odysseus's tricks, Troy becomes food for the torch.

14. Craft betrays the city, the city walks into peril,
    Gluttonous flame shaves Pergamum bare: Troy falls.

15. The wealth of the mangled city provided food for fires,
    The flames put an end to walls, to barricades and bolts.

16. Despised by the Argives, Ilium dies, formerly happy,
    Renowned, and beautiful; the rose is now a bramble-bush.

17. Surviving the fire, Troy, begotten by you, Cytherea,
    Depending on its strong fleet, flees, ready to suffer all.

18. The destined land is sought in flying ships,
    Which meet the angry plague, the evil and fury of the sea.

19. The sea stirred up the plague, the waves began to rise,
    The foam stole over the ships, the wind roared.

20. The mad south wind blows, the unholy whirlwind gathers force,
    The Trojan sailor relies on his hands.

21. Here it is as though the sea's mad anger is armed;
    Dreadful death is near, there is no music here.

22. Having endured the storm in the turn of fateful events,
    Aeneas heads for desired realms, relying on navigation.

23. He looks for peace but the dreadful struggle fatigues him,
    And madness holds sway and a new battle ties him up.

24. In battle he plunders, he rages against Turnus and wins,
    His sword-point, sated with blood, digs into entrails.

25. Atoning for crime undertaken, confess yourself, Turnus, defeated;
    Eclipsed, you die by the sword and are prey and food for the beasts.

26. Victory comes to Aeneas, the battle is ended,
    Glory succeeds the battle, and peace returns.

27. Under the bond of trust, following his famed achievements,
    The princess a maiden favored by god, is wedded to him.

EIA DOLOR!

I.

1a.   Eia sadness!
      Now I comfort myself
      like the
   white swan dying.
      Abject, I grieve,
      despised, I die,
      cut off, I pine.

1b.   Venus burns
      in my heart, she
      whom neither the Rhine
nor the mighty Euphrates
      can extinguish
      Only she can save
      or destroy me.

2a.   Why, livid Envy,
born of the Stygian night,
babbling with impious tongue,
do you confound my joys,
bolting shut doors that once
were opened to me,
    denying to one man,
    me, one woman, the dark
     Florula,
    neither pallid
    nor marked by a
     blemish,
    rivalling a chaste
    flower and the dew
     of heaven,
    a golden vessel,
    a wand
     of spices?

2b.   Maiden, the equal of Helen,
look favorably on your Paris!
Rose of the flowering meadow,
show no resistance to Venus!
Filled with troubled grief
from the bite of envious teeth,
    Venus burns,
Amor rages against
[. . .]
    one accustomed,
and seizes for himself
your devoted
    servant.
I yield to you,
I bend my knee
    to you.

3a.   Have pity on a suppliant!
In the role of a healer
    soothe the fevered,
    acquit the accused,
    loosen one who is bound
by a double chain!

3b.   The Muse is pleased
to be refreshed with trifles

of rhythmic song;
hoarsely she pleads
that the singer be restored
to his Eurydice!

II.

1a.   Splendor of life!
I lust in my heart
for you, blinded
by the beam of your sun,
kindled by your
radiant face, I burn
as though I die.

1b.   May you wish to end
your spear-throwing!
Then in the heavens
I would assume Jove's throne,
wiser than Plato,
stronger than Samson,
richer than Augustus!

2.   Maiden, the equal of Helen,
look favorably on your Paris!
Rose of the flowering meadow,
show no resistance to Venus!
Filled with troubled grief
from the bite of envious teeth,
Venus burns,
Amor rages against

[. . .]

one accustomed,
and seizes for himself
your devoted
servant.
I yield to you,
I bend my knee
to you.

3a.   With my wound healed
by your grace,
may life return,
may the fire die
which would consume us
with unbridled love!

3b.   Having learned to make love
   in a partnership,
     bathe my wound,
     lovely maid,
     do not set me under
the weight of death!

III.

1a.   The force of love
   is within me; on the outside
   it harasses me
with the whips of its madness.
   O golden Venus!
     you are a harsh goddess,
     with your flaming torch

1b.   You burn me up.
   Why do you rage?
   Why have you wounded
me with your bitter javelins?
   I am destroyed by love's fire;
   death is better for me
   than more of this life!

2.   I burn incessantly
   bound in a fiery clasp.
   I strive with every effort
   to drink the water of
   love from Venus's well,
   but I do not succeed.
     Corinna, worthy
   of Jove, has
     entwined me,
   has subdued me
   with her halters
     and bridles.
   May she who has
   conquered and tightly
     constrained me,
   relieve me somewhat
   of the force of fires
     very soon!

3a.   My head aches,
   my heart pounds,

62

       burns, breaks,
       shakes, and quakes
[…]
       under your Venus.

3b.   Why am I driven?
     Why am I racked?
      Help one who prays,
      spare one who pleads
      after weeping for a long
     time in your prison!

VIRENT PRATA HIEMATA

1. Freed of winter's fury
    the meadows grow green
and, given to a world of flowers,
    smile with beauteous face.
    With the sun's ray
they gleam, they beam, they blush, they glow,
they spread the power of the rites of spring
    in various forms of birth.

2. Chattering birds break into
    sweet melody
with holy voice, and they fly
    everywhere busily;
    and within the grove
are budding flowers, scents, and
fronds; all that is young is at
    this time in heat.

3. A crowd of young men collects
    and grows in size;
a chorus of maidens gathers
    together and unites;
    and under the linden
a mother leaps into the dances
of Venus, in the midst of which
    her daughter is.

4. There is one woman whom,
    as luck would have it, I adore;
as bright as the unclouded moon,

she wounds me and
my sighs are all for her.
Desirable, artless, shapely,
she had assailed my heart
and drives out its sadness.

5. When I see her I think that she
is something out of heaven.
I am disregarding everything until
I have lain with her alone in love.
I want her bound
and fastened by my arms
when I have got into
her happy private place.

TEMPUS TRANSIT GELIDUM

1. The freezing season passes away,
the world is renewed,
and flowing spring returns;
nature takes on beauty.
The bird trills
and, trilling, is made happy
[. . .]
a clearer
and milder
air now becomes serene;
in flower
and in leaf
the forest foliage thickens.

2. Maidens frolic graciously
upon the grassy land;
new songs issue melodiously
from their pretty lips.
Birds show their approval
with singing of their own;
the flower-painted earth
gives off propitious scent.
And so the heart
is bound
and touched by love,
as virgins

64

    and birds
    are resonant in voice.

3. The boy with arrows now
        is spreading his nets;
    to him whose mastery
        has gone too far
        the gods' assembly
        tenders slavery;
        having won with Cupid's help,
        I've also suffered wounds:
        I had fought
        and at first
    I had prevailed,
        but again
        Cupid threw
    me prostrate before Venus.

4. I loved one woman, who seriously
        wounded me;
    I bound her to myself
        in steadfast covenant.
        I never breached
        the faith I vowed;
        I dedicated my whole being
        to such a sweet affair.
            How luscious
            your kisses are,
        sweetheart! I've tasted them
            and neither cinnamon
            nor balsamed
        honey would be so sweet!

VIRGO QUEDAM NOBILIS, DIV GIE ZE HOLCE UMBE RÎS

1. A certain noble virgin
        went to the woods to gather twigs.
        And, as she tied her bundle up,
    Refr.   Heia, heia, how she sang!
        Cicha, cicha, how she sang!
            The bands,
            the bands,

    she broke the bands.

2. A certain young man came along,
    handsome and very likable,
    and he untied her bodice.
Refr.   *Heia, heia, how she sang!*
        Cicha, chica, how she sang!
            The bands,
            the bands,
        he broke the bands.

3. *He grasped her by the white hand,*
    he took her into Birdsongland.
[. . .]
Refr.   *Heia, heia, how she sang!*
        Cicha, cicha, how she sang!
            The bands,
            the bands,
        he broke the bands.

4. A Swabian north wind came along
    and tossed her in the bushes
    and tossed her in the woods.
Refr.   *Heia, heia, how she sang!*
        Cicha, cicha, how she sang!
            The bands,
            the bands,
        it broke the bands.

ICH WAS EIN CHINT SO WOLGETAN

1. *I was such an attractive child*
        while I bloomed as a virgin,
    all the world praised me,
        I was pleasing to everybody.
Refr.   *Hoy and oe!*
        shame upon the linden trees
        that stand beside the road!

2. *I wanted to go out to the meadow*
        to gather flowers,
    and there was a scoundrel wanted to
        deflower me.
Refr.   *Hoy and oe!*

shame upon the linden trees
that stand beside the road!

3.   *He took me by my pale white hand*
      but not improperly,
   he led me to the meadow's edge
      quite deceitfully.
Refr.   *Hoy and oe!*
   shame upon the linden trees
   that stand beside the road!

4.   *He laid his hands on my white dress*
      quite improperly,
   and pulled me forward by the hand
      very forcefully.
Refr.   *Hoy and oe!*
   shame upon the linden trees
   that stand beside the road!

5.   *He said "Lady, let's get going!*
      the grove's a good way off."
   Cursed be that way to me!
      I wept, but that was all.
Refr.   *Hoy and oe!*
   shame upon the linden trees
   that stand beside the road!

6.   *There was a stately linden tree*
      not far from the road.
   That's where I had left my harp,
      and with my harp my tambour.
Refr.   *Hoy and oe!*
   shame upon the linden trees
   that stand beside the road!

7.   *When he reached the linden tree*
      he said "Let's sit down,"
   —love made him quite restless—
      "let's play a game!"
Refr.   *Hoy and oe!*
   shame upon the linden trees
   that stand beside the road!

8.   *He laid his hands on my white flesh,*
      not without timidity;
   he said, "I'll make a woman of you;

you have a lovely mouth!"
Refr.   *Hoy and oe!*
          shame upon the linden trees
          that stand beside the road!

9. *He removed my underthings,*
      my body was exposed,
    he broke into my little door
      with his upright lance.
Refr.   *Hoy and oe!*
          shame upon the linden trees
          that stand beside the road!

10. *He took his quiver and his bow,*
       the hunting went quite well!
    The hunter had betrayed me.
       "Let the game be ended!"
Refr.   *Hoy and oe!*
          shame upon the linden trees
          that stand beside the road!

SUSCIPE, FLOS, FLOREM, QUIA FLOS DESIGNAT AMOREM

I. Flower, pluck my flower, because a flower stands for love!
    By that flower I am quite caught up in love.
    Smell this flower, sweetest Flora, ever fragrant!
    Let your loveliness become as beauteous as the dawn.
    Look upon the flower, Flora! When you see it, smile at me!
    Speak kindly to the flower !Your voice is the song of the nightingale.
    Give kisses to the flower! A flower suits a rose-red mouth.

II. A flower in a picture is not a flower, just a figure;
    whoever paints a flower, paints not the fragrance of a flower.

SECTION 3

Selections from LYRICS OF THE MIDDLE AGES; CARMINA BURANA (*Continuation*)

ESTUANS INTRINSECUS IRA VEHEMENTI[1]

1. As my inner self's on fire
        With a raging flame,
    In a blaze of bitter ire
        I address my brain:
    Manufactured out of matter,
        Air my element—
    I'm a bough the breezes batter
        With a playful bent.

2. Wise men who heed imprecations
        When their reason talks
    Carefully place their foundations
        On the mighty Rock.
    Idiot me! Shall you compare me
        To the river's run?
    A path pursued will never bear me
        Back where I've begun.

3. No, I'm swept on ocean foam
        Skipperless and drifting,
    A bird that flies skyways alone,
        Flitting, ever shifting.
    Chains will never fetter fast,

---

1. Confessions of Golias. Continues for about 14 stanzas as the speaker runs through his sins in a rather exhaustive way. Attributed to a certain Archpoet (*ca.* 1130–1167), an otherwise unknown German who was a friend of Rainald of Dassel, the Archbishop of Cologne. Ed. Schmeller, No. 172.

Locks not last long whiles.
I hunt friends of my own cast
    And bind me to—the vile!

4.   Affairs high-serious belabor
        Hearts, too little funny.
    I love jokes; to me their savor's
        Sweeter far than honey.
    Labor bearing Venus' stamp
        Seems suavely empowered;
    She has never pitched her camp
        In the breasts of cowards.

5.   Down life's open road meandering
        In the guise of youth,
    Ever given to philandering,
        Never shriven to truth,
    Greedy to try all lustful fare
        More than health to win—
    Dead in soul, O God! my care
        Is only for my skin! . . .

OLIM LACUS COLUERAM[2]

1.   Once I skimmed over inland seas;
    Once my white down was fine to see;
    I lived my swan-life peacefully—
        Poor me! Poor me!
        Now basted blackly
        And roasted totally!

2.   Turn me, turn me now the sculleries;
    Burn me, burn me the rotisseries;
    Here comes the serving boy to offer me—
        Poor me! Poor me!
        Now basted blackly
        And roasted totally! . . .

5.   Now on a serving-plate stretched out I lie,
    Thinking in vain of flying through the skies;

---

2. Dirge of the Roasted Swan; ed. Schmeller, No. 92. *Lacus* in title preferred to *latin,* Hilka-Schumann, No. 130.

Now gnashing molars start to catch my eye—
    Poor me! Poor me!
    Now basted blackly
    And roasted totally!

EGO SUM ABBAS CUCANIENSIS[3]

    I am the Abbot of Cuckoo-Ninny
And my counsel is always with drinkers like me,
And I follow the sect of Decius, Lord of the Dice,
And whoever runs after me mornings in taverns
    At nightfall will issue naked
    And stripped of his shirt will cry:
    Wafna! Wafna!
Bitter Chance, O why hast thou forsaken me?
All the pleasures of this life
You have stolen away!

IN TABERNA QUANDO SUMUS[4]

1.   In the tavern when we're toping
No one sits with death-sighs moping—
To the gambling we go rushing,
Sweating from the heavy crushing;
If you have a lust for mastering
How we pass our time in casting
(There where Penny summons schooners)
Listen to these random rumors.

2.   This one's slurping, that one's sporting,
Someone's foolishly cavorting,
But of those who stay for gambling
Some will exit nudely scrambling,
Some will put on fine apparel,
Others sackcloth or a barrel;
There where death is all forgotten
With Bacchus they toss dice all sodden.

3. Gambling Song. *Cucaniensis* can be Cockaigne, a fictional land of luxurious life is an emergency cry for help.
4. Drinking Song. Ed. Schmeller, No. CLXXII.

3.   First throw says who pays for wine,
That liquid of the libertine.
Next to prisoners toasts they're giving,
Thrice saluting then the living;
Four times for each Christian head,
Five times for the faithful dead,
Six for sisters who are bolting;
Seven's a soldier who's not revolting.

4.   Eight's for all the Brothers Perverse;
Nine's for all those monks dispersed;
Ten is for the sailor at sea;
Eleven for brawlers constantly;
Twelve for the truly penitent;
Thirteen for men on missions sent.
Here's to the Pope! Here's to the King!
Everyone drink no end to the thing!

5.   Drinks the mistress, drinks the master;
Drinks the soldier with the pastor;
Drinks the Madame with Monsieur;
Drinks the maid-girl with the steward;
Drinks the slinker, drinks the slack one,
Drinks the pinkie with the black one;
Drinks the set man, drinks the bummer;
Drinks the genius with his dumber.

6.   Drinks the pauper and the weak one;
Drinks Old Prelate with the Deacon;
Drinks the exile, drinks the cipher;
Drinks teen-ager with long-lifer;
Drinks the sister, drinks the brother,
Drinks old grandma with your mother;
This girl's swilling; that churl's plundered—
Thousands drinking—yes, and hundreds!

7.   Six-hundred coins could not remotely
Fill the bill, for there's no quota
To this drink that knows no measure.
And though nothing gives more pleasure,
Still are some who pick and carp,
Hoping to make our guilt pangs sharp.
Let those carpers go depraved—
Write their names not with the saved!

STETIT PUELLA[5]

1. There stood the girl
      In the crimson dress—
      At the softest press,
   How that tunic rustled:
                Eia!

2. There stood the girl,
      Rosebud on a vine;
      Face ashine,
   Mouth a reddish bloom.
                Eia!

3. There stood the girl *by a tree;*
   She wrote of love *on a leaf,*
   Then came Venus very quickly—
   Great charity,
   Highest love;
   She gave herself to her man.

TEMPUS EST IOCUNDUM[6]

1. Pleasant is the weather—you maidens!
   Now rejoice together—with young men!
         O! O! O!
         I flower from head to toe!
         I'm all on fire
         For the girl I desire;
         New's this love I cherish:
         New, new, new by which
               I perish . . .

4. O the better solace—accepted!
   O the bitter malice—rejected!
         O! O! O! . . .

7. In cold Winter's fling—man's trusty!

---

5. Parody of hymns to Mary (see No. 8). The third stanza mixes German and Latin with the German italicized here. It equates "great charity" in Latin *(caritatem magnam)* with *hohe Minne* ("high love") in German. Ed. Schmeller, No. 138.
6. Verses so arranged by Orff. Ed. Schmeller, No. 140.

Comes the sudden breath of Spring—lusty!
    O! O! O! . . .

5.   Virginity quite jestfully—speeds me;
    And yet simplicity—impedes me.
       O! O! O! . . .

8.   Come with joy, my lady—abounding;
    Come, O come, my beauty—I'm floundering!
       O! O! O! . . .

AVE, FORMOSISSIMA[7]

Hail, most beautiful and good,
    Jewel held most dear by us;
Hail, honor of maidenhood,
    Virgin ever glorious—
Hail, thou light above all lights,
    Hail, rose of the world—
    Blancheflor
    And Helen,
        Venus,
        Venus,
        Venus noble-souled!

ALTE CLAMAT EPICURUS[8]

1.   Epicurus cries aloud:
    "A belly full is surer.
    Belly is my own true god—
    Throat is his procurer;
    Kitchen is his sacred shrine
    Where are fragrant goods divine.

2.   "Behold! this god is awfully good;
    Fasts he does not cherish;
    And before the morning food,

---

7. Parody of *Ave, Maria*. This stanza is the opening address of a man to a woman in a longish pastourelle: *Si linguis angelicis,* ed. Hilka-Schumann, No. 77.

8. Hymn to the Belly. Epicurus is the Greek philosopher whom thinkers of the Middle Ages associated with hedonism and a denial of immortality. Ed. Schmeller, No. CLXXXV.

There's a burp of sherry;
To him tables and big bowls
Are the truly heavenly goals.

3.   "Yes, his flesh is always bulging
Like a bloated jug of sack:
Ruby cheeks show his indulging;
Lunch meets dinner back to back;
When his desire stirs the veins
It is stronger than a chain."

4.   This religious cult expresses
Devotion in its belched excesses;
Belly folds in agony;
Beer is battling burgundy;
Yet life is blesséd with much leisure
When its center's belly's pleasure.

5.   Belly speaks now: "Not one damn
Care I for anything but me;
I just quietly want to jam
Plenty of stuff inside of me,
And then above the chow and wine
To sleep, to rest in peace divine."

ISTE MUNDUS[9]

1.   This old world
In fury furled
Sets false joys before our eyes—
These all spill,
Run downhill
As the lily quickly lies.

2.   Worldly schemes,
Life's vain dreams
Steal away the truer prize;
They impel
Man to Hell
Where he fully buried lies.

---

9. Poem reflects the *contemptus mundi* or "contempt of the world" tradition. Ed. Schmeller, No. VI.

3.   Carnal matters,
Law that shatters
Truly full of frivolousness
Falters, fades
Like a shade
That has lost its mesh of flesh.

4.   All we spy,
Hold close by
In our fatherland today
We'll dismiss,
Slowly miss
As the oak leaves drift away. . . .

6.   Let us batter,
Let us scatter
All desires of the skin;
Stand erect
Among the elect
And the justest of all men.

7.   Heavenly pleasure
We shall treasure
Through the ages that never end!
                Amen.

SECTION 4

Selections from THE LETTERS OF HÉLOISE AND ABELARD

Introduction by Albrecht Classen

Although we know many details of the two correspondents' lives, and are well informed about their love affair and brief marriage, many questions pertaining to the authenticity of their letters remain open. Abelard (1079–1142) was a highly acclaimed teacher and philosopher in Paris who founded the University, the Sorbonne, in 1132, and wrote a famous autobiographical account, the *Historia Calamitatum* (1132). Many of his philosophical texts laid the foundation for "modern" thinking, such as his rational *Sic et Non*. But his 133 Latin hymns also gained him considerable respect as a poet. Abelard fell in love with one of his female students, Héloise (1100 or 1101–1163 or 1164), who, as an orphan was living with her uncle, the canon Fulbert. After Héloise's uncle had found out that his niece had secretly married this cleric and had delivered a child, one night he broke into Abelard's quarters together with his friends, attacked him violently, and castrated him as a punishment for his "sin." Marriage was not really forbidden for members of the higher clergy, but it was certainly considered an impediment and viewed very negatively. But at that time the Church was the only institution that offered a career in higher education.

Realizing the shame brought upon them, and also aware that their marriage had been a betrayal of their own values and ideals, even in terms of love, Héloise and Abelard parted from each other, she more or rather less voluntarily retiring into a convent, he returning to his teaching duties. After years of separation she heard or read his *Historia* and began with her famous correspondence in which she and her husband explored fundamental questions of marriage and love in face of God's commands and the teachings of the Church.

These letters have gained a great and long-lasting reputation, but scholars have not yet reached an agreement as to whether these letters were actually written by these two people, or whether Abelard made them up as a literary enterprise, or whether a later writer falsified them altogether. One of the crucial questions always was whether Héloise could and would have written so openly about her sexuality, frustrations, and thinking in letters which were evidently supposed to be published.

BIBLIOGRAPHY

R. W. Southern, *The Letters of Abelard and Héloise.* Medieval Humanism and Other Studies (Oxford: Blackwell, 1970).

The Letters of Abelard and Héloise. Trans. with an Introduction by Betty Radice (Harmondsworth: Penguin, 1974).

Peter Dronke, "Excursus: Did Abelard Write Héloise's Third Letter?" *Women Writers of the Middle Ages: A Critical Study of Texts from Perpetua (+203) to Marguerite Porete (+1310)* (Cambridge: Cambridge University Press, 1984), 140–143.

Glenda McLeod, "'Wholly Guilty, Wholly Innocent': Self-Definition in Héloise's Letters to Abélard," *Dear Sister. Medieval Women and the Epistolary Genre,* ed. Karen Cherewatuk and Ulrike Wiethaus. Middle Ages Series (Philadelphia: University of Pennsylvania Press, 1993), 64–86.

Listening to Heloise. The Voice of a Twelfth-Century Woman. Ed. Bonnie Wheeler (New York: St. Martin's Press, 2000).

Letters of Peter Abelard, Beyond the Personal, trans. Jan M. Ziolkowski (Washington, D.C.: The Catholic University of America Press, 2008).

THE FIRST LETTER WHICH IS FROM HÉLOISE TO ABELARD, INTERCEDING WITH HIM

Argument: Héloise, *first Abelard's mistress, then his wife, and later set by him over the monastery of Paraclete, which he for himself with the wealth of his disciples had raised from its foundations, having read his letter to his friend, writes him this, praying that he will write back to her of his perils or deliverance, whereby she may be made a partner in his sorrow or in his joy. She expostulates also that he has not written to her since her monastic profession, when previously he had sent her many letters of love. She expounds her love for him, both in time past when it was base and carnal, and at the present time when it is chaste and spiritual: and bitterly complains that she is not loved equally by him in return.*

It is a letter full of great affection and querulous complaints, in the feminine way, a letter which a woman's heart may be discerned, abounding in great erudition.

To her master, nay father, to her husband, nay brother; his handmaid, nay daughter, his spouse, nay sister: to *Abelard, Héloise.*

Your letter written to a friend for his comfort, beloved, was lately brought to me by chance. Seeing at once from the title that it was yours, I began the more ardently to read it in that the writer was so dear to me, that I might at least be refreshed by his words as by a picture of him whose presence I have lost. Almost every line of that letter, I remember, was filled with gall and wormwood, to wit those that related the miserable story of our conversion, and thy unceasing crosses, my all. Thou didst indeed fulfil in that letter what at the beginning of it thou hadst promised thy friend, namely that in comparison with thy troubles he should deem his own to be nothing or but a small matter. After setting forth thy former persecution by thy masters, then the outrage of supreme treachery upon thy body, thou hast turned thy pen to the execrable jealousy and inordinate assaults of thy fellow pupils also, namely *Alberic* of Rheims and *Lotulph* the Lombard; and what by their instigation was done to that famous work of thy theology, and what to thyself, as it were condemned to prison, thou hast not omitted.

From these thou comest to the machinations of thine Abbot and false brethren, and the grave detraction of thee by those two pseudo apostles, stirred up against thee by the aforesaid rivals, and to the scandal raised by many of the name of Paraclete given to the oratory in departure from custom: and then, coming to those intolerable and still continuing persecutions of thy life, thou hast carried to the end the miserable story of that cruellest of extortioners and those wickedest of monks, whom thou callest thy sons. Which things I deem that no one can read or hear with dry eyes, for they renewed in fuller measure my griefs, so diligently did they express each several part, and increased them the more, in that thou relatedst that thy perils are still growing, so that we are all alike driven to despair of thy life, and every day our trembling hearts and throbbing bosoms await the latest rumour of thy death.

And so in His Name Who still protects thee in a certain measure for Himself in the Name of Christ, as His handmaids and thine, we beseech thee to deign to inform us by frequent letters of those shipwrecks in which thou still art tossed, that thou mayest have us at least, who alone have remained to thee, as partners in thy grief or joy. For they are wont to bring some comfort to a grieving man who grieve with him, and any burden that is laid on several is borne more easily, or transferred. And if this tempest should have been stilled for a space, then all the more hasten thou to write, the more pleasant thy letter will be. But whatsoever it be of which thou mayest write to us, thou wilt confer no small remedy on us; if only in this that thou wilt shew thyself to be keeping us in mind.

For how pleasant are the letters of absent friends *Seneca* himself by his own example teaches us, writing thus in a certain passage to his friend *Lucilius:* "Because thou writest to me often, I thank thee. For in the one way possible thou shewest thyself to me. Never do I receive a letter from thee, but immediately we are together." If the portraits of our absent friends are pleasant to us, which renew our memory of them and relieve our regret for their absence by a false and empty consolation, how much more pleasant are letters which bring us the written characters of the absent friend. But thanks be to God, that in this way at least no jealousy prevents thee from restoring to us thy presence, no difficulty impedes thee, no neglect (I beseech thee) need delay thee.

Thou hast written to thy friend the comfort of a long letter, considering his difficulties, no doubt, but treating of thine own. Which diligently recording, whereas thou didst intend them for his comfort, thou hast added greatly to our desolation, and while thou wert anxious to heal his wounds hast inflicted fresh wounds of grief on us and made our former wounds to ache again. Heal, I beseech thee, the wounds that thou thyself hast given, who art so busily engaged in healing the wounds given by others. Thou hast indeed humoured thy friend and comrade, and paid the debt as well of friendship as of comradeship; but by a greater debt thou hast bound thyself to us, whom it behoves thee to call not friends but dearest friends, not comrades but daughters, or by a sweeter and a holier name, if any can be conceived.

As to the greatness of the debt which binds thee to us neither argument nor evidence is lacking, that any doubt be removed; and if all men be silent the fact itself cries aloud. For of this place thou, after God, art the sole founder, the sole architect of this oratory, the sole builder of this congregation. Nothing didst thou build here on the foundations of others. All that is here is thy creation. This wilderness, ranged only by wild beasts or by robbers, had known no habitation of men, had contained no dwelling. In the very lairs of the beasts, in the very lurking places of the robbers, where the name of God is not heard, thou didst erect a divine tabernacle, and didst dedicate the Holy Ghost's own temple. Nothing didst thou borrow from the wealth of kings or princes, when thou couldst have obtained so much and from so many, that whatsoever was wrought, here might be ascribed to thee alone. Clerks or scholars flocking in haste to thy teaching ministered to thee all things needful, and they who lived upon ecclesiastical benefices, who knew not how to make but only how to receive oblations, and had hands for receiving, not for giving, became lavish and importunate here in the offering of oblations.

Thine, therefore, truly thine is this new plantation in the divine plan, for the plants of which, still most tender, frequent irrigation is necessary that they may grow. Frail enough, from the weakness of the feminine nature, is this plantation; it is infirm, even were it not new. Wherefore it demands more diligent cultivation and more frequent, after the words of the Apostle: "I have planted, *Apollos* watered; but God gave the increase." The Apostle had planted, by the doctrines of his preaching, and had established in the Faith the Corinthians, to whom he wrote. Thereafter *Apollos*, the Apostle's own disciple, had watered them with sacred exhortations, and so by divine grace the increment of virtues was bestowed on them. Thou art tending the vineyard of another's vine which thou didst not plant, which is turned to thine own bitterness, with admonitions often wasted and holy sermons preached in vain. Think of what thou owest to thine own, who thus spendest thy care on another's. Thou teachest and reprovest rebels, nor gainest thou aught. In vain before swine dost thou scatter the pearls of divine eloquence. Who givest so much thought to the obstinate, consider what thou owest to the obedient. Who bestowest so much on thine enemies, meditate what thou owest to thy daughters. And, to say nothing of the rest, think by what a debt thou art bound to me, that what thou owest to the community of devoted women thou mayest pay more devotedly to her who is thine alone.

How many grave treatises in the teaching, or in the exhortation, or for the comfort of holy women the holy Fathers composed, and with what diligence they composed them, thine excellence knows better than our humility. Wherefore to no little amazement thine oblivion moves the tender beginnings of our conversion, that neither by reverence for God, nor by love of us, nor by the examples of the holy Fathers hast thou been admonished to attempt to comfort me, as I waver and am already crushed by prolonged grief, either by speech in thy presence or by a letter in thine absence. And yet thou knowest thyself to be bound to me by a debt so much greater in that thou art tied to me more closely by the pact of the nuptial sacrament; and that thou art the more beholden to me in that I ever, as is known to all, embraced thee with an unbounded love. Thou knowest, dearest, all men know what I have lost in thee, and in how wretched a case that supreme and notorious betrayal took me myself also from me with thee, and that my grief is immeasurably greater from the manner in which I lost thee than from the loss of thee.

And the greater the cause of grief, the greater the remedies of comfort to be applied. Not, however, by another, but by thee thyself, that thou who art alone in the cause of my grief may be alone in the grace of my comfort. For it is thou alone that canst make me sad, canst make me joyful or canst comfort me. And it is thou alone that owes me this great debt, and for this reason above all that I have at once performed all things that thou didst order, till that when I could not offend thee in anything I had the strength to lose myself at thy behest. And what is more, and strange it is to relate, to such madness did my love turn that what alone it sought it cast from itself without hope of recovery when, straightway obeying thy command, I changed both my habit and my heart, that I might shew thee to be the one possessor both of my body and of my mind. Nothing have I ever (God wot) required of thee save thyself, desiring thee purely, not what was thine. Not for the pledge of matrimony, nor for any dowry did I look, nor my own passions or wishes but thine (as thou thyself knowest) was I zealous to gratify.

And if the name of wife appears more sacred and more valid, sweeter to me is ever the word friend, or if thou be not ashamed, concubine or whore. To wit that the more I humbled myself before thee the fuller grace I might obtain from thee, and so also damage less the fame of thine excellence. And thou thyself were not wholly unmindful of that kindness in the letter of which I have spoken, written to thy friend for his comfort. Wherein thou hast not disdained to set forth sundry reasons by which I tried to dissuade thee from our marriage, from an ill-starred bed; but wert silent as to many, in which I preferred love to wedlock, freedom to a bond. I call God to witness, if *Augustus,* ruling over the whole world, were to deem me worthy of the honour of marriage, and to confirm the whole world to me, to be ruled by me for ever, dearer to me and of greater dignity would it seem to be called thy strumpet than his empress.

For it is not by being richer or more powerful that a man becomes better; one is a matter of fortune, the other of virtue. Nor should she deem herself other than venal who weds a rich man rather than a poor, and desires more things in her husband than himself. Assuredly, whomsoever this concupiscence leads into marriage deserves payment rather than affection; for it is evident that she goes after his wealth and not the man, and is willing to prostitute herself, if she can, to a richer. As the argument advanced (in *Aeschines*) by the wise *Aspasia* to *Xenophon* and his wife plainly convinces us. When the wise woman aforesaid had propounded this argument for their reconciliation, she concluded as follows: "For when ye have understood this, that there is not a better man nor a happier woman on the face of the earth; then ye will ever and above all things seek that which ye think the best; thou to be the husband of so excellent a wife, and she to be married to so excellent a husband." A blessed sentiment, assuredly, and more than philosophic, expressing wisdom itself rather than philosophy. A holy error and a blessed fallacy among the married, that a perfect love should preserve their bond of matrimony unbroken, not so much by the continence of their bodies as by the purity of their hearts. But what error shows to the rest of women the truth has made manifest to me. Since what they thought of their husbands, that I, that the entire world not so much believed as knew of thee. So that the more genuine my love was for thee, the further it was removed from error.

For who among kings or philosophers could equal thee in fame: What kingdom or city or village did not burn to see thee: Who, I ask, did not hasten to gaze upon thee when thou appearedst in public, nor on thy departure with straining neck and fixed eye follow thee? What wife, what maiden did not yearn for thee in thine absence, nor burn in thy presence: What queen or powerful lady did not envy me my joys and my bed: There were two things, I confess, in thee especially, wherewith thou couldst at once captivate the heart of any woman; namely the arts of making songs and of singing them. Which we know that other philosophers have seldom followed. Wherewith as with a game, refreshing the labour of philosophic exercise, thou hast left many songs composed in amatory measure or rhythm, which for the suavity both of words and of tune being oft repeated, have kept thy name without ceasing on the lips of all; since even illiterates the sweetness of thy melodies did not allow to forget thee. It was on this account chiefly that women sighed for love of thee. And as the greater part of thy songs descanted of our love, they spread my fame in a short time through many lands, and inflamed the jealousy of many women against me. For what excellence of mind or body did not adorn thy youth: What woman who envied me then does not my calamity now compel to pity one deprived of such delights:

What man or women, albeit an enemy at first, is not now softened by the compassion due to me?

And though exceeding guilty, I am, as thou knowest, exceeding innocent. For it is not the deed but the intention that makes the crime. It is not what is done but the spirit in which it is done that equity considers. And in what state of mind I have ever been towards thee, only thou, who hast knowledge of it, canst judge. To thy consideration I commit all, I yield in all things to thy testimony. Tell me one thing only, if thou canst, why, after our conversion, which thou alone didst decree, I am fallen into such neglect and oblivion with thee that I am neither refreshed by thy speech and presence nor comforted by a letter in thine absence. Tell me, one thing only, if thou canst, or let me tell thee what I feel, nay what all suspect. Concupiscence joined thee to me rather than affection, the ardour of desire rather than love. When therefore what thou desiredst ceased, all that thou hadst exhibited at the same time failed. This, most beloved, is not mine only but the conjecture of all, not peculiar but common, not private but public. Would that it seemed thus to me only, and thy love found others to excuse it, by whom my grief might be a little quieted. Would that I could invent reasons by which in excusing thee I might cover in some measure my own vileness.

Give thy attention, I beseech thee, to what I demand; and thou wilt see this to be a small matter and most easy for thee. While I am cheated of thy presence, at least by written words, whereof thou hast an abundance, present to me the sweetness of thine image. In vain may I expect thee to be liberal in things if I must endure thee niggardly in words. Until now I believed that I deserved more from thee when I had done all things for thee, persevering still in obedience to thee. Who indeed as a girl was allured to the asperity of monastic conversation not by religious devotion but by thy command alone. Wherein if I deserve nought from thee, thou mayest judge my labour to have been vain. No reward for this may I expect from God, for the love of Whom it is well known that I did not anything. When thou hastenedst to God, I followed thee in the habit, nay preceded thee. For as though mindful of the wife of *Lot*, who looked back from behind him, thou deliveredst me first to the sacred garments and monastic profession before thou gavest thyself to God. And for that in this one thing thou shouldst have had little trust in me I vehemently grieved and was ashamed. For I (God wot) would without hesitation precede or follow thee to the Vulcanian fires according to thy word. For not with me was my heart, but with thee. But now, more than ever, if it be not with thee, it is nowhere. For without thee it cannot anywhere exist. But so act that it may be well with thee, I beseech thee. And well with thee will it be if it find thee propitious, if thou give love for love, little for much, words for deeds. Would that thy beloved, had less trust in me, that it might be more anxious! But the more confident l have made thee in the past, the more neglectful now I find thee. Remember, I beseech thee, what I have done, and pay heed to what thou owest me. While with thee I enjoyed carnal pleasures, many were uncertain whether I did so from love or from desire. But now the end shews in what spirit I began. I have forbidden myself all pleasures that I might obey thy will. I have reserved nothing for myself, save this, to be now entirely thine. Consider therefore how great is thine in, justice, if to me who deserve more thou payest less, nay nothing at all, especially when it is a small thing that is demanded of thee, and right easy for thee to perform.

And so in His Name to whom thou hast offered thyself, before God I beseech thee that in whatsoever way thou canst thou restore to me thy presence, to wit by writing me some word of comfort. To this end alone that, thus refreshed, I may give myself with more alacrity to the service of God. When in time past thou soughtest me out for temporal pleasures, thou visitedst me with endless letters, and by frequent songs didst set thy *Héloise* on the lips of all men. With me every public place, each house resounded. How more rightly shouldst thou excite me now towards God, whom thou excitedst then to desire. Consider, I beseech thee, what thou owest me, pay heed to what l demand; and my long letter with a brief ending I conclude. Farewell, my all.

THE SECOND LETTER WHICH IS THE REPLY OF PETER TO HÉLOISE

Argument: Abelard *answers the last letter from* Héloise *and frankly excuses himself, protesting that his not having written to her for so long a time proceeded in no way from want of interest in her; on the contrary, he had such confidence in her prudence, learning, piety and devotion that he did not imagine that she required either exhortation or comfort. He bids her write again to him, saying what in the way of exhortation or divine comfort she wishes to have from him; and he himself will answer according to her desire. He asks her that both she and her community, the choir of holy virgins and widows, shall help him before God with their prayers, admirably expounding from the authority of the Scriptures what force prayer has with Him, and especially the prayers of wives for their husbands; and, reminding her of the prayers which are already being offered to God for him in that monastery by the holy women at each of the canonical Hours, prescribes others which may be said for his safety when he is absent. Furthermore he requires of her that, in whatsoever manner or place he may be destined to pass from this life, she will have his body brought to the Community of the Paraclete, and there buried.*

To Héloise his dearly beloved sister in Christ, ABELARD her brother in the Same.

If since our conversion from the world to God I have not yet written thee any word of comfort or exhortation, it must be ascribed not to my negligence but to thy prudence, in which always I greatly trust. For I did not suppose it to be necessary to her on whom divine grace has abundantly bestowed all things needful, so that both by words and by examples thou art able to teach the erring, to comfort the weak, to exhort the lukewarm, as thou wert long since wont to do when under the Abbess thou didst obtain the priorship. Wherefore if now thou watch over thy daughters with as great diligence as then over thy sisters it is enough, we believe, that now we may consider any teaching or exhortation from us to be wholly superfluous. But if to thy humility it appear otherwise, and in those things also which pertain to God thou have need of our teaching and writings, write to me of what thou requirest, that I may write again to thee as God may be pleased to grant me. But thanks be to God Who, inspiring in your hearts solicitude for my most grave and assiduous perils, has made you partners in my affliction, and may divine mercy by the suffrage of your prayers protect me, and swiftly crush Satan beneath our feet. And to this end especially the Psalter which thou hast solicitously required of me, sister once dear in the world, now dearest in Christ, I have made haste to send thee. Whereon for our great and many excesses, and for the daily imminence of our perils, mayest thou offer a perpetual sacrifice of prayers to the Lord.

For of how great a place before God and His Saints the prayers of the faithful obtain, and especially the prayers of women for their dear ones and of wives for their husbands, many testimonies and examples occur to us. Which diligently observing, the Apostle bids us pray without ceasing. We read that the Lord said to *Moses:* "Let me alone that my wrath may wax hot" And to *Jeremy* He said: Therefore pray not thou for this people, neither make intercession to me." By which words the Lord Himself manifestly professes that the prayers of the Saints are set as it were a bridle upon His wrath, whereby it may be checked, and He rage not against sinners to the fulness of their deserts. As a man whom justice leads almost spontaneously to vengeance the supplication of his friends may turn aside. So it is said to him who is praying or about to pray: "Let me alone, neither make intercession to me." The Lord ordains that prayer be not made to Him for the impious. The righteous man prays when the Lord forbids him, and obtains from Him what he demands and alters the sentence of the irate Judge. For thus it is added of *Moses:* "And the Lord repented of the evil which he thought to do unto his people." It is written elsewhere of the universal works of God: "He commanded, and they were created." But in this passage it is recorded also that He had said that the people had deserved affliction, and that prevented by the virtue of prayer He did not perform what He had said.

Take heed therefore how great is the virtue of prayer, if we pray as we are commanded, when that for which the Prophet had been forbidden by God to pray he nevertheless obtained by prayer, and turned Him aside from that which He had said. To Whom also another Prophet says: "In wrath remember mercy." Let them hear this and give heed, the Princes of the Earth who in the execution of the justice they have decreed and published are found obstinate rather than just, and blush to appear remiss should they be merciful, and untruthful if they alter their edict or do not execute what with little foresight they have decreed, or emend the words to fit the matter. Who indeed I might rightly say were comparable to *Jephthah* who, what he had foolishly vowed more foolishly performing, slew his only daughter. But who so desires to be a member of Him, says with the Psalmist: "I will sing of mercy and judgment: unto Thee, O Lord, will I sing." "Mercy," as it is written, "exalteth judgment," according to what elsewhere the Scripture threatens: "He shall have judgment without mercy that hath shewed no mercy." Which the Psalmist himself diligently considering, at the supplication of the wife of *Nabal* the Carmelite, in mercy brake the oath which he had sworn in justice, to wit against her husband and for the destruction of his house. And so he set prayer above justice, and what the man had done amiss the supplication of the woman wiped clean.

Wherein for thee indeed, sister, is an example set, and assurance given; that if this woman's prayer obtained so much from a man thou be taught how much thy prayers for me may prevail before God. Inasmuch as God, Who is our Father, loves His children more than *David* loved a suppliant woman. And he indeed was reckoned pious and merciful, but Piety itself and Mercy is God. And this woman who then besought him was secular and lay, nor was she bound to the Lord by the profession of holy devotion. For if in thyself thou suffice not to secure it, the holy convent, as well of virgins as of widows, which is with thee will obtain what by thyself thou canst not. For when the Truth says to the Disciples: "Where two or three are gathered together in my name, there am I in the midst of them"; and again: "If two of you shall agree on earth as touching anything that they shall ask, it shall be done for them of my Father which is in Heaven"; who does not see how greatly the frequent prayer of a holy congregation prevails before God: If, as the Apostle asserts: The effectual prayer of a righteous man availeth much," what is to be expected from the multitude of a holy congregation: Ye know, dearest sister, from the eight, and twentieth Homily of Saint *Gregory* what aid the prayer of his brethren speedily brought to an unwilling or resisting brother. Of whom, in the extremity to which he had been brought, in what an anxiety of peril his wretched soul was labouring, and with what desperation and weariness of life he recalled his brethren from their prayers, it is there diligently written and cannot have escaped thy wisdom.

And may that example invite thee and the convent of holy sisters to prayer, that it may keep me alive for you through Him from Whom, as *Paul* bears witness, women have received their dead raised to life again. For if thou turn the pages of the Old Testament and the New thou wilt find that the greatest miracles of resuscitation were displayed only or principally to women, and for them or in their persons were wrought. The Old Testament records two dead men who were raised to life at the supplication of their mothers, namely by *Elias* and by his disciple *Eliseus*. And the Gospel contains the resurrection of three dead men only, wrought by the Lord, which things being displayed to women strongly confirm by their example that Apostolic saying which we have quoted above: "Women received their dead raised to life again." It was to a widow at the gate of the city called Nain that He restored a son to life and gave him back to his mother, touched with compassion for her, and *Lazarus* also, His friend, at the entreaty of his sisters *Mary* and *Martha,* He raised from the dead. When He also accorded the same grace to the daughter of the ruler of the synagogue, paying heed to her father's petition, "women received their dead raised to life again." For she being raised to life received her own body again from death, as they the bodies of their dead. And with but few intercessions these resurrections were accomplished. So that the manifold prayers of your devotion will easily obtain the preservation of my life. The more the abstinence or the chastity of women consecrated to God is pleasing to Him, the more propitious will it find Him. And the better part of those who were raised from the dead were not of the faithful; thus we do not read that the widow aforesaid, to whom without her asking it the Lord restored her son, had lived in the faith. Whereas with us, not only does the integrity of our faith draw us together but our profession of the same vows unites us.

But, to leave now out of account the sacrosanct congregation of your college, in which the devotion of so many virgins and widows bears the yoke of the Lord, let me come now to thee alone, whose great sanctity I doubt not is effectual before the Lord, nor do I doubt that thou art bound to do all that thou canst for me above all men, especially when I am labouring in the toils of such great adversity. Remember therefore always in thy prayers him who is specially thine, and so much the more confidently watch in prayer as thou dost recognise it to be more righteous, and accordingly more acceptable to Him to whom prayer is made. Listen, I beseech thee, with the ear of thy heart to what thou hast heard so often with thy bodily ear. It is written in the Proverbs: "A virtuous woman is a crown to her husband." And again: "Whoso findeth a wife findeth a good thing, and obtaineth favour of the Lord." And another time: "House and riches are the inheritance of fathers: and a prudent wife is from the Lord." And in Ecclesiasticus: "Blessed is the man that hath a virtuous wife." And a little later: "A good wife is a good portion." And according to Apostolic authority: "The unbelieving husband is sanctified by the wife." An example whereof indeed in our own realm, that is France, divine grace has specially displayed, to wit when by the prayers of his wife rather than by the preaching of the saints *Clovis* the King being converted to the Faith of Christ placed his whole realm under the divine law, that the lesser folk might be encouraged by the example of the great to persevere in prayer. To which perseverance indeed the Lord's parable vehemently invites us, that if a man persevere in knocking: "I say unto you, Though he will not rise and give him, because he is his friend, yet because of his importunity he will rise and give him as many as he needeth." By which, to continue still of importunity in prayer, *Moses* relaxed the severity of divine justice and altered its sentence.

Thou knowest, beloved, what ardours of charity in my presence your convent was aforetime wont to exhibit in prayer. For every day at the conclusion of each of the Hours they used to offer this special supplication to the Lord for me, and, a proper response with its versicle having been first said and sung, added prayers to them and a collect as follows:

Response: Forsake me not, O Lord: O my God, be not far from me.

Versicle: Make haste, O God, to deliver me.

Prayer: Save thy servant, O my God: whose hope is in Thee. Lord, hear my prayer, and let my cry come unto Thee. *(Let us pray.)* God, Who through Thy servant hast been pleased to gather Thy handmaids together in Thy Name, we beseech Thee to grant that both he and ourselves may persevere in Thy Will. Through our Lord, *etc.*

But now, when I am absent, there is all the more need of your suffrage for me, in that I am fast bound by the anxiety of a greater peril. Beseeching you therefore I demand, and demanding beseech that I may find, now that I am absent, how far your true charity embraces the absent, by your adding this form of proper prayer at the conclusion of each Hour:

Response: O Lord, Father and Governor of all my whole life, leave me not to their counsels, and let me not fall by them.
Versicle: Take hold of shield and buckler, and stand up for my help. Leave me not.

Prayer: Save thy servant, O my God, whose hope is in Thee. Send him, Lord, help from Thy Sanctuary, and watch over him from Sion. Be unto him, O Lord, a tower of strength from the face of his enemy. Hear my prayer, O Lord, and let my cry come unto Thee. *(Let us pray.)* God, Who through Thy servant hast been pleased to gather Thy handmaids together in Thy Name, we beseech Thee that Thou wilt protect him from all adversity and restore him in safety to Thy handmaids. Through our Lord, *etc.*

And if the Lord should deliver me into the hands of mine enemies, so that they prevail over me and slay me, by whatsoever chance I may go the way of all flesh while absent from you, wheresoever, I beseech you, my body, either exposed or buried, may lie, have it brought to your cemetery, where our daughters, nay, sisters in Christ, seeing every day our sepulchre, may be encouraged to pour out prayer more fully for me to the Lord. For I deem no place to be safer or more salutary for a soul grieving for its sins and made desolate by transgression than that which to the true Paraclete, that is to the Comforter, is properly consecrated, and is specially distinguished by His Name. Nor do I think that there is a fitter place for Christian burial among any of the faithful than among women devoted to Christ. Women they were who, solicitous for the sepulchre of the Lord Jesus Christ, came to it with precious ointments, and went before and followed, diligently watching about His sepulchre and bewailing with tears the death of the Bridegroom, as it is written: "The women sitting over against the sepulchre lamented the Lord." And there before His Resurrection they were comforted by the apparition and speech of an angel, and thereafter were found worthy to taste the joy of His Resurrection, He appearing to them twice, and to touch Him with their hands. But this lastly above all things I demand of you, that whereas now ye labour in too great solicitude for the welfare of my body, then being solicitous especially for the salvation of my soul ye shew to the dead man how greatly ye loved the living, to wit by a special and proper suffrage of your prayers.

Live, prosper, and thy sifters too with thee.
Live, but in Christ be mindful, pray, of me.

THE THIRD LETTER WHICH IS THE REPLY OF HÉLOISE TO PETER

Argument: *Filled with griefs and lamentations is this letter. For* Héloise *laments her own wretched plight, and that of the nuns her sisters, and* Abelard's *also, taking an occasion for her lamentations from the latter part of the preceding letter, in which* Abelard *reminds her that he must depart from this life. She makes use of many tender appeals, whereby she moves the reader to compassion for her own lot and for* Abelard, *so as haply to draw tears from his eyes. She deplores also the mutilation of* Abelard. *She complains greatly, too, of those burning carnal desires in the body, which aforetime she had known with* Abelard. *Then, not incongruously, she makes light of the outward and open firm of her religion, and ascribes it to feint rather than to piety; she begs for the help of* Abelard's *prayers, and humbly rejects his praise of herself.*

To her all, after Christ, his all in Christ.

I marvel, my all, that, against the custom in writing letters, nay against the natural order of things, at the head of the greeting in thy letter thou hast made bold to set my name before thine, to wit the woman before the man, the wife before the husband, the handmaid before the master, the nun before the monk and priest, the deaconess before the Abbot. Right indeed is the order and honourable that they who write to their superiors or to their equals place the names of those to whom they are writing before their own. But if they write to their inferiors, those take precedence in the order of writing who take precedence in rank. This also we received with no little amazement, that whereas thou shouldst have brought us the remedy of comfort thou hast increased our desolation and hast provoked tears which thou shouldst have dried. For who among us could hear with dry eyes what thou hast put towards the end of thy letter, saying: "If the Lord should deliver me into the hands of mine enemies, so that they prevail over me and slay me," and the rest?

O, dearest, with what mind didst thou think that, with what lips couldst thou endure to say it? Never may God so forget His handmaids as to keep them to survive thee. Never may He concede that life to us which is harder to bear than any kind of death. It is for thee to celebrate our obsequies, for thee to commend our souls to God, and those whom thou hast gathered together for God to send first to him, that thou be no more disturbed by anxiety for them, and so much the more joyfully follow us the more assured thou already be of our salvation. Spare, I beseech thee, master, spare us words of this sort, whereby thou makest wretched women most wretched, and take not from us before our death that which is our life. "Sufficient unto the day is the evil thereof," and that day, wrapped about with every bitterness, will bring to all whom it shall find enough solicitude with itself. "For to what end," says *Seneca*, "anticipate evil, and before death lose one's life?" Thou askest us, my all, that, by whatsoever fate, if absent from us, thou mayest end this life, we shall have thy body brought to our cemetery, that there thou mayest gather a richer fruit of our prayers from our assiduous memory of thee. But how couldst thou suspect that thy memory could ever fail among us? Or what time will then be suitable for prayer when our extreme perturbation allows us no peace: When neither the soul retains the sense of reason nor the tongue the use of speech: When the maddened mind enraged, if I may so speak, against God Himself rather than appeased, will not so much placate Him by prayer as anger Him by complaints: Then there will be time only for the wretched to weep, pray they may not, and must hasten rather to follow than to bury thee, for we shall be more fit to be buried with thee than able to bury thee. Who, when in thee we shall have lost our life, will not at all be able to live with thee removed from us. Oh that we may not be able to live even until then! The very thought of thy death is as death to us.

But what will be the reality of that death if it find us living: Never, God grant, may we pay that debt to thee as thy survivors, may we yield thee that assistance which in the last hour we expect from thee. In this may we precede, not follow thee! Spare us, therefore, I beseech thee, spare at least her who is thine alone, namely by ceasing from the use of such words, wherewith as with swords of death thou piercest our souls, so that what comes before death is harder to bear than death itself. The heart overwhelmed by grief knows no rest, nor can the mind occupied by perturbations be given sincerely to God. Do not, I beseech thee, hinder that service of God to which especially thou didst devote us. Every inevitable thing which when it comes will bring with it the greatest grief we must desire to come suddenly, lest it torment us long beforehand with vain fears which no foresight can remedy. Which also the poet well considering, prays to God, saying:

May whatso'er Thou hast in store
Be swift and sudden. Let the human mind
To future destiny be ever blind.
Allow our fears to hope.

But with thee lost what hope remains to me? Or what reason for remaining in this pilgrimage when I may have no remedy save thee, nor aught else in thee save this that thou art alive, all other pleasure from thee being forbidden me to whom it is not allowed even to enjoy thy presence, that at times I might be restored to myself. O—if it be right to say so—cruel to me in all things God! O inclement clemency! O fortune unfortunate, which has already so spent all the arrows of its whole strength on me that it has none now wherewith to assail others; it has emptied its full quivers on me so that vainly do others now fear its onslaughts. Nor if any arrow still remained to it would it find in me a spot to wound. One thing amidst so many wounds it has feared, lest I end my torment by death. And albeit it does not cease to destroy me, it fears that destruction which it is bringing rapidly to pass.

Ah me, most wretched of the wretched! Unhappiest of the unhappy, who when I had been raised to so lofty a pinnacle, being preferred to all other women in thee, have now, fallen from thence, suffered as great a prostration in thee and in myself alike! For, the higher the step of advancement, the heavier is the fall. Whom among great and noble women did fortune ever set above or equal with me? Whom has it so cast down and crushed with grief? What glory did it give me in thee; what ruin has it brought me in thee! How vehement has it been to me in either direction, so as neither in good nor in evil to shew any mean. Which that it might make me the most wretched of all women first made me happier than any. That in thinking of how much I have lost the lamentations that consume me might be increased to equal the losses that have crushed me; that as great regret might follow for what I have forfeited as was previously my enjoyment of what I possessed, and that the supreme sadness of despair might terminate the joys of supreme pleasure.

And in order that from the injustice a greater indignation may arise, all the rights of equity are equally turned against me. For while anxiously we enjoyed the delights of love, and, to use a viler but more expressive word, abandoned ourselves to fornication, divine severity spared us. But when we corrected the unlawful with the lawful, and covered the vileness of fornication with the honesty of marriage, the wrath of the Lord vehemently increased the weight of His Hand upon us, nor did He allow an immaculate couch Who had long endured one polluted. For men taken in the most flagrant adultery that would have been sufficient punishment which thou didst suffer. What others might merit by adultery thou didst incur by a marriage whereby thou thoughtest that thou hadst given satisfaction for all thy wrongdoing. What adulteresses bring to their lovers thine own wife brought to thee. And not while we were indulging still in our old pleasures, but when, already separated for a time, we were living chastely, thou indeed presiding over thy school in Paris, and I at thy command dwelling at Argenteuil among the nuns. When we were thus divided, that thou the more studiously mightest devote thyself to thy school, I the more freely to prayer or the meditation of holy books, while we were living thus, as in greater holiness so in greater chastity, thou alone didst pay in thy body the penalty for what we both alike had committed. Alone wert thou in punishment, two were we in the fault; and thou who wert the less guilty hast borne all. For inasmuch as thou hadst given fuller satisfaction by humiliating thyself for me, and hadst exalted me and all my race alike, so thou hadst given less cause for punishment both to God and to those traitors.

Unhappy that I am, born to be the cause of so great a crime! O constant bane of women, greatest against the greatest men! Wherefore is it written in the Proverbs to beware of women: "Hearken unto me now therefore, O ye children, and attend to the words of my mouth. Let not thine heart decline to her ways, go not astray in her paths: for she hath cast down many wounded; yea, many strong men have been slain by her. Her house is the way to hell, going down to the chambers of death." And in Ecclesiastes: "All things have I seen in the days of my vanity . . . and I find more bitter than death the woman, whose heart is snares and nets, and her hands as bands: whoso pleaseth God shall escape from her; but the sinner shall be taken by her." For the first woman drave the man from Paradise, and she who had been created for him by the Lord as a helpmeet was turned to his supreme destruction. That strongest Nazarite of the Lord, conceived by the message of an angel, *Delilah* alone overcame, and when he was betrayed to his foes and deprived of his eyes, grief at length carried him to such a pass that he brought down himself also in the overthrow of his enemies. The wisest of all men, *Salomon,* a woman alone whom he had taken to himself infatuated and drove him to such insanity that she plunged him, whom the Lord had chosen to build a Temple to Himself, after his father *David,* who was a righteous man, had been rejected for that task, in idolatry until the end of his days, abandoning that service of God which in his words as in his writings he preached and taught. *Job,* the most holy of men, endured the supreme and heaviest of blows from his wife, who urged him to curse God. And the most cunning tempter knew this well, for that he had often found it, to wit that the ruin of men was most easily effected through their wives. Who also into our time extending his wonted malice, him whom he could not bring down by fornication tried by marriage: and used a good thing ill who was not permitted to use an evil. Thanks be to God for this at least, that the tempter did not draw me into guilt by my consent, like the women aforesaid, albeit he turned me, from my affection, into a cause of the wickedness that was done.

But even though innocence may purge my heart, nor does consent incur me the guilt of that crime, yet many sins went before it which do not allow me to be altogether immune from the guilt of it. For indeed long before that time, ministering to the delights of carnal snares, I then deserved that which I now bewail, and the sequel is made a fitting punishment of my previous sins. Evil beginnings must lead to an untoward end. Oh, that I may have the strength to do fit penance for this fault, especially that I may be able in some measure to recompense by the long contrition of penitence that punishment of the wound inflicted on thee, and what thou to the present hour hast borne in thy body may I all my life long, as is right, take upon my mind and in this way satisfy thee at least, if not God. For, if I am truly to set forth the infirmity of my most wretched heart, I and no penance wherewith I may appease God Whom always for that outrage I charge with the utmost cruelty, and, refractory to His dispensation, offend Him rather by my indignation than appease Him by my repentance. For what repentance of sins is that, however great the mortification of the body, when the mind still retains the same will to sin, and burns with its old desires? Easy is it indeed for anyone by confessing his sins to accuse himself, or even in outward satisfaction to mortify his body. But it is most difficult to tear away the heart from the desire of the greatest pleasures. Wherefore and with reason Holy *Job,* after first saying: "I will leave my complaint upon myself," that is, "I will let loose my tongue and will open my mouth in confession to accuse myself of my sins," straightway added: "I will speak in the bitterness of my soul." Which Saint *Gregory* expounding says: "Some there are who in open speech confess their faults, and yet in confession know not how to weep, and say lamentable things rejoicing. Wherefore if any detesting his faults speaks, it is necessary that he speak thus in the bitterness of his soul, and that this same bitterness punish whatsoever the tongue accuses by the judgment of the mind." But this bitterness indeed, how rare it is, Saint *Ambrose* diligently studying says: "They are easier to find who have kept innocence than they who have made repentance." So sweet to me were those delights of lovers which we enjoyed in common that they cannot either displease me nor hardly pass from my memory. Whithersoever I turn, always they bring themselves before my eyes with the desire for them. Nor even when I am asleep do they spare me their illusions. In the very solemnities of the Mass, when prayer ought to be more pure, the obscure phantoms of those delights so thoroughly captivate my wretched soul to themselves that I pay heed to their vilenesses rather than to my prayers. And when I ought to lament for what I have done I sigh rather for what I have had to forego. Not only the things that we did, but the places also and the times in which we did them are so fixed with thee in my mind that in the same times and places I reenact them all with thee, nor even when I am asleep have I any rest from them. At times by the very motions of my body the thoughts of my mind are disclosed, nor can I restrain the utterance of unguarded words.

Oh, truly miserable I, and most worthy to utter that complaint of a stricken soul: "O wretched man that I am! Who shall deliver me from the body of this death?" Would that I might truthfully add also what follows: "I thank God through Jesus Christ our Lord." That grace, beloved, came to thee unsought, and by healing thee from these goads a single injury to thy body has cured many in thy soul, and in that wherein God is thought to be more adverse to thee, He is found to be more propitious. After the manner of a most faithful physician who does not spare pain that he may shew the way to health. But in me these goads of the flesh, these incentives of lust the very fervour of my youth and my experience of the sweetest pleasures greatly stimulate, and all the more oppress me with their assaults the weaker the nature is that they are assaulting. They preach that I am chaste who have not discovered the hypocrite in me. They make the purity of the flesh into a virtue, when it is a virtue not of the body but of the mind. Having some praise among men, I deserve none before God, Who tries out the heart and the reins and sees in the secret places. I am judged religious at this time, in which but a little part of religion is not hypocrisy, when he is extolled with the highest praise who does not offend the judgment of men. And this is peradventure in some measure praiseworthy, and seems in some measure acceptable to God, to wit if any by the example of his outward works, whatever his intention, is not a scandal to the Church, and if by his life the Name of God is not blasphemed among the infidels, nor the Order of his profession defamed among the carnal. And this also is a certain gift of divine grace, to wit one by the aid of which he comes not only to do good but to abstain from evil. But in vain does the former precede when the other follows not; as it is written: "Depart from evil, and do good." And in vain is either done, which is not done in the love of God.

But in the whole period of my life (God wot) I have ever feared to offend thee rather than God, I seek to please thee more than Him. Thy command brought me, not the love of God, to the habit of religion. See how unhappy a life I must lead, more wretched than all others, if I endure all these things here in vain having no hope of reward in the future. For a long time thou, like many others, hast been deceived by my simulation, so as to mistake hypocrisy for religion; and thus, strongly commending thyself to our prayers, what I expect from thee thou demandest from me. Do not, I beseech thee, presume so highly of me, nor cease by praying to assist me. Do not deem me healed, nor withdraw the grace of thy medicine. Do not believe me to be not in want, nor delay to succour my necessity. Do not think this strength, lest I fall before thou hold up the falling. False praise of themselves has injured many, and has taken away the support that they needed. Through *Esaias* the Lord cries: "O my people, they which lead thee cause thee to err, and destroy the way of thy paths." And through *Ezekiel* he says: "Woe to the women that sew pillows to all armholes, and make kerchiefs upon the head of every stature, to hunt souls!" Whereas by *Solomon* it is said: "The words of the wise are as goads, and as nails fastened by the masters of assemblies," nails, to wit, which cannot touch wounds softly but must pierce them. Cease, I beseech thee, from praise of me, lest thou incur the base mark of adulation and the charge of falsehood. Or, if thou suspect in me any good thing, the breath of vanity blow it away when it is praised. No one having skill in medicine judges an inward disease by inspection of the outward appearance. Nor do things obtain any merit before God which are common to the reprobate equally with the elect. And these things are they which are done outwardly, which none of the Saints so zealously performs as do hypocrites. "The heart is deceitful above all things, and desperately wicked: who can know it?" And "there is a way which seemeth right unto a man; but the end thereof are the ways of death." Rash is the judgment of man upon that which is reserved for divine scrutiny alone. Wherefore also it is written: "Judge none blessed before his death." To wit, praise not a man at that time when by praising him thou mayest make him no longer praiseworthy. And so much the more perilous is thy praise to me, the more pleasing it is: and so much the more am I taken and delighted by it, the more I study to please thee in all things.

Always, I beseech thee, be fearful for me rather than place thy trust in me, that I may ever be helped by thy solicitude. But now especially must thou fear, when no remedy is left in thee for my incontinence. I wish not that, exhorting me to virtue, and provoking me to fight, thou say: "Strength is made perfect in weakness"; and: "Yet is he not crowned, unless he strive lawfully." I seek not a crown of victory. It is enough for me to avoid danger. It is safer to avoid danger than to engage in battle. In whatsoever corner of heaven God may place me, He will do enough for me. For none there will envy any, since what he shall have will be sufficient for each. And indeed, that I may add the strength of authority also to this my counsel, let us hear Saint *Jerome:* "I confess my weakness, I wish not to fight in the hope of victory, lest peradventure I lose the victory." What need to abandon things certain, and to follow things uncertain?

THE FOURTH LETTER WHICH IS PETER'S REPLY TO HÉLOISE

Argument: *He divides the whole of* Héloise's *last letter into four heads, and replies clearly: he follows the reasoning of each, not so much to excuse himself as to teach, to exhort and to comfort* Héloise. *And first of all he gives the reason why in his last letter he set her name before his own. Secondly, if he made mention of his own perils and death, he explains that he had been adjured by her to do so. Thirdly, he approves her rejection of the praise that is given her: only she must do this sincerely and without any desire of praise. Fourthly, he pursues at length the occasion of their several conversion to the monastic life. The injury to a base part of his body, which she deplored, he thus extenuates, declaring it to be most salutary to them both, and a source of many good things in comparison with the lewd actions of the said shameful part: and on that account he extols the wisdom and clemency of God. Many other things also are included in the letter for the teaching and exhortation and comfort of* Héloise. *He includes also a short prayer wherewith the nuns of Paraclete may propitiate God towards* Abelard *and* Héloise.

To the Bride of Christ, the servant of the Same.

In four points, I observe, in which the body of thy last letter consists, thou hast expressed the commotion of thy grief. And first of all thou complainest of this, that against the custom in letters, nay against the natural order of things even, our letter to thee placed thy name before mine in the greeting. Secondly, that when I ought rather to have offered thee a remedy for thy comfort, I increased thy desolation and provoked the tears that I should have shyed, by adding in that letter: "If the Lord should deliver me into the hands of mine enemies, so that they prevail over me and slay me," etc. And thirdly thou hast added thine old and assiduous complaint against God, of the manner of our conversion to God and of the cruelty of that betrayal which was practised upon me. Lastly, thou hast made an accusation of thyself against our praise of thee, with no mean supplication that henceforth I presume not so. And each of these points I have decided severally to answer, not so much in excuse of myself as for thine instruction or exhortation, that thou mayest more readily assent to our petitions when thou hast understood that they are based upon reason, and may give ear to me more fully in thine own case when thou findest me less reprehensible in mine, and be the more reluctant to despise me the less deserving thou seest me to be of reproach.

Of the unnatural (as thou sayest) order of our greeting, that was done, if thou examine it closely, according to thine opinion also. For it is common knowledge, as thyself hast shewn, that when any writes to his superiors their names are put first. And thou must understand that thou didst become my superior from that day on which thou becamest to me my lady, becoming the bride of my Lord, according to the words of Saint *Jerome,* writing thus to *Eustochium:* "For this reason I write 'my lady,' *Eustochism.* For I must call her my lady who is the bride of my Lord." Right happy is such an exchange of wedlock; that being formerly the wife of a wretched man thou art now exalted to the bed of the King of Kings. Nor, by the privilege of this honour art thou set over thy former husband only, but, over all and sundry the servants of that King. Marvel not therefore if both alive and dead I commend myself especially to thy prayers, since it is established by the common law that with Lords their wives can more prevail by intercession than the rest of their households, ladies rather than slaves. As a type whereof that Queen and Bride of the King of Kings is diligently described, where it is said in the Psalm: "Upon thy right hand did stand the Queen." As though, to speak openly, she being joined to his side adheres most intimately to her spouse and goes by his side, all the rest standing apart or following. Of the excellence of this prerogative the bride in the Canticles, exulting, that Ethiopian, so to speak, whom *Moses* took to wife, says: "I am black, but comely, O ye daughters of Jerusalem. The King hath brought me into his chambers." And again: "Look not upon me, because I am black, because the sun hath looked upon me." In which words, albeit generally the contemplative soul is described which is called especially the Bride of Christ, yet that they more expressly pertain to you your outward habit shews. For that outward cult of black or coarse garments, in the likeness of the mournful vesture of good widows lamenting the husbands whom they loved, shews you in this world, according to the Apostle, to be widows indeed and desolate, such as are to be relieved at the charge of the Church. The grief of which widows for their spouse that was slain the Scripture commemorates, saying: "The women sitting over against the sepulchre and weeping lamented the Lord."

The Ethiopian woman also has an outward blackness in the flesh, and in so far as pertains to outward things appears less comely than other women; whereas she is not unlike them inwardly, but in many things is more comely and more white, as in her bones or her teeth. The whiteness of which teeth is commended in the husband himself where it is said: "His teeth shall be white with milk." And so she is black in outward things, but in inward things comely; because in this life afflicted in the body by frequent tribulations of adversities, she darkens outwardly in the flesh, as is said by the Apostle: "Yea and all that will live godly in Christ shall suffer persecution." For as by white prosperity, so not incongruously by black is indicated adversity. But inwardly, as in the bones, she is white, because her soul is rich in virtues, as it is written: "The King's daughter is all glorious within." For the bones, which are within, surrounded by the outward flesh, and of that flesh which they bear or sustain are the strength and fortitude, fitly express the soul which gives life to the flesh itself, within which it is, sustains it, moves it, governs it, and ministers to it all well-being. Whereof the whiteness or the comeliness are those virtues wherewith it is adorned.

And she is black also in outward things because, while she is still an exile in this pilgrimage, she keeps herself vile and abject in this life, that in the other she may be made sublime, which is hidden with Christ in God, entering then into her inheritance. So indeed the true sun changes her colour, because the heavenly love of the bridegroom so humiliates her or torments her with tribulations, left prosperity puff her up. He changes her colour thus, that is, he makes her unlike the rest of women who pant for earthly things and, seek the glory of the world, that she may truly be made a lily of the valley by her humility: not indeed a lily of the mountains, like those foolish virgins who from purity of the flesh or from outward abstinence growing puffed up in themselves, are become parched by the fire of temptation. And rightly, in addressing the daughters of Jerusalem, that is the more imperfect of the faithful who deserve rather to be called daughters than sons, she says: "Look not upon me, because I am black, because the sun hath looked upon me." As who should say more openly: "If I thus humiliate myself or endure adversities in so manly a wise, it is not by my virtue but by His grace, whom I serve." Not thus is the use of heretics or hypocrites, who looking to the sight of men, in the hope of earthly glory, vehemently humiliate themselves or endure many evils to no good end. Whose abjection or tribulation of this sort, which they endure, is greatly to be marvelled at, since they are more wretched than all men, who enjoy the good things neither of this present life nor of the life to come. This also the bride diligently considering says: "Marvel not that I do so." But we must marvel at them who, vainly burning with the desire of earthly praise, deprive themselves of earthly riches, impoverishing themselves here as in the world to come. Which indeed is the continence of the foolish virgins, who are shut out from the door.

Rightly also does she say that because she is black, as we have said, and comely, she is beloved and taken into the chamber of the King, that is into the secret place or quiet of contemplation and to that bed whereof she says elsewhere: "By night on my bed I sought him whom my soul loveth." For the

98

uncomeliness of her colour chooses the hidden rather than the open, and the secret rather than the public. And whoso is such a wife desires the secret enjoyment of a husband rather than the open, and will more readily be felt in bed than seen at table. And it often happens that as the flesh of black women is more uncomely, so is it sorer to the touch, and so the enjoyment of them is greater and comes more easily in secret pleasures than in public, and their husbands, to enjoy them, take them in rather to their chambers than out before the world. According to which metaphor this spiritual bride fitly, when she said: "I am black but comely," straightway added, "therefore the King hath loved me and hath brought me into his chambers," relating each to each, namely that because she is comely he has loved her, and because she is black he has brought her into his chambers. Comely, as I have said, with inward virtues, which the bridegroom has loved; black outwardly from the adversity of bodily tribulations. Which blackness indeed, that to wit of bodily tribulations, easily turns away the minds of the faithful from the love of things earthly, and attaches them to the longing for life eternal, and often leads them from the tumultuous life of the world to the secret places of contemplation.

Thus Saint *Jerome* writes that in *Paul* was wrought the beginning of our, that is of the monastic, life. This abjectness also of coarse garments seeks retirement rather than publicity, and is eminently in keeping with the humility and the more secret place which befits our profession. For that nothing more provokes us to display in public than a costly garment, which is sought by none save for vainglory and the pomp of the world, Saint *Gregory* proves to us in these words: "For none adorns himself thus in secret but where he may be seen." As for the aforesaid chamber of the bride, it is that to which the Bridegroom himself in the Gospel invites whoso prays, saying: "But thou, when thou prayest, enter into thy closet, and when thou hast shut the door pray to thy Father which is in secret." As who should say: "Not in the streets and public places like the hypocrites." And so His chamber He calls a place that is secret from the tumults and from the sight of the word, where one may pray more quietly and more purely. Such are surely the secret places of monastic solitudes where we are bidden to close the door, that is to stop up every approach, lest the purity of prayer be any way obstructed, and our eye ravish the unhappy soul. And many of our habit, scorners of this counsel, nay this divine precept, we still find it hard to endure, who when they celebrate the divine offices, opening their cloisters or their quires, shamelessly comport themselves in the public view of women and men alike, and then especially when on solemn feasts they have decked themselves with precious ornaments, are made like unto those to whom they display themselves, profane men. In whose judgment a feast is the better celebrated, the richer it is in outward ornaments and more abundant in offerings. Of whose most wretched blindness, wholly contrary to the religion of Christ, which is of the poor, it is the more honourable to keep silence, the more scandalous it is to speak. Who utterly Judaizing, follow their own custom in place of a rule, and have made God's commandment vain by their tradition attending not to what they ought but to what is their wont. When, as Saint *Augustine* also reminds us, the Lord has said: "I am the Truth," not, "I am the custom." To the prayers of these, which to wit are made with an open door, let him commend himself who will. But ye who in the Chamber of the Heavenly King, led thither by Himself and resting in His embrace, with the door ever shut give yourselves up wholly to Him, the more intimately are joined to Him, according to the words of the Apostle: "He that is joined unto the Lord is one spirit," so much the purer and the more efficacious we believe you to be in prayer, and therefore the more vehemently we demand your aid. Which prayers also we believe are to be made the more devoutly for me, the more closely we are bound by a tie of mutual charity.

But if by the mention of the perils in which I labour, or of the death which I fear, I have distressed you, it was done at thine exhortation, nay adjuration. For so the first letter which thou didst address to me, contains in a certain passage the words: "And so in His Name Who still protects thee in a certain measure for Himself, in the Name of Christ, as His handmaids and thine, we beseech thee to deign to inform us by frequent letters of those shipwrecks in which thou still art tossed, that thou mayest have us at least, who alone have remained to thee, as partners in thy grief or joy. For they are wont to bring some comfort to a grieving man who grieve with him, and any burden that is laid on several is borne more easily, or transferred." Why therefore dost thou complain that I have made you partners in my anxiety, when thou didst, by adjuration compel me: Did it behove thee, in so great a desperation of life, whereby I am tormented, to rejoice: Partners not in grief but in joy only do ye wish to be; nor to weep with them that weep but to rejoice with them that do rejoice? For there is no greater difference between true friends and false than that the former associate themselves with adversity, the latter with prosperity. Cease, I beseech thee, from saying such things, and forbear from complaints of this sort, which are worlds apart from the bowels of charity! Or if thou art still offended in this respect, it behoves me nevertheless, being placed in such a nick of peril, and in daily despair of life, to be solicitous for the welfare of my soul, and to provide for it while I may.

Nor wilt thou, if thou truly love me, find this provision odious. Nay rather, if thou hadst any hope of divine mercy towards me, so much the more wouldst thou wish me to be set free from the hardships of this life as thou seest them to be more intolerable. Thou at least knowest that whoso may deliver me from this life will snatch me front the greatest torments. What I shall hereafter incur is uncertain, but from what I shall be absolved is in no question. Every wretched life has a happy ending, and whoso truly feel compassion for the anxieties of others, and grieve for them, desire that they may be ended; and to their own hurt, even, if those whom they see to be anxious they truly love, and look not so much to their own advantage as to their friends'. Thus when a son has long been lying sick his mother desires his sickness to end even in death, a sickness which she herself cannot endure, and bears more easily to be robbed of him than to have him as a fellow-sufferer. And whosoever most delights in the presence of a friend yet prefers that his absence should be happy than his presence wretched. For hardships which he is unable to remedy he cannot endure. But to thee it is not given to enjoy our presence, wretched as it may be. Nor can I see why, when thou mightest provide anything in me for thine own advantage, thou shouldst prefer me to live most wretched rather than more happily to die. For if thou desirest to prolong our miseries for thine own advantage, thou art proved an enemy rather than a friend. If thou art reluctant so to appear, cease, I beseech thee, as I have said before, from these complaints.

But I approve thy reproval of praise; because in this thou shewest thyself to be the more praiseworthy. For it is written: "He that is first in his own accusation is just"; and: "He that humbleth himself shall be exalted." May it be so in thy heart as in thy writing! If it be so, thine is true humility, nor will it vanish away at our words. But see, I beseech thee, left in this very matter thou be seeking praise when thou seemest to be fleeing it, and reprove that with thy mouth which thou desirest in thy heart. Whereof to *Eustochium* the virgin thus among other things writes Saint *Jerome:* "We are led by our natural evil. We give ear willingly to our flatterers, and albeit we reply that we are unworthy and a cunning blush suffuse our cheeks, yet inwardly the soul rejoices in its own praise." Such cunning also in the wanton, *Galathea Virgil* describes, who what she desired drew after her by flight, and by the feint of a repulse incited her lover more hotly towards her: "And she flies to the willows," he says, "and wishes first to be seen." Before she hides herself she wishes to be seen, in that by that very flight whereby she seems to repulse the company of the youth, she may the more certainly obtain it. Thus it is that, when we seem to be shunning the praise of men, we excite it more warmly towards ourselves, and when we pretend that we wish to hide, lest any, forsooth should discover what there is in us to praise, we excite more hotly to our praise the imprudent, because we seem more worthy of that praise. And this we say because it often occurs, not because we suspect such things of thee, being in no doubt as to thy humility. But from these words also we wish thee to refrain, lest thou appear to those who know thee less, as *Jerome* says, to be seeking fame by shunning it. Never will, my praise puff thee up, but it will provoke thee to better things, and thou wilt embrace all the more zealously those things that I shall have praised, the more anxious thou art to please me. Our praise is not to thee a testimony to thy piety wherefrom thou mayest derive any pride. Nor ought we to believe our friends in their praise of anything, as we ought not to believe our enemies in their vituperation.

It now remains for us to come to that old, as we have said, and assiduous complaint on thy part, that namely wherein thou rather presumest to accuse God for the manner of our conversion than seekest to glorify Him as is fitting. I had thought that this bitterness of thy heart at so manifest an act of divine mercy had long since vanished. Which bitterness, the more perilous it is to thee, wearing out thy body and soul alike, is so much the more miserable and grievous to me. Since thou seekest to please me in all things, as thou professest, in this one thing at least, that thou mayest not torment me, nay that thou mayest supremely please me, lay aside this bitterness. Wherewith neither canst thou please me nor attain with me to blessedness. Wilt thou endure my proceeding thither without thee, I whom thou dost profess thy willingness to follow to the Vulcanian fires: In this one thing at least seek piety, lest thou sunder thyself from me who am hastening, as thou believest, to God; and all the more readily, the more blessed is the goal to which we shall come, that our fellowship may be the more pleasant the more happy it also is. Remember what thou hast said. Call to mind what thou hast written, to wit that in this manner of our conversion, wherein God is believed to have been more thoroughly against me, He shewed Himself to be, as is manifest, more propitious to me. In this one thing at least let His disposition be pleasing to thee, that it is most salutary to me, nay to thee and me alike, if the force of grief admit reason. Neither grieve that thou art the cause of so great a good, for which thou needst not doubt that thou wert principally created by God. Neither lament that I have borne this loss, save when the blessings of the passions of the martyrs and of the death of Our Lord Himself shall make thee sad. Had it befallen me justly, wouldst thou have borne it any more easily, or would it offend thee less? Of a surety, if it were so, the consequence would be that it would be more ignominious for me and more praiseworthy for mine enemies, since justice would acquire praise for them and transgression contempt for me. Neither would any now reproach what has been done, so that he might be moved to compassion for me.

Yet, that in this way we may mitigate the bitterness of this grief, we shall shew that it befell us as justly as profitably, and that God was avenged more righteously upon the wedded than upon the fornicators. Thou knowest that after the pact of our marriage, when thou didst retire to Argenteuil with the nuns in cloister, I on a certain day did come to thee privily to visit thee, and what the intemperance of my desire then wrought with thee, even in a certain part of the refectory itself, since we had no place else whereto we might repair. Thou knowest, I say, how shamelessly we then acted in so hallowed a place, and on consecrated to the Most Holy Virgin. Which, all other shameful acts apart, must be a token of a far more dire punishment. Need I recall our earlier fornications and most shameful pollutions which preceded our marriage? Or shall I then recall my supreme betrayal whereby I turned away from thee thine uncle, with whom I was living constantly in his own house. Who would not consider that I was justly betrayed by him whom so shamelessly I myself had first betrayed? Dost thou think that the momentary pain of that wound suffices for the punishment of such crimes? Nay, for such wrongdoing is such a payment fitting? What wound dost thou imagine to satisfy the justice of God for so great a contamination, as we have said, of the most consecrated abode of His Mother? Of a surety, unless I am greatly in error, it was not that most wholesome wound that was turned to a punishment of those crimes, but the wounds which daily without ceasing I now endure. Thou knowest also how, when I carried thee pregnant to mine own country, thou didst put on the sacred habit and feign thyself to be a nun, and by such a pretence irreverently cozen the religion which now thou holdest. Wherefore consider how fitly to that religion divine justice, nay grace has led thee against thy will, which thou wert not afraid to cozen; wishing thee to expiate in the same habit the profanation that thou hadst made of it, and that the truth of the event should furnish a remedy for the lie of thy pretence, and correct the falsehood. And if thou wilt add to the divine justice wrought upon thee the thought of our own interest, thou wilt be able to call what God then did to us not so much His justice as His grace.

Take heed, therefore, take heed, beloved, with what drawnets of His mercy, from the depths of this so perilous sea the Lord has fished us up, and from the gullet of what a Charybdis He has saved our shipwrecked albeit unwilling souls, so that each of us may fitly break out in that cry: *"Yet the Lord thinketh upon me."* Think, and think again in what dangers we were placed, and from what dangers the Lord plucked us out; and repeat always with the utmost thanksgiving what things the Lord has done for our soul; and comfort by our example any unrighteous who may despair of God's bounty, that they all may know what things are given to those that supplicate and pray, when such benefits are conferred upon the sinful and reluctant. Perpend the supreme designs of divine piety towards us, and how mercifully the Lord has turned His judgment into regeneration, and how prudently He has made use of the evil also, and piously deposed impiety, that the most just injury to one part of my body might heal two souls. Compare the danger and the manner of deliverance. Compare the sickness and the medicine. Examine the cause—our deserts, and marvel at the effect—His mercy.

Thou knowest to what great infamies my immoderate lust had sacrificed our bodies, until no reverence for honour, nor for God even, for the days of Our Lord's Passion or of any solemnity soever could recall me from wallowing in that filth. And thee also unwilling and to the utmost of thy power resisting and dissuading me, being weaker by nature, often with threats and blows I drew to consent. For with such ardour of concupiscence I was attached to thee that those wretched and most obscene pleasures which even to name confounds us, I preferred both to God and to myself; nor could divine clemency seemingly decide otherwise than by forbidding me those pleasures utterly, without any hope. Wherefore most justly and most clemently, albeit with the supreme treachery of thine uncle, that I might grow in many things, of that part of my body have I been diminished wherein was the seat of lust, and the whole cause of this concupiscence consisted, that rightly that member might mourn which had committed all in us, and might expiate in suffering what it had misdone in enjoyment, and might cut me off from those filthinesses wherein as in the mire I had immersed myself wholly, circumcising me in mind as in body; and so make me more fit to approach the holy altar, in that no contagion of carnal pollutions might ever again call me thence. With what clemency also did He wish me to suffer so greatly in that member, the privation of which would both aid the salvation of my soul and not degrade my body, nor prevent me in any ministration of mine office. Nay, it would make me so much more prompt to all things that are honourably done, the more wholly it set me free from the heavy yoke of concupiscence.

When therefore of these vilest members which from their practice of the utmost filthiness are called shameful, nor bear their proper name, divine grace cleansed me rather than deprived me, what else did it do than, to preserve the purity of cleanness, remove the sordid and vicious: This purity of cleanness indeed we have heard that sundry wise men most vehemently desiring have laid hands also upon themselves, that they might remove utterly from themselves this disgrace of concupiscence. For the removal of which thorn in the flesh the Apostle also is recorded to have besought the Lord, and not to have been heard. An example is that great philosopher of the Christians, *Origen,* who, that he might wholly extinguish this fire in himself, was not afraid to lay hands upon himself; as if he understood in the letter that they were truly blessed who for the Kingdom of Heaven's sake made themselves eunuchs, and believed such to be truthfully fulfilling what the Lord enjoins about the members by which offence cometh, that we should cut them off and cast them from us, and as if he interpreted that prophecy of *Esaias* as history rather than as mystery, wherein the Lord prefers eunuchs to the rest of the faithful, saying: "The eunuchs that keep my sabbaths, and choose the things that please me, and take hold of my covenant; even unto them will I give in mine house and within my walls a place and a name better than of sons and of daughters: I will give them an everlasting name, that shall not be cut off." And yet *Origen* incurs no small blame when in the punishment of his body he seeks a remedy for his fault. Having zeal, doubtless, for God, but not according to knowledge, he incurs the guilt of homicide, by laying a hand upon himself. By the suggestion of the devil or by the greatest of errors, plainly he wrought this upon himself which through the mercy of God was perpetrated upon me by another. I escape blame, I incur it not. I deserve death, and I obtain life. I am called, and I hold back. The Apostle prays, and is not heard. He persists in prayer, and prevails not. Truly the Lord thinketh upon me. I will go and declare what the Lord hath done for my soul.

Approach then also, my inseparable comrade, in a common thanksgiving, who hast been made a partner both in the fault and in the grace. For of thy salvation also the Lord is not unmindful, nay He is most mindful of thee, Who, by a sort of holy presage of His Name, marked thee down to be especially His, to wit when he called thee *Héloise,* after His Own Name which is *Elohim;* He, I say, in His clemency has resolved to aid two in one, which two the devil strove in one to extinguish. For, but a little while before this befell us, He had bound us mutually by the indissoluble law of the nuptial sacrament, when I desired to retain thee, beloved beyond measure, for myself for all time, nay when He Himself was already preparing to convert us both to Himself by these means. For if thou hadst not been joined to me already in matrimony, easily on my withdrawal from the world, either at the suggestion of thy kindred or in thy relish for carnal pleasures, thou mightest have clung to the world. See, therefore, how solicitous the Lord was for us, as though He were reserving us for some great ends, and as though He were indignant, or grieved, that those talents of literary knowledge which He had entrusted to us both should not be dispensed to the glory of His Name; or as though, even, He feared for His most incontinent servant what is written in the Scripture: "that women make even the wise to fall away." As it is known of the wisest of men, namely *Solomon.*

But the talent of thy prudence, what usury it returns daily to the Lord, thou who hast already borne many spiritual daughters to the Lord, while I remain utterly barren, and labour in vain among the sons of perdition! Oh, how detestable a loss, how lamentable a misfortune, if, given over to the filthiness of carnal pleasures, thou were to bring forth a few children with pain for the world who now art delivered of a numerous progeny with exultation for heaven! Nor wouldst thou then be more than a woman, who now transcendest men even, and hast turned the curse of *Eve* to the blessing of *Mary.* Oh, how indecently would those holy hands, which now turn the pages of sacred books, serve the obscenities of womanly cares! He Himself has deigned to raise us up from the contagion of this filth, from the pleasures of this mire, and to draw us to Himself by force, wherewith He chose by striking him to convert Saint *Paul,* and by this example, haply, wrought in us, to deter others, skilled also in letters, from similar presumption. Let not this, therefore, distress thee, sister, I beseech thee, neither trouble thou the Father Who paternally corrects us; but pay heed to what is written: "Whom the Lord loveth He chasteneth, and scourgeth every son whom He receiveth." And elsewhere: "He that spareth his rod hateth his son." This punishment is momentary, not eternal; one of purgation, not of damnation. Hear the prophet, and take courage: "What do ye imagine against the Lord? He will make an utter end; affliction shall not rise up the second time." Hearken to that supreme and mighty exhortation of the Truth: "In your patience possess ye your souls." Wherefore also *Solomon:* "He that is slow to anger is better than the mighty; and he that ruleth his spirit than he that taketh a city." Does He not move thee to tears or to compunction, the Only-begotten Son of God, innocent, for thee and for all mankind taken by the hands of most impious men, led, beaten, and with veiled face mocked and buffeted, spat upon, crowned with thorns, and finally on what was then so ignominious a gibbet, the Cross, hung between thieves, and by that then horrible and execrable form of death slain? Hold Him ever, sister, as thy true Spouse, and the Spouse of all the Church before thine eyes, bear Him in thy mind. Behold Him going out to be crucified for thee, and Himself bearing the Cross. Be of the people, of the women who wept and wailed for Him, as *Luke* relates in these words: "And there followed Him a great company of people, and of women, which also bewailed and lamented him." To whom indeed graciously turning, with clemency He foretold the destruction that was to come in vengeance of His death, which indeed, if they were wise, they might avoid by following this counsel: "Daughters of Jerusalem," He said, "weep not for Me, but weep for yourselves, and for your children. For, behold, the days are coming, in the which they shall say, Blessed are the barren, and the wombs that never bare, and the paps which never gave suck. Then shall they begin to say to the mountains, Fall on us; and to the hills, Cover us. For if they do these things in a green tree, what shall be done in the dry?"

Have compassion upon Him Who suffered willingly for thy redemption, and look with compunction upon Him Who was crucified for thee. Be present ever in thy mind at His Sepulchre, and with the faithful women bewail and lament. Of whom also, as I have said, it is written: "The women sitting over against the sepulchre lamented the Lord." Prepare with them the ointments for His burial, but better ointments, spiritual indeed not corporeal; for he requires the former fragrance who did not accept the latter. Be compunctious over these duties with the whole force of thy devotion. To which compunction of compassion indeed Himself also, through *Jeremy*, exhorts the faithful, saying: "Is it nothing to you, all ye that pass by? behold, and see if there be any sorrow like unto my sorrow, which is done unto me." That is, if there be any suffering for whom ye ought to grieve in compassion when I alone, for no fault, pay the penalty for the wrong-doing of others. He Himself is the Way whereby the faithful out of exile pass into the promised land. Who also raised up the Cross, wherefrom He thus cries, as a ladder for us to that end. Here for thee is slain the Only-begotten Son of God, as a free will offering. Over Him alone grieve with compassion, be compassionate with grief. And that which was prophesied by *Zachary* the Prophet of devout souls, do thou fulfil: "They shall mourn for him, as one mourneth for his only son, and shall be in bitterness for him, as one that is in bitterness for his first born."

See, sister, what a lamentation arises among those who love the King, over the death of his first-born and only-begotten son. Consider with what lamentation the household, with what sorrow the whole court is consumed; and when thou comest to the bride of the only-begotten who is dead, thou shall not endure her intolerable wailings. This lamentation, sister, be thine; this wailing be thine, who hast given thyself in happy matrimony to the Bridegroom. He bought thee not with His wealth but with Himself. With His own Blood He bought thee and redeemed thee. What right He has over thee see, and behold how precious thou art. This price, indeed, which was paid for him the Apostle considering, and perpending how small a part of this price he was worth for whom it was paid, and attaching what return he should make for such a grace, says: "God forbid that I should glory save in the Cross of our Lord Jesus Christ, by Whom the world is crucified unto me, and I unto the world." Thou art greater than the heaven, thou art greater than the world; of whom the Creator of the world is Himself become the price. What, I ask, has He, Who lacketh nothing, seen in thee, that to purchase thee He should strive even unto the agony of so horrid and ignominious a death: What, I say, does He seek in thee save thyself? He is a true friend Who desires thyself, not what is thine. He is a true friend Who when about to die for thee said: "Greater love hath no man than this that a man lay down his life for his friends."

He truly loved thee, and not I. My love, which involved each of us in sin, is to be called concupiscence, not love. I satisfied my wretched desires in thee, and this was all that I loved. For thee, thou sayest, I have suffered, and peradventure that is true; but rather through thee, and that unwillingly. Not from love of thee but by compulsion of myself. Neither for thy salvation, but for thy grief. But He for thy salvation, He for thee of His own Will suffered, Who by His suffering heals all sickness, takes away all suffering. In Him, I beseech thee, not in me, be thy whole devotion, thy whole compassion, thy whole compunction. Grieve for the iniquity of such cruelty perpetrated upon One so innocent, not for the just punishment in righteousness of me, nay the supreme grace, as has been said, given to us both. For thou art unrighteous, if thou lovest not righteousness; and most unrighteous, if thou knowingly art adverse to the will, nay to the so great grace of God. Weep for thy Saviour, not for thy seducer; for thy Redeemer, not for thy defiler; for the Lord dead for thee, not the servant living, nay now for the first time truly freed from death. Beware, I beseech thee, lest what *Pompey* said to the mourning *Cornelia* be most basely applied to thee:

> *After the combat still the Hero lives:*
> *His fortune perishes; thy tears are shed*
> *For that which thou didst love.*

Pay heed, I pray thee, to this, and blush, lest what thou hast in mind be our former most shameless filthiness. Accept, therefore, sister, accept, I beg of thee, with patience such things as mercifully have befallen us. This is the rod of the father, not the sword of the persecutor. The father strikes that he may correct, lest the enemy wound that he may kill. With a wound He prevents death, He deals it not; He thrusts in the steel that he may cut off the disease. He wounds the body, and heals the soul. He should have slain, and He makes to live. He withers up the uncleanness, that He may make clean. He punishes once that He may not punish always, one suffers by the wound that two may be spared from death. Two were in the fault, one in the punishment. This also is granted by the divine commiseration to the infirmity of thy nature, and in a measure justly. For inasmuch as naturally thou wert the weaker in sex and the stronger in continence, thou wert less liable to punishment. I give thanks to the Lord for this, Who thee then both set free from punishment, and preserved for a crown, and together with me, by the suffering of my body, cooled once and always from all the heat of this concupiscence, in which I had been wholly absorbed by my unbounded incontinence, lest I be destroyed; many passions of the heart, too strong for thy youth, from the assiduous suggestion of the flesh, He has reserved for the crown of martyrdom. Which albeit it may wean thee to hear, and thou forbid me to say, yet the truth is manifest. For to whom there is ever the strife, remains the crown; for he shall not be crowned, except he strive lawfully. But for me no crown remains, since there remains no cause for strife. The matter for the strife is lacking in him from whom is plucked out the thorn of concupiscence.

Yet I esteem it to be something if, though I may hereafter receive no crown, I may nevertheless escape some punishment, and by the pain of one momentary punishment may haply be forgiven many and eternal. For it is written of the men, nay the beasts of this most wretched life: "The beasts have rotted in their dung." Also I complain less that my merit is diminished, while I doubt not that thine increases. For we are one in Christ, one flesh by the law of matrimony. Whatsoever is thine cannot, I consider, but be mine also. But thine is Christ, for thou art become His Bride. And now, as I have said, thou has me for thy servant, whom formerly thou knewest as thy lord; yet more joined to thee now by spiritual love than subjected by fear. Wherefore also in thy patronage of us before Him we greatly trust, that I may obtain that by thy prayer which I cannot by mine own. And now especially, when the daily pressure of perils or perturbations allows me neither to live nor to find leisure for prayer. Nor to imitate that most blessed eunuch in authority under *Candace* Queen of the Ethiopians, who had the charge of all her treasure, and had come from so far to Jerusalem for to worship. To whom as he was returning there was sent by an angel *Philip* the Apostle, that he might convert him to the faith: Which he had merited already by his prayer or assiduity in holy reading. Whereby indeed, that not even then upon his journey might he be idle, albeit very rich and a Gentile, it befell by a great benefit of divine dispensation that the passage in the Scripture was before him which should furnish to the Apostle a most opportune occasion for his conversion. But that nothing may prevent this our petition, nor delay its fulfilment, I have studied to compose a prayer also, which ye may repeat as suppliants for me to the Lord, and to send it to thee.

GOD, Who from the first beginning of the human creation, with woman formed from the rib of man didst sanctify the great sacrament of the nuptial bond, and Who hast raised marriage to the greatest honour, as well by being born of a Virgin given in marriage, as by the first of Thy miracles, and for the incontinence of my frailty, when it phased Thee, hast aforetime granted this remedy, despise not the prayer of Thine handmaid, which for mine own excesses and for those of my beloved in the sight of Thy Majesty I pour forth in supplication. Pardon, O most bountiful, nay bounty itself: pardon our so great offences, and may the ineffable immensity of Thy Mercy make trial of the multitude of our faults. Punish, I beseech Thee, in this world the guilty, that Thou mayest spare them in the world to come. Punish for the time, punish not in eternity. Take to Thy servants the rod of correction, not the sword of wrath. Afflict our flesh, that Thou mayest preserve our souls. Be a purifier, not an avenger; bountiful rather than just; the Merciful Father, not the Austere Lord. Prove us, O Lord, and try us, as the Prophet asks Thee of himself, as though to say: First examine my strength, and according thereto moderate the burden of temptations. Which also Saint *Paul* promising to Thy faithful, says: "God is faithful, Who will not suffer you to be tempted above that ye are able; but will with the temptation also make a way to escape, that ye may be able to bear it." Thou hast joined us together, O Lord, and Thou has put us asunder when it pleased Thee and in the manner that pleased Thee. Now, O Lord, what Thou hast mercifully begun most mercifully finish. And these whom Thou hast divided one from another once upon earth join perennially to Thyself in heaven. Our hope, our portion, our expectation, our comfort, Lord Who art Blessed, world without end. AMEN.

Farewell in Christ, Bride of Christ, in Christ fare well, and in Christ dwell. AMEN.

SECTION5

Selections from LYRICS OF
THE TROUBADOURS AND TROUVÈRES

Introduction by Albrecht Classen

Troubadours were the courtly singers active first in Southern France since the late eleventh century, and the trouvères were the poets active in the Northern part of France. "Troubadour" derives from Old Occitan, meaning "the finder" or composer of songs about *fin'amor*. This term means the desire to gain unrequited love, bestowable only by a lady, mostly not identified by name. This kind of courtly and aristocratic poetry was presented orally in the language of the Occitan region. There are about 350 composers known by their names, many of whom also served as patrons for other singers dependent on money for their performances. Whereas one of the earliest troubadours, Duke William IX of Aquitaine (1071–1127), grandfather of the famous Eleanor of Aquitaine, often formulates rather earthly and sexually explicit ideas about love, most of his followers and contemporaries elaborated a highly refined and abstract concept of love, the idea of courtly love. Guillem de Petieus, as he was also called, initiated one of the most important intellectual games for the troubadours, by challenging his audience to decipher the true meaning of his poem.

We have no clear idea where the idea to compose troubadour poetry came from, but a number of theories exist which suggest either that the Arabs in Spain and in Palestine influenced the Christian crusaders with their own love poetry, or that a new form of Marian veneration since the early twelfth century spreading all over Europe might have inspired the worldly poets to transfer the religious imagery to the secular sphere. Possibly the rise of court life in Southern France triggered the development of troubadour poetry, possibly it was influenced by popular love songs, but were refined and transformed into courtly love poetry with the new wealth and power of the aristocracy.

Many different styles and imageries can be found in troubadour poetry. Mostly, the male lover is desperate and longs for his beloved, but does not know how to overcome the physical distance and her resistance. In other types of

110

songs, the dawn songs, the lovers have spent a night together and now, with the coming of dawn, must part from each other. In spring songs the beginning of spring and the return of love are celebrated. In the *pastourella* the male lover encounters a peasant woman, for instance a shepherdess, and more or less forcefully convinces her to make love. In some cases, though, the male lover is angered and criticizes his lady for being so recalcitrant or inattentive.

The troubadours soon influenced their Northern contemporaries, and they in turn or in tandem with them later exerted an influence on the German *Minnesänger* and the Italian poets of the *Dolce stil nuovo*.

BIBLIOGRAPHY

A Handbook of the Troubadours. Ed. F. R. P. Akehurst and Judith M. Davis (Berkeley-Los Angeles-London: University of California Press, 1995).

Medieval France: An Encyclopedia, ed. William W. Kibler and Grover A. Zinn (New York and London: Garland, 1995.

Words of Love and Love of Words in the Middle Ages and the Renaissance, ed. Albrecht Classen. Medieval and Renaissance Texts and Studies, 347 (Tempe: Arizona Center for Medieval and Renaissance Studies, 2008).

GUILLAUME (1071–1127)

Guillaume, the seventh Count of Poitiers and the ninth Duke of Aquitaine, was the lord of an immense realm. He succeeded his father in 1086, and from that moment to the end of his life his rule involved him in interminable conflicts with his own vassals, the lords of other domains, the King of France, and the Church. In 1101 he led a disastrous crusade into the Holy Land. In 1120 he aided the King of Aragón in a victorious battle against the Moors. Guillaume is depicted by contemporary chroniclers as witty, boisterous, riotous, salacious, "as though he believed all things were moved by chance, and not ruled by Providence"; and he was excommunicated many times for various reasons: many disputes with the Church regarding rights, and a liaison with the Vicomtesse de Châtellerault that he refused to terminate. He told the papal legate, who was bald: "The comb will curl the hair on your head before I put aside the Vicomtesse."

Guillaume is the first troubadour whose songs are extant, and he is sometimes regarded as the originator of the courtly love lyric. In any case, whether he is really the first troubadour or rather the first whose work survives, this boisterous misruler of his realm was a first-rate poet. In eleven little lyrics, which are all that we have today, he shows his mastery of the basic metrical forms and the essential themes that would hardly vary in the troubadour lyric in the following generations; and, most important of all, he perfects the technique of composing a song for performance before an audience. For versification and theme are of the essence of all poetry; but the special distinction of the troubadour lyric is that it depends for its coherence and effect on a live relation between the poet, or the singer, and an attending audience.

My companions, I am going to make a *vers* that is refined,
and it will have more foolishness than sense,
and it will all be mixed with love and joy and youth.

Whoever does not understand it, take him for a peasant,
whoever does not learn it deep in his heart.
It is hard for a man to part from love that he finds to his desire.

I have two good and noble horses for my saddle,
they are good, adroit in combat, full of spirit,
but I cannot keep them both, one can't stand the other.

If I could tame them as I wish,
I would not want to put my equipment anywhere else,
for I'd be better mounted then than any man alive.

One of them was the fastest of the mountain horses,
but for a long time now it has been so fierce and shy,
so touchy, so wild, it fights off the currycomb.

The other was nurtured down there around Confolens,
and you never saw a prettier one, I know.
I won't get rid of that one, not for gold or silver.

I gave it to its master as a grazing colt;
but I reserved the right
that for every year he had it, I got it for more than a hundred.

You knights, counsel me in this predicament,
no choice ever caused me more embarrassment:
I can't decide which one to keep, Na Agnes or Na Arsen.

Of Gimel I have the castle and the fief,
and with Niol I show myself proud to everyone,
for both are sworn to me and bound by oath.

2

My companions, I have had so much miserable fare,
I cannot keep from singing and from feeling vexed.
Still, I do not want my little doings known in great detail.

And I shall tell you my thoughts:
these things do not please me: a cunt under guard, a fishpond without fish,
and the boasting of worthless men when there is never to be any action.

Lord God, King and Ruler of the universe,
why did he who first set a guard on cunt not perish?
For no servant or protector ever served his lady worse.

But I shall tell you about cunt, what its law is,
as one who has done badly in this matter and suffered worse:
as other things diminish when you take from them, cunt increases.

And those who will not believe my advice,
let them go and behold in a private preserve near the woods:
for every tree that gets cut down, two or three grow up in its place.

And as the wood is cut, the thicker it grows,

and the lord does not lose any property or dues.
A man is wrong to cry damaged goods when there is no loss.
It is wrong to cry loss when there's no damaged goods.

3

I will make a *vers* of exactly nothing:
there'll be nothing in it about me or anyone else,
nothing about love or youth
or anything else.
It came to me before, while I was sleeping
on my horse.

I do not know the hour of my birth.
I am not cheerful or morose,
I am no stranger here and do not belong in these parts,
and I can't help being this way,
I was turned into this, one night, by some fairy
high on a peak.

I don't know when I slept
or wake, if someone doesn't tell me.
My heart is almost broken
from the grief in it,
and I swear by Saint Martial, to me the whole thing
isn't worth a mouse.

I am sick and shiver at death
and don't know it except when I'm told.
I will look for the doctor I have in mind,
I don't' know who he is.
He's a good doctor if he can make me well,
but not if I get worse.

I have my little friend, I don't know who she is,
because I've never seen her, so help me God;
she's done nothing to make me feel good, or bad,
and I don't care,
because there's never been a Frenchman or a Norman yet

inside my house.

I have never seen her and love her a lot,
she has never yet done right by me, or wrong.
When I do not see her, I enjoy myself.
And I don't care a cock,
because I know a nicer one, better looking,
and worth more.

I do not know the region where she dwells,
whether it's in the heights or on the plains.
I dare not tell how she wrongs me,
it hurts me in advance.
And it pains me to stay on here,
and so I go.

I have made this *vers,* I don't know what about;
and I shall send it to someone
who will send it for me with someone else
to someone in Anjou there;
let him send me from his little box the key
to what we have here.

4

I shall make a *vers,* since I am sleeping,
and walking around, and standing in the sun.
Well, there are ladies who are all wrongheaded,
and I can say who:
the ones who turn down the love of a knight
and treat it badly.

A lady who does not love a loyal knight
commits a great mortal sin.
But if she loves a cleric or a monk
she is in error:
her they should burn by right
with firebrands.

In Auvergne, beyond Limousin,
I was walking alone, on the sly.
I met the wives of En Garin
and En Bernard.
They greeted me modestly in the name
of Saint Leonard.

One of them says to me with her high-class speech:

"God save you, my lord pilgrim,
you look to me like a gentleman,
as far as I can tell;
but we all see crazy fools too often
walking through the world."

Now you are going to hear how I answered them:
I didn't say but or bat to them,
didn't mention a stick or a tool,
but only this:
"Babariol, babariol,
barbarian."

Then Agnes says to Ermessen:
"We've found what we are looking for.
Sister, for the love of God let us take him in,
he is really mute,
with this one what we have in mind
will never get found out."

One of them took me under her mantle
and brought me to her chamber, by the fireplace.
Let me tell you, I liked it,
and the fire was good,
and I gladly warmed myself
by the big coals.

To eat they gave me capons,
and you can be sure I had more than two,
and there was no cook or cook's boy there,
but just the three of us,
and the bread was white, and the wine was good,
and the pepper plentiful.

"Sister, this man is tricky,
he's stopped talking just for us.
Let us bring in our red cat
right now,
it'll make him talk soon enough,
if he's fooling us."

Agnes went for that disgusting animal,
and it was big, it had a big long mustache,
and I, when I saw it, among us, there,
I got scared,
I nearly lost my courage

and my nerve.
When we had drunk and eaten,
I took my clothes off, to oblige them.
They brought the cat up behind me,
it was vicious.
One of them pulls it down my side,
down to my heel.

She gets right to it and pulls the cat down
by the tail, and it scratches:
they gave me more than a hundred sores
that time;
but I wouldn't have budged an inch
if they killed me.

"Sister," Agnes says to Ermessen,
"he's mute, all right.
So, Sister, let us get ourselves a bath
and unwind."
Eight days and more I stayed
in that oven.

I fucked them, you shall hear how many times:
one hundred and eighty-eight times. C.LXXX.VIII.
I nearly broke my breeching strap
and harness.
And I cannot tell the vexation,
it hurt so bad.

No, no, I cannot tell the vexation,
it hurt so bad.

5

I want everyone to tell
whether there's good color to this *vers*
that I have brought out of my workshop:
because I'm the one that gets the flower in this craft,
and that is the truth,
and I will call this *vers* to witness
when it is all laced up.

I know what wisdom is, and foolishness,
and I know what honor is, and shame,
I can tell bravery and fear;
and set before me a game of love,

I am no such fool
but I can tell the best chances
from the worst.

I know which man speaks courteously to me,
yes, and which one seeks my harm,
and I know the one who smiles at me,
and whether valiant men take pleasure in my company;
I understand,
I too must try to get their trust
and solace.

A blessing on the man who brought me up,
for my portion he gave me such great skill,
I have never disappointed anyone;
because I know how to play, on a cushion,
every winning roll;
I know more than anyone around,
this man you see before you.

I praise God for it, and Saint Julian,
I have learned that sweet game so well,
I have a winning hand over all the others;
and whoever wants advice from me,
I will not deny him,
no one will ever part from me
unadvised.

For they call me the old reliable master:
that's right, my little friend will never have me for a night
without wanting to have me again next day;
for in this craft—that's right, I boast of it—I am
so expert,
I could earn my bread by it
in any exchange.

But, friends, you don't hear me bragging
that I wasn't shaken up the other day.
I was playing at a game that was gross
and enjoying it enormously, at first—
till I took my place at the gaming table:
I took one look, and I lost the whole craft,
I was that unnerved.

But she gave me this reproach:
"My Lord, your dice are too small,

I challenge you to start again."
I said, "If they gave me Montpellier,
I shall not fail."
And I raised her gaming table a little
with my two arms.

And when I had raised the gaming table
I threw the dice,
and two of them rolled,
and the third sank.

And I made them strike that table hard,
and it was played.

6

Now when we see the meadows once again
in flower and the orchards turning green,
streams and fountains running clear,
the breezes and the winds,
it is right that each man celebrate the joy
that makes him rejoice

Now I must not say anything but good of Love.
Why do I get not one bit of it?
Maybe I wasn't meant for more.
And yet how freely
it gives great joy to any man who upholds
its rules.

This is the way it has always been with me:
I never had the joy of what I loved,
and I never will, as I never did.
For I am aware,
I do many things and my heart says,
"It is all nothing."

And so I know less than anyone what pleasure is,
because I want what I cannot have.
And yet, one wise saying tells me
the certain truth:
"When the heart is good, its power is good,
if a man knows patience."

Surely no one can ever be Love's
perfect man unless he gives it homage in humility
and is obliging to strangers

and acquaintances,
and to all the people of that realm
obedient.

A man who wants to be a lover
must meet many people with obedience,
and must know how to do
the things that fit in court,
and must keep, in court, from speaking
like a vulgar man.

Concerning this *vers* I tell you a man is all the more noble
as he understands it, and he gets more praise;
and all the strophes are built exactly
on the same meter,
and the melody, which I myself am happy about,
is fine and good.

Let my *vers*, since I myself do not,
appear before her,
Mon Esteve, and let it be the witness
for my praise.

7

I shall make a new song
before the wind blows and it freezes and rains.
My lady is trying me, putting me to the test
to find out how I love her.
Well now, no matter what quarrel she moves for that reason,
She shall not loose me from her bond.

Instead, I become her man, deliver myself up to her,
and she can write my name down in her charter.
Now don't go thinking I must be drunk
if I love my virtuous lady,
for without her I have no life,
I have caught such hunger for her love.

For you are whiter than ivory,
I worship no other woman.
If I do not get help soon
and my lady does not give me love,
by Saint Gregory's holy head I'll die
if she doesn't kiss me in a chamber or under a tree.

What shall it profit you, my comely lady,

if your love keeps me far away?
I swear, you want to become a nun.
And you better know, I love you so much
I'm afraid the pain will prick me to death,
if you don't do right by me for the wrongs I cry against you.

MARCABRU (fl. 1129–1150)

Marcabru was a Gascon, born in the first decade of the twelfth century. One of the vidas makes him a foundling, while he himself says he was the son of a poor woman named Marcabruna. He had many patrons throughout the Midi and Spain, including Guillaume X of Aquitaine, the son of "the first troubadour," and Alfonso of Castile and León.

The low birth and noble patronage are reflected in his point of view and in the variety of his style. No one equals him in the furor with which he denounces the effeminacy and depravity of the courtly life and the conventions of courtly love. From this moral urgency and highly idiomatic style arises some of the most difficult poetry in the whole Troubadour canon, the first instance of *trobar clus*, the hermetic style. But these moralizing lyrics are only one mark of his range. At the other end are songs extolling true love; and other songs, such as *A la fontana* and the *pastorela*, which dramatize a profoundly medieval view of right order— they are among the most civilized utterances in Provençal poetry.

His influence was great, not only on the practitioners of the hermetic style, but on others who chose from the wide variety of his forms, or who took up his moral stance. But no one could ever re-create his irascible and exalted tone. About forty-two lyrics are extant.

The most frequent theme in his songs is the distinction between true love and false love: true love is joyful, intense, in harmony with the welfare of a community and with divine intentions; false love is bitter, dissolute, self-regarding, and destructive. He denounces the courtly class for its preciousness and lust—it is on the way to ruin because it is infested with its own bastards, the women trick their husbands into raising the children of others, the men are cuckoos who lay their eggs in someone else's nest. And pandering to this cupidity are the troubadours, a vile crowd (*gens frairina*) of liars and madmen who defame love and glorify lust.

In the songs of Marcabru we see for the first time the figure of the singer who takes a stand against the "false lovers," the *fals amador*, whom he identifies as the other poets of the court. From this position Marcabru distinguishes different kinds of people in the society he addresses: they will become the characters whom future poets will identify as their audience—besides the false lovers, the flatterers, the slanderers, the spies, the envious, the vulgar; and the true lovers, who will be the singer's "friends."

The poets who followed Marcabru retained all these designations, though they did not take up Marcabru's religious values or his prophetic stance. For they were concerned with defining the values of courtliness in terms of a fictional love relation, and they stood before their audience as constituents and spokesmen. The differences between their poetry and Marcabru's reflect the differences of their poetic task and their performing attitude.

However, these differences are not so great as has sometimes been made out. What Marcabru means by true love is a secular experience: it is not *caritas*, or the love of God and of all things in God; it is love between man and woman. This love is good because it is involved in a larger life, the life of a society, a noble class that has a certain ethical and religious mandate, in Marcabru's eyes. True love is of this earth and this life, and it is intense and full of joy; but in a wonderful way, because the lovers themselves are good and have courtly virtues, like steadfastness and restraint, their love inevitably realizes a divine intention, the calling of their class.

This is made very clear in *A la fontana* (no. 10), for example, where the speaker's voice of carnality is silenced by the young girl's unanswerable lament. She calls down a curse on King Louis for commanding the crusade and complains to Jesus that her sorrow is great because of Him; and in her final words she brushes aside the very thought of eternal joy in the world to come: that means nothing to her, because right now her one joy is far away. Now that is hardly what the Fathers of the Church meant by charity. And yet, with all her indifference to religion, she speaks, in the rapture of her loyalty and grief, with the voice of true love. The narrator is blinded by his carnality and cannot speak except in carnal terms: too much weeping makes the flesh grow pale, the color fade; there is no need to despair, God can provide plenty of joy, he tells her— hoping she will notice him. But she, in her purity and faithfulness, does not understand his meaning, she thinks he must be referring to the life in heaven. Oh, yes, she says, there is that—but that has nothing to do with me right now. Now this is not *caritas*, and to call it that would not only degrade divine love, which truly is greater than this, but also diminish the dignity of her grief. Her love is *Amors*, good love; the narrator's love is *Amars*, bitter love, the bitterness of lust, cupidinous and humiliating. And both are of this earth.

10

By the fountain in the orchard,
where the grass is green down to the sandy banks,
in the shade of a planted tree,
in a pleasant setting of white flowers
and the ancient song of the new season,
I found her alone, without a companion,
this girl who does not want my company.

She was a young girl, and beautiful,

the daughter of a castle lord.
And just as I reckoned the birds
must be filling her with joy, and the green things,
in this sweet new time,
and she would gladly hear my little speech,
suddenly her whole manner changed.

Her eyes welled up beside the fountain,
and she sighed from the depths of her heart,
"Jesus," she said, "King of the world,
because of You my grief increases,
I am undone by your humiliation,
for the best men of this whole world
are going off to serve you, that is your pleasure.

"With you departs my so
handsome, gentle, valiant, noble friend;
here, with me, nothing of him remains but the great distress,
the frequent desiring, and the tears.
Ai! damn King Louis,
he gave the orders and the sermons,
and grief invaded my heart."

When I heard how she was losing heart,
I came up to her beside the clear stream.
"Beautiful one," I said, "with too much weeping
your face grows pale, the color fades;
you have no reason to despair, now,
for He who makes the woods burst into leaf
has the power to give you joy in great abundance."

"Lord," she said, "I do believe
that God may pity me
in the next world, time without end,
like many other sinners,
but here He wrests from me the one thing
that made my joy increase. Nothing matters now,
for he has gone so far away."

11

For this I praise God
and Saint Andrew:
no man has more senseI
than I have, that's what I think,
and I'm not just making noise.
And I'll tell you why.

It is very unpleasant
when you get involved in arguing something
and you can't reach the light at the end,
and it is not good
to make judgments on any subject
you can't explain.

I am so rich
in brilliant ideas,
I am very hard to make a fool of;
I eat the bread
of the fool while it is soft
and warm, and let my own cool down.

As long as his bread lasts
I swear to him, I pledge
that nothing could ever make me part from him,
and when he's out of his,
let him stare at mine with his mouth open
and long for it;

because I think it is right
that a fool act like a fool
and a wise man watch out for what he can come away with;
for he is doubly stupid
and brainless
who lets a fool make a fool of him.

With a Breton stick
or any weapon
or a sword, no one's better:
because I hit the other man
and keep him from hitting me,
and he—he can't take cover from my blow.

In another man's woods
I go hunting every time I feel like it,
and I set my two little dogs barking
and my third, my hound,
thrusts forward,
all bold and fixed on the prey.

My own private place
is so safe
no one can enjoy it but me:
I've got it so locked up
and barricaded,
no one can force his way in.

I'm teeming
with the snakiest tricks,
with a hundred false colors to choose the best from.
I carry fire here,
water there,
that I can use to put out the flame.

Let everyone watch out,
for with such art
I play at living and dying.
I am the bird
that gets the starlings
to feed my little ones,

12

Starling, take flight:
tomorrow at daybreak
you go to a land
where I thought I'd have a friend.
You will find her
and see her—
here's why you go:
you will tell her,
spell out to her,
right on the spot
why she goes beyond all bounds.

I don't know, maybe she was fated
to get my love without loving me;
but one single time,
what a great day,
if it pleased her,
if she wanted
me to do it;
for one month
is worth three,
to the man
who breaks bread with her.

Ai! how convincing it is,
this falsehood covered with gold:
"She is chosen among all women"
he is crazy who puts his trust there—
watch out
for the dice

she has leaded,
she has taken
in so many,
I tell you,
and left them on the road.

You can look at her and tell she has more tricks
than an old fox being chased.
The other day she made me wait around with my mouth open
the whole night long till day.
Her desire
is flighty
and full of devices,
but every child
makes songs of her,
punishing such
women for their cruelty.
The man to whom her love was given—
a pagan fairy marked him out;
no baptized woman was ever like her
between here and the cave of Elijah.

Fly, go
straight there,
tell her
I will die
unless I know
how she lies
down at night, naked or dressed.

Her beauty was born when she was,
without vapors of cress, or fomentation of herbs.
She has a thousand friends on supply,
and of a thousand lords is the friend.
Marcabru
says the door
is never closed.
Let him gape and waste his time
who looks for more in her—
he'll back off
and walk away from that treacherous bitch.

She has one many-colored flower, always changing,
of perfect love long desired,
better placed with her than any other woman.

A little fool soon commits great foolishness.
I forgive her the thanks
of the Abbot
of St. Privat.
I figured,
surely
when she tells me Checkmate,
love will quickly swell forth.

The wrong
she did me
I forgive
and hand myself over;
only, underneath me
let her lie down on her back
and bind me and tie me up.

16

I say he's a wise man, no doubt about it,
who makes out, word for word,
what my song signifies,
and how the theme unfolds:
for I myself take pains
to cast some light on the obscurity

of those troubadours with childish minds
who worry honest men:
they scourge and improve
what Truth itself puts forth,
always taking pains to make their words
tangled up and meaningless.

And they put up that false love of theirs
against true love, as though it were as good.
And I say: whoever settles down with Lust
wars against himself;
for afterwards, when his wallet is empty,
Lust shows such fools its cruelty.

It fills me with anger and grief
to hear that pack of perjurers telling us
that Love deceives and tortures
a man by cooling down his lust.
They are liars, for the happiness of lovers
is Joy, Patience, Restraint.

Such lovers, if they don't go off

in two directions, bear witness,
since good Love is their neighbor,
to the one single longing of two desires,
in trust that is firm,
white, precious, true, pure.

For Love has the meaning
of emerald and sard,
it is the top and root of joy,
it is a lord who rules with truth,
and its power overcomes
every creature.

By its word, its action, and its look,
it comes from a true heart
when it gives its promise and pledge—
if only it does not befoul its gifts;
and whoever does not hasten to it
bears the name of fool.

No sermon, no preaching
is worth a hen's egg
with this fool—they say foolishness
has to do vile things and belts are made of leather;
for I know, when Lust is the mode of their desiring,
it is false to many men, and full of tricks.

The fool, since everything he hears he sings to others,
does not follow reason, he just makes noise,
for his love lives on what it grabs.
Well, I'll agree: his love really loves,
and Costans is constancy,
and cheating is justice.

The end of this *vers*
takes its stand and turns
on a vile people, dogs
whom an evil star keeps in the dark,
all pompous with their dumb ideas,
barren of the deeds that bring happiness.

May the ideas they're so proud of
make them miserable.

BERNART DE VENTADORN (fl. 1150–1180)

Nothing certain is known about Bernart's life. The absence of any verifiable biographical information has spurred the invention of many stories about him, beginning with the *vida*. According to these stories, he rose from his low birth as the son of a serf and a baker in the castle of Ebles II of Ventadour to become the great lover of three noble ladies, including Eleanor of Aquitaine; and, after the death of his protector, ended his days in the monastery of Dalon. It is clear that these stories originated in a literal-minded response to a strophe in Peire d'Alvernhe's playful poem about the troubadors, and to some passages in Bernart's lyrics. The only certain fact about him is that he was one of the most popular poets of his own day, judging from the numerous manuscripts of his songs, and from the many poets who allude to, or imitate, his work. He wrote songs about love exclusively; apart from three *tensos,* all his poems are *cansos.*

With Bernart, the troubadour technique of playing on the perspectives of an audience reaches a level that was never to be surpassed. What began to take shape in the songs of Guillaume is now completely developed.

We have seen how Guillaume, in his new song, continually acknowledges the powerful presence of his old companions, and thus of his own carnality, all during his lyric vow of service to the lady. That was how he saved his song from the jeers and snickers of those who had Agnes and Ermessen in their minds. The lyric audience of Bernart de Ventadorn contains this same element: the *gens vilana,* the vulgar ones. They keep their place, for no poet, especially one who values refinement, would ever want to dislodge them.

21

Of course it's no wonder I sing
better than any other troubadour:
my heart draws me more toward love,
and I am better made for his command.
Heart body knowledge sense
strength and energy—I have set all on love.
The rein draws me straight toward love,
and I cannot turn toward anything else.

A man is really dead when he does not feel
some sweet taste of love in his heart;
and what is it worth to live without worth,
except to irritate everyone?
May the Lord God never hate me so
that I live another day, or even less than a day,
after I am guilty of being such a pest,
and I no longer have the will to love.

In good faith, without deceit,
I love the best and most beautiful.
My heart sighs, my eyes weep,
because I love her so much, and I suffer for it.
What else can I do, if Love takes hold of me,
and no key but pity can open up
the prison where be has put me,
and I find no sign of pity there?

This love wounds my heart
with a sweet taste, so gently,
I die of grief a hundred times a day
and a hundred times revive with joy.
My pain seems beautiful,
this pain is worth more than any pleasure;
and since I find this bad so good,
how good the good will be when this suffering is done.

Ah, God! if only true lovers
stood out from the false;
if all those slanderers and frauds
had horns on their heads.
I'd give all the gold in the world,
and all the silver, if I had it to give,
just so that my lady knew
how I love her with the love of a courtly man.

Whenever I see her, you can see it in me,
in my eyes, my look, my color,
because I shake with fear
like a leaf in the wind.
I don't have the good sense of a child,
I am so taken over, ruled by love;
and when a man is overcome like this,
a lady may let herself feel great pity.

Good lady, I ask you for nothing
but to take me for your servant,
for I will serve you as my good lord,
whatever wages come my way.
Behold me at your command, a man to rely on,
before you, o noble, gentle, courteous, and gay.
You are not, after all, a bear or a lion,
you would not kill me if I give myself to you.

To Mon Cortes, down there, where she dwells,
I send this song, and let her not be vexed
that I have been so far away.

22

My heart is so full of joy
it changes every nature.
The winter that comes to me
is white red yellow flowers;
my good luck grows
with the wind and the rain,
and so my song mounts up, rises,
and my worth increases.
I have such love in my heart,
such joy, such sweetness,
the ice I see is a flower,
the snow, green things that grow.

I could walk around undressed,
naked in my shirt,
for perfect love protects me
from the cold north wind.
But a man is a fool when he does things out of measure
and doesn't hold himself with courtesy.
Therefore I have kept a watch upon myself
ever since I begged her,
my most beautiful, for love,
and I await such honor
that in place of her riches
I don't want Pisa.

Let her make me keep my distance from her love—
there's still one thing I'm sure of:
I have conquered nothing less
than her beautiful image.
Cut off from her like this I have
such bliss,
that the day I see her again,
not having seen her will not weigh on me.
My heart stays close to Love,
my spirit runs to it there,
but my body is here, in another place,
far from her, in France.

I get good hope from her;
but that does me little good,
because she holds me like this, poised
like a ship on the wave.
I don't know where to take cover

from the sad thoughts that pull me down.
The whole night long I toss and turn
on the edge of the bed.
I bear more pain from love
than Tristan the lover,
who suffered many sorrows
for Isolt the blonde.

Ah, God! couldn't I be a swallow
and fly through the air
and come in the depths of the night
into her dwelling there.
O gentle lady, o joyful,
your lover dies.
I fear the heart will melt within me
if this lasts a little longer.
Lady, for your love
I join my hands and worship.
Beautiful body of the colors of youth,
what suffering you make me bear.

For in this world no enterprise
so draws my thought,
that when I hear any talk of her
my heart does not turn to it
and my face light up,
so that no matter what you hear me saying,
you will always think
I want to laugh.
I love her so with such good love,
that many time I weep for it,
because for me the sighs
have a sweeter taste.
Go, messenger, run,
and tell her, the one most beautiful,
of the pain and the sorrow
I bear for her, and the willing death.

23

Down there, around Ventadorn, all my friends
have lost me, because my lady does not love me;
and so, it is right that I never go back there again,
because always she is wild and morose with me.
Now here is why the face she shows me is gloomy and full of anger;

because my pleasure is in loving her, and I have settled down to it.
She is resentful, and complains, for no other reason.

Like a fish that rushes to the bait
suspecting nothing till it is caught on the hook,
I rushed into too much loving one day
and took no care till I was in the middle of the flame
that burns me now more hotly than a furnace fire;
and for all that I can't move away the width of a hand,
that's how her love holds me captive, puts me in chains.

I do not wonder that love of her holds me bound,
because I do not think you can see a nobler body in the world:
she is beautiful and white, young and gay and soft,
altogether as I want her, long for her.
I cannot say anything bad about her, because nothing bad is in her—
if I knew of anything, I would tell it with joy,
but I do not know one bad thing about her, and so I say nothing.
I shall always desire her honor and her good,
and I shall be her man, and her lover, and her servant,
and I shall love her whether it pleases her or grieves her,
for no one can constrain a heart without killing it.
I don't know one woman that I could not love,
if I wanted to, whether she wanted it or not.
But anything can be set down as a bad thing.

And so I have now become available to all other women—
anyone who wants to can get me to come to her,
on one condition: let her not sell me at too dear a price
the honor and the good she has it in her heart to do me;
for it is wearisome to beg, if it all turns out for nothing.
I tell you this from my own case, because much suffering has come my way,
that beautiful lady there, with that vicious nature, has betrayed me.

To Provence I send joy and well-being
and a greater blessing than I can specify;
and thus I do heroic deeds, miracles, prodigies,
for I send them in abundance what I scarcely have myself,
for I have no joy except what comes
from my Bel Vezer, and from En Fachura, my friend,
and En Auvergnat, the lord of Beaucaire.

My Bel Vezer, for your sake God performs this miracle:
no man beholds you without getting carried away
by the pleasant things you know how to do and say.

24

When the new grass and the leaves come forth
and the flower burgeons on the branch,
and the nightingale lifts its high
pure voice and begins its song,
I have joy in it, and joy in the flower,
and joy in myself, and in my lady most of all;
on every side I am enclosed and girded with joy,
and a joy that overwhelms all other joys.

Ah, weary, how I die from thinking—
for many times I am so lost in thought of her,
robbers could come and carry me away,
and I wouldn't even know what they were doing.
By God, love, you find me an easy victim,
a man with few friends and no other lord.
Why don't you press on my lady like this one time,
before I am destroyed by my desiring?

It makes me wonder, how I can go on
not letting her know what I want.
When I see my lady, when I gaze on her,
her beautiful eyes become her so well,
I can hardly keep myself from running to her;
and I would do it, if I weren't so afraid,
for I never saw a body so well cut and colored
for the work of love be so slow and hard to move.

I love her and cherish her so much,
fear her and attend to her so much,
I have never dared to speak to her of myself,
and I ask her for nothing, and I send her nothing.
But she knows my sorrow and my pain,
and when it pleases her, she gives me comfort and honors me,
and when it pleases her, I make do with less,
so that no blame should touch her.

If I only knew how to put a spell on people,
my enemies would turn into babies,
so that none of them could pick us out
and say anything to hurt us.
I know I would see my most noble then,
her beautiful eyes, her young color,
and I would kiss her mouth in all directions,
so that for a month the mark of it would show.

I would like to find her alone,
sleeping, or pretending to,
so I could steal a soft kiss off her,
because I am not worth enough to ask for it.
By God, lady, we get little loving done,
times passes, and we lose the best of it.
Let us talk in secret signs,
and, since being direct can't help us, let our cunning help us.

A lady deserves blame
when she makes her lover wait too long,
for endless talk of love
is a great vexation, and seems like a trick,
because one can love, and pretend to everyone else,
and nobly lie when there are no witnesses.
Sweet lady, if only you would deign to love me,
no one will ever catch me when I lie.

Messenger, go, and may she not think less of me,
if I am afraid to go to her.

BERTRAN DE BORN (b.ca. 1140)

Bertran de Born was one of the minor noblemen whose fortunes depended entirely on war, and his loyalty to this group never wavered. He may have switched allegiances among the mighty lords, but he was always the spokesman for the noble mercenaries who saw their holdings, if they had any, confiscated if they fought for the losing side, and who languished in poverty whenever there was a prolonged period of peace.

The life and the position of these petty nobles are lucidly described by Marc Bloch in his classic work, *Feudal Society.* Commenting on Bertran's *Be•m platz lo gais temps de Pascor,* Bloch writes:

> The accurate observation and the fine verve, in contrast with the insipidity of what is usually a more conventional type of poetry, are the marks of an uncommon talent. The sentiment, on the other hand, is in no way extraordinary; as is shown in many another piece from the same social world . . . In war . . . the noble loved first and foremost the display of physical strength, the strength of a splendid animal, deliberately maintained by constant exercises, begun in childhood. "He who has stayed at school till the age of twelve," says a German poet [Hartmann von Aue], repeating the old Carolingian proverb, "and never ridden a horse, is only fit to be a priest."
>
> . . . Fighting was also, and perhaps above all, a source of profit—in fact, the nobleman's chief industry.

Bertran de Born made no secret of the less creditable reasons which above all disposed him "to find no pleasure in peace." "Why," he asks, "do I want rich men to hate each other?" "Because a rich man is much more noble, generous and affable in war than in peace." . . . The poet belonged to that class of petty holders of fiefs, the "vavasours"—he so described himself—for whom life in the ancestral manor-house lacked both gaiety and comforts. War made up for these deficiencies by stimulating the liberality of the great and providing prizes worth having.

The baron, of course, out of regard for his prestige as well as his interest, could not afford to be niggardly in the matter of presents . . . Finally, in the face of the growing inadequacy of the vassal contingents, there was soon no army which could dispense with the assistance of that wandering body of warriors to whom adventure made so strong an appeal, provided that there was a prospect of gain as well as of mighty combats . . .

If the propensity to bloody deeds was prevalent everywhere—more than one abbot indeed met his death as the victim of a cloister feud—it was the conception of the necessity of war, as a source of honour and as a means of livelihood, that set apart the little group of "noble" folk from the rest of society.

Bertran de Born thus expresses the viewpoint of the lower nobility, of the hired fighting hands whose gentle birth could not always be proved, and whose fortunes were uncertain; he speaks for those who had to look to the great ones higher up to sustain them and to make use of them. Bertran had his own castle, though he had earlier shared it with a brother whom he eventually managed to drive out. But the young men of this class who were in attendance in the courts of the mighty lords because they had no share in the ancestral fief owned nothing but a hereditary claim to nobility, and sometimes not even that. It was the interests and the aspirations of this inferior segment of courtly society, according to Erich Köhler, that formed the ethical and the sociological basis of the courtly love lyric. The relations in the love song reflect the social structure in which these aspiring young men wanted to find a dignified place. And the song, in representing true courtliness as an ethical condition that transcended all material distinctions, was thus intended to legitimize the position of these newcomers and to foster their integration into that privileged society.

Bertran joined a party of nobles in a revolt against Henry and his son Richard Couer de Lion. The revolt was led by the King's own eldest son, who was called "The Young King," and later generations believed that Bertran's songs were a major cause of this uprising of son against father, and brother against brother. In *Inferno* XX, 113–142, Bertran appears with his head separated from his body, thus punished for pressing discord upon the members of the royal family. Whatever else it may signify, this grisly apparition is a great tribute to the power of

Bertran's poetry. Dante's admiration is explicit in *De vulgari eloquentia*, II, 2, where he cites Bertran as the sole paragon of martial poetry.

The revolt failed. The Young King died in 1183, Bertran's castle of Hautefort was besieged and burned, and he became Richard's prisoner. Later, he managed to win Richard's pardon, and everything was restored to him; he always championed Richard's cause thereafter. The author of the *razo* has invented the following scene, erroneously substituting Henry II (who was not at the siege) for his son Richard:

> And En Bertran, with all his people, was led to the pavilion of King Henry, and the King received him very badly, and King Henry said to him, "Bertran, Bertran, you have said that you never needed even half of your wit at any time, but know that today you truly need the whole of it."—"Lord," said En Bertran, "it is very true that I said it, and, indeed, I said the truth." And the King said, "I do believe that that wit of yours is failing you now."—"Lord," said En Bertran, "indeed, it is failing me."—"And how is that?" said the King.—"Lord," said En Bertran, "the day the valiant Young King, your son, died, I lost my wit, and my knowledge, and my understanding." And the King, when he heard what En Bertran said to him, weeping, about his son, great grief came to his heart, from pity, and to his eyes, and he could not keep from fainting with grief. And when he came out of the faint, he cried out and said, weeping: "En Bertran, En Bertran, you are right, and you have good cause, if you have lost your wit for my son, because he loved you more than any man in the world. And I, for love of him, set free your body, and your goods, and your castle, and I give you back my love and my grace, and I give you five hundred marks of silver for the losses you have suffered." And En Bertran fell at his feet, thanking him. And the King, with all his host, went away.

Bertran was one of the most exciting and original poets of the Middle Ages. The conventional troubadour themes are rethought in his poetry—note, for example, what happens to the *Natureingang* in no. 45, He celebrated the ritual beauty and horror of medieval warfare, with none of the vicious and sentimental archaism that now distinguishes the language of hawks; for war made a man and made money.

The planh that Bertran de Born made for the Young King bears no other explanation but that the Young King was the best man in the world, and En Bertran loved him more than any man in the world, and the Young King loved and trusted him more than any man in the world, wherefore King Henry, his father, and Count Richard, his brother, bore ill will against En Bertran. And for the Young King's excellence and the great grief over him among all the people, he made the planh for him which says . . .

I end my song in grief and misery,

I hold it ended forever,
for I have lost my cause and my pleasure,
losing the greatest king ever born of woman,
large-handed, nobly spoken,
well riding,
graceful in his form
and meek in his manner
of giving great honors.
I feel the grief drawing tight
around me, putting out my life
even as I speak of it.
I give him in trust to God,
may He put him in the dwelling of Saint John.

King of the courtly and emperor of the valiant
you would have been, Lord, if you had lived,
for you came to be called the Young King,
you were the guide and the father of all who are young.
Hauberks and swords
and handsome fabrics,
helms and gonfalons,
quilted doublets, rich garments,
and joy, and love,
these things have no one to preserve them,
no one to keep them here—
no, they will follow you there,
they will go away with you,
with every right and noble act.

Gentle receptions, giving without a changing heart,
handsome replies, and "Be Welcome,"
grand lodgings accorded and nobly kept,
gifts, bestowals of garments, abiding without doing wrong,
repasts to the noise
of viol and song
with a brave companion
valiant and strong,
among all the best—
I want all these things to stay with you,
let nothing remain
in this rabble world
in this forsaken year,
that once made us think it was beautiful.

Lord, in you not one thing was missing,

for all the world had chosen you
the greatest king that ever carried shield,
the best, the bravest fighter in tournaments,
from the time of Roland,
and before that time,
I never saw a man so brave,
so warlike,
nor whose renown
so presses through the world
and restores it,
seeking it forth
in every corner, keeping vigil,
from the Nile to the sunset.

Lord, for you I want to wrest myself away from joy,
and everyone who saw you
now must stand mad with grief for you, and mute,
and never again will joy light up my gloom.
Men of England and Normandy,
Brittany and Ireland,
Gascony and Aquitaine,
and Anjou suffer this loss.
And Maine and Tours,
all France to Compiègne
cannot keep from weeping,
and Flanders from Ghent
to the port of Wissant,
and the Germans, too, let them weep.

The men of Lorraine and Brabant
when they are in the jousts
will have grief when they do not see you.

It is not worth a cent,
not the cup of an acorn,
the world of those here who remain,

now, after the sad death
of the glorious Young King,
for whom we suffer loss and pain.

I shall make a half *sirventes* about both kings,
for soon we shall see who will have more riders:
the valiant king of Castile, En Alfons,
who is coming, I hear, and will want soldiers for pay; I
Richard will pay by the bushel and the pail

gold and silver, and he thinks he is lucky
to pay out and give, and he wants no treaties,
no, he wants war more than a hawk wants quail.
If both of the kings are brave and spirited,
soon we shall see the fields bestrewn with fragments,
helms and shields and swords and saddlebows,
and corpses cloven through the trunk to the cinctures,
and the coursers we shall see running wild,
and in sides and breasts many lances,
and joy and weeping and grief and celebration:
the loss will be great, but the winnings will be greater.

Trumpets and tabors, ensigns and pennons,
banners and horses white and black
we shall soon see, and life will be good,
we shall pillage the stores of the usurers,
and on the roads the sumpters will not go

safely in the light, nor the burgher without wondering,
nor any merchant traveling from France,
no, but he will be rich who will gladly take.

If the King comes, I put my faith in God
I shall be alive or in pieces.

And if I am alive, it will be great luck,

and if I am dead, a great deliverance.

. . . It pleases me to see the lordship change
and the old relinquishing their mansions to the young;
every man can leave in his lineage
enough sons so that one, at least, is brave:
it is this, and not some flower or the twittering of birds,
makes me feel the earth is new again.
And if a man wants to change his old lord or lady
for a young one, he will be in his best days again.

I say a lady is old when her hair falls out,
and she is old when no knight attends her;
old if she is pleasured by more than one lover,
old if some common brute does it to her,
old if she only grants her favors at home,
old if she must use witchcraft and little tricks,
and I consider her old when singers vex her,
and she is old when she likes to talk too much.

A lady is young when she honors her class,

and she is young in her good deeds, when she does them,
and stays young by her honest heart,
when she does not abuse good merit and fame,
young when she cares for her beauty,
and a lady is young when she bears herself well,
stays young when she isn't just dying to find something out,
and when she holds back, with some handsome youth, from doing wrong.

A man is young when he stakes everything he has,
and young when he has nothing left,
young when his hospitality costs him a fortune,
young when he makes reckless gifts,
young when his money burns a whole in his pocket,
and he wants to hold court and tournaments:
and he stays young when he loves to sit down to a game,
and he is young when he knows how to serve a lady well.

A man of means is old when he won't risk a thing,
and he hoards up grain and wine and bacon;
and I consider him old when he puts eggs and cheese on the table
for himself and his friends on meat-eating days,
old when he has to wear a hood on top of his cloak,
old when he owns a horse another man has trained;
he is old when he wants to sit one day in peace,
and old when he can pull out before he squanders everything.

Arnaut jongleur, take my *sirventes* about young
and old to Richard, let it guide him,
may he never want to pile up old-man's treasure
when he can win glory with the riches of the young.

45

I love the joyful time of Easter,
that makes the leaves and flowers come forth,
and it pleases me to hear the mirth
of the birds, who make their song
resound through the woods,
and it pleases me to see upon the meadows
tents and pavilions planted,
and I feel a great joy
when I see ranged along the field
knights and horses armed for war.

And it pleases me when the skirmishers
make the people and their baggage run away,
and it pleases me when I see behind them coming

a great mass of armed men together,
and I have pleasure in my heart
when I see strong castles besieged,
the broken ramparts caving in,
and I see the host on the water's edge,
closed in all around by ditches,
with palisades, strong stakes close together.

And I am as well pleased by a lord
when he is first in the attack,
armed, upon his horse, unafraid,
so he makes his men take heart
by his own brave lordliness.

And when the armies mix in battle,
each man should be poised
to follow him, smiling,
for no man is worth a thing
till he has given and gotten blow on blow.

Maces and swords and painted helms,
the useless shields cut through,
we shall see as the fighting starts,
and many vassals together striking,
and wandering wildly,
the unreined horses of the wounded and dead.
And once entered into battle
let every man proud of his birth
think only of breaking arms and heads,
for a man is worth more dead than alive and beaten.

I tell you there is not so much savor
in eating or drinking or sleeping,
as when I hear them scream, "There they are! Let's get them!"
on both sides, and I hear riderless
horses in the shadows, neighing,
and I hear them scream, "Help! Help!"
and I see them fall among the ditches,
little men and great men on the grass,
and I see fixed in the flanks of the corpses
stumps of lances with silken streamers.
Barons, pawn your castles,
and your villages, and your cities
before you stop making war on one another.

Papiols, gladly go
fast to my Lord Yes-and-No

and tell him he has lived in peace too long.

LE CHATELAIN DE COUCI (d. 1203)

The poet has been identified with Guy, the châtelain of Coucy, who died at sea during the Fourth Crusade. As his title indicates, he was important: a châtelain was high up in the feudal hierarchy, being a vassal of the king or of a duke or a count, the governor of a castle, and the justice of the region; and Coucy (in Vermandois, in southern Picardy) was a powerful and well-known castellany—one of the most powerful in the twelfth century, according to the poet's editor, Alain Lerond. The poet became even more famous as the hero of a thirteenth-century romance; he dies at sea in that, too, and his heart is sent to his beloved, the lady of Fayel, and fed to her by her jealous husband.

His lyrics are clearly modeled on troubadour themes and forms, but he innovates also, quite in the spirit of their pride in technique (*Li nouviauz tanz*, no. 8, for example, which, as published by Lerond, has an unprecedented strophic order, with identical rhymes in i, ii, and iv, and in iii, v, and vi; note that these strophes can be rearranged into *coblas ternas*, three successive strophes with identical rhymes). The mournful lover's tone of his lyrics hardly varies, but within that range he is unsurpassed.

6

To you, lovers, more than all the others,
it is right that I lament my grief,
for I must, absolutely, go away
and part from my true love;
and when I lose her, I have nothing left.
Now, Love, take note of this and do not doubt it:
if a man ever died from a grieving heart—
there will not be another song from me, not one strophe.

Dear Lord God, what will happen, and how?
Shall I have to take my leave at last?
Yes, by God, it can't be otherwise:
I must go, without her, into a strange land;
Now I do not think I shall lack big sorrows,
for I shall not have her comfort or her words,
and I look for my joy to no other love
but the love of her and do not know if that shall ever be.

Dear Lord God, must I do without
that great delight and company
and those always gentle words of her

who was my lady, my friend, my love?
When I remember her gentle presence
and the pleasures she revealed to me,
how can the heart in my body keep
from breaking out? It must be a poor thing.

God does not want to give me free
all the pleasures I have had in my life,
but makes me pay dear;
now I fear this toll will destroy me.
Love, pity! If ever God did something base,
he has, like a brute, broken true love in two:
I cannot put this love away from me,
and yet I must leave my lady.

Now the slanderers will celebrate
who used to groan under the weight of my joys;
I will never be pilgrim enough
to wish them well;
and so I may waste this voyage,
for those traitors have done me so much harm,
if God commanded me to love *them*
He couldn't weigh me down with a heavier burden.

I go, Lady. To God the Creator
I commend you, wherever I find myself.
I do not know whether you will ever see my return:
perhaps I shall never see you again.
In God's name I ask you, wherever I may be,
keep our promises, whether I return or stay,
and I pray God give me honor as surely
as I have loved you faithfully.

7

The season when no rose or leaf
or flower can come forth,
when I hear no bird chanting
in the woods in the morning or night—
that is when my heart flowers in one desireI
for perfect love, which has me in its power,
which I do not want to be free of;
and if there is anyone who wants to get me out of it,
I do not want to know him, and may God not want it!

I am right when I grieve,
because I want my suffering,

and I love more than ever
what I cannot have
and know I shall never reach;
if Love does not overcome Reason, I have to fail,
I speak the truth.
For God's sake, Love, let Reason lose
its influence till she accepts me.

Lady, I have no torment
that is not my joy,
for without you I could not
live and do not want to.
Without loving you my life has no use—
unless I want to get on everyone's nerves
or walk around dying.
Mother of God, let me not live long enough
to annoy the world and lose true love.

Many times Love
scares me and fills me with thoughts,
yet often she restores my peace
and gives me a heart full of joy;
thus she makes me live in a wild disorder
of grief and happiness, and I don't know whether
she does this to try me,
whether she does it for pleasure, to torture me,
to see if the pain makes me give up.

Many a long week
I drag out far from her,
and in my suffering
I curse and curse the days away from her.
There is nothing I can do, alas, for I want
to win her, whose words and ways
I do not forget,
no, I think of her and behold her in my mind,
and that is my comfort when she is far away.

GACE BRULÉ (fl. 1180–1213)

The poet was a knight of Champagne (see no. 14). Brulé is derived from *burelé*, banded—barred in gules and silver, the design on his escutcheon. He had several patrons among the highest nobility, among them Marie de France. He probably took part in the Third Crusade and possibly in the Fourth. He is last attested in 1213.

He was venerated in his own time and long after his death. Dante cites *Ire d'amors* (no. 19) in DVE, II, 6, though he attributes this song to the King of Navarre, Thibaut de Champagne. Probably no other northern French poet adhered more closely to the themes and techniques of the troubadours. His resemblance to Bernart de Ventadorn is unmistakable, and it has been suggested that he was personally acquainted with Bertran de Born, Gaucelm Faidit, and Guiraut de Calanson. He also resembles Guillaume IX in explicitly distinguishing the songs addressed to a male audience from those intended for the full court: several of his lyrics begin with *Compaignons,* or *Seigners.*

14

The little birds of my country
I have heard in Brittany.
When their song rises up, I think
I used to hear them, once,
in sweet Champagne,
if I am not mistaken.
They have put me in such gentle thought,
I have set myself to sing
till I at last attain
what Love has long been promising.

I am troubled by long hope
and must not complain.
That takes away my joy and laughter,
for no one tormented by love
is mindful of anything else.
I find my body
and face poised on the thought of her so many times,
that now I have the look of a madman.
Others have done other wrongs in love,
but my great fault is to show my suffering.

My sweet gentle lady
kissing me stole away my heart;
it was crazy to quit me
for her who torments me.
Alas, I never felt it
leaving me;
she took it so gently,
she drew it to her as I sighed;
she covets my mad heart

but will never have pity for me.

That one kiss, which is always on my mind,
is over, I now realize—
it has betrayed me,
I do not feel it on my lips.
When she permitted,
God! what I am telling of,
why didn't she furnish me against my death.
She knows I am killing myself
in this long expectation,
my face is pale and colorless.

And so she takes away my joy and laughter
and makes me die of longing,
Love makes me pay dearly
again and again for her obligingness.
Alas, I don't dare go to her,
because I have this crazy look
which these false lovers get me blamed for.
I am dead when I see them talking to her there,
because not one of them will find
any of their treachery in her.

15

Most have sung of Love
as an exercise and insincerely;
so Love should give me thanks
because I never sang like a hypocrite.
My loyalty kept me from that,
and Love, which I have in such abundance
it is a miracle if I hate anything,
even that crowd of pests.

The truth is, I have loved with a loyal heart
and will never love another way;
my lady could have put this to the test

19

Grief of love that sojourns in my heart
has such a hold on me, I keep from singing.
It would be a great miracle if I could draw out a song,
and I do not know where the cause could come from,
for desire and constant readiness

trouble me and fill me with many thoughts,
and so have brought me to the point—I can tell you this—
where I can hardly tell joy from grief.

And yet my whole heart brightens
with one good hope—God let it come true.
For I think my lady would be much displeased
if this love kills me—what good could it do her!
I have been slain by the grace and ornament of her figure,
and her sweet face the color of youth,
and her beauty, which cannot be described.
Why did God give her the beauty to destroy me?

I am angered by that bad crowd
more than by any suffering I endure for Love;
But it won't help them, they won't be able to undo
the truth that Love possesses me and takes hold in my heart.
This is how I have given myself to her:
I do not believe I will ever part from her except by dying.
A man who acquits himself well before Love—
should he not be the one chosen lover?

Faithful desires, of which I have more than a hundred pair,
will surely kill me before that joy comes
long promised me—as bait.
I do not think my lady, whom God gave goodness
and much beauty, will remember.
Pride is up in arms against me,
and I don't have the strength to denounce this wrong,
since my heart wants to kill me over her.

This great love makes me act foolishly
and will do so, I'm afraid, for a long time;
but I cannot take my heart back.
I like things as they are, whatever happens to me.
And so I am poorly contented,
for I want what harms me most,
and dismay makes me laugh and play:
I have never seen martyrdom so deceitful.

Ah, Count of Blois, you who would be loved,
keep this in your memory;
for if a man withdraws his heart from love,
it is doubtful he longs for great honor.

The other day in an orchard
I heard two ladies talking quietly,
till they began to quarrel
and raise their voices.
I was resting near a rosebush
underneath a grafted tree in flower.
One said to the other: "I want advice
about a bad man who loves me and begs
for requital;
should I love this knight, the way he is,
a coward, for his money?

"Now there's somebody else who keeps begging me,
he is honest and courteous and well spoken,
and when he goes back to tourney
in his country, I won't want a better man.
He is prudent, and dignified,
and he is not proud or foolish.
But you don't need love
if you want money.
From the first
I was mean to him when I received him,
for the other bad one who keeps begging me."

The good lady says, "I think it is right
that a beautiful lady should love
a good knight, if she finds one
true and loyal to her.
And any woman seduced by wealth
I will never call a lady;
she's a slut, because everyone knows, everyone sees
she has dishonored herself for a price.
Whoever trusts her
is a fool and will taste his foolishness
when she gets a hold of his money."

The dishonest lady says, "Whoever followed your advice
would die of misery and hunger.
I will not love a knight who keeps going on tourneys
and wanders around, and spends a lot, and borrows on credit,
and in winter dies of cold
when his credit goes;
I don't want my lover to shatter

a big lance for his little friend.
You take
honor any day and I'll take income,
and we'll see who has more in the end."

"Shut up, whore, go to a whorehouse,
I can't stand listening to you any more.
Since you want to go to the devil,
no one could stop you.
How will you be able to stand
having such trash in your bed?"
She wanted to scratch out one of her eyes,
but Gace kept it from happening
as he was going away,
he went and stopped her fists:
and in this he did a bad thing.

RAIMBAUT DE VAQUEIRAS (fl. 1180-1205)

LEUS SONETZ

1. I seek forthwith in my song a simple melody, as is my wont, for I wish to compose a *sirventes* worthy of praise. Let no man think, however, that in my song or outside it I shall conceal base dissension, for it seems to me a shameful, damaging and cowardly thing when a noble family is disunited and one member abandons another. I see that the lord of Baux is attacking and destroying and being destroyed; yet he has many kinsmen, rich and taking their ease, and many other sworn allies, who are lacking in courage and valour.

2. But justice does not admit that one should reject one's friends in time of war, as the relatives of the Baux are doing, one with another. For Sir Ademar of Poitiers shuns them from the outset, so great an ordeal is it for him to wage war and offer sureties. Instead, he sent word of the agreement and then freed himself from anxiety. Seeing this example, Sir Gerald Ademar his brother-in-law censures him (since Barri is demolished), and so do I, for he (Sir Ademar) is an intimate friend of the Count who is depriving him (Sir Gerald) of his inheritance.

3. The younger Gerald Amic has my leave to amuse himself this year, for it is but meet that a child should store away his weapons when his most honoured friends are being ruined and destroyed. He and Rostan, than whom no lawyer is more talkative, are remaining hostages during the war,

Eor never have they carried pendant pieces (of a banner) or bell, nor worn hauberk with hood of mail, nor clad their horses, nor taken or given blows. Thus it is that the Count holds undisturbed the castle of Mornas.

4. If the young Count does not make stronger protest touching the insolence which the Count is showing him, you must know that I will not support him, but will rather reject him, for at the present time he is a handsome, full-grown person, and promises to be fierce towards his enemies. Power and high birth must be equalled by great merit, and he must fight and quarrel like an impetuous youth. A warlike, violent man is feared, and let the disinherited man who is submissive and peace-loving take to himself henceforth whom he pleases.

5. I shall sing, too, of wrongs of another kind, for the great lords are forswearing themselves. Sir William of Montpellier amuses himself, though before our eyes he swore by sacred objects to wage war and create havoc. It was his duty to follow the lord of Baux in his journeys, but his thoughts have taken a different turn; and yet neither the Count nor his county has been enriched one iota. Sir Bernard of Anduze amuses himself also, though he is despoiled and challenged, and he has violated and forgotten his compact with the lord of Baux.

6. The young hero of Nanteuil wielded his sword to better purpose than Sir Dragonet has done this year. Let the lord of Baux turn his thoughts elsewhere, for this man neither strikes at once and without delay nor is he struck. Alas! how many successes he was wont to achieve, how many fine feats of valour to perform, and it is a pity that he lapses so easily into indolence, since he sees that his most honoured kinsmen are being assailed, and he takes his ease nearby! Sir Williarn Arnaud is resting; he has conducted himself so ill in this affair that men consider him rotten.

DOMNA, TANT VOS AI PREIADA

1. Lady, I have so entreated you to consent, if it please you, to love me that I have become your vassal, for you are noble and well-bred and you set the seal on fair fame everywhere, so that your friendship delights me. And because you are courtly in all your acts, my heart is now held fast in you more than in any other lady of Genoa, and so it will be a kindness if you love me. Then shall I be more satisfied than if the city of the Genoese belonged to me, with all the wealth amassed in it.

2. Minstrel, you aren't courteous, to importune me in this way: I'll have naught to do with it. I would rather you were hanged! I won't be your rnis-

tress. To be sure, I'll do you in, you ill-omened Provencal! I'll give you this insult: "You nasty, foolish, crop-headed fellow!" I won't love you at all, because I have a husband who is handsomer than you are, that I know. Your ways, brother, I have a happier time (with him).

3. Lady, you who are gracious, distinguished, joyous, excellent and wise, may your good breeding avail me, for joy and youth and courtliness and merit and wisdom guide you, and fair deportment in all things. It is because of this that I am unreservedly your faithful suitor, candid, humble and suppliant, so mightily am I constrained and vanquished by the love I bear you, so that it is a delight to me. Hence it will be an act of mercy if I become your follower and your lover.

4. Minstrel, you seem out of your senses, making speeches like this. May you meet misfortune in your cornings and goings ! You haven't the sense of a cat, and you don't please me one whit, for you look a bad lot. And I don't want this thing, even if you were the son of a king. Do you think I have lost my senses? Upon my word, you won't have me. If you pledge yourself to have my love, you will die of cold this year! The Provencals have very bad habits!

5. Lady, be not so cruel to me, for it is not meet and it becomes you ill. Rather, if it please you, it behoves me to pursue you earnestly and to love you sincerely, as it behoves you to end my pain, since I am your liegeman and your servant. For I see and recognise and know, when I contemplate your beauty, fresher than the rose in May, that in all the world there is no lady more beautiful. That is why I love and shall love you, and if true faith betrays me, it will be a sin.

6. Minstrel, so may I have joy of my person as I value this Provencal speech of yours less than a Genoese coin. I don't understand you any more than I do a German or Sardinian or Berber, nor do I care about you. Do you want to scuffle with me? If my husband learns of this, you will have an unpleasant argument with him. Fair Sir, I tell you truly: I don't want this talk. Brother, I assure you this is so. Be off with you, you ragged Provencal, let me be.

7. Lady, you have cast me into painful sadness and distress; but once more I shall beseech you to allow me to show you how a Provencal does the deed, when he is mounted.

8. Minstrel, I shall not be with you, since you are troubled way. It will be better if, for the feast of Saint Martin, you go to Lord Obizino, who will perhaps give you a pack-horse, as you are a minstrel.

ARAIM DIGATZ, RAMBAUT, SI VOS AGRADA

1. Now tell me Raimbaut, I pray you, if it has indeed befallen you as rumour says, that your lady, here in Tortona, has behaved ill towards you, she for whom you have composed many a song in vain. She in turn has addressed to you a *sirventes* of such a kind that you are thereby dishonoured and she covered with shame; your love brought her neither honour nor profit, and that is why she has renounced you in this fashion.

2. Marquis Albert, it is true that I have loved the deceiver in whose name you have challenged me, and who has parted both from me and from fair fame. But I bear no blame for this, for I have in no wise failed her, rather have I ever served and honoured her. But I hope that you and she are punished for the faith you have broken, and which you have violated a hundred times for lucre; indeed, the Genoese complain about you on this score, for you assail them on the highway despite their protests.

3. By Heaven, Raimbaut, I can assure you that if I have robbed on many an occasion it was not in order to enrich myself or to amass a treasure, but through a desire to give. But I have seen you a hundred times wandering on foot through Lombardy, like the most wretched of minstrels, poor in worldly goods and unfortunate in love, and any man would have done you a service if he had offered you a meal; remember, too, how I found you in Pavia.

4. Marquis Albert, insult and outrage come easily to you in speech and still more easily in deeds, and in you one may find every kind of deceit and treachery and malice, but little valour and knightly virtue. Hence it is that they took Val di Taro from you without protest on your part, and by your folly you are losing Pietracorva; and Niccolo and Lanfranco da Mar have good reason to accuse you of perfidy.

5. By Heaven, Raimbaut, in my estimation you acted foolishly when you abandoned the occupation from which you derived honour and ease, and he who promoted you from minstrel to knight brought you grief, torment, misfortune, anxiety, sorrow and embarrassment, and robbed you of joy, valour and gaiety; for since you rose from the pack-horse to the charger you have struck not a single blow with sword or lance.

6. Marquis Albert, your sole hope lies in betrayal and in practising deception: towards all those who have an agreement with you and who serve you loyally and sincerely, you keep neither oath nor faith. And if, in respect of arms, I am not an Oliver, neither are you a Roland, it seems to me.

For Piacenza does not leave you Castagnero: she despoils you of that territory and yet you do not wreak vengeance.

7. Raimbaut, provided God preserves for me my Squire, in whom I have placed my heart and my hope, I care naught for your versifying or Sir Peter's, scabby wether's face, fat paunch !

8. Marquis Albert, all your enemies have such fear and distrust of you that they call you the whoring Marquis, disinherited, disloyal and untrustworthy!

KALENDA MAIA

1. Neither May Day nor leaf of beech-tree nor song of bird flower can please me, noble lady and gay, until from your fair person there comes to me a speedy messenger telling me of some fresh delight that love and joy bring me, and I repair to you, true-hearted lady, and the jealous one falls stricken, ere I depart thence.

2. My fair one, pray God that the jealous one may never rejoice at my hurt, for he would sell his jealousy dearly if he separated two such lovers; never more would I be joyful, nor without you would joy profit me. I would take that road whereby no man would ever see me more; excellent lady, the very day I lost you, I should die.

3. How shall I lose a lady or regain her, if first I have not possessed her? No man or woman becomes a lover by thought alone. But when the wooer changes to a lover, the honour which has accrued to him thereby is great, such is the fame produced by a sweet glance. Yet I have not held you naked, nor won aught else from you. I have desired you and put my trust in you, without any rewart.

4. Enjoyment would come hardly to me, Fair Knight, lf I should depart from you in sorrow, for nowhere else does my heart turn or my desire draw me, since it desires naught else. Lady, I know that the slanderers would be well pleased, for not otherwise could their malady be cured. Such a one would see and feel my misfortune who would be beholden to you for it, as he contemplates you and medihtes on you in his presumption, for which my heart sighs.

5. Lady Beatrice, your worth blossoms and grows so exquisitely, and surpasses that of all other ladies. As I believe, you adorn your might with merit and pleasant words. You are the source of deeds which please. You

have knowledge, indulgence and judgnent, and beyond all dispute you clothe your worth in kindness.

6. Amiable lady, everyone praises and proclaims your worth which gives such pleasure. and he who forgets you prizes his life but little, and so I worship you, distinguished lady; for I have chosen you as the most gracious and the best of all, perfect in merit, and I have wooed you and served you better than Eric did his Enid. Lord *Engles,* the "estampida" I have composed is ended.

ERAS QUAN VEY VERDEYAR
Multilingual descort

1.   Eras quan vey verdeyar
pratz e vergiers e boscatges,
vuelh un descort comensar
d'amor, per qu'ieu vauc aratges;
q'una dona m sol amar,
mas camjatz l'es sos coratges,
per qu'ieu fauc dezacordar
los motz e.ls sos e.ls lenguatges.

2.   Io son quel que ben non aio
ni jamai non l'averò,
ni per april ni per maio,
si per ma donna non l'ò;
certo que en so lengaio
sa gran beuta dir non sò,
chu fresca qe flor de glaio,
per qe no m'en partirò.

3.   Belle douce dame chiere,
a vos mi doin e m'otroi;
je n'avrai mes joi' entiere
si je n'ai vos e vos moi.
Mot estes male guerriere
si je muer per bone foi;
mes ja per nulle maniere
no.m partrai de vostre loi.

4.   Dauna, io mi rent a bos,
coar sotz la mes bon' e bera
q'anc fos, e gaillard' e pros,

ab que no•m hossetz tan hera.
Mout abetz beras haisos
e color hresc' e noera.
 Boste son, e si•bs agos
no•m destrengora hiera.

5.   Mas tan temo vostro preito,
todo•n son escarmenhdo.
Por vos ei pen' e maltreito
e meo corpo lazerado:
la noit, can jatz en meu leito,
so mochas vetz resperado;
e car nonca m'aprofeito falid ei en mon cuitado.

6.   Belhs Cavaliers, tant es car
lo vostr' onratz senhoratges
que cada jorno m'esglaio.
Oi me lasso! que farò
si sele que j'ai plus chiere
me tue, ne sai por quoi?
Ma dauna, he que dey bos
ni peu cap sanh Quitera,
mon corasso m'avetz treito
e mot gen favlan furtado.

1. Now when I see the meadows and orchards and woods turn green, I would begin a "discord" on love, on whose account I am distraught. For a certain lady was wont to love me, but her heart has changed, and so I produce discordance in the rhymes, melodies and languages.

2. I am one who has no happiness, nor shall I ever have it, either in April or in May, if I do not have it from my lady. Certain is it that in her own language I cannot describe her great beauty, which is fresher than the gladiolus flower, and that is why I shall not part from her.

3. Fair, sweet, dear lady, I give and commit myself to you. Never shall I krlow perfect bliss if I have not you and you me. You are a most treacherous enemy if I die through my good faith; yet I shall in no wise depart from my obedience to you.

4. Lady, I surrender to you, for you are the kindest and fairest that ever was, and joyous and worthy, if only you were not so cruel to me. Your features are

most fair and your complexion fresh and youthful. I am yours, and if I possessed you, nothing would be lacking to me.

5. But I so fear your anger that I am in complete despair. For your sake I endure pain and torture, and my body is racked. At night, as I lie in my bed, I wake again and again; and since I gain no advantage for myself thereby, I have failed in my intent.

6. Fair Knight, so precious to me is your noble sovereignty that each day I am dismayed. Ah me! what shall I do, if she whom I cherish most slays me, I know not why? My lady, by the faith I owe you and by the head of Saint Quiteria, you have wrested my heart from me and stolen it with your most sweet discourse.

SECTION 6

Selections from
THE WOMEN TROUBADOURS

Translated by Meg Bogin

Introduction by Albrecht Classen

Rarely do we hear of medieval women poets who participated in the public discourse on secular love because they seem to have enjoyed lesser freedom than men in the world of aristocracy. Nevertheless, during the early twelfth century a handful of female voices could be heard who joined the debates about courtly love and claimed their right to fight for their personal happiness. These noble ladies lived in Southern France in an area today known as the Provence. Similar to their male colleagues, these women poets are called "trobairitz" because they searched for melodies and images for their erotic themes ("trobar"). The trobairitz are relatively unique figures in medieval literature because we know of no other women writers throughout the entire period who discussed courtly love in the public in similarly terms as they did. Their names are the following: Tibors, the Comtessa de Dia, Almucs de Castelnau, Iseut de Capio, Azalais de Porcairagues, Maria de Ventadorn, Alamanda, Garsenda, Isabella, Lombarda, Castelloza, Clara d'Anduza, Bieris de Romans, Guillelma de Rosers, Domna H., Alais, Iselda, and Carenza. Certainly, we know of many religious women writers in Germany, Italy, France, and England, and often those women reflect some of the courtly love poetry in their religious visions (mystics), but this does not change the observation that the trobairitz were the only representatives of medieval women who joined their male colleagues in this debate. Some of the trobairitz can be identified in historical documents, others are only known through their names and texts, which is not untypical for most medieval literature.

The significance of the trobaritz poetry appears to be that these women raised their voices to express ever so slightly but yet noticeably different opinions about love and the relationship between the sexes. Some historians argue that the trobairitz reflect a unique socio-economic and political situation in the early Middle Ages. Until ca. 1100 there were many more female than male saints, and the family structure did not yet display the typical patriarchal features. On a broad scale, since then a new patrilinear kinship system emerged which forced women out of the public sphere back into the family. This process was completed by about 1500, when economic factors played their part to transform the family-run workshops to capital-based companies which only men were entitled to operate. Around 1200 women fared worse in the Church because the public debate increasingly focused on the inherited guilt of Eve and increased its misogynistic pitch. Nevertheless, the situation in the Provence was different from the rest of Europe because women could still inherit fiefs and rule over their lands without necessarily being married. We might even say that between 1180 and 1230 women had regained a similar position as their sisters had enjoyed until the eleventh century. The historical documents demonstrate that women acted as guardians for their sons, received and gave homage for their fiefs, executed their husbands' will, and received inheritance equal to those of their brothers. In light of these conditions, it is not totally surprising that the Provence saw the emergence of *trobairitz poetry*, whereas in other parts of Europe women could not enjoy this type of literary freedom.

Once the *Roman Law* became known and was widely accepted in medieval Europe from ca. 1230 onwards, this unique freedom for women changed radically. From then on they were much more subjected under their husbands and fathers, and also lost access to literature. This might be one of many possible explanations why *trobairitz poetry* came to an end during that time, and why similar love poems were not composed by any of their European sisters.

The only literary outlets from then on would be the world of mysticism (see Mechthild von Magdeburg) and letters (see Heloise). The process of suppressing women was, however, not a fast one, and there was no uniformity to it either. The real drastic transformation took place not until the end of the fifteenth century when an economic crisis, new forms of "industrial" production, and a modern system of financing replaced the traditional family-based medieval economy. Moreover, when Martin Luther launched the Protestant Reformation in 1517 with his 99 theses, this was indirectly also an attack against women's independence in the arts and literature. With the closure of vast numbers of convents and nunneries, women lost their access to an advanced level of education and their traditional learning and art centers. From then on particularly aristocratic women had basically only one choice, that is, to marry and to have children, or to work as maids within their family. This generalization also applies to a large extent to the Catholic areas where the same economic factors affected women's lives.

BIBLIOGRAPHY

The Voice of the Trobairitz. Perspectives on the Women Troubadours. Ed. William D. Paden. Middle Ages Series (Philadelphia: University of Pennsylvania Press, 1989).

William D. Paden, "Rape in the Pastourella," *Romantic Review* 80, 3 (1989): 331–349.

Songs of the Women Troubadours, ed. and trans. by Matilda Tomaryn Bruckner, Laurie Shepard, Sarah White. The Garland Library of Medieval Literature (New York-London: Garland, 1995).

Medieval Woman's Song. Cross-Cultural Approaches. Ed. by Anne L. Klinck and Ann Marie Rasmussen (Philadelphia: University of Pennsylvania Press, 2002).

TIBORS

TIBORS *is probably the earliest of the women troubadours. She was the sister of the troubadour Raimbaut d'Orange and the wife of Bertrand de Baux, who was an important patron of troubadours and lord of one of the most powerful families of Provence. This fragment is the only poem of hers to survive.*

Sweet handsome friend, I can tell you truly
that I've never been without desire
since it pleased you that I have you as my courtly lover;
nor did a time ever arrive, sweet handsome friend,
when I didn't want to see you often;
nor did I ever feel regret,
nor did it ever come to pass, if you went off angry,
that I felt joy until you had come back;
nor. . . .

THE COUNTESS OF DIA

THE COUNTESS OF DIA *was probably from Die, northeast of Montèlimar. She was descended from seigneurial families of the Viennois and Burgundy and was married to a lord of Die. Four of her poems have survived.*

I

I thrive on youth and joy,
and youth and joy keep me alive,
for my friend's the very gayest,
which makes me gay and playful;

and since I'm true,
he should be faithful:
my love for him has never strayed,
nor is my heart the straying kind.

I'm very happy, for the man
whose love I seek's so fine.
May God with joy richly repay
the man who helped us meet.
If anyone should disagree,
pay him no heed; listen only
to the one who knows one often picks the blooms
from which one's own broom's made.

The lady who knows about valor
should place her affection
in a courteous and worthy knight
as soon as she has seen his worth,
and she should dare to love him face to face;
for courteous and worthy men
can only speak with great esteem
of a lady who loves openly.

I've picked a fine and noble man,
in whom merit shines and ripens—
generous, upright and wise,
with intelligence and common sense.
I pray him to believe my words
and not let anyone persuade him
that I ever would betray him,
except I found myself betrayed.

Floris, [2] your worth
is known to all good men;
therefore I make this request:
please, grant me your protection.

II

Of things I'd rather keep in silence I must sing:
so bitter do I feel toward him

---

1. Probably a proverb. Literally, "For one often picks the brooms with which one sweeps oneself:" *i.e.*, "One is often responsible for one's own undoing."
2. Probably a *senhal;* Floris was the hero of a popular romance, now lost (see Countess of Dia, poem III).

whom I love more than anything.
With him my mercy and fine manners are in vain,
my beauty, virtue and intelligence.
For I've been tricked and cheated
as if I were completely loathesome.

There's one thing, though, that brings me recompense:
I've never wronged you under any circumstance,
and I love you more than Seguin loved Valensa.
At least in love I have my victory,
since I surpass the worthiest of men. ← *better than men*
With me you always act so cold,
but with everyone else you're so charming.
I have good reason to lament
when I feel your heart turn adamant
toward me, friend: it's not right another love   ← *another women*
take you away from me, no matter what she says.
Remember how it was with us in the beginning
of our love! May God not bring to pass
that I should be the one to bring it to an end. ← *she doesn't want to break it off*

The great renown that in your heart resides
and your great worth disquiet me,
for there's no woman near or far
who wouldn't fall for you if love were on her mind.
But you, my friend, should have the acumen
to tell which one stands out above the rest. ← *he has to choose*
And don't forget the stanzas we exchanged.

My worth and noble birth should have some weight,
my beauty and especially my noble thoughts;
so I send you, there on your estate,
this song as messenger and delegate.
I want to know, my handsome noble friend,
why I deserve so savage and so cruel a fate.
I can't tell whether it's pride or malice you intend.

But above all, messenger, make him comprehend
that too much pride has undone many men.

III

I've lately been in great distress
over a knight who once was mine,

---

3. Hero and heroine, respectively, of a lost romance.

162

and I want it known for all eternity
how I loved him to excess.
Now I see I've been betrayed   4
because I wouldn't sleep with him;
night and day my mind won't rest
to think of the mistake I made.

*he left her
b/c she wouldn't
sleep with him*

How I wish just once I could caress
that chevalier with my bare arms,
for he would be in ecstasy
if I'd just let him lean his head against my breast,
I'm sure I'm happier with him
than Blancaflor with Floris.[6]
My heart and love I offer him,
my mind, my eyes, my life.

*wants to
give him herself*

Handsome friend, charming and kind,
when shall I have you in my power?
If only I could lie beside you for an hour
and embrace you lovingly—
know this, that I'd give almost anything
to have you in my husband's place,
but only under the condition
that you swear to do my bidding.

IV   7

Fine joy brings me great happiness,
which makes me sing more gaily,
and it doesn't bother me a bit
or weigh my spirit down   8
that those sneaky *lauzengiers*
are out to do me harm;
their evil talk doesn't dismay me,
it just makes me twice as gay.

*she is now
sleeping around*

Those nasty-worded *lauzengiers*
won't get an ounce of trust from me,
for no one will find honor

4. Some scholars see in this line a classic reference to the *épreuve*, or test of chastity, which required the lovers to sleep together naked with a sword between them.

5. Literally, "in bed and when I'm dressed."

6. Heroine and hero, respectively, of a lost popular romance.

7. "Fine" in the sense of "courtly, "as in *fin' amors*, courtly love

8. Omnipresent characters in troubadour love poetry, *Lauzengiers* were spies in the employ of the jealous husband; they not only eavesdropped on the lovers but did everything possible to thwart their secret meetings. The figure of the *lauzengier* probably corresponds to the very real difficulty of finding privacy in the courtly setting.

who has anything to do with them.
They are like the cloud that grows
and billows out until
the sun loses its rays:
I have no use for such as them.

And you, gossiping *gelos*,[9]
don't think I'm going to hang around,
or that joy and youth[10] don't please me:
beware, or grief will bring you low.

AZALAIS DE PORCAIRAGES

AZALAIS DE PORCAIRAGES *was from the modern town of Portiragnes, just outside Béziers. Nothing definite is known about her life, but she appears to have moved in courtly society.*

Now we are come to the cold time
when the ice and the snow and the mud winter
and the birds' beaks are mute
(for not one inclines to sing);
and the hedge-branches are dry—
no leaf nor bud sprouts up,
nor cries the nightingale
whose song awakens me in May.[11]

My heart is so disordered
that I'm rude to everyone;
I know it's easier to lose
than gain; still, though I be blamed
I'll tell the truth:
my pain comes from Orange.[12]
That's why I stand gaping,
for I've lost the joy of solace.

A lady's love is badly placed
who argues with a wealthy man,

9. *Gelos* is almost always used in Provencal to designate the jealous husband, an indispensable third party to any properly conducted courtly liaison.
10. *Iois e iovenz* may here he taken as a single term designating courtly love. "Joy" and "youth" were the essential qualities of any courtly lover, male or female.
11. This line recalls the May songs of the popular tradition.
12. Perhaps a reference to Raimbaut d'Orange.

one above the rank of vassal:
she who does it is a fool.[13]
For the people of Vélay
say love and money do not mix,
and the woman money chooses
they say has lost her honor.

I have a friend of great repute
who towers above all other men,
and his heart toward me is not untrue,
for he offers me his love.
And I tell you I reciprocate,
and whoever says I don't,
God curse his luck—
as for myself, I know I'm safe.

Handsome friend, I'd gladly stay
forever in your service—
such noble mien and such fine looks—
so long as you don't ask too much;
we'll soon come to the test,
for I'll put myself in your hands:
you swore me your fidelity,
now don't ask me to transgress.

To God I commend Bel Esgar
and the city of Orange,
and Gloriet' and the Caslar,
and the lord of all Provence,
and all those there who wish me well, [14]
and the arch where the attacks are shown.
I've lost the man who owns my life,
and I shall never be consoled.

Joglar, you of merry heart,
carry my song down to Narbonne,[15]
with its *tornada* made for her
whose guides are youth and joy.

---

13. Corresponds to the southern part of the Auvergne.

14. The Roman arch of Orange was one of the outstanding monuments of medieval Provence. The other references in the stanza are to now unknown landmarks, presumably also in the area of Orange.

15. Probably the Viscountess Ermengarda of Narbonne, a major political and cultural figure over a period of fifty years.

ALAMANDA

ALAMANDA *may have been a Gascon. Our only knowledge of her comes from the vida of Guiraut de Bornelh, one of the major troubadours of the classical period, with whom she exchanged her tenson.*

conversation

If I seek your advice, pretty friend Alamanda,
don't make things hard for me, for I'm a banished man.
For that's what your deceitful mistress told me,
that now I've been expelled from her command:
and what she gave me she retracts now and reclaims.
What should I do?
I'm so angry that my body's
all but bursting into flame.

In God's name, Guiraut, a lover's wishes
count for nothing here, for if one partner fails
the other should keep up appearances
so that their trouble doesn't spread or grow.
If she tells you that a high peak is a plain,
believe her,
and accept the good *and* bad she sends:
thus shall you be loved.

I can't keep from speaking out against her pride,
even if you're young and beautiful and blond.
The slightest pain hurts me, the smallest joy overwhelms,
and still I'm not in first or second place.
I'm worried that this anger will destroy me:
you praise me,   17
but I can tell—I'm closer to the waves
and I think you're leading me astray.

If you come to me with questions so profound,
my God, Guiraut, I don't know what to say.
You call to me with a joyful, easy heart,   18
but I want to mow my field before someone else tries;
if I wanted to arrange a peace

---

16. In other words. "I'm sensitive the way a courtly lover is supposed to be, and still it gets me nowhere with her." The Provencal uses "you" *(vos)* in the sense of "one."

17. *Onda*—wave—is probably a misreading of *ongla*, fingernail; this would be less interesting but a much more common metaphor in Provencal.

18. The exact meaning of this line is obscure.

I would have looked for you,
but since she keeps her lovely body hidden so,
I think you're right that you've been ditched.
Now don't start yakking, young girl,
for she lied to me first, more than five times.
Do you think I can put up with this much more?
I'd be taken for an ignoramus.
I have a mind to ask about another friendship
if you don't shut up;   19
I got much better counsel from Na Berengeira
than I ever got from you.

Now I see, Guiraut, that she's capable of everything,
since you call her fickle and unfaithful;
still, do you think she wants to patch things up?
I doubt she's that tame yet:
from now on she'll keep courtesy in last place,
no matter what you say.
She's so angry with you that she'll suffer
neither peace nor oath nor treaty.

Beauty, for God's sake, don't let me lose your aid—
you already know how it was granted me.
If I've done wrong in being so irate,
don't hold it against me; and if you've ever felt how fast
a lover's heart can change, or if you've ever loved,
think of some way;
for I'm as good as dead if I have lost her—
but don't tell her that.

Seigneur Guiraut, I didn't want your love to end,
but she says she has a right to be enraged,
because you're courting someone else in front of everyone
who next to her's worth nothing, clothed or nude.
If she didn't jilt you she'd be acting weak,
since you're courting someone else.
But I'll speak well of you to her—I always have—
if you promise not to keep on doing that.

Beauty, for God's sake, if she has your trust,
promise her for me.

---

19. Unknown noblewoman. Perhaps the wife of one of the many Raimon Berengars of Provence.

I'll gladly do so, but when she's given you her love again,
don't take yours back.

LOMBARDA

LOMBARDA *appears to have been from Toulouse. She is one of the few women troubadours to write in* trobar clus, *the hermetic, "closed" style of some of the best Provencal poets. Her* tenson *with Barnat Arnaut d'Armagnac is in two sections, rather than the customary alternating stanza pattern. Part I is spoken by Bernart Arnaut, part II by Lombarda.*

I

I'd like to be a Lombard for Lombarda,
for I like her more than Alamanda or Giscarda;
I like the way her pretty eyes regard me,
as if to offer me her love—but how she makes me wait!

> For beauty, laughter,
> and my pleasure
> she has under lock and key
> where nobody can get.

Lord Jordan, if I leave you Germany,
France, Poitiers, Normandy and Brittany,
then you should leave me without argument
Lombardy, Livorno and Lomagna.

> And if you're worthy
> I'll increase your worth
> tenfold with her who's foreign
> to all evilness.

> Merit's mirror,
> who hath honor,
> don't let that good-for-nothing
> break the love that binds us.

II

I'm glad I wasn't called Bernarda for Bernart,
and that I wasn't named Arnauda for Arnaut;
but many thanks, lord, since it gives you pleasure
to name me side by side with two such ladies.

I want to know
your true opinion:
which one you prefer, and what's
the mirror where you stare.

For the mirror with no image so disrupts
my rhyme that it almost interrupts it;
but then when I remember what my name records,
all my thoughts unite in one accord.

But I wonder
where your heart is,
for it's house and hearth
are hid, and you won't tell

CASTELLOZA   *unrequited love*

CASTELLOZA was from the Auvergne, from the region of Le Puy. She was probably the wife of a nobleman who fought in the Fourth Crusade. Three of her poems have survived.

I

Friend, if you had shown consideration,
meekness, candor and humanity,
I'd have loved you without hesitation;
but you were mean and sly and villainous.
Still, I make this song to spread your praises
wide, for I can't bare to let your name
go on unsung and unrenowned,
no matter how much worse you treat me now.

she will praise him even though he hurts her

I won't consider you a decent man
nor love you fully nor with trust
until I see if it would help me more
to make my heart turn mean or treacherous.
But I don't want to give you an excuse
for saying I was ever devious with you;
something you could keep in store
in case I never did you wrong.

---

20. Alamanda's reply makes fun of Bernart Arnaut's precious first stanza. Occitanian women often took their husband's name when they married; Lombarda plays on this and makes herself into two "wives" of Bernart Arnaut—they are unreal, like "the mirror with no image" of her third stanza. He, she seems to say, is in love with his own image.

It greatly pleases me
when people say that it's unseemly
for a lady to approach a man she likes
and hold him deep in conversation;
but whoever says that isn't very bright,
and I want to prove before you let me die
that courting brings me great relief
when I court the man who's brought me grief.
Whoever blames my love for you's
a fool, for it greatly pleases me,
and whoever says that doesn't know me;
I don't see you now at all the way I did
the time you said I shouldn't worry,
since at any moment I might
rediscover reason to rejoice:
from words alone my heart is full of joy.

— girl don't usually go after a guy they like

All other love's worth naught,
and every joy is meaningless to me
but yours, which gladdens and restores me,
in which there's not a trace of pain or of distress;
and I think I'll be glad always and rejoice
always in you, friend, for I can't convert;
nor have I any joy, nor do I find relief,
but what little solace comes to me in sleep.

still in love with him

cannot love another

— dreams about him

I don't know why you're always on my mind,
for I've searched and searched from good to evil
your hard heart, and yet my own's unswerving.
I don't send you this; no, I tell you myself:
if you don't want me to enjoy
the slightest happiness, then I shall die;
and if you let me die, you'll be a guilty man;
I'll be in my grave, and you'll be cruelly blamed.

— about to kill herself because of her one-sided love

II

God knows I should have had my fill of song—
the more I sing
the worse I fare in love,
and tears and cares
make me their home;
I've placed my heart and soul
in jeopardy,

song $\stackrel{?}{=}$ partners

and if I don't end this poem now
it will already be too long.

Oh handsome friend, just once before I die
of grief, show me
your handsome face;
the other lovers say *← other women*
you are a beast—
but still, though no joy
comes to me from you,
I'm proud to love you always
in good faith, with an unfickle heart.

Nor ever from me a treacherous heart
toward you will turn—
though I be your inferior, *← she is of lower class*
in loving I excel; *or sexual class*
this I believe,
and this I think
even when I ponder your great worth,
and I know well that you deserve
a lady higher born that I. *← thinking of him, not herself*

Since I first caught sight of you I've been
at your command; and yet, friend,
it's brought me naught,
for you've sent neither
messages nor envoys.
And if you left me now,
I wouldn't feel a thing,
for since no joy sustains me
a little pain won't drive me mad.

If it would do me any good, I'd remind you singing
that I had your glove—
I stole it trembling;
then I was afraid
you might get scolded
by the girl who loves you now:
so I gave it back fast, friend, *← tried to get back at him. Failed*
for I know well enough
that I am powerless.

Knights there are I know who harm themselves
in courting ladies

more than ladies them,
when they are neither
higher born nor richer;
for when a lady's mind
is set on love, she ought
to court the man,
if he shows strength and chivalry.

[handwritten: women are better at courting]

Lady Almucs,[21] I always
love what's worst for me,
for he who's most deserving
has the heart most fleeting.
Good Name,[22] my love for you
will never cease,
for I live on kindness,
faith and constant courage.

[handwritten: guys who want her are flickle]

III

You stayed a long time, friend,
and then you left me,
and it's a hard, cruel thing you've done;
for you promised and you swore
that as long as you lived
I'd be your only lady:
if now another has your love
you've slain me and betrayed me,
for in you lay all my hopes
of being loved without deceit.

[handwritten: broke up with her]

Handsome friend, as a lover true
I loved you, for you pleased me,
but now I see I was a fool,
for I've barely seen you since.
I never tried to trick you,
yet you returned me bad for good;
I love you so, without regret,
but love has stung me with such force
I think no good can possibly
be mine unless you say you love me.

[handwritten: she still loves him but sees her mistake]

21. Unknown reference. Castelloza could not have known Almucs de Castelnau, who died ca. 1180.
22. A *senhal*.

172

I would have compared poorly
with the other women in your life,
for it's proper to send words
and messages selected with great care:
but I'm content, friend, by my faith,
to speak to you in person—
it suits me best;
for even highborn women are enriched
if from you they have some show
of kisses or affection.

May evil strike me down if ever
I was fickle or displayed
a flighty heart, or ever
wanted any other lover;
no, if I'm sad and mournful
it's because you don't remember me.
And if still I have no joy from you,
you'll soon come upon me dead:
for when unhappiness persists
a woman dies, unless her man speeds joy.

← she is going to die (metaphoricly?)

All the abuse and suffering
that's been my lot because of you
have made my family adore you,[23]
and my husband most of all;
and if you ever did me wrong
I pardon you in all good faith
and beg you to come back to me
now that you've heard my song:
for here, I promise you,
you'll find a fine reception.

← family enjoys fame from poems

← married now

still wants him

---

23. That is, suffering has made her write poems, which brings fame to her family.

SECTION 7

THE UNFORTUNATE LORD HENRY/HEINRICH

Hartmann von Aue

Introduction by Albrecht Classen

We know only little about Hartmann von Aue because the chronicles are silent about him. According to his language, however, we may assume that he lived in Southwestern Germany, Swabia, and was connected with the influential Hohenstaufen family. The precise location of "Aue" is unknown, because there are too many towns and places with the same name, meaning "meadow" or "pasture." He claimed to be of the rank of a knight but seems to have received the training similar to that of a cleric.

Hartmann von Aue was one of the most significant poets of the Middle High German period and was highly praised for his work by Gottfried von Strassburg in his *Tristan*. His earliest text appears to have been a theoretical treatise on love and its physiological and spiritual dimension, his *Klagebüchlein*, in which heart and soul debate the nature of love and its social value. Next Hartmann wrote two major Arthurian romances, *Erec* and *Iwein*, the first around 1170/80, the other around 1200. Both texts he translated from models provided by his French contemporary Chrétien de Troyes. But in *Erec* he exercised considerable poetic freedom, whereas *Iwein* is much more closely connected with the French romance, though the term "translation" would not fully capture the character and poetic quality of this work. In the earlier romance the protagonist has to learn how to combine private and public life and to exercise sympathy and pity, and to apply chivalry for the good of society ("Joie de la curt"); the later romance reverses this problem and shows how Iwein forgets about his personal obligations over his overly passionate interest in chivalry. He also has to recover his social identity and to reform, and only once when his chivalric deeds have become functional elements for courtly society, does Iwein gain forgiveness and love from his wife.

Hartmann also composed a religious tale, "Gregorius," which is strongly characterized by an Oedipal theme. It treats the life of a man who, after his parents had committed the crime of incest, innocently falls to the same sin, but is later redeemed by God who chooses him as the next pope as a reward for his extreme self-afflicted penance on a lonely rock in a lake. In addition Hartmann wrote a number of courtly love poems—*Minnelieder*.

The short novella "The Unfortunate Lord Henry" encapsulates many of Hartmann's literary themes and serves well to gain a solid understanding of courtly culture as could be found in Germany during the late twelfth century. The text was copied in seven manuscripts (four complete manuscripts and three fragments), and many later poets referred to this novella or quoted from it, thus testifying to its considerable popularity far into the fourteenth and fifteenth centuries.

BIBLIOGRAPHY

Frank Tobin, "Middle High German," *A Concise History of German Literature to 1900*. Ed. Kim Vivian. *Studies in German Literature, Linguistics, and Culture* (Columbia, S.C.: Camden House, 1992), 21–57.

W. H. Jackson, *Chivalry in Twelfth-Century Germany: the Works of Hartmann von Aue*. Arthurian Studies, 34 (Cambridge-New York: D.S. Brewer, 1994).

Will Hasty, "Hartmann von Aue," *German Writers and Works of the High Middle Ages: 1170–1280*, ed. James Hardin and Will Hasty (Detroit, Washington, D.C., and London: Gale Research, 1994), 27–43.

Will Hasty, *Adventures in Interpretation: the Works of Hartman von Ave and Their Critical Reception*. Literary Criticism in Perspective. (Columbia, SC: Camden House, 1996).

Hartman von Aue, *Der arme Heinrich*. Ed. Hermann Paul. 16th, newly revised ed. Kurt Gärtner. Altdeutsche Textbibliothek, 3 (Tübingen: Niemeyer, 1996).

Marion E. Gibbs, Sidney M. Johnson, *Medieval German Literature. A Companion* (New York and London: Garland, 1997).

Encyclopedia of Medieval Literature, ed. Jay Ruud (New York: Facts on File, 2006).

THE UNFORTUNATE LORD HENRY

There was a knight so learned
that he read in books
whatever he found written there.
His name was Hartmann and
he was a vassal of the House of Aue.
He began searching around
in various kinds of books,
looking through them to see
whether he might find something
with which he could make

oppressive hours more pleasant,
things of such a nature
which would do honor to God
and with which he could
endear himself to his fellow men.
Now he will begin to interpret for you
a tale which he found written.
It is for this reason that he has mentioned his name
so that he would not be
without reward for the work
which he has expended on it
and so that whoever might hear it recited or might read it
after his [Hartmann's] death
might pray
to God for the salvation of his soul.
One says that he is his own intercessor
and redeems himself thereby
who intercedes for the sins of another.

The story which he read tells of a lord living in Swabia in whom no quality was lacking that a knight in the flower of manhood should have to win full esteem. No one in all those lands was connected so highly. He had at his disposal lineage as well as power and wealth. Also, he possessed capabilities in many areas. However sufficient his possessions were, however flawless his ancestry, which was doubtless comparable to that of princes, still he was not nearly so rich by reason of birth and possessions as he was because of his sense of dignity and noble attitude.

His name was very well known. He was called Lord Heinrich and was born of the House of Aue. His heart had foresworn duplicity and ill-breeding, and he kept this oath with constancy to the end of his days. His honor and conduct were without the slightest fault. That abundance of worldly honors one could rightly wish for had been lavished upon him. And he knew how to increase these honors through his many sterling qualities. He was a flower of young manhood, a mirror of the joy of the world, a diamond of constant loyalty, a full crown of courtly behavior. He was a refuge to those in need, a shield of protection for his kin. His generosity weighed the amount to be given against the need. Both excess and lack were foreign to him. He carried the wearisome burden of honors upon his back. He was a bridge stretching forth help and was well-versed in singing of courtly love. Thus he knew how to gain the honor and glory of the world. He embodied all the qualities of the courtly gentleman and showed mature wisdom.

When Lord Heinrich had thus attained the enjoyment of honor, possessions, a happy heart, and earthly joy—he was praised and esteemed as the first among his kinfolk—his lofty existence was turned into a life of utter humiliation. In his case, as also with Absalom was made clear, as Holy Scripture has told us, the empty crown of worldly sweetness falls from its place of highest esteem into dust under foot. There it says, *media vita in morte sumus,* which means we are hovering in the midst of death when we think we are living to the fullest.

The stability of this world, its constant and best wealth, power, and majesty can be mastered by no one. We can see a true picture of that happening with the candle which turns to ashes in the act of giving forth light. We are made of fragile stuff. Just look how our joy dissolves in tears. Life's sweetness is mixed with bitter gall. Our blossom must fail just when it seems to be thriving best. Heinrich's fate made very evident that he who lives on this earth in great esteem is despised in the sight of God. Through God's command he plunged from his esteemed position into a despicable state of misery: he fell victim to leprosy. When the grave chastisement became evident on his body, he was repulsive to everyone. However pleasant all the world found him before, now he was so repulsive that people avoided looking at him. The noble and wealthy Job met with this fate, too. In the midst of good fortune he piteously found himself on a dung heap.

When poor Heinrich first began to realize that the world found him repugnant, he behaved as most people in a similar situation do. His reaction to his bitterly felt anguish differed greatly from the patience of Job. The good man Job suffered with patient bearing all the afflictions that came his way so that his soul might find joy. The disease and tribulations which he suffered from the world were occasions for him to praise God and he was happy. Alas, poor Heinrich did not at all react in this manner. He was gloomy and dejected. His soaring heart sank, his buoyant joy went under. His self-esteem tumbled. Honey turned to gall. A sudden dark thunderclap shattered his noontime. A cloud, thick and sullen, enveloped the radiance of his sun. Many a sigh escaped him at the thought of having to leave such honor behind. Repeatedly he cursed and damned the day of his birth.

And yet a little joy was left to him. He still had one consolation. He had often heard that there were several different strains of the disease and some of them were curable. Hence his hopes and thoughts were quite mixed. He thought that he could perhaps be cured, and so he hurried off to Montpellier to seek medical advice. Here he quickly found nothing but the sad news that he would never recover. He received the news with disappointment and rode off toward Salerno and here also sought the skills of experienced doctors in the hope of being cured.

The best physician whom he found there immediately gave him a strange answer: he was curable and yet he would never be cured. "How can that be?" asked Heinrich. "What you are saying is quite impossible. If I am curable, then I'll recover. And whatever is imposed upon me in the way of a fee or however strenuous the treatment might be, I'm quite confident that I can accomplish it." "Give up your hopes," the doctor replied. "I'll tell you the nature of your sickness, although my explanation won't do you any good. For a cure a certain medicine is all that is necessary. Hence you are curable. However, no one is so wealthy or has such keen intellectual powers that he can attain it. Thus you will forever remain uncured, unless God wishes to be your physician."

"Why are you trying to discourage me?" asked poor Heinrich. "I have a great amount of wealth at my disposal. Unless you want to act contrary to your medical skills and medical ethics, not to mention that you would be turning down my silver and gold, I'll make you so favorably disposed toward me that you will quite readily heal me." "It's not that my good will is lacking," replied the doctor. "And if the medicine were of such a kind that one could find it for sale or that one could acquire it by any means, I would not let you languish. But that is unfortunately not the case. Hence you must of necessity remain without my help. You would have to find a virgin of marriageable age who would be willing to suffer death for your sake. Now it is not the usual state of affairs among people that someone freely takes such an act upon himself. Nothing else is necessary for a cure than the blood from the heart of such a girl. This would be a cure for your disease."

Now poor Heinrich saw clearly that it would be impossible for anyone to find a person who would willingly die for him. Thus the one consolation which had made him undertake the journey was taken from him. And from this time on, he had no hope left concerning his recovery. Because of this the pain of his heart was so great and strong that it infuriated him most of all that he should go on living. He journeyed home and began distributing his lands as well as his personal effects according to his own feelings and the judicious advice of others as to where it would do the most good. With discrimination he increased the means of his poor relatives and also gave material comfort to poor people who were strangers to him so that God might have mercy on his soul. Monasteries received the rest. Thus did he free himself from all his major possessions except for a farm on cleared land. Hither he fled from people. Heinrich was not the only one to bewail his tragic affliction. In all the lands where he was known and even in foreign lands where he was known only by reputation people grieved for him.

The man who had already been farming this land for a long time was a free peasant who never had any of the great troubles which other peasants had whose lords were worse and did not spare them taxation and other fees. Whatever this farmer did willingly seemed good enough to his lord. What is more, he protected him from any violence inflicted by outside parties. Because of this no one of his class in the whole land was as well off as he. To this peasant came his lord, poor Heinrich. Whatever Heinrich had spared him earlier, how that was now repaid! How handsomely he reaped the benefits of this! The farmer was not at all bothered by what he had to do for Heinrich's sake. Out of loyalty he was determined to endure willingly the burdensome task that was now his lot because of his lord. He spared no means to make Heinrich comfortable.

God had given the peasant a good life according to his class. He was capable of strenuous physical labor, and he had a hardworking wife. In addition, he had beautiful children who really bring joy to a man's life. One of the children, as one says, was a girl, a child eight years old. Her actions revealed her real goodness.

She would never budge from her lord even a foot. To gain his favor and greeting she served him constantly in every way she could with her kind attention. She had such a pleasing way about her that she could have fittingly been the child of the emperor in her loveliness.

The others were smart enough to know how to avoid him without being too obvious. But she fled to him all the time and nowhere else. She alone made the time pass quickly for him. With the pure goodness of a child she had opened her heart to her lord so she could always be found at his feet. With pleasing eagerness she attended her lord. He, in turn, tried to please her in whatever way he could. Her lord gave her in abundance whatever fitted in with her childhood games. Also in his favor was the fact that children are so easy to win over. He got for her whatever he found for sale—a mirror, hair ribbons—whatever children find nice—a belt and a ring. By means of these attentions he brought things to the point that she became so close to him that he called her his bride. The dear child never let him remain alone. She thought of him as a completely healthy person. However strongly she was influenced by the gifts and playthings, still it was before all else a sweet disposition, a gift of God, which made this way of acting please her. Her devotion manifested great kindness.

Once, when the unfortunate Heinrich had already spent three years there and God had tormented him with great bodily suffering, the peasant, his wife, and the girl I have already mentioned were one day sitting together with him as they worked. They were lamenting over the sufferings of their lord, and they had every reason to be sad. For they feared that his death would work great harm for them in that they might lose their good standing and their property, and that a different lord would be much more severe with them. These thoughts kept running through their minds until the peasant thus began to inquire, saying, "My dear lord, I would like to ask a question, if I may do so with your favor. There are so many doctors of medicine in Salerno. Why is it that none of them was able to find help for you with his skill? Sir, that is what surprises me." Poor Heinrich emitted a sigh of bitter anguish from the bottom of his heart. Such was the sadness with which he spoke that sobs punctuated his speech: "I deserved this shameful humiliation at God's hands. For you saw very well how formerly my gate stood wide open to worldly joy and that no one among his family and relatives had his wish fulfilled better than I. This was impossible since I always had my way completely. During this time I took very little notice of Him who in His goodness had given me this life. My attitude was that of all fools of this world who are persuaded that they can have honor and possessions without God. Thus did my foolish notion deceive me. For I very seldom looked to Him from whose favor many honors and possessions came my way. When, then, the Heavenly Gatekeeper had enough of my arrogance, He closed the gates of happiness to me. Now I'll never enter there! My foolish attitude spoiled that for me. As punishment God imposed an infirmity upon me of such a nature that no one can free me of it. Now I have become repugnant to the common people. Those of prominence take no notice of me. However lowly the man who looks at me, I am still more lowly than he. He shows me his contempt by casting his eyes from me. Now the loyalty in you really becomes evident for the first time—that you let me stay with you in my wretched condition and that you do not in the least flee from me. But although you do not shun me, although I am loved by you, if by no one else, and however much you have me to thank for your prosperity, still you would easily resign yourself to my death. Who in the world was ever so worthless and so wretched? I used to be your lord, now I am your suppliant. Dear friend, by keeping me here in my sickness you are earning for yourself, your wife, and my bride life everlasting.

"I'll gladly tell you what you asked me. In Salerno I was not able to find a doctor who dared or wanted to take me into his charge. For the means by which I was to recover from my sickness was to be of such a kind that no one in the world is at all able to gain it. I was told nothing else but that I would have to find a virgin fully able to marry who would be willing to suffer death for my sake, that the doctor would cut her open to the heart, and that nothing else could help me than the blood from her heart. Now it is obviously impossible that any such girl would willingly suffer death for my sake. Hence I must bear shameful misery till my death. May God send it to me quickly!"

The innocent girl heard what he told her father, for the dear child had the feet of her dear lord resting in her lap. One could easily compare her childlike attitude to the goodness of the angels. She understood what he said and forgot not a word. She kept thinking about it in her heart until she went to bed that night where she lay at the feet of her father and mother as she was accustomed to do. After they had both fallen asleep, she pressed many a deep sigh from her heart. Her sadness because of the sufferings of her lord became so great that the flood from her eyes poured over the feet of her sleeping parents. Thus did the dear child awaken them.

When they felt the tears, they awoke and asked her what was the matter with her and what kind of distress it could be that caused her to weep so quietly. At first she did not want to tell them anything. But when her father repeatedly begged and threatened her saying she had to tell them, she spoke: "You could well weep with me. What can cause us more trouble about our lord but that we shall lose him and with him give up our possessions and good standing? We shall never again get a lord so good that he would treat us the way he does." They said, "Daughter, you are right, but sorrowing and lamenting are not going to help us one bit. Dear child, don't talk about it. We are just as sorry as you are. Unfortunately, we are not able to help him in the least. God is the one who has taken him from us. If anyone else had done it, we would have to curse him."

Thus did they silence her. That night as well as the whole next day she remained dejected. Whatever anyone else did, these thoughts never left her heart. Then finally everybody went to bed the following night. When she had lain down on her usual place for sleeping, she again bathed everything with the tears from her eyes, for she bore hidden in her heart the greatest amount of goodness that I ever heard of in a child. What child had ever acted as she did? One thing she was completely resolved to do: if she was still alive the next day, she would in fact give her life for her lord.

This thought made her happy and light-hearted. She had not a care in the world except for one irritating fear: when she told her lord her intention, he might back down; and if she made her plans known to all three of them, she would not find any constancy in them and they would not let her go through with it. So greatly was she disturbed about this that her mother and father were awakened by it as in the previous night. They sat up facing her and said, "Look, what is the matter with you? It is very foolish for you to take this sad situation so completely to heart since no one can do anything about it anyway. Why don't you let us sleep?" Thus did they begin to take her to task: what good did her crying do since no one could prevent or make good the misfortune? And so for a second time they thought they had silenced the dear girl. But they little realized what she had resolved to do. The girl replied to them, "As my lord told us, he is quite able to be healed. And unless you want to keep me from it, I am suitable medicine for him. I am a virgin and have the right disposition. Before I see him go to ruin, I would rather die for him." When they heard this, both mother and father became sad and troubled. The father asked his daughter to put such thoughts out of her mind and to promise her lord only what she could really carry out, for her present plan was out of the question for her. "Daughter, you are just a child and your devotion in such matters is too great. You are not able to go through with it the way you have just proclaimed. You have no idea what death is like. When it comes to such a pass that there is no way out and that you must die, then you would much prefer to go on living if you could bring it about. For you have never entered into a more deplorable pit. So, shut your mouth. If you ever in the future talk about such things again, you'll get what's good for you!" And so he thought that by pleas and intimidation he had silenced her. But he was not able to do it.

His daughter answered him, "Dear father, however young and inexperienced I may be, I still have sense enough to understand from what I've heard the harsh fact that death of the body is violent and severe. But whoever lives a long life filled with trials and hardships doesn't have it very easy either. For after a person has struggled and made it to a ripe old age through much hard work, then he still has to suffer death anyway. If he then suffers the loss of his soul, it would be better for him never to have been born. I have the opportunity, and because of it I shall always praise God, of being able to give my young body in return for eternal life. Now, you should not try to make it hard for me. I want to do the best thing for you as well as for me. I alone am able to preserve us from suffering and harm, as I shall now explain to you. We have honor and possessions. These come from the favorable disposition of my lord. For he has never spoken a command to cause us suffering, and he never took away any of our possessions. As long as he remains alive, things will go well for us. If we let him die, we shall also go to ruin. I want to keep him alive for our sakes through a well thought-out plan so that things will go well for all of us. Now let me do it, for it has to be."

When the mother saw how serious her daughter was, she began to cry and said, "Remember, dear child, how great the hardships were that I suffered for your sake, and let me receive a better reward than the words I hear you speaking. You are going to break my heart. Make your words a little more pleasant for me to hear. You are going to forfeit salvation by God by what you are doing to us. Don't you remember his commandment? He certainly commanded and asked that one show father and mother love and honor, and as a reward he promised that the soul would be saved and one would enjoy a long life on earth. You say you want to offer your life for the joy of both of us. But you will actually be filling our lives completely with suffering. Your father and I enjoy living because of you. What good to us are life, property, earthly well-being if we have to do without you? You should not cause us to worry. My dear daughter, you ought to be a joy for the both of us, our pleasure unmixed with suffering, a bright delight for us to look upon, the cheer of our life, a flower among your kin, a staff for our old age. And if through your own fault we have to stand at your graveside, you will be forever cut off from God's favor. That is what you will earn in regard to us! Daughter, if you wish to be good to us, then for the sake of our Lord's favor, change your attitude and forget these ideas I have heard from you."

"Mother," she replied, "I give you and father full credit for how well you have provided for me, as a mother and father should provide for their child. This attention I experience from your hands day after day. From your good favor I have a soul and a beautiful body. Everyone who sees me says in praise that I'm the most beautiful child he has seen in his whole life. To whom should I attribute this favor besides God, if not to the two of you. For this reason I shall always stand ready to obey your command. How great is my obligation in this!

"Mother, wonderful woman, since I have you to thank for both body and soul, let it be with your approval that I deliver both of them from the devil that I may give myself to God. Certainly the life of this world is nothing but loss to the soul. Besides, until now worldly desires have not touched me. I want to thank God now that he has granted me the insight, young though I am, to look with contempt upon this fragile life. I wish to deliver myself into God's dominion as pure as I am now. If I were to continue living, I'm afraid that the sweetness of the world would drag me down under foot as it has done to many whom its sweetness has also deceived. Then I must even be kept from God. To Him we should bewail the fact that I must live even till tomorrow. I don't find the world a nice place at all. Its comfort is great hardship, its pleasure great suffering, its sweet reward bitter want, its long life a sudden death. Nothing is more certain than that today's joy will be followed by tomorrow's suffering. And finally at the end is always death. That is an anguish to make you weep. Neither noble birth, nor riches, nor beauty, nor strength, nor exhilaration can protect one. Virtue and honor help one in the face of death no more than lowliness and vice. Our life and our youthful vitality have no more substance than clouds or dust. Our stability trembles like a leaf. Whether man or woman, whoever likes to fill himself with smoke is a very misguided fool who doesn't know how to think things out rightly and who simply follows the world. For over the foul dung is spread for us a silk cloth. He whom this splendor leads astray is born for hell and has lost nothing less than both body and soul. Now call to mind, dear woman, the love you as a mother owe to me and temper the sorrow which you have because of me. Then father will think things over in similar fashion. I well know he doesn't begrudge me salvation. He is a man honest enough to recognize well that you could not long enjoy having me even if I remain alive. If I were to remain here with you unmarried for two or three years, then my lord is probably dead, and we shall very likely suffer such distress from poverty that you will not be able to give any suitor a sufficient dowry on my behalf, and I would have to lead such an impoverished existence that you would rather see me dead. But let us forget about this problem for a minute. Even if nothing were causing us distress and my dear lord were to be preserved for us and went on living until I were wed to a man who was well-off and respected—this is what you want to happen—you would then think that everything had turned out for the best for me. My heart has told me otherwise. If it turns out that I love him, that would bring distress. If I find him repulsive, that is as bad as being dead. In either case my lot is one of suffering, a life filled with hardship and far from comfort with all sorts of things that cause women trouble and lead them astray from joy.

"Now put me in possession of that full abundance that never dwindles. A Free Yeoman seeks my hand to whom I give myself gladly. You should certainly give me to Him. Then my life is really well taken care of. His plow works very well for him, his farm is filled with all provisions. There neither horse nor cattle die. There one is not vexed by crying children. There it is neither too warm nor too cold. There no one grows old as the years pass: older people become younger. There one finds neither frost nor hunger. There suffering of any kind is absent. There one finds complete happiness without any hardship. To Him I wish to go and flee such fields that rain and hail destroy and floods wash away, fields with which one struggles and always has. What one is so tediously able to gain through toil in the course of a year is suddenly destroyed in half a day. These are the farm lands I wish to leave. Let them receive my curse. You love me. That is as it should be. Now I would gladly see that your love does not turn out to be the opposite. If you can come to see that I have the right understanding of the situation, and if you wish me to have possessions and honors, then let me go to our Lord Jesus Christ whose grace is so constant that it never fades, and who has as great a love for me, poor as I am, as for a queen. God willing, I shall never through my own fault lose your favor. It is certainly His commandment that I be obedient to you, for I have my life from you. This I do without regret. But at the same time I must not be disloyal to myself. I have always heard people say that whoever makes someone else happy in such a way that he himself becomes unhappy and whoever treats someone else like a king and shows only contempt for himself—that this is too much devotion. I certainly want to be obedient to you by showing you devotion, but above all else I must be true to myself! If you want to keep me from my salvation, then I would rather let you weep a bit over me than not to be clear about what I owe to myself. I constantly long to go where I shall find complete happiness. Besides, you have other children. Let them be your joy and thus console yourselves over losing me. No one can keep me from saving my lord and myself! Mother, I heard you complain just now saying it would cause your heart great pain if you should have to stand at my grave. You will most certainly be spared this. You will not stand at my grave because no one will let you see where I shall die. This will take place in Salerno. There death shall free us four from every kind of misery. Through death we shall all be saved, I much more so than you."

When they saw the child so eager for death speaking so wisely and acting in contradiction to all human norms, they began to consider that no tongue in a child's mouth could manifest such wisdom and such insight. They were convinced the Holy Spirit must be the cause of these ideas, who also was active in St. Nicholas as he lay in the cradle and taught him wisdom so he turned his child-like goodness toward God. They considered in their hearts that they did not want to and should not at all prevent her from doing what she had taken upon herself to do. The idea must have come to her from God.

The peasant and his wife turned cold with grief. They sat there in bed and for love of their child so forgot their tongue and were so out of their senses that neither of them could then speak a single word. The mother was torn by a fit of weeping in her suffering. Thus they both sat sad and dejected until they realized what little good their grieving was doing them. Since nothing was able to change her mind, the only sensible thing for them to do was to grant her wish willingly because they could never lose her in a better way. If they showed opposition to her plan, it could get them into a lot of trouble with their lord and other than that they would accomplish nothing by it. With a show of agreement they then said they were happy with her plan.

This made the innocent girl happy. When it had barely become day she went to where her lord was sleeping. His bride called to him saying, "Lord, are you asleep?" "No, I'm not, my bride, but tell me, why are you up so early today?" "Lord, my grief over your illness forces me." He said, "My bride, you show very well in the way you treat me that you are sorry. May God repay you accordingly. But there is nothing that can be done about it." "Truly, my dear lord, there is help for you. Since you can be helped, I shall not let you wait another day. Lord, you told us that if you had a virgin who would willingly suffer death on your account, you would thereby be healed. I myself want to be that girl, so help me God. Your life is more useful than mine."

The lord thanked her very much for her intentions and in sorrow his eyes filled unnoticed with tears. He said, "My bride, death is by no means a pleasant affair as you perhaps picture it to yourself. You have made it very clear to me that you would help me if you could. That is enough for me from you. I know your affectionate heart. Your intentions are pure and good. I desire nothing more from you. You are not able to carry out for me what you have just said. May God reward you for the devotion you have shown toward me. Since I have already tried several remedies, I would be the laughing stock of the people here if this didn't do any good and my disease continued as before. My bride, you act like children do when they are impulsive. They act immediately on whatever comes to mind, whether it be good or bad, and regret it afterwards. My bride, you are acting that way, too. You are convinced of what you are saying now. If, however, someone were to take you up on it so that your intention would be carried out, you would very probably regret it." He asked her to think it over a little more. "Your mother and father," he said, "cannot easily do without you. I should not desire something that would cause suffering to people who have always been good to me. Whatever the both of them advise, dear bride, that you should do." In saying this he smiled broadly for he had no idea what would then take place. Thus did the noble man speak to her.

The father and mother said, "Dear lord, you have been very good to us and shown us great respect. The only fitting response for us is to repay you in kind. Our daughter desires to suffer death for your sake. We are quite happy to give her our blessing, so completely has she convinced us. It was not a quick decision on her part. For three days now she has been constantly urging us to give our blessing to her plan. This she has now achieved. May God let you be healed through her. We are willing to give her up for your sake."

His bride was offering to die in order to deliver him from his illness, and her determination was evident. This caused much joylessness and displays of sorrow. Quite different were the worries they had, the three of them on the one hand and the girl on the other. The father and mother began to weep bitterly, and they had every right to weep over the death of their very dear child. The lord also began to think about the devotion of the child, and such sadness took hold of him that he wept much and could not at all make up his mind whether it was better to go through with it or let things be. Because of fear the girl also cried. She was afraid he would become faint-hearted and not go through with it. Thus they were all dejected and sought no cheer. Finally their lord, poor Heinrich, pulled himself together and thanked all three of them for their loyalty and generous care. The girl was exuberant that he was willing to go along with her plan. He prepared himself as quickly as possible for the trip to Salerno. What was suitable for the girl was quickly ready. Beautiful horses and expensive clothes which she had never worn before: ermine, velvet, and the best sable one could find. These were the girl's clothes.

Now who could fully express the deep sorrow and lamenting, the bitter suffering of her mother and the misery of her father? The departure of their dear child would have been a torment for them as they sent her away healthy to her death never to be seen by them again, except that the pure goodness of God which gave the child's heart the determination to die willingly relieved their distress. It had come about without any help from them. Hence they were spared all self-incrimination and depression. For otherwise it would have been a miracle that their hearts did not break. Their sorrow turned to joy so that afterwards they suffered no distress about the child's death.

And so the girl rode off toward Salerno happily and willingly with her lord. What could now trouble her except that the journey was so long and her life was thus prolonged? And when he had finally brought her there as he had planned, he found his doctor and with great elation told him he had found the kind of girl he had told him to get. Then he let him have a look at her. This seemed unbelievable to the doctor. He said, "Child, did you reach this decision on your own or were you influenced in your plan by entreaties and threats from your lord?" The girl answered that these ideas came from her heart.

This surprised him greatly and he took her aside and begged her in all seriousness to tell him whether her lord had persuaded her by means of threats. He said, "Child, you must seriously consider the matter further and I'll tell you exactly why. If you were to die and you didn't do it willingly, then your young life would be at an end, but unfortunately it would not help us the least little bit. Now keep nothing concerning your decision from me. I'll tell you what is going to happen to you. I undress you. Then you stand there completely unclothed, and the shame that you certainly will feel as you stand there naked before me will be great indeed. Then I bind your arms and legs. If you have any regard for your physical well-being, then consider the suffering yet to come. I cut into you all the way to your heart and tear it still beating from you. Now, young lady, tell me how you feel about all this. Never has a child so suffered as you are going to suffer under my hands. That I should carry it out and witness it fills me with great trepidation. Consider how your body will be treated. And if you regret it the least little bit, then I have performed my work and you have lost your life in vain." Again he entreated her in all seriousness that unless she knew she had great determination, she should forget the whole idea.

The girl said cheerfully, for she well understood that on this day death would help her escape from worldly cares, "May God reward you, dear sir, that you have told me the complete truth. As a matter of fact, I am a little hesitant. A certain doubt has arisen in me. I want to tell you exactly what kind of doubt it is that has taken hold of me. I am afraid that our efforts will not be brought to completion because of your cowardice. You talk like a woman. You have about as much courage as a rabbit. Your qualms about my dying are excessive. It's certainly true that you are not taking care of things very well with your great skill. I am a woman and have the nerve. If you are not afraid to cut me open, I certainly have the courage to suffer it. The gruesome details of the operation which you have just explained to me—I was aware of all that apart from you. I certainly would not have come here if I didn't know that I am so firm of purpose I can easily endure it. I have lost all paleness, if you please, and the firmness of my resolve has so increased that I'm standing here about as fearful as if I were about to go dancing. For no bodily suffering that is over with in one day is so great that I should think that this one day was too high a price to pay for eternal life which never passes away. Nothing should make you uneasy concerning me since my mind is made up. If you are confident you can give my lord his health again and give me eternal life, then for heaven's sake, do it soon. Show what kind of doctor you are. He in whose name it shall be done is urging me on, and I well know for whose sake I am doing it. He gives due recognition to service and lets nothing go unrewarded. I know well that He Himself says that whoever performs great service, such a person's reward will accordingly be the greatest. Hence I shall consider this way of dying a sweet affliction because of such certain reward. It would certainly be a foolish attitude if I were to turn my back on the heavenly crown. Then I would certainly be silly, for I am of humble origin."

Now he had heard that she was completely unshakeable and he led her out again to the sick man, her lord, and said to him, "Nothing can stop us. Your girl is completely suitable. Be happy, I shall soon make you healthy." Again he led her to his private room where her lord saw nothing and closed and bolted the door to him. He did not want to let him see how her end would come about. In the room that was well supplied with suitable medicines he ordered the girl to undress immediately. This made her happy and joyful. She tore the garments at the stays. Almost at once she stood there undressed and was naked and bare, but was not the least bit ashamed.

When the doctor looked at her, he realized in his heart that a creature more beautiful than she was rare in the whole world. He felt so completely sorry for her that his heart and mind almost made him hesitate. The generous girl saw a high table standing there. He commanded her to climb upon it. He tied her to it tightly and took in his hands a sharp knife that was lying there that he used for such operations. It was long and broad, but it did not at all cut as well as he would have wished. Since she was not to survive, her suffering saddened him and he wanted to make her death as pleasant as he could. Next to him a very good whetstone was lying. He took the knife and began stroking it across the stone very carefully, thereby sharpening the knife. Poor Heinrich, who was standing there in front of the door and who disturbed her joy, heard this and it saddened him greatly that he should never see her alive again. And so he began to look around and he searched until he found a hole going through the wall. Through the crack he caught a glimpse of her bound and naked. Her body was very lovely. Then he looked at her and at himself, and a whole new attitude took hold of him. What he had thought before no longer seemed good to him. And in an instant his former attitude was transformed to one of new goodness.

As he saw her in all her beauty, he said to himself, "You are really harboring a foolish thought in that you desire to live one day apart from His approval against whom no one can accomplish anything. Since you certainly have to die, you really don't know what you are doing in not bearing with great willingness this wretched existence God has given you. Besides, you do not really know whether the child's death will cure you. Whatever God has assigned for you, that you must always let happen. I will not witness the death of the child."

He made up his mind immediately and began pounding on the wall and asked to be let in. The doctor said, "I don't have the time to open up for you." "No, doctor, I must talk to you." "Sir, I can't. Wait until this is finished." "No, doctor, we must talk before that." "Well, tell me what you want through the wall." "It's really not that sort of thing." Immediately he let him in. Then poor Heinrich went to where he saw the girl bound. He said to the doctor, "This child is so lovely. I just cannot see her die. May God's will in my regard be done. We must let her up again. I shall give you the silver in accordance with our agreement, but you must let the girl live." This the doctor of Salerno was happy to hear and he obeyed, immediately untying the girl.

When the girl realized she was not going to die, she took it with a heavy heart. She acted not at all as she usually did nor in accordance with her upbringing. She had her fill of sorrow, beat her breast, tearing and pulling at herself. No one could have looked at her without crying, so dolefully did she behave. With great bitterness she shrieked, "Woe is me, poor me! What is going to happen to me now? Have I then lost the splendid heavenly crown? It was to be given to me as my reward for this ordeal. Now I am really dead. Alas, powerful Christ, what honor has been taken from us, my lord and me! We are both bereft of the honors which were predestined for us. If this had been completed, his body would have been restored to health and I would have been eternally blessed."

Thus did she again and again ask to die. But no matter how desperately she longed for it, her pleadings were in vain. Since no one did as she wanted, she began to scold, saying, "I have to suffer because of my lord's timidity. People didn't tell me the truth. That I've found out for myself. I always heard people say you were upright and good and had the steadfastness of a man. So help me God, they lied! The world has always been deceived in you. You always were and still are a great big coward. This is obvious to me through the fact that, even though I am brave enough to suffer, you don't have the courage to permit it. Lord, what caused you to become afraid when I was being bound? After all, there was a thick wall between you and me. My lord, don't you have enough backbone to be able to stand another person's death? I can promise you explicitly nobody is going to do anything to you. And the whole affair is to your advantage."

However much she pleaded and begged and even scolded, it did not help her a bit. She still had to go on living. However much she scolded, poor Heinrich accepted it calmly and with good grace, as an able knight should who never was lacking in refinement and good breeding. After the luckless visitor had dressed the girl again and had payed the doctor as he had agreed to do, he rode straight home again to his own country although he well knew that at home he would find nothing but ridicule and sarcasm from all sides. All this he put in God's hands.

In the meantime, the dear girl had scolded and cried herself almost to death. Then He, *Cordis Speculator,* for whom the gate of the heart is never locked, saw clearly her devotion and her distress. Since He in His sweet providence had thought it best to try them both just as completely as He had tried the wealthy Job, Holy Christ made manifest how dear devotion and compassion are to Him. He freed them both from all their miseries and at that very moment cleansed Heinrich and made him completely healthy. Good Lord Heinrich improved to the extent that while still on the journey he regained full health under the treatment of God our Lord and was just as he had been at the age of twenty. When they had thus been made happy, he had it announced at home in his own country to those who he knew would in their good will and sympathy rejoice in their hearts at his good fortune. Justly they would have to be joyful because of the favors God had shown him.

Those closest to him who knew he was coming rode out or went on foot three days toward him to welcome him. They would believe no one's word, only their own eyes. They saw the mysterious working of God manifested in the handsomeness of his body. Concerning the peasant and his wife, one can certainly presume, unless one wants to do them an injustice, that they did not remain at home. The joy they experienced can never be expressed in writing, for God provided them with a tasty feast for their eyes, namely, their daughter and their lord. Never did anyone experience joy equal to theirs when they saw both of them were healthy. They did not know how to act. Their greetings were a strange assortment of unusual ways of behaving. The happiness in their hearts was so great that a rain of tears from their eyes flooded their merriment. The report is certainly true that they kissed their daughter's lips well over three times.

The Swabians received him with a splendid gift, namely, a greeting filled with good will. God knows that an honest man, who has seen them at home, has to admit that no greater good will was ever shown than when they, his countrymen, welcomed him on his journey home. What happened afterwards? What more needs be said? He was better off than before in material wealth and honor. All this he referred to God with great constancy and acted according to His commandment much more than he had previously. For this reason his honor rests on a solid foundation.

The peasant and his wife had well-earned possessions and honor for the way they had taken care of him. Nor was he so dishonest as to prevent them from having them. He gave them as their own on the spot the extensive farm, both the land and the people, where he had stayed while he was sick. His bride he treated as a courtly lady or even better, giving her all sorts of things and seeing to her pleasure. Justice demanded this of him.

At this time his counsellors began to advise him to marry and praised this institution. But their suggestions diverged. Then he told them what he planned to do. If it seemed good to them, he would send for those nearest him and bring the matter to a conclusion according to what they might advise him. He had invitations and summonses sent to whoever might be of help. When he had gotten them all there, both relatives and vassals, he explained his intentions to them. With one voice they said it was proper and opportune for him to marry. A lively dispute arose among them as they were giving their advice. One counselled in one direction, another in the opposite direction, as always happens when people are called upon to render advice. They could not agree at all.

Then Lord Heinrich spoke, "You all well know that a short time ago I was greatly repugnant and disgusting to people. Now no one shuns me. God's commandment has given me a sound body. Now tell me, in God's name, how can I repay the person whom I have to thank for the favor which God has bestowed on me; namely, that I have regained my health?" They said, "Promise that you and what you own shall ever be at this person's service." His bride was standing near by. He looked at her lovingly, and embracing her he said, "You have certainly all been told that I have this wonderful girl standing here by me to thank for having my health again. She is just as freeborn as I am. My every thought tells me to take her as my wife. May God grant that this seem fitting to you. Then I shall have her as my wife. Truly, if this cannot be, I will die without marrying, for I owe her my life and good standing. By God's grace I bid you all that this may find your favor."

All spoke at once that it would certainly be fitting. Priests were readily found who gave him to her in marriage. After a long and happy life they both gained possession of the eternal kingdom. May the same thing fall to the lot of us all at the end! May God help us to attain the reward which they received. Amen.

Translated by Frank Tobin

SECTION 8

Selections from GERMAN LYRICS
OF THE MIDDLE AGES
Middle High German Minnesong

Translated by Frederick Goldin

Introduction by Albrecht Classen

By about 1170 the ideals of courtly love poetry became known in the German speaking areas as well. To some extent the Middle High German "Minnesang" (minnesong) was an indigenous product, first expressed in the area of the upper and lower Danube, in Southeastern Bavaria and Upper Austria, but later the French influence ("troubadours" and "trouvères") became a strong factor in the development of the "classical" minnesong. Predominantly the German minnesinger came from Southwestern Germany and reflected the strong impact of the royal family of Hohenstaufen through its role as patrons on contemporary culture. Mostly nothing more than the names of the minnesingers are known, which is, however, not untypical of medieval literature. In the modern anthology, first prepared by Karl Lachmann in 1857, and published under the title *Des Minnesangs Frühling*, we find poets such as Der von Kürenberg, Der Burggraf von Rietenburg, Dietmar von Eist, Friedrich von Hausen, Rudolf von Fenis, Albrecht von Johansdorf, Bligger von Steinach, Heinrich von Morungen, Reinmar der Alte, and Wolfram von Eschenbach.

Although German Minnesang flourished at the end of the twelfth century, these songs were not copied in parchment manuscripts until the early fourteenth century, and then until the late fifteenth century. There are about 40 manuscripts extant, many of them, though, only in fragmentary form. The most important manuscripts are the "Kleine Heidelberger Liederhandschrift"(A), the "Weingartner" or "Stuttgarter Liederhandschrift" (B), and the "Grosse Heidelberger Liederhandschrift"(C). The latter is also known as the "Manessische Liederhandschrift" because the Zurich family Manesse had commissioned this manuscript, which was also richly illuminated. These illustrations show idealistic images of the poets, but have nothing in common with realistic portraits. Most of these manuscripts are art works in themselves as calligraphically trained scribes, rubricators, and miniaturists collaborated to create these codices.

Only beginning with the fourteenth century do we find musical notations in the manuscripts, beginning with the famous "Jenaer Liederhandschrift." Many songs were simply contrafacta, that is, songs which copied the melodies from religious songs, for instance, but now applied for worldly, erotic themes.

The minnesinger use, as their themes, the unrequited love to a noble lady; dialogues between lovers about the nature and value of love; the transmission of love letters to the beloved; the crusade and the necessity to part from the admired lady; the coming of dawn when the lover has to leave his mistress, and even complaints about the lack of love or the coldness of the lady.

Most of the German minnesinger were of noble origin, some of them belonging even to the royal house. Others seem to have been *ministeriales*, or lower-ranking nobility, whereas only few lacked nobility.

BIBLIOGRAPHY (7.1)

William T. H. Jackson, *The Literature of the Middle Ages* (New York: Columbia University Press, 1960).

Peter Dronke, *Medieval Latin and the Rise of European Love-Lyric.* Vol. 1 (Oxford: Clarendon, 1965).

Olive Sayce, *The Medieval German Lyric 1150–1300* (Oxford: Oxford University Press, 1982).

Stephen J. Kaplowitt, *The Ennobling Power of Love in the Medieval German Lyric.* University of North Carolina Studies in the Germanic Languages and Literatures, 106 (Chapel Hill-London: The University of North Carolina Press, 1986).

Des Minnesangs Frühling, ed. Hugo Moser and Helmut Tervooren. Vol. I. 38th, newly revised ed. (Stuttgart: Hirzel, 1988).

Günther Schweikle, *Minnesang.* Sammlung Metzler, 244 (Stuttgart: Metzler, 1989).

Will Hasty, "Hartmann von Aue," *German Writers and Works of the High Middle Ages: 1170–1280*, ed. James Hardin and Will Hasty (Detroit, Washington, D.C., and London: Gale Research, 1994), 27–43.

Marion E. Gibbs, Sidney M. Johnson, *Medieval German Literature. A Companion* (New York and London: Garland, 1997).

7.1 GERMAN MINNESANG

Der von Kürenberg (ca. 1170–1190)

1

Bad luck brings sorrow, good luck rejoicing.
Once I got to know a lordly man:
the busybodies and their envy took him from me then.
Because of that my heart will not rejoice again.

2

Late at night I stood on a battlement:
then I heard a knight singing well
a melody of Kürenberg amidst the crowd.
Let him clear out of my land, or let him be mine.

Now bring me my horse and armor, fast,
for I must clear out of a lady's land:
she wants to make me bow and serve.
She will have to live without my love.

3

When I stand alone in my shift
and think, noble knight, of you,
my color flowers up like the rose on the thorn,
and my heart gathers sorrows.

4

It has often caused my heart great pain
that I craved a thing I could not have
and can never get. That hurts.
Now I don't mean gold or silver: this thing looks like people.

5

I trained me a falcon, for more than a year.
When I had him tamed the way I wanted him
and set gold among his feathers,
he rose up high and flew away to wildness.

Since then I have seen the falcon in lordly flight:
he bore silken jesses on his legs,
and gold and red in his feathers.
God bring together all people who want to be lovers.

6

The morning star goes under cover.
Beautiful and high born, do the same when you see me
and let your eyes turn to another.
No one will guess what we have together.

7

The joy of all women still goes a maid.
When I send my dear messenger to her,
I'd gladly bring it myself, if that would not injure her.
I don't know how she likes it: no woman was ever so dear before.

8

Woman and falcons—they are easily tamed.
If a man knows how to lure them right, they come flying.
Just so, to try to win a splendid lady, a handsome knight set out.
My spirit rises when I think of that.

HEINRICH VON VELDEKE. (fl. last quarter of the twelfth century)

The poet's name derives from the village of Veldeke, west of Maastricht in
Belgian Limburg. His chief work is his romance *Eneit,* which he completed,
probably between 1187 and 1189, in the court of the great patron Landgraf
Hermann of Thuringia. This work was widely celebrated in its own day, and in
its manner of exemplifying courtly values it was a determining influence on the
courtly romance in German-speaking areas.

His lyrics are very clearly influenced by French poetry (the *Eneit* is based
on the Old French *Roman d'Eneas* as well as on Vergil). From this source come,
for example, the tripartite structure of the strophe, the precise rhymes and
regular meter, and such themes as the imperious rule of the beloved lady and
the ennobling effect of Minne—metrical and thematic innovations that would
have a tremendous vogue in the later Minnesang. In both the romance and the
lyric Heinrich von Veldeke was thus a pioneer for courtly poetry.

Heinrich wrote in Limburg dialect, but in the manuscripts nearly all of his
poetry has been transposed into High German. In 1947 Theodor Frings
published his reconstruction of the original texts, and it is Frings's edition that
MF follows.

Text: *Des Minnesangs Frühling.*

9

Tristan had no choice
but to be faithful to the Queen,
for poison drove him to it

more than the power of love.
Therefore, let The Good One be grateful
to me, for I never drank
such spiced wine and I love her
more than he loved, if that might be.
O beautiful and faultless,
let me be yours,
and you be mine.

10

I beg Minne, who has won everything
from me, and warn her:
move that beautiful lady
to increase my pleasure.
For if it goes with me as with the swan
that sings about to die,
she will lose too much when I am gone.

I never drank of the potion
that poisoned Tristan,
but my pure heart and my entire will
make me love more than he loved.
Therefore, mine should be the thanks for this,
for nothing forced me to love
except that I trusted my eyes,
through which I set out on the path
I shall never stray from and have never renounced.

11

I would rather seven years
of misery than speak
one word against her will.
She has understood this very well
yet wants me to complain some more.
Love is the same as it was before.

12

Whoever hurts my favor with my lady,
I wish him the dead branch
on which thieves snatch death.
Whoever helps me with her faithfully,
I wish him paradise
and fold my hands to him.
If anyone asks who she is,

let him know her this way:
it is The Beautiful One.

Lady, pity me.
To you I yield the sun:
then let the moon have light for me.
Were my misery more bearable,
I could reach to pleasure after pain,
to joys and joys,
for I hear lovely news:
the flowers are springing on the heath, tra la,
the birds are singing in the woods;
where snow once lay
green clover grows,
covered with dew in the morning.
So, whoever wants to, let him rejoice—
but let him not press me.
I am unfree of sorrows.

13

In April when the flowers spring,
the lindens leaf out, the beeches turn green,
with a will the birds begin to sing,
for they all find love where they seek it,
in their mates, so their joy is great—
which I never minded, for all winter long they keep still.

When they saw on the branches the blossoms
springing among the leaves, then they were rich
in the varied songs they always sang.
They started to sing, joyfully and loud,
low and high. My mind, too, is such
that I want to know joy. I ought to praise my luck.

If I could win my lady's grace,
could seek it as becomes her!
I shall die, and it will be my fault
unless she consents to accept
a penance other than death for her grace; and so it must be,
for God never commanded any man be glad to die.

14

They have said it is true, for many a year,
that women hate gray hair.
That makes it hard for me—

and a shame for them
if they prefer their lovers
clumsy rather than wise.
As much or as little as I am gray,
a feeble wit in women is what I hate—
they'd rather have
new tin than old gold.
They say they favor the young ones
because they cannot wait.

FRIEDRICH VON HAUSEN (ca. 1150–1190)

A member of a baronial family, the poet dwelt near Kreuznach in the neighborhood of Worms. He was part of the most intimate circle around Friedrich Barbarossa and his son Heinrich VI, and his presence at several important events between 1171 and 1190 is attested. He participated in the Third Crusade with Barbarossa and died in battle in Asia Minor in 1190.

He cultivated French and Provencal themes and metrical forms to a greater degree than any German poet before him. Frank publishes seven of his lyrics together with French and Provencal models. Many familiar motifs from this source are found in his poetry: the distant longing, the personification of love, the fulfilling dream and the rude awakening, the constant threat from spies and slanderers and hypocrites, "die valschen diet."

Text: *Des Minnesangs Frühling.*

15

In my dream I saw
a very beautiful woman
the whole night long till day,
then I awoke.
Then, alas, I was bereft of her
and do not know where she might be,
from whom my joy should come.
My own eyes did this to me.
I wish I did not have eyes.

16

When I parted from my Good
and did not tell her
how she was dear to me,
I suffer for it now.
I left it out because of all those hypocrites

198

whose envy ruined my pleasure.
I wish them nothing else
but that the One who harried Hell
make them hurt and yell.

"They think they can spy on me,
though this is none of their business,
and show their envy,
but it does them little good.
They could sooner make
the Rhine flow into the Po
before I'd give him up
who served me,
no matter how things go."

17

Help! How Minne has deserted me—
she made me give my soul up
to a dream that will destroy me
if I am not relieved by kindness from that one woman,
the cause why I so often have no sense.
I would think I'd gotten something if she were willing
to know the distress that has settled in my mind.

Help! What dishonor have I done
that the Good does not let me have her greeting?
This way she can lead my heart into a trap.
Behold my mad faith: that I could never find a better
woman
in this world. As my faith I shall uphold it
and serve her loyally,
this good woman who scourges me hard without whips.

What may that be which the world calls Minne,
which makes me feel continual pain
and deprives me of so much sense?
I don't think anyone can really find it out.
If I could claim that I had seen it,
the cause of so much sorrow come my way,
then I would believe in it ever more.

Minne, God let me get revenge on you
How many joys have you detoured away from my heart
And if I could stick out that squinting eye of yours,
I would be right to do it, because you make no end

to the distress you commanded against me,
and if you were dead, I would think I was rich,
yes, only now I have to live beneath your power.

18

I think sometimes about
what I would tell her
if I were near enough.
It makes the miles shorter
to call my sorrow out
to her, with thoughts.
Often the people here
see in me the figure
of a carefree man,
for so I let it seem.

Had I not taken on
such lofty love,
I might be saved.
I did it without thinking.
And every moment now I suffer
pain that presses deep.
Now my own constancy
has tied down my heart
and will not let it part
from her, as things are now.

It is a great wonder:
she whom I love with greatest torment
has always acted like my enemy.
Now may no man ever get to know
what such a burden is,
it weighs down hard.
I thought I knew what it was before,
now I know it better.
Over there, where home is, I was sad,
and here three times more.

However little good it does me,
still I have this pleasure:
no one can stop me
from thinking close to her,
wherever on earth I turn.
This comfort she must let me have.
If she takes it well,

that gives me joy forever,
for I, more than any other man,
was always hers.

19

My heart and my body want to separate,
that have ridden together all my life.
The body wants to strike against the heathen,
but the heart has chosen out a woman
before all the world. It has weighed on me ever since,
that one will not go in the steps of the other.
My eyes have brought me to grief.
May God alone break up that strife.

I had hoped to be free of this great weight
when I took the cross for the glory of God.
It would be right if the heart were in it too,
but its own faith held it back.
I would truly be a living man again
if it would stop its ignorant desiring.
I see now, to the heart it's all one
how I shall fare at last.

Heart, since I cannot turn you back
from deserting me so sadly,
I pray God reach down to send you
where they will welcome you in.
Alas, poor Heart, how will it go with you?
How could you dare to go boldly into this danger all
alone?
Who will help you end your cares
with such loyalty as I have shown?

20

My heart believes:
if any man could rightly stay behind
for pleasure or for Minne's sake,
then I would still be on the Rhine.
For the parting I had from dear friends
moves me deeply.
But whatever happens to me,
Lord God, let me commend
to your grace the one
I left for You.

I do not allow of good women
that the day could ever come
when they would love a man
who shrank from the way of God.
How could he ever serve them?
It would be a blow to their honor.
Therefore I send them this song,
and I warn them as best I can.
If my eye were never more to see them,
their dishonor still would cause me pain.

HEINRICH VON MORUNGEN, (d. 1222)

Heinrich von Morungen came from a family that was settled near Sanger-
hausen in Thuringia. He was in the service of Landgraf Hermann's son-in-law,
Dietrich von Meissen. Nothing else is known for sure about him, except that in
1217 he made over his possessions to the Thomaskloster in Leipzig, where he
finished out his days. He died in 1222. It is generally assumed that his literary
activity flourished in the 1190s.

Heinrich's language has the same apparent simplicity that generally charac-
terizes the classic Minnesang; but his lyrics are distinguished by the sharp
contrast between this surface clarity and the resonating complexity of the scenes
he depicts. That moment (in no. 26) when the lady leads him in his solitude high
over the battlements, consoling him in his grief; and the complementary moment
when be stands on the ground beneath her window gazing up at her radiance
and she withdraws, awakening his grief, are often cited, among many other
examples, as evidence of the poet's dramatic effect and the sense of inexhaustible
meaning that he evokes. His continual elaboration of the imagery of light across
the whole body of his work is an example of the way he rethinks conventional
themes. The power of his imagination is made all the more effective by his
mastery of a great variety of metrical forms. . .

21

I heard on the meadow
bright voices and sweet tones
and was at once
rich in joys, in sorrows poor.
The one toward whom my thoughts have struggled and
soared—
I found her in the dance, singing.
Free of sorrow, I danced too.

I found her withdrawn,

by herself, and her cheeks wet,
in the morning where
she fathomed my death.
I would rather the hate of my beloved than how it felt
kneeling before her where she sat
and let go of all her pain.

I found her on the battlement, alone,
and I had been sent for—
and could have taken, quite without uncourtliness,
the proof of her love from her hand.
I thought I had burnt up the land,
it was only that love with its gentle hand
had darkened my mind.

22

Glances that hurt and overwhelming grief
have nearly destroyed my heart and body.
I would raise a new lament for ancient suffering
if I did not fear the rage of those who mock me.
But if I sing for her who once rejoiced me,
let no man then, by God, defame my loyalty,
for I was born into the world to sing.

Many a one of them says, "Aha! look at him singing!
If he suffered, he wouldn't do that."
A man like that cannot know what drives me to sing.
But now, as in former days, I shall raise my voice.
When I stood mute in sorrow, I was worth nothing to her.
That is the anguish that oppresses me:
sorrow is despised where men rejoice.

She is my heart's one joy, the crown
above all women I have seen,
beautiful, more beautiful, beautiful above the most
beautiful
is she: that I must affirm.
Now let the whole world beg her, by her beauty:
"It is time now, lady, for you to requite him,
or else he speaks foolishness with his praise."

When I stand before her and look upon the wonder
God created in her beauty,
I see something so extraordinary,
I want to stand forever in her sight.

Ah, but then I have to go away, cast down:
a dark cloud comes between us
and I have nothing of her light.

23

Alas, why do I follow that childish dream
that leads me so sorely into misery?
I parted from her barren of all joy,
because she sent no sign of comfort or help.

Yet the color on her was the white of lilies, the red of
roses,
and that beloved and beautiful lady sat before me
in flowering radiance like the full moon.

That was joy to my eyes, death to my heart.
My mind is firm, it is not like the wind:
I am still as I was when she left me—
loyal to this moment since my childhood
with all the grief she has given me so long,
forced to be silent about the hidden dream,
no matter how many times I take on this foolishness:
standing before her full of glorious utterance,
and going away without a word.

I have said so much in melody and verse,
I am hoarse from lamenting, and out of breath.
I am driven by nothing but the dream,
for she will not believe what I speak:
how I love her, and bear a heart that she commands.
I have not been rewarded as I have deserved.
Had I struggled toward God with half so great a will,
He would take me to Him before my death.

24

Many a man gets bewitched by the elves.
I have been bewitched with love
by the best a man ever won as friend.
If she wants to be my enemy for that
and destroy me, let her get her vengeance
by doing what I ask: then she delights me so sorely
I pass away with pleasure.

She commands and in my heart
is Lady, her rule is mightier than mine.
O if I could get the power over her somehow

and she stayed with me obediently
three full days, and some night
My body's strength would not be ebbing away.
But now she is all too free of me.

The light of her eyes burns me up
like fire on dry tinder.
Her distance clamps my heart
like water on a rising flame.
And her rejoicing spirit, her beauty, and her worth,
and the miraculous virtues that have won her fame—
it's my sickness now, but maybe it will be my health.

When her glowing eyes turn
and she looks through my heart,
the fool that steps between us then and gets in my way,
may all his pleasures evaporate,
because I am standing there looking out for her,
like the little bird that waits for day.
I wait for joy—how long must I wait?

7.2 WALTHER VON DER VOGELWEIDE (ca. 1170–ca. 1230)

Although he is mentioned in only one extant contemporary document—an item in the accounts of Bishop Wolfger of Passau, dated November 12, 1203, recording an amount given to buy a fur coat for the singer Walther von der Vogelweide—the important periods in Walther's life can be inferred from his poetry. He writes that he learned to be a poet in Austria—*Ze Osterrîche lernte ich singen unde sagen;* at the Babenberger court in Vienna he became the rival of Reinmar von Hagenau. His stay in Vienna ended in 1198 with the death of his patron, the elder son of Leopold V. He then began a life of wandering from court to court in German speaking lands.

He was rewarded with patronage by Philip of Swabia for his support in Philip's struggle against the Papist candidate for Emperor, Otto of Brunswick. Afterwards, he was in the court of Landgrave Hermann of Thuringia, where he knew Wolfram von Eschenbach. There were several other patrons. He revisited the Viennese court—in 1203, with Bishop Wolfger—hoping, in vain, to find a place there again.

Walther continued to side with his patrons in the political disputes that arose in German-speaking areas at this time. After the death of Phillip, Otto was crowned Emperor and was soon in a struggle against the Pope over land holdings in Italy. Walther supported Otto at first but later rebuked him for his stinginess and switched his support to Friedrich II, who was now also supported for Emperor by Pope Innocent III. Friedrich defeated Otto in 1214; in 1220 he gave Walther the fief which the poet asks for so piteously in 39a and exults in so deliriously in 39b. In October 1227, Friedrich was excommunicated by the Pope for failing to carry through the crusade he had begun. Walther refers to the *unsenfte brieve* from Rome—the Bull of Excommunication—in 50, which is his last datable poem.

His earliest lyrics presumably were written under the influence or tutelage of Reinmar. These vary in quality, but almost always when he wrote in the mode of Reinmar he was inferior to his master and rival. In the wonderful elegy for Reinmar (42) he gives the old man his due: "You never got tired of praising noble ladies." After his initial efforts, however, Walther apparently rebelled against the poetic tradition of which Reinmar was the paragon. He attacked every telling quality of Reinmar's poetry: the fruitless devotion, the willing pain, the self-mocking timidity. All this Walther found foolish and unnatural. It was foolish because, as Walther saw it, the poet felt unworthy of a lady whose glorious virtue was really his invention: it was he who had conceived of it and chosen her to grace with it; she would be nothing without him. It was in fact the lady who needed the poet, for his song alone distinguished her: it endowed her with a beautiful life that the whole courtly world had to venerate. So Walther turns Reinmar's Minne completely around. Where Reinmar declares, *stirbet si, sô bin ich tôt,* if she perishes, I am dead, Walther responds with a boldness that shows how far he departed from Reinmar's style: *ir leben hât mînes lebennes êre: stirbe ab ich, sô ist si tôt,* her life receives glory from my life: and if I should perish, she is dead.

Hôhe Minne, one-sided love celebrated by a boasting poet within a small circle of friends, was also unnatural to Walther. Love is supposed to be simple, effortless, mutual—*zweier herzen wünne,* one pleasure of two hearts; it bears no resemblance to that wake of self-praise and self-mortification that the poets held in court. Therefore, Walther repudiated that overwrought conscience of theirs; he stepped out of their circle, out of that enclosure with its secrets and intrigues, and into the free and open air of nature—or what he called nature. The lyrics that depict what he at this time regards as true love are set in outdoor scenes full of birds and trees and dancing troupes. The woman he discovers there is a carefully created alternative to Reinmar's imperious lady: a sweet and artless girl, grateful for love, undemanding, altogether present, all involved in pleasure; she might be of noble birth, but she has no tutelary power, and not one wrinkle of moral concern. The lover just leads her gently to a bed of roses. It is all very easy and uncomplicated, like love in the *pastourelle* (see for example, pt. II, no. 33), from which Walther's girl is descended. The veil of distances that surrounds the courtly lady is completely removed; the young woman that appears is not ringed with silences or made attractive by obstacles, she is right there; anyone passing the spot can tell by the broken flowers just where she lay with her lover, who, she proudly recalls, was gentle and respectful.

The difference between the *lady*—a personage of lofty station, unapproachable, cruelly virtuous—and the woman—unenhanced, immediate, shining with human qualities like passion, innocence, and trust—underlies a famous strophe by Walther, written in the full swing of his revolt against the familiar courtly style:

> Wîp muoz iemer sîn der wîbe hôhste name
> und tiuret baz danne frowe, als ichz erkenne.
> swâ nû deheiniu sî diu sich ir wîpheit schame,
> diu merke disen sanc und kiese denne.
> under frowen sint unwîp,
> under wîben sint si tiure.
> wîbes name und wîbes lîp
> die sint beide vil gehiure.
> swiez umb alle frowen var,
> wîp sint alle frowen gar.
> zwîvellop daz hoenet,
> als under wîlen frowe:
> wîp daz ist ein name der si alle kroenet.

> "Woman" will always be the highest name of women,
> and is higher praise than "lady," to my mind.
> If there is one ashamed of her womanhood,
> let her listen to this song and then decide.
> Among ladies are those who are unwomanly,
> among women they are rare
> The name of woman and the figure of woman
> are both full of grace.
> However it may be with all these ladies,
> all true women are ladies.
> Equivocal praise is mockery—
> like "lady," for instance, at times.
> "Woman" is a name that sets on them all a crown.

It does seem, at first, that Walther finds a perfect escape from *hôhe Minne*, a serene and mutual love that thrives in fields with birds and flowers. But there are lots of snags in this green world of his. He has to wonder about the moral substance of this lovely girl, who is unspoiled but also undefined by all those indoor virtues that made the courtly lady so distant and yet so admirable, and the struggle to reach her so ennobling. *Hast du triuwe unde staetekeit:* an earlier poet, speaking in the role of courtly lover, never had to wonder whether his lady possessed these noble qualities, for the simple reason that he himself had given them to her. But Walther's future is uncertain, because the staying power of a plain woman is unknown. Gradually it comes to him that Reinmar's lady cannot be replaced by the vrowelîn, for this serene and easy loving will never come true: every man may dream of it, but it lacks the one crucial thing that made a courtier's love for the unattainable lady, with all its anguish, an expression of his nobility: the dignity of obstacles. Noble men and women cannot love like birds without becoming less than noble; they will always long for a love that is rare and difficult, and fosters worthiness. As things turn out, it was nowhere but in his sleep that Walther found this willing and perfect girl, and when he wakes he has to go round and round looking for her. He does not have much chance of finding her. His green girl is a wonderful dream: pure pleasure unadulterated by conscience; but she must remain a dream forever, the goal of an unfulfillable longing, like the brilliant lady of the minnesingers. The love of her is no escape from uncertainty.

So Walther wakes from one dream only to fall into another. The exalted lady who sends down nothing but demands, and the sweet girl of the open meadows—the *vrowe* and the *vrowelin* both vanish in the daily light. Each is the center of a different play circle, for Walther's nature is really a man-made enclosure, like the court. The object in the game of *hôhe Minne* is to act out courtliness, and the player has to endure the strain of endless reformation; in *nidere Minne* the lover impersonates "natural man" and has to withstand great moral hunger. For Walther it is a choice of one game or the other: no. 41 makes this clear. A man encounters a woman on plain ground—and steps immediately into this circle or that. In the end, Walther returns to *hôhe Minne,* and this return after a long rebellion is the greatest confirmation of the values of courtly love.

Thus Walter's apparent "revolt" against Reinmar and the courtly style in fact corroborates the old values. That is what it was meant to do. Walther's great achievement was not to discover a "natural" love, but to find in nature a new way to confirm the nobility of courtly love, which Reinmar had extolled, and to reveal its unreality and impossible demands, which Reinmar had laughed at. Whatever they may have felt about each other, and however great the differences between their styles, they took the same stand.

Walther does seem to have come upon one innovation, as a result of the setting of *nidere Minne.* In his songs on this theme, nature is really endowed with the dimensions of a realm and becomes a ground of experience: it is not, as in the *Natureingang,* simply a mirror of the speaker's feelings.

Walther gave the tradition of courtly love poetry a new turn, but in his political and moral poetry he created something that had never existed before among German poets. Before Walther there had been a kind of proverbial poetry called *Spruchdichtung,* consisting of sentences of folk wisdom in short single strophes. Walther took this over, introduced the tripartite structure from Romantic poetry and the Minnesang, and the telling references to contemporary events such as he found in the *sirventes* and in Latin satiric poetry. He also introduced a very sure dramatic touch, as for example the Pope's laughter and mocking boast (38).

Walther wrote a good number of single strophes in this manner. However, his greatest poems go far beyond this: they are long, dignified, oracular utterances, conveying a tone of great moral elevation but full of specific details vividly dramatized. From the earliest ones to the latest there are prophetic, elegiac, tragic tones that had never before been possible in German poetry.

Walther's pre-eminence was recognized from the very beginning. Gottfried praises him lavishly in *Tristan*. For five hundred years after Walther's death—until Goethe—no German lyric poet was his equal.

BIBLIOGRAPHY (7.2)

Text: Friedrich Maurer, ed. *Die Lieder Walthers von der Vogelweide unter Beifügung erhaltener und erschlossener Melodien.* 3d ed. 2 vols. Altdeutsche Textbibliothek, 43 & 47. (Tübingen: Max Niemeyer, 1967/69.) Marks indicating vowel length added.

Olive Sayce, *The Medieval German Lyric 1150–1300* (Oxford: Oxford University Press, 1982).

Tim McFarland/Silvia Rawanake, eds., *Walther von der Vogelweide. Twelve Studies.* Oxford German Sudies 13 (1982).

Gerhard Hahn, *Walther von der Vogelweide: eine Einführung.* Artemis Einführungen, 22 (Munich: Artemis, 1989).

Frank Tobin, "Middle High German," *A Concise History of German Literature to 1900.* Ed. Kim Vivian. Studies in German Literature, Linguistics, and Culture (Columbia, S.C.: Camden House, 1992), 21–57.

Walther von der Vogelweide: Werke. Gesamtausgabe. Vol. 1: *Spruchlyrik.* Ed., trans. and commented by Günther Schweikle (Stuttgart: Reclam, 1994).

Horst Brunner, Gerhard Hahn, Ulrich Müller, Franz Viktor Spechtler, *Walther von der Vogelweide. Epoche-Werk-Wirkung* (Munich: Beck, 1996).

Hubert Heinen, "Walther von der Vogelweide," *German Writers and Works of the High Middle Ages: 1170–1280,* ed. James Hardin and Will Hasty (Detroit, Washington, D.C., and London: Gale Research, 1994), 158–69.

42

Will anyone tell me what Minne is?
Though I know a little, I gladly would know more.
Whoever understands it better,

let him tell me why it causes pain.
Minne is minne if it gives pleasure:
if it causes misery, it isn't right to call it minne—
then I don't know what it should be called.

If I guess right
what Minne is, say "Yes":
Minne is one joy between two hearts.
If they share alike, there is Minne:
but if it isn't shared,
one heart alone cannot contain it.
Alas, my lady, if you would only help me.

Lady, I bear a little too much.
If you want to help me, help in time.
But if I do not mean a thing to you,
say so once and for all: then I'll give up the struggle, and become a free man.
But, lady, understand one thing:
no other man can sing your praise so well.

Can my lady turn the sweet to sour?
Does she dream I'll give her pleasure in exchange for
misery?
Should I lend her all that value
just to have her set it against my unworthiness?
That way I must see things wrong.
O lord what am I saying, deaf and blind?
A man dazzled by Minne—how can he see?

43

To be long silent was my thought:
now I shall sing once again as before.
Gentle people brought me back to it:
they have the right to command me.
I shall sing and make up words,
and do what they desire; then they must lament my grief.

Listen to this wonder, how I fared
for all my hard work:
a certain woman will not look at me—
and it was I that brought her up to that esteem
which makes her so high-minded now.
She does not know: when I leave off singing, her praise
will die away.

Lord what curses she'd endure,

were I now to stop my song!
All those who praise her now, I know
they'll rebuke her then—against my will.
A thousand hearts were made happy
by her kindness to me; they will suffer for it if she lets me
perish.

When it seemed that she was gentle,
who was more devoted then than I?
But that's all over: whatever she does to me,
she can expect the same—
if she frees me from this distress,
her life receives the glory of my life; if I perish, she is dead.

If I grow old in her service,
she won't get much younger in that time.
Maybe then my hair'll have such a look
she'll want a young man at her side.
So help you God, avenge me,
you young man, and have a go with switches on her
ancient hide.

NOW HAS THE WINTER BROUGHT HARM TO US ALL

(Uns hat der winter geschat uber al)

Now has the winter brought harm to us all,
meadow and forest are both in his thrall,
where many voices still sang in the fall.
If I were watching the maidens play ball,
soon I'd be hearing the forest birds call.

Could I but slumber the whole winter long!
When I'm not sleeping he does me much wrong,
great is his might and malice is strong,
yet is he conquered when Mary sings its song.
Where the frost now glistens shall flowers then throng.

BLISSFULLY HE LAY

Blissfully he lay,
the lusty cavalier,
upon a lady's arm. He saw the morning light

as, gleaming from a distance, through the mist it broke.
With grief the lady spoke,
'I wish you woe, O Day.
for I can stay no longer with my handsome knight.
What's known as love is only a longing and a fear.'

'Lady, I implore
you not to sorrow so.
It's better for us both that I should now depart,
I see the silver gleam of the morning star above.'
'O stay with me, my love,
and let us speak no more
of leaving, that you may not so distress my heart.
Indeed, it is not right. Why need you haste to go?'
'Lady, it shall be,
I'll stay a while with you,
Now tell me what you wish, but still it must be brief,
that we may now deceive the watchers once again.'
'My heart is filled with pain.
Before I shall be free
to lie with you once more I'll have so much of grief.
Don't stay away too long! Such nights are all too few.'
'I'll come whene'er I may,
so do not be forlorn.
Though I must now depart and leave you for a while,
my heart shall still remain and shall not stir from here.'
'Obey me now, my dear;
you will not stay away
if you are true to me without deceit or guile.
Alas, the night is gone. I see the breaking morn.'
'Lady, I must fly!
Permit me now to ride
away from here, to save your name must I take leave.
So loud and near the watchman sings his morning song.'
'He will be here ere long,
so we must say goodbye,
but how this sad departure causes me to grieve!
May God in heaven be your guardian and your guide!'
The lover soon was gone,
and all his joy had flown.
He left the pretty lady weeping bitter tears.
But he was always loyal because he shared her bed.
'Whene'er I hear,' she said,

a melody at dawn,
my heart shall always be distressed with pain and fears.
A sad and longing woman I lie here now alone.'

Although Walther often sang of courtly love, he once declared that 'woman' was a more complimentary term than 'lady,' that femininity was preferable to lofty pride. And the naively charming 'courtly' young woman who here describes a meeting with her lover well supports his claim.

In the song, 'How Beautiful Her Form and Face,' Walther plays a joke on his listeners. The song follows almost to the end the standard pattern for a particular type of minnesong in which all of the beauties and virtues of the lady are enumerated (a device probably borrowed from several of the Songs of Solomon) and at the end the complaint is made that the lady does not reward her admirer for his many services. Walther, however, at the last minute substitutes a peeping Tom for the forlorn lover with very gratifying results.

UNDER THE LINDEN

(*Under der linden*)

Under the Linden
I and my lover
softly were bedded in grass and shade.
And if you should wander
there, you'll discover
many a broken bloom and blade.
By the forest, in the dale,
'tandaradei!'
sweetly sang the nightingale.

I went to our meeting
and did not tarry,
for he I loved had gone before.
Oh, what a greeting!
Holy Mary,
I'll be blessed for evermore!
Did he kiss me? Yes, and how!
'Tandaradei.'
See how red my lips are now.

My lover had laid
with care meanwhile
a lovely bed of flowers for me.
The village maid
will slyly smile
who walks there past the linden tree
and sees the spot where on that day
'tandaradei'
my head among the roses lay.

If anyone guesses
that we were together
(May God forbid!), I'd surely die.
Of his caresses,
hid by the heather,
may no one know but he and I
and the bird that sang so well:
'tandaradei.'
I can trust it not to tell.

HOW BEAUTIFUL HER FORM AND FACE

(*Si wunderwol gemachet wîp*)

How beautiful her form and face,
may she give thanks to me ere long,
for both of them I now shall place
with loving care within my song.
I serve the ladies, one and all,
but I have chosen her alone.
To other men may others fall,
I care not how they praise their own,
though they use song and air
that I composed; as I praise here, may they praise thee.

Her head is so exceeding fair
as only heaven e'er may be,
with it can nothing else compare
in splendor truly heavenly.
Two stars are there and gleaming clear,
I'd like to see myself therein,
would she but hold those stars so near
then might a miracle begin
to make me young once more

and fill with joy the one whose heart
with love is sore.

God made her cheeks a true delight
in which his richest color glows,
the deepest red, the purest white,
here, like a lily, there, a rose.
I hope it's not a sin to say
I'd rather watch her blushes than
admire the starry Milky Way,
but why should I, O foolish man,
place her so high above me?
My praise would cause me pain, were she too proud to love me.

Such lips she has, so full and red,
if I could bring them close to mine
I would arise as from the dead
and nevermore would faint or pine
Whose cheek she touches with those lips
would gladly have them stay for hours,
for from them such a fragrance drips,
as balsam or perfume of flowers
If she would lend a kiss
I'd give it back whene'er she wished,
be sure of this.
Her throat, her hands, her feet I've seen
and found how greatly all excelled,
and should I praise what lies between,
I'd but relate what I beheld.
I must confess, no warning cry
was uttered when I saw her bare.
She saw me not when she let fly
the Cupid's dart which still I wear.
I praise the blissful state
in which the lovely woman left her bath of late.

Although Walther could compose non-courtly lovesongs and could use the conventional minnesong for humorous purposes, he accepted the chivalric concept of faithful service to a high-born lady and most of his lovesongs follow the general courtly tradition. Even here, however, Walther's sense of humor and his inability to play convincingly the role of a grief-stricken lover lend a very distinctive mood to his verse. Chivalric poetry in general presents love not merely as a highly idealized emotion, but also as a powerful, capricious, often destructive force, against which the individual struggles in vain. The classic example of such a presentation is found in Gottfried's *Tristan and Isolde*. In 'Who Made You, Love, So Fierce and Bold' Walther acknowledges this fatal power of love, but is happy that he is chained to one who meets his complete approval. The song 'When From the Grass the Meadow Flowers Spring' is also a happy one, but it belongs to a type of minnesong, the spring song or May-day song, which was customarily lighthearted. This is a dance song and was doubtless performed to accompany dancing in the open air, perhaps as a part of a spring festival. The personification of May greatly antedates Walther and probably goes back to his pagan ancestors and their worship of various phenomena of nature.

WHO MADE YOU, LOVE, SO FIERCE AND BOLD

(*Wer gab dir, minne, den gewalt*)

Who made you, love, so fierce and bold;
who gave you power so immense
that you should conquer young and old,
and wisdom offers no defense?
Well, I'll thank God because, at last,
your chains (which I have known so well) now bind me fast
to one whom I adore and praise.
I'll never more be free, so grant me, queen, this favor,
that I may serve you all my days.

WHEN FROM THE GRASS THE MEADOW FLOWERS SPRING

(*Sô die bluomen ûz dem grase dringent*)

When from the grass the meadow flowers spring
and turn their laughing faces toward the sun
upon a May-day in the morning dew,
and all the birds of field and forest sing
their sweetest songs—for who would be outdone,
what shall I then compare such rapture to?
To half the joys of Paradise.
And yet, if you should ask what can entice
me more than this, I should avow
what pleased my sight most in the past,
and still would, if I saw it now.

For when a lovely and a noble lady,
attired in finest clothes and with her hair
done up in stately manner, walks with friends
of courtly bearing in a garden shady,
and looks about at times with such an air
as might become the sun as it ascends
among the stars, then May can bring
us all its wealth, and beauty, yet what thing
shall with this lovely form compare?
We leave May's flowers where they stand
and gaze upon the lady fair.
If you would know the truth, then take my arm
and let us join the festival of May
that now is here with all its joyful treasure.
Look well! Then look upon the ladies' charm
and tell me who will bear the prize away,
and say which wonder gives you greater pleasure.
I know, if I were forced to choose
the one to keep, the other one to lose,
I'd make my choice with no ado.
Sir May, you would be March before
I'd sacrifice my love for you.

SECTION 9

DER WILDE ALEXANDER
(*Late Thirteenth Century*)

Introduction by Albrecht Classen

The name of the "Wild Alexander" is given to a Middle High German poet whose songs were copied in several fourteenth century manuscripts. He seems to have been a late thirteenth–century goliard, travelling from court to court to find patrons for his art. Three of his five songs are of a religious nature, among them his famous "Strawberry Song" included in our collection. Notwithstanding the evident allusions to a sinful lifestyle and warnings to stay away from worldly temptations (New Testament, Galatians 4:3), this song has also been interpreted in many different ways, not the least being an analysis as a highly erotically charged love poems describing the process of growing up and entering adulthood. The imagery and tone of voice indicates the extent to which the religious and the erotic could be quickly combined to create innovative literary texts.

The Wild Alexander composed, in addition, twenty four stanzas and one lay ("Leich") in which he discusses the vicissitudes of fortune, the hardship of the goliardic life style, and the art of composing poetry.

The poet did not belong to the noble class, as the title meister in one manuscript makes clear. The adjective "wilde" means "wandering," "vagabond": the poet traveled from place to place. His dialect is Alemannic.

He wrote a number of religious lyrics, of which the following is the best and most famous—this is no fond recollection of the simple joys of childhood. The other meaning of the forest, the children, the snake, the warden, etc., can be easily inferred. The conclusion refers to the parable of the five foolish virgins and to the bride's search for the bridegroom in the Song of Songs (5, 6–7).

BIBLIOGRAPHY

Text: Carl von Kraus, ed. *Deutsche Liederdichter des 1373. Jahrhunderts,* 2nd ed. revised by Gisela Kornrumpf (Tübingen: Niemeyer, 1978) with parts of the following lines restored from J: 1, 4, 9, 15, 21, 23, 39, 42, 46, 47.

Olive Sayce, *The Medieval German Lyric 1150–1300* (Oxford: Oxford University Press, 1982).

William C. McDonald, "A Pauline Reading of Der Wilde Alexander's 'Kindheitslied,'" *Monatshefte* 76, 2 (1984): 156–175.

TEXT

Years ago when we were children
and at an age
where we'd run across the meadows,
from one to another and back,
where sometimes
we'd find violets—
you see cattle plagued by flies there today.
I remember how we sat
among flowers and compared
which one was fairest.
our childhood shone
with the garlands we wore
at the dance.
So the time passes on.
See how we ran then looking for strawberries
from the fir to the beech,
over fences and stones,
as long as the sun would shine.
Then a man who watched in the woods
called through the branches,
"Now, children, go home now."
We all got covered with red spots
yesterday, when we picked strawberries.
To us it was all great fun for children.
Then we heard our shepherd
calling loud,
and grieving,
"Children, there are many snakes in there!"
One child went into the high grass

and started, and screamed,
"Children, a snake's rushed in here
and bit our comrade,
and he can't be saved,
he'll be black
and sick forever!"
Well then, get out of the woods!
And if you don't hurry soon,
I'll tell you what will happen:
if you don't take careVI
to leave the woods by day,
your joy will turn
to grief, for you will stay too long.
Do you know five virgins
tarried in the meadows,
and the king went in to his betrothed
and locked the hall? They were horrified.
The watchman tore
their garments from them,
and they had to stand unclothed.

SECTION 10

NEW DIRECTIONS IN THE GERMAN COURTLY LYRIC

Translated by J. W. Thomas

BIBLIOGRAPHY (9.1)

A. T. Hatto, Ronald Taylor, *The Songs of Neidhart von Reuental; 17 Summer and Winter Songs Set to Their Original Melodies* (Manchester, England: Manchester University Press, 1958).

Olive Sayce, *The Medieval German Lyric 1150–1300* (Oxford: Oxford University Press, 1982).

Eckehard Simon, *Neidhart von Reuental*. Twayne's World Authors Series; TWAS 364 (Boston: Twayne Publishers, 1975).

9.1 NEIDHART (ca. 1200–1240)

Walther refers disparagingly to Neidhart's uncouth themes and Wolfram mentions his pretentious peasants; otherwise we know no more of Neidhart than can be derived from the occasional personal references in his songs. These tell of a Bavarian knight who had a very modest estate and sang at the court of Duke Ludwig I of Bavaria. He took part in a crusade, either that of 1217-19 or that of 1227-28. About the year 1233 he fell out of favor with the new ruler, Duke Otto II, lost his property, and was obliged to leave Bavaria in order to find a new sponsor. He went to Austria and was granted a small fief by Duke Friedrich II, who was himself a minnesinger. Later he apparently entered the service of the Austrian nobleman Otto von Lengenbach. Neidhart must have been born about 1190 and he died after the year 1236.

The influence of goliard and *Spielmann* songs which is sometimes apparent in the verse of Walther von der Vogelweide is much more obvious in the compositions of Neidhart. Although the latter employs for the most part the sophisticated forms and frequently the chivalric expressions of the traditional mimesong, he uses them to treat peasants and peasant scenes, especially those having to do with indoor and outdoor dances. He thus creates a new type of lyric, which has been called the courtly village song. In lively dance rhythms Neidhart sings of village people and events with the superior, often mocking tones of the nobleman, and spices his colorful reality with burlesque humor. All but one of his songs fall into two groups, the summer songs and the winter songs. The former were perhaps written in the early part of Neidhart's career and, in keeping with the season and the poet's youth, are generally more lighthearted and spirited than the latter. Most of the winter songs were composed while the poet was living in Austria. The two groups of songs differ with regard to structure. Although at first glance it may seem complex, the basic pattern of the summer songs is quite simple and actually represents little more than ingenious variations of the rhymed couplets which the *Spiellute* had been using for generations. The winter songs have the traditional tripartite structure of the minnesong, made up of two *Stollen* and an *Abgesang*, and have metrical and rhyme patterns which are often rather complicated and more characteristic of the courtly song of his day. Both summer and winter songs usually begin with a stanza which describes the season and is followed by stanzas which dramatically relate, often in dialogue form, some village incident. Several of the summer songs consist merely of arguments between a village lass and her mother as to whether the former is to go to the dance. This situation and its treatment is drawn from the Latin *altercatio,* or argumentative song, and was especially popular among the goliard composers. Whatever the incident or situation, however, its narration frequently does not carry over into the last stanza, which deals rather with the poet's own hopes, joys, or sorrows, and often contains his name. In keeping with the accepted summer: joy—winter: sadness symbolism the final stanza of the summer songs shows a happy mood, that of the winter a sorrowful one. In the case of a love song, the narrator's prospects look good in the summer and rather bleak in the winter. Although the narrator takes part in the village activities and even competes with the rude farmers for the favor of rustic maidens, it should not be assumed that these accounts are autobiographical. Neidhart played and sang for dances, it is true, but these were held in the halls or gardens of castles, and the dancers were knights and ladies.

The mixture of chivalric and popular elements in Neidhart's verse often produces incongruous, almost grotesque effects. The ethereal and melancholy longing of the minnesong can change abruptly to the coarse expression of the goliard song; the lovely and remote lady of courtly verse becomes the simple, all-too-human peasant girl; the romantic illusion is destroyed by an almost brutal reality. The impression is frequently one of satire and caricature: the sharp contrasts sometimes make the peasants and the peasant scenes ridiculous; sometimes it is chivalric romanticism which is made to look foolish. Neidhart composed for an audience which knew and was perhaps surfeited with the traditional minnesong, and they would have immediately recognized the incongruity and humor of using courtly expressions and metrics to treat peasants.

Neidhart's songs were very popular in his day and were frequently imitated by composers throughout the entire subsequent history of courtly verse. Nearly six hundred of Neidhart's stanzas are extant and more of his melodies have survived than those of any other secular lyric composer of his century. Five manuscripts have songs attributed to him. Those containing most of the texts believed to be genuine (there are many pseudo-Neidhart songs) date from the fourteenth and fifteenth centuries, the earliest one from about a century after his death.

The first five songs given here are summer songs, composed to be sung at outdoor dances, probably in the court-yard or garden of a castle. Neidhart perhaps sang the first stanza while the dance leaders were going through the first step of the dance, paused while the step was performed by the entire group, sang the second stanza while the leaders demonstrated the second step, etc. These outdoor dances were performed by the company as a whole, whereas the indoor dances were executed in smaller groups of two to four members. Each of the songs begins by welcoming the spring which has brought the young people out into the fields. In 'Such Delightful Meadows' the narrator follows this nature introduction by inviting all of the girls to come out and dance. His invitation is followed by an 'argument' between two girls in which the peasant boys are unfavorably compared with the Knight of Reuenthal. The song 'Barren Were the Meadows and Forsaken' follows a similar pattern except that the narrator does not enter directly into the discussion and that the dispute is between a maid and her mother. The incongruity of the beautiful descriptions of nature and the rather earthy language of the village maiden is particularly striking. The third song, 'Field, Meadow, Forest, as You See,' is distinctive in that the nature theme is carried through the entire song in a consistent development: the beauties of nature lead to the beauty of the young people in their bright spring clothing, which leads in turn to the singer, whose duty it is to teach them to enjoy life. The metrical pattern with its spritely rhythm shows how close Neidhart adheres to the folk tradition: if the last three lines of the stanza are combined there is a simple four-line stanza consisting of two couplets. The reference to the 'vale of tears' in the last strophe is a play on the author's name, Reuenthal, which it translates. The following song, 'The Woods Were Bare and Gray,' begins with a description of nature and an invitation by the singer for the girls to come and dance. Once more the charms of nature are associated with those of the narrator's sweetheart. In this song are no discordant notes: the leafy trees, the meadow flowers, the singing of the birds, the warm rays of the sun, and the dancing village maiden combine to produce a harmonious, idyllic scene. The last of the summer songs is more typical. After describing the beauties of spring, Neidhart presents the contrasting picture of the ugly old peasant woman and her wild, ungainly dancing.

224

SUCH DELIGHTFUL MEADOWS

(INE GESACH DIE HEIDE)

Such delightful meadows I've never seen,
such changing shades and shadows of forest green.
May reveals itself in wood and heather.
Come, maidens, all together
and dance a merry roundelay to greet the
　　　summer weather.

Praise from many voices
now hails the May,
and field and wood rejoices
in colors gay,
where before were seen no leaves or flowers.
Beneath the linden bowers
a group of youths and pretty maidens dance
　　　away the hours.

No one's heart is laden
with grief or care.
Come, each shapely maiden,
so sweet and fair,
deck thyself as Swabians desire thee,
Bavarians admire thee,
with silken ribbons on thy blouse from neck
　　　to hips attire thee.

'Why bother?' answered, weeping,
a village maid.
'The stupid men are sleeping,
so I'm afraid.
Honor and delight are but a fable,
the men are all unstable,
to court a woman faithfully and well, they're
　　　quite unable.'

'Let's hear no more of sadness,'
thus spoke her friend,
'We'll all grow old with gladness,
for there's no end
of suitors for a maid whose good, and jolly.
Such mournful talk is folly;
I have a lover that can drive away all melancholy.'

'If thou canst show a lover
for whom I'd care,
this belt thy waist shall cover
which now I wear.
Tell his name whom thou art thus commending,
whose love is so unending.
I dreamed of thee last night and learned that
    thou art just pretending.'

'Everybody knows him
as Reuenthal.
His merry songs disclose him
to one and all.
I like him and repay him for his singing.
For him shall I be springing
about in all my finery. But hark, the bell is
    ringing.'

BARREN WERE THE MEADOWS AND FORSAKEN

(BLÔZEN WIR DEN ANGER LIGEN SAHEN)

Barren were the meadows and forsaken
until the summer came to warm and waken,
flowers pressed through grass and clover then.
Once again
summer now is opening the roses
and making lovely heath and glen.

Nightingale and thrush, we hear them singing,
with the sound the hills and vales are ringing.
They sing their songs of joyous summertime
as they climb.
May has brought us happiness and beauty:
the heath is blooming in its prime.

Spoke a maid, 'The dew is on the heather,
see the splendor summer brings together.
The trees that in the wintertime were bare
everywhere
wave their leafy branches in the breezes.
The nightingales are singing there.

'Losa, hear the songs of birds resounding,
they greet the May from all the trees surrounding.

I fancy, we are free of winter now.
Wierat, thou
must dance more spritely, wouldst thou gain my favor,
beneath the linden's leafy bough.

'Spring's the time for each to choose a lover,
Roses blossom 'neath the forest's cover
and I shall have a crown of roses red
on my head
when I'm dancing hand in hand so gaily
with such a handsome knight,' she said.

'Daughter, think no more of bold advances.
Should'st thou disturb the nobles at the dances,
who are not the sort for folk as we,
I forsee
thou willst have a lot of pain and trouble.
A sturdy farmer covets thee.'

'Let a heifer wed the worthy farmer!
My hope is for a stately knight in armor.
Why should I take a farmer as my man?
Never can
I be happy with a rustic lover.
A knight alone will suit my plan.'

'Daughter, don't despise his lowly station
to win a stupid noble's admiration.
This has caused your friends distress and pain.
All in vain
are thy promises, I tell thee truly,
thy wilfulness I never could restrain.'

'Mother mine, stop scolding, and believe me,
I would love him though my friends should leave me,
I never hid my wishes, I recall.
One and all
may the people know whom I have chosen,
for he's the knight of Reuenthal.'

FIELD, MEADOW, FOREST, AS YOU SEE

(HEID ANGER WALT IN FRÖDEN STAT)

Field, meadow, forest, as you see,

have restively adorned themselves in all the finery
that May has placed at their command.
Let us sing,
glad with spring:
summer has come into the land.

Come out of your rooms, you pretty maids,
and onto the streets; no bitter wind will chill
your promenades,
and ice and snow have gone away.
Come together
to the heather;
birds are singing, once more gay.

They all are now repaid for pain.
But heed what I have said and come and look
upon the plain;
and see how summertime can bless,
as a friend,
it will send
every tree a leafy dress.

But those of you who can aspire
to something better, now put on your holiday attire
and show us what your silver buys.
We shall see,
gay and free,
many flowers before our eyes.

Though I possess a vale of tears,
this lovely summer sets me free from all my pain
and fears.
And now that winter's rage is spent,
I shall teach
youth to reach
for joy, such is my firm intent.

THE WOODS WERE BARE AND GRAY

(DER WALT STUONT ALLER GRISE)

The woods were bare and gray,
in ice and snow they lay,
but warmer skies have clothed each bough.
See them now,

maidens fair,
and dance among the flowers there.

From many tiny throats
I heard the silver notes
of little birds in sweetest song.
Flowers throng
in grass and briar,
the meadow dons her spring attire.

I love the charms of May;
I saw my darling play
and dance beneath the linden's crown.
Its leaves bent down,
every one,
to shade her from the radiant sun.

ON THE MOUNTAIN AND IN THE GLEN

(UF DEM BERGE UND IN DEM TAL)

On the mountain and in the glen
swells the music of bird's again.
Now are seen
fields in green.
Away with you, Winter, your breath is too keen.

Trees which were standing so long in gray
have all new leaves and among them play
birds of the wood.
This does one good:
they greet the May as warblers should.

A wrinkled old hag who had fought with death
days and nights for life and breath
danced like a sheep
with a bound and a leap
and knocked the younger ones down in a heap.

The three winter songs which are given here are fairly representative of Neidhart's winter songs in general. Like the summer songs, they were composed to be sung at dances, but the dancing was done inside and the dances themselves were of a different kind. The descriptions are somewhat more realistic than in the summer songs; the humor is more pronounced, much sharper, and directed not only at the pretentious and boorish farm boys, but also at the timid, quite unheroic knight who serves as narrator. It is not entirely coincidence that two of the three songs consist of seven stanzas, for this was a favorite number with Neidhart which produced the type of symmetry of which he strove. The first song, 'Children, Ice is Here, So Ready Up a Sleigh,' well illustrates his symmetrical treatment of a situation. The first stanza gives the nature introduction, the next two describe the preparations for the dance. In the third stanza the singer makes some personal (and slightly risque) comments about women's clothing, the following two stanzas tell of an amusing, slapstick episode, and the last stanza presents the singer's lament, in this case about the trials of a property owner. The peasant Engelmar appears in several of the winter songs as the rival of the singer . . .

SING, MY GOLDEN COCK, I'LL GIVE THEE GRAIN

[SINC AN, GULDIN HUON! ICH GIBE DIR WEIZE)

'Sing, my golden cock, I'll give thee grain!'
(at her voice
I rejoice)
spoke the pretty maid for whom I sigh.
Thus a dunce's hopes are raised in vain
seasons through.
Were it true,
no one's spirit then would be so high,
no one else's heart would beat so light.
Will her careless gaiety ever free
me from all the sorrows of my plight?

Listen! Hear the dancing at the inn!
Every man
go who can,
there the women wait, a merry throng.
Soon we'll see the ridewanz begin.
Tarradiddle
goes the fiddle,
lusty peasant youths break forth in song.
Each in turn sings out his verse with pride,
shakes the room with lungs of brass.
Noblegrass
dances with a maid on either side.

Move out all the chairs and clear the floor;
take the tables
to the stables

and we'll dance till feet and ankles hurt.

Open up the windows and the door;
let the breeze
cool their knees,
blowing through each village wench's skirt.
When the leaders stop to rest a little,
then we'll all, great and small,
short and tall,
step a courtly dance once to the fiddle.

Gozbreht, Willebolt, Gumpreht, and Eppe,
Willebrand,
hired hand,
Werenbolt and also youngster Tutze,
Megenbolt, the farmer's son, and Reppe,
Irenwart,
Sigehart,
Giselher and Frideger and Utze—
he's the stupid oaf from Holingare.
He goes courting every day,
so they say,
but the girls don't like him anywhere.

Never has a bumpkin looked so grand,
nor so flighty;
God Almighty,
how he struts in line before the rest!
More than two hands wide the leather band
of his sword,
like a lord
in his new and gaily-colored vest,
scraps of every shape and hue are there,
fancy shirt, embroidered pants,
see him prance
in a garb no other fool would wear.

His attire is rustic as can be,
it's absurd.
So I've heard,
he's been wooing Engel's daughter, Pearl.
All such hopes are futile, I foresee.
She's a prize of shape and size
to win the admiration of an earl.
Good advice I'll give him: let him try

someone else; for all his pain
what he'll gain
he can take to Mayence in his eye.

Though his clothes are colorful and gay
and he's dressed
in his best,
he should know she simply can't abide him.
He has hung around her every day;
I became
red with shame
when I saw her sitting down beside him.
If I win this maid who looks so pretty,
I shall give to her my all,
Reuenthal,
for her own: this is my fabled city.

WINTER'S EVIL ART

[WINTER DINIU MEIL]

Winter's evil art
strips the forest of its leaves
and flowers from the blooming earth.
Summer, joy has vanished from thy merry retinue.
Many a happy heart
now in bitter sadness grieves
which was made for only mirth.
How could a maid whom I before all others would pursue
still appear
not to hear
the serenade with pleasure
which I sang with all the fervor I possess
and yet today preserve and treasure
that she may never find a limit to my faithfulness.

Should my constancy
and devotion through the year
afford me naught but her rejection,
then might I repent, and rightly, this unhappy quest.
It was told to me,
who was always faithful here
would gain in fortune and affection.
With thee to comfort, Lady Luck, my hope is for the best:

that she may mend
and show her friend
less extreme vexation.
Could this be, perhaps the end might still be good.
Grant her evil temper moderation!
Woe, that women never treat their lovers as they should.

For this love of mine
many wish me only ill.
Now hear my plaint with sympathy,
never have I needed wise and prudent counsel more.
Erph and Adelwine
cause me trouble still,
before my time this ages me.
No one can imagine what I've suffered heretofore.
All this year,
so I hear,
they have sought her favor
whom I'll always love and wish to be my own.
Mistress of a heart that ne'er shall waiver,
thou shallst never comfort any man but me alone.

Thou must lock the door
which will close those ears of thine,
that they no jealous words may hear
which might make me seem to thee otherwise than good.
Mark such talk no more,
oh my darling, lady mine,
that is not fitting for thy ear.
Listen lo a faithful friend's advice, as each one should.
Kuenebrecht
Engeknecht,
forward and deceiving,
sue for thy affection, Lady, have them go.
They are why my loving heart is grieving,
they have ever been the source of secret, bitter woe.

Only see my hair,
it is colored like the snow!
Despite my age it makes me gray
that I suffer grief from peasant louts because of her.
There is Engelmare;
he's a reason I am so.
The mirror he still has today
which he once did take from Vriderun, the villager.

From then on
I have gone
courting her no longer.
save with timid steps and timid heart and fear,
and my sorrow waxes ever stronger
that my aching heart desires the maid whom he holds dear.

Westward to the Rhine,
from the Elbe to the Po,
I know the countries an around.
All their borders do not hold so many brazen louts
as a county line
here in Austria, you know.
Many new ones every day are found.
See, there's one who's caused a lot of trouble hereabouts.
Wankelbolt,
he's a dolt,
me he would discredit
(he's a leader there in Lyingdale, it's said),
and the bastard really will regret it.
If he gets too saucy, I'll put holes right through his head.

Love once came to me:
Oh, if Love had but remained!
I came and found the roses fair.
See, I plucked a rose, but soon it lost its loveliness.
Pain and misery
drove away the joy I gained.
I'll tell what I discovered there:
I broke the rose, a wretched thorn then caused me sore distress,
so that I,
though I sigh,
let no roses prick me,
neither look to see what roses I may find.
Many roses raise their thorns to stick me,
but I know there still are roses which are kind.

9.2 TANNHÄUSER

Although the influence of the classical and pre-classical mimesong on the thirteenth century was significant, the strongest influence to be exerted by courtly singers was that of Walther and Neidhart. Their songs and the *Spielmann* songs from which they drew provided new material and new attitudes for the courtly lyric and encouraged a closer relationship between literature and life. The new directions of the verse of the century were mainly toward an increased realism which gave it different values, expressions, and symbols and frequently led to parody and satire. Walther had many followers in his use of courtly verse forms to tell of the love of a village maiden, to discuss political affairs, or to advise the youth. Neidhart's peasant dances and parody of chivalric manners were imitated and echoed by his contemporaries and successors. But much of that which was new in the courtly lyric was doubtless taken from the popular songs of the *Spielleute:* animal stories, fairy tale material, fabulous Oriental creatures, problems of village society, Marian themes, and harvest festivals. It was doubtless the influence of the *Spielleute* as well as that of Walther and Neidhart which caused an increase in the amount of humorous verse, and much of the humor was the result of ridicule of ideals and themes which a previous generation had taken very seriously.

Very much in keeping with the spirit of the times were the songs of the hero of the Venus Mountain ballad and Wagner's opera, *Tannhäuser.* He was born about the year 1200 as the younger (and therefore propertyless) son of Bavarian or Austrian nobility. He appears in no historical records and our knowledge of him is derived solely from personal references in his works. These tell of an adventurous, exuberant, and wastrel life. In the early part of his career, Tannhäuser was a protege of Friedrich II of Austria and his two sons, Heinrich and Konfid. From Friedrich the singer received extensive properties, including a residence in Vienna, which enabled him to carry on a gay existence at the court, interrupted by his participation in the crusade of 1228–29 and the Cyprian War two years later. With the death of Friedrich in 1246 Tannhäuser's carefree life was over, and the hardships of the penniless minstrel began. For he long before had wasted away the property which Friedrich had given him. From then on until his death around 1266 Tannhäuser wandered from court to court, supporting himself meagerly with his songs.

The style and general content of Tannhäuser's love songs, *Leiche* and Sprüche is courtly, but one can readily see that the singer does not take the courtly ethic or the ideal of *minne* seriously. In a humorous and often ironic manner he parodies chivalric themes: his grand lady turns out to be a simple peasant girl, his knightly deeds are exaggerated to the impossible, his languishing lover becomes ridiculous. Two contrasting moods predominate in his works, the one a jovial affirmation of the life of the senses, the other a sad regret that such good times as he had experienced should end. Most of his love songs and five of his six *Leiche* are composed to dance rhythms, not to those of courtly dances, but to those of lively, even tumultuous village dances. The dance songs, like those of Neidhart (by whom he was influenced), are divided into summer songs and winter songs.

Tannhäuser was by nature a realist, not only in his burlesques of outworn themes, but also in his keen interest in the world about him. The songs of no other courtly singer contain so much factual and detailed information as do his. They reveal, too, a broad knowledge of literature and contain allusions to Arthurian legends, Germanic heroic verse, and even to classical figures.

Tannhäuser's familiarity with the *Spielmann* lyric is seen in his use of riddles as well as his treatment of peasants. Only two of his songs deal with courtly love and even there in a rather off-hand manner. The singer is not one to waste his time with plaints about wooing in vain, his suit is more often than not successful. Tannhäuser was obviously not interested, either immediately or symbolically, in the ethical aspects of courtly love. Nor is there idealism revealed in his one crusade song. In it he tells of his experiences and hardships, but says little about any religious purpose or goal. He was, however, capable of sincere religious feeling and expression, as several of his poem demonstrate.

In the song, 'My Lady Wishes to Reward,' Tannhäuser parodies the extravagant promises made by lovers in the earlier minnesong and ridicules the chivalric idea of service to a noble lady. He here reveals his most characteristic mood. The second song, 'How Delightful is this Lovely Day,' is not typical of Tannhäuser and the question has been raised as to whether he is really the author. It may be that this song was the cause of his becoming associated with the Venus Mountain legend. It is also possible, however, that the song was altered in the process of oral transmission to conform with an already established folk tradition such as appears in the Tannhäuser ballad.

BIBLIOGRAPHY (9.2)

J. W. Thomas, *Tannhäuser: Poet and Legend, with Texts and Translations of His Works*. University of North Carolina Studies in the Germanic Languages and Literatures, 77 (Chapel Hill: University of North Carolina Press, 1974).

U. M. Clifton-Everest, *The Tragedy of Knighthood: Origins of the Tannhäuser-Legend* (Oxford: Society for Mediaeval Languages and Literatures, 1979).

Olive Sayce, *The Medieval German Lyric 1150–1300* (Oxford: Oxford University Press, 1982).

MY LADY WISHES TO REWARD

(MIN FROWE DIU WIL LONEN MIR)

My lady wishes to reward
my service and my loyalty.
Let's thank her, all with one accord,
for having been so kind to me.
I only need to cause the Rhine
to flow no more through Coblenz land
and she will grant a wish of mine.
She'd also like some grains of sand

from out the sea where sets the sun,
then she'll give heed to my request.
She wants a star, the nearest one
will do, it need not be the best.
My love is strong,
whate'er her song
I will not think she does me wrong,
my own.
To God alone
and no one else is this fair lady known.

If from the moon I steal the glow,
then may I have this noble wench.
And she'll reward me well, I know,
if 'round the world I dig a trench.
If like an eagle I might fly,
then would she welcome my advances
(that is, if none could soar so high),
or if I broke a thousand lances
within a day, as did the sire
of Parzival to win the prize,
she'd gladly do what I desire,
't will cost me plenty otherwise.
My love is strong
whate'er her song
I will not think she does me wrong,
my own.
To God alone
and no one else is this fair lady known.

If I the Elbe's waters bound,
I'd be rewarded; could I make
the Danube flow without a sound,
she'd love me well for custom's sake.
A salamander I must bring
to her from searing fire and flame,
then she will grant me anything
that any loving knight might claim.
When I can turn aside the rain
and snow, I've often heard her say,
and make the summer wax and wane,
then I shall have a lover's pay.
My love is strong,
whate'er her song

I will not think she does me wrong,
my own.
To God alone
and no one else is this fair lady known.

HOW DELIGHTFUL IS THIS LOVELY DAY

(EZ IST HIUTE EYN WUNNICHLICHER TAC)

How delightful is this lovely day!
Now care for me who over all disposes,
that I may ever live with blessing
and may do penance for my worldly blindness.
For he indeed will be my stay
and through His aid my soul secure reposes.
May I be healed of all transgressing
and may I yet obtain God's loving kindness.
Grant me a will which shall not bend
and which deserves His love so well
that God may well reward me!
May I but have a happy end,
and may my soul in rapture dwell,
a gentle death afford me.
May I be saved by purity,
that hell may be no danger.
What I require, give unto me,
that I to highest joy be not a stranger.
Here must I have no family,
that friends I may have yonder
who take such pleasure in my songs
that I shall be renowned among the knights
        who heavenward wander.

SECTION 11

Selections from THE LAIS OF MARIE DE FRANCE

Introduction by Albrecht Classen

Although Marie's identity has never been determined, we can be certain that she lived in the second half of the twelfth century, either at the court or in the vicinity of the English king, or maybe in France. In the manuscripts she is only referred to as Marie, but posterity has labelled her 'Marie de France' since 1581 when Claude Fauchet referred to her under this name in a collection of French poetry. We know of at least four different personalities with the name of Marie who could have composed these *lais*, but it is impossible to reach any further conclusions. The choice would be: Marie, King Henry II's half sister, the illegitimate daughter of Geoffrey Plantagenet; Marie de Champagne; Marie de Boulogne; Marie de Meulan, and a nun at Reading (England) named Marie. The epithet "de France" probably means that Marie was born in France but had left her homeland.

Marie authored, apart from these twelve poems (*lais*), also a collection of fables and a religious narrative of *Saint Patrick's Purgatory*. She might also have translated from Latin *La vie Seinte Audree*.

Marie's *lais* are short verse narratives in which the theme of love is examined from many different angles. These twelve poems, preceded by a fifty-six-line Prologue, appear in the manuscript British Library, Harley 978 in the following sequence: *Guigemar, Equitan, Le Fresne, Bisclavret, Lanval, Deus Amanz, Yonec, Laüstic, Milun, Chaitivel, Chevrefoil,* and *Eliduc*. Marie explains repeatedly that she is simply retelling tales of adventures which had happened in the past and were captured by Breton writers in prose narratives. She translated these into verse and presented them to the king as valuable literary lessons on love, virtue, and honor.

BIBLIOGRAPHY

Judith Rice Rothschild, "A Rapprochement between *Bisclavret* and *Lanval*," *Speculum* XL VIII, 1 (1973): 78–88.

The Lais of Marie de France. Trans. with an Introduction by Glyn S. Burgess and Keith Busby (London: Penguin, 1986).

Glyn S. Burgess, *The Lais of Marie de France. Text and Context* (Athens: The University of Georgia Press, 1987).

Chantal Marechal, ed., *In Quest of Marie de France, a Twelfth-Century Poet.* Medieval and Renaissance Series, 10 (Lewiston: Edwin Mellen Press, 1992).

Marie de France, *Lais*. Ed. by Alfred Ewert. With Introduction & Bibliography by Glyn S. Burgess (Bristol: Bristol Classical Press, 1995).

Sharon Kinoshita, "Colonial Possessions: Wales and the Anglo-Norman Imaginary in the *Lais* of Marie de France," *Discourses on Love, Marriage, and Transgression in Medieval and Early Modern Literature,* ed. Albrecht Classen (Arizona Center for Medieval and Renaissance Studies, 2004), 147–62.

R. Howard Bloch: *The Anonymous Marie de France* (Chicago and London: The University of Chicago Press, 2003).

"Marie de France," *The Literary Encyclopedia,* ed. Robert Clark, online version only, 2003 Albrecht Classen, (http://www.litencyc.com/php/speople.php?rec=true&UID=5494); there is a charge to read after 600 words.

Elisa Narin van Court, "Marie de France," *Encyclopedia of Medieval Literature,* ed. Jay Ruud (New York: Facts on File, 2006), 439–40.

MARIE DE FRANCE: PROLOGUE

Whoever has received knowledge
and eloquence in speech from God
should not be silent or secretive
but demonstrate it willingly.
When a great good is widely heard of,
then, and only then, does it bloom,
and when that good is praised by many,
it has spread its blossoms.
The custom among the ancients—
as Priscian testifies—
was to speak quite obscurely
in the books they wrote,
so that those who were to come after
and study them
might gloss the letter
and supply its significance from their own wisdom.
Philosophers knew this,
they understood among themselves
that the more time they spent,
the more subtle their minds would become[1]

and the better they would know how to keep themselves
from whatever was to be avoided.
He who would guard himself from vice
should study and understand
and begin a weighty work
by which he might keep vice at a distance,
and free himself from great sorrow.
That's why I began to think
about composing some good stories
and translating from Latin to Romance;
but that was not to bring me fame:
too many others have done it.
Then I thought of the *lais* I'd heard.
I did not doubt, indeed I knew well,
that those who first began them[2]
and sent them forth
composed them in order to preserve
adventures they had heard.
I have heard many told;
and I don't want to neglect or forget them.
To put them into word[3] and rhyme
I've often stayed awake.
In your honor, noble King,
who are so brave and courteous,
repository of all joys
in whose heart all goodness takes root,
I undertook to assemble these *lais*
to compose and recount them in rhyme.
In my heart I thought and determined,
sire, that I would present them to you.
If it pleases you to receive them,
you will give me great joy;
I shall be happy forever.

---

1. In this reading we have followed Mickel's suggestion, to ignore the emendation of *trespassereit* and take the (H) reading *trespasserunt* ("The Unity and Significance of Marie's Prologue"). The other way, these lines would mean "the more time went by, the more difficult the sense became, and the more care they must take to find what might be overlooked."

2. The order of the next four lines has been shifted; in the French ll. 37-38 precede ll. 35-36.

3. *Ditié* can be a moral saying or a song. It may refer to the *surplus,* the glossed meaning, what Robertson calls the doctrinal content, or to the fact that the *lais* were sung, cf. *Guigemar,* ll. 885-86.

Do not think me presumptuous
if I dare present them to you.
Now hear how they begin.

GUIGEMAR

Whoever deals with good material
feels pain if it's treated improperly.
Listen, my lords, to the words of Marie,
who does not forget her responsibilities when her turn comes.[4]
People should praise anyone
who wins admiring comments for herself.
But anywhere there is
a man or a woman of great worth,
people who envy their good fortune
often say evil things about them;
they want to ruin their reputations.
Thus they act like
vicious, cowardly dogs
who bite people treacherously.
I don't propose to give up because of that;
if spiteful critics or slanderers
wish to turn my accomplishments against me,
they have a right to their evil talk.

The tales—and I know they're true—
from which the Bretons made their *lais*
I'll now recount for you briefly;
and at the very beginning of this enterprise,
just the way it was written down,
I'll relate an adventure
that took place in Brittany,
in the old days.

At that time, Hoel ruled Brittany,
sometimes peacefully, sometimes at war.

---

4. The French *en sun tens* could also be rendered, "in her day"; Rychner opts for this sense, seeing in it an implied contrast between Marie as a modern writer and the ancient writers and sages referred to in the Prologue to the whole collection.

The king had a vassal
who was lord of Leonnais;
his name was Oridial
and he was on very intimate terms with his lord.
A worthy and valiant knight,
he had, by his wife, two children,
a son and a beautiful daughter.
The girl's name was Noguent;
they called the boy Guigemar.
There wasn't a more handsome youngster in the kingdom.
His mother had a wonderful love for him,
and his father a great devotion;
when he could bring himself to part with the boy,
his father sent him to serve the king.
The boy was intelligent and brave,
and made himself loved by all.
When his time of probation was at an end,
and he was mature in body and mind,
the king dubbed him knight,
giving him luxurious armor, which was exactly what he desired.
Guigemar left the court,
but not before dispensing many rich gifts.

He journeyed to Flanders to seek his fame;
there was always a war, or a battle raging there.
Neither in Lorraine nor in Burgundy,
in Anjou nor in Gascony,
could one find, in those days,
Guigemar's equal as a fine knight.
But in forming him nature had so badly erred
that he never gave any thought to love.
There wasn't a lady or a maid on earth,
no matter how noble, or how beautiful,
who wouldn't have willingly granted him her love,
had he asked her for it.
Many maids asked him,
but he wasn't interested in such things;
no one could discover in him
the slightest desire to love.
Therefore both friends and strangers
gave him up for lost.

At the height of his fame,

this baron, Guigemar, returned to his own land
to visit his father and his lord,
his good mother and his sister,
all of whom were most eager to see him.
Guigemar stayed with them,
I believe, an entire month.
Then he was seized by a desire to hunt;
that night he summoned his companions in arms,
his huntsmen, and his beaters;
next morning he set out for the woods
to indulge in the sport that gave him much pleasure.
They gathered in pursuit of a great stag;
the dogs were unleashed.
The hunters ran ahead
while the young man lingered behind;
a squire carried his bow,
his hunting knife, and his quiver.[5]
He wanted to fire some arrows, if he had the opportunity,
before he left that spot.
In the thickest part of a great bush
Guigemar saw a hind with a fawn;
a completely white beast,
with deer's antlers on her head.
Spurred by the barking of the dogs, she sprang into the open.
Guigemar took his bow and shot at her,
striking her in the breastbone.[6]
She fell at once,
but the arrow rebounded,
gave Guigemar such a wound—
it went through his thigh right into the horse's flank—
He collapsed on the thick grass
beside the hind he'd struck.
The hind, wounded as she was,
suffered pain and groaned.
Then she spoke, in this fashion:
"Alas! I'm dying!
And you, vassal, who wounded me,
this be your destiny:

---

5. As practiced by the medieval aristocracy, the hunt proceeded according to precise, complicated rules that governed the actions of each participant.

6. "Breastbone": so Rychner glosses *esclot*; Ewert reads, "front hoof" that he had to dismount.

may you never get medicine for your wound!
Neither herb nor root,
neither physician nor potion,
will cure you
of that wound in your thigh,
until a woman heals you,
one who will suffer, out of love for you,
pain and grief
such as no woman ever suffered before.
And out of love for her, you'll suffer as much;
the affair will be a marvel
to lovers, past and present,
and to all those yet to come.
Now go away, leave me in peace!"
Guigemar was badly wounded;
what he had heard dismayed him.
He began to consider carefully
what land he might set out for
to have his wound healed.
He didn't want to remain there and die.
He knew, he reminded himself,
that he'd never seen a woman
to whom he wanted to offer his love,
nor one who could cure his pain.
He called his squire to him;
"Friend," he said, "go quickly!
Bring my companions back here;
I want to talk to them."
The squire rode off and Guigemar remained;
he complained bitterly to himself.
Making his shirt into a bandage,
he bound his wound tightly;
Then he mounted his horse and left that spot.
He was anxious to get far away;
he didn't want any of his men to come along,
who might interfere, or try to detain him.
Through the woods he followed
a grassy path, which led him
out into open country; there, at the edge of the plain,
he saw a cliff and a steep bank
overlooking a body of water below:
a bay that formed a harbor.
There was a solitary ship in the harbor;

246

Guigemar saw its sail.
It was fit and ready to go,
called outside and in—
no one could discover a seam in its hull.
Every deck rail and peg
was solid ebony;
no gold under the sun could be worth more.
The sail was pure silk;
it would look beautiful when unfurled.

The knight was troubled;
he had never heard it said
anywhere in that region
that ships could land there.
He went down to the harbor
and, in great pain, boarded the ship.
He expected to discover men inside,
guarding the vessel,
but he saw no one, no one at all.
Amidships he found a bed
whose posts and frame
were wrought in the fashion of Solomon,[7]
of cypress and ivory,
with designs in inlaid gold.
The quilt on the bed was made
of silken cloth, woven with gold.
I don't know how to estimate the value of the other bedclothes,
but I'll tell you this much about the pillow:
whoever rested his head on it
would never have white hair.
The sable bedspread
was lined with Alexandrian silk.
Two candelabra of fine gold—
the lesser of the two worth a fortune—
were placed at the head of the cabin,
lighted tapers placed in them.

7. Rychner notes that this term referred during the Middle Ages to a certain type of inlaid work. There is, however, also a widely diffused medieval legend about a marvelous ship made by Solomon that intrudes into some versions of the story of the Grail, and moreover the description of the bed contains reminiscences of the biblical Song of Solomon (see Ewert's note).

Guigemar, astonished by all this,
reclined on the bed
and rested; his wound hurt
Then he rose and tried to leave the ship,
but he couldn't return to land.
The vessel was already on the high seas,
carrying him swiftly with it.
A good, gentle wind was blowing,
so turning back now was out of the question.
Guigemar was very upset; he didn't know what to do.
It's no wonder he was frightened,
especially as his wound was paining him a great deal.
Still, he had to see the adventure through.
He prayed to God to watch over him,
to use his power to bring him back to land,
and to protect him from death.
He lay down on the bed, and fell asleep.
That day he'd survived the worst;
before sundown he would arrive
at the place where he'd be cured—
near an ancient city,
the capital of its realm.

The lord who ruled over that city
was a very aged man who had a wife,
a woman of high lineage,
noble, courteous, beautiful, intelligent;
he was extremely jealous,
which accorded with his nature.
(All old folk are jealous;
every one of them hates the thought of being cuckolded,
such is the perversity of age.)
The watch he kept over her was no joke.
The grove beneath the tower
was enclosed all around
with walls of green marble,
very high and thick.
There was only one entrance,
and it was guarded day and night.
On the other side, the sea enclosed it;
no one could enter, no one leave,
except by means of a boat,
as the castle might require it.

Inside the castle wails,
the lord had built a chamber—
none more beautiful anywhere—to keep his wife under guard—
At its entrance was a chapel.
The room was painted with images all around;
Venus the goddess of love
was skillfully depicted in the painting,
her nature and her traits were illustrated,
whereby men might learn how to behave in love,
and to serve love loyally.
Ovid's book, the one in which he instructs
lovers how to control their love,
was being thrown by Venus into a fire,
and she was excommunicating all those
who ever perused this book
or followed its teachings.[8]
That's where the wife was locked up.
Her husband had given her
a girl to serve her,
one who was noble and well educated—
she was his niece, the daughter of his sister.[9]
There was great affection between the two women.
She stayed with her mistress when he went off,
remaining with her until he returned.
No one else came there, man or woman,
nor could the wife leave the walls of the enclosure.
An old priest, hoary with age,
kept the gate key;
he'd lost his nether member
or he wouldn't have been trusted.
He said mass for her
and served her her food.

That same day, as soon as she rose from a nap,
the wife went into the grove;

8. The book in question is Ovid's *Remedia amoris* (Remedies for Love), a companion volume to the Roman poet's equally tongue-in-cheek *Ars amatoria*. E.J. Mickel notes the irony of this old mural, presumably, commissioned by the husband to encourage his wife to love him, but, as Marie describes is predictive of the coming relationship between Guigemar and the young wife.

9. The French text is ambiguous as to whether the girl is the niece of the husband or the wife.

she had slept after dinner,
and now she set out to amuse herself,
taking her maid with her.
Looking out to sea,
they saw the ship on the rising tide
come sailing into the harbor.
They could see nothing guiding it.
The lady started to flee—
it's not surprising if she was afraid;
her face grew red from fear.
But the girl, who was wise
and more courageous,
comforted and reassured her,
and they went toward the water, fast as they could.
The damsel removed her cloak,
and boarded the beautiful ship.
She found no living thing
except the sleeping knight.
She saw how pale he was and thought him dead;
she stopped and looked at him.
Then she went back
quickly, and called her mistress,
told her what she'd found,
and lamented the dead man she'd seen.
The lady answered, "Let's go see him!
If he's dead, we'll bury him;
the priest will help us.
If I find that he's alive, he'll tell us all about this."

Without tarrying any longer, they returned together,
the lady first, then the girl.
When the lady entered the ship,
she stopped in front of the bed.
She examined the knight,
lamenting his beauty and fine body;
she was full of sorrow on his account,
and said it was a shame he'd died so young.
She put her hand on his breast,
and felt that it was warm, and his heart healthy,
beating beneath his ribs.
The knight, who was only asleep,
now woke up and saw her;
he was delighted, and greeted her—

he realized he'd come to land.
The lady, upset and weeping,
answered him politely
and asked him how
he got there, what country he came from,
if he'd been exiled because of war.
"My lady," he said, "not at all.
But if you'd like me to tell you
the truth, I'll do so;
I'll hide nothing from you.

I come from Brittany.
Today I went out bunting in the woods,
and shot a white hind;
the arrow rebounded,
giving me such a wound in the thigh
that I've given up hope of being cured.
The hind complained and spoke to me,
cursed me, swore
that I'd never be healed
except by a girl;
I don't know where she might be found.

When I heard my destiny,
I quickly left the woods:
I found this boat in a harbor,
and made a big mistake: I went on board.
The boat raced off to sea with me on it;
I don't know where I've arrived,
or what this city's called.
Beautiful one, I beg you, for God's sake,
please advise me!
I don't know where to go,
and I can't even steer this ship!"
She answered him, "My dear lord,
I'll be happy to advise you;
this is my husband's city,
and so is the region around it.
He is a rich man of high lineage,
but extremely old;
he's also terribly jealous.
On my word of honor,
he has locked me up in this stronghold.

There's only one entrance,
and an old priest guards the gate:
may God let him burn in hell!
I'm shut in here night and day.
I'd never dare
to leave except at his command,
when my lord asks for me.
Here I have my room and my chapel,
and this girl lives with me.
If it pleases you to stay here
until you're better able to travel,
we'll be happy to put you up,
we'll serve you willingly."
When he hears this,
Guigemar thanks the lady warmly,
and says he'll stay with her.
He rose from the bed;
with some difficulty they supported him,
and the lady brought him to her chamber.
The young man lay down
on the girl's bed,
behind a drape that was hung
across her room like a curtain.
They brought him water in a golden basin,
washed his thigh,
and with a fine, white silk cloth
they wiped the blood from his wound.
Then they bound it tightly.
They treated him very kindly.
When their evening meal came,
the girl left enough of hers
for the knight to have some;
he ate and drank quite well.

But now love struck him to the quick;
great strife was in his heart
because the lady had wounded him so badly
that he forgot his homeland.
His other wound no longer bothered him,
but he sighed with new anguish.
He begged the girl, who was assigned to take care of him,
to let him sleep.
She left him and went away,

since he had requested it,
returning to her mistress,
who was also feeling somewhat scorched
by the same fire Guigemar felt
igniting and consuming his heart.

The knight was alone now,
preoccupied and in distress.
He didn't yet know what was wrong,
but this much he could tell:
if the lady didn't cure him,
he was sure to die.
"Alas!" he said, "what shall I do?
I'll go to her and tell her
that she should have mercy and pity
on a poor, disconsolate wretch like me.
If she refuses my plea,
shows herself so proud and scornful,
then I'll have to die of grief,
languishing forever in this pain."
He sighed; but a little later
formed a new resolution,
and said to himself he'd have to keep suffering;
you have to endure what you can't change.
He lay awake all night,
sighing and in distress.
He turned over in his mind
her words and appearance,
the bright eyes, the fair mouth
whose sweetness had touched his heart.[10]
Under his breath he cried for mercy;
he almost called her his beloved.
If he only knew what she was feeling—
how love was torturing her—
I think he would have been very happy;
that little bit of consolation
would have diminished the pain
that drained him of his color.
If he was suffering from love of her,
she had nothing to gloat about, either.

Next morning, before dawn,
the lady arose.
She'd been awake all night, that was her complaint.
It was the fault of love, pressing her hard.
The damsel, who was with her,
noticed from the appearance of her lady
that she was in love
with the knight who was staying
in her chamber until he was healed;
but her mistress didn't know whether or not he loved her.
The lady went off to church
and the girl went off to the knight.

She sat down by the bed;
he spoke to her, saying,
"My dear friend, where has my lady gone?
Why did she rise so early?"
He paused, and sighed.
The girl spoke frankly:
"My lord," she said, "you're in love;
take care not to hide it too well!
The love you offer
may in fact be well received.
Anyone whom my lady chooses to love
certainly ought to think well of her.
This love would be suitable
if both of you were constant:
you're handsome and she's beautiful."
He answered the girl,
"I'm so in love with her
that if I don't get relief soon
I'll be in a very bad way.
Advise me, dear friend!
What should I do about my passion?"
The girl very sweetly
comforted the knight,
promised to help him
in every way she could;
she was very good-hearted and well bred.

When the lady had heard mass
she returned; she was anything but neglectful:
she wanted to know whether the man

whom she couldn't help loving
was awake or asleep.
The girl called her
and brought her to the knight;
now she'll have all the time she needs
to tell him what she's feeling,
for better or for worse.
He greeted her and she him;
they were both very scared now.
He didn't dare ask anything from her,
for he was a foreigner
and was afraid, if he told her what he felt,
she'd hate him for it, send him away.
But he who hides his sickness
can hardly be brought back to health;
love is a wound in the body,
and yet nothing appears on the outside.
It's a sickness that lasts a long time,
because it comes from nature.
Many people treat it lightly,
like these false courtiers
who have affairs everywhere they go,
then boast about their conquests;
that's not love but folly,
evil and lechery.
If you can find a loyal love,
you should love and serve it faithfully,
be at its command.
Guigemar was deeply in love;
he must either get help quickly
or live in misery.
So love inspires bravery in him:
he reveals his desires to the lady.

"Lady," he said, "I'm dying because of you;
my heart is full of anguish.
If you won't cure me,
I'll have to perish sooner or later.
I beg you to love me—
fair one, don't deny me!"
When she had heard him out,
she gave a fitting answer.
She laughed, and said, "My love,

I'd be ill advised to act too quickly
in granting your prayer.
I'm not accustomed to such a request."
"My lady," he replied, "for God's sake, have mercy!
Don't be annoyed if I speak like this to you.
It's appropriate for an inconstant woman
to make some one plead with her a long time
to enhance her worth; that way he won't think
she's used to such sport.
But a woman of good character,
sensible as well as virtuous,
if she finds a man to her liking,
oughtn't to treat him too disdainfully.
Rather she should love and enjoy him;
this way, before anyone knows or hears of it,
they'll have done a lot that's to their advantage.
Now, dear lady, let's end this discussion."
The lady realized he was telling the truth,
and immediately granted him
her love; then he kissed her.
From now on, Guigemar is at ease.
They lie down together and converse,
kissing and embracing often.
I hope they also enjoy whatever else
others do on such occasions.

It appears to me that Guigemar
stayed with her a year and a half.
Their life was full of pleasure.
But Fortune, who never forgets her duty,
turns her wheel suddenly,
raising one person up while casting another down;
and so it happened with the lovers,
because suddenly they were discovered.

One summer morning,
the lady was lying beside her young lover;
she kissed his mouth and eyes,
and said to him, "Dear, sweet love,
my heart tells me I'm going to lose you.
We're going to be found out.
If you die, I want to die, too,
but if you can escape,

you'll go find another love
while I stay here in misery."
"Lady," he said, "don't say such a thing!
I would never have any joy or peace
if I turned to another woman.
You needn't be afraid of that!"
"Beloved, I need your promise.
Give me your shirt;
I'll make a knot in the tail.
You have my leave to love the woman,
whoever she may be,
who will be able to undo it."
He gave her the shirt, and his promise;
she made the knot in such a way
that no woman could untie it
except with scissors or knife.
She gave him back the shirt,
and he took it on condition
that she should make a similar pledge to him,
by means of a belt
that she would wear next to her bare flesh,
tightened about her flanks.
Whoever could open the buckle
without breaking it or severing it from the belt,
would be the one he would urge her to love.
He kissed her, and left it at that.

That day they were discovered—
spied upon and found out
by an evil, cunning chamberlain,
sent by the husband.
He wanted to speak with the lady,
and couldn't get into her chamber;
he looked in a window and saw the lovers,
he went and told his lord.
When heard about it,
the lord was sorrier than he'd ever been before.
He called for three of his henchmen
and straightaway went to the wife's chamber;
he had the door broken down.
Inside he found the knight.
He was so furious
that he gave orders to kill the stranger.

Guigemar got up,
not at all afraid.
He grabbed a wooden rod
on which clothes were usually hung,
and waited for his assailants.
Guigemar will make some of them suffer for this;
before they get close to him,
he'll have maimed them all.

The lord stared at him for a long time,
and finally asked him
who he was, where he came from,
how he'd gotten in there.
Guigemar told him how he'd come there
and how the lady had received him;
he told him all about the adventure
of the wounded hind,
about his wound and the ship;
now he is entirely in the other's power.
The lord replied that he didn't believe him,
but if it really was the way he had told it
and if he could find the ship,
he'd send Guigemar back out to sea.
If he survived, that would be a shame;
he'd be happier if Guigemar drowned.

When he had made this pledge,
they went together to the harbor,
and found the ship; they put Guigemar on it—
it will take him back to his own land.
The ship got under way without waiting.
The knight sighed and cried,
often lamenting his lady
and praying to almighty God
to grant him a quick death,
and never let him come to port
if he couldn't regain his mistress,
whom he desired more than his own life.
He persisted in his grief
until the ship came to the port
where he'd first found it;
he was now very near his native land.
He left the ship as quickly as he could.

A boy whom Guigemar had raised
came by, following a knight,
and leading a war-horse.
Guigemar recognized him and called to him;
the squire looked at him,
recognized his lord, dismounted,
and presented the charger to him.
Guigemar went off with him; all his friends
rejoiced that they had found him again.
He was highly honored in his land,
but through it all he was sad and distracted.
His friends wanted him to take a wife,
but he refused them altogether;
he'll never have to do with a woman,
for love or money,
if she can't untie
his knotted shirt without tearing it.
The news traveled throughout Brittany;
all the women and girls
came to try their luck,
but none could untie the knot.

Now I want to tell you about the lady
whom Guigemar loved so dearly.
On the advice of one of his barons,
her husband had her imprisoned
in a dark marble tower.
There she passed bad days, worse nights.
No one in the world could describe
the pain, the suffering,
the anguish and the grief,
that she endured in that tower.
She remained there two years and more, I believe,
without ever having a moment of pleasure.
Often, she mourned for her lover:
"Guigemar, my lord, why did I ever lay eyes on you?
I'd rather die quickly
than suffer this lingering torture.
My love, if I could escape,
I'd go to where you put out to sea
and drown myself." Then she got up;
in astonishment she went to the door

and found it unlocked;
by good fortune, she got outside—
no one bothered her.
She came to the harbor, and found the boat.
It was tied to the rock
where she had intended to drown herself.
When she saw it there, she went aboard;
she could think of only one thing—
that this was where her lover had perished.
Suddenly, she couldn't stand up.
If she could have gotten back up on deck,
she would have thrown herself overboard,
so great was her suffering.
The boat set out, taking her with it.
It came to port in Brittany,
beneath a strong, well-built castle.
The lord of the castle
was named Meriaduc.
He was fighting a war with a neighbor,
and had risen early that morning
because he wanted to dispatch his troops
to attack his enemy.
Standing at a window,
he saw the ship arrive.
He went downstairs
and called his chamberlain;
quickly they went to the ship,
climbed up its ladder;
inside they found the woman
who had a fairylike beauty.
He took her by the cloak
and brought her with him to his castle.
He was delighted with his discovery,
for she was incredibly beautiful;
whoever had put her on the boat,
he could tell she came from high lineage.
He felt for her a love
as great as he'd ever had for a woman.

He had a young sister,
a beautiful maiden, in his care;
he commended the lady to her attention.
So she was waited on and made much of;

the damsel dressed her richly.
But she remained constantly sad and preoccupied.

The lord often came to speak with her,
since he wanted to love her with all his heart.
He pleaded for her love; she didn't want it,
instead she showed him her belt:
she would never love any man
except the one who could open the belt
without breaking it. When he heard that,
Meriaduc replied angrily,
"There's another one like you in this land,
a very worthy knight,
who avoids, in a similar manner, taking a wife
by means of a shirt
the right tail of which is knotted;
it can't be untied
except by using scissors or a knife.
I think you must have made that knot!"

When the lady heard this, she sighed,
and almost fainted.
He took her in his arms,
cut the laces of her tunic,
and tried to open the belt.
But he didn't succeed.
There wasn't a knight in the region
whom he didn't summon to try his luck.

Things went on like this for quite a while,
up to the time of a tournament
that Meriaduc had proclaimed
against the lord he was fighting.
He sent for knights and enlisted them in his service,
knowing very well that Guigemar would come.
He asked him as a special favor,
as his friend and companion,
not to let him down in this hour of need,
but to come help him.
So Guigemar set out, richly supplied,
leading more than one hundred knights.
Meriaduc entertained him
as an honored guest in his stronghold.

He then sent two knights to his sister,
and commanded her
to prepare herself and come to him,
bringing with her the woman he so much loved.
The girl obeyed his order.
Lavishly outfitted,
they came hand in hand into the great hall.
The lady was pale and upset;
she heard Guigemar's name
and couldn't stand up.
If the damsel hadn't supported her,
she'd have fallen to the ground.
Guigemar arose when the women entered;
he looked at the lady and noticed
her appearance and behavior;
involuntarily, he shrank back a bit.
"Is this," he said, "my dear love,
my hope, my heart, and my life—
my beautiful lady who loved me?
Where did she come from? Who brought her here?
Now, that was a foolish thought!
I know it can't be she;
women often look alike—
I got all excited for no reason.
But because she looks like the one
for whom my heart aches and sighs,
I'll gladly speak to her."
Then the knight came forward,
kissed her and sat her down beside him;
he didn't say another word,
except that he asked her to sit down.
Meriaduc looked at them closely,
upset by the sight of them together.
He called Guigemar cheerfully:
"My lord," he said, "please
let this girl try
to untie your shirt,
to see if she can manage to do it."
Guigemar answered, "Certainly."

He summoned a chamberlain
who was in charge of the shirt
and commanded him to bring it.

It was given to the girl,
but she couldn't untie it at all.
The lady knew the knot very well;
her heart is greatly agitated,
for she would love to try to untie it,
if she dared and could.
Meriaduc saw this clearly;
he was as sorry as he could be.
"My lady," he said, "now try
to untie it, if you can."
When she heard his order,
she took the shirttail
and easily untied the knot.
Guigemar was thunderstruck;
he knew her very well, and yet
he couldn't bring himself to believe firmly it was she.
So he spoke to her in this way:
"Beloved, sweet creature,
is that you? Tell me truly!
Let me see your body,
and the belt I put on you."
He put his hands on her hips,
and found the belt.
"My beautiful one," he said, "what a lucky adventure
that I've found you like this!
Who brought you here?
She told him about the grief,
the great pains, the monotony
of the prison where she was held captive,
and everything that had happened to her—
how she escaped,
how she wished to drown, but found the ship instead,
and how she entered it and was brought to this port;
and how the lord of the castle kept her in custody,
guarding her in luxury
but constantly asking for her love.
Now her joy has returned:
"My love, take back your beloved!"

Guigemar got up.
"My lords," he said, "listen to me!
Here I have the mistress
I thought I had lost forever.

Now I ask and implore Meriaduc
to give her back to me out of kindness.
I will become his vassal,
serve him two or three years,
with one hundred knights, or more!"
Meriaduc answered,
"Guigemar," he said, "my handsome friend,
I'm not so harried
or so afflicted by any war
that you can bargain with me about this.
I found this woman and I propose to take care of her
and defend her against you."
When Guigemar heard that, he quickly
commanded his men to mount.
He galloped away, defying Meriaduc.[11]
It upset him to leave his beloved behind.
Guigemar took with him
every knight who had come
to the town for the tournament.
Each declared his loyalty to Guigemar;
they'll accompany him wherever he goes.
Whoever fails him now will truly be dishonored!
That night they came to the castle
of Meriaduc's opponent.
The lord of the castle put them up;
he was joyful and delighted
that Guigemar came over to his side, bringing help with him.
Now he's sure the war's as good as over.

The next morning they arose,
and equipped themselves at their lodgings.
They departed from the village, noisily;
Guigemar came first, leading them.
Arriving at Meriaduc's castle, they assaulted it;
but it was very strong and they failed to take it.
Guigemar besieged the town;
he won't leave until it has fallen.
His friends and other troops increased so greatly
that he was able to starve everyone inside.

11. The *defi* was a formal gesture, renouncing feudal bonds of alliance or dependency and making it possible for one knight to attack another (or a vassal his former lord) without incurring charges of treason.

He captured and destroyed the castle,
killed its lord.
Guigemar led away his mistress with great rejoicing;
all his pain was now at an end.

From this story that you have heard
the *lai* of Guigemar was composed,
which is now recited to the harp and rote;
the music is a pleasure to hear.

EQUITAN

Most noble barons
were those Bretons of Brittany.
In the old days they were accustomed, out of bravery,
courtliness, and nobility,
to create *lais* from the adventures they heard,
adventures that had befallen all sorts of people;
they did this as a memorial,
so that men should not forget them.
They made one that I heard—
it should never he forgotten—
about Equitan, a most courtly man,
the lord of Nauns, a magistrate and king.[12]
Equitan was a man of great worth,
dearly loved in his own land.
He loved sport and lovemaking;
and so he kept a body of knights in his service.
Whoever indulges in love without sense or moderation
recklessly endangers his life;
such is the nature of love
that no one involved with it can keep his head.[13]
Equitan had a seneschal,

---

12. The meaning and location of Nauns are subjects of scholarly dispute. Conjectures range from Nantes, in Brittany, to the kingdom of the dwarfs *(nains)*. Equitan's name may, as Mickel suggests, contain a play on the Latin word for horse *(equus)*, appropriate for a huntsman. Cf. further the endnote to *Milun* (note 3).

13. There is a play in the text on two meanings of *mesure*, rendered "moderation" in 1.17 and "nature" in 1.19.

a good knight, brave and loyal,
who took care of his land for him,
governed and administered it.
Unless the king was making war,
he would never, no matter what the emergency,
neglect his hunting,
his hawking, or his other amusements.

This seneschal took a wife
through whom great harm later came to the land.
She was a beautiful woman
of fine breeding,
with an attractive form and figure.
Nature took pains in putting her together:
bright eyes in a lovely face,
a pretty mouth and a well-shaped nose.
She hadn't an equal in the entire kingdom:
The king often heard her praised.
He frequently sent his greetings to her,
presents as well;   *king*
without having seen her, he wanted her,
so he spoke to her as soon as he could.

For his private amusement
he went hunting in the countryside,
where the seneschal dwelt;
in the castle, where the lady also lived,
the king took lodging for the night
after he had finished the day's sport.
He now had a good chance to speak to the wife,
to reveal to her his worth, his desires.
He found her refined and clever,
with a beautiful body and face,
and a pleasing, cheerful demeanor.
Love drafted him into his service:
he shot an arrow at the king
that opened a great wound in the heart,
where Love had aimed and fixed it.
Neither good sense nor understanding were of use to the king now;
love for the woman so overcame him
that he became sad and depressed.
Now he has to give in to love completely;
he can't defend himself at all.

That night he can't sleep or even rest,
instead he blames and scolds himself:
"Alas," he says, "what destiny
led me to these parts?
Because I have seen this woman
pain has struck at my heart,
my whole body shivers.
I think 1 have no choice but to love her—
yet if I love her, I'm doing wrong;
she's the wife of my seneschal.
I owe him the same faith and love
that I want him to give me.
If, by some means, he found out about this
I know how much it would upset him.
Still, it would be a lot worse
if I went mad out of concern for him.
It would be a shame for such a beautiful woman
not to have a lover!
What would become of her finer qualities
if she didn't nourish them by a secret love?[14]
There isn't a man in the world
who wouldn't be vastly improved if she loved him.
And if the seneschal should hear of the affair,
he oughtn't be too crushed by it;
he certainly can't hold her all by himself,
and I'm happy to share the burden with him!"
When he had said all that, he sighed,
and lay in bed thinking.
After a while, he spoke again:"Why
am I so distressed and frightened?
I still don't even know
if she will take me as her lover;
but I'll know soon!
If she should feel the way I do,
I'd soon be free of this agony.
God! It's still so long till morning!
I can't get any rest,
it's been forever since I went to bed."
The king stayed awake until daybreak;

making himself believe it isn't to bad of an act

can't sleep out of excitement

---

14. The French text refers to *druerie*, extramarital passion that would, of course, be kept secret from the husband.

he could hardly wait for it.
He rose and went hunting,
but he soon turned back
saying that he was worn out.
He returns to his room and lies down.
The seneschal is saddened by this;
he doesn't know what's bothering the king,
what's making him shiver;
in fact, his wife is the reason for it.

The king, to get some relief and some pleasure,
sends for the wife to come speak with him.
He revealed his desire to her,
letting her know that he was dying because of her;
that it lay in her power to comfort him
or to let him die.
"My lord," the woman said to him,
"I must have some time to think;
this is so new to me,
I have no idea what to say.
You're a king of high nobility,
and I'm not at all of such fortune
that you should single me out
to have a love affair with.
If you get what you want from me,
I have no doubt about it:
you'll soon get tired of me,
and I'll be far worse off than before.
If I should love you
and satisfy your desire,
love wouldn't be shared equally
between the two of us.
Because you're a powerful king
and my husband is your vassal,
I'm sure you believe
your rank entitles you to my love.
Love is worthless if it's not mutual.
A poor but loyal man is worth more—
if he also possesses good sense and virtue—
and his love brings greater joy
than the love of a prince or a king
who has no loyalty in him.
Anyone who aims higher in love

than his own wealth entitles him to
will be frightened by every little thing that occurs.
The rich man, however, is confident
that no one will steal a mistress away
whose favor he obtains by his authority over her."

Equitan answered her,
"Please, my lady! Don't say such things!
No one could consider himself noble
(rather, he'd be haggling like a tradesman)
who, for the sake of wealth or a big fief,
would take pains to win someone of low repute.
There's no woman in the world—if she's smart,
refined, and of noble character,
and if she places a high enough value on her love
that she isn't inconstant—
whom a rich prince in his palace
wouldn't yearn for
and love well and truly,
even if she'd nothing but the shirt on her back.
Whoever is inconstant in love
and gives himself up to treachery
is mocked and deceived in the end;
I've seen it happen many times like that.
It's no surprise when someone loses out
who deserves to because of his behavior.
My dear lady, I'm offering myself to you!
Don't think of me as your king,
but as your vassal and your lover.
I tell you, I promise you
I'll do whatever you want.
Don't let me die on your account!
You be the lord and I'll be the servant[15]—
you be the proud one and I'll be the beggar!"

The king pleaded with her,
begged her so often for mercy,
that she promised him her love
and granted him possession of her body.
Then they exchanged rings,

---

15. The French text has *dame* and *servant*.

and promised themselves to each other.
They kept their promises and loved each other well;
they died for this in the end.

Foreshadowing

Their affair lasted a long time,
without anyone hearing of it.
At the times set for their meetings,
when they were to speak together at the king's palace,
the king informed his followers
that he wanted to be bled privately.
The doors of his chamber were closed,
and no one was so daring,
if the king didn't summon him,
that he would ever enter there.
Meanwhile, the seneschal held court
and heard pleas and complaints.
The king loved the seneschal's wife for a long time,
had no desire for any other woman;
he didn't want to marry,
and never allowed the subject to be raised.
His people held this against him,
and the seneschal's wife
heard about it often; this worried her,
and she was afraid she would lose him.
So when she next had the chance to speak to him—
when she should have been full of joy,
kissing and embracing him
and having a good time with him—
she burst into tears, making a big scene.
The king asked
what the matter was,
and the lady answered,
"My lord, I'm crying because of our love,
which has brought me to great sorrow:
you're going to take a wife, some king's daughter,
and you will get rid of me;
I've heard all about it, I know it's true.
And—alas!—what will become of me?
On your account I must now face death,
for I have no other comfort than you."
The king spoke lovingly to her:
"Dear love, don't be afraid!
I promise I'll never take a wife,

will not marry

270

never leave you for another.
Believe me, this is the truth:
If your husband were dead,
I'd make you my lady and my queen;
no one could stop me."
The lady thanked him,
said she was very grateful to him;
if he would assure her
that he wouldn't leave her for someone else,
she would quickly undertake
to do away with her lord.
It would be easy to arrange
if he were willing to help her.
He agreed to do so;
there was nothing she could demand of him
that he wouldn't do, if he possibly could,
whether it turned out well or badly.
"My lord," she says, "please
come hunting in the forest,
out in the country where I live.
Stay awhile at my husband's castle;
you can be bled there,
and on the third day after that, take a bath.[16]
My lord will be bled with you
and will bathe with you as well;
make it clear to him—and don't relent—,
that he must keep you company!
I'll have the baths heated
and the two tubs brought in;
his will be so boiling hot
that no man on earth
could escape being horribly scalded
as soon as he sat down in it.
When he's scalded to death,
send for his men and yours;
then you can show them exactly how
he suddenly died in his bath."
The king promised her
that he'd do just as she wished.

going to kill

plan to kill

16. Baths were taken much less frequently in the Middle Ages than now and would normally be planned in advance.

Less than three months later,
the king went out into the countryside to hunt.
He had himself bled to ward off illness,
and his seneschal bled with him.
On the third day, he said he wanted to bathe;
the seneschal was happy to comply.
"Bathe with me," said the king,
and the seneschal replied, "Willingly."
The wife had the baths heated,
the two tubs brought;
next to the bed, according to plan,
she had them both set down.
Then she had boiling water brought
for the seneschal's tub.
The good man got up
and went outside to relax for a moment.
His wife came to speak to the king
and he pulled her down beside him;
they lay down on her husband's bed
and began to enjoy themselves.
They lay there together.
Because the tub was right before them,
they set a guard at the bedroom door;
a maidservant was to keep watch there.
Suddenly the seneschal returned,
and knocked on the door; the girl held it closed.
He struck it so violently
that he forced it open.
There he discovered the king and his own wife
lying in each other's arms.
The king looked up and saw him coming;
to hide his villainy
he jumped into the tub feet first,
stark naked.
He didn't stop to think what he was doing.
And there he was scalded to death,
caught in his own evil trap,
while the seneschal remained safe and sound.
The seneschal could see very well
what had happened to the king.
He grabbed his wife at once
and thrust her head first into the tub.

king dies after being caught

she dies as well

Thus both died,
the king first, the wife after him.
Whoever wants to hear some sound advice
can profit from this example:
he who plans evil for another
may have that evil rebound back on him.

It all happened just as I've told you.
The Bretons made a *lai* about it,
about Equitan, his fate,
and the woman who loved him so much.

LE FRESNE (THE ASH TREE)

I shall tell you the *lai* of Le Fresne
according to the story as I know it.
In olden days there lived in Brittany
two knights who were neighbors;
both were rich men,
brave and worthy knights.
They lived close by, within the same region;
each was married.
Now one of the wives became pregnant;
when her time came
she gave birth to twins.
Her husband was absolutely delighted;
in his joy at the event
he sent word to his good neighbor
that his wife had had two sons—
he had that many more children now.
He would send one to him to raise,
and name the child after him.
The rich neighbor was sitting down to eat
when the messenger arrived;
he knelt before the high table
to announce his news.
The lord thanked God for it
and rewarded him with a fine horse.
The knight's wife laughed
(she was seated next to him at dinner)
because she was deceitful and proud,

evil-tongued and envious.
She spoke very foolishly,
saying, for all her household to hear,
"So help me God, I can't imagine
where this worthy man got such advice
to announce to my lord,
to his own shame and dishonor,
that his wife has had twin sons.
Both he and she are disgraced by this;
we know the truth of the matter all too well:
it never was and never will be
possible for such a thing to happen[17]—
that a woman could have
two sons in one birth—
unless two men had lain with her."
Her lord stared fiercely at her,
reproached her bitterly for what she said.
"Wife," he said, "stop that!
You mustn't talk that way!
The fact is that she's a woman
who's always had a good reputation."
But the people in the household
repeated the wife's words;
the matter was widely spoken of
and became known throughout Brittany.
The slanderous wife was hated for it,
and later made to suffer for it.
Every woman who heard about it,
rich or poor, hated her.
The messenger who had brought the news
went home and told his lord everything.
When he heard the messenger's report,
he became so sad he didn't know what to do.
He hated his worthy wife because of it,
strongly suspected her,
and kept her under strict guard,
even though she didn't deserve it.

The wife who had spoken so evilly

---

17. Marie uses the word *aventure* here and throughout the *lai* to refer to unexpected circumstances of the kind that test the endurance and moral worth of human beings, and bring them to happiness if they deserve it.

became pregnant herself that same year,
and was carrying twins—
now her neighbor has her vengeance.
She carried them until her time came;
then she gave birth to two daughters; she was extremely upset,
and terribly sad about the situation.
She lamented bitterly to herself:
"Alas!" she said, "what shall I do?
I'll never get any honor out of this!
I'm in disgrace, that's certain.
My lord and all his kin
will never believe me
when they hear about this bad luck;[18]
indeed, l condemned myself
when I slandered all womankind.
Didn't I say it never happened—
at least, we've never seen it happen—
that a woman could have twins
unless she had lain with two men?
Now that I have twins, it seems to me
my words have come back to haunt me.
Whoever slanders another
never knows when it will rebound on him;
he may speak badly about someone
who's more deserving of praise than he.
Now, to keep from being disgraced,
I'll have to kill one of my children!
I'd rather make that up to God
than live in shame and dishonor."
Those of her household who were in the bedchamber with her
comforted her and said
they wouldn't allow her to do it;
killing somebody was no joke.

The lady had an attendant
who was of noble birth;
the lady had raised and taken care of her
and was very attached to her.
This girl heard her mistress crying,
bemoaning her situation;

---

18. The French text has *aventure.*

it bothered her terribly.
She came and comforted her:
"My lady," she said, "it's not worth carrying on so.
Stop grieving—that's the thing to do.
Give me one of the babies;
I'll take care of her for you,
so that you won't be disgraced;
you'll never see the child again.
I'll abandon her at a convent,
to which I'll carry her safe and sound.
Some good person will find her,
and, God willing, he'll raise her."
The lady heard what she said;
she was delighted with the idea, and promised her
that if she did her this service
she'd be well rewarded for it.

They wrapped the noble child
in a linen garment,
and then in an embroidered silk robe,
which the lady's husband had brought back to her
from Constantipole, where he had been.
They had never seen anything so fine.
With a piece of ribbon
she tied a large ring onto the child's arm;
it contained a full ounce of pure gold,
and had a ruby set in it,
with lettering around the rim of the setting.
Wherever the little girl might be found,
everyone would know beyond doubt
that she came from a noble family.

The damsel took the baby
and left the chamber with her.
That night, after dark,
she left the town
and took the highroad
that led into the forest.
She went right through the woods
with the baby, and out the other side,
without ever leaving the road.
Then, far off to the right, she heard
dogs barking and cocks crowing;

she knew she would be able to find a town over there.
Quickly, she went in the direction
of the barking.
Soon she came
to a fine, prosperous town.

There was an abbey there,
a thriving, well-endowed one;
I believe it held a community of nuns
supervised by an abbess.
The damsel saw
the towers, walls, and steeple of the abbey,
and she hastened toward it,
stopping at the front gate.
She put down the child she was carrying
and knelt humbly
to say a prayer.
"O God," she prayed, "by your holy name,
if it is your will,
protect this infant from death."
When she'd finished praying,
she looked behind her,
saw a broad-limbed ash tree,
its branches thick with leaves;
its trunk divided into four boughs.
It had been planted as a shade tree.
The girl took the baby in her arms
and ran over to the ash tree,
placed the child up in its branches and left her there,
commending her to the true God.
Then the girl returned to her mistress
and told her what she'd done.
There was a porter in the abbey,
whose job it was to open the abbey gate,
to let in the people who had come
to hear the early service.
That morning he rose as early as usual,
lit the candles and the lamps,
rang the bells and opened the gate.
He noticed the clothes up in the ash tree,
and thought that someone must have stolen them,
and then left them there.
He didn't notice anything else.

As quickly as he could, he went over to the tree,
touched the clothes, and found the child there.
He gave thanks to God;
he did not leave the child, but took her with him
to his own dwelling.
He had a daughter who was a widow;
her husband was dead and she had a child,
still in the cradle, whom she was nursing.
The good man called her:
"Daughter," he said, "get up!
Light the candle, start the fire!
I've brought home a baby
that I found out there in the ash tree.
Nurse her for me,
then get her warm and bathe her."
The daughter obeyed him;
she lit the fire and took the baby,
made her warm and gave her a good bath,
then nursed her.
On the child's arm they discovered the ring,
and they saw her costly, beautiful clothes.
From these they were certain
that she was born of noble lineage.

The next day, after the service,
when the abbess came out of the chapel,
the porter went to speak to her;
he wanted to tell her how, by chance,
he had found the child.
The abbess ordered him
to bring the child to her
just as she was found.
The porter went home,
willingly brought the child back,
and showed her to the abbess.
She examined the baby closely
and said she would raise her,
would treat her as her niece.
She strictly forbade the porter
to tell the truth about the child's discovery.
She raised the child herself,
and because she had been found in the ash tree
the abbess decided to name her "Fresne" [Ash].

And so people called her.

The abbess did indeed treat her as a niece,
and for a long time she grew up in privacy;
she was raised
entirely within the walls of the abbey.
When she reached the age
where nature creates beauty,
in all of Brittany there wasn't such a beautiful
or so refined a girl;
she was noble and cultivated
in appearance and speech.
Everyone who saw her loved her,
praised her to the skies.
Now at Dole there lived a good lord—
there's never been a better, before or since—
whose name I'll tell you here:
they called him Gurun in that region.
He heard about the young girl
and he fell in love with her.
He went to a tournament,
and on his way back passed the abbey,
where he stopped to ask after the damsel.
The abbess introduced her to him.
He saw that she was beautiful and cultivated,
wise, refined, and well educated.
If he couldn't win her love
he'd consider himself very badly off indeed.
But he was at a loss about how to proceed;
if he came there often,
the abbess would notice what was going on,
and he'd never lay eyes on the damsel again.-
He hit upon a scheme:
he would become a benefactor of the abbey,
give it so much of his land
that it would be enriched forever;
he'd thus establish a patron's right to live there,
so that he could come and stay whenever he chose.
To be a member of that community
he gave generously of his goods—
but he had a motive
other than receiving pardon for his sins.

He came there often
and spoke to the girl;
he pleaded so well, promised so much
that she granted him what he desired.
When he was sure of her love,
he spoke seriously with her one day.
"Beautiful one," he said, "now that
you've made me your lover,
come away from here and live with me.
I'm sure you know
that if your aunt found out about us
she'd be upset,
especially if you became pregnant right under her roof.
In fact, she'd be furious.
If you'll take my advice,
you'll come away with me.
I'll never let you down—
and I'll take good care of you."
Since she loved him deeply,
she willingly granted what he desired.
She went away with him;
he took her to his castle.
She brought her silk swaddling cloth and her ring with her;
that could turn out to be very fortunate for her.
The abbess had given them to her
and told her the circumstances
in which she had been sent to her:
she was nestled up in the ash tree,
and whoever had abandoned her there
had bestowed on her the garments and the ring.
The abbess had received no other possessions with her;
she had raised her as her niece.
The girl kept the tokens,[19]
locked them in a chest.
She took the chest away with her;
she'd no intention of leaving it behind.

The knight who took her away
loved and cherished her greatly,
and so did all his men and servants.

---

19. The translation follows Rychner's emendation of *l'esgardat* to *les gardat*.

There wasn't one, big or little,
who didn't love her for her noble character,
and honor her as well.

She lived with him for a long time,
until the knight's vassals
reproached him for it.
They often urged him
to marry a noble woman,
and to get rid of this mistress of his.
They'd be pleased if he had an heir
who could succeed to
his land and inheritance;
it would be much to their disadvantage
if he was deterred by his concubine
from having a child born in wedlock.
They would no longer consider him their lord
or willingly serve him
if he didn't do what they wanted.
The knight agreed
to take a wife according to their wishes,
so they began to look about for one.
"My lord," they said, "quite near by
lives a worthy man of your rank;
he has a daughter who is his heiress.
You'll get much land if you take her.
The girl's name is Codre [Hazel];
there isn't one so pretty in this region.
In exchange for the ash, when you get rid of her,
you'll have the hazel.
The hazel tree bears nuts and thus gives pleasure;
the ash bears no fruit.
Let us make the arrangements for the daughter;
God willing, we will get her for you."

They arranged the marriage,
obtained everyone's promise.
Alas! what a misfortune
that these good men didn't know
the real story about these girls[20]—

they were twin sisters!
Fresne was hidden away,
and her lover was to marry the other.
When she found out that he had done this,
she didn't sulk about it;
she continued to serve her lord well
and honored all his vassals.
The knights of the household,
the squires and serving boys
were all very sad on her account;
sad because they were going to lose her.

On the day of the betrothal,
her lord sent for his friends.
The archbishop of Dole,
another of his vassals, was there as well.
They all brought his fiancée to him.
Her mother came with her;
she worried about this other girl
whom the lord loved so much,
because she might try to cause trouble, if she could,
between Codre and her husband.
The mother wants her expelled from the house;
she'll tell her son-in-law
that he should marry her off to some good man;
that way he'll be rid of her, she thinks.

They held the betrothals in grand style;
there was much celebrating.
Fresne was in the private chambers.
No matter what she saw,
it didn't seem to bother her;
she didn't even seem a bit angry.
She waited on the bride-to-be
courteously and efficiently.
Everybody who saw this
thought it a great marvel.
Her mother inspected her carefully,
and began to love and admire her.
She said to herself that if she'd known
what kind of a person Fresne was,
she wouldn't have let her suffer on account of her daughter Codre,
wouldn't have taken Fresne's lord away from her.

That night, Fresne went
to make up the bed
in which the new bride was to sleep;
she took off her cloak,
and called the chamberlains to her.
She instructed them concerning the manner
in which the lord liked things done,
for she had seen it many times.
When they had prepared the bed,
they threw a coverlet over it.
The cloth was some old dress material;
the girl looked at it,
it seemed to her poor stuff;
that bothered her.
She opened a chest, took out her birth garment,
and put it on her lord's bed.
She did it to honor him;
the archbishop would be coming there
to bless the newlyweds in bed.
That was part of his duty.
When the chamber was empty,
the mother led her daughter in.
She wished to prepare her for bed,
and told her to get undressed.
She looked at the cloth on the bed;
she'd never seen such a fine one
except the one she'd given
to her infant daughter when she abandoned her.
Then she suddenly remembered the castaway;
her heart skipped a beat.
She called the chamberlain:
"Tell me," she said, "on your honor,
where was this fine silk cloth found?"
"My lady," he replied, "I'll tell you:
the girl brought it,
and threw it over the coverlet
because the coverlet didn't seem good enough to her.
I think the silk cloth is hers."
The mother now called Fresne,
and Fresne came to her;
she removed her cloak,
and the lady began questioning her:

"My dear, don't hide anything from me!
Where did you find this beautiful cloth?
How did you come by it? Who gave it to you?
Tell me at once where it came from!"
The girl answered her,
"My lady, my aunt, who raised me—
she is an abbess—gave it to me
and ordered me to take good care of it;
whoever sent me to be raised by her
had given me this, and also a ring."
"Fair one, may I see the ring?"
"Yes, my lady, I'll be happy to show you."
Then Fresne brought her the ring;
she examined it carefully.
She recognized it very well,
and the silk cloth too.
No doubt about it, now she knew—
this was her own daughter.
She didn't hide it, but cried out for all to hear,
"My dear, you are my daughter!"
Out of pity for Fresne
she fell over in a faint.
When she regained consciousness,
she quickly sent for her husband,
and he came, all in a fright.
When he entered the bedroom,
his wife threw herself at his feet,
hugged and kissed him,
asked his forgiveness for her crime.
He didn't know what this was all about;[21]
"Wife," he said, "what are you talking about?
There's been nothing but good between us.
I'll pardon you as much as you please!
Tell me what's bothering you."
"My lord, since you've forgiven me,
I'll tell you—listen!
Once, in my great wickedness,
I spoke foolishly about my neighbor,
slandering her because she had twins.
I was really wronging myself.

284

The truth is, I then became pregnant
and had twin daughters; so I hid one,
had her abandoned in front of an abbey,
wrapped in our brocaded silk cloth,
wearing the ring that you gave me
When you first courted me.
I can't hide this from you:
I've found the ring and the cloth,
and also discovered our daughter,
whom I lost through my folly;
and this is she, right here,
the brave, wise, and beautiful girl
loved by the knight
who has married her sister."
Her husband said, "I'm delighted by this news;
I was never so pleased.
Since we've found our daughter,
God has given us great joy,
instead of doubling the sin.
My daughter," he said, "come here!"
The girl was overjoyed
by the story she'd heard.[22]
Her father won't wait any longer;
he goes to get his son-in-law,
and brings in the archbishop too—
he tells him the adventure.
When the knight heard the story
he was happier than he'd ever been.
The archbishop advised
that things should be left as they were that night;
in the morning he would separate
the knight from the woman he had married.
They agreed to this plan.
Next morning, the marriage was annulled
and the knight married his beloved;
she was given to him by her father,
who was well disposed toward her;
he divided his inheritance with her.
The father and his wife remained at the festivities,
for as long as they lasted, with their daughter.

When they returned to their land,
they took their daughter Codre with them;
later, in their country, she made a rich marriage too.
When this adventure became known
just as it happened,
the *lai* of Fresne was made from it.
It was named after its heroine.

BISCLAVRET (THE WEREWOLF)

Since I am undertaking to compose *lais,*
I don't want to forget Bisclavret;
In Breton, the *lai*'s name is *Bisclavret*—
the Normans call it *Garwaf [The Werewolf].*
In the old days, people used to say—
and it often actually happened—
that some men turned into werewolves
and lived in the woods.
A werewolf is a savage beast;
while his fury is on him
he eats men, does much harm,
goes deep in the forest to live.
But that's enough of this for now:
I want to tell you about the Bisclavret

In Brittany there lived a nobleman
whom I've heard marvelously praised;
a fine, handsome knight
who behaved nobly.
He was close to his lord,
and loved by all his neighbors.
He had an estimable wife,
one of lovely appearance;
he loved her and she him,
but one thing was very vexing to her:
during the week he would be missing
for three whole days, and she didn't know
what happened to him or where he went.
Nor did any of his men know anything about it.

One day he returned home
happy and delighted;
she asked him about it.
"My lord," she said, "and dear love,
I'd very much like to ask you one thing—
if I dared;
but I'm so afraid of your anger
that nothing frightens me more."
When he heard that, he embraced her,
drew her to him and kissed her.
"My lady," he said, "go ahead and ask!
There's nothing you could want to know,
that, if I knew the answer, I wouldn't tell you."
"By God," she replied, "now I'm cured!
My lord, on the days when you go away from me
I'm in such a state—
so sad at heart,
so afraid I'll lose you—
that if I don't get quick relief
I could die of this very soon.
Please, tell me where you go,
where you have been staying.
I think you must have a lover,
and if that's so, you're doing wrong."
"My dear," he said, "have mercy on me, for God's sake!
Harm will come to me if I tell you about this,
because I'd lose your love
and even my very self."
When the lady heard this
she didn't take it lightly;
she kept asking him,
coaxed and flattered him so much,
that he finally told her what happened to him—
he hid nothing from her.
"My dear, I become a werewolf:
I go off into the great forest,
in the thickest part of the woods,
and I live on the prey I hunt down."
When he had told her everything,
she asked further
whether he undressed or kept his clothes on [when he became a werewolf].
"Wife," he replied, "I go stark naked."
"Tell me, then, for God's sake, where your clothes are."
"That I won't tell you;

for if I were to lose them,
and then be discovered,
I'd stay a werewolf forever.
I'd be helpless
until I got them back.
That's why I don't want their hiding place to be known."
"My lord," the lady answered,
"I love you more than all the world;
"you mustn't hide anything from me
or fear me in any way:
that doesn't seem like love to me.
What wrong have I done? For what sin of mine
do you mistrust me about anything?
Do the right thing and tell me!"
She harassed and bedeviled him so,
that he had no choice but to tell her.
"Lady," he said, "near the woods,
beside the road that I use to get there,
there's an old chapel
that has often done me good service;
under a bush there is a big stone,
hollowed out inside;
I hide my clothes right there
until I'm ready to come home."

The lady heard this wonder
and turned scarlet from fear;
she was terrified of the whole adventure.
Over and over she considered
how she might get rid of him;
she never wanted to sleep with him again.
There was a knight of that region
who had loved her for a long time,
who begged for her love,
and dedicated himself to serving her.
She'd never loved him at all,
now pledged her love to him,
but now she sent a messenger for him,
and told him her intention.
"My dear," she said, "cheer up!
I shall now grant you without delay
what you have suffered for;
you'll meet with no more refusals—

288

I offer you my love and my body;
make me your mistress!"

He thanked her graciously
and accepted her promise,
and she bound him to her by an oath.
Then she told him
how her husband went away and what happened to him;
she also taught him the precise path
her husband took into the forest,
and then she sent the knight to get her husband's clothes.
So Bisclavret was betrayed,[23]
ruined by his own wife.
Since people knew he was often away from home
they all thought
this time he'd gone away forever.
They searched for him and made inquiries
but could never find him,
so they had to let matters stand.
The wife later married the other knight,
who had loved her for so long.
A whole year passed
until one day the king went hunting;
he headed right for the forest
where Bisclavret was.
When the hounds were unleashed,
they ran across Bisclavret;
the hunters and the dogs
chased him all day,
until they were just about to take him
and tear him apart,
at which point he saw the king
and ran to him, pleading for mercy.
He took hold of the king's stirrup,
kissed his leg and his foot.
The king saw this and was terrified;
he called his companions.
"My lords," he said, "come quickly!"
Look at this marvel—
this beast is humbling itself to me.

23. Hereafter Bisclavret will be treated as a proper name, and the definite article omitted.

It has the mind of a man, and it's begging me for mercy!
Chase the dogs away,
and make sure no one strikes it.
This beast is rational—he has a mind.
Hurry up: let's get out of here.
I'll extend my peace to the creature;
indeed, I'll hunt no more today!"
Thereupon the king turned away.
Bisclavret followed him;
he stayed close to the king, and wouldn't go away;
he'd no intention of leaving him.

The king led him to his castle;
he was delighted with this turn of events,
for he'd never seen anything like it.
He considered the beast a great wonder
and held him very dear.
He commanded all his followers,
for the sake of their love for him, to guard Bisclavret well,
and under no circumstances to do him harm;
none of them should strike him;
he should be well fed and watered.
They willingly guarded the creature;
every day he went to sleep
among the knights, near the king.
Everyone was fond of him;
he was so noble and well behaved
that he never wished to do anything wrong.
Regardless of where the king might go,
Bisclavret never wanted to be separated from him;
he always accompanied the king.
The king became very much aware that the creature loved him.
Now listen to what happened next.
The king held a court;
to help him celebrate his feast
and to serve him as handsomely as possible,
he summoned all the barons
who held fiefs from him.
Among the knights who went,
and all dressed up in his best attire,
was the one who had married Bisclavret's wife.
He neither knew nor suspected
that he would find Bisclavret so close by.

As soon as he came to the palace
Bisclavret saw him,
ran toward him at full speed,
sank his teeth into him, and started to drag him down.
He would have done him great damage
if the king hadn't called him off,
and threatened him with a stick.
Twice that day he tried to bite the knight.
Everyone was extremely surprised,
since the beast had never acted that way
toward any other man he had seen.
All over the palace people said
that he wouldn't act that way without a reason:
that somehow or other, the knight had mistreated Bisclavret,
and now he wanted his revenge.
And so the matter rested
until the feast was over
and until the barons took their leave of the king
and started home.
The very first to leave,
to the best of my knowledge,
was the knight whom Bisclavret had attacked.
It's no wonder the creature hated him.

Not long afterward,
as the story leads me to believe,
the king, who was so wise and noble,
went back to the forest
where he had found Bisclavret,
and the creature went with him.
That night, when he finished hunting,
he sought lodging out in the countryside.
The wife of Bisclavret heard about it,
dressed herself elegantly,
and went the next day to speak with the king,
bringing rich presents for him.
When Bisclavret saw her coming,
no one could hold him back;
he ran toward her in a rage.
Now listen to how well he avenged himself!
He tore the nose off her face.
What worse thing could he have done to her?
Now men closed in on him from all sides;

they were about to tear him apart,
when a wise man said to the king,
"My lord, listen to me!
This beast has stayed with you,
and there's not one of us
who hasn't watched him closely,
hasn't traveled with him often.
He's never touched anyone,
or shown any wickedness,
except to this woman.
By the faith that I owe you,
he has some grudge against her,
and against her husband as well.
This is the wife of the knight
whom you used to like so much,
and who's been missing for so long—
we don't know what became of him.
Why not put this woman to torture
and see if she'll tell you
why the beast hates her?
Make her tell what she knows!
We've seen many strange things
happen in Brittany!"

The king took his advice;
he detained the knight.
At the same time he took the wife
and subjected her to torture;
out of fear and pain
she told all about her husband:
how she had betrayed him
and taken away his clothes;
the story he had told her
about what happened to him and where he went;
and how after she had taken his clothes
he'd never been seen in his land again.
She was quite certain
that this beast was Bisclavret.
The king demanded the clothes;
whether she wanted to or not
she sent home for them,
and had them brought to Bisclavret.
When they were put down in front of him

292

he didn't even seem to notice them;
the king's wise man—
the one who had advised him earlier—
said to him, "My lord, you're not doing it right.
This beast wouldn't, under any circumstances,
in order to get rid of his animal form,
put on his clothes in front of you;
you don't understand what this means:
he's just too ashamed to do it here.
Have him led to your chambers
and bring the clothes with him;
then we'll leave him alone for a while.
If he turns into a man, we'll know about it."

The king himself led the way
and closed all the doors on him.
After a while he went back,
taking two barons with him;
all three entered the king's chamber.
On the king's royal bed
they found the knight asleep.
The king ran to embrace him.
He hugged and kissed him again and again.
As soon as he had the chance,
the king gave him back all his lands;
he gave him more than I can tell.
He banished the wife,
chased her out of the country.
She went into exile with the knight
with whom she had betrayed her lord.
She had several children
who were widely known
for their appearance:
several women of the family
were actually born without noses,
and lived out their lives noseless.

The adventure that you have heard
really happened, no doubt about it.
The *lai* of Bisclavret was made
so it would be remembered forever.

LANVAL

I shall tell you the adventure of another *lai*,
just as it happened:
it was composed about a very noble vassal;
in Breton, they call him Lanval.

Arthur, the brave and the courtly king,   5
was staying at Cardoel,
because the Scots and the Picts
were destroying the land.
They invaded Logres[24]
and laid it waste.   10
At Pentecost, in summer,[25]
the king stayed there.
He gave out many rich gifts:
to counts and barons,
members of the Round Table—   15
such a company had no equal[26] in all the world—
he distributed wives and lands,
to all but one who had served him.
That was Lanval; Arthur forgot him,
and none of his men favored him either.   20
For his valor, for his generosity,
his beauty and his bravery,
most men envied him;
some feigned the appearance of love
who, if something unpleasant happened to him,   25
would not have been at all disturbed.
He was the son of a king of high degree
but he was far from his heritage.
He was of the king's household
but lie had spent all his wealth,   30
for the king gave him nothing
nor did Lanval ask.
Now Lanval was in difficulty,

24. Logres is England.

25. In medieval poetry, only two seasons are usually recognized, summer and winter. The feast of Pentecost is frequently the starting point of an Arthurian adventure.

26. Equal in number as well as in worth: cf. Ewert, "There was no equal number of such knights in all the world" (p. 173).

depressed and very worried.
My lords, don't be surprised: 35
a strange man, without friends,
is very sad in another land,
when he doesn't know where to look for help.
The knight of whom I speak,
who had served the king so long,   40
one day mounted his horse
and went off to amuse himself.
He left the city
and came, all alone, to a field;
he dismounted by a running stream   45
but his horse trembled badly.
He removed the saddle and went off,
leaving the horse to roll around in the meadow.
He folded his cloak beneath his head
and lay down.   50
He worried about his difficulty,
he could see nothing that pleased him.
As he lay there
he looked down along the bank
and saw two girls approaching;   55
he had never seen any lovelier.
They were richly dressed,
tightly laced,
in tunics of dark purple;
their faces were very lovely.   60
The older one carried basins,
golden, well made, and fine;
I shall tell you the truth about it, without fail.
The other carried a towel.
They went straight   65
to where the knight was lying.
Lanval, who was very well bred,
got up to meet them.
They greeted him first
and gave him their message: 70
"Sir Lanval, my lady,
who is worthy and wise and beautiful,
sent us for you.
Come with us now.
We shall guide you there safely.   75
See, her pavilion is nearby!"

The knight went with them;
giving no thought to his horse
who was feeding before him in the meadow.
They led him up to the tent,   80
which was quite beautiful and well placed.
Queen Semiramis,
however much more wealth,
power, or knowledge she had,
or the emperor Octavian   85
could not have paid for one of the flaps.
There was a golden eagle on top of it,
whose value I could not tell,
nor could I judge the value of the cords or the poles
that held up the sides of the tent;   90
there is no king on earth who could buy it,
no matter what wealth he offered.
The girl was inside the tent:
the lily and the young rose
when they appear in the summer   95
are surpassed by her beauty.
She lay on a beautiful bed—
the bedclothes were worth a castle—
dressed only in her shift.
Her body was well shaped and elegant;   100
for the heat, she had thrown over herself,
a precious cloak of white ermine,
covered with purple alexandrine,
but her whole side was uncovered,
her face, her neck and her bosom;   105
she was whiter than the hawthorn flower.
The knight went forward
and the girl addressed him.
He sat before the bed.
"Lanval," she said, "sweet love,   110
because of you I have come from my land;
I came to seek you from far away.
If you are brave and courtly,
no emperor or count or king
will ever have known such joy or good;   115
for I love you more than anything."
He looked at her and saw that she was beautiful;
Love stung him with a spark
that burned and set fire to his heart.

He answered her in a suitable way.   120
"Lovely one," he said, "if it pleased you,
if such joy might be mine
that you would love me,
there is nothing you might command,
within my power, that I would not do,   125
whether foolish or wise.
I shall obey your command;
for you, I shall abandon everyone.
I want never to leave you.
That is what I most desire."   130
When the girl heard the words
of the man who could love her so,
she granted him her love and her body.
Now Lanval was on the right road!
Afterward, she gave him a gift: 135
he would never again want anything,
he would receive as he desired;
however generously he might give and spend,
she would provide what he needed.
Now Lanval is well cared for.   140
The more lavishly he spends,
the more gold and silver he will have.
"Love," she said, "I admonish you now,
I command and beg you,
do not let any man know about this.   145
I shall tell you why:
you would lose me for good
if this love were known;
you would never see me again
or possess my body."   150
He answered that he would do
exactly as she commanded.
He lay beside her on the bed;
now Lanval is well cared for.
He remained with her   155
that afternoon, until evening
and would have stayed longer, if he could,
and if his love had consented.
"Love," she said, "get up.
You cannot stay any longer.   160
Go away now; I shall remain
but I will tell you one thing:

when you want to talk to me
there is no place you can think of
where a man might have his mistress   165
without reproach or shame,
that I shall not be there with you
to satisfy all your desires.
No man but you will see me
or hear my words."   170
When he heard her, he was very happy,
he kissed her, and then got up.
The girls who had brought him to the tent
dressed him in rich clothes;
when he was dressed anew,   175
there wasn't a more handsome youth in all the world;
he was no fool, no boor.
They gave him water for his hands
and a towel to dry them,
and they brought him food.   180
He took supper with his love;
it was not to be refused.
He was served with great courtesy,
he received it with great joy.
There was an entremet   185
that vastly pleased the knight
for he kissed his lady often
and held her close.
When they finished dinner,
his horse was brought to him.   190
The horse had been well saddled;
Lanval was very richly served.
The knight took his leave, mounted,
and rode toward the city,
often looking behind him.   195
Lanval was very disturbed;
he wondered about his adventure
and was doubtful in his heart;
he was amazed, not knowing what to believe;
he didn't expect ever to see her again.   200
He came to his lodging
and found his men well dressed.
That night, his accommodations were rich
but no one knew where it came from.
There was no knight in the city   205

who really needed a place to stay
whom he didn't invite to join him
to be well and richly served.
Lanval gave rich gifts,
Lanval released prisoners,   210
Lanval dressed jongleurs [performers],
Lanval offered great honors.
There was no stranger or friend
to whom Lanval didn't give.
Lanval's joy and pleasure were intense;   215
in the daytime or at night,
he could see his love often;
she was completely at his command.

In that same year, it seems to me,
after the feast of St. John,   220
about thirty knights
were amusing themselves
in an orchard beneath the tower
where the queen was staying.
Gawain was with them   225
and his cousin, the handsome Yvain;
Gawain, the noble, the brave,
who was so loved by all, said:
"By God, my lords, we wronged
our companion Lanval,   230
who is so generous and courtly,
and whose father is a rich king,
when we didn't bring him with us."
They immediately turned back,
went to his lodging   235
and prevailed on Lanval to come along with them.
At a sculpted window
the queen was looking out;
she had three ladies with her.
She saw the king's retinue,   240
recognized Lanval and looked at him.
Then she told one of her ladies
to send for her maidens,
the loveliest and the most refined;
together they went to amuse themselves   245
in the orchard where the others were.
She brought thirty or more with her;

they descended the steps.
The knights came to meet them,
because they were delighted to see them. 250
The knights took them by the hand;
their conversation was in no way vulgar.
Lanval went off to one side,
far from the others; he was impatient
to hold his love, 255
to kiss and embrace and touch her;
he thought little of others' joys
if he could not have his pleasure.
When the queen saw him alone,
she went straight to the knight. 260
She sat beside him and spoke,
revealing her whole heart:
"Lanval, I have shown you much honor,
I have cherished you, and loved you.
You may have all my love; 265
just tell me your desire.
I promise you my affection.
You should be very happy with me."
"My lady," he said, "let me be!
I have no desire to love you. 270
I've served the king a long time;
I don't want to betray my faith to him.
Never, for you or for your love,
will I do anything to harm my lord."
The queen got angry; 275
in her wrath, she insulted him:
"Lanval," she said, "I am sure
you don't care for such pleasure;
people have often told me
that you have no interest in women. 280
You have fine-looking boys
with whom you enjoy yourself.
Base coward, lousy cripple,
my lord made a bad mistake
when he let you stay with him. 285
For all I know, he'll lose God because of it."
When Lanval heard her, he was quite disturbed;
he was not slow to answer.
He said something out of spite
that he would later regret. 290

"Lady," he said, "of that activity
I know nothing,
but I love and I am loved
by one who should have the prize
over all the women I know.   295
And I shall tell you one thing;
you might as well know all:
any one of those who serve her,
the poorest girl of all,
is better than you, my lady queen,   300
in body, face, and beauty,
in breeding and in goodness."
The queen left him
and went, weeping, to her chamber.
She was upset and angry   305
because he had insulted her.
She went to bed sick;
never, she said, would she get up
unless the king gave her satisfaction
for the offense against her.   310
The king returned from the woods,
he'd had a very good day.
He entered the queen's chambers.
When she saw him, she began to complain.
She fell at his feet, asked his mercy,   315
saying that Lanval had dishonored her;
he had asked for her love,
and because she refused him
he insulted and offended her:
he boasted of a love   320
who was so refined and noble and proud
that her chambermaid,
the poorest one who served her,
was better than the queen.
The king got very angry;   325
he swore an oath:
if Lanval could not defend himself in court
he would have him burned or hanged.
The king left her chamber
and called for three of his barons;   330
he sent them for Lanval
who was feeling great sorrow and distress.
He had come back to his dwelling,

knowing very well
that he'd lost his love,   335
he had betrayed their affair.
He was all alone in a room,
disturbed and troubled;
he called on his love, again and again,
but it did him no good.   340
He complained and sighed,
from time to time he fainted;
then he cried a hundred times for her to have mercy
and speak to her love.
He cursed his heart and his mouth;   345
it's a wonder he didn't kill himself.
No matter how much he cried and shouted,
ranted and raged,
she would not have mercy on him
not even let him see her.   350
How will he ever contain himself?
The men the king sent
arrived and told him
to appear in court without delay:
the king had summoned him   355
because the queen had accused him.
Lanval went with his great sorrow;
they could have killed him, for all he cared.
He came before the king;
he was very sad, thoughtful, silent;   360
his face revealed great suffering.
In anger the king told him:
"Vassal, you have done me a great wrong!
This was a base undertaking,
to shame and disgrace me   365
and to insult the queen.
You have made a foolish boast:
your love is much too noble
if her maid is more beautiful,
more worthy, than the queen."   370
Lanval denied that he'd dishonored
or shamed his lord,
word for word, as the king spoke:
he had not made advances to the queen;
but of what he had said,   375
he acknowledged the truth,

about the love he had boasted of,
that now made him sad because he'd lost her.
About that he said he would do
whatever the court decided. 380
The king was very angry with him;
he sent for all his men
to determine exactly what he ought to do
so that no one could find fault with his decision.
They did as he commanded, 385
whether they liked it or not.
They assembled,
Judged, and decided,
than Lanval should have his day;
but he must find pledges for his lord 390
to guarantee that he would await the judgment,
return, and be present at it.
Then the court would be increased,
for now there were none but the king's household.
The barons came back to the king 395
and announced their decision.
The king demanded pledges.
Lanval was alone and forlorn,
he had no relative, no friend.
Gawain went and pledged himself for him, 400
and all his companions followed.
The king addressed them: "I release him to you
on forfeit of whatever you hold from me,
lands and fiefs, each one for himself."
When Lanval was pledged, there was nothing else to do. 405
He returned to his lodging.
The knights accompanied him,
they reproached and admonished him
that he give up his great sorrow;
they cursed his foolish love. 410
Each day they went to see him,
because they wanted to know
whether he was drinking and eating;
they were afraid that he'd kill himself.
On the day that they had named, 415
the barons assembled.
The king and the queen were there
and the pledges brought Lanval back.
They were all very sad for him:

I think there were a hundred   420
who would have done all they could
to set him free without a trial
where he would be wrongly accused.
The king demanded a verdict
according to the charge and rebuttal.   425
Now it all fell to the barons.
They went to the judgment,
worried and distressed
for the noble man from another land
who'd gotten into such trouble in their midst.   430
Many wanted to condemn him
in order to satisfy their lord.
The Duke of Cornwall said:
"No one can blame us;
whether it makes you weep or sing   435
justice must be carried out.
The king spoke against his vassal
whom I have heard named Lanval;
he accused him of felony,
charged him with a misdeed—   440
a love that he had boasted of,
which made the queen angry.
No one but the king accused him:
by the faith I owe you,
if one were to speak the truth,   445
there should have been no need for defense,
except that a man owes his lord honor
in every circumstance.
He will be bound by his oath,
and the king will forgive us our pledges   450
if he can produce proof;
if his love would come forward,
if what he said,
what upset the queen, is true,
then he will be acquitted,   455
because he did not say it out of malice.
But if he cannot get his proof,
we must make it clear to him
that he will forfeit his service to the king;
he must take his leave."   460
They sent to the knight,
told and announced to him

that he should have his love come
to defend and stand surety for him.
He told them that he could not do it: 465
he would never receive help from her.
They went back to the judges,
not expecting any help from Lanval.
The king pressed them hard
because of the queen who was waiting.   470
When they were ready to give their verdict
they saw two girls approaching,
riding handsome palfreys.
They were very attractive,
dressed in purple taffeta,   475
over their bare skin.
The men looked at them with pleasure.
Gawain, taking three knights with him,
went to Lanval and told him;
he pointed out the two girls.   480
Gawain was extremely happy, and begged him
to tell if his love were one of them.
Lanval said he didn't know who they were,
where they came from or where they were going.
The girls proceeded   485
Still on horseback;
they dismounted before the high table
at which Arthur, the king, sat.
They were of great beauty,
and spoke in a courtly manner: 490
"King, clear your chambers,
have them hung with silk
where my lady may dismount;
she wishes to take shelter with you."
He promised it willingly   495
and called two knights
to guide them up to the chambers.
On that subject no more was said.
The king asked his barons
for their judgment and decision;   500
he said they had angered him very much
with their long delay.
"Sire," they said, "we have decided.
Because of the ladies we have just seen
we have made no judgment.   505

Let us reconvene the trial."
Then they assembled, everyone was worried;
there was much noise and strife.
While they were in that confusion,
two girls in noble array,   510
dressed in Phrygian silks
and riding Spanish mules,
were seen coming down the street.
This gave the vassals great joy;
to each other they said that now   515
Lanval, the brave and bold, was saved.
Gawain went up to him,[27]
bringing his companions along.
"Sire," he said, "take heart.
For the love of God, speak to us.   520
Here come two maidens,
well adorned and very beautiful;
one must certainly be your love."
Lanval answered quickly
that he did not recognize them,   525
he didn't know them or love them.
Meanwhile they'd arrived,
and dismounted before the king.
Most of those who saw them praised them
for their bodies, their faces, their coloring;   530
each was more impressive
than the queen had ever been.
The older one was courtly and wise,
she spoke her message fittingly:
"King, have chambers prepared for us   535
to lodge my lady according to her need;
she is coming here to speak with you."
He ordered them to be taken
to the others who had preceded them.
There was no problem with the mules.[28]   540
When he had seen to the girls,
he summoned all his barons

27. Ewert gives Yweins; Warnke, Walwains. Gawain seems more likely, since he is the one most concerned with Lanval throughout and since he always moves with his companions, as in this case.

28. The following two lines are added in (S) to explain this remark: "There were enough men to care for them / and put them into the stables."

to render their judgment;
it had already dragged out too much.
The queen was getting angry   545
because she had fasted so long.29
They were about to give their judgment
when through the city came riding
a girl on horseback:
there was none more beautiful in the world.   550
She rode a white palfrey,
who carried her handsomely and smoothly:
he was well apportioned in the neck and head,
no finer beast in the world.
The palfrey's trappings were rich;   555
under heaven there was no count or king
who could have afforded them all
without selling or mortgaging lands.
She was dressed in this fashion:
in a white linen shift   560
that revealed both her sides
since the lacing was along the side.
Her body was elegant, her hips slim,
her neck whiter than snow on a branch,
her eyes bright, her face white,   565
a beautiful mouth, a well-set nose,
dark eyebrows and an elegant forehead,
her hair curly and rather blond;
golden wire does not shine
like her hair in the light.   570
Her cloak, which she had wrapped around her,
was dark purple.
On her wrist she held a sparrow hawk,
a greyhound followed her.30
In the town, no one, small or big,   575
old man or child,
failed to come look.
As they watched her pass,
there was no joking about her beauty.

---

29. Warnke and Rychner give *jeünot*; Ewert, *atendeit*, "waited," which is not quite as callously selfish.

30. (S) adds the following attractive if doubtful lines: "A noble youth led her / carrying an ivory horn. / They came through the street very beautiful. Such great beauty was not seen / in Venus, who was a queen, / or in Dido, or in Lavinia."

She proceeded at a slow pace.   580
The judges who saw her
marveled at the sight;
no one who looked at her
was not warmed with joy.
Those who loved the knight   585
came to him and told him
of the girl who was approaching,
if God pleased, to rescue him.
"Sir companion, here comes one
neither tawny nor dark;   590
this is, of all who exist,
the most beautiful woman in the world."
Lanval heard them and lifted his head;
he recognized her and sighed.
The blood rose to his face;   595
he was quick to speak.
"By my faith," lie said, "that is my love.
Now I don't care if I am killed,
if only she forgives me.
For I am restored, now that I see her."   600
The lady entered the palace;
no one so beautiful had ever been there.
She dismounted before the king
so that she was well seen by all.
And she let her cloak fall   605
so they could see her better.
The king, who was well bred,
rose and went to meet her;
all the others honored her
and offered to serve her.   610
When they had looked at her well,
when they had greatly praised her beauty,
she spoke in this way,
she didn't want to wait:
"I have loved one of your vassals: 615
you see him before you—Lanval.
He has been accused in your court—
I don't want him to suffer
for what he said; you should know
that the queen was in the wrong.   620
He never made advances to her.
And for the boast that he made,

if he can be acquitted through me,
let him be set free by your barons."
Whatever the barons judged by law   625
the king promised would prevail.
To the last man they agreed
that Lanval had successfully answered the charge.
He was set free by their decision
and the girl departed.   630
The king could not detain her,
though there were enough people to serve her.
Outside the hall stood
a great stone of dark marble
where heavy men mounted   635
when they left the king's court;
Lanval climbed on it.
When the girl came through the gate
Lanval leapt, in one bound,
onto the palfrey, behind her.   640
With her he went to Avalun,
so the Bretons tell us,
to a very beautiful island;
there the youth was carried off.
No man heard of him again,   645
and I have no more to tell.

LES DEUS AMANZ (THE TWO LOVERS)

There happened once in Normandy
a famous adventure
of two young people who loved each other;
both died because of love.
The Bretons composed a *lai* about it;   5
and they gave it the title, *The Two Lovers*.

The truth is, that in Neustria,
which we call Normandy,
there's a wondrously great, high mountain:
the two youngsters lie buried up there.   10
Near one side of that mountain,
with much deliberation and judgment,
a king who was lord of the Pistrians
had a city built;

he named the city after the Pistrians— 15
he called it Pistre.
The name has lasted ever since;
the town and its dwellings still remain.
We know the region well:
it's called the valley of Pistre. 20

The king had a beautiful daughter,
an extremely gracious girl.
He found consolation in the maiden
after he had lost his queen.
Many reproached him for this— 25
even his own household blamed him.[31]
When he heard that people were talking about his conduct
he was saddened and troubled;
he began to consider
how he could avoid 30
anyone's seeking to marry his daughter.
So he sent word far and near, to this effect:
whoever wanted to win his daughter
should know one thing for certain:
it was decreed and destined that he 35
would have to carry her in his arms
to the summit of the mountain outside the city
without stopping to rest.
When the news was known
and spread throughout the region, 40
many attempted the feat,
but couldn't succeed at all.
There were some who pushed themselves so hard
that they carried her halfway up the mountain;
yet they couldn't get any farther— 45

---

31. The reason for this attitude on the part of the household is made clearer by the
following lines added after 24 in MSS (S) and (N):

Except for her he had neither son nor daughter;
he cherished her and loved her deeply.
She was wooed by rich men
who would willingly have wed her,
but the king didn't want to give her away
for he could not do without her.
The king had no other solace;
she was near him night and day.

they gave up there.
So, for a long time, he put off giving her away,
because no one wanted to ask for her.

There was a young man in that country,
the son of a count, refined and handsome;   50
he undertook great deeds
to win renown beyond all other men.
He frequented the court of the king
He stayed there quite often
and he came to love the king's daughter,   55
and many times he pleaded with her
to grant him her love
and become his mistress.
Because he was brave and refined,
and because the king thought highly of him,   60
she granted him her love
and he humbly thanked her for it.
They often conversed together
and they loved each other truly,
and as much as they could they hid their love   65
so that no one would discover it.
This restraint disturbed them greatly;
but the young man made up his mind
that he would rather suffer such hardships
than be too hasty in his love and thus lose everything.   70
He was hard pressed by love for her.

So it chanced one day
that the young man—who was so wise, so brave, and so handsome—
came to his beloved
and made his complaint to her: 75
he earnestly begged her
to run away with him
he couldn't stand the pain any longer;
if he asked her father for her,
he knew that the king loved her so much   80
that he'd refuse to give her up,
unless the suitor could carry her
in is arms to the summit of the mountain.
The maiden answered him:
"Dearest," she said, "I know very well   85
that you couldn't carry me up there for anything:

you aren't strong enough.
If I ran away with you,
my father would be grief-stricken and angry;
he would suffer the rest of his life.   90
Certainly, I love and cherish him enough
that I would never want to upset him.
You'll have to think of another scheme,
because I don't want to hear any more of this one.
I have a relative in Salerno,   95
a rich woman with lots of property;
she's lived there more than thirty years.
She's practiced the medical arts for so long
that she's an expert on medicines.[32]
She knows herbs and roots so well   100
that if you want to go to her
bringing a letter from me with you,
and tell her your problem,
she'll take an interest in it;
then she'll make up such prescriptions   105
and give you such potions
that they'll fortify you,
give you lots of strength.
When you return to this region,
you'll ask my father for me;   110
he'll think you're just a child,
and he'll tell you the agreement
that he won't give me away to any man,
whatever pains he may take,
if he can't carry me up the mountain   115
in his arms, without stopping to rest."

The youth listened to the idea
and the advice of the maiden;
it delighted him, and he thanked her.
He took leave of his mistress,   120
and went off to his own country.
Quickly he supplied himself

---

32. According to many medieval writers, women studied and practiced medicine at Salerno from the eleventh century onward. A gynecological treatise from this period, the *Trotula*, has frequently (but not without objection) been attributed to a Salernitan woman doctor. See A. B. Cobban, *The Medieval Universities* (London, 1975), 40, and works cited in Cobban's notes.

with rich clothes, money,
palfreys and pack mules;
only the most trustworthy of his men   125
did the youth take with him.
He went to stay in Salerno,
to consult his beloved's aunt.
On her behalf he gave her a letter.
When she had read it from one end to the other,   130
she kept him with her
until she knew all about his situation.
She strengthened him with medicines
and gave him such a potion that,
no matter how fatigued he might be,   135
no matter how constrained, or how burdened,
the potion would still revive his entire body—
even the veins and the bones—
so that he would have all the strength he needed,
the moment he drank it.   140
She poured the potion into a bottle;
he took it back to his own land.[33]

The young man, joyful and happy,
wasted no time at home
on his return.   145
He went to the king to ask for his daughter:
if the king would give her to him, he would take her
and carry her to the summit of the mountain.
The king made no attempt to refuse him,
though he took him for a great fool,   150
because the lover was so young.
Many great men, hardy and wise,
had undertaken this task
and none could accomplish it at all!
The king named and set a date;   155
then sent for his vassals, his friends,
everybody he could get;
he wouldn't let anyone stay behind.
Because of his daughter, and the young man
who was taking the chance   160
of carrying her to the mountain's top,

33. We follow Rychner, who reverses 141 and 142 in MS (H).

they came from everywhere.
The damsel prepared herself:
she fasted and dieted,
cut down on her eating,   165
because she desired to help her lover.

On the day when everyone arrived,
the youth was there first;
he didn't forget to bring his potion.
Toward the Seine, out in the meadow,   170
and into the great crowd assembled there
the king led his daughter.
She wore nothing except her chemise
her suitor lifted her into his arms.
The small phial containing his potion   175
he gave her to carry in her hand:
he knew well she'd no desire to cheat him.
But I'm afraid the potion did him little good,
because he was entirely lacking in control.
Off he went with her at top speed,   180
and he climbed until he was halfway up the mountain.
In his joy for his beloved
he forgot his potion.
She noticed he was growing weak:
"Love," she said, "drink!   185
I can tell you're getting tired—
now's the time to regain your strength!"
The youth answered:
"Sweetheart, my heart is very strong;
I wouldn't stop for any price,   190
not even long enough to take a drink,
so long as I can still move an inch.
The crowd below would raise a racket,
deafen me with their noise;
soon they'd have me all confused.   195
I don't want to stop here."
When they had gone two thirds of the way up,
he was on the verge of collapsing.
Again and again the maiden begged,
"Dearest, take your medicine!"   200
But he wouldn't listen or take her advice;
in great anguish he staggered on.
He reached the top of the mountain in such pain

that he fell there, and didn't get up;
the life went out of his body.   205
The maiden looked down at her lover,
she thought he had fainted.
She knelt beside him,
attempting to give him his potion;
but he couldn't respond to her.   210
That's how he died, as I've told you.
She grieved for him with loud cries;
she emptied and threw away
the bottle that contained the potion.
The mountain got well doused with it,   215
and the entire region and countryside
were much improved thereby:
many a fine herb now found there
owes its start to the potion.

Now I'll tell you about the damsel: 220
when she knew she had lost her lover,
you never saw anyone so sad;
she lay down and stretched out beside him,
took him in her arms, pressed him to her,
kissed his eyes and lips, again and again;   225
sorrow for him struck deep in her heart.
She died there too,
that maid who was so brave, so wise, so beautiful.
The king and the others who were waiting for them,
when they saw that they weren't returning,   230
went after them and found them.
The king fell down in a faint.
When he could speak again, he grieved greatly,
and so did all the strangers.
They stayed there mourning for three days.   235
Then they ordered a marble tomb
and placed the two youngsters inside it.
On the advice of everyone present
they buried them on the mountain's summit,
and at last they went away.   240

Because of the sad adventure of the young folk,
the place is now called the Mount of the Two Lovers.
It happened just the way I've told you;
the Bretons made a *lai* about it.

ELIDUC (in the original Anglo-Norman this text was also composed in verse)

I shall tell you the story and the whole substance of a very old Breton lay, in so far as I understand the truth of it.

In Brittany there was a knight, worthy and courtly, brave and fierce: Eliduc was his name, I believe, and there was no man so valiant in the land. His wife was noble and wise, of good family and high-born. They lived together for a long time and loved each other with great loyalty, but then it happened that he went in search of paid military service. There he loved a maiden, the daughter of a king and queen, whose name was Guilliadun, and none in the kingdom was more beautiful. His wife, whose name was Guildelüec, remained in her country. From these two the lay of *Guildelüec and Guilliadun* takes its name. It was first called *Eliduc*, but now the name has been changed, because the adventure upon which the lay is based concerns the ladies. I shall relate to you the truth of it as it happened.

Eliduc's lord, the King of Brittany, loved him dearly and cherished him. He served the king loyally and, whenever the king was away, the land was Eliduc's to guard. The king retained Eliduc for his prowess and as a result many advantages accrued to him. He could hunt in the forest and no forester was bold enough to oppose him or even grumble at him in any way. The envy of his good fortune, which often possesses others, caused him to be embroiled with his lord, to be slandered and accused, so that he was banished from the court without a formal accusation. Eliduc did not know why and often beseeched the king to hear his defence and not to believe slander, for he had served him long and willingly. But the king did not answer him and, since his lord refused to listen, he was obliged to depart. He returned to his house, summoned all his friends and told them of the anger which his lord, the king, felt towards him. He had served him to the best of his ability and ought not to have deserved his ill-will. The rustics say in a proverb that when he admonishes his ploughman a lord's love is no fief. He who is loyal to his lord and loves his good neighbours is wise and sensible. Eliduc did not want to stay in the country and said that he would cross the sea to the kingdom of Logres to take his ease for a while. He would leave his wife at home and order his men to look after her faithfully, and all his friends likewise. He kept this counsel and equipped himself richly. His friends were very sad that he was leaving them. He took only ten knights with him, and his wife, who bewailed her husband's departure, escorted him at his leaving, but he assured her that he would keep good faith with her. Thereupon he parted from her and pursued his path onwards. Coming to the sea, he crossed it and arrived at Totnes.

There were a number of kings in that land and there was great strife and war between them. In this country, near Exeter, lived a very old and powerful man, who had no male heir of his own, just a daughter of marriageable age. Because he refused to give her to one of his peers, this latter was making war upon him and laying waste all his lands. The enemy had surrounded him in a castle where no man was bold enough to resist and engage in single combat or in mêlée, but when Eliduc heard of this he would proceed no further now that he had found a war. He wanted to remain in that country to help as best he could the king who was most afflicted and discomfited, and remain in his service. He sent messengers and informed the king in a letter that he had left his own country and come to his aid, asking him to make known his wishes and, if he did not want to retain him, to grant him safe conduct through the land. He would then go further in search of service. When the king saw the messengers, he received them eagerly and honourably. He called his constable and quickly ordered him to prepare an escort to bring the baron there, to prepare hostels where they could lodge and to give them as much as they would need for a month's expenditure. The escort was prepared and sent to fetch Eliduc, who was received with great honour and made very welcome by the king. His lodging was with a very wise and courtly burgess, who turned over to him his fine chamber hung with curtains. Eliduc ensured that he was well-served and had all the poor knights who were lodged in the town—come to his table. He forbade all his men to be so bold as to accept any gift or money during the first forty days. On the third day of their stay the cry went up in the city that their enemies had come and were spread throughout the land intending to assault the town and come right up to the gates. Eliduc heard the tumult of the frightened people and armed himself without delay, as did his companions. There were forty mounted knights staying in the town—a number were wounded and there were many prisoners—and when they saw Eliduc mount they went to their lodgings to arm themselves. They left with him by the gate, not waiting to be summoned. 'Lord,' they said, 'we shall go with you and do as you do!' He replied: 'I thank you. Does anyone know of a narrow pass or defile where we can ambush the enemy? If we await them here, we could join battle with them, but this would not be to our advantage if anyone knows a better plan.' They said to him: 'Lord, truly, near this wood, in a thicket, is a narrow cart-track along which they must return. When they have captured their spoils, they will return thence. They often come back unarmed on their palfreys, thus openly courting death. It would be easy to inflict losses on them, humiliate them and make them suffer.' Eliduc said to them: 'Friends, I pledge my faith to you in this matter: he who does not some-times go where he surely thinks he will lose will gain little and never rise in esteem. You are all vassals of the king and should thus remain loyal to him, so come with me wherever I go and do as I do. I promise you faithfully that you will meet no obstacle as long as I can help it, and, if we can win anything, the discomfiting of our enemies will increase our reputation.' They accepted his pledge and took him to the wood, hiding in the bushes near the path until the enemy returned. Eliduc showed them exactly how to engage the enemy and how to shout at them. When the enemy had entered the pass, Eliduc shouted after them and called to all his companions, exhorting them to do well. They struck vigorously and did not spare the enemy, who were quite astounded, quickly routed and their ranks split, being vanquished in a short time. Their constable and many other knights were held and entrusted to the keeping of the squires. Twenty-five men on Eliduc's side captured thirty of the enemy. They quickly seized the equipment, took much booty and then returned joyfully, having achieved much. The king was in a tower, much afraid for his men, and lamented Eliduc loudly for he thought and feared that he had abandoned his knights. But they arrived back in a body, loaded with booty, their number greater upon their return than it had been when they left; because of this, the king failed to recognize them and harboured doubts and suspicions. He ordered the gates shut and told his people to climb on to the walls to shoot at them and bombard them. They would have no need of this, however, for the party had sent in advance a souire on a swift steed, who related the adventure to them, told them of the soldier, how he had defeated the enemy and how he had conducted himself. There was never such a knight, they said. He had taken the constable, captured twenty-nine of the others, and killed and wounded many more. When the king heard the news, he was exceedingly joyful and came down from the tower to meet Eliduc. He thanked him for his kindness and Eliduc surrendered the prisoners to him, distributing the arms to the others and keeping for his own use only three horses, which were highly praised. He shared and gave away everything, including his own portion, to both the prisoners and the others.

After this deed I have related to you, the king loved and cherished Eliduc greatly, retaining him for a whole year along with his companions. He received his allegiance and made him custodian of his land.

Eliduc was courtly and wise, a fine knight, worthy and generous, and the king's daughter heard tell of him and his virtues. She sent her personal chamberlain to him to request and summon him to come and relax for a while with her, so that they might talk and become acquainted. She was most surprised that he had not come to her, but Eliduc replied that he would go and make her acquaintance willingly. He mounted his steed, taking a knight with him, and then went to talk to the maiden. Before he entered the chamber he sent the chamberlain on ahead and delayed a little until the latter returned. With gentle mien, honest expression and very noble demeanour, he spoke with much breeding and thanked the damsel, Guilliadun, who was very beautiful, for having sent for him to come and talk to her. She took him by the hand and they sat down on a bed and spoke of many things. She looked at him closely, at his face, his body and his appearance, saying to herself that there was nothing unbecoming about him and forming a great admiration for him. Love dispatched its messenger who summoned her to love him. It made her go pale and sigh, but she did not want to discuss the matter with him lest he blame her for it. He stayed there a long while, then took his leave and left. She granted him leave very unwillingly, but he nevertheless departed and returned to his lodging. He was very sad and pensive, and anxious because this beautiful girl, the daughter of his lord the king, had addressed him so gently and sighed. He considered himself most unfortunate to have been in the country for so long and to have seen her so little. Having said this, he repented of it, for he remembered his wife, and how he had assured her that he would be faithful and behave loyally.

When she had seen him, the maiden wanted him for her lover. She had never esteemed anyone as much and wanted to keep him with her if she could. Thus she stayed awake the whole night and neither rested nor slept. She arose the next morning, went to a window, calling her chamberlain in whom she confided fully. 'By my faith,' she said, 'how unfortunate I am! I have fallen into a sorry plight, for I love the new soldier, Eliduc, the good knight. I had no rest last night and could not close my eyes to sleep. If he wishes to love me truly and will pledge himself to me, I shall do whatever he wants; he could benefit greatly from it and be king of this land. He is so exceedingly wise and courtly that, if he does not love me truly, I shall have to die a mournful death.' When she had spoken thus, the chamberlain whom she had summoned gave her some loyal advice with which he should not be reproached. 'Lady,' he said, "if you love him, send someone to ask him to come and send him a girdle, a ribbon or ring, for this will please him. If he receives it gladly and is happy about the summons, then you will be sure of his love. There is no emperor on earth who ought not to be glad if you wanted to love him.' When she had heard his advice, the maiden replied: 'How shall I know from my present whether he is inclined to love me? I have never seen a knight who received such a request, whether he felt love or hate, who did not willingly keep any present sent to him. I should hate him to mock me. But we may nevertheless learn something of the man from his mien. Get yourself ready and go.' 'I am ready now,' he replied. 'You will take him a gold ring and give him my girdle. Greet him a thousand times on my behalf.' The chamberlain departed and she remained thus. Although she almost called him back, she nevertheless let him go and began to lament: 'Alas, how my heart has been taken unawares by a man from another country! I do not even know if he is of a noble family. He will soon leave and I shall be left behind to mourn, for I was foolish to set my mind on this. I only spoke of it yesterday and now already I am begging him for his love. I think he may blame me, but if he is courtly, he will be grateful. Now the die is cast and, if he does not care for my love, I shall consider myself unfortunate and shall have no joy for the rest of my life.'

While she was lamenting, the chamberlain hurried to Eliduc and greeted him secretly, telling him the maiden had asked to see him. He presented Eliduc with the ring and the girdle and the knight thanked him, put the golden ring on his finger and the girdle around him. The young man said no more, nor did Eliduc inquire further, but only offered him a present of his own. He left, refusing to take anything. He returned to his lady and found her in her chamber, and when he had greeted her on Eliduc's behalf and thanked her for the gift, she said: 'Come now, hide nothing from me! Does he want to love me truly?' He replied: 'This is my opinion: the knight is not fickle. I consider him courtly and wise, and he knows well how to conceal his feelings. I greeted him on your behalf and gave him your gifts. He put on your girdle, attaching it securely around his waist and put the ring on his finger. I said nothing more to him, nor he to me.' 'Did he not receive it as a love-token? If not, then I am betrayed.' He replied: 'By my faith, I do not know, but listen to what I am about to tell you: if he did not wish you well, then he would want nothing of yours. "You jest,' she said. 'I know he does not hate me, for I never did him any harm, except by loving him so deeply. If he still wants to hate me, he deserves to die. I shall never ask anything else of him through you or anyone else until I speak to him. I want to show him myself how my love for him afflicts me, but I do not know if he will stay.' The chamberlain replied: 'Lady, the king has retained him on oath for a year to serve him faithfully. Thus you will have enough opportunity to show him your desire.' When she heard he would be remaining, she rejoiced greatly, very glad he was staying. She knew nothing of the sadness he had felt since seeing her, but he had no joy or pleasure, except when thinking of her. He considered himself unfortunate, for he had promised his wife, before leaving his own country, that he would love only her. Now his heart was firmly trapped, for he wanted to remain faithful, but could not refrain from loving the maiden Guilliadun, who was so beautiful, from looking at her and talking to her, kissing and embracing her. However, he would never ask her for her love, which would redound to his dishonour, both in order to keep faith with his wife, and because he was in the king's service. In great distress, Eliduc mounted up and delayed no longer, calling his companions to him. He went to the castle to talk to the king and wanted to see the maiden if he could, as she was the reason why he had set out. The king rose from the table, went into his daughter's rooms and began to play chess with a knight from over the sea, who sat at the other side of the chessboard and whose duty it was to teach his daughter. Eliduc approached, and the king welcomed him warmly, making him sit down beside him. He then called his daughter and said to her: 'Damsel, you should become well acquainted with this knight and show him great honour. There is none better in five hundred.' When the girl had listened to what her lord had commanded, she was very glad, and she arose and spoke to Eliduc. They sat well apart from the others, both caught in love's grip, but she dared not address him and he was fearful about talking to her, apart from thanking her for the present she had sent him: he had never cherished any possession more. She answered the knight that she was glad of this and that she had sent him the ring, and the girdle as well, because she had granted him possession of herself. She loved him so much and wanted to make him her husband and, if she could not have him, he truly ought to know that she would have no man alive. Now, she said, he ought to tell her his wishes. 'Lady,' he replied, 'I am very grateful to you for your love and it gives me much joy. Since you esteem me so much, I ought to be very glad of this and will not forget it. I have agreed to remain one year with the king who took my oath—that I would not leave until his war was over. Then I shall return to my country, as I wish to remain no longer, providing you will give me leave.' The maiden answered him: 'Beloved, I thank you profusely! You are so wise and courtly that before then you will have decided what to do about me. I love and trust you above anything else.' They pledged each other their troth and spoke no more on that occasion. Eliduc went to his lodgings and was very happy, for he had achieved much. He could often speak with his beloved and great was the love between them. His efforts in the war were so successful that he captured and retained the king's adversary, and freed the whole land. He was greatly valued for his prowess, his wisdom and his generosity. Good fortune had befallen him.

While all this was taking place, his own lord had sent out three messengers to look for him, to say that he was being set upon and injured. He was losing all his castles and all his land was being laid waste. He had often regretted that Eliduc had left him and had been ill-advised to view him with disfavour. He had cast out of the country and exiled for ever those traitors who had accused Eliduc, who had blamed him and caused him to be embroiled with his lord. In his dire need he summoned and required Eliduc by the promise he had made when he had accepted his homage to come and help him, for he stood in great need.

Eliduc heard the news and was much disturbed for the maiden's sake, for he loved her dearly and she him as much as possible. There was no foolishness between them, nor fickleness, nor wickedness, as their love consisted entirely of courting and talking, and exchanging fair gifts when they were together. It was her intention and her hope to make him hers completely and keep him if she could, but she did not know that he had a wife. 'Alas,' he said, 'I have behaved badly! I have been too long in this country. Alas that ever I saw it! Here I have deeply loved a girl, Guilliadun, the king's daughter, and she has loved me. If I must leave her thus, one of us will have to die, or perhaps even both. But nevertheless I must go, for my lord has summoned me in a letter and required me by my oath, and my wife as well. Now I must take care. I can remain no longer and must leave. If I were to marry my beloved, the Christian religion would not accept it. Things are going badly in all respects. God, parting is so hard! But whoever may blame me for it, I shall always do right by my beloved. I shall do as she wishes and act according to her advice. The king, her lord, is now at peace and henceforth I think no one will make war upon him. In my own lord's interests I shall seek to depart before the day set to mark the end of my stay here with the king. I shall go and talk with the maiden and inform her fully about my situation. She will tell me her wishes and I shall carry them out as best I can.'

The knight delayed no more and went to take leave of the king. He told him what had happened and read him the letter sent by his lord, who was summoning him in great distress. When the king heard the summons, he realized Eliduc would not remain and was very sad and disturbed. He offered him a large share of his possessions and surrendered to him his treasure and a third of his heritage. He would do so much to make him stay that Eliduc would thereafter always be grateful to him. 'God,' he said, 'since my lord is in distress and has summoned me from such a distance, this time I shall go to his aid; nothing would keep me here. If you need my service, I shall willingly return to you with a great force of knights.' The king thanked him for this and gladly gave him leave, putting all the wealth of his house at his disposal, gold and silver, dogs and horses, and silken clothes, fine and fair. Eliduc took a moderate quantity and then, as was fitting, said he would go and speak with his daughter, if he agreed. The king replied: 'That would please me.' The king sent ahead a squire to open the chamber door. Eliduc went to talk with her and when she saw him she spoke to him and greeted him six thousand times. He consulted her about the matter and briefly explained to her his journey, but before he had told her everything, or begged or taken his leave, she fainted with grief and lost all her colour. When Eliduc saw her faint he began to moan and kissed her mouth often and wept most tenderly. He took her and held her in his arms until she recovered from her swoon. 'Ah God,' he said, 'sweet love, let me tell you something: you are my life and my death, in you is all my comfort! I consulted you because of the pledge between us, but of necessity I must go to my country. I have taken leave of your father, but I shall do what you wish, whatever may befall me.' 'Take me away with you,' she said, 'since you will remain no longer! If not, I shall kill myself and never have joy or happiness again.' Eliduc replied gently that he loved her deeply and truly: 'Fair one, in truth I belong by an oath to your father up to the appointed time—if I were to take you away with me, I should betray my faith. Loyally I swear and pledge to you that, if you give me leave, grant me a postponement and set a day by which you wish me to return, nothing on earth will keep me from doing so, providing I am alive and well. My life is completely in your hands.' She had great love for him and so set a period and fixed the day on which he was to return and take her away. They grieved much on parting, exchanged their golden rings and kissed each other affectionately.

He came to the sea, where the wind was good, and soon crossed. When Eliduc had arrived, his lord was joyful and glad, as were his friends, relations and everyone else, above all his good wife, who was very beautiful, wise and worthy. But he was still distracted by the love that had taken him unawares, and he displayed no joyful or friendly mien, whatever he saw, nor would he indeed be joyful until he saw his beloved. He behaved most secretively and his wife was sad in her heart because of this, not knowing what it meant. She lamented to herself and often asked him whether someone had told him that she had misbehaved or done wrong while he had been out of the country, for she would willingly defend herself in front of his people, if he wished. 'Lady,' he said, 'I do not accuse you of any crime or misdemeanour, but in the country where I have been I pledged and swore to the king that I should return to him; now he has great need of me. If my lord the king were at peace, I should not stay another week. Great torment will come my way before I can return, and nothing will make me happy until I have done so, for I do not want to break my word.' At this the lady let the matter rest. Eliduc was with his lord, whom he aided greatly. The king acted on his advice and took steps to safeguard the whole land, but when the time approached which the maiden had appointed, Eliduc strove to make peace. He reconciled the king with all his enemies, and then prepared himself for departure together with those he wished to take with him. He took only two of his nephews whom he loved, a chamberlain of his (who had been privy to their plans and had borne the message) and his squires, for he wanted no others. He made these pledge and swear to keep his affair secret.

Waiting no longer, he put to sea and they were soon on the other side. He arrived in the region where he was greatly desired, but Eliduc was very sensible and took lodging far from the harbour, for he did not want to be seen, discovered or recognized. He prepared his chamberlain and sent him to his beloved to inform her of his arrival and that he had kept his covenant. That night, when all was dark, she was to leave the city; the chamberlain would go with her and Eliduc himself would come to meet her. The chamberlain had changed all his garments and went swiftly on foot to the city where the king's daughter was. He sought and inquired until he found his way into her chamber, where he greeted the damsel and said that her beloved had come. Whereas she had been mournful and dismayed before, when she heard the news she wept tenderly for joy and kissed the chamberlain several times. He told her that she would have to leave with him at nightfall and thus they remained the whole day, planning their route well. At night, when all was dark, she and the young man left the town, the two of them alone, but she was still frightened lest anyone see her. She was dressed in a silken garment finely embroidered with gold, with a short cloak attached.

A bow's shot from the gate was a wood surrounded by a beautiful pasture. Her beloved, who had come on her account, waited for them at the foot of the palissade, towards which the chamberlain led her. Eliduc dismounted and kissed her and they were most joyful at their reunion. He made her mount a horse and then mounted himself, taking the reins. He quickly departed with her and came to the harbour at Totnes, where they boarded the ship straightaway. There was no one on board, save his own men and his beloved Guilliadun. They had a good wind and settled weather, but as they were about to arrive, they encountered a storm at sea and a wind arose before them that drove them far from the harbour. Their mast broke and split and the sail was completely torn. They solemnly called upon God, St Nicholas and St Clement, and upon the Virgin Mary to beseech her son to help them and save them from destruction and so enable them to reach the harbour. They sailed back and forth along the coast and came extremely close to being shipwrecked. Then one of the sailors cried aloud: 'What are we doing? Lord, you have with you the woman who will cause us to perish. We shall never make land! You have a loyal wife and now with this other woman you offend God and his law, righteousness and the faith. Let us cast her into the sea and we shall soon arrive safely.' Eliduc heard what he said and almost went demented with anger. 'Son of a whore,' he said, 'wicked and evil traitor, say no more! If I had abandoned my love, you would have paid dearly for it.' But he held her in his arms and comforted her as best he could against her sea-sickness and because she had heard that he had a wife in his own country. She fell face down, quite pale and wan, in a swoon in which she remained, for she did not come round or breathe. He who was taking her away with him truly believed that she was dead. He lamented greatly and then arose, went quickly up to the sailor and struck him with the oar so that he knocked him out flat. Then with his foot he pushed him overboard and the waves bore the body away. When he had cast him into the sea, he went to take charge of the helm, steering the boat and holding it on course so that he reached the harbour and land. When they had arrived, he put down the gangway and dropped anchor. Guilliadun still lay in a swoon, seemingly dead, and Eliduc lamented loudly, for he would gladly have died with her. He asked each of his companions for advice on where he could bear the maiden, for he would not leave her. She would be interred and buried with great honour and with a fine service in a consecrated cemetery, for she was a king's daughter and had a right to this. They were quite forlorn, unable to give him any advice, and so Eliduc began to think where he could take her. His dwelling was close to the sea and he could be there by dinner time. All around it was a forest, thirty leagues in circumference, where a holy hermit, who had been there for forty years, lived and had a chapel. Eliduc had spoken with him many times. He decided to take her to him and have her buried in his chapel. He would provide a large portion of his land to found an abbey there and establish a convent of monks, nuns or canons who would always pray for her. May God be merciful to her! He had his horses brought and ordered his companions to mount, making them swear that they would not betray him. He carried his beloved before him on, his palfrey.

They rode straight onwards until they entered the wood and came to the chapel, where they called and knocked, but found no one to answer them—or to open the door, so Eliduc sent one of his men inside to unlock and open it. Eight days earlier, the holy, saintly hermit had passed away, and when Eliduc found the newly dug tomb, he was most aggrieved and upset. The others wanted to dig the grave where he was to place his beloved, but he made them draw back and said to them: 'This is not correct, for I shall first take counsel with the wise men of the country about how I can glorify the place either as an abbey or as a church. We shall lay her before the altar and commend her to God.' He had sheets brought and they made a bed for her at once, laying the girl on it and leaving her for dead. But when it came to parting, he thought he would die of grief, and he kissed her eyes and her face, saying. 'Fair one, may it never please God for me to bear arms again or live and endure in this world! Fair love, how sad that you ever laid eyes on me! Sweet darling, how sad that you followed me! Fair one, you would soon have been a queen, but for the loyal and pure love with which you loved me so faithfully. My heart grieves because of you and the day I bury you I shall take holy orders. On your tomb every day I shall make my grief resound.' Then he left the maiden and closed the chapel door.

He had sent a messenger home to tell his wife that he was coming, but that he was weary and upset. When she heard this, she was very glad and prepared to meet him. She received her lord properly, but little joy awaited her, for he showed no friendly mien nor spoke fair words, and no one dared address him. He was in the house for two days and then heard mass in the morning and set off. He went to the chapel in the woods where the damsel lay and found her still in a swoon, for she neither recovered nor even breathed. It seemed astonishing to him to see the colour in her cheeks still, for she had lost little of it and was only a trifle paler. He wept in anguish and prayed for her soul. When he had finished his prayer, he returned to his house.

One day his wife had one of her servants spy on Eliduc as he left the church. She promised him a large reward if he followed at a distance and took note of which direction her lord took. If he did this, she would give him horse and arms. He obeyed her command, taking to the woods and following Eliduc without being noticed. He saw how he entered the chapel and heard the lamentation he made, but before Eliduc came out he had returned to his lady, telling all he had heard, the lamentation, the noise, and the cries that her husband had made in the hermitage. She was disturbed by this and said: 'We shall go straightaway and search the hermitage thoroughly. My husband has to go out, I think, for he is going to court to talk to the king. The hermit died some time ago, and even though I know that my husband loved him well, he would not do this on his account, nor show much grief' Such was her conclusion on this occasion.

On the afternoon of the same day, when Eliduc went to talk to the king, the lady took the servant with her and he led her to the hermitage. When she entered the chapel and saw the bed of the maiden who was like a new rose, she raised the coverlet and saw the body so slender, the long arms, the white hands, the fingers, slim, long, and full. Then she knew why her husband had grieved. She called the servant and showed him the marvel: 'Do you see this woman,' she said, 'who in beauty resembles a gem? This is my husband's beloved for whom he laments so, and, in faith, it is no wonder when such a beautiful woman has perished. Either pity or love will prevent me from ever knowing joy again.' She began to weep and lament the damsel and, as she sat weeping in front of the bed, a weasel, which had come out from beneath the altar, ran past, and the servant struck it because it passed over the body. He killed it with a stick and threw it on the floor. It did not take long for another to run up which, seeing the first one lying there, walked around its head, touching it often with its foot. Unable to rouse its partner, it seemed distressed and left the chapel, going into the woods in search of herbs. With its teeth the weasel picked a flower, bright red in colour, and then quickly returned, placing it in the mouth of its companion, whom the servant had killed, with the result that it quickly recovered. The lady noticed this and shouted to the servant: 'Catch it! Throw your stick, good man, do not let it escape!' And he threw it and hit the weasel so that the flower fell from its mouth. The lady arose, picked it up and quickly came back, placing the beautiful flower inside the maiden's mouth. After a short while she revived and breathed. Then she spoke and opened her eyes: 'God,' she said, 'I have slept so long!' When the lady heard her speak, she began to thank God and asked her who she was. The girl said: 'Lady, I was born in Logres, the daughter of a king of that country. I deeply loved a knight, Eliduc, the good soldier, who took me away with him. He sinned when he tricked me, for he has a wife and never told me or even gave any indication of this, and so, when I heard about his wife, my grief caused me to faint. He has wickedly left me forlorn in another land and has betrayed me. I do not know what to think. She who trusts a man is extremely foolish.' 'Fair one,' the lady replied, 'nothing on earth could make him joyful, you may be assured of that, for he thinks you are dead and is terribly distressed. He has come to look at you every day, but I assume he found you in a swoon. Truly, I am his wife and my heart grieves for him. Because of the grief he displayed, I wanted to know where he went, and came after him and found you. I am overjoyed that you are alive and shall take you with me and return you to your beloved. I shall set him free completely and take the veil.' The lady comforted the girl until she was able to take her away with her.

She made her servant ready and sent him for her husband. He searched until he found him and then greeted him courteously, telling him the story. Eliduc mounted on a horse, but did not wait for his companions and returned that night to his house. When he found his beloved alive, he thanked his wife gently. Eliduc was extremely happy, and had never been so joyful. He often kissed the maiden and she him tenderly, for together they were very happy. When the lady saw how they looked, she spoke to her husband and asked him for permission to leave and to separate from him, for she wanted to be a nun and serve God. He could give her some of his land, on which she could found an abbey, and then marry the girl he loved so much, for it was neither right nor proper to keep two wives, nor should the law allow it. Eliduc granted his wife this and willingly gave her leave, for he would do everything she wanted and give her some land. Near the castle in the woods, where the hermitage chapel stood, she had her church and houses built. It was endowed with much land and great possessions and would have everything it needed. When everything had been properly prepared, she took the veil, as did thirty nuns with her. Then she established her way of life and the rules of her order.

Eliduc married his beloved. On the wedding day the celebrations were conducted with great honour and a fine service. They lived together for many a day and the love between them was perfect. They distributed great alms and great wealth until such time as they themselves turned to God. Near the castle, on the other side, Eliduc wisely and carefully built a church, which he endowed with most of his land and all his gold and silver. There he placed his own men and other pious persons to uphold the order and maintain the house. When everything was ready, he hardly delayed, but joined himself to them in order to serve almighty God. He placed his dear wife together with his first one and the

326

latter received her as her sister and showed her great honour, urging her to serve God and teaching her the order. They prayed that God might show their beloved His sweet mercy and Eliduc in turn prayed for them, sending his messenger to see how they fared and how their spirits were. Each one strove to love God in good faith and they came to a good end thanks to God, the true divine.

From the story of these three the ancient courtly Bretons composed a lay to be remembered, so that it should not be forgotten.

SECTION 12

THE FRENCH FABLIAUX

Introduction by Albrecht Classen

The Old French *fabliaux* represent, at least for some modern readers with strict moral standards, a highly problematic literary genre because of their explicit erotic content, and some might say, pornographic quality. The word *fabliaux* is the plural of *fabliau*, which is the diminutive of Old French *fable*, meaning *fable* or 'narrative.' They are rhymed verse novellas consisting of 200 to 500 verses and mostly deal with comical aspects of marital life, adultery, treachery, deception, breaking of monastic vows, conflicts between lovers, wooing, etc. From a medieval point of view it would be inappropriate to cast them as obscene, as the anonymous authors intended to provoke laughter, to teach their audiences a funny lesson about human behavior, relate examples of witticism, little tragedies, and often even to convey a moral exhortation. Generally, women are portrayed from a misogynistic point of view, but also praised as ruseful and intelligent who outsmart their husbands and enjoy their adulterous relationships. Clerics are mostly sharply criticized for their lax morality and disregard of the law of celibacy. In a number of cases the *fabliaux* satirize peasants and burghers, and seem to be written from an urban perspective. In total circa 150 *fabliaux*, written in Northern France and modern Belgium, partly also in England, have come down to us. The earliest *fabliaux* were composed around 1170. We know the names of some *fabliaux* authors, such as Henri d'Andeli, Huon le Roi, Philippe de Remi, Sire de Beaumanoir, Rutebeuf, but mostly these texts have been preserved anonymously. Despite—but perhaps because of—their seemingly crude appearance, they enjoyed a considerable popularity among the aristocratic and urban audiences, as they powerfully served as parodies of courtly romances and courtly ideals. *Fabliaux* transgressed and transformed traditional literary standards and ideals and opened the reader's/listener's eyes towards the material realities of medieval life. Similar tales were also written in medieval Germany, the so-called *maeren*, and in Italy, see Poggio Bracciolini's *Facetiae*. Geoffrey Chaucer imitated several *fabliaux* in his *Canterbury Tales* (1399). In the early modern age, especially during the age of the Renaissance, writers happily welcomed these narratives and imitated or copied them profusely, such as Boccaccio, Rabelais, and Molière.

BIBLIOGRAPHY

Charles Muscatine, *The Old French Fabliaux* (New Haven: Yale University Press, 1986).

Mary Jane Stearns Schenck, *The Fabliaux*: *Tales of Wit and Deception*. Purdue University Monographs in Romance Languages, 24 (Amsterdam-Philadelphia: Benjamins, 1987).

Kathryn Gravdal, *Vilain and Courtois. Transgressive Parody in French Literature of the Twelfth and Thirteenth Centuries.* Regents Studies in Medieval Culture (Lincoln-London: University of Nebraska Press, 1989).

Norris J. Lacy, Reading Fabliaux. Garland Reference Library of the Humanities, 1805 (New York: Garland, 1993).

Texts from:

The French Fabliaux B.N. MS. 837. Ed. and trans. Raymond Eichmann and John Du Val. Vol II (New York-London: Garland, 1985), pp. 27, 29, 31, 33, 35 (Wife), 37, 39, 41, 43 (Partridges), 49, 51, 53, 55 (Judgment), 63, 65, 67 (Priest), 79, 81, 83, 85, 87 (Young Man).

R. Howard Bloch, *The Scandal of the Fabliaux* (Chicago: University of Chicago Press, 1986).

B. J. Levy, *The Comic Text: Patterns and Images in the Old French Fabliaux* (Amsterdam and Atlanta: Editions Rodopi, 2000).

Old French Fabliaux: Essays on Comedy and Context, ed. Kristin L. Burr, John F. Moran, and Norris J. Lacy (Jefferson, NC, and London: McFarland & Company, 2008).

THE WIFE OF ORLEANS

Now I will tell you a fairly courtly
Adventure about a bourgeois' wife.
She was born and reared in Orleans,
And her husband, who was born in Amiens,
Was an excessively rich landowner.   5
He knew all the tricks and points
Of merchantry and usury,
And whatever he held in his fists
Was held very tightly.
     Into the town came   10
Four fresh scholar clerks;

They carried their sacks hanging down from their necks.
The clerks were big and fat,
Because they ate very well, no fooling.
They were very well thought of in the town   15
Where they were lodged.
One of them, who was much esteemed,
Frequented a bourgeois' house;
People considered him very courteous;
He wasn't full of pride or buffoonery,   20
And his acquaintance
Greatly pleased the lady;
And he came and went there so often,
That the bourgeois decided,
Whether by deception or by speech,   25
That he would teach him a lesson,
If he could manage
Some way of doing it.
      In his house he had one niece,
Whom he had reared for a long time;   30
He secretly called her to him
And promised her a petticoat
If she would spy concerning this business
And tell him the truth about it.
Meanwhile, the scholar begged the bourgeois' wife   35
So much, out of friendship,
That she granted him what he wanted;
And all the time, the girl
Was listening well enough to hear
How they had made a pact   40
She went straight to the bourgeois
And told him what the arrangement was;
And the arrangement was this:
The lady would send for him
As soon as her lord left.   45
Then he would come to the two bolted gates
Of the orchard, which she showed him,
And she would be there to meet him
When it would be completely dark.
The bourgeois heard it and was very happy.   50
Then he went to his wife:
"Lady," he said, "I must go
To do my business as a merchant;
Take care of the house, my dear friend,

Just as a good wife ought to do.   55
I don't know when I'll be coming back."
"Sir," she said, "I certainly will."
He got his drivers ready
And said that in order to get
A head start he would go and lodge   60
As far as three leagues from the town.
The lady did not catch onto the trick,
But let the clerk know about the business.
He who intended to deceive them
Had his people go and take lodging,   65
While he went to the gate of the orchard,
For the night was blending with the day.
And the lady, all on the sly,
Came to meet him, opened the door for him,
And welcomed him into her arms,   70
Believing that he was her friend.
But hope deceived her.
"Welcome," she said.
He refrained from speaking out loud
And returned her greeting in a low voice.   75
They directed their steps through the orchard,
But he kept his face very much turned to the side,
And the wife bent over a little
And looked at him beneath the hat.
She realized there was some treason going on.   80
She recognized and perceived
That it was her husband who was deceiving her.
From the moment she perceived him,
She meditated how to deceive him.
(A woman got the best of Argus;   85
Wise men ever since the time of Abel
Have been fooled by their trickery.)
"Sir," she said, "I'm very pleased
To be able to hold you and have you;
I will give you some of my money   90
To help you get back the things you've pawned,
If you keep this affair secret.
Now let's go along;
I'll put you secretly
in an upstairs room that I have the key to.   95
There you will wait for me very quietly
Until our people have eaten;

And when they've all gone to bed,
I will lead you beneath my bed curtain.
Nobody will know what we've agreed to."   100
"Lady," he said, "you have spoken well."
(God! How little he knew
What she was thinking and intending!
The ass-driver thinks one thing,
And the ass thinks something entirely different.)   105
He would soon have bad lodging,
Because when the lady had closed him up
In the upstairs room, from which he couldn't get out,
She returned to the orchard gate.
There she found her lover and took him   110
And embraced and hugged and kissed him.
The second man, I think,
Was more comfortable than the first.
The lady let the clod in the upstairs room
Cool his heels for a long time.   115
Soon they passed through the orchard
And they came into the bedroom,
Where the sheets were pulled back.
The lady led her lover
And brought him all the way into the bedroom   120
And put him under the covers;
And he soon threw himself into
The game which love commanded him to play
So that he wouldn't have given an almond
For all the other games, unless love had a part   125
And she was appreciating it.
They enjoyed themselves for a long time.
When they had hugged and kissed,
She said, "Friend, now you will stay here
A little while and wait for me,   130
Because I'm going in there
To see that our people get to eat,
And we'll have supper, you and I,
Later tonight, all by ourselves."
"Lady, whatever you say."   135
She walked away very nicely
And went to the servants' quarters
And did her best to make the people happy.
When the meal was ready,
They ate and drank quite a bit.   140

And when they had all eaten,
Before they had dispersed,
The lady called her people
And spoke very skillfully.
Two nephews of the lord were there   145
And a boy who carried water,
And there were three chambermaids;
And the niece of the bourgeois was there,
And two rascals and a rogue.
"Lords," she said, "as God may save you,   150
Now listen to my talk:
Lately you've seen,
Coming into this house, a clerk,
Who does not let me live in peace;
For a long time he has been begging me for love;   155
I've refused him thirty times.
When I saw that I wouldn't get out of it,
I promised him that I'd do
All his pleasure and all his will
As soon as my lord had gone away.   160
Now he's gone—may God lead him!—
And I have indeed kept my part of the bargain
With this man, who bothers me every day.
Now his time has come:
He's waiting for me up in that room.   165
I'll give you each a large cup
Of the best wine that's here
If I can be avenged.
Go upstairs to him in that room,
And beat him well with sticks,   170
Down on the floor and standing up.
Give him so many bruising blows
That never again will he care
To woo a woman of worth."
          When the people understood their task,   175
All jumped up; none waited there.
One took a stick, another a club,
Another a pestle big and solid;
The wife gave them the key.
(I'd say anyone who could tally   180
All the blows would be a good teller.)
"Don't let him get out of there;
But attack him in the high room."

"By God," they said, "Sir Student,
You will be disciplined!"   185
One of them threw him to the floor
And seized him by the throat;
He squeezed him so tightly by the hood
That he couldn't utter a word.
Then they got him ready so they could lay into him;   190
They were not stingy with their beating.
If he had paid a thousand marks,
He wouldn't have had a better beating.
Many times his two nephews
Took pains to strike well,   195
First above and then below;
It did him no good to cry for mercy.
They dragged him out like a dead dog
And flung him on a manure pile.
Then back into the house they went.   200
They had plenty of good wines,
All the best in the house,
White wines and wines of Auvergne,
Just as if they had been kings.
And the lady got cakes and wine   205
And a white linen cloth
And a large wax candle.
She held council with her lover
All night until the dawn.
As he left, Love required her   210
To give him as much as ten marks
And to entreat him to come back
Every time he could.
            And the one who was lying in the manure pile
Bestirred himself as well as he could   215
And went to where he had his equipment.
When his people saw him so beaten up,
They were greatly grieved and astonished.
They asked him how things were going.
"Badly," he said, "is how they're going with me.   220
Take me back to my house
And don't ask me anything more."
Immediately they raised him up.
They didn't wait any longer.
But it was a great comfort to him   225
And put him out of his bad mood

To realize that his wife was so loyal;
He didn't count his pain worth an egg,
And he decided that if he could be healed,
He would always cherish her.   230
                    Then he went back to his house,
And when the lady saw him
She made a bath of good herbs for him
And completely cured him of his hurt.
She asked him how all this had happened to him.   235
"Lady," he said, "I had
To travel through some grave dangers,
Where somebody broke my bones."
The people in the house told him
About the student and how they had fixed him,   240
And how the lady delivered him up to them.
By my head, she got herself out of this
Like a decent and a wise woman:
Never again in his whole life
Did her husband blame or mistrust her,   245
Nor did she ever fail
To love her friend always,
Until he went back to his own country.

THE PARTRIDGES

Since I am used to telling fabliaux,
Instead of a fable, I want to tell
An adventure which is true,
Of a peasant who happened to catch
Two partridges behind his hedge.   5
He put his care into preparing them:
He had his wife put them on the fire;
She knew how to prepare them right.
She fixed the fire and turned the spit,
And then the peasant left   10
And went off running to get the priest.
But he took such a long time coming back
That the partridges were cooked first.
The lady put the spit down
And pinched off a bit of skin,   15
Because she really enjoyed being a glutton.
When God gave her something to have,

She didn't long to have a lot,
But to consume what she did have.
She hastily attacked one partridge,   20
And ate both wings,
Then went out to the road
To see if her lord was coming.
When she didn't see him coming,
She would eat the other one;   25
And disposed of the rest in the same manner:
Fie on any bite that remained!
Then she thought to herself and said
She would eat the other one;
She knew very well what to say   30
If anyone asked her what had happened:
She would say some cats had come
When she had pulled the birds out;
They had suddenly seized them from her hands,
And each had carried a bird off for himself;   35
Thus, she said, she would escape.
Then she went to stand in the middle of the road
To look out for her husband,
And when she didn't see him coming,
Her tongue started quivering   40
For the partridge she had left.
She would go absolutely mad
If she didn't get just one little bit more.
She pulled its neck off very delicately,
And ate it with great pleasure.   45
She licked her fingers all around.
"Oh my!" she said, "What shall I do?
If I eat it all, what shall I say?
And how can I stop?
I have a very, very great desire.   50
Now come what may,
I have to eat it all!"
      The time passed until
The lady was full.
And the peasant didn't delay.   55
He came to the house and cried out:
"Hey! Tell me! Are the partridges done?"
"Sir," she said, "everything's gone wrong,
Because the cats ate them."
At once the peasant leapt   60

And ran at her like a madman.
He would have torn her eyes out
But she cried out, "It's a joke, it's a joke!
Get away from me," she cried, "Satan!
They're covered to keep warm."   65
"I would have sung you some stinking Lauds,"
Said he, "by the faith I owe Saint Lazarus!
Here! My good wooden mug
And my finest white table cloth;
I'll spread it out over my cape,   70
Under the trellis in that little meadow."
"But why don't you take your knife,
Which really needs sharpening,
And sharpen it a little
On that rock in the yard."   75
The peasant stripped and ran,
Holding the bare knife in his hand.
          Here came the chaplain after a while,
Who was coming there to eat.
Without hesitation, he came to the lady   80
And embraced her very sweetly.
And she spoke to him quite simply:
"Sir," she said, "flee! Flee!
I won't stand by while your body
Gets shamed and maimed.   85
My lord has gone outside
To sharpen his great knife,
And he said he's going to cut
Your balls off, if he can catch hold of you."
"Think about God!"   90
The priest said; "what are you saying?
We're supposed to eat two partridges
That your husband caught this morning."
She answered him: "By Saint Martin,
There's not a partridge here, not a bird!   95
It would be fine with me for you to eat,
And I'd be sorry about your misfortune;
But now look down there,
How he's sharpening his knife."
"I see him!" he said; "by my hat,   100
I really think you've told the truth."
He didn't stay much longer,
But left in a great hurry,

And right away she cried out:
"Come here, Sir Gombaut!"   105
"What's the matter," he asked, "God save you?"
"What's the matter? You'll know soon enough!
But if you can't start running,
You're going to lose out, that's what I think,
For by the faith I owe you,   110
The priest is carrying off your partridges."
The good man was really angry.
He grabbed the knife in his hand
And ran after the chaplain.
When he saw him, he cried out: 115
"You won't carry them off like that!"
Then he shouted with all his might:
"You're carrying them away good and hot.
You'll leave them here with me if I catch you!
You'd be a bad friend   120
If you ate them without me."
The priest looked back
And saw the peasant running;
When he saw the knife in his hand,
He thought he'd be a dead man if he caught him   125
He didn't fail to run full speed,
And the peasant, who believed he was rescuing
The partridges, was concentrating on running too.
But the priest hurriedly
Locked himself in his house.   130
          The peasant returned home
And had a talk with his wife:
"Speak up," he said, "and tell me
How you lost the partridges."
She answered him: "As God's my help,   135
As soon as the priest saw me,
He begged me, if I really loved him,
To show him the partridges,
Because he wanted very much to see them.
Well, I led him straight there   140
Where I had them covered up.
Right away he had his hands open,
And he took them and ran away;
But I didn't follow him;
Instead I let you know right away."   145
He answered, "You must be speaking the truth.

Now let him be for now."
And so the priest was fooled,
And Gombaut, who caught the partridges.
      This fabliau illustrates   150
How a woman is made to deceive:
She turns lies into truth,
And truth into lies.
He who made this fabliau and this *dit*
Doesn't want to make it longer.   155
Here ends the fabliau of the partridges.

THE JUDGMENT ON CUNTS

This fabliau tells and informs us
That there was once, beneath the authority of the Count
Of Blois, a man who had
Three daughters, whom he very much wanted
To attain honor.   5
They were in love with
A very handsome and noble young man
Who was of a very good family;
But he was not very rich,
And he was not miserly or stingy.   10
He put on a good show for all three:
He was engaged to each of them
To take them each as his wife.
All three held him very dear.
Now I will tell you about their affair.   15
      The eldest couldn't keep quiet any longer,
So she told her sister that she loved
A handsome young man.
The other replied, "Who is he then?"
"He's Robin from over the bridge."   20
"Alas!" said she, "I was born to evil,
Since my sister has gone so crazy
That she loves the man who loves me!"
"May the evil bellyache bind you!"
Said the youngest; "he loves me!"   25
And so all three were in great
Confusion over only one man.
      Here came the good man
Who was the girls' father.

And the eldest of the three maidens   30
Went straight to her father
And courteously said to him,
"Father, I want to get married.
If you would give me
The man who has loved me for a long time,   35
Our family and our lineage
Would all be greatly honored."
"Daughter, as God may bless me,"
Said the father, "you are greatly wrong."
"Right! May God strike me dead first!"   40
Said the one who was born next;
"I am loved three times as much by the man
She's boasting about and taking credit for."
"Why should I be put last?"
Said the last-born; "I boast indeed   45
That he loves me more eagerly
Than he does either of you two."
The father was completely amazed:
When he heard them argue,
He began to get very angry.   50
The father said: "This cannot be!
No clerk or priest would judge
That all three of you could have one man.
But before the month is out,
I'll get some advice about this."   55
They said, "Do it now,
For we would like to know soon
Which one should have him."
            The good man went to church
To hear mass. On the way back,   60
He met his full brother,
Seized him by the hand,
And drew him aside for some advice.
"Brother," he said, "as God may protect me,
You are my brother, and you ought to   65
Advise me if I have the need."
"Yes," said the brother, "that's only right."
"Brother," he said, "very great discord
Has come into my house:
My daughters are having a great quarrel.   70
They love a young man,
All three, without let-up;

Each one declared that she would have him."
Their uncle said: "There won't be a one of them
Who will be sure she can have him,   75
If I can act wisely!"
          The two brothers went off
Into the house, it seems to me,
Where the three maidens were
Who were involved with the young man.   80
Their uncle called them:
"Nieces," he said, "come here!
Tell me about your business."
Immediately the maidens
Came before their uncle;   85
They weren't quiet or speechless,
But spoke up very loudly.
First of all, the eldest
Told him that she had a boyfriend,
Handsome and courteous and very cute,   90
And that she wanted to marry him.
The second couldn't contain herself any longer,
But said, "You're lying, really. I will have him,
Because I met him before you did."
The youngest didn't know what to say.   95
She was full of anger and wrath;
She took a stick in both hands,
Beat her sister with it right in the kidneys,
And tumbled her to the ground.
Their uncle went to separate them.   100
"Nieces," he said, "settle down!
The judgment of which one
Should have him will soon be made,
And she will have some of my money, too:
I'll give her one hundred Tournai sous,   105
And I'll award her lover
To the one who can best reply
To what I'm going to say."
They all replied together:
"We agree to it entirely.   110
Ask! We'll answer."
"Very well," said the good man.
          He called on three of the most accomplished
Municipal leaders from among his neighbors
To make a rightful judgment   115

Concerning what each girl would say.
First he asked the eldest:
"Niece, there is no concealing anything;
Who is older, you or your cunt?"
"Uncle, by God and by his name,   120
My cunt is, in good faith,
So help me God, older than I:
It has a beard; I don't have one.
If I have answered well,
Judge right and faithfully."   125
The town leaders heard
What the maiden said.
          Then, without arguing, the second girl came forward.
Her uncle put her to the test:
"Now tell me about your cunt,   130
If it's older than you, my niece!"
"Uncle," said she, "I am a great
Deal older than my cunt,
For I have large and long teeth,
And my cunt still doesn't have any.   135
Now don't refuse me Robin
If I'm the one who should have him."
          Now the two had spoken what they knew.
Then the last born was called.
Her uncle spoke to her: 140
"Niece," he said, "now you must tell me
If your cunt is older than you
Or you are older than it?"
"Uncle," said she, "I would not hold back
From telling you for anything;   145
Let whoever wishes think it foolish:
My cunt is younger than I.
And I will tell you the reason why:
I am weaned from the breast;
My cunt has a hungry mouth: 150
It is young and wants to suckle.
Now I dare to affirm
That I have found a good reason.
May his soul be honored
Who will judge these words justly!"   155
"Young lady, with good judgment
You have answered with this reasoning.
You have completely won,"

The town leaders said to her.
Then, without any argument, they gave her   160
The one who had loved her for a long time.
       Now I go seeking throughout the country
To find whether the judgment is well made.
May God pardon you for your wrong doings!
If you know any way to improve on it,   165
I come to ask you for it.

THE PRIEST WHO WAS CRUCIFIED

I would like to begin a tale
Which I learned about my lord Rogier,
A fine free master workman
Who knew how to make statues
And fashion crucifixes skillfully.   5
He was no apprentice,
But made good and beautiful statues.
But his wife had fallen
Desperately in love with a priest.
Her husband led her to believe   10
That he had to go to market
And take a statue with him,
For which, he said, he would get money,
And the lady very willingly
Let him, and was very happy about it.   15
When he saw her face light up,
Then he could well perceive
That she intended to deceive him,
Just as she had become accustomed to doing.
Then he threw upon his neck   20
A crucifix chosen for that occasion
And left the house.
He went to town and stayed there
And waited until that time
When he thought that they would be together.   25
His heart trembled with anger.
He arrived back home.
Through a peekhole he saw them,
Seated for a meal.
He called, but it was   30
Too risky to open the door.

The priest had nowhere to flee.
"God," said the priest, "what shall I do"
The lady said, "I'll tell you:
Take your clothes off and go   35
In there and stretch out
With these other crucifixes."
Whether he wanted to or not,
The priest did it—note it well.
Soon the priest was undressed.   40
He stretched out among the wooden statues,
Just as if he were one of them.
When the good man didn't see him,
Right away he realized
That he had gotten in among the statues.   45
But he acted very wisely concerning this,
Because he took his time and drank
Plenty before he made a move.
When he had gotten up from eating,
He began to sharpen   50
His knife on a big tail-strap.
The gentleman was strong and valiant.
"Lady," he said, "quickly light
A candle and come inside
With me where I have some work to do."   55
The lady didn't dare hold back.
She lighted a candle
And went with her lord
Quickly into the workshop.
And the good man immediately   60
Saw the priest all stretched out,
And he marked him well.
He saw the balls and the prick hanging down.
"Lady," he said, "I've blundered
Badly with this statue.   65
I was drunk, that's what I think,
When I left that thing there.
Light up, and I'll fix it."
The priest didn't dare to move.
And I tell you this in truth: 70
That he cut off the prick and balls,
So that he didn't leave a thing
That he didn't completely cut away.
When the priest felt himself wounded,

He left, fleeing,   75
And the good man at once
Cried out with loud cries:
"Lords, catch my crucifix
Which just now escaped from me!"
Then the priest encountered   80
Two young men who were carrying a bucket;
And it would have been better for him to be in Arles,
Because there was a rogue
Who had a crowbar in his hand;
He struck him so hard on the neck   85
That he threw him into a soft mud-pit.
When he had beaten him to the ground,
Along came the good man,
Who brought him back to his house again:
Fifteen pounds in ransom   90
He immediately made him give,
So that he was never short of money.
      This tale shows us well
That no priest for any reason whatsoever
ought to love another man's wife,   95
Or come or go around her;
Nor should anyone get involved in a quarrel,
Lest he leave either balls or forfeit,
Just as the priest, Constant, did,
Who left his hanging there.   100

THE YOUNG MAN WITH TWELVE WIVES

Lords, would you like me to tell you
What happened once in Normandy?
The man I learned about this from
Said that a well-respected young man
In that country wanted to get married.   5
But he declared and swore
That he would never in his life take a wife
Unless he got twelve of them in hand.
      "Son," said the father, "what are you talking about?
One wife has been so hard on me   10
That I'm exhausted.
I'd gladly say whoa,
If I could get away with it;

But one has worn me out so much
That I can't help myself any more. 15
Son, take one wife,
And try that and see how it goes
Until the end of the year.
If she doesn't serve you to your liking,
I'll let you have two, 20
Or three or four or five or six
Or seven or eight or nine or ten,
Or however many more you want.
Never have any doubts about that."
"Father," said the son, "this isn't right: 25
Just one wouldn't do a thing.
And what good would that be?" But his parents
Lectured him and guided him so much
That they gave him one maiden,
Who was very attractive and beautiful. 30
The 'young lady had often heard
The young man's boast
That he would never take a wife
Unless he got ten or twelve of them;
But she said to herself 35
That within one year she would tame him so thoroughly
(If she got him in her arms)
That she would make him cry, "Enough!"
        When the young man had married her,
His wife urged him 40
[And took great pains to serve him well;
And he who expected to conquer her,
Sought her just as eagerly,
And night and day contended with her,
Until he was in great agony. 45
Before half a year had passed,
He was so much worse off
That he couldn't stand on his feet,
For his body wasted away,
And his neck, which used to be 50
Big and stout, became frail;
Now he was in such bad shape
That it seemed that he had pined away.
And his wife solicited him again]
Day and night to make love, 55
To embrace and kiss.

"Sir," said she, "what's wrong with you?
You used to be so hardy,
So sharp and so active,
And so vigorous and so helpful   60
That you wouldn't let me sleep.
And now I see you keep so still
That I really believe in my heart
That you love someone else."
"Oh, alas!" he said; "By faith, let God have   65
Nothing to do with this jealousy!
A lot I need to be in love,
And a lot you're worried about it!"
"I am, sir, as God's my help,
Because you don't take any pleasure with me any more."   70
"That's not it," he said; "it's because I'm dying.
I have nothing left but skin and bones.
For the love of God, leave me alone!
Do you want to be sporting now?
A curse on that kind of sport!"   75
"This," she said, "is a fine song!
Now tell me what you would have done
If you had had twelve wives?
If the one had had her pleasure from you,
The next would have wanted hers.   80
There would have been a great fight over it.
Each one in turn would have wanted
To have her joy and comfort.
But you're so worn out from me,
You can't even move your loins.   85
Now I can really see
That you would have been a lot worse off
If you had had twelve wives."
          That's how it was for a while.
The young man's father was a worthy man.   90
One day he came to speak to him:
"Son," he said, "today you must
Wed a wife before God,
And tomorrow another one. Now decide on a place
Where you can have your wedding.   95
I have looked after your interests very well.
You have one. I have eleven more for you.
You must have twelve!"
"Twelve," he cried, "to hell with that!

A hundred men couldn't satisfy them!   100
[I have too many already, I swear to you.
Leave me in peace, for the love of God.]"
       That's how matters stood for a long time,
Until it happened—I don't know how
Or by what chance—   105
That somebody caught a wolf in the field
In the town where this man lived.
It had been causing great damage.
Someone judged that it should be skinned;
Someone else judged it should be drowned;   110
A third, that it be burned to ashes,
And a fourth judged that it should be hanged—
Until the young man came along,
Who was very thin and pale.
The husband, the one I've told you about,   115
Who used to be so gay of heart,
Spoke up and told them this:
"Give him a wife, I beg you,
And he'll be ruined just the way I was
And so cruelly confined   120
That he'll never be happy in his life.
That way you'll deprive him of his life."
When they heard that, everybody laughed.
Along came his wife, who told them,
"Lords, believe him,   25
For no one is more ruined than he is."
       [Everyone considered this to be a good judgment.
They gave the wolf to a wife then,
But it didn't belong to her for a month
Before its skin, which had been so furry,   130
Was everywhere as thin
As if it had been torn out,
Because she led it such a life
That the wolf went so mad
That at last it had to die   135
And depart from this world.
And so they had vengeance on the wolf
By the advice of the man who had married foolishly.
       By this story I want to warn
Braggarts who marry foolishly   140
Not to do any bragging before marriage;
And to make sure that pride doesn't humble them,

Let them take care of one wife;
For one wife would take on
A hundred men, one by one,
And would tell them "Checkmate in the corner!"]   145

Lines 128–147 in the Hamilton 257(C) are so dissimilar that we offer below
the version of that manuscript:

There wasn't a cow in the country
Or a pig or a sheep
Or a single mare that he didn't kill.
The town was terrified,
And they were very happy when they caught him.   5
And I believe they took him
Just as fast as they could
To the town leaders and the provost.
One of them judged that he should be maimed.
Another condemned him to be skinned,   10
The third condemned him to be tied
To a chain and swung from it,
And the fourth condemned him to be hanged,
And the fifth, to be burned to ashes.
When they had said everything they wanted,   15
Skin him or burn him
Or leave him to starve,
Then along came the young man,
The husband I told you about
Who used to be so light-hearted.   20
There was never such a marvel:
Now his flesh had changed so much
That he could hardly brush off
The flies that ran around over him.
He spoke up after they had all spoken: 25
"Gentlemen, now listen a little,
And I'll gladly tell you
And instruct you very well
How you can ruin this wolf,
All without even beating or striking him.   30
If you skin him or kill him,
His martyrdom will soon be over:
Let him stay alive in a kind of pain
That lie will never escape from."
And they said, "Well, tell us how!"   35

"I will tell you," he said, "briefly:
As God may grant me joy,
Make him marry a wife right away,
And you'll have him so ruined
That he was never so bad off in his life."   40
Then they all started laughing,
And his wife spoke up:
"Let's go, my dear friend,
You have just taught some good advice!"
She who was both wise and clever,   45
Enlightened and well put together,
Took her husband and led him away
And very gently bathed him.
She had him drink and eat plenty
And shaved and barbered him regularly   50
And let him rest and sleep
And have all his pleasures
Until he filled out
And got his strength back   55
          Now he got his pay
For the outrage he had been demanding:
The twelve wives whom he wanted
But whom his wife wanted to deny him.
          This fabliau says in the end   60
That anyone who believes his wife more than he does himself
Will often have pain and sorrow.
Therefore, nobody should boast
Of anything he cannot accomplish,
Because it is right that anyone who chases after trouble   65
Should have trouble done to him.

SECTION 13

MORIZ VON CRAÛN

Introduction by Albrecht Classen

Shortly after 1500 the German Emperor Maximilian I commissioned his custom official Hans Ried, probably because of his calligraphic skills, to collect a large number of medieval heroic epics. Ried began with his task in 1504 and copied many of the most famous Middle High German heroic epics, but also courtly romances, and verse novellas, until the manuscript was completed in 1516. Because this manuscript was deposited in the library of castle Ambras near Innsbruck, it is called the "Ambraser Heldenbuch," although today it is housed in the National Library of Austria, Vienna. Many of the text contained in this manuscript were copied only once, although we are certain that they enjoyed a considerable popularity throughout the centuries. They were either transmitted orally for all those years, or all other manuscripts containing them have been lost.

Moriz von Craûn is one of those texts in the "Ambraser Heldenbuch" for which we have no other written documents. The date of the original could have been either ca. 1170/80 or, as the majority of scholar believe, ca. 1220/30. We know nothing about the author, but believe that he came from the Western Rhine region near Strassburg. He (she?) used, as his model, an anonymous French *fablel* (short entertaining narrative) "Du chevalier qui recovra l'amour de sa dame," but expanded and changed it considerably. The true meaning of this text has remained obscure and provoked many scholars to explore the enigmatic intricacies of this text. Obviously the author was intrigued by the question of how to determine guilt in the case of the two lovers in his narrative. *Moriz von Craûn* casts a highly ambivalent light on both the male hero Moriz and the Countess of Beaumunt. But the text also seems to be a parody of courtly culture, of tournaments, and the entire concept of courtly love. Andreas Capellanus' love treaties might well have exerted influence on this German novella because the dominant issue seems to be to provide a complex casuistic case of a conflict between lovers. The idea would be to discuss both sides and use the literary text as a basis for a highly sophisticated debate among the audience.

BIBLIOGRAPHY

Ruth Harvey, *Moriz von Craûn and the Chivalric World* (Oxford: Clarendon, 1961).

J. Wesley Thomas, "Structure and Interpretation in Four Medieval German Novellas,"*Spectrum Medii Aevi. Essays in Early German Literature in Honor of George Fenwick Jones.* Ed. William C. McDonald. Göppinger Arbeiten zur Germanistik, 362 (Göppingen: Kümmerle, 1983), 509–520. *Moriz von Craûn Mittelhochdeutsch/Neuhochdeutsch.* Übersetzung, Kommentar und Nachwort von Albrecht Classen (Stuttgart: Reclam, 1992).

Albrecht Classen, "Moriz, Tristan, and Ulrich as Master Disguise Artists: Deconstruction and Reenactment of Courtliness in *Moriz von Craûn, Tristan als Mönch, and Frauendienst,* in *Journal of English and German Philology* 103, 4 (2004): 475–504.

ANONYMOUS (either ca. 1170 or ca. 1220)

Translated by J. W. Thomas

You have often heard and have come to know with certainty this truth: that knighthood always was and always should be esteemed. We learn from books where it began and where it moved to later. The land in which the art of chivalry first appeared is called Greece, but it has since vanished from there. Knighthood sprang up in Greece when its armies besieged Troy because of a woman. One could indeed see there, so the story goes, many Greeks who constantly strove with like zeal for knightly fame.

Bold and stalwart warriors—Hector, Paris, Helenus, Deiphobus, and their brother Troilus—often defended the plain before their walls from the invaders and responded to the haughty Greeks in such a manner that the latter brought dead and wounded back to their camp. They struggled many years, for truly the attacks and defense of the Greeks never ceased. I would tell you still more about Troy, but what good would that do? We can let it go, because no one is able to relate it all. Even Dares—who was there, who wrote down and recited at night what had happened during the day, as he had seen it with his own eyes—could not tell the whole story of how the Trojans defended their land as long as Hector lived and protected them. However, when he perished, their renown faded greatly, day by day, for his heart was the heart of all.

Pandarus and Aeneas also contended fiercely for all to see, in the vanguard where heroic deeds were performed. Often there were so many fearless contests being fought before Troy that one could hardly see between the gleaming swords. That was no place for a coward, where warriors from many lands had to fight the defenders of the city constantly, for they struggled furiously then. Many fainthearted men would have died without a wound because of their ceaseless fear. When the Trojans lost Hector, whom they had chosen as their protector, the position of the city worsened daily until it lay desolate. Wondrous things happened at Troy. That is a special story which I would be glad to tell in full if I could. Why haven't I done so? I don't know it well enough.

Knighthood can thrive only where it is loved, as was seen in Greece. It soon flees from the one who hates it, and did so from this land. When it tired of the decay there, it left. One must pay dearly when one gains honor through knightly deeds. That is a very old custom which, however, has lost nothing because of age, but renews itself daily, grows, and spreads afar. Honor and disgrace avoid one another. What the esteemed Alexander conquered for the Greeks, they gave up against their will, and their own worthlessness was to blame for their injury: they who once received tribute now pay it. A man should therefore hold fast to honor; it rewards without deceit.

Later there was no city in all the lands that could compare with Rome in power and splendor. It was famous. The proud Romans began to practice chivalry and realized at once that it afforded a noble enjoyment that became greater day by day. Knighthood abode in Rome after it was driven from Greece. As soon as it arrived there, Julius Caesar received it in knightly manner and conquered all the lands, so that they paid him tribute. His hand won greater praise than anyone else will ever gain as long as the world endures. Whoever is taught by his heart to do his very best gladly will surely succeed, but I see many men in this world living with no more honor than a beast. What good is life to such a man? He wastes both the happiness and the stores that God has given us all.

Rome's fame lasted until King Nero became ruler of the lands. He was a very wicked man who did everything, good or evil, that came into his head: nothing could prevent him from carrying out whatever his arrogance counseled. He had himself treated as a woman and indeed preferred men to women. Hear how he lay one day thinking about what it would be like for a woman to carry and give birth to a child. Since King Nero was most eager to know, he sent at once for his physician and asked, "How can you treat me so that I may have a child? You had better think of a way, for you will die if you don't."

"There is a very good medicine for that," the physician answered, "I shall fully carry out your order," and he gave him a powder that caused a toad to grow in his stomach. The king then started to bear a very heavy burden, although he might easily have been spared it, and when the toad commenced to grow large in him, he looked like a woman in front. Now he constantly regretted that he had ever begun this, for he feared the pains of labor. He therefore told the physician to abort the child and cure him. The physician did as he was ordered and helped the king to come out of it well and recover.

Nero was a tall man with large bones, and his mother was small. He thus always wondered where there could ever be a place in her so big that she could give birth to him. He had to find that out also and wouldn't rest until he ordered her cut open. She had to suffer this because of his wicked pleasure. He looked under the breasts and found countless wonders all the way down the body.

The king committed many outrages. Just hear what he did to destroy Rome. When he was told what had happened at the conquest of Troy, he sent for all his men and complained: "The Romans have wronged me so gravely that I indeed cannot rest until I see to it that they atone to me with their own ruin. Whoever helps avenge my grievance I promise to make very powerful and rich before I am through." Then his troops began a great battle against the lords of the city, as the king had commanded: he bade them set fires in many streets. He acted so unseemly because he wanted to see what had occurred at Troy. Rome was laid waste by the flames, and all the gallant men on both sides lay dead. Never in a thousand years had so much cruelty and shame appeared in their land as at that time: one still sees many deserted palaces. All Rome burned down because of a single man.

Knighthood then had to leave Rome, for it was poor in body and goods and had been robbed of its high spirits like an orphan by bitter hardships. It came to France in wretched state and lived there meagerly for a long time, until Charlemagne began to conquer the lands with his armies. Because of their bold courage, Oliver and Roland chose it as a comrade and practiced it in a knightly manner, for which they were highly praised. When their countrymen saw what fame the two had won, they followed their example, and thus all began to profit.

No one ever lived in a country which embraced joy more than France does, for their chivalry is noble. It is well-known and esteemed, and many other lands have greatly improved their knightly customs through its guidance. There they serve the ladies for pay in a most refined manner, because they are better rewarded in France than anywhere else.

Not long ago a knight lived there whose thoughts all turned to the love of a lady and whose heart counseled him to serve the countess of Beaumont at all times, for he found no one more highly regarded. This man, who is still famous, was named Moriz, and his ancestral home was at Craûn. He served her a long time eagerly and loyally, for journeying and presenting gifts were his whole life, and he was always hoping to be rewarded. When he came into the borderland of France to take part in tournaments, there was no one on either side who did better or won more praise for it. He was handsome, well-mannered, courtly, prudent, and worldly-wise. He therefore behaved commendably, and everyone was rightly pleased with him.

Since things were going so well with him, he did as light-hearted gentlemen often do who love and gladly accept whatever they get in exchange. To be sure, the constant lover frequently wins both pain and distress. Still, if his faithfulness helps him to gain a reward that he has sincerely desired, then he is fully repaid for what he suffered before. That is now sweet and good, because he is richly compensated and is never pained by regret at having begun his suit.

Many people say with respect to this matter that all living things on earth, wild or tame, are destined to be subject to man and his wisdom. I thought so too before I learned that it can indeed not be. Without a blow Love forces a man to greater loyalty than an emperor could. So this man too was compelled to believe that he had to do and leave undone whatever Love commanded, whether it brought him comfort or distress.

Who is well acquainted with Love knows that she burns the heart in her fire: a man needs to be careful and consider how he can save himself from disgrace. Whatever harm befalls him, he must treat it as if it were nothing. You should know the truth of this, that one can never pay the price of honor by sparing oneself. Nobody now alive would expect to love without harm—he wouldn't have good sense, for Harm is the counselor of Love. If he is to carry out his affair to a happy ending, he who turns to Love should display much constancy until he persuades her to let him succeed with her.

I advise him who is in love and is wise to flee inconstancy and appeal to faithfulness. He will thus quickly take on a sweet burden, and all will end as he desires. There is much inconstancy in the world. I compare him who becomes fond of it to thieves: when one is hanged, the other does not consider limiting or giving up his stealing because of it. However often an unfaithful man sees a faithful one succeed, it means no more to him than a splash in the sea, for he wants nothing better.

I could warn you against much here, and must lament one thing more. Through the world a modish pair is moving that conquers many noble lovers, which is a wound to honor. Pray now that our Savior may turn them from the two! I'll tell you their names: Vanity and Error. May God keep them away from good people, who go to ruin because of them—I ask nothing for evil men, who will act according to their natures. Whoever becomes a companion of the pair because of inconstancy I call a faithless creature. They are not better together and become more wanton all the time: Vanity gives and Error takes. (No one could get me to do anything, even for pay, if it cost me some of my wealth.) A woman behaves the same way and soon creates want: who pays for shame with his property doubles the offense. Many people find fault with this price and rightly so, for it is a crime to forsake honor because of lust.

The nature of many men is such that, rather than suffer any kind of difficulty because of a good woman, they prefer to avoid them all. These men lack sense and think loss is profit. I would count it gain if, to further my happiness, I were to strive through service for honor or reward in courtly love. I claim this right for myself.

Sir Moriz knew how to maintain himself in a most courtly manner and therefore was sure to win honor from noblewomen, whose company he enjoyed: the reward of the vulgar is small. He chose one of them and served her a long time. Whoever serves and is able to profit by service, let him serve so as to benefit himself most and where one can reward him. Whatever rewards evil women give, they often make a man's soul and body joyless and of little worth. The good women give us high spirits and repay us with fame for whatever our service has cost. It is right that a courtly man who knows how to win their favor should serve them.

No matter what the faithful Sir Moriz had always earned from his lady, he still had to wait for his reward until he began to be uncertain and very unhappy. One night while lying alone and thinking about his trouble, he said, "I am sorry I was ever born. Am I to lose completely the hope I have always had? She whom I have served so much does not accept my efforts and is too late with her pay. I can therefore never be happy." Then he spoke again, "I am not prudent in this. From one land to another my service has brought me such praise that people have esteemed me as being noble, and my lady rewards me thus. What pay could be better! On the other hand I have to suffer some distress. How could I avoid it, for he who wants to strive for honor must give up ease. Still, if he wishes to escape sorrow, a man should consider carefully, and then everything will turn out well no matter how grievous his situation is. Taking thought is the best protection against trouble.

"It is quite clear that I am foolish and am wasting my time to no purpose. God knows that no one was ever so tormented as I, and I'll tell you how. I have always faithfully loved one who treats me as an enemy: as often as I implore her, I get only threats. How could I rejoice because of her, when I see myself in the distressing state where I can obtain neither a reward nor a promise from her for whom I have given up all other women? I serve and strive until it is the ruin of me. That is wretched grief. I would rather have a gentle death than to be chained like this. But it is she who must cure me; I must remain unrewarded by all women except her."

He thought thus about his lament: "What good does it do for me always to endure such terrible sorrow? I am the more foolish because of it. Whoever has become accustomed to care does not mind grieving, and that has happened to me. In this respect I must admit in truth that my heart has always been a coffer filled with sadness, that I have never lacked for pain, and that happiness has been a stranger to me. Indeed, my heart still knows nothing of joy except that I have often heard what has brought it to others. When I thought of it, I would gladly have done the same. This would make a Bavarian shilling out of each of my thousand sorrows. How could I endure them if my lady will not save me?

"It will be shameful if she will not tell me her intentions: I won't give her my life in exchange for death from longing. First, I'll see if she will allow me to be free of my trouble. Should her sweet comfort console me, then I would be forever proud and happy at last. However, considering what has happened up till now, I must be prepared for one thing (if I ever see the day I can speak to her): her heart may pay for my service with anger, for it is hard as flint. That is why fate has played vexing tricks on me with respect to her. But lack of faith robs me of comfort, and a most unwise resolve causes me to accuse a fate that still lies ahead of ill-treatment. If fortune had been kinder, it would have spared me half of what I have suffered. Perhaps she will think better of it. Oh, if I could only know that before I see her!"

Filled with these misgivings, he came to where the lady stood. Listen to what happened as soon as he saw her: fear made him pale, then flush, then pale again. He changed color several times before he could say a single word, long or short, which annoyed the lady. "Why are you acting this way?" she demanded.

"Lady, I am unhappy."

"For what reason, or shouldn't you tell me?"

"No, lady, I just have to endure it."

"Speak. What is wrong with you?"

"Lady, do I have permission to say?"

"Yes. Tell me what troubles you."

"Lady, I am disconsolate."

"That can be very distressing for you."

"It is indeed, my lady."

"Is anything else the matter with you?"

"Yes, lady, I feel bad."

"Where?"

"All over."

"Then you should rub an ointment on yourself."

"I can't, for I know nothing of such things."

"But you are a strong man."

"Lady, my strength is gone."

"Would you like my advice?"

"Yes, lady, very much."

"Go to Salerno. There are many doctors in that place; if you are to recover, they will cure you. You may be sure of that."

"Lady, it is high time to stop this arguing, for I need a respite. I have lost my senses because of you, as you probably know, and you are now robbing me of my happiness. This is pillage that I am eager to avoid. Mistress of my joy, show me your kindness—which I greatly need—or I must die. I want you to reward me with death or with confident expectation; that is why I have come. Now I would like to hear how I am to leave, rich or very poor."

"Although I am not to blame for this," the lady replied, "I admit being indebted to you. All your life you have served me well and so much that I shall gladly pay you. You should know that I would do what might harm me forever, rather than remain the warden of your happiness any longer. For some time I have wanted to reward you as well as I can. A dependable man will become a thief for love of good pay. Because of your service, I must risk my honor from now on. It can't be helped, since 'thou art mine and I am thine.' Therefore do one thing for me," the countess continued, "and I shall never cease to repay you." He could hardly wait to learn what she wanted.

"Hold a tournament just outside the town," she said, "so that I can watch it here. Now arrange this soon, because I have never seen one. Be my knight here, and I'll reward you when I can." He then became a happy man. Without anyone noticing, she drew a fine ring with a precious stone from her finger and placed it on one of Sir Moriz's. The noblewoman wanted to indicate that she was marking him with it according to the customs of ladyloves. He took leave at once. She raised her beautiful arms, embraced him most tenderly, kissed him on the lips, and commended him to God's care. Her love put an end to his worry and distress and made up for all he had suffered because of her.

My lord Moriz von Craûn got himself many pages, who proclaimed this tournament in all the lands around. If I were able, I would now tell you just how the lord prepared for it. Using strange materials, he had a ship made that was to move over the fields without hindrance as if on the sea. This was done to excite wonder; the ship's master would have to have great wealth and knowledge to complete it.

Listen to how he devised the ship; I wish I could do it justice. Its keel was a wagon that held light beams, shaped in the form of a ship that might sail to Cologne, The master builder ordered these joined together and a deck laid. In it many holes were bored all around both sides where spears were to stand. So that the ship which was thus made could move, he constructed it as follows: a framework was built around it—on which it rested like a large building on a high foundation—so that one could drive it along on wheels.

The master had sent to Flanders for a fine, red fabric which made up all the outer walls. He went around and fastened it to the beams with good, long nails that were as white as silver: a ship needs many nails. He built this cloth ship with great care so that people would be pleased with it and ordered that the bow, the stern, and the high mast that was soon raised be solidly plated with gold. He attached a large rudder, as would be done with a real ship. He wanted to have still more gear for his vessel, as if it were to journey across the sea, so brass anchors and a railing of silk line were added. This was most unusual, and he could easily have dispensed with them as a vain waste, because the ship stood on a dry shore.

The people from far and near who saw this ship said, "What might that be? There is no Meuse or Rhine here: how will he send it on its way? Unless he is afraid of the Flood and wants to save himself in it, it is property lost. Of what other use could it be?" This news spread widely before the time of departure arrived.

When the ship was ready, it was decked out all over with the lord's coat of arms. All the helmsmen and seamen were dressed in his colors and looked as if their clothing had been made by the same tailor. I wish I could describe it to you rightly. He now ordered that the oars be carried on board and after them a wagon-load of spears. Three hundred of them, the color of the mast, had been kept separate from the others so that none would be lost. To each of these a costly pennon, like the sail, was tied at once. The lord ordered that they be placed upright in their holes and adjusted in the same way. The other spears were white. It was strange that he should want to use all of them up in one day in honor of the lady.

Without many people knowing it, he slyly brought into the ship the horses that were to pull it when they wanted to set out. Harnesses had been arranged between the cloth walls and the board floor, and the horses were hitched up there. That no one outside could see what was going on inside was a clever idea. The horses were so concealed that whosoever observed with his own eyes the ship moving would swear it was a dream. His shield was hung in the middle of the mast so that he would be recognized. The sail gleamed far across the land like a Lombard banner.

When the skipper came aboard, he directed the men to avoid completely the roads themselves, for easier passage, and to travel at all times over the open fields. The people then followed him, just as if it were a wedding celebration, and looked at everything there was to see. His sailors sang and rowed, but their labor went for nothing, because their strokes did not make the ship go any faster.

In this so knightly manner he journeyed through France to where the tournament was to be held. Many people gathered there—knights and ladies, old and young—to see the ship. A fair wind drove him to the field before the castle; he disembarked at once, and a tent was set up. His harbor was above a running spring by a meadow. It was not long until all the people came out of the castle with festive clamor and gazed at the skipper as at a strange beast.

His coat of arms was sewn to the cloth of the protective covering of his splendid tent. He would have been sorry to have left this behind because he could display it with honor. It was pitched on the grass with fine ropes. The knob was a mirror and the studs on the tent poles were of very hard sapphires. Beneath the tent lay long, broad quilts of splendidly ornamented sendal and gold on which the guests were to sit. Those who wished to enjoy his plenty were well received. A full cask of wine, as clear as could be, stood there, with a wooden cup floating in it so that everyone who was thirsty could get his own drink.

No other lord had ever treated the minstrels who came there so well: enough of these wanderers were in and before his tent to have carried off a house. When daylight was gone, so many large, wound candles were lit that they seemed to the people up in the castle a fire, as if a barn were burning. His tent gleamed in splendor. Had he been wearing the country's crown, it would not have been disgraced. Early in the morning the knights decided to come to the ship for mass. They did this, all together, which so pleased the skipper that he hardly knew what to do. A hen was roasted for each two knights. After they had eaten them and each had drunk his fill, the mass was sung and all hurried forth to arm themselves.

As soon as the lord of Craûn had the time and the room to do so, he put on a goathair doublet and asked for a soft felt cloth which he tied in front of his knees to protect them. He then had his legs enclosed in stockings of white mail. These were firm but not heavy, for he preferred light armor: he could spring about like a roe. He bound a fine girdle around his hips and fastened the stockings to it. They brought him a helmet which completely covered his forehead so that no one could even scratch the skin underneath. At last he drew on a hauberk, white as snow, and had the thongs tied very firmly with knots.

When all this was done, he boarded the ship with those whom he wanted to accompany him. A squire went to get his strong, handsome horse, brought it secretly to the door, and concealed it in the ship. The knight ordered that the others be led to a nearby hill where they were to wait for him. Then he had the sail turned toward the castle walls and set out with great pomp. They beat tambourines and sounded flutes and horns. No man was ever so angry but that this joyous music would have dispelled his ill humor. They blew long trumpets, and many notes rang out from pipes and rotes, as if the knight were leading a band of pirates and about to attack a ship on the sea.

Up in the castle, close to the gate, stood the countess's stately palace, which was beautifully adorned with marble. The windows were filled with ladies, in the midst of whom sat the one who had caused all this. "Do you know what is coming there?" she asked. "It is beautiful. I think that Saint Brandan has journeyed here to see miracles. However, let no one be dismayed if it is the Antichrist, because Judgment Day is near. Therefore do not listen to his words: we must have more faith in God."

The lord ordered that his craft be driven up to the mountain and near the palace. There he dropped anchor in order to hold fast to the land. When the knights learned that the ship had anchored, they rode onto the field. Why make a long story of it? There was such a crowd around the ship that they hardly had room to contend. The tournament had attracted many knights, who were evenly divided between the two sides. As soon as it began, the count came down from the castle and, while his wife was looking on, happened to kill an opponent with his spear. This made them both very sad. The count clearly showed his grief, weeping bitterly that he should ever become laden with guilt because of knighthood, and took off his armor at once. He rode to the castle, disheartened at his sin.

Everyone was unhappy at the distressing event, but the skipper who had sailed there over land urged them to continue. "My ship and I have come to be present," he said. "See what an honor that is for you. You would never live down the shame if I were to drown on dry land." Then one after another said that it would be most unusual if the tournament should be ruined. "What if a man has died? Let us commit his soul to Saint Michael and joust." All advised as he had desired.

A great clamor arose from the lists as many helmets and shields resounded and many men were unhorsed. When the lord in the ship saw a host of bold knights wielding swords and spears out on the field, he put on a surcoat of fine samite that shown brightly. It was wide, well-cut, and displayed a skillfully wrought coat of arms that had the most elegant border you have ever heard of.

He tied on a helmet that suited him well. It was artfully decorated and embellished with so much gold that one could see it gleaming from afar. Anybody would think from his appearance that it was a king sitting there. They brought the knight a horse that was white as a swan and that wore a coat of sendal—he had eight others outside with equally fine trappings. He then ordered his men to bring the ship quickly to the thick of the conflict. Forward in the bow of the ship a door had been cut from which the knight now rode alone and in splendor. His company had been small when he sailed across the land, but later it had become much larger. Some of his squires came running up with one or two spears in their hands as a real battle began. He hurriedly seized his shield and a colored spear, spurred his horse forward in a fearful rage, and fell on the enemy just like an eagle on a flock of small birds.

The knight struck down one man, another, and then the third and fourth together. He unhorsed the fifth with great force, the sixth with even more, and went on to strike down the seventh and eighth. He knocked the ninth far from his horse in the midst of his friends and the tenth onto the grass. Everything fell before him. He fought with such success that all around him there were horses running riderless like a herd of breeding stock. As soon as his steed began to sweat, he gave it away and mounted another; and when he moved on to the next horse, somebody appeared at once to accept the one he had left. The skipper thereby earned the noisy support of all the wandering minstrels, through his gifts as well as his prowess.

After using up all his colored spears in regular jousts—as the lady had requested when she kissed him—the knight started on the white ones. She indeed owed him thanks, for no man ever won such great praise as he received then from both sides. Even if he had been a real heathen, outside of Christianity, whoever saw him that day would have granted him the honors, and rightly so. While he was flying around like a ball, he had the heralds announce everywhere that those who wanted gifts should go to the ship. Throughout the day they were given there whatever they desired of the things he had brought.

When evening approached, the knight retired to his tent to rest, because he was weary from wielding sword and spear. Since he knew how to satisfy with his wealth and good will anyone who asked him for a present, he was praised everywhere. He told the pages to take the ship in which he had ridden there, saying, "Who could deserve it more than you?" But as soon as they laid hands on it, a host of wanderers also hurried up. So many that no one could count them. The first got two yards of cloth, the second and third three, and the fourth enough for a coat. The fifth broke the head of the sixth, the seventh seized the mast, and the eighth the rudder. The ninth obtained the cloth for a vest, and the tenth only enough to make an ornamental hem. With such honors it was divided among them. You never before heard of so famous a ship that was never in the water.

Some time after the tournament was over, a man who had been taken captive came and begged for something from the knight. The latter pulled off his hauberk, gave it to him as a present, and received his heartfelt thanks. On removing the hauberk, he quickly drew his surcoat over his shoulders because of the cold. He waited to see if somebody would appear to take his stockings too, but no one came. He then untied the thongs on one leg. Those who had accompanied him had left him entirely alone since they had heard him say that they were to give whatever they had to whoever asked for it. For this reason no attendants were there to care for him.

While he was taking off the stocking, a messenger arrived and, finding him alone, said, "My lady has sent for you. Come now, the time is here. She told me to tell you to come to her just as you are." The knight was most happy to do this: he mounted the squire's horse and rode forth as he had been ordered. Now listen to where the squire left him—in an orchard. Waiting here at the lady's command was a pretty maiden who asked him to go with her to a room which the two women had secretly chosen for the assignation. The maiden led the hero there. On every side the walls were so covered with fine murals that the place had the splendor of a cathedral, and the ceiling was decorated with mosaics until it was as bright as a mirror inside both night and day: as if the ceiling had windows of precious stones.

The two went in alone. A bed was standing in the middle of the room; hear how it was made. The posts were large, round, and inlaid with the raised, ivory figures of every kind of beast on earth. They were framed by the gold in which the ivory had been mounted. The crosspieces were of a wood Vulcan cannot burn, and over them were stretched four leopard skins—that only very rich people have—held together by seams. All this is true, although I can't prove it. On the skins lay much large, soft bedding which was covered with elegant silk from Greece. On top of it was a quilt—I don't think Lady Cassandra or any of her race ever made a better—and a bedspread of fine, white linen. this had a border of coal-black sable a span wide above and a down fur below that was splendid and costly. The beast from which the pelts came is called an alfurt and is caught only in a land named Carthage, far across the sea, that was once ruled by Lady Dido and now belongs to the king of Morocco. Where the heads lay, the bed was made higher with a silk bolster.

The bed could well be finer than I have described, but I can do no better than to leave it as it is. In splendor it was like the one that Heinrich von Veldeke made so well for King Solomon, on which he was lying asleep when Lady Venus called and awakened him. She startled him out of his sleep with her bow when she shot him in the heart, causing pain that distressed him the rest of his life. However wise he might have been, he had to submit to her fetters because she robbed him of his senses. It was very little better with this man, who was sitting beside the maiden under such intimate and strange conditions.

Grass, leaves, and rushes were strewn on the flagstones. The two entertained each other with conversation, speaking in turn. At times she would ask him questions, and then he would inquire about all sorts of things. "This is certainly a splendid palace," the knight said, "lovely and delightful. It truly seems to me that it would be just what I would ask for, could I get my wish: that my lady were here. But I would think any house on earth, however humble, to be better than this if I once saw her go into it."

"As bad as things are with her husband," replied the maiden, "she will come as soon as she can. My lord has been in bed all day, weeping bitterly. He doesn't think he will ever be happy again since, because of you, he had the great misfortune to kill a knight. He therefore sorely laments the fact that your journey was ever undertaken and constantly curses the building of the ship. So it is that my lady must be very careful if you two are to carry out your agreement in all respects."

"My journey didn't harm your lord," said the knight, "nor has it helped me yet. But I know one thing indeed: as far as I can judge, he is a man of courtly manners who, if he were told of all I have done for his wife and knew that I were here, would command her to go to me, however much he might miss her and even though he had killed nine men." The knight sat there—sad and weary, angry and sullen—and made a motion as if he were about to lie down and be comfortable for a while. Seeing that he was annoyed, the maiden said kindly, "Why don't you lay your head in my lap and rest until my lady comes? Since you are tired and weak, it will perhaps do you good."

"I would do it if I could be sure of awakening before my lady came and found me asleep. If my nap were to cost me her favor, I would never be happy again."

"Leave it to me," answered the maiden. "I'll take care of it."

"Will you?"

"Yes."

"Then I'll go to sleep." Since she had given her permission, he then laid his head in her lap and at once fell asleep. His trouble was that he had spent so many long nights thinking about how to carry out his wasteful project with the ship and how to gain honor from that to which he had devoted a great deal of thought.

He had not lain there long when the noblewoman, who could easily have come sooner, arrived in secrecy and fear. The maiden started to awaken the weary man as soon as she heard her lady's steps, but the latter saw her and, hurrying up, ordered her not to disturb him. Then they discussed the tired knight. "I know it is true," said the beautiful lady, "that no one ever served a woman better than this man has served me: if I were to leave him unrewarded, it would be a sin for which I could never atone. I therefore heeded his lament to the extent that I was going to pay him today for his labors. Here I am, ready to do so, and he lies there like a dead sheep. He prefers sleep to me. If he had been able to do without it, I could have depended on him: I have learned that. As it is, I am not going to take the risk. If I had been so dear to him as he claimed, he would have waited better for me. No rest will cost him as much this year: whatever good it may do him later, his sleep has taken me away from him."

"I lament this before God, dear knight," spoke the maiden, "for my lady has given a hard sentence. You went to sleep trusting in me! How can I ever make up for my failure? I shall always deeply regret that you, tired and battle-scarred, were placed in my care, since you are to lose the reward for all your service because of me. Oh that I was ever fated to harm you so! Believe me, lady, should people learn of this shameful deed, you will never regain your honor: you may be sorry if you behave in such an uncourtly manner. I don't believe any man alive will serve any more for a lover's pay when he hears about this. Your anger is not well directed.

"It is displeasing to us women that this evil should burden the world because of you: that men will rely on none of us any longer. Now see how that would become you. You shouldn't make him suffer for it. It is in the nature of men that they do less for women than suits us. For God's sake, lady, consider well: there is no one here but us three. Bid him get up. If he has lost, then perhaps sixty more have lost, knights who would gladly endure hardships for noblewomen if they were to get a reward. Should they be robbed of it because of you, it is most unfortunate that you came when you did. What is the world without the wages women give? Were King Solomon living, he could not offer better advice than mine: if the knight is asleep, what of it?"

"I am sorry I ever became so much involved with courtly love," replied the countess. "I am afraid it will bring me harm. This is quite likely to follow the one who is too eager to pursue courtly love, I'll tell you what happens to those who give way to sexual passion: they make themselves prisoners, just like the man who spreads a net and falls into it himself. I intend to guard against that. I would rather be free than belong to a man, for men are disloyal. Whatever I were to do for this knight would amount to a public confession. Tomorrow probably three or four people would learn of our 'wedding' and very soon after thirty more: my honor would thus be sacrificed for nothing. Therefore I'll remain just as I am."

"You have spoken of the worst thing that can happen to you later," the maiden replied, "when you should expect the best: it would be proper for him to avoid them all. We, however, must still observe the old custom and do as women have always done. Now wake him, for it is getting late. Even though you are still unconquered, you know that in the end Love is the master of all reason."

"I am not afraid of her power and do not believe she will ever overcome me either by entreaty or by force. So see to it that the man lies here until I am gone, after that tell him to get up and go home. Bid him be more careful: it will profit him in the future." With this she departed. The good maiden was sad that the esteemed lord had not benefited from his devotion and fearful because he was to leave, unrewarded and forsaken, after having asked her to watch for him.

Just then the knight awakened from a dream and, as soon as he looked up, said to her, "I never had such an oppressive sleep. I fancied that my lady was here and would not speak to me. How could I ever get over that? If I were to lose her favor now through my own fault, I would grieve the rest of my life."

"Oh!" cried the maiden. "One tired and the other unfit, we both have failed. My lady has behaved poorly and may have harmed herself forever because of it:

a woman's anger has cost her her honor. But I indeed hope that she has since regretted her command. She came on me very quickly and without warning. Truly, I was afraid she would be offended and was looking all around, but she slipped up on me just like an incubus. She was pale with fear, but it may have been wrath that made her vacillate."

"You should have wakened me."

"I would gladly have done so if she had not strictly forbidden it. I was frightened almost to death."

"Why couldn't she have acted kindly! Now for the first time I clearly see her disloyalty. My service has been in vain," said the highly praised knight, "and I must always endure the burden of the injury done me. But what did she tell you to say to me?"

"She said only that I should let you lie for a moment and then bid you go back to your quarters.

"It would be strange indeed if I were to get any rest now that this has happened to me. Because of sleep, my misfortune will truly be awake for a long time. Lady, since you are at fault, do just one thing for me."

"Lord, I shall do it if it can possibly be done."

"My lady has made me unhappy, believe me. In the name of God go back to her and beg her for the sake of every woman's honor to restrain her anger and not leave me like this. It will be a painful story if she won't have pity on poor me. The pay she has given me too rashly for my error is more than I can bear." He urged her with pretty entreaties until she did it for him.

With tears flowing onto her hands and sleeves, the maiden sadly returned to her lady. However, although she bitterly lamented the latter's shameful deed, she acted prudently, as the knight had asked her to do: she tiptoed very quietly up to the bed in which the lady lay, lifted the covers, and gently touched her hand. As soon as the lady felt the touch, she said, "Where did you come from and what do you want now?"

"Lady, I am his messenger and want to beg you in the name of the God who gave you soul and body to honor all women and not let him lose his suit thus. You can calm the anger of the three of us by going to him, as becomes you. However hard a heart might be—though it be as unyielding as a diamond—it would become soft if it saw the grievous harm you have done him and heard his laments."

"Now believe what I tell you: his injury can easily worsen. Should my lord wake up and find him here, the knight will never leave alive. So if he is wise, let him go back as he came. You don't know what you are chattering about and are making a fool of yourself. Now be still, for I am going to stay here and sleep until morning." Vexed, she turned over and acted as if she were sleeping. The maiden sighed deeply and silently walked away, weeping because of this affront.

Annoyed at the delay, the knight had followed her to the door and was waiting there for her. When he heard her story, his heart was deeply troubled, but he spoke out as an upright man: "Lady, I commend myself to God, for life means nothing to me. I'll speak with her myself or leave it here. I shall go in there to her and find out how I have done wrong." He pushed the door open with a hard shove and quickly entered the bedroom. This night, as always, a candle was burning there in a glass.

The knight did not make a splendid appearance, as I shall explain. He had been so hard pressed by blows that the blood had run from his forehead down over his eyes, with much collecting on his brows. In his wrath the esteemed nobleman looked like a lion creeping up on his prey when he moved stealthily toward the two sleepers. Greatly distressed, the count had lain there as a troubled man who cannot sleep for grief. He had struggled so with his thoughts that he had often started up and looked around in terror. Afterwards, he slept fitfully but not for long.

As Sir Moriz came closer to the lady—in a bloody surcoat that had been slashed and stabbed almost to pieces—one of his mail stockings, the one on the right leg, rang out against the stone floor. The count looked up and cried out, too frightened to utter an incantation. He woke his wife with his clamor: "Wherever he came from, the devil is here with us, or the raging host. If God doesn't save us, we shall die." He was more afraid than his wife, who knew the hero at once. "Who goes there?" cried the count.

"I'll be glad to tell you: I am the one you killed. You must be my companion in hell forever. Since you dispatched me thither, it cannot be helped." When this apparition appeared to him, the lord of the castle sprang up from his bed in great alarm and bumped his shin so hard that he lay in a faint the rest of the night. Seeing what had happened, the knight went to the bed and said, "This is half empty. I don't know who should be here, but it is where I shall rest." Then he drew back the covers and slipped in with the lady. She was greatly surprised and, moreover, in this distressing situation did not know whether her husband were alive or dead. She dared not go to him, for the bold knight had robbed her of her wits, but she did answer.

"You are the most daring man I ever heard of," she said, "to attempt such a risky venture. You didn't ask if I wanted you to do this or not. It seems to me so strange that people will be talking about it until Judgment Day." However she was thinking, "Since things have turned out this way, it can't be helped: I'll have to let him do his will with me. Well, I'll submit in a friendly manner and dispel his anger." She kissed him once and then again. Then she spoke to him, but when he did not reply to any of her questions she tired of this and put her arms around him. The knight too began to warm up now and he did something with the lady: I don't know what. At any rate, why should I tell you? You are quite aware of what goes on under such conditions, and it might as well be left unsaid.

Afterwards the bold warrior stood up and quickly took from his white hand a ring the lady had given him. "Take back your gold," he said, "for I shall not be your lover. You are ruthless. Until now I have always been devoted to you and have gladly done everything I could to serve you. If all were like you, I would never serve a woman again. Now go to your ailing husband and live without honor. I won't punish you anew for having robbed me so shamefully of my reward." The knight thus took his leave. Later he travelled about even more than before, when he was trying to gain the lady's favor, and won praise and honor with all sorts of extravagance.

Since people spoke highly of him, she began to regret having caused him pain. Indeed, she felt such remorse that everyone noticed the change in her color. "It is only just that I should suffer," she thought, "and have sorrow instead of great love. I brought this grief on myself. If I should once again wish for a man to serve me, how could he be more suitable for a woman or more highly born than the one I have lost? I therefore curse the day when my unjust quarrel harried me until it conquered me. I have brought shame on myself that I would gladly do without. However, I shall endure the disgrace as long as I live unless God grants me such wisdom and good fortune that the knight will really love me. The maiden could see this and acted in all loyalty. How one honors oneself who gives aid to a friend for whom things are going badly! And help in time is better than that given after the man has perished."

This was at the beginning of summer. The birds in the forest sang clearly and boldly with many voices, and the roses and heather outdid each other in blooming. It was just the season when one cannot endure sorrow. The forest had again decked itself out to greet the summer in beautiful attire. Green foliage, grass resplendent with a mass of all kinds of blossoms, the sweet song of the birds: these fill with cheer everyone who is looking forward to happiness.

Early one morning when she could not sleep for care and remorse, the lady got up and, driven by her sorrow, went alone to a gallery that hung over the castle wall. She stood there at a window, as pining women often do who, like her, have endured sorrow because of love: one can see them grieving. She laid her cheek in her lovely white hand and listened to the beautiful song of the nightingale. "Happy is he who is destined to live joyfully," she said, "as I would be doing if I had allowed myself to. However, now I must waste my entire youth with great loss of honor. Whom do I have to blame that from now on I must be subject to a tiresome life and serve it to no purpose? The one who caused it: myself, and I can only cry out to God in sorrow."

Meanwhile the maiden, who also had gone out for a walk, quietly approached and heard the lady's lament. However much at fault her mistress might be, the maiden nevertheless was so troubled by her grief that she could not remain there, but wanted to go back in: her complaint was too pitiful. Just then the lady looked around and quickly spoke: "Have you been here long?"

"Yes. I heard all that was in your heart, and it distresses me. What I told you was true. You couldn't believe it, but remember how I advised you."

"I do, and I know in truth that the only one who could make me joyful now is He who blots out my sin just as He quiets the waves of the sea. I shall always be sad unless it should happen that He destines me for happiness and in kindness appeases the man for whom I grieve day and night. I am sorry I ever caused him pain, but my remorse comes too late. I should have taken your advice. He who acts on his own, according to his own desires, and without seeking counsel, will regret it just as I do. I used to think that the causes of women should rightly prevail, and that is why I have come to grief. However, I have not done what is right, and he has avenged himself by leaving me. My heart will be filled with sorrow and distress as long as I live. It was my fault that I fell into this snare. I therefore advise all of you who may undertake a love affair in the future to consider my sorrow and take care not to suffer the same fate."

Well let us bring this story to an end. The German language is not rich, and whoever wants to compose in it must tend to his rhymes, splitting some words apart and putting others together. I would do this more skillfully if I could.

S E C T I O N 14

WOLFRAM VON ESCHENBACH: TITUREL

Introduction by Albrecht Classen

Next to Gottfried von Strassburg, Hartmann von Aue, and the anonymous author of the heroic epic *Nibelungenlied*, Wolfram von Eschenbach (ca. 1175/80–after 1220) was one of the greatest writers in the history of Middle High German Literature. There are no references to him in the chronicles, but we can deduce from allusions in his texts much about his life. He was born in Eschenbach, today Wolframs–Eschenbach near Ansbach and might have been of noble descent. He was dependent on literary patronage and often appealed to his audience to be more generous with their payment. Wolfram explicitly states that he was illiterate, what might be confirmed with the entire lack of references to the canonical school authors. But his claim must be understood as tongue–in–cheek because in his literary work he displays a remarkable range of knowledge about natural and medical science, occult sciences, theology, astronomy and astrology, and philosophy. Some scholars believe that Wolfram studied at the famous university of Toledo, Spain, where both Hebrew and Arabic studies were pursued.

In his grail romance, *Parzival (ca. 1205–1210)*, Wolfram claims that he heard this tale from a teacher called Kyot of Toledo, and Kyot again had, according to Wolfram, heard about it from a Syrian called Flegetanis. But Wolfram's major source was, to be sure, Chrétien de Troye's *Perceval* (ca. 1180/90), although he changed the Old French text considerably, expanding and enriching it in many ways.

Wolfram's other great work was his version of a French *chanson de geste*, *Willehalm* (ca. 1218–1220) which deals with the battle between Christians and Saracens after Willehalm had gained the love of the Moslem Queen Arabel. The lovers had escaped to France, but then must defend themselves against her father's, husband's, and brother's armies. Eventually all of Christian France assembles and defeats the threat. *Willehalm* is a remarkable representative of its genre because Wolfram incorporated, despite the military theme, in the end of the narrative clear elements of religious tolerance and a message against war.

370

Moreover, Wolfram composed a handful of love songs which are, to a large extent, unique in their concern to discard the traditional concept of the courtly, but illegitimate love affair in favor of marital love.

In *Titurel*, which was composed around 1218–1220, Wolfram picked up a narrative thread from his *Parzival* and continued to spin it for a while, without providing us with a completion of the tale. A thirteenth–century poet Albrecht (von Scharfenberg?) took it upon himself to write a continuation of *Titurel*, today known as the *Jüngere Titurel*. Albrecht expanded Wolfram's short text consisting of only 170 four–line stanzas (680 verses) to a monumental epic of about 50,000 verses.

In the first fragment Wolfram's narrator describes the religious origin of the Grail and the history of the Grail family down to its last descendants. The reader knows from *Parzival* that the young woman Sigune will lament throughout her life the death of her lover Schionatulander. In the course of his trials and tribulations the protagonist Parzival had encountered his aunt Sigune at regular intervals and marvelled at her deep sorrow and mourning of her lover, thus assuming the figure of a *pietà*. In *Titurel* the narrator looks backwards and examines the role of the family as the essential unit within medieval society, and then moves on to a discussion about the dangers of courtly love if encountered at a too early age. In particular, the themes of reading and the danger of misunderstanding a text's message dominate the second fragment. The external, physical fragment (manuscript) is uncannily repeated within the text with the dog leash escaping with the dog. With the leash, however, the text also escapes the reader who then sends her lover in pursuit of both the dog and the leash. This search will, as we know from *Parzival*, lead Schionatulander directly to his death.

BIBLIOGRAPHY

Margaret F. Richey, "The 'Titurel' of Wolfram von Eschenbach: Structure and Character," *Modern Language Review* 56 (1961): 180–93.

Wolfram von Eschenbach, *Titurel and the Songs*. Texts and Translations with Introduction, Notes and Comments by Marion E. Gibbs and Sidney M. Johnson. Garland Library of Medieval Literature, Series A, 57 (New York-London: Garland, 1988)

Albrecht Classen, *Utopie und Logos. Vier Studien zu Wolframs von Eschenbach Titurel*. Beiträge zur älteren Literaturgeschichte (Heidelberg: Winter, 1990).

Marianne Wynn, "Wolfram von Eschenbach (circa 1170–after 1220)," *German Writers and Works of the High Middle Ages: 1170–1280*. Ed James Hardin and Will Hasty. Dictionary of Literary Biography, 1038 (Detroit-Washington, D.C.,-London: Gale Research, 1994), 185–206.

Alexander Sager, *Minne von maeren: Of Wolfram's "Titurel"*. Transatlantische Studien zu Mittelalter und Früher Neuzeit, 2 (Göttingen: V&R unipress, 2006).

TITUREL I

1. When mighty Titurel could still engage in knightly combat, he was daring enough to lead his men personally into the fray. Later when he was old he said: "I am coming to realize that I must lay down my lance which I once wielded with skill and pleasure.

2. "If I could still bear arms," the courageous man said, "the air would be blest with the crash of spear from my hand, and splinters would provide shade from the sun. Many a helmet decoration has been set on fire by the edge of my sword.

3. "If ever I received the solace of noble Love or if the sweetness of Love ever exerted its rapturous power over me; if I ever received a sign of recognition from a lovely lady, all that has now become completely foreign to me as I yearn in lamentation.

4. "My bliss, my purity, my constancy of mind, and if my hand ever gained high renown by bestowing gifts, or in battle, that can bring nothing but credit to my young heirs. Indeed, all my descendants must evermore inherit true love with real devotion.

5. "I know for sure that he who is welcomed by a woman's smile will always have purity and constancy as close companions of his heart. These two things can never leave him save in death alone: no one can lead them astray otherwise.

6. "When I received the Grail by the authority bestowed upon me by the holy angel with his mighty power, I found all my commandments written on it. This gift had never passed into human hands until it came into mine.

7. "The Lord of the Grail must be pure and chaste. Alas, Frimutel, my sweet son, I have you alone of my children remaining here for the Grail! Now, my fair son, receive the crown of the Grail and the Grail itself.

8. "Son, in your time you have practiced chivalry, charging into combat. On one occasion your wheel was stuck, and I had to pull you out of the fray. Now defend yourself alone, my son, for my strength is deserting both of us.

9. "God has endowed you, my son, with five noble children. They make up a blessed noble company for the Grail as well. Anfortas and Trevrezent, the fleet of foot,—I hope to live to hear them acclaimed above all others.

10. "Your daughter, Schoysiane, holds firmly in her heart so many good things that the world enjoys a blessing from that. Herzeloyde is likewise inclined, and no other praise can silence praise for Repanse de Schoye."

11. Knights and ladies heard what he said, and much heartfelt grief could be seen in the Templars, whom he had often saved from many a difficult situation when he was defending the Grail with his own hand and with their aid.

12. Thus strength was lost to mighty Titurel, both through old age and through the ravages of sickness, and Frimutel held sway in true nobility over the Grail at Munsalvaesche. This was the greatest and best that one could wish for, beyond all earthly realms.

13. Two of his daughters were of an age to be eligible for noble love in the arms of a lover. Many a king from many a land had sought Schoysiane's love in fitting fashion, and yet it was a prince to whom she granted it.

14. Kyot of Katelangen won the hand of Schoysiane. No more beautiful maiden was seen before or since under the sun or by the light of the moon. Kyot was full of fine qualities. His heart was never daunted in striving for high renown, no matter what it cost in substance or in deeds of valor.

15. She was brought to him in great splendor and was received lavishly. King Tampunteire, Kyot's brother, came to Katelangen too, and countless powerful princes were there. Not for years had anyone seen such a costly wedding.

16. Kyot, the lord of the land, had gained renown both for his generosity and his courage: all his activity was very successful wherever fierce fighting was going on and also where jousting was taking place in full array for the reward of ladies.

17. If any prince won for himself a dearer wife, what heartfelt love he must have known! That is just what Love intended for these two! But alas, sorrow is drawing near to him now. This is how things end in the world: all our sweetness must always turn bitter at the last.

18. In due time his wife presented him with a child. (May God spare *me* from having in *my* house such a companion, if I should have to pay so dearly for him! As long as I have my wits about me I'll never wish for that.)

19. Sweet Schoysiane, radiant and constant as she was, died in giving birth to a daughter who was endowed with many blessings. All maidenly honor had its source in her. She had so much loyalty that they still speak about it in many lands.

20. Thus was the sorrow of the prince mingled with joy: his young daughter was alive, her mother dead. This was what he had from the two of them. Schoysiane's death helped him to purchase his loss of true joys and the lasting gain of sorrows.

21.   Then, grieving, they commended the lady to the earth. Before that she had to be perfumed with spices and embalmed appropriately. They had to wait for some time for many kings and princes to come from far and wide for the burial.

22.   The prince, Kyot, held his land in fief from Tampunteire, from his brother, the King of Pelrapeire, as he was called. Now he requested that the fief should pass to his little daughter, and he proceeded to renounce sword, helmet, and shield.

23.   Duke Manfilot suffered greatly when he looked at his noble brother; it was a sorrowful sight. He too laid down his sword in grief so that henceforth neither of them sought noble Love nor jousting.

24.   The child, whom her father Kyot had purchased at so high a price since through her he had lost her mother, was baptized Sigune. Schoysiane was the first woman allowed by the Grail to be its bearer.

25.   King Tampunteire took little Sigune to his own daughter Condwiramurs. When Kyot kissed her in parting many tears were shed. Condwiramurs was still a tiny baby, and the two grew up as playmates. Never was anything reported that diminished their reputation.

26.   It was at that time that Castis died. He had won the hand of lovely Herzeloyde at Munsalvæsche, and he duly bestowed Kanvoleiz on the lady, and Kingrivals too. In both these lands he ruled over other princes.

27.   Castis never consummated his marriage to Herzeloyde. She came to Gahmuret's arms a virgin, but even so she was queen of two lands, gentle Frimutel's child, who had been sent forth from Munsalvæsche.

28.   When Tampunteire died and handsome Kardeiz—he had ruled in Brobarz; Sigune had been there nearly five years—then the two young playmates, not yet grown up, had to part.

29.   Queen Herzeloyde thought of Sigune and took great pains to see that she was brought to her from Brobarz. Condwiramurs began to weep at the prospect of having to do without Sigune's companionship and firm affection.

30.   The child Sigune said: "My dear Papa, have my chest filled with dolls brought along for me when I travel from here to my aunt's. That way I'll be well equipped for the journey. There are many knights alive who will bind themselves to my service in the future."

31.   "How fortunate I am to have so fine a child and one so sensible! May God long grant Katelangen such a splendid lady as you! My cares can sleep so long as your blessed fortune is awake. If this were the Black Forest, it would be turned completely into lance shafts on your account."

32. Thus Kyot's child, Sigune, grew up in her aunt's household. Whoever beheld her, preferred her to the splendor of May with its dewy flowers, for blessed fortune and honor blossomed forth from her heart. (Just let her grow up a little, and I'll sing her praises even more!)

33. Whatever virtues constitute perfection in a pure woman were not forgotten in her sweet person by as much as a hair. O perfect fruit, completely pure, without fault, noble Schoysiane's child, of the same lineage, chaste, young, and pure!

34. Now we should also think of Herzeloyde, the pure. She was incapable of damaging *her* reputation. In truth, she is the lovely one I have in mind now. Well-spring of all womanly honor, she deserved to have her fame increase throughout the lands.

35. Wherever one sang the praise of ladies in their youth, none resounded so clearly as that of the virgin widow, child of Frimutel. Her praise traveled afar into many lands, until her love was earned at Kanvoleiz with clashing lances.

36. Now listen to strange and wondrous things about the maiden Sigune: when her little breasts became round and her fair, curling hair turned darker, an awareness of herself stirred in her heart. She began to act with pride and buoyant high spirits, yet even so with womanly virtue.

37. I'll not mention here how Gahmuret left Belakane and how he won Schoysiane's sister in noble fashion and how he broke with the French woman, rather I'll tell you of the love of a young girl.

38. The French queen, Ampflise, was entrusted with a child, of princely stock and of such lineage as can be preserved from anything damaging to fame. Of all princes ever to be born, not one will strive harder for renown.

39. When Gahmuret received his shield from Ampflise, the noble queen entrusted this boy to him. We shall have cause to praise him in the future because he possessed the true sweetness of a child. He is to be the lord of this tale, and I am right to praise all young people because of him.

40. This very child, then, traveled with the Angevin across the sea to heathendom to the Baruc Ahkarin, and Gahmuret brought him back from there to Waleis. If boys witness deeds of valor, this is said to help them, if they ever grow to manhood.

41. Let me tell you something of the lad's lineage. His grandfather—Gurnemanz of Graharz by name—could split iron and did so in jousting with many a charge. His father was called Gurzgri. He died at Schoydelakurt.

42.   His mother was Mahaute, the sister of Ehkunat, the mighty Count Palatine, named after the fortress city of Berbester. The boy himself was called Schionat-ulander. No one else ever achieved such high renown, however long he lived.

43.   I did not name noble Gurzgri's son before I named the maiden Sigune because her mother had been sent out from the protection of the pure Grail. Her noble birth gives her precedence too, as does her family of fair appearance.

44.   All the people of the Grail are chosen ones, ever blessed in this world and in the next, numbered among the ranks of those of unshakable renown. Now Sigune too was from that selfsame seed, which came from Munsalvaesche and was sown throughout the world, received by those blessed by fortune.

45.   Wherever this very seed was brought from the land of the Grail it became fruitful for those people and a veritable hailstorm against disgrace for them. Because of this, Kanvoleiz is known far and wide, and it was ever called the capital of fidelity in many tongues.

46.   Hail to you, Kanvoleiz, how often does one speak of your constancy and the ardent affection which soon arose within your walls! Love grew up there early between two children. It developed with such purity that all the world could find none of its own murkiness in it.

47.   Proud Gahmuret raised these children together under his own roof. While Schionatulander was still lacking in maturity of mind he was already in the grip of heartfelt misery because of his love for Sigune.

48.   Alas, that they are still too young and inexperienced for such anguish, for where love begins in youth it lasts longest of all. Even if old age can free itself from love, youth still remains in its bondage, and love is not robbed of its powers at all.

49.   Alas, Love, of what use is your power among children, except only for the fact that someone with no eyes, a truly blind person, could see you there? Love, you come in all too many forms. Not even all the scribes in the world could ever completely describe your lineage or your estate.

50.   Even though the proper monk and also the true hermit are called upon to do many things in the name of Love which are difficult enough for them, no matter how obedient their spirits, Love really afflicts the helmeted knight. Yet Love occupies a very small space.

51.   Love holds all things in its embrace, the great and the small. Love dwells here on earth, and in heaven it leads the way in purity to God. Love is every-where save in hell. Strong Love's powers are crippled when doubt and inconstancy are its companions.

52. The maiden Sigune and Schionatulander had neither inconstancy nor doubt. Yet still they knew suffering. It was interlaced with great joy. I could tell you many wondrous things about their young love, but it would take too long.

53. Their good breeding and the nature of their lineage—born as they were of pure love—made conflicting claims on them so that they did not reveal their love outwardly in their handsome features but inwardly were tormented with pain in their hearts.

54. Schionatulander had also gained experience as the result of many a sweet message which the French Queen Ampflise had sent secretly to the Angevin. He carried the messages and many times turned their misery aside. Now turn his aside!

55. Schionatulander very often noticed how his kinsman Gahmuret could speak with fine sensibility and how he could shake off his troubles. Many Christians over here attributed this ability to him, as did many noble heathens over there.

56. All of you who have loved and have assumed the burden of love, listen now to a maiden's cares and to manliness in toil. I'll tell a tale about that for the real lovers who have ever suffered the pangs of heartfelt love.

57. Sweet young Schionatulander plucked up his courage. Pressed on by his relationship with her which was causing him abundant sorrow, he said: "Sigune, helpful lady, help me, noble lady, out of my sorrow: this will be help indeed.

58. *"Duchesse* of Katelangen, give me a chance! I hear tell that you are born of the race that never tired of being helpful in rewarding anyone who suffered distress on its account. Confirm your blessedness now in your behavior toward me."

59. *"Bel ami,"* she replied, "now tell me, my fair friend, what you mean. Let me hear whether you are of a mind to make a proper request of me, which will ensure that your plea may not go unheard. Unless you know this for sure, you should not be too hasty."

60. "One should seek grace where it dwells. My lady, I desire your grace. May you deign to give it to me through your grace. Noble companionship is fitting indeed for children. Who can find true grace where it has never exercised its right?"

61. She said: "To find comfort you should make your suffering known where people can help you better than I can. Otherwise you may be misguided if you are asking *me* to relieve your pain, for I am indeed an orphan, far from my relatives and the people of my country."

62. "I know full well that you are the mistress of a country and a people. Of that I desire nothing, but only that your heart may look at me through your eyes so that it may notice my distress. Now help me quickly before my love for you destroys my heart and my joy."

63. "If someone has a love that is dangerous to any friend so dear as you to me, I shall never again call it by the inappropriate name of Love. God knows that I have never had the loss nor gain of Love.

64. "Love, is that a he? Can you explain Love to me? Is it a she? How shall I show my love for Love if Love comes to me? Must I keep it with my dolls? Or does Love, untamed as it is, not like to fly to the hand? I know well enough how to lure Love."

65. "My lady, I have heard from men and women that Love knows how to span its bow to shoot at young and old, inflicting wounds with thoughts. It unfailingly hits everything that runs, crawls, flies or swims.

66. "Indeed, sweet maiden, until now I have known of Love only by hearsay. Love exists in our thoughts; I can prove that now in my own case. Steadfast loving makes it like that. Love steals joy from my heart more surely than any thief."

67. "Schionatulander, my thoughts force me to be bereft of joy whenever you are out of my sight until I look at you secretly again. Because of this I am sad not just once during the week but all too many times."

68. "Then you don't need to ask me about Love, sweet maiden. You will know well enough about the losses and gains of Love without asking. See now how Love turns from joy into grief. Do as Love requires before Love destroys both our hearts."

69. Sigune asked: "If Love can steal into hearts so that neither man, woman, nor maiden can avoid it, however quick they may be, doesn't anyone know why Love is taking revenge on people who never sought to harm Love, and is shattering their joy?"

70. "Certainly it exerts its power over the inexperienced young and wise old men alike. There is no one alive skilled enough to praise its marvels fully. Let us both strive for Love's help with flawless affection. No one can deceive Love, capricious as it is."

71. "Alas, if only Love could demonstrate its helpful nature in some other way than by my surrendering myself, free as I am, into your power and into your service! Your youth has not yet earned me properly. You must first serve me with sword and shield: be warned of this."

72. "Madam, between now and the time when I can bear arms with strength, I shall be seen in bitter-sweet travail, striving in service for your help. I was born to receive your help. Now help me to succeed with you."

73. This was the beginning of their love, albeit only in words, at the time when Pompeius and noble Ipomedon had announced a campaign to attack Baldac in full force. Many a new lance from their army was broken to smithereens.

74. Gahmuret made his way there very secretly with just his own one shield. Yet there is no denying that he had forces aplenty, after all he was king in three lands. Thus did Love chase him to his death, which he received at the hand of Ipomedon.

75. Schionatulander was reluctant to take part in the journey, because his love for Sigune had deprived him completely of his high spirits and his joy. Nevertheless, he departed with his kinsman. That was heartfelt misery for Sigune and for him. Love had entrapped the two of them.

76. The young prince took leave of the maiden secretly. He said: "Alas, how shall I live so that Love will quickly make me rich in joys and preserve me from death? Wish me well, sweet maiden: I must leave you and go to fight the heathens."

77. "I am very fond of you, my faithful friend, but tell me, is that Love? As things are, I shall always be wishing for that success which will gain great joy for both of us. All the waters shall be consumed by fire before my love shall wane."

78. Much love remained there: love departed thence. You have never heard tell of maidens or women, nor of stout-hearted men who knew how to love each other more devotedly. Parzival realized this later when he met Sigune at the linden tree.

79. Gahmuret, the King of Kingrivals, stole away from his relatives and vassals so that his journey was completely kept from them. He had picked out just twenty courtly lads of noble birth to travel with him, and eighty squires in armor but without shields.

80. Five handsome steeds, much gold and precious stones from Azagouc accompanied him on the way, his shield all alone without companions. (A shield should choose companions for itself so that another shield could say "Bless you," if the first shield were to sneeze.)

80a. His panther insignia was concealed. An expensive anchor of sable was affixed to his shield, when that splendid man rode in the manner of an unattached knight. Thus was he decorated, that man rich in renown, and under such decorations will he meet his end at Baldac in a fierce joust.

80b. Noble Gahmuret took leave of Herzeloyde. A tree so completely bountiful in loyalty will never be produced again on earth, nor will a more loyal woman than she proved to be. Sorrow arose from the parting of the two of them. Many an eye shed tears over that later.

81. His heartfelt affection and her love had never yet turned to strangeness through force of habit. The queen gave him her shift, silken white, just as it was when it had touched her white skin. (It had also touched something brown at her hips). He wore it during the attack at Baldac.

82. He headed from Norgals toward Spain, as far as Seville, that son of brave Gandin. He caused many tears to be shed when people heard how his journey ended. His lofty renown will never be banished from the thoughts of Christians or heathens.

82a. They must recognize it. It can't grow old. Bold Hermann of Thuringia, who commanded all one could wish in terms of renown, earned honors. When one hears tell of the likes of Hermann who died before he did, how his renown stands far out beyond them!

83. I say this in truth. This is by no means just a supposition. Now let us turn our thoughts back to the young prince from Graswaldan and to how Sigune, his chaste *amie,* caused him anguish. She drew joy from his heart as the bee sucks sweetness from the flowers.

84. The sweet sickness that he suffered on account of Love, the loss of his high spirits and his gain in sorrows forced much pain on the Graharzois. He would have been better off dead like Gurzgri at the hand of Mabonagrin.

85. Even if he will at some time attack an opponent's shield with the crash of breaking lance, he is still physically too weak for such suffering. Strong Love is making him weak, and the fact that his thoughts are so intent on his lovely love, whom he cannot forget.

86. Whenever other squires were practicing at arms and wrestling on the fields and in the roadways, he did not join in because of his painful longing. Love caused his steadfast joy to ail. Before children learn to climb up on chairs, they have to crawl towards them.

87. Now let him seek noble love, but he must also think about how he will raise himself on high and how his lasting fame can destroy all falsity for him in his youth and in old age. I know princes who are so stupid that one might more easily teach the psalter to a bear than have them learn these things.

88. Schionatulander bore his many sufferings secretly until noble Gahmuret detected his concealed sorrows and realized that his favorite kinsman was struggling with grief like this. He continued in torment through all the months as the seasons changed, in winter and in summer.

89. His perfect figure, the product of his noble birth, his complexion, his bright eyes, his radiant countenance, whatever one could see of him—all this lost its pure brilliance on account of his suffering. No faulty wavering was paining him, but strong and perfect love.

90. Gahmuret's heart, too, was oppressed by the heat of Love; and its fire had scorched his fair complexion from time to time and made it look murky. He had experienced something of Love's help, but he also knew its painful hours.

91. However cunning Love may be, it must reveal itself. If someone turns all-seeing, trained eyes towards Love, its power cannot conceal itself. It is also a square, I hear tell. Love designs and weaves very cleverly, even better than weaving tablet and knife.

92. Gahmuret became aware of the secret misery and of the fact that the young dauphin from Graswaldan was so bereft of joy. He took him aside into a field, away from the road, saying: "What's wrong with Ampflise's page? Your sorrow doesn't suit me.

93. "I have proper concern for all your distress. The Roman Emperor and the Admirat of all the Saracens would not be able to alleviate it with all their wealth and power. Whatever has brought you to this lamentable misery must also make me forfeit my joy."

94. Now you should readily believe that the noble Angevin would like to help the lovelorn young dauphin if he could. He cried: "Alas, why has your countenance shed its glowing look? Love is robbing itself in robbing you.

95. "I detect Love in you: its tracks are all too large and clear. You should not conceal your secrets from me since we are such close kinsmen and are one flesh of special lineage, more closely related than through Mother Eve, who grew out of a stolen rib.

96. "You well-spring of Love, you fruitful sap of Love's own flower! Now I must have compassion for Ampflise, who entrusted you to me in her womanly virtue. She had raised you as if she had borne you herself and regarded you as her own child. This is how dear you always were to her and still are now.

97. "If you keep your secrets from me, then my heart, which has always been your heart too, will be wounded, and your loving devotion will have become dishonored if you keep such great distress from me. I can't believe that your constancy would allow you to behave in such a fickle way."

98. Troubled, the young lad replied: "Then let my hope reside in your protection and in your grace, and let me hope that you will never again direct your anger toward me. It was out of courtesy and self-restraint that I kept all my

pangs from you. Now I must mention to you the name of Sigune. She it is who has conquered my heart.

99. "You can, if you will, lighten my monstrous burden. Now let me remind you of the French queen: if I ever carried any of your cares, lift me out of my infirmity for her sake. No steeping lion ever became so heavy as my waking thoughts.

100. "Remember how many lands and seas I have traversed out of love for you, not out of need. I have left behind kinsmen and vassals and Ampflise, my noble lady. For all this I should benefit now from you. Let me see your help.

101. "You can surely release me from the bonds that hold me tight. If I ever become master of a shield with helmet on my head, demonstrating my generosity in all the lands, my helping hand will fight to gain renown. Meanwhile be my guardian so that your protection will preserve me from Sigune's oppression."

102. "Alas, poor young boy, how many forests must be laid waste by your hand in jousts before you can experience the love of the *Duchesse!* Noble Love is requited according to definite rules. It is won by the fortunate man through bravery rather than by the cowardly, wealthy one.

103. "Yet even so, I am glad to hear that your heart rises up so high. Where else did a tree trunk ever have such fine twigs growing from its branches? Radiant flower that she is, on the heath, in the woods, in the field! If my little niece has conquered you, then congratulations on this happy news!

104. "Schoysiane, her mother, was acclaimed for the fact that her beauty was created quite deliberately by God Himself and by His artistry. Sigune, Kyot's child, has the sunlike radiance of Schoysiane, as the familiar stories tell of her.

105. "Thus, I truly salute the child of the two of them, of Kyot, Prince of Katelangen, who sought renown in fierce battle until Schoysiane's death deprived him of joy: Sigune, the victor in the contest in which the virtue and sweetness of maidens are judged.

106. "By fighting victoriously in devoted service to her love you shall gain the one who has conquered you. And I shall delay no longer in my intention of involving her noble aunt in helping you. Sigune's splendor will make your complexion bloom like the dazzling flowers."

107. This is how Schionatulander replied: "Now your comforting words and your loyalty will completely sever the bonds of all my cares since I have your consent to love Sigune, who for so long now has been robbing me of joy and happy thoughts."

108. So Schionatulander could be sure of help if Gahmuret wanted to provide it. However, we should not forget the great distress endured by the child of Kyot and Schoysiane. Before she received consolation, she had to go without joy.

109. How the Princess of Katelangen had been afflicted by relentless Love! Her thoughts had been struggling hard for too long for her to be able to conceal it from her aunt. The Queen's heart skipped a beat as she realized what Sigune was suffering.

110. Sigune's eyes had become just like a dewy rose, red and wet with tears. Her mouth and the whole of her face bore witness to her sufferings. Then even her pure reserve could not conceal the tender love within her heart, which was agonizing for her young hero.

111. Then the queen spoke out of love and loyalty, saying: "Alas, fruit of Schoysiane, I was already bearing much sorrow of quite a different kind on account of the Angevin. Now since I detect such pain in you, a new thorn is growing in my grief.

112. "Tell me what in all the world is bothering you! Or is my support and that of my other kinsmen so remote from you that their help cannot reach you? What has become of your sunny glow? Alas, who has stolen that from your cheeks?

113. "Wretched waif, your unhappiness does indeed arouse my pity. Even though I am queen of three lands, I should always be counted among the poor unless I live to see your sorrow disappear and find out the true story of all your woes."

114. "Then I must recount to you with trepidation all my distress. If you think any the less of me, you will be violating your good breeding through your treatment of me since I cannot rid myself of that distress. Let me keep in your good graces, sweet love! That will be right for both of us.

115. "May God reward you! If ever a mother treated her child with loving tenderness, then, bereft of joy as I am, I have found in you the same unfaltering devotion. Indeed, you have kept me from feeling lonely, and I thank your womanly virtue for that.

116. "I need your counsel, your consolation, and your kindness, all of them, since I am suffering misery and torture, yearning eagerly for my beloved. That is unavoidable. He tortures my free thoughts and shackles them. All my mind is fettered to him.

117. "Many an evening I have gazed out of windows across the heath, onto the roadway, and toward the lovely meadows, but all in vain. He never comes to me. And so my eyes must pay dearly with tears for the love of my friend.

118. "Then I leave the window and go onto the battlements. There I keep watch to the east and to the west, to see whether I can catch sight of the man who has long oppressed my heart. I can well be counted among the old lovers, not the young.

119. "I sail out a while on the wild waters. There I keep watch far and wide, more than thirty miles, in the hope of hearing any tidings that would rid me of the misery I am feeling because of my handsome young friend.

120. "What has become of my playful joy, or how is it that high spirits have deserted my heart like this? A cry of woe which I had meant to suffer on my own for him must follow both of us now. I am sure that yearning grief will drive him back again to me, though now he may be far away.

121. "Alas, he just never comes! I often get cold chills because of him and afterwards it is as if I were lying in a crackling fire, for Schionatulander makes me glow like that. Love for him fills me with fire as Agremuntin does the dragon Salamander."

122. "Alas," replied the queen, "you are talking like someone with experience in such matters. Who has misled my Sigune? Now I am afraid the French queen, Ampflise, has taken out her anger on me. All your wise talk comes from *her* mouth.

123. "Schionatulander is a very powerful prince. His nobility, his courtly restraint would never have dared make him so bold as to ask for your love, young as he is, if the envy of proud Ampflise were not taking revenge on me out of spite.

124. "It was she who raised that child since he was weaned. If she did not with malicious intent give you the advice which has hurt you so cruelly, you may gain much joy for him and he for you. If you are favorably disposed to him, don't allow your perfect beauty to become spoiled.

125. "Do this for him: see to it that your eyes, your cheeks, your chin become radiant again. How does it suit your youthful years to let such a beautiful complexion lose its glow? You have mixed much sorrow too painfully into the fleeting joys of youth.

126. "If the young Dauphin has ruined your joys, he can increase them for you too. He has inherited much good fortune and love from his father and the Dauphine, Mahaute, who was his mother, and from his aunt, Queen Schoette.

127. "I am only sorry that you have become his *amie* too early. You will inherit the sorrow that Mahaute experienced with the Dauphin Gurzgri. Her eyes often discovered that he had won renown in many lands with helmet in place.

128. "Schionatulander can only rise to fame, born as he is of those who do not let their fame decline. It increased for them in length and breadth. Now hold fast to him in joy and consolation and let him not inflict cares upon you.

129. "I'm not surprised that your heart is rejoicing in your breast at the thought of him. How handsome he looks when he is wearing his shield! Many tears will flow down upon him, sparks which leap from helmets by sword strokes when it is pouring fiery rain.

130. "He is made for the joust. Who could have designed him so? Never was so little left out of man's countenance in any mother's child, to earn the love of a lady, as far as I know. The sight of him will delight your eyes. I'll commend your love to him in the hope that it will be returned."

131. Then and there love was permitted and sealed with love. Both their hearts were eager to match love with love and not to falter. "How fortunate I am, dear aunt," said the Duchess, "that I can now love the Graharzois like this, with your consent before all the world!"

TITUREL II

132. Thus they had been encamped there for only a short time when they heard all at once a hunting dog coming toward them baying loudly, with a clear, pleasing bark, hot on the blood-red spoor of a wounded animal. The hound was detained for just a while, and because of that I am still lamenting them, for they are my friends.

133. When they heard the forest resounding like that, Schionatulander—he was known from childhood to be in the forefront of the fleet of foot, only surpassed by Trevrizent the pure, who ran and leaped ahead of all of those who did that as knights—

134. thought to himself now: "If someone can catch that dog, he'll need the legs of a knight." He will sell his joy and in doing so receive lasting sadness in return. Up he leaped and ran towards the bark, intending with his speed to catch the hound.

135. Since the fleeing game was not able to head into the wide woods but instead went straight for the Dauphin, his suffering will increase. It brought him future sadness. Now he hid himself in a thicket, and dragging its leash behind it, along came

136. the hound of the prince from whose hands it had slipped when it had been set down on the trail made by the blood from the arrow wounds. (May she never send another dog: I mean the woman who sent it to that great-spirited

knight from whom it raced away, right up to the proud Graharzois! This later caused him to lose much lofty joy.)

137. When it thus broke through the thicket following the spoor, its collar was an Arabian band, woven very tightly by beating down with a weaving knife. Precious and brilliant jewels could be seen on it. They sparkled through the forest like the sun. It was not just the hound that Schionatulander seized.

138. Let me tell you what else he laid hold of along with the hound. He had to experience unflinchingly grief lined with toil and great striving for combat ever more. The hound's leash was indeed for him the source of joyless times.

139. He carried the dog in his arms to the lovely Sigune. The leash was a good twelve fathoms long, made up of band-silk of four colors: yellow, green and red, with brown the fourth, fastened together ornamentally wherever one span ended.

140. At such points there were rings decorated with pearls. Regularly between the rings at a good span's length, enhanced by precious stones, were four layers, in four colors, a good finger in width. (If I ever catch a dog on such a leash, it will stay in my possession, even if I let the dog go!)

142. When it was unfolded between the rings you could see an inscription of costly material outside and inside. Listen to this wondrous tale, if you order me to tell it. The gems were firmly fastened to the leash with golden nails.

141. The letters were emeralds mixed with rubies. There were diamonds, chryso-lites, and garnets too. Never did leash have better dog to wear it, and the dog was well leashed too. (You can surely guess which I would take, if it came to a choice between the dog and the leash.)

143. The collar was a band stitched to velvet, green as the woods in May, with many precious stones of numerous varieties affixed to it. A lady had commissioned the inscription. The dog's name was Gardeviaz. That means in German: "Keep on the trail!"

144. Duchess Sigune read the beginning of the inscription: "Even though this may be the name of a hound, the saying is appropriate for noble people. Let men and women stay on the right trail! Then they will enjoy favor in this world, and bliss will be their reward in the next."

145. She read further on the collar, not yet on the leash itself: "Whoever knows how to stay on the right trail will never have his renown put up for sale. It will dwell in a pure heart so strengthened that no eye will ever disregard it on the unstable, fickle market-place."

146. The hound and the leash had been sent to a prince out of love. She who sent them was a young queen of royal lineage, reigning in her own right. Sigune

read some of the information on the leash, who the queen was, also the prince. They were both named there.

147. The queen was born in Kanadic, the sister of Florie, who gave to Ilinot the Breton, as her *ami*, her heart, her thoughts and her whole self, everything she had, except her actual body. She had trained him from the time they were children until he ventured forth on knightly journeys, and she loved him above all possessions.

148. He met his end too in service under arms for her love. If it were not a violation of my sense of propriety, I should still be cursing the hand that caused his death in a joust. Florie died in that joust too, although she never came close to the point of a lance.

149. She left behind a sister who inherited her crown. Clauditte was the name of this maiden. As a reward for her purity and virtue, stranger and friend alike accorded her praise. Thus her renown was acclaimed in many lands, and no one denied it to her.

150. On the leash the Duchess read about this maiden. The princes of her realm demanded on the basis of a judgment that she should furnish them with a lord. She summoned them to court at Beauffremont. Countless people came there, the rich and the poor. They charged her to make a choice without delay.

151. She had been carrying Duc Ehkunat de Salvasch Florien in her heart all the while and had selected him as her *ami*. As a result of this his heart soared higher than her crown. Ehkunat sought the goal of all princes, and he did follow the spoor very nicely.

152. His youth swayed her, as did the law of the land. Since she had been told to choose, the noble maiden made her choice. Do you wish to know the name of her beloved in German? Duc Ehkunaver von der blühenden Wildnis (of the flowering wilderness), so I have heard him called.

153. Since he was named "of the wilderness," she sent this "wild letter" toward the wilderness, the hunting dog, who followed the spoor in fields and forest, as was his nature. Moreover the inscription on the leash declared that she herself should keep on the proper trail for a woman.

154. Schionatulander was catching graylings and trout with an artificial fly, while Sigune was reading, but he landed a loss of joy as well, so that he was never happy afterwards. The Duchess was loosening the knot in order to read the whole of the inscription on the leash.

155. The dog was tied securely to the tent pole. It grieves me that she loosened the knot. Alas, if only she had not done so! Gardeviaz stretched and strained

forward before the Duchess could order some food for him. She was wanting to give him something to eat.

156. Two servant girls rushed out in front of the tent. I shall bewail the Duchess' soft white hands, if the leash should lacerate them. What can I do about that? It had hard stones on it. Gardeviaz tugged and leaped in order to chase off on the spoor of the game he had been following.

157. This was how he had run away from Ehkunat too that same day. Sigune called out to her servant girls, who had been fetching the hound's food. They rushed back into the tent very quickly. Meanwhile the hound had slipped out through the tent wall and was soon heard far off in the forest.

158. You see, he had ripped out some of the tent pegs. When he got back onto the fresh red track, he did not keep it a secret; rather he followed the spoor openly and without stealth. This was why the son of noble Gurzgri had much pain to suffer later.

159. Schionatulander was catching large and small fish with a lure, standing with bare white legs in the swift, clear brook to enjoy the coolness. Now he heard the baying of Gardeviaz, resounding to his misfortune.

160. He threw the lure aside and raced swiftly over tree stumps and through brambles, yet even so he could not get anywhere near the hound. The trackless forest had let the dog get so far away from him that he could locate neither game nor dog, and the wind was playing tricks on his hearing too.

161. His bare legs were badly scratched by the brambles and his white feet were somewhat wounded too by running over the sharp tree stumps. You could see his wounds more easily than those on the wounded animal. He had them washed before he entered the tent where he found Sigune.

162. The palms of her hands were grey, as though covered with hoarfrost, like the hand of a jouster whose lance slips back through his hand upon impact and scrapes across the bare skin. In just that way the leash had run through the hand of the Duchess.

163. She could see that he had many wounds on his legs and feet. She lamented for him, and he for her. Now this story is about to turn bitter, as the Duchess began to talk to him about the inscription on the leash. This loss will now cause many lances to break.

164. He said: "I have never heard of leashes with writing on them, but I do know about books of love letters *en français*—art of this kind is not unfamiliar to me—and I could read what might be written in them. Sigune, my sweet maiden, don't bother about the inscription on the leash!"

165. She replied: "But there was a wondrous story written on the leash. If I don't get to read that to the end, my whole land of Katelangen will be meaningless to me. No matter what wealth anyone might offer me, always assuming that I were worthy to accept it, I would rather have the inscription than all that.

166. "I'm not saying this to hurt you or anyone else, my noble friend. If we two young people are to live out our further years and if you will still be seeking to serve to gain my love, you must first obtain for me the leash with which Gardeviaz was tied in here."

167. He said: "Then in that case I shall gladly try to gain the leash. If it is to be won by combat, then I must either forfeit my life and honor, or bring it back into your hands. Be gracious, sweet maiden, and don't hold my heart in bondage for that long!"

168. "Grace and everything that ever maiden is supposed to grant to her noble, handsome beloved I shall give to you, and no one can ever keep me from doing so, if you are determined to get the leash which the hound was dragging along the trail when you caught it and brought it to me."

169. "My service will always strive after that with constancy. You offer a rich reward. How shall I ever pass the time until my hand can accomplish that by which I shall retain your favor? I shall attempt that both near and far. May Fortune and your love protect me!"

170. Thus they had recompensed one another with their words and with their good will too. The beginning of much sorrow: how did that end? The wise man and the fool alike will indeed find out whether the undaunted man, thus pledged, will rise or sink in renown.

SECTION 15

THE TALE OF THE HEART

Konrad von Würzburg (died 1278)

Introduction by Albrecht Classen

Konrad was a professional writer of Middle High German narratives and poems who was born shortly after Walther von der Vogelweide's death (ca. 1220) in Würzburg (ca. 1230). He does not appear to have been of noble origin, as he once expressed his desire to be a member of the aristocracy, and depended entirely on the income from his literary output. His name began to appear in the chronicles of Strassburg and Basel from 1260 onwards, and in 1287 he died in Basel a rather wealthy man. Obviously he had received a solid training in Latin, but was also well versed in French. His earliest text was the verse novella *Der Schwanenritter* (ca. 1257/58), soon followed, or perhaps even preceded by *Das Herzmaere* and *Die Klage der Kunst*. Soon after followed his political poem *Das Turnier von Nantes* and the romance *Engelhard* (ca. 1260), a tale of true love and friendship. His novella *Heinrich von Kempten* treats a historical theme, whereas his *Goldene Schmiede* is an allegorical poem celebrating the Virgin Mary. Konrad's most important works were his verse romance *Partonopier und Meliur* (ca. 1277) and the historical romance *Trojanerkrieg* (ca. 1281–1287), the latter a major examination of the accounts of the Trojan war characterized by Konrad's efforts to maintain objectivity and not to take the Trojans' side, as was typical in the entire Middle Ages.

In addition Konrad composed a number of courtly love songs and verse novellas in the vein of Marie de France and the author of *Moriz von Craûn*.

He died on August 31, 1287 a highly acclaimed writer, who excelled both through his versatility in using various genres and themes, and his highly artistic language. The Meistersinger (mastersinger), the fifteenth- and sixteenth-century craftsmen-turned-poets all over Germany, among them Hans Sachs, praised him as one of their twelve masters.

BIBLIOGRAPHY

David M. Blamires, "Konrad von Würzburg's Verse *Novellen*," *Medieval Miscellany. Festschrift for Eugene Vinaver*, ed. Frederick Whitehead et al. (Manchester/England: Manchester University Press, 1965), 28–44.

Timothy R. Jackson, "Konrad von Würzburg (circa 1320–1287)," *German Writers and Works of the High Middle Ages: 1170–1280.* Ed. James Hardin and Will Hasty. Dictionary of Literary Biography, 1038 (Detroit-Washington, D.C.,- London: Gale Research, 1994), 58–71.

THE TALE OF THE HEART BEGINS

I am well aware that pure love has become scarce in the world. Therefore, knights and ladies should take an example from this tale, for it tells of absolute love. We have it on the good authority of Master Gottfried von Strassburg that whoever wants to set his foot straight upon the path of love must listen to the recounting and singing of things of the heart, which have previously happened to those who have gazed upon one another with loving eyes. It is undeniable: He who hears something of love sung or read always loves all the better. Therefore I intend to take pains that I render this beautiful tale faithfully so one will be able to find therein a model of love which will be pure and bright and free from all falsity.

A knight and lady had heart and spirit so interwoven in each other that both their spirits and their hearts had become as one. What was distressing for the lady was for the knight as well. As a result of that their end was bitter. Love had become so sovereign over both that it made their hearts ache intensely. Yes, sweet love caused their hearts great pain. It had inflamed them to the depths with its fire and so pierced them with its glow that words could never describe its power. No one could fully relate their devotion. Never was greater faithfulness borne by man or by woman as they bore for each other. Yet, according to proper convention, they could not come to one another so they might share in the duties of love. The most gracious, beautiful woman was married to a worthy man—which caused her much grief. Her beauty was so well guarded that her noble friend could never still the desire of his wounded heart which was torn out of love to her. This was the affliction endured by them; it was harsh and dreadful. He began to grieve so terribly for the sake of her wondrous love that he could not conceal his torment from her husband. He rode to the fair one whenever possible and, with woeful cries, made known to her his heart's lament. Because of this, misfortune befell him in the end and crushed him. The woman's husband observed both of them very carefully until he, unfortunately, realized from their behavior that love had completely entangled them in its snare and that both were withering away for want of each other. The good lord was filled with sorrow and thought, "If I do not take care with my wife, I see clearly that I shall regret it later since she is brewing up disgrace for me with this worthy nobleman. Indeed, if I can arrange it I will bring her out of his power. I shall journey with her over the wild sea so that in this way I can guard her until he turns his heart's desire away from her and she her mind from him. I have often heard it said that the beloved gradually becomes estranged from the lover if both are separated for a long time. Thus I am willing to go with her to Christ's Holy Sepulcher until she has forgotten entirely the great love which she bears the worthy knight."

Thus he decided to turn love into sorrow for the two lovers who would never have wanted to part of their own accord and he determined that he and his lady would visit Jerusalem in the Holy Land. When the knight, who burned for her gracious love, learned of this, he, in his melancholy, quickly resolved to follow her swiftly over the sea. For he would surely die at home should he decide to do without her. The heavy burden of love crushed him so forcefully he would have sought out grim death itself for her sake. Thus he delayed no longer in going to her. As the sweet virtuous one perceived his intention, she summoned him to her in secret. "My friend, my lord, my life," she spoke, "my husband, as you have heard, intends to take me from you in flight. Now mark what I say, dear friend: for the sake of your happiness prevent this journey which he is planning over the wide, wild ocean. Go there yourself before he does so he will remain here. For when he learns you have gone before him, he will stay and the suspicion he harbors will be averted and he will think, 'Were there anything to those tales which concern my good and beautiful wife, as I believe, then the proud and spirited knight would not have left the land.' In this manner he will be freed of the mistrust he bears me in his heart. You should also not regret being there for a while until the talk about us which is flying across the land has ceased. And, when the most pure Christ has sent you back here, you then may have your will with me, indeed on every occasion as soon as the rumors stop. Alas, that you cannot always be with me in accord with your will and I with you in accord with my desire! Now farewell, dear lord, and receive this ring from me. It will serve at all times as a reminder of the sorrow I suffer when my eyes see you not, for whatever happens to me, I will think of you. Your going sinks aching desire into the very depths of my heart. Give me a kiss of sweet friendship on my mouth and do, for my sake, that which I bid." With a troubled heart he said to her, "Gladly lady, regardless of what I may gain by it, I will do whatever you wish. I have so lost both heart and soul in my desire for you that I am bound to you like a vassal. Now grant me leave, dear lady, and know that my desire for you causes me great tribulation. Indeed, I am so completely bound up in you that I greatly fear I shall be borne a dead man to the grave before I have the good fortune ever to see you again."

With this the talk which they had about their hearts' sorrow was at an end. The two lovers parted in agony and bound themselves together in their hearts at that moment much more intensely than I could ever express to you. Both their hearts were dead to worldly joy and their bright, rosy mouths yielded sweet, gentle kisses after which they renounced all pleasure between them. The worthy knight departed at once with aching heart to the sea and set sail in the first ship he found there. He knew with certainty he would never be of joyful mind or truly happy again, unless God saw to it that he came home and heard news about his beloved. For that reason the pain in his heart was unrelenting and bitter. The virtuous knight began to pine away for her and wall up piteous regret in his heart. His old cares for the sake of her love became ever new. Indeed he displayed the manner of the turtle dove, for in longing for his beloved he avoided the green bough of happiness and dwelt constantly on the withered branch of care. He longed for her unceasingly and his sorrow became so great that the pain pierced him to his marrow, to the very depths of his soul; such were the deep sorrow and the inner burden which wounded him. Love's martyr spoke many an hour with a sigh on his lips, "Honored be the pure woman, whose life and sweet body requires such heartache of me. Truly, through her dominion, that dear lady of mine knows how to send bitter misery into my heart! How can she, perfect beyond measure, inflict such pain! If she does not ease this life of mine, I will surely die." Because of his heart's distress, grief was with him all the days and he lamented for so long until at last he fell into such a consuming sickness that he no longer wished to live. One saw clearly on him the grim misery and hidden sorrow which he bore within. And, when the noble knight saw with painful certainty that he was dying, he said to his squire, "Hear me, dear companion. I find that I must die out of love for my lady, for she has wounded me to death with longing sorrow. Thus, do as I tell you. When it is over and l lie dead, cut open my body and take from it my heart, bloody and etched with pain. Cover it entirely with balsam so it will long remain fresh. Heed now what else I have to tell you. Prepare a little coffin adorned with gold and jewels. Place my dead heart therein and put in the ring which my lady gave me so that both are together, closed and sealed and locked in this fashion. Bring them both to my lady that she may see what I have suffered for her and how my heart was wounded for the sake of her gentle love. She is so pure and faithful that her aching desire for me will ever remain in her heart, when she considers the pain I had to suffer for her. Thus do well and fulfill my command. May God, who never abandons a noble heart, through his intercession take pity on me, poor wretch. And may he grant to her for whose sake I must lie here dead much love, happiness, and a joyful life."

With this mournful sorrow the knight met his end. The squire wrung his hands in grief and ordered him to be cut open at once and fulfilled the knight's wish. What the noble man had earlier asked of him, he did then and left, a joyless man with the lifeless heart. He brought it, as ordered, to the same castle where he knew he would find her for whom his dear lord had suffered the pain of death.

When he came to the castle where the noble lady was at that time, her husband chanced upon him in an open field, where, as the story tells us, he intended to do some falconing. This caused the squire great misfortune. For when the knight saw him there, he thought at once, "Surely this one is sent here for no other reason than to bring my wife some word of his master who yearns for her love." He thereupon rode to the squire and intended to question him at once. Then he espied the box of beautiful design wherein the squire carried the heart and the lady's ring, for he had hung it upon his belt as if it were nothing special.

When the knight looked upon it, he greeted the squire and asked what he was carrying in it. The most clever and loyal youth then said, "Lord, it is only a little thing which has been sent with me from afar." "Let us see," the knight quickly spoke, "what lies hidden within." The squire spoke with great distress, "In truth, I shall not do it. No one may ever see it except the one who has a right to do so." "No, that is not the way it will be," the knight said. "For I shall take it from you by force and look at it against your will." After that it was not at all long until he had torn the little box from the squire's belt.

He opened it and saw the heart and with it found the lady's ring. By these two tokens he realized that the knight was dead and that both were to be a sign to his beloved of his distress. The knight said, "Squire, I will tell you what to do. Take any road you wish and I will keep this little gem for myself." He then rode home and ordered the cook to prepare a special dish from the heart with great care. The cook did this gladly. He took the heart and prepared it so well that no one will ever enjoy any other delicacy so excellently made with precious spices as the noble heart. When all was ready, there was no more waiting. The lord went to dine at the table and had the meal quickly brought to his wife. "Lady," he spoke most sweetly, "this is a little dish that you alone must eat and not share." Thus, the noble lady took and ate her friend's heart entirely without being aware of its origin. That sorrowful little morsel seemed so sweet in her mouth that she had never before at any time eaten a dish whose taste had pleased her better. When the faithful lady had eaten the heart, the knight quickly spoke, "Now tell me lady, how this food has pleased you. I suspect that in all your days you have never tasted a sweeter dish than this one." "Dear Lord," she said, "never shall I be as happy, even if I should partake of food that might seem as sugarsweet and as pure as this dainty morsel which I have just enjoyed. Truly, I consider it to be the best of all meals. Speak, my lord, was this noble food wild or tame?" "Lady," he spoke again, "hear well what I now reveal to you. This morsel was both tame and wild, so help me God! Wild, because it was free of all joy, and tame because it was oppressed by unceasing care. You have eaten the heart of the knight who has endured more than enough heartaches for your sake all of his days. Believe me when I tell you: he is dead from the longing of his suffering heart for your sweet love and has sent you his heart and the little ring as a sign into this land with his servant."

With this tale of woe the noble lady took on the appearance of a dead woman. Believe me, her heart grew cold within her body. Her white hands fell together in her lap and blood gushed forth from her mouth as the true debt demanded of her. "Yes," she spoke with great distress, "if I have eaten the heart of him who has borne faithfulness toward me never ceasing, I will now tell you truly that after this nourishment I shall never more partake of any other food. God, in his justice, will prevent me from eating any lesser food after such good and worthy sustenance. I will not partake of anything except of that ill fate called death. I shall sacrifice my poor life in grievous heart's torment for him who has given up his life for me. I would be an unfaithful woman, if I did not remember that he, most virtuous man, sent his dead heart to me. Alas, that after his bitter end I had even one more day of life! Truly, it will not be long now that l live alone without him, who never concealed his fidelity from me and who is held in the thrall of death." Her distress was very great and out of true sorrow she folded her beautiful white hands together and her heart broke from painful desire. The young one brought her sweet life to an end and thus balanced perfectly the heavy burden which her beloved had assumed for her. She repaid him with full constancy and great faithfulness.

May God grant that whatever I take, I may return it with less effort and better than her most pure heart did. I believe that at no time was love ever requited so completely, nor will it ever be. I can see this in the people who live today. For the separation which is caused by Lady Love does not burden them so harshly so that man and woman are bound together in such a way they would now suffer the pain of death for one another's sake. One must use more force to pluck a straw from the meadow by hand than to undo the band of love where two lovers lie. Those who would now bear burdensome suffering for the sake of each other are easily separated without the pain of death. Lady Love gives them a good buy these days. In times past she never stole off to unvirtuous folk for a lesser reward; formerly her sweetness seemed so good that many a noble mind was consumed unto death by her. Now her ways are changed and her order is so weak she can easily be bought for a mere pittance by the stingy. Thus hardly anyone suffers for her sake today. One no longer cares to heed and scarcely holds in esteem that which has made itself available to one and all, for by so doing it is of little value. So it is with love; if she could arrange things so she would become even dearer, there would be a burden of heartache placed on man and woman more firmly than now. There would be such contest on her account and such suffering for each other that one would see it gladly.

I, Konrad of Würzburg, can tell you nothing more. Whoever has pure feelings so that he does what is best, will happily place this tale in his heart in order to learn to bear love purely. No noble heart will ever fail!

Translated by Ernst Hintz

SECTION 16

FLORIS AND BLAUNCHFLOUR
[*13th century*]

Although the opening lines of the English manuscript are missing, this gap can be filled in by summarizing the opening lines of the French work:

King Felix, pagan ruler of Almería in Spain, makes a predatory raid in Gallicia. All the pilgrims whom he attacks surrender without resistance, except a French noble and his daughter. Felix kills the noble, and takes the daughter, a young widow, as captive to Almería, where she is treated with the respect due a lady of her rank. Placed under the control of the queen, this young widow soon wins the love and respect of the entire court by reason of her gentilesse. On Palm Sunday, both she and the queen bear children: the queen bears a son; the widow, a daughter. Because that day is the festival of flowers (Pasque-florie), King Felix commands that the boy be named Floris and the girl Blaunchflour, and places their upbringing under the care of the young widow.

Two finer children, fair and grand,
Could not be found in any land.
The Christian woman nursed these two;
That she well loved them both is true;
Both of them she fed and reared,
Until these two were seven years.
The King summoned his own dear son,
And told him that the time had come,
Because 'twould be an evil thing
Not to start his own learning,
That he should letters in a book well know,
As true men do—both high and low.
"Fair son," he said, "thou now shalt learn;
Make sure your letters you don't spurn."
Floris said with tearful tone
As he stood before the throne,
Weepingly, then answered he,

15

"Shall not Blaunchflour learn with me?
To school I do not want to go
Without Blaunchflour." His voice was low.   20
"I do not wish to go to school
Without Blaunchflour to share my stool."
The king then sighed, with glance above,
"She too shall learn, for thy deep love."
So then for schooling did they sit;   25
Both of them were quick of wit.
A wonder it was to see their lore,
Because their love improved it more.
So much they loved each other's heart,
They hoped they'd never have to part.   30
When they to school five years had gone
To learn, each was a paragon.
In Latin[1] they grew competent,
And how to write on parchment.
     The king watched close this deep amour   35
Between his son and fair Blaunchflour,
And realized when they were grown
Their love also would be full blown;
How then could Floris his love withdraw
When he must take wife by law?[2]   40
The king spoke to the queen of this,
These thoughts that he could not dismiss,
And of his worry and his care,
And how it would with Floris fare.
"Madam," he said with heavy breath,   45
"Blaunchflour must soon be put to death,
So that when she has been slain
And in her tomb she has been lain,
Then Floris will not sigh nor fret,
For quickly then he'll her forget;   50
Then may he wed as we tell him."
The queen she answered sad and grim;
She thought perhaps to intercede
To save the maiden from this deed.
"Sir," she said, "we ways must find,   55

---

1. Latin: universal language of scholars in the Middle Ages; it long remained the chief subject taught in shcools, even to the very young children.
2. Mohammedan law required the boy to marry the girl his parents chose for him.

Young Floris' life to honor bind,
That loss of honor he'll not incur
For the maiden Blaunchflour!
Someone could take her away,
So she would not lose life this day.   60
With this we'd all be happier
Than if we slay the sweet Blaunchflour."
    Reluctantly the king agreed:
"Madam, please tell us what we need."
"Sir," she said, "well send Floris   65
Into the land of Montargis;[3]
Happy will my sister be,
Who is the lady of that country,
And when she understands why we
Have sent him there by our decree,   70
She shall do all within her might
To help us both, by day and night;
To love anew, she'll him persuade,
So soon he will forget this maid.
And furthermore, I thee appraise,   75
The maiden's mother should feign malaise;
That gives to us a perfect chance,
By reason of that circumstance
The maid may not from her mother go."
    This news filled both the youths with woe;   80
Their parents they could not deter;
Sadder children never were.
Floris wept before the king,
And said, "Dear sir, without lying,
To my regret you sent me away,   85
My love may not beside me stay;
Nor may we out together go.
All my joy is turned to woe."
The king said to his son outright:
"Son, within the next fortnight,   90
Be her mother alive or dead,
Surely," the king to Floris said,
"That fair maid then shall come to thee."
"Oh, sire," he said, "I pray it be.
If you will send her by my side,   95

---

3. Montargis: in Loiret, central France.

I care not where I then abide."
That his child agreed the king was fain,[4]
And entrusted him to his chamberlain.
    With honor were they welcomed there,
As fitting for a rich king's heir;   100
Well were they met by Duke Orgas,
Who met them with his court en masse.
His aunt also was comforter;
But Floris yearned for his Blaunchflour.
Though glad and merry they were with him,   105
He felt no joy, stayed always grim;
He would not join in games or laugh,
His thoughts were on his love's behalf.
His aunt set him to learn anew
As other children had to do;   110
Often he sighed, but naught he learned,
For Blaunchilour evermore he yearned.
If anyone ever to him spake, :
His gloomy heart would almost break;
His love increased with each heartbeat—   115
Young love is always dear and sweet.[5]
Both galingale and licorice[6]
Were not so sweet as her love is,
Nor nothing else, nor bloom or myrrh,
So much he missed his own Blaunchflour;   120
To him each day became as three
When he could not his true love see.
Thus he lived, depressed, downcast,
Until the fourteen nights had passed.
When he saw that she did not come,   125
His sorrow deepened, his mind grew numb;
He bothered not with food or drink,
And so his strength began to sink.
The chamberlain sent the king in haste
A letter telling of Floris' waste.   130
    The king ripped off the sealing wax
To learn good news and then relax,

---

4. Fain: happy.

5. Sweets were rare and expensive in the Middle Ages. This, then, suggests value and pleasure, not cloying sentiment.

6. Galingale: an aromatic East Indian root much loved in the Middle Ages.

But when he read, he changed his mind,
And realized that he'd been unkind.
Angrily he called the queen,   135
And told her they must intervene;
With fury in his heart he said,
"Go now and bring to me the maid,
Before nightfall her head shall go."
At this the queen was crushed with woe.   140
But then she spoke, that lady good,
"Have mercy, sir, for God's dear blood!
At the harbor nearest here,
There are merchants rich, my dear,
Merchants come from Babylon,⁷   145
Who will buy her and be gone.
Thus may you for that lovely maid
Receive much chattel and brocade,
And so she may from us depart
Without her death upon our heart."   150
          Reluctantly the king agreed,
And thus, in truth, was done this deed.
The king summoned this burgess,
Who was both kind and courteous;
This man could buy to meet demands,   155
And speak the tongues of many lands.
Soon the maid by him was bought,
And to the haven was she brought.
The price for which the maid was sold
Was twenty marks of heavy gold,   160
And a cup with precious stone—
In all the world it stood alone.
Never was one so well engraved;
He that made it was no knave.
On it was portrayed the scene,   165
How Paris led away the queen;⁸
And on the covercle⁹ above,
Also engraved was their deep love,
And on the pommel¹⁰ diadem

---

7. Babylon: not the Babylon of the Old Testament, but the old city of Cairo in Egypt, the ruins of which are still known as Baboul.

8. This refers to the abduction of Helen by Paris, which led to the Trojan war.

9. Covercle: the lid of the vessel mentioned in line 161.

10. Pommel: ornamental knob on the lid.

Was fastened a carbuncle[11] gem— 170
No cellar in the world so low
But that this stone's bright light would show
The butler how to pour the wine
In cup of gold or silver fine.

. . . . [Gap in manuscript]

Aeneas, the king, that noble boy,
In battle won it while at Troy,
And brought it into Lombardy
To give Lavinia,[12] his ami.
This cup from Caesar's treasure dole, 180
One dreary night a thief then stole.
This selfsame thief, so boldly brave,
This cup for Blaunchflour then he gave.
In his country he knew he'd trade
Three times its worth for this fair maid. 185
This merchant then sailed out to sea
With the sad maid to his country.
They traveled long by night and day,
As to Babylon they made their way.
To the emir of Babylon 190
They sold this beautiful paragon.
These two agreed on terms precise;
The emir paid the merchant's price.
He paid for her, as she stood sedate,
Seven times in gold her weight; 195
He thought, when he saw her arrayed,
His queen to make this fair young maid.
Amidst his harem with his wives
From her much honor he'd derive.
. . . .Now let us with sweet Blaunchflour be, 200
And speak of Floris in his country.
In his church the king had made
An ornate tomb for this sweet maid,
And ordered to be placed thereon
A newly graven broad headstone 205
On which the letters, without a chip,

---

11. Carbuncle: often used to refer to any red stone. there was a widespread belief in the
Middle Ages that precious stones gave off light at night. See Appendix A.
12. Lavinia: daughter of Latinus whom Aeneas married in Italy.

Were carved with clever workmanship.
Whoever could these letters read
Would see they spoke of this sad deed:
"Here lies the sweetest Blaunchflour
Whom Floris loved as his amour." 210
Meanwhile had Floris traveled home,
Straight to his father he had come;
He hailed his father on the throne,
And kissed the king as one unknown;
The queen he seemed a stranger to, 215
For he knew what he had to do.
Demanding his sweet lass, Blaunchflour,
He left without their sad answer.
Straight to her chamber forth he strode, 220
He prayed she was in her abode.
To Blaunchflour's mother he appeared,
"Where's Blaunchflour, my sweetest dear?"
"Sire," she answered cautiously,
"I do not know where she can be." 225
That crafty dame remembered well
The king's stern order not to tell.
"You lie! You lie!" he cried at her.
"Your lies strike deep, you gossiper!
Tell me, quick, where can she be?" 230
Weepingly then answered she,
"Dead" she murmured. "Dead? 'Tis true?"
"Sire," she said, "I swear it's true."
"Alas ' he sobbed, "when died my sprite?"
"Sire, within this last fortnight, 235
The earth on her was laid above,
And dead she was for thy deep love."
Floris, that was so young and fair,
Swooned;[13] that news he could not bear.
The Christian woman made loud plea 240
To Jesu Christ and Saint Mary.
When king and queen then heard that cry,
Into the chamber they did fly;
The queen saw him as in a sleep,
Heartbroken she began to weep. 245
The king's heart soon began to melt

---

13. Swooning lovers were commonplace in French and English romances.

As by his quiet son he knelt.
    ....Floris awoke and tried to speak,
And sobbed as tears rolled down his cheek;
He spoke to them with tear-filled eyes,   250
"Show me where my true love lies."
They took him gently for his sake,
For fear his tender heart would break.
When he approached the silent tomb,
And stood before it sunk in gloom,   255
He saw the epitaph thereon,
And read aloud, so gaunt and wan,
"Here lies the sweetest Blaunchflour
Whom Floris loved as his amour."
Three times he swooned, three times he stirred;   260
He could not move or speak a word.
At last his grief-stilled tongue he tried,
As freely he wept and sadly sighed:
"Blaunchflour, Blaunchflour, my love!" he wept,
"So sweet a love should ere be kept.   265
In all the world was none so fair,
As thee, my sweet, whose love I bear;
Great and small alike loved thee,
For thy boundless courtesy.
If death were dealt out fair and right,   270
We should have met it on the same night,
For born we were on the same day,
And should meet death in the same way.
Oh, Death, how full; of treachery,
And spiteful envy you must be!   275
You stole from me my own true dame.
In truth," he sobbed, "you are to blame.
She should have lived, you know full well;
Truly I'd die with her to dwell.
Those that seem the best to live,   280
Them you treat as fugitive;
And if there be a long-lived soul
Who for his life gives not a dole,
And fain would die to ease his lot,
For him you care not one small jot.   285
Thus I for life no longer care.
I shall tonight be with my dear.
No more on death will I then call,
But end my sadness by nightfall."

His dagger drew he from silver sheath,   290
Himself he would have done to death,
To plunge it deep within his heart,
Had not his mother seen him start.
She snatched from him his gleaming knife,
And by so doing she saved his life.   295
Out ran the queen then, sadly weeping,
Until she came unto the king.
To him spake this sad lady,
"For God's love, Sire, I beg mercy.
Of our twelve children have we none   300
Alive now but our own dear son;
So better the marriage they undertake
Then he be dead for his loved one's sake."
 . . . ."Madam, thou speak the truth," said he,
"Since it may not different be,   305
I'd rather have her as his wife
Than lose my only son's dear life."
At this word, then, the queen was fain,
And to her son she ran again.
"Floris, harken well to me.   310
Thy love, my son, you soon will see;
Thy proud father, this country's king,
And also I, we did this thing;
We had engraved upon the stone
Thy love's sad death to be made known.   315
We did it, son, for your own sake,
So as your wife you'd gladly take
A woman we would choose for you,
And thus our counsel you'd pursue."
Soon every word she had him told,   320
Of how the maiden they had sold.
"Is this the truth, my mother dear?"
"It's true, my son. She is not here."
 . . . .The graven stone was then unearthed
And Floris saw the empty berth   325.
"Now, Mother, I think that live I may.
But I shall not rest for night or day,
Night or day on any ground,
Till I my own true love have found.
To seek her out, my way I'll wend   330
If need be to the whole world's end."
To the king he strode to say farewell,

But his father begged him there to dwell.
"I will not stay for any price,
To ask me thus I deem a vice."   335
Then said the king, "Thus be it so.
Since now you feel you have to go,
All you will need we will provide.
May Jesus be ever by your side!"
   . . . ."Father dear," the lad replied,   340
I'll list what you shall me provide.
Give to me at my advice,
Seven horses of highest price:
Two well packed, and stout and bold
Both with silver and with gold;   345
And two with silver coins packed well,
To rent a wayside room to dwell;
Three with clothes both gay and rich,
The best your courtly tailors stitch.
Seven horses and seven men,[14]   350
And three knaves[15] to accompany them,
And your aged chamberlain,
Who truly is a noble swain:
He can both counsel us and guide,
For dressed as merchants we shall ride."   355
His father added a gracious thing;
The cup of gold he did him bring,
That selfsame beauteous cup of gold,
For which sweet Blaunchflour had been sold.
"Have this, my son," then said the king,   360
"With which you may that sweet young thing
Win back to make her soon your bride,
And evermore be at your side—
   Sweet Blaunchflour, so fair to see."   365
The knaves brought forth the staunch palfrey,
One-half white, as white as milk,
The other half as red as silk.[16]
No words have I to tell you aught
How richly was the saddle wrought:

14. Men: men-at-arms.
15. Knaves: servants.
16. This strange horse is from the French romance. Such brightly colored horses were common in the gay world of French romance.

The saddlebows of gold were made,   370
With stones of virtue[17] in them laid,
And trimmed around with orfreis.[18]
The queen was kind and courteous;
Her fingers on her hand did grasp,
A rich gold ring[19] which she did clasp.   375
"My son, I give you now, this ring.
While you wear it fear no thing;
No fire will burn you, no sea you drown,
No iron nor steel will bring you down,
And be it early or be it late,   380
Your needs will be filled with scarce a wait."
     Weepingly Floris took his leave,
And told his parents not to grieve.
They made for him such little cheer,
As if they saw him on his bier;   385
They feared him never again they'd see,
As thus in time it came to be.
     Forth he went with all his men,
Floris beside the chamberlain.
Silently they rode along,   390
And found a haven at evensong,
The selfsame place Blaunchflour had stayed,
For them a splendid meal was laid.
Full courteous was the master there,
He placed young Floris next to his chair,   395
And sat him in the fine guest seat.
Refreshed they were to drink and eat.
All the others were free from fear;
They reveled in the host's glad cheer.
They ate and toasted to each other,   400
But Floris' thoughts were on another.
Nor food nor drink would he partake,
For Blaunchfiour did his heart still ache.
     The lady of the house perceived
That Floris only sat and grieved.   405
She said to her lord in quiet tone,
"Sire," she said, "why does he moan?

---

17. Stones of virtue.
18. Orfreis: rich, embroidery.

Why are his spirits sunk so low?
Why meat and drink does he forego?
Little he eats, and less does drink;   410
He is no merchant, I really think."
        To somber Floris then spoke she,
"You're full of mourning, as well I see.
In this chair the other day
Sat fair young Blaunchflour, on her way,   415
Journeying to Babylon,
Brought by merchants, woebegone;
Herein they brought that maiden sweet
To sell the emir when next they meet.
To Babylon they will her bring,   420
To sell her to a prince or king.
You are like her in all your ways,
In your grief and in your face,
But you are a man, and she a maid."
Thus the wife to Floris said.   425
        When Floris heard his sweetheart's name,
Joyous then he soon became;
His spirits soared, his heart leaped up;
With wine he filled a silver cup,
And said, "Madam, this drink is thine;   430
Both the silver cup and wine,
For of my loved one you did speak;
On her I think, for her I seek.
I knew not where to seek her out,
But now your news has left no doubt.   435
I won't be stopped from going on
To find my love in Babylon."
        Floris rested there all night,
But he arose before daylight.
He then embarked on azure sea,   440
Good wind and weather both had he.
To the mariners he gave largess,
Who took him, with complete success,
To the land where he should find
His fair young maiden, sweet and kind.   445
As soon as he had come to shore,
Our Lord he did on knees adore.
In the land where his loved one lies,
He thought he was in Paradise.
        Immediately was Floris told   450

About the feast the emir would hold.
Kings and dukes would come in band,
All who from him hold their land,
Come to honor this emir,
And also him to see and hear.   455
When Floris heard this glad tiding,
Then he was pleased in every thing,
For in his heart he knew that he
Would certainly at that feast be;
For well he dreamed when in the hall,   460
Her he would see among them all.
     Floris traveled far and wide,
Until at last a town he spied.
Men gave him their benison,
As fitting to a rich king's son,   465
And at an inn incomparable,
The host set a rich table full.
For them he lavished many a fee
To ensure that plenty there should be
Of fish, of flesh, of tender bread,[20]   470
And both of white wine and of red,
For this lord, too, had traveled wide.
He sat young Floris by his side,
In the finest high guest seat.
Gladly did they drink and eat,   475
Yet Floris drank and ate naught;
On Blaunchflour, still, was all his thought.
The host of the inn then understood
Why this child sat in mourning mood.
Then up he spoke, this kind burgess,   480
That gracious was, and courteous:
"Child, I think your thoughts do dwell
Too much on your own chattel."
     "Nay, on my chattel my thoughts are naught,
On other things is all my thought.   485
My mind, I say, contrariwise,
Is centered on my merchandise;[21]
For, sir, that is my greatest woe,
That if I find it, I must forego."

---

20. Stock category of foods in the romances.

21. Merchandise: what he had come to buy (Blaunchflour) rather than what he carried to sell (chattel), for which he cared nothing.

Then said the host of that fine inn,   490
"There sat a recent day herein,
A sad fair maid named Blaunchflour.
Both in this hall and in her bower,
Ever she wore a mourning face
For she could not her love embrace;   495
She had no thought of joy and bliss;
Her dreams were ever on Floris."
    When Floris heard his loved one's name,
Glad he was, his heart aflame.
A silver cup he gave the lord,   500
And scarlet mantle as reward,
Paneled rich with miniver,[22]
He gave them to his host so fair.
"Have these," he said, "to your honor.
For them you should thank Blaunchflour.   505
Stolen she was, to my dismay;
Here I seek her by the way.
You would make my sad heart swell
If you could tell where she does dwell."
    "Child, to Babylon she was brought,   510
And the rich emir hath her bought;
He gave for her, as she stood bold,
Seven times her weight in gold;
For her beauty, bright and clear,
This rich emir bought her so dear.   515
For he thought, as could be seen,
This fair young maid to make his queen;
Among the maidens in his tower,
With much honor, he placed Blaunchflour."
    Floris rested there all night;   520
At dawning when it was daylight,
Up he rose in early light,
A hundred shillings he gave the knight;
From his host and his hostess,
He took his leave, gave them a kiss.   525
Eagerly as he told his plight,
He asked for help if that they might,
If in the town they had friend wise,
Who could direct and well advise

---

22. Miniver: gray fur (suirrel?)

How he might with some strategy   530
That fair maid for himself set free.
     "Soon a bridge you will approach,
You'll find its porter without reproach.
His home is at the bridge's end.
This courteous man is my good friend,   535
Sworn brother is he to me, and wise,
He well can counsel and advise;
If you will give to him this ring
As a symbol of my tokening,
Then he will help in every way;   540
You should listen and obey."
     Floris felt his heart grown free,
And thanked his host most gratefully.
He took the ring and began to ride,
He should no longer there abide.   545
By the time that the sun was high,
Toward the stone bridge he drew nigh.
As he to this stout bridge did wend,
He found the burgess at the end,
Sitting on a marble seat,   550
A fair and gracious man to greet.
This noble man was named Dayre,
And Floris greeted him with cheer.
He handed him the ornate ring
The lord had given him to bring;   555
Through the token of that ring,
Floris then got everything:
Fish and flesh and tender bread,
And flasks of wine both white and red.
     As Floris throughout the meal did sigh,   560
Dayre watched with careful eye,
"My dear young man, what troubles thee?
So full of care are you I see;
Don't you like my company,
Or perhaps this locality?"   565
     Floris moaned with glance above,
"Yes, kind sir, by God's dear love,
Such welcome have I ne'er before,
I hope I can in some small way,
Find the means to you repay,   570
But all of my thoughts in this wise,
Are always on my merchandise,

For which I've traveled far, my friend,
Lest I not find it at the end;
And thus it is my greatest woe   575
That I will it find but then must forego."
    Answered Dayre, the fair burgess,
Who was so kind and courteous:
"Child, please tell me of your grief;
To help you now is my belief."   580
Then every word he Dayre told,
How the maid from him was sold;
How he was a fine king's son,
And for the maid he'd hither run
To find how with some sly attack   585
That maid he could at last win back.
As Dayre this young boy beheld,
He thought him fool unparalleled.
"Child," he said, "I know your gloom,
Truly, though, you court your doom.   590
The emir has beneath his wing
Half a hundred wealthy kings,
And the best of such a worthy breed
Would never try such daring deed
As this fair maid from him to wrest,   595
Neither with guile nor strength obsessed.
For should the emir this perceive,
Soon of their life he'd them relieve.
For Babylon is large and strong:
Sixty miles its walls are long,   600
And in these walls, inviolate,
Are seven times twenty well-wrought gates,
And each gate has twenty towers strong.
Beneath them daily is such a throng
That no fair in all the year   605
Attracts more people there, I fear.
Seven hundred towers are there also,
Which overlook the town below.
The feeblest tower of all of these
Would challenge anyone with ease,   610
The emir, too, to try to come in;
By no means could the challenger win.
If all the strong men ever born,
Were joined as one, and oath had sworn,
They would win the maid as soon,   615

As from heaven they'd win the sun or moon.
"In the middle of that city strong,
There stands a tower, I am not wrong;
A hundred fathoms it is high,
For all to see and to terrify;   620
A hundred fathoms it is wide,
And made with careful workmen's pride.
It's built of lime and marble stone;
In all the world it stands alone.
The mortar for it was mixed so well   625
As to withstand a mangonel;[23]
And on the tower's finial,[24]
A carbuncle[25] set with such great skill
That no one needs at night to burn
Either torch or bright lantern;   630
Such a finial was never done,
It shines as bright as noonday sun.
"Deep within that same rich tower,
Live twenty-four maidens in a bower;
One who sees that bower nice   635
Would never wish for Paradise!
He never would relinquish this,
Ever to seek for greater bliss.
Now there are servants in this hall
To serve these maidens of beauty all;   640
No servant may ever enter there
Who in his breeches is no mare,[26]
Neither by night nor by the day,
But he be capon, as I say.
At the gate is a gateward,   645
Who is no fool nor a coward.
If there approaches any man
Within that selfsame barbican,[27]
Unless he has this man's consent,
Then will he have his body rent.   650
That porter stands in broad gateway;

---

23. Mangonel: a military device for hurling heavy stones and other projectiles.
24. Finial: an ornament at the top of a spire.
25. Carbuncle: see line 170, and Appendix A.
26. Mare: servants must be eunuchs.
27. Barbican: a defensive tower at a gate leading to a castle or a town.

Each day he wears a rich array.
Now the emir is so strange a man
That every year it is his play
To choose himself a fresh new wife,   655
Though he loves his queen as much as life.
When he would a new wife choose,
This is the method he does use:
His men fetch down from in the tower
The noble maidens from the bower,   660
And lead them all to the orchard
The fairest grove in Middlehard.[28]
Merry birds there sing their song,
There men might live their whole life long;
About the orchard stands a wall   665
That has been built of fine crystal.
There one may see within the stone
The world's wisdom shown to him alone.
      "A well springs up within this year,
A perfect well, it stands unmarred;   670
This well is held in great esteem,
From Paradise the waters stream;
The gravel is of precious stone,
And of high virtue is each one:[29]
Sapphires and sardoines,[30]   675
And ultrarich calsidoines,[31]
Jacinths and also topace,[32]
Onyx, too, of highest grace,
And many other beauteous stones
The names of which are not well known.   680
About this well there is much fear,
For if unchaste maiden[33] comes it near,
When she bows low unto the pool,
To wash her hands in water cool,
The water churns as in a flood   685

28. Middlehard: middle earth—the old Teutonic conception of the earth as the middle
ground between the heavens and the lower regions.

29. Stones of virtue: see note to line 371 above.

30. Sardoines: sardonyx.

31. Calsidoines: chalcedony.

32. Topace: topaz.

33. Medieval romances offer abundant examples of the "chastity test," the most famous
of which, undoubtedly, is in *Sir Gawain and the Green Knight*.

And on the maid it turns to blood.
On whom the water thus turns so,
Her life she must, in truth, forego.
Yet if she is a maiden clean,
The well does not then intervene, 690
And it runs both still and clear,
And does not fill the maid with fear.
　　"Beside the well there stands a tree,
The fairest that on earth may be.
It is called the tree of love, 695
It flowers and blooms forever above.
As soon as the old blooms be done,
New ones spring forth in the sun.
Maidens who from stain are free,
Men bring them beneath the tree, 700
And on whom falls the first fair bloom,
A queen she'll be with the king her groom;
And if there is a maiden bold,
Who in high esteem the emir holds,
The blossom then on her shall be, 705
Through magic and through conjury.
Thus he chooses by the flower;
We think this year 'twill be Blaunchflour."
　　Three times Floris swooned low,
Before his words began to flow. 710
When he awoke and turned aside,
Sorely he wept and sadly sighed.
"Dayre," he said, "I'll lose my prize,
Unless you help me and advise."
　　"Dear child, full well I see and know, 715
That thou unto thy death will go.
This is the best counsel that I can give,
I give it freely while I live:
Tomorrow to the gate draw near,
As if thou were an engineer, 720
And take a square and scantiloun,[34]
As if you were a famed mason,
And examine the tower all around;
But beware the porter where he's found.
Quickly will he come to demand, 725

34. Scantiloun: a builder's measuring rod.

What brings you to his alien land;
And work on you his felony,
And accuse you that you are a spy.
You should answer readily,
And speak to him both bold and free,   730
And say you are an engineer
Who's come to see that tower near,
For to measure and to find,
How to build one of its kind.
Soon he'll come with artfulness,   735
And ask that you with him play chess;
To play he will be anxious,
And to win from you quite covetous.
When you are to the chess game brought,
To play for money you must give thought;   740
You should have ready in your hand
Thirty marks at your command;
If he wins nothing then from you,
Leave it all with him, pray do!
And if from him you nothing win,   745
Consider it not worth a pin;
Greatly will he then thank you,
And greatly wonder at you, too.
He will ask you to remain,
Or that you return to play again;   750
You should say that you agree,
And take tomorrow twice your fee,
But always keep safe by your side
The good gold cup which now you hide,
That selfsame cup of finest gold,   755
For which Blaunchflour from you was sold.
The third day take a hundred pounds,
And the cup all whole and sound.
If his marks and money fail,
Let your money then prevail,   760
Because the cup you'll let him see,
And he will show cupidity;
He will be covetous and keyed up,
And eager then to buy the cup.
Remember he will on that same day   765
Honor you as much as he may!
He then will lead you to his hall,
The cup of gold to win with all.

Eagerly will he bid and pray
That you for that fine cup will play.   770
You shall then to him exclaim,
You care no more to play his game.
For the cup he'll offer more,
The further to increase his store.
You shall it not from him withhold,   775
Though it be of purest gold,
And say, I give this gift to thee,
Though it be worth as much as three.
Say also that you have no lack
Of gold and silver in your sack;   780
Say that much to him you'll give,
So he'll be rich while he does live;
For then he will so much love thee,
That you shall truly hear and see,
That he will grovel at thy feet;   785
To be your man, he'll you entreat.
His homage then accept you must,
And also take his hand in trust;
When he has thus become your man
He will help you with some plan."   790
     Floris followed this advice,
Just what Dayre did devise;
Thus through his gold and clever game,
The porter then his man became.
"Now," said Floris, "thou art my man,   795
And thee I trust to make a plan,
For you to help me easily;
To save me from death you must agree."
Then every word he hath him told,
How Blaunchflour was from him sold,   800
And how he was a king's bold son,
And for her love he'd thither run
To find how with some crafty game
The maiden to him he could reclaim.
     The porter listened and sorely sighed,   805
"I am betrayed; I am denied.
Through thy chattel I am betrayed,
And for my life I am dismayed;
Now I quake with anxious breath,
Through thee I fear to suffer death;   810
Nonetheless, I'll not fail thee,

While I may ride or live or see;
My agreement I will keep for all,
Whatever to me may befall.
Go thou home unto thine inn,   815
While I devise some sly engine
Between now and the third day,
And I will do whatever I may."
        Floris wept and sang no song;
The porter's term he thought too long.   820
The porter, though, thought what could be:
He had flowers gathered on the lea;
Because he knew the maiden's will,
Two baskets of flowers he had filled.
This was the device he thought to use,   825
Floris in one basket with his ruse.
Two servants bore the baskets both—
Such heavy loads that they were wroth;
They asked their God to give him pain
Who such a load did them ordain,   830
So they should have a heavy woe.
Not knowing where they were to go,
They turned to left once in the tower,
And thus ignored sweet Blaunchflour's bower;
To Clarice' bower the baskets they bore   835
With the sweet flowers that therein were.
There the basket they set down,
And gave them both a curse and frown
That so many flowers they had to bring;
They left the basket, muttering.   840
        Clarice to the basket raced
To see the blooms and them embrace.
Floris thought his love was near,
And stood upright to kiss his dear.
The startled maiden then grew pale,   845
And she began to shriek and wail,
And when he saw it was not she,
Into the basket in fear sprang he,
And felt he was betrayed and lost,
And for his life gave not a ghost.   850
Maidens came to Clarice' side,
By ten, by twenty, from far and wide,
And asked of her what was the matter
That she made such a fearful chatter.

Clarice understood immediately   855
That this was Blaunchflour's sweet ami,
For close to each they did reside,
Always they were side by side;
Each other's story they often heard,
Each other's sadness they often shared.   860
She gave the maidens this answer so
That back into their rooms they'd go:
"To this basket I came to see
The flowers to handle lovingly;
Before I knew it, I admit,   865
A butterfly toward me did flit.
So startled and afraid was I,
That I shrieked aloud and began to cry."
The maidens laughed and had much glee,
Then turned to go and let her be.   870
    As soon as the maidens all were gone,
To Blaunchflour's room Clarice went anon,
And said with laughter to Blaunchflour,
"Would you care to see a fine young flower?
Indeed, a flower for your delight   875
You have not seen for many a night!
It grew not in this dreary land,
This flower for thy dear sweet hand."
    "Away, damselle," cried Blaunchflour,
"To scorn me thus in small honor.   880
I know, Clarice, without strife,
The emir will have me to wife;
But that same day shall never be,
When men shall grieveously chastise me
For being to my one love untrue,   885
Nor change my love to someone new,
For dreaded fear, or new ami,
As does sweet Floris in his country.
Forever I yearn for sweet Floris,
None other shall have my lasting bliss."   890
    Clarice stood and saw with ruth
The constancy of her sad truth.
Laughingly, she told Blaunchflour,
"Come with me now to see my flower!"
To the basket they both drew near;   895
Rapturous was Floris without a fear,
For overheard them had this boy;

Out of the basket he leaped with joy.
Blaunchflour instantly changed hue
As soon as they each other knew.   900
Without a word they together leaped;
They clung and kissed and deeply wept.
Their kissing lasted a long, long while,
But to them it was a moment's smile.
    Clarice stood back and watched all this,   905
Their countenance and their sweet bliss,
And smiling said to sweet Blaunchflour,
"Lass, know you now this tender flower?'
A moment ago you would not see,
And now you will not set it free.   910
He must know much of cunning art,
If you present him with your heart."
"In truth," said Blaunchflour to Clarice,
"This is my own, my sweet Floris."
Both these sweet children in their bliss,   915
Knelt down to Clarice her feet to kiss,
And begged her mercy, all weeping,
Not to betray them to the king;
To the king she'd not them betray
Or else they would meet death that day.   920
    Then spoke Clarice to Blaunchflour,
Words full of fine and true amour,
"Doubt not that you are as safe with me,
As if to myself this had come to be;
Know you well for certainty,   925
That your secret love is safe with me."
Then to one bed these two she led,
That was of silk and linen thread;
They lay themselves there softly down,
As Clarice drew the curtains round.   930
Then these two embraced and kissed
And made much joy and lovers' bliss.
    At length to speak Floris began,
And said, "Dear Lord, who made me man,
I humbly thank thee, dear God's son;   935
For all my care I have overcome;
Now again my love I've found,
And of all my care I am unbound."
    Then each other they did tell
Of sorrows which to each befell.   940

Their griefs and cares they whispered low,
How separation had caused their woe.
Clarice served them secretly,
As they wished it, quietly.
To no other heaven could they aspire,   945
But to their bed of bliss retire.
Clarice could not them long protect,
Far soon the emir would them detect.
        Now had the emir such a way,
That there should come forth every day   950
Two fair maidens from their bower
To serve him well within his tower:
One with towel and gold basin,
For him to wash his hands within;
The other brought a comb and mirror,   955
To serve him thus with great honor.
Thus they served him ever fair;
Each day should serve another pair.
The two most called for in the tower
Were sweet Clarice and Blaunchflour.   960
So long had others served this route
That this pair's service had come about.
On the morning when came Floris,
It fell to Blaunchflour and Clarice.
Clarice—may blessings be on her! —   965
In the morning light did stir,
And called forth sweet Blaunchflour
To wend with her into the tower.
Blaunchflour mumbled, "I will come,"
But sleep then did her mind benumb;   970
So Clarice goes her way alone,
While Blaunchflour sleeps, to Clarice known.
As soon as Clarice came to the tower
The emir asked for sweet Blaunchflour.
"Sire," then Clarice said outright,   975
"She was awake this whole past night,
And knelt and gazed in meditation,
And read her book in exhortation.
She made to God her orison,[35]
That to you He give His benison,[36]   980

---

35. Orison: prayers.

And grant a long full life to you;
Thus now she sleeps in sleep so true.
Blaunchflour, that maiden sweet,
She could not come to you to greet."
     "How touching," murmured then the king,   985
"Is she not a sweet young thing,
The type that I should have as wife,
When she offers prayers for my long life?"
     Clarice arose the following day,
And scolded Blaunchflour for her delay,   990
That she had almost brought them woe,
"Arise, together we must go."
Blaunchflour murmured, "Yes, I come."
But Floris began to get venturesome;
They fell asleep, their love so dear.   995
Clarice to the pillar's brook,
The golden basin then she took,
And called aloud for young Blaunchflour,
To go with her into the tower;   1000
She answered neither yea nor no,
So Clarice alone then had to go.
     As soon as Clarice entered the tower,
The emir asked for sweet Blaunchflour,
Demanded why she was not there,   1005
And how she dared to be elsewhere.
"Before me, she arose with cheer;
I thought to find this young lass here.
Yet she has not come to you?
"She does not give to me my due!"   1010
Forth he called his chamberlain,
And bade him go with all his main,
To learn why she was still away,
Since he had ordered her that day.
     The chamberlain ran to the tower   1015
To mount the stairs of Blaunchflour's bower,
And stood outside her covered bed,
And found the two youths, head to head,
Mouth to mouth, and face to face;
Quite soon he will their joy erase!   1020
Back to the emir then he sped,

---

36. Benison: blessing.

To tell his lord about the bed!
    The outraged emir grabbed his sword;
This news, he felt, must be explored.
Forth he stalks with all his main,   1025
The emir with his chamberlain,
Until they came where these two lay,
Sleeping soundly after love play.
He yanked the covers with a will,
And exposed two figures lying still.   1030
Then he saw on that divan,
That one was woman, and one was man.
He quaked with anger where he stood;
To kill them both was first his mood.
He paused, though, ere he'd have them slain,   1035
So they could to him their acts explain,
And afterward he'd have their heads.
Soon these two awoke in dread
To see a sword above them shine;
To death they did themselves resign.   1040
The emir to Floris began to speak,
Words that made these two feel weak:
"Tell me quick, impetuous one,
Who advised this deed be done,
To steal your way into my tower,   1045
To lie there by my sweet Blaunchflour?
To dismal fate you must be born;
You both shall die before the morn."
Then said Floris to Blaunchflour,
"Of our poor lives there is no succor."   1050
For mercy they begged with such sobbing breath
That he gave brief respite from their sad deaths,
Until he had for his barons sent,
To avenge him through their wise judgment.
He had them rise from their love bed,   1055
And quickly dress, weak-spirited,
And then he ordered them bound fast,
And into prison rudely cast,
Until he had for his barons sent
To advise him through their wise judgment.   1060
It is no help to pad a tale,
So I will thus my words curtail.
Now all his barons have come to meet,
And the proud emir they humbly greet.

His hall he'd had so richly built, 1065
With kings and dukes it soon was filled.
He promptly stood up in the hall,
His angry face was seen by all;
He spoke, "My lords of high honor,
You have heard of my Blaunchflour, 1070
How I bought her to behold,
For seven times her weight in gold;
For her beauty and her cheer,
I bought this child to bring her here.
And I intended for my demesne[37] 1075
That I should have her as my queen;
And yet today on her divan,
I found her with a naked man.
The fury in my heart was hot,
I thought to kill them on the spot; 1080
Enraged was I with what I saw,
And yet their deaths I did withdraw,
Until for you word could be sent,
To avenge me through your wise judgment.
Now you know why you are come; 1085
Avenge me of this odium!"
. . . . Then spoke a king from distant land,
"This your shame we understand;
Before your vengeance on them we wreak,
We should hear the children speak, 1090
What they will say in their defense,
Of their ingratitude immense. ·
It would not be a judgment fair,
Without the answer of this pair."
. . . . A Nubian[38] king then answered bold, 1095
"Their answers false shall not be told.
It is just for every fact,
That felons caught right in their act
Should suffer then their punishment,
Without an answer or argument." 1100
. . . . After the children then they sent,
To burn them was the court's intent.

---

37. Demesne: the lord's domain.

38. Nubian: from Nubia, an ancient country in northeastern Africa between the Red Sea and the Sahara Desert. This seems to confirm the indentification of Babylon as Cairo rather than the more famour Near Eastern city.

Two servants brought them from their cell,
Toward their doom; their spirits fell.
Sorrowful were these children two;   1105
Each grieved the most for the other's due.
Floris said to fair Blaunchflour:
"For our life there is no succor;
But mine is the guilt, and mine the fault;
Grim death should not you now assault.   1110
If human nature would allow,
Two deaths for you I'd die somehow,
One for myself and one for thee,
Your death is near because of me!
For if I never here had come,   1115
Your life here would be frolicsome."
    ....Blaunchflour answered quickly, though,
"The guilt is mine for our deep woe."
Floris then drew forth the ring,
"While it is yours, death shall not sting."   1120
    ....Blaunchflour quickly answered him,
"Never shall it be so grim
That this bright ring shall save but me,
Nor may I no death on you see."
The ring she handed to her lover,   1125
But he thrust it back again to her;
Back to her the ring he thrust,
But then she cast it in the dust.
A duke saw it lying on the ground
And glad he was the ring he'd found.   1130
    ....In this way these sad children came,
Weeping to their doom in flame.
Before the court these two were brought;
Sorrow was their only thought.
Never was there so stern a man   1135
Who these sad children could then scan,
That he would not have willingly
Withdrawn the judgment and set them free,
To use great treasure them to buy,
If only they dared speak or sigh.   1140
For Floris was so fair a lad,
And Blaunchflour such a sweetness had,
Of men and women, now alive
That walk and speak and ride and thrive,
None were so lovely in their glee   1145

As were these two in misery.
No one who saw these two in woe
Could help be changed by their love-filled glow,
And by the tears that they had shed.
....The emir still was so outraged   1150
That he would not his wrath assuage.
He ordered the children bound fast,
And into the fire then be cast.
The duke who found the ring of gold,
His pity made him speak out bold.   1155
He felt he must help them survive,
And told how they for the ring did strive.
The emir, when he heard this plea,
Had the two brought instantly.
He asked Floris what was his name,   1160
And Floris answered him without shame.
"Sire," he said, "if it be thy will,
There is no need this maid to kill;
All the guilt belongs to me;
I ought to die, and she go free.   1165
So, Sire, I beg, put me to death,
But let the maiden keep her breath."
Blaunchflour spoke up in his defense,
"The guilt is mine for this offense.
If it weren't for love of me,   1170
He never would have crossed the sea."
Said the emir in reply,
"Truly, then, you both shall die.
My vengeance on you will I wreak
You both now nevermore shall speak."   1175
.... His sword he brought forth from its sheath,
The children he would put to death.
Blaunchflour first put forth her neck,
But Floris held her close in check.
"I am a man; I shall go first.   1180
To suffer the first death is worst."
Floris then thrust forth his head,
But Blaunchflour pulled him back instead.
Neither wished the other woe,
To receive the first death blow.   1185
All that saw this devotion
Felt deep and sad emotion,
And said, "How sorry now are we,

When we such love in children see."
....The emir, although angry still,   1190
Changed both his mood and his ill-will.
He saw how each for love would die,
And also many a weeping eye
For he, too, loved this maid so gay,
So weeping, too, he turned away,   1195
And his sword fell from his grasp,
He could not hold it in his clasp.
....The same duke who had found the ring
Spoke to him, compassioning,
"Sire," he said, "it is little worth,   1200
To lay these children in the earth.
It far more will you avail
For you to learn from Floris' tale
Who taught to him that crafty scheme
To steal within your staunch regime,   1205
And find out who had brought him there;
The better of others you might beware."
....All that heard this analysis
Beseeched the youths be granted this.
The emir said to Floris, "Quick,   1210
Tell me who taught you this trick."
"That," said Floris, "I'll never do,
Unless he be forgiven, too.
Then shall I tell you what you desire,
Else, you shall never learn, good Sire."   1215
When all the men begged this be done,
The emir finally was won.
So all details then Floris told,
How the maid from him was sold,
And how he was a rich king's son,   1220
And for her love what he had done,
To find how with some sly attack
That fair young maiden to win back.
And how through his gold the servingman
Had recently become his man;   1225
And how he was in the basket borne;
At this the others laughed with scorn.
....Now the emir, God bless him well,
Called Floris to beside him dwell,
And ordered him to stand upright,   1230
And on the spot dubbed him a knight,

And bade that he should with him be
In the foremost of his company.
Floris fell to the emir's feet,
And begged him for his love so sweet.
The emir granted this wish so dear,
And all the others he thanked sincere.
To a church he had them led,
And with his own ring he had them wed.
Now both the children in their bliss,
Bent down the emir's feet to kiss;
And through the advice of Blaunchflour,
Clarice was set free from the tower,
And the emir wedded her as queen,
At the finest feast as ever seen:
I cannot name the viands all,
But never richer feast was set in hall.
It wasn't long in that far land,
That tidings came to Floris' hand
That his father the king was dead;
Then all the barons to him said,
That he should make the journey home,
To receive his own kingdom.
From the emir he took sad leave,
To leave this land did Floris grieve.
Then spoke up the emir, wise,
"If you will do as I advise,
Dwell with us, and my man become,
And I will give thee a kingdom,
Just as long and just as wide
As where thy father did reside."
"My heritage I'll keep for any price;
To ask me not to is bad advice."
The emir then besought our Lord
That He help them return as wards.
Floris then was crowned as king,
And she as queen, the sweet young thing,
And accepted Christ did all the land,
And thanked our God for his kind hand.
Now they both are dead indeed—
May Christ of Heaven our souls lead
Now this tale is brought to end,
Of Floris and his little friend,
How they were blissful after woe;

God grant to us that it happens so,
That we may love Him all so well,
That will our Lord save us from hell.

SECTION 17

ITALIAN COURTLY LOVE POETRY
[*13th century*]

Introduction by Albrecht Classen

About hundred years after courtly love poetry had first appeared in Southern France (*troubadours*), these love songs were imitated in Italy as well. It is not fully clear whether these so-called poets of the *dolce stil nuovo* were directly influenced by the troubadours, but the assumption is highly likely because of the many connections between all continental European poets. After the German Emperor Frederick II had been coronated in 1220, he established a new court life in Sicily and a highly structured administration, helping the entire region to experience a considerable economic, social, and cultural growth. In the wake of these new developments courtly love poetry found its way to Southern Italy as well. Whereas the *troubadours* preferred the *canso* as the basic poetic form for their songs, the representatives of the *dolce stil nuovo* primarily turned to the *sonnetto* (sonnet). There is no information available why this different poetic form gained such a popularity in Italy, but had no followers in the Provence. We know that in the thirteenth century Petrarch perfected the *sonnetto* and laid the foundation for the modern version of this poetic model.

In contrast to the *troubadours* and the Minnesänger, for instance, the poets of the *dolce stil nuovo* emphasized the religious component of courtly love in that they often equated their beloved with the *Madonna*, the Virgin Mary.

The term *dolce stil nuovo* was coined by Dante in his *Divina Commedia, Purgatorio* 24, 57, but by that time this courtly love poetry had found many followers and enthusiasts in Northern Italy as well. For these poets love assumed a quasi religious character, as to love meant to grow mentally, spiritually, ethically, and morally. Dante illustrated the fundamental nature of the *dolce stil nuovo* in his "autobiographical," perhaps metapoetic narrative *Vita Nuova* (ca. 1293).

BIBLIOGRAPHY

Ronald Martinez, "Italy," *A Handbook of the Troubadours*. Ed. F. R. P. Akehurst and Judith M. Davis (Berkeley-Los Angeles-London: University of California Press, 1995), 279–95.

Hans-Erich Keller, "Italian Troubadours," ibid., 295–304.

Medieval Italy: An Encyclopedia, ed. Christopher Kleinhenz. 2 vols. (New York and London: Routledge, 2004).

Il Dolce Stil Nuovo

BONAGIUNTA DA LUCCA[1]

VOI, CHE AVETE MUTATA LA MAINERA

To Guido Guinizelli

You, who have changed the style
Of writing pleasing love songs
From the form and essence of before
In order to surpass all other poets,
Have acted like a beacon
Casting your light into dark quarters,
But not here where a sublime sphere illuminates,
Which surpasses everything else with its splendor.

You so surpass all other writers in your subtlety
That there isn't anyone who can explain you,
Since your style is so obscure!
It seems to me very strange that from Bologna,
Which has long been noted for its rational sense,
You squeeze love songs out of turgid prose.

GUIDO GUINIZELLI

VEDUT'HO LA LUCENTE STELLA DIANA[2]

I have seen the blazing morning star
Appear before day hands us dawn,

---

1. Bonagiunta Orbicciani of Lucca (*fl.* 1242–1257). With Guittone, helped to bring earlier modes of poetry to northern Italy. In this *sirventtes*, he criticizes his father of the " new style," but Dante makes him atone for this in *Purgatorio* XXIV.20 ff. Text in Edwards, *Poetry of Guido Guinizelli* (Garland, 1987), No. 19a.

Shaped like a woman standing afar,
More splendid than any other one—
Snow-white face with scarlet glow,
Gay, sparkling eyes, full of love for earth;
No worldly Christian girl I know
Can march her beauty and her worth.

By the love of her I'm so assailed
With a battle of sighs that rages fierce,
Before her I'd stand by fear impaled:
O if she knew how desires pierce
And, wordlessly, would get me some gain
From the pity she should pass upon my pain!

IO VOGL' DEL VER LA MIA DONNA LAUDARE

I truly wish to give my lady praise
And liken her to lily and to rose:
Brighter than morning star she comes and glows
And makes me think of all that heavenly blaze.
Green banks I compare with her, I compare the skies,
Flowers of every color, yellow and green,
Azure and gold, the richest jewels to be seen;
Through her even Love feels his value rise.

She passes in the streets, noble, adorned;
She humbles the pride of any with her greeting,
And skeptics to believers quickly are turned;
No wicked man with her would risk a meeting;
And still I say: her powers are even keener.
No man thinks evil once that he has seen her.

AL COR GENTIL REMPAIRA SEMPRE AMORE[3]

1. Love always repairs to the noble heart
       Like a bird winging back into its grove:
   Nor was love made before the noble heart,
       Nor did nature, before the heart, make love.
   For they were there as long as was the Sun,

---

2. Or Guido Guinizelli (*ca.* 1230–1276). Acknowledged father of the *dolce stil nuovo.* Judge in Bologna, descended from wealthy Ghibellines; driven into exile after the Guo victory in 1274. Died near Padua. Immortalized by Dante in *Purgatorio* XXVI, where introduces Arnaut Daniel. Texts in Robert Edwards, *Poetry of Guido Guinizelli* (Garland, 1987), No. 7; next poem, No. 10.

3. Original text appears in Section IX, taken from Edwards, No. 4.

Whose splendor's ever bright;
Never did love before that shining come.
Love nestles deep inside nobility
    Exactly the way
  One sees the heart within the fiery blaze.

2. Fire of love in noble heart is caught
     Like power gleaming inside a precious stone.
  The value does not come down from the stars
     Until the Sun has blenched the stone all pure.
  Only after the might of the Sun
     Has drawn out all that's vile
  Does the star bestow its noble power.
     Just so a heart transformed by nature pure,
  Noble and elect,
     A woman starlike with her love injects.

3. Love for this reason stays in noble heart
     Like a waving flame atop a burning brand,
  Shining, its own delight, subtle and bright;
     It is so proud, it knows no other way.
  Yet a nature which is still debased
     Greets love as water greets the fire,
  With the cold hissing against the heat.
  Love in noble heart will find a haven
     Like the shine
  Of a diamond glinting in ore within the mine.

4. Sun beats against the mud the livelong day;
  Mud it remains; Sun does not lose its ray;
  The haughty one says: "I am noble by my tribe."
     He is the mud; Sun is the noble power.
  Man must never believe
     That nobility exists outside the heart
  In the grandness of his ancestry,
  For without virtue, heart has no noble worth;
     It's a ray through a wave;
  The heavens retain the sparkle and splendor they gave.

5. Shines among the powers of heaven
     God the creator, more than Sun in our eye;
  Each angel knows the Maker beyond its sphere,
     And turning its circle, obeys God's noble power.
  And thus it follows at once:
     The bléssed tasks of the Master transpire.

In the same way, in all truth, the beautiful lady
Should behave, for in her eyes reflects the desire
    Of a noble man
  Who will turn his every thought to her command.

6.   Lady, God will ask me: "Why did you presume?"
    When my soul stands before his mighty throne.
"You passed the heavens, came all the way to me,
    And cheapened me in the light of profane love.
To me is due all the praise
    And to the Queen of the Royal Realm
Who makes all fraudulence cease."
I'll tell him then: "She had an angel look—
    A heavenly face.
What harm occurred if my love in her was placed?"

GUIDO CAVALCANTI

IN UN BOSCHETTO TROVA' PASTURELLA

1.   Once within a little grove a shepherdess I spied;
    More than any star of sky beauteous did she prove.

2.   Ringlets she had, blonde and curly locks,
    Eyes filled with love, a face of rosy hue,
    And with her staff she led her gentle flocks,
    Barefoot, with their feet bathed by the dew.
    She sang, indeed, as if she were enamored;
    She had the glamour of every pleasing art.

3.   I greeted her, and asked her then at once
    If she had any company that day;
    She answered sweetly: "For the nonce,
    Alone throughout this grove I make my way."
    And added: "Listen, but when the gentle bird is heard,
    A friend should have my heart."

4.   And when she told me of this state of mind,
    Suddenly I heard birdsongs in the wood.
    I said to myself: "This surely would be the time
    To take from this shepherdess what joy I could."
    Grace I requested—just to kiss her face—
    And then embrace if she should feel like me.

5.   She took my hand, seized with love's old power,
    And said she'd give me her heart too;

She led me then into a fresh green bower,
And there I saw flowers of every hue.
And I was filled so full of sweetened joy
Love's godlike boy there too I seemed to see.

FRESCA ROSA NOVELLA

1. Fresh newborn rose,
   My beauteous Spring,
   Through field, by river,
   Gaily singing,
   Your noble worth I set, In nature.

2. Your truly noble worth
   Renews itself with joy
   In agéd man or boy
   With every setting forth;
   Birds chant to it their vows,
   Each in his own Latin,
   From vespers into matins,
   On their greenish boughs.
   The whole world's now with song,
   Since it's your season,
   And, with proper reason,
   Hymns your majesty,
   For you're the most heavenly Of creatures.

3. Heavenly features
   In you, my lady, rest;
   O God, how wondrous blessed
   Now seems my desire.
   Lady, your glad expression,
   Whenever it comes and passes,
   Nature and custom surpasses
   In wonderful expression.
   Together women admire
   Your truly godlike form,
   For you are so adorned,
   Your beauty's not transcribed,
   For can't it be described: Beyond nature?

4. Beyond our human nature
   God made your excellence
   To show by its very essence
   That you were born to rule.
   Now, so your noble face

May stay forever near,
To me keep ever dear
Your most abundant grace,
And if I seem a fool
To set you as my queen,
Know that I don't blaspheme,
For Love makes me courageous
Which still no force assuages
          Nor measure.

CHI È QUESTA CHE VÈN, CH'OGN'OM LA MIRA

Who is it comes whom every man admires,
Who sets the air with clarity atremble?
Bringing Love too, so no man dare dissemble,
By speech, but each can only now suspire?
O how to catch her from the eye's swift gyre?
Love tells me: "No, you'd only bumble,
Because of women she's so far most humble
That any other you must then call 'ire.'"

No one could count her many charms, though modest,
For toward her bends every noble power;
Thus Beauty sets her forth to be her goddess.
Still my mind is not so high and grand,
Nor have I felt the grace at any hour
To encompass her and say, "I understand."

AVETE 'N VO' LI FIOR' E LA VERDURA

You have in you the flowers and the verdure
And all that's light or beautiful to sight,
So far outshining Sun, that nurture
No man knows who knows not your delight.
In this world live no ther creatures
So full of beauty or of countless pleasures;
Whoever fears Love needs but view your features,
To rest assured of all his many treasures.

The ladies who now lend you company
Much please me because of their respect for you,
And so I beg them, for their courtesy:
Whatever they can, that much honor show
And hold with love your loving mastery;
Because of all the rest, you are the best.

DONNA ME PREGA, PER CH'IO VOGLIO DIRE

1. A lady asks me; therefore, I'd explain
    An accident that often fiercely smarts
    And is so high it claims Love for its name.
    Now who'd deny, let him hear its fame,
    Though I can't hope to teach a lowly heart;
    I'd reach some men with knowledge in their brains,

2. Who bring to reason some intelligence.
    Because without a bit of natural science
    I have no will or wit to try to prove
    Where Love is born, or who created Love,
    What is his virtue or his potency,
    How he might move or what his essence be,
    His delights which by "to love" are known
    Or if Love's ever to men's sight been shown.

3. In that part where memory has its locus
    He takes his state and there he is created,
    Diaphanous by light, out of that dark
    That comes from Mars and then takes lasting focus;
    And once he's made, he has a name sensate,
    Taking desire from heart, from mind his mark.

4. He comes from an image seen and comprehended
    That's apprehended in the Possible Intellect;
    There he waits in subject, without wandering,
    And in that part his vigor has no force,
    For Love's never from pure quality descended;
    And yet he shines, himself his own effect,
    Without delight, unless it's that of pondering,
    Because he cannot breed from his own source.

5. Love is not virtue, but he takes his course
    From what we call perfection—
    Not rational but emotional, I say:
    Outside of health he steers his judgment's force,
    Lets ecstasy gain reason's predilection,
    Choosing poorly friends to vice's way,
    Pursuing his power often to death's end.

6. Yet if by chance his power is turned aside
    To guide instead along the other way,
    He was not made by nature to go astray:
    However far from the perfect good he bend,

By that much is the lover life denied:
Stability can fall the mastery it's gotten;
Love can't prevail when reason's all forgotten.

7. Love comes to be whenever desire's so strong
It can't keep bearing nature's measures;
Then leisure can't long please, and so Love veers,
Changing complexions, turning smiles to tears,
Twisting the face with fear; his pleasures
Last but a little, for he stays not long.

8. And yet you'll find him most in men of worth
Where his new qualities create new sighs
And make men gaze at uncreated spaces,
Arousing ire to burn in fiery faces
(No man can imagine it until he tries).
Love does not move, though arrows whistle forth;
He does not twist to find his jests at all;
Nor does he search for great wisdom, or small.

9. Like looks and tempers attract their kindred parts,
And make Love's pleasures then appear the surer.
No man can ever cower from his spear.
Never was nymphlike Beauty like his darts,
For coyer passions expire in such furor.
Still, a reward awaits the spirit speared—

10. Though not a trace appears on the lover's face.
For Love's no object, neither black nor white;
Look at a lover; you find no form for seeing
Unless some emotion from Love's form takes its being.
Outside of color, likewise cut off from space
This form out of darkness sheds faint light;
Beyond all fraud, says one who to truth is sworn,
So that only by this Love is true compassion born.

11. Go now, my song, where you aspire,
Securely, for I've so upraised
You, you'll be praised
Most highly for your sense
By all who own intelligence:
To stand with others you have no desire.

PERCH'I' NO SPERO DI TORNAR GIAMMAI[4]

1. Because I never hope to go once more,
   Ballata, into Tuscany—

You go soft and gently
    Straight to my lady's door,
    And she, from her high courtesy,
    Will do you honor.

2.   Go, and carry with you tales of sighings,
    Filled with long pain and grievous fear;
Beware only of hostile spyings
    From those who hold nobility not dear.
For certainly from my estate so low,
    To see you ill-dispatched
    Or by cruel hands snatched,
Which cause me now so many anguished breaths,
    Would cause me after death
    Grief and fresher woe.

3.   You feel, Ballata, now how death
    Forces me to put my life behind;
You feel my heart pounding with every breath,
    Sensing the end of every reasoning mind.
    Now my body's so totally torn apart
      That pain's not even fervent;
      If you would be my servant,
I ask: take my spirit with you
    (And this I beg you too:)
    Soon, when it leaves my heart.

4.   Alas, Ballata, to your kindly company
    This soul that trembles I too recommend:
Take it along, out of your piety,
    To that sweet lady where I send.
    Alas, Ballata, say with sighings more
      When you've at last drawn near,
      "I am your servant here,
And I have come to stay
    From one who's gone away,
    But was Love's servant long before."

5.   You, my voice, now weakened and dismayed,
    Which issues crying from this saddened heart,
With soul, and with this song that I have made,

---

4. Commonly called the *"Farewell Ballata,"* probably written in exile at Sarzan before death. Adapted by T.S. Eliot in "Ash Wednesday." Ed. Nelson, No. 35.

From ruined mind now reason wide apart.
You'll find that lady pleasing to the sense
   For her sweet intellect;
    And out of charmed respect
You'll always stand before her;
    Spirit, you too adore her
   Forever for her excellence.

DANTE ALIGHIERI

GUIDO, I' VORREI CHE TU E LAPO ED IO[5]

Guido, I wish that you and Lapo and I,
Spirited on the wings of a magic spell,
Could drift in a ship where every rising swell
Would sweep us at our will across the skies;
Then tempest never, or any weather dire
Could ever make our blissful living cease;
No, but abiding in a steady, blessèd peace
Together we'd share the increase of desire.

And Lady Vanna and Lady Lagia then
And she who looms above the thirty best
Would join us at the good enchanter's behest;
And there we'd talk of Love without an end
To make those ladies happy in the sky—
With Lapo enchanted too, and you and I.

AL POCO GIORNO E AL GRAN CERCHIO D'OMBRA[6]

1. To slender daylight and a vast circle of shade
I've come, alas! and to whitening of the hills,
Where all the coloration is lost from the grass;
And yet my desire has thus not lost its green,
For it is founded on a hard, hard rock
Which speaks and hears as if it were a woman.

2. Similarly this most extraordinary woman

---

5. Dante Alighieri (1265–1321), author of the monumental *Divine Comedy.* Wrote many lyrics in his youth, some collected in his youthful biography, the *Vita Nuova* (N Life); No. 15 in *Dante's Lyric Poetry,* ed. K. Foster and P. Boyde, an Invitation to Laa Gianni (with Lagia) and Guido Cavalcanti (with Giovanna) to ride in a magic ship with Merlin (11) and Beatrice (10).

6. Sestina to a mysterious "Rock Lady," No. 78 in the Foster-Boyde edition.

Stands frozen like the snow beneath the shade;
She's never moved, unless it's like a rock,
By the sweet season that heats up all the hills
And makes them turn from whitening into green,
Because it covers them with flowers and grass.

3. Whenever she wears a garland hat of grass
    She draws attention from every other woman,
    Because the blend of curly gold and green
    Is beautiful; Love stands within their shade,
    And locks me in between these little hills
    More tightly than the limestone locks the rock.

4. Her beauty exerts more power than magnetic rock,
    And her blows cannot be cured by any grass;
    For I have fled through fields and over hills
    To try to escape the clutches of such a woman;
    And yet her light won't grant me any shade,
    Under mound or wall or any frond of green.

5. I've seen her already dressed up in her green
    So stunningly that she would have moved a rock
    With the love I offer even to her shade;
    And so I've wanted her in a pretty field of grass
    To fall in love like me, like any woman,
    Surrounded by a circle of the highest hills.

6. But the rivers will run upward to the hills
    Before this wood that's dewy and is green
    Takes fire, as would any pretty woman;
    I'd take my life and sleep out on a rock
    And go around pasturing on the grass
    Just to see where her garments cast their shade.

7. Whenever the hills cast down a blackened shade
    In a fair green this youthful woman makes them
    Disappear, like a rock that's hidden under grass.

DONNE CH'AVETE INTELLETTO D'AMORE[7]

1. Ladies who have intelligence of love
    With you about my lady I'd discourse,
    Not that by talk I'd reckon up her worth,

---

7. Canzone from the *Vita Nuova* XIX. Original text appears in Section IX, taken from Foster and Boyde, No. 33.

But speech can often ease the burdened mind.
I say: whenever her worth looms high above,
Love makes me feel his presence sweetly, so
That if I didn't gradually lose his glow,
I'd teach the entire world to feel her love.
And yet I should not be talking overmuch,
For later fear will make me vilely quake;
No, I shall treat her most genteel estate,
Compared to what she is, with light-handed touch
In talk to you, my loving ladies and lasses—
It's not a thing for sharing with the masses.

2. An angel proclaims to the divine intellect,
Saying, "My Master, upon the earth I heed
A miracle in act that now proceeds
Out of a soul which this far casts its splendor."
Heaven, which has suffered no other defect
Except the lack of her, to its Lord exclaims
And every saint cries out in mercy's name.
Pity is my only staunch defender,
Saying in God, who my lady comprehends,
"Delights of mine, suffer now in peace,
For although your hope is one that can only please,
Still there's a man who's waiting for her end
And he will say in Hell: 'O spirits hexed,
These eyes have seen the great hope of the blessed.'"

3. My lady is desired in highest Heaven.
Ladies, become acquainted with her power:
I say: she is the gentle lady's endower,
So go with her whenever she passes by.
Love casts a frost upon hearts which are craven,
And every thought then icily petrifies;
But he who can stand and fix on her his eyes
Will become a noble thing—or else, will die.
Whenever she finds a man who shows his worth
For seeing her, he experiences her grace;
She humbles him, all injuries to erase,
And changes into happiness all that hurts.
For even more grace God has given a donation:
Certain salvation after her conversation.

4. Love says about her: "How can she possibly be
A mortal thing, since she's beautiful and pure?"
He looks at her and inwardly is sure

God wants to set her forth as something new.
Almost the color of pearl she has, to the degree
A woman should, certainly within measure;
She has all good that lies in nature's treasure;
Her very existence proves that Beauty is true.
Out of her eyes, whenever she moves them round,
Issue spirits of Love encased in blaze
Which strike the eyes of all who on her gaze
And penetrate till the heart of each is found:
Love you will see upon her visage painting;
No one dare look there long or he'll be fainting.

5. Song, I know that talking you'll make your way
To many ladies, once I've set you free.
Now I admonish: I've reared you up to be
A little daughter of Love, sweet and simple,
And wherever you go, you must always say:
"Show me the road; for I am being sent
To one whose praise explains my embellishment."
And if you don't want to act like an imbecile,
Stay away from people who are base,
Contriving, if you can, to show true grit
Only to ladies and to gentlemen of wit
Who will guide you quickly over the straightaways.
When you find Love in her company,
Never forget to offer him greetings from me!

AMORE E 'L COR GENTIL SONO UNA COSA[8]

Love and the noble heart are a single thing
(So said wise Guinizelli in his rhyme):
One without the other can have no fling,
As reason and soul are joined forever in time.
Nature creates them when with love it abounds,
Love is the sire, his mansion is the heart;
Deep inside he lies with sleep wrapped round;
Sometimes it's long or soon before he starts.

Beauty appears as a lady seeming wise,
Wakening desire from his heavy sleep,
Striking the heart through windows of the eyes.
Desire has lasted so long within the deep

---

8. Sonnet from the *Vita Nuova*, XX. Strongly indebted to Guinizelli; ed. Foster and Boyde, No. 34.

It rouses the spirit of Love as best it can.
Thus too a lady is acted on by a man.

OLTRE LA SPERA CHE PIÙ LARGA GIRA[9]

Beyond the sphere that circles us most wide
Passes a sigh that issues from my heart.
A new intelligence that Love imparts
With tears will be its upward guide.
When it arrives where it most desires,
A lady receiving honor it will see,
Shining with a splendor so dazzlingly
The pilgrim spirit will marvel at her fire.

Such he sees. But when he crosses the breach,
I can't comprehend; he talks with subtlety
To my mourning heart, which demands his speech.
I know only: he describes that noble lady
Because he often utters, "Beatrice . . . "
That, my dear women, is one thing I can reach.

BEN TI FARANNO IL NODO SALAMONE[10]

Solomon's knot will soon be wrapping you in,
Bicci Junior, with those precious necks of quail.
Those expensive cuts of mutton will make you wail
Your sins duly recorded on the dead sheepskin.
Your house'll be even closer to St. Simon's Jail,
Unless, of course, you make a quick getaway.
But now (I fear) it's just too late to repay
Those debts—unless that appetite should fail;

They tell me, though, you've got a clever hand.
Well, if it's true, maybe you'll be like new
Because you can make a hoist of some thousand grand.
Perhaps this art will ease your gluttony's grief:
You'll pay your debts, and stay in Florence too.
What's better, Bicci? To be glutton or be thief?

---

9. Final Sonnet of the *Vita Nuova*, XLII, affirming the ascension of Beatrice in Paradise; ed. Foster and Boyde, No. 57.

10. Debate Poem *(Tenzone)* with Forese Donati. "Solomon's knot" is a symbol. The last line is freely rendered; in Foster and Boyde, No. 73: "But thievery Stagno's sons(?)." For Forese's poems, Foster and Boyde, Nos. 72a, 73a, 74a.

444

CECCO ANGIOLIERI

S'I' FOSSE FOCO, ARDEREI 'L MONDO[11]

If I were fire, I would burn the world,
If I were wind, I'd buffet it wide.
If I were sea, I'd drown it in swirls.
If God, I'd boot it on the Devil's side.
If I were Pope, what a gay thing I'd be!
I'd toss all those Christians into jail.
If Emperor, know what would pleasure me?
To slice off every head from every tail.

If I were Death, I'd go to visit Papa;
If I were Life, I'd bid him fond adieux.
And frankly I'd do the same for dear ole Mamma.
If I were Cecco, as I am and cannot choose,
I'd snatch the chicks who are young and happy too,
And all the old ugly broads I would leave to you.

BECCHIN' AMOR!—CHE VUO', FALSO TRADITO?

"Becchina, my love!" "What do you want, you lout?"
"Pardon me!" "You don't deserve it a bit."
"Please! O God!" "You're looking all washed-out."
"I'll serve forever—" "What do I get for it?"
"My good faith." "Ha! That you've got in droves."
"Always for you." "Peace! I know what's fraud."
"How'd I go wrong?" "A bird told me in the grove."
"Tell me, my love!" "Go! in the wrath of God!"
"Want me to die?" "It'd take a thousand years."
"Ah, you talk bad." "*You* want to teach me good?"
"No. I'll just die." "God, you're a screw-up, dear!"
"God pardon you!" "O hell! go—like you should!"
"Ah, if I could . . . " "Shall I lead you by your seat?"
"You've got my heart." "And with torment that I'll keep."

LA STREMITÀ MI RICHER PER FIGLIUOLO

Misery calls out to me: "Hi, Sonny!"

---

11. Cecco Angiolieri (fl. 1281–1312). Cynical poet of Siena. Member of an aristocratic family. Military deeds documented from 1281; known dead in 1313. Wrote only Figures as a duped character in *Decameron* IX.4. Texts in Maurizio Vitale, *Rimato realistici del Due e Trecento* (UTET, 1968), pp. 398, 351, 391, 420.

I answer back: "How goes it, Mother, there?"
I was bred by a stud named Grief—not funny!—
And Melancholy delivered me from the mare.
My swaddling clothes were woven from a thread
That's called Disaster by the common folk.
From the bottoms of my soles up to my head
There's not a thing in me that's not a joke.

When I grew up, to make a restoration,
They gave me a wife; she's the one who yells
As far as the starry heavens feel vibrations:
Her yap's a thousand tympanums with bells.
A man whose wife is dead enjoys purgation:
He who takes another goes straight to Hell.

DANTE ALLEGHIER, S'I' SO BON BEGOLARDO

Dante, if I'm a big loud-talking cuss,
It's 'cause you've got your sword against my guts;
If I have lunch with someone, you have dinner;
I feed on fat, while lard-sucking makes you thinner;
If I shear out the cloth, you squeeze the carder;
If I run at the mouth, you gallop harder;
If I play gentleman, then you're downtrod;
If I'm the man of Rome, then you're a Lombard.

Okay! thank God at least we know we two
Are both to blame, me as much as you.
It's misery or bad sense that makes us run.
But if you want to carry on this fun—
Dante, I'll go until you're in the box;
For I'm the gay gadfly, and you're the ox.

FOLGORE OF SAN GIMIGNANO

I'DOTO VOI, NEL MESE DE GENNAIO

In the month of January I will bear
Courtyards with the snap of kindled hay,
Warm rooms with beds of the loveliest array:
Silken sheets and coverlets of vair,
Asti spumante, sugared nuts, and sweets,
The finest clothes from Arras and Douai
To ward the chill and bitter blasts away

Of winter wind and rain, of snow and sleet.

We'll go out sometimes in the course of day
And toss some glistening, shiny snowy balls
At the little girls who'll follow on our way;
And when we're tired of all those skids and falls,
Back to the court we'll troop in disarray,
And with fine friends make restful festival.

D'APRIL VI DONO LA GENTIL CAMPAGNA

For April I offer the gentle countryside
All flowering with blossoms bright and fresh,
Fountains of water that never can depress,
Maids and ladies over whom you can preside;
Stallions from Spain, chargers which boldly prance,
Company coutured in the latest Parisian style,
Instruments from Germany, lutes and viols
For tunes of old Provence and for the dance.

SECTION 18

Aucassin et Nicolette (either ca. 1230 or ca. 1270)

Introduction by Albrecht Classen

The date of *Aucassin et Nicolette* is very unclear. Some scholars argued for the first half of the thirteenth century because of an allusion to a twenty-year war could refer to the Albigensian Crusade, which would definitely place the text beyond 1229. Others suggested a date around 1270 on paleographical grounds and because of a reference to a new kind of coin minted only after 1266.

The author demonstrates an extraordinary sense of humor, mixed with a remarkable contempt of the Church's teaching, such as when he mentions that harpists and jongleurs provide entertainment to the evil sinners in Hell which to Aucassin, kept in prison by his father because of his love for Nicolette, seems much more preferable to Paradise. Whereas the latter is a place where "old priests go, and old cripples, and the maimed who grovel day and night in front of altars and in old crypts . . . dying of hunger, thirst, cold, and misery," Hell to him appears much more appealing: "That is where beautiful courtly ladies go, because they have two or three lovers as well as their husbands . . . I want to go with them, provided I have with me Nicolette, my very sweet friend" (VI). Nicolette, however, who quickly proves to be the main character in this tale—obviously the only one truly active and competent enough to strategize how to realize her love for Aucassin—had been kidnapped from her royal parents in Carthage and sold as a slave girl by some Saracen traders. The Viscount of Beaucaire had bought and baptized her, and taken her on as his godchild. Aucassin's father, the Count Garin of Beaucaire, involved in a war with the Count Bougar of Valence, desperately tries to convince his son to get knighted and lead his troops, so he strikes a deal with him, offering him the permission to talk with his beloved and kiss her once if he takes up arms for his father. But the latter breaks his promise once his son has defeated the opponent, and then imprisons Aucassin because he insists on his love for Nicolette. The latter manages to escape and hides in a forest where she creates a bower where Aucassin, in the meantime released from prison by his father, eventually finds her again with the help of a group of children. The lovers depart together and travel across the sea until they reach the curious country of Torelore where everything has turned to its opposite, the king lying in childbed and his wife waging war using rotten crab-apples, eggs, and fresh cheeses like her opponent. When Aucassin gets involved and kills many of the enemies, the King of Torelore stops him, saying: "It is not our custom to kill each other" (XXXII). But when a Saracen pirate ship arrives, they are all taken prisoners, and the lovers are placed on two different ships. Aucassin accidentally returns to Beaucaire where he is liberated and entrusted with the land because his parents have died already three years ago. Nicolette, in the meantime, is taken to Carthage (today in Tunisia; older scholarship tended to identify the town with Cartagena near Murcia, Spain, but there are no absolutely convincing reasons), where her parents do no longer recognize her until she reveals the secret to them. In order to find her lover, she soon dons a minstrel's garb and secretly returns to the Provence, disguised as a man. After she has tested Aucassin's love for her, she recovers her true appearance, and the two people marry.

Although the narrative seems to be just very light, facetious, even nonsensical entertainment, the satirical author offers profound criticism of military operations, explores the significance of gender roles, seriously critiques the medieval practice of marriage arrangements according to social, financial, and political criteria in total disregard of the young people's feelings and desires, and also examines the possibility of interracial marriages. This *chantefable* also proves to be interesting because it operates with both prose and verse, opens up many different perspectives toward the new money-based economy (Nicolette pays five sous to the children in return for their help to direct Aucassin to her hiding place in the woods; Aucassin also gives money to a man in the woods), discusses the danger of piracy and kidnapping, and emphasizes the significance of truthfulness and keeping promises (see Aucassin's father). Finally, the poet also sheds light on the life of minstrels and jongleurs.

BIBLIOGRAPHY

Ed.: *Aucassin et Nicolette*, ed. par Jean Dufournet (Paris: Garnier-Flmaarion, 1984).

Ed. and Trans.: *The Pilgrimage of Charlemagne* and *Aucassin and Nicolette*, ed. by Anne Elizabeth Cobby, with a Translation and Introduction by Glyn S. Burgess (New York and London: Garland 1988).

Lit.: Eugene Vance, "The Word at Heart: Aucassin et Nicolette as a Medieval Comedy of Language," *Yale French Studies* 45 (1970): 33-51.

Jane Gilbert, "The Practice of Gender in *Aucassin et Nicolette*," Forum for Modern Language Studies 33, 3 (1997): 217-28.

Roberta L. Krueger, "Beyond Debate: Gender in Play in Old French Courtly Fiction Author(s)," *Gender in Debate from the Early Middle Ages to the Renaissance*, ed. Thelma S. Fenster, Thelma and A. Clare Lees (New York: Palgrave; 2002), 79–95.

'TIS OF AUCASSIN AND OF NICOLETTE

WHO would wish good verse to hear,
Made to please an old man's ear,
Where two children fair stand set,
Aucassin and Nicolette;
Of the great pains were his load,
And the prowess that he showed
For his dear, so blithe of cheer?
Sweet's the song and fair's the word,
Courteous to the ear when heard.
No man can be so distraught,
Grieving so, so lost in thought,
Or in so great malady,
But at sound he cured must be,
And his heart for gladness beat;
It is so sweet!

HOW the Count Bougars of Valence made war on Count Garin of Beaucaire, so great and so wonderful and so deadly, that never a day dawned but he was about the gates and walls and barriers of the town, with a hundred knights and ten thousand soldiers, foot and horse; and he burned his land, and wasted his country, and killed his men.

The Count Garin of Beaucaire was old and frail, and had outstayed his time. He had no heir, neither son nor daughter, save an only boy, of such sort as I shall tell you. Aucassin was the young lord's name; fair he was, shapely and fine, and well formed in legs and feet and body and arms. His hair was yellow and close curled, his eye merry and grey, and his face clear and keen, with a high nose firmly set. He was so charged with good points that nothing bad, or that was not good, was to be found in him. But so overthrown was he by Love, the all-conqueror, that he wished not to be knight nor to take arms, nor to go into tourney, nor to do anything which he ought to have done.

His father and his mother say to him: "Son, now take thine arms, and mount thy horse, and fight for thy land, and bring aid to thy men! If they see thee among them, the better will they defend their bodies and their belongings, and thy land and mine."

"Father," replies Aucassin, "of what do you speak now? May God never give me anything that I ask, if as knight I mount horse, or go into fray or battle where I may strike knight, or he me, unless you give me Nicolette, my sweet friend, whom I so love!"

"Son," says the father, "that could not be. Let Nicolette alone, seeing that she is a slave-girl come from a strange land; the Viscount of this town bought her from the Saracens, and brought her to this place, and has reared her, and baptized, and made her his god-daughter; and one of these days he will give her to some young man, who will earn honourable bread for her. With this thou hast nothing to do. And if thou art after a wife I will give thee a King's or a Count's daughter. There is no man so rich in France but, if thou desire his daughter, thou shalt have her."

"Alas, father!" says Aucassin, "where is there now such high honour on earth, but if Nicolette, my most sweet friend, had it, it were well placed in her? Were she Empress of Constantinople or of Germany, or Queen of France or of England, it would be little enough for her, so noble is she, and courteous and debonair, and abounding in all good graces."

Now one sings.

Aucassin from Beaucaire came,
Courtly castle of high fame.
From the fair-made Nicolette
None may win a heart so set;
Though his father stands between,
And his mother harsh of mien:
"Out, alack! what fool's way's this?
Nicolette right winsome is:
Carthage town cast out the maid,
Saxon folk of her made trade.
If to wed thy heart is bent,
Take a dame of high descent!"
"Mother, naught for none I care!
Nicolette is debonair:
Her fair body, her bright eyes,
Hold my heart in enterprise.
Well is me, her love seems meet:
It is so sweet!"

Now they tell and narrate and the tale goes on.

WHEN the Count Garin of Beaucaire saw that he would not be able to draw Aucassin his son back from the love of Nicolette, he went to the Viscount of the town, who was in his service, and thus spake to him:

"Come you, Sir Count, and get rid of Nicolette your god-daughter! Evil be to the land from which she was fetched into this country! For now through her I lose Aucassin, that will not be a knight or do anything that he ought to do. And know well that, if I can get hold of her, I will burn her in a fire, and you yourself might have every reason to fear."

"Sire," said the Viscount, "it grieves me that he goes to her, or comes to her, or has speech with her. I had bought her with my money, and had reared her, and baptized and made her my god-daughter, and would have given her to a young man who would have earned honourable bread for her. With this would your son Aucassin have had nothing to do. But since it is your will and pleasure, I will send her to such a land and such a country that nevermore shall he set eyes on her."

"Keep you to it!" says the Count Garin. "Great evil might come to you of it !They went each his way. And the Viscount was a very rich man, and he had a rich palace looking upon a garden. There in a chamber on a high storey caused he Nicolette to be placed, and with her an old woman to give her countenance and fellowship; and there he let put bread and meat, and wine, and whatsoever was needful. Then he let seal the door, so that one could by no way go in there or go out, save that there was one window opening upon the garden, and quite small, through which came to them a little fresh air.

Now one sings.

Nicolette, for prison close,
To a vaulted chamber goes;
Cunning art had there made be
Paintings wonderful to see.
By the window's marble wall
Leaned herself the maid in thrall.
Bright blond locks her hair let go,
Shapely were her brows below;
Fair and clear without a flaw,
Such sweet face you never saw.
She looked out on forest-bower,
There she saw the rose in flower,
And the birds that singing went.
Then from orphan came lament:
"Me alas! ah, wretched me!
Why should I in prison be?
Aucassin, my lord and liege,

Love of you has me in siege,
Me, whom now you cannot hate,
That for you bear captive state
In this vaulted chamber high,
Where through weary days I lie.
But by Mary's Son I pray
Hence ere long to make my way,
       If I but may I!"

Now they tell and narrate and the tale goes on.

NICOLETTE was in the prison-chamber, as you have heard and had it told. The cry and the rumour went through all the land and through all the country that Nicolette was lost. Some say that she is fled forth from the country, and some that the Count Garin of Beaucaire has caused her to be slain. Whosoever had joy of it!"Aucassin was not glad, but went to the Viscount of the town and thus spake to him:

"Sir Viscount, what have you done with Nicolette, my most sweet friend, the thing in all the world that I most loved? Have you ravished her away, or stolen her from me? Know well that if I die of it, the penalty will be on you; and very rightly will that be so, since with your two hands you will have slain me; for you have taken from me the thing in this world that I most loved."

"Fair Sir," said the Viscount, "now let be! Nicolette is a captive whom I brought from a strange land; with my own money I bought her of the Saracens, and reared her, and baptized and made her my god-daughter, and have nourished her; and one of these days I would have given her to a young man, who would have earned honourable bread for her. With this you have nothing to do. But take you a King's or a Count's daughter to wife. Moreover, what would you think to have gained if you had taken her for paramour and brought her to your bed? Much of little would you have got by it, for all the days of the world would your soul be in Hell for it, since into Paradise never could you win."

"In Paradise what have I to do? I seek not to enter there, but only to have Nicolette, my most sweet friend, whom I so love! For into Paradise go none but such folk as I shall tell you. There go these old priests, and the old cripples and the maimed, who all day and all night crouch in front of the altars and in the old crypts, and those who are clad in old worn-out coats and tattered rags, who go naked and barefoot and full of sores, who die of hunger, and hardship, and cold, and wretchedness. All these go into Paradise; with them I have nothing to do. But into Hell I am willing to go; for to Hell go the fine clerks and the fair knights who have fallen in jousts and in ripe wars, and the skilled warriors and the brave men. With these I am fain to go. There also go the fair and courteous ladies who have two lovers or three, and their lords beside. And there go the gold and the silver, and the ermines and the grey furs; there, too, the harpers and the rhymers and the kings of the world. With these will I too go, so that I may have with me Nicolette, my most sweet friend."

"Certes," said the Viscount, "tis for nought that you shall speak thereof, for never will you see her. And if you spoke to her, and your father knew it, he would burn both me and her in a fire, and you yourself might have everything to fear."

"That is my grief" said Aucassin.

He departs from the Viscount sorrowfully.

Now one sings.

"Aucassin has turned away,
Sorrowful, in sore dismay
For his love so bright of brow.
None can give him comfort now,
Nor in counsel aught can say.
To the palace then he fares,
Up and up he mounts the stairs,
Then into a chamber creeps,
Where he throws him down and weeps;
And great dole his heart lets go
For the love he longs for so;
"Nicolette, oh fair to show,
Fair to come, and fair to go,
Fair to please, and fair to say,
Fair to jest, and fair to play,
Fair to kiss, and fair to press,
Sore for thee is my distress!
And my grief's so ill to mend,
Sure it brings me to my end,
        Sweet sister, friend!"

Now they tell and narrate and the tale goes on.

WHILE Aucassin was in the chamber and was mourning for Nicolette, his friend, the Count Bougars of Valence, who had his war to achieve, was in no wise forgetting it: and so, having marshalled his men, foot and horse, he went against the castle to storm it. And the cry arose and the clamour; and the knights and the soldiers arm themselves, and run to the gates and to the walls to defend the castle; and the burghers go up to the alleys of the ramparts and hurl quarrels and pointed stakes.

So while the assault was great and in full fling, the Count Garin of Beaucaire came into the chamber where Aucassin made dole and mourning for Nicolette, his most sweet friend whom he so loved.

"Ha! son," says he, "what a caitiff and unworthy thou art, to look on while they storm thy castle, the best and the strongest of all! And know, if thou lose it, thou art without inheritance! Son, come now, take arms and mount horse, and defend thy land, and carry aid to thy men, and go into the fray! Never smite a man there, nor let other smite thee; yet if they see thee among them they will the better defend their bodies and their belongings, and thy land and mine. And thou art so big and strong that thou canst well do it, and so oughtest to do."

"Father," replied Aucassin, "of what do you speak now? May God never give me anything that I ask Him, if I do as knight, or mount horse, or go into fray where I may strike knight or he me, unless you give me Nicolette, my sweet friend whom I so love!"

"Son," said the father, "that cannot be ! Rather would I suffer myself to be wholly despoiled, and to lose all that I hold, than that thou shouldest ever have her to bed or to wed."

He turned away. And when Aucassin saw him going, he called him back.

"Father," said Aucassin, "come forward! I will make a fair covenant with you."

"What is it to be, fair son?"

"I will take arms, and go into the fray, on this covenant, that if God bring me back safe and sound you will let me see Nicolette, my sweet friend, so long as to have two or three words with her, and until I have once kissed her."

"I grant it," said his father.

So he agreed with him, and Aucassin was glad.

Now one sings.

Aucassin has heard the kiss
On returning shall be his.
Hundred thousand marks full weight
Could not make his heart so great.
Calling for his harness bright
Soon he stood accoutred right:
Hauberk lined his breast encased,
On his head his helm he laced,
Sword gold-hilted girds he on,
Lightly up to horse has gone,
Takes in hand his shield and lance,
At his two feet casts a glance,
Well the stirrup-irons they tread:
Wondrous high he holds his head.

Of his fair one thinking yet,
To his steed his spurs he set;
Fain and fast he rode away,
Making for the gate which lay
     Toward the fray.

Now they tell and narrate and the tale goes on.

AUCASSIN was armed and horsed, as you have heard and had it told. God! how well sat the shield at his neck, and the helm on his head, and the sword-belt upon his left side. And the boy was big and strong, and fair, finely bred and well formed; and the horse whereon he sat was fiery and swift, and finely had the youth ridden him through the gate.

Now might you not think that his mind had been to take beeves or kine or goats, and that he would have struck knight, and had other strike him? None of that; not once did he think of it! But he thought so much of Nicolette, his sweet friend, that he forgot his reins and all that he had to do; and the horse that had felt the spur bore him away into the press, and hurled right into the midst of his foes; and they laid hands on him all round and caught him fast. Then they took from him shield and lance, and forthwith led him away prisoner, and already were consulting by what death to make an end of him. This when Aucassin heard:

"Ah, God!" quoth he, "sweet Maker! are these my mortal enemies that here have hold of me, and will now be cutting off my head? And when once I have my head cut off, nevermore shall I speak to Nicolette, my sweet friend, whom I so love! Yet have I here a good sword, and I ride a goodly fresh steed. If now I defend me not for her sake, may God never help her if she love me more!"

The boy was big and strong, and the horse whereon he sat was mettlesome. And he claps hand to sword, and starts smiting to right and to left, and cuts through helmets and arms and face-pieces and fists, and makes havoc about him, even as the wild board when hounds set on him in the forest. And so he smites down ten knights of them and wounds seven, and so drives straight out of the *melée*, and so returns full speed back again, sword in hand.

The Count Bougars of Valence heard tell how they would be hanging Aucassin his enemy; and he came to that quarter, and Aucassin mistook him not. He gat his sword into his hand and smote him over the helm, so that he cleft him to the head. So stunned was he that he fell to earth; and Aucassin puts out his hand and takes him, and leads him away a prize by the nose-guard of his helmet and delivers him to his father.

"Father," said Aucassin, "see here your enemy, who has so long warred on you and done you despite. For twenty years now has this war endured, and never by man could it be brought to an end."

"Fair son," said the father, "such feats of youth you ought to do, and not bay after folly."

"Father," said Aucassin, "give me no sermons, but keep your covenants with me!"

"Bah! what covenants, fair son?"

"Alas, father! have you forgotten them? By my head, whosoever forgets them, I will not so forget them, so greatly have I them at heart. Did you not make covenant with me, when I took arms and went to the fray, that if God brought me back safe and sound, you would let me see Nicolette, my sweet friend, so long as to have two or three words with her, and until I had once kissed her? This you had in covenant with me, and this will I that you hold to."

"I?" said the father. "Never may God help me if ever I keep covenant with you in this! And if she were here now I would burn her in a fire, and you yourself might have everything to fear!"

"Is this the full end?" said Aucassin.

"So help me God," replied his father, "yes!"

"Certes," said Aucassin, "I am much grieved when a man of your age lie!— Count lValence," said Aucassin, "I took you prisoner?"

"Surely, sir, you did!" said the Count.

"Give me your hand on it!" said Aucassin.

"Sir, right willingly!" He put his hand into his.

"You pledge me this," said Aucassin, "that on no day while you have life shall you be able to do my father dishonour or disturbance in his person or his property, but you will do it him!"

"Sir, for God's sake," said he, " mock me not, but put me to ransom! You will not know now how to ask of me gold or silver, horses or palfreys, ermine or grey, hawks or hounds, that I will not give you."

"What?" says Aucassin; "know you not that I have taken you prisoner?" "Sir, I do!" replies the Count Bougars.

"Never may God help me," says Aucassin, " if, an' you pledge me not, I do not now make that head fly off you ! "

"In God's name," said he, "I promise you whatsoever you please!"

He gives him his word; and Aucassin makes him mount on a horse, and himself mounts another, and so leads him back into safety.

Now one sings.

Now when sees the Count Garin
How that his son Aucassin
Never can let leave him now
Nicolette, the bright of brow,
Into ward he sends him bound,
To a dungeon underground,

Which of dark grey stone was wrought.
Here when Aucassin was brought,
Sad as none could sadder be,
Loudly into grief brake he:
You shall hear him,—how distraught.
"Nicolette, thou fleur-de-lis,
Sweet, and dear, and fair to see,
Sweeter than the clustered vine,
Sweeter than the sop in wine!
Once a pilgrim did I see,
Out of Limousin came he:
Dizziness so laid him low,
Off his bed he might not go:
Sore on him was that disease,
Sick with many maladies.
Passing by where he lay down,
Thou did'st gather thy long gown,
And thy cloak of ermine bright,
And thy smock of linen white,
Till thine ankle they revealed.
Straightway was the pilgrim healed;
Ne'er till then so sound of limb
From his bed he lifted him;
Off to his own land he ran,
Sane and sound, a mended man!
Sweet my dear, my lily-bloom,
Fair to go, and fair to come,
Fair at play, and fair at flight,
Fair to speak, and fair delight,
Soft to kiss, and sweet to hold,
None to you could ere grow cold!
I for you in ward am bound,
In this dungeon underground,
Where I make an evil end:
Now I may but death attend
      For you, sweet friend!"

Now they tell and narrate and the tale goes on.

AUCASSIN was put in prison, as you have heard and had it told; and Nicolette, on the other hand, was in the chamber. It was summer-time, the month of May, when the days are warm, and long, and clear, and the nights still and serene. Nicolette lay one night on her bed, and saw the moon shine clear through a window, and heard the nightingale sing in the garden, and she remembered Aucassin her friend, whom she loved so well. Then she began to concern herself with the Count Garin of Beaucaire, who hated her to death, and bethought her that she would no longer remain there, since, if she were reported and the Count Garin knew of it, he would cause her to die an evil death.

She saw that the old woman who was with her was asleep; so she got up and put on a gown of silk cloth that she had, very fine, and took bedclothes and towels, and knotted them the one to the other, and made a cord as long as she could and bound it to the window-post, and let herself down into the garden. And she took her gown in one hand before and in the other behind, and tucked it up from the dew which she saw lying heavy on the grass, and went her way down the garden. IIer hair was yellow and closely curled, and her eyes grey and laughing; her face fairly formed, her nose high and well-set, her lips more red than a cherry or a rose in summertime, and her teeth white and small; and her little breasts were so firm they lifted up her bodice as if they had been two walnuts; and she was slender in the waist, so that in your two hands you could have clasped her. And the heads of the daisies which she broke with the tips of her feet, and which fell upon her instep above, were dead black against her feet and limbs, so white was the small maiden.

She came to the postern and unlocked it, and passed forth through the streets of Beaucaire under cover of shadow, for the moon shone out bright, and wandered on till she came to the tower where her friend lay.

The tower was flawed in places, and she hid herself alongside one of the buttresses, and wrapped herself in her mantle, and laid her head into a crevice of the tower, which was old and time-worn, and heard Aucassin who there within wept and made great dole, sorrowing after his sweet friend whom he loved so well. And when she had hearkened to him long enough she began to speak.

Now one sings.

Nicolette, so blithe of cheer,
Leaned herself against a pier;
Aucassin there heard she mourn,
All for love of heart forlorn.
Then from thought her words came right:
"Aucassin, thou noble knight,
Fair lord of unshamed renown,
What avails to be cast down?
What are woe and weeping worth?
Ne'er of me shalt thou get mirth;
As thy father hates me true,
So thy kinsfolk likewise do.
Now for thee o'er seas I'll go,

Life in other lands to know."
From her locks a tress she clipt,
And within the crevice slipt;
Aucassin, with this to touch,
May not honour it too much;
Oft he kissed it, and caressed,
Oft he clasped it to his breast,
Then again to weeping brake
    For her dear sake.

Now they tell and narrate and the tale goes on.

WHEN Aucassin heard Nicolette tell how she would go away into another land, there was in him naught but rage.

"Fair, sweet friend," said he, "go you shall not, for then will you be my death! And the first that saw you or could come by you would take you forthwith and bring you to his bed, and have you for his paramour. And once you had lain in a man's bed other than mine, do not think that I would rest till I had found a knife wherewith I might strike me to the heart and make an end of me! Nay, surely, so long would I not wait, but would speed me to where I saw a wall or a grey stone, and there would I hurl my head so hard that I would make my eyes start out of it, and beat out all my brains. Far rather would I die such a death than know that you had lain in a man's bed other than mine."

"Alas! said she, "I think not that you love me so much as you say; but I love you more than you do me!"

"Alack!" said Aucassin, "fair, sweet friend, it could not be that you should love me so much as I do you! Woman cannot so love man as man loves woman. For the love of the woman is in her eye and upon the nipple of her breast, and upon the tip of her foot; but the love of the man is planted within-the heart whence it cannot get f'orth."

There while Aucassin and Nicolette were speaking together, down the street came the town-guard, and they had their swords drawn under their cloaks, for the Count Garin had charged them, if they could take her, that they should kill her. And the warder who was on the tower saw them coming, and heard that they went talking of Nicolette, and that they were threatening to slay her.

"God" said he, "how great a loss were so fair a maiden were they to kill her! And very great kindness would it be if I could tell her by some means that they perceived not, and she be on her guard against them. For if they kill her then will Aucassin, my young lord, die, of whom grievous were the loss."

Now one sings.

Brave the warder stood to view,

Valiant, wise, and courteous too.
He began to chant a rhyme,
Fair it went, and sweet to time:
"Little maid, of heart so light,
Shaped so well, a comely sight,
Comely blond thy tresses show,
Grey thine eyes, thy face aglow;
Well I see, by that bright mien,
Thou hast with thy lover been,
Who for thee is like to die.
Listen, now, to what say I!
Let thy watch on traitors be
Who this way come seeking thee;
Under cloak do brands made bare
Grievous harm for thee prepare.
Lest with thee it soon go hard,
    Be on thy guard!"

Now they tell and narrate and the tale goes on.

Ha! " said Nicolette, "may the soul of thy father and of thy mother be in blessed repose, since so fairly and courteously thou hast given me word of it! If it please God, I will keep me well, and may God also guard me from them!"

She wraps herself in her cloak under shadow of the buttress till they have passed by: and she takes leave of Aucassin and goes her way until she is come to the castle-wall. The wall was battered about, and had been shored up; and she climbed thereby and made on until she was between the wall and the moat; and she looked down, and saw the moat very deep and sheer, and was sorely afraid. "Ah God," said she, "sweet Maker! If I let myself fall I shall break my neck; and if I remain here, to-morrow they will take me and burn me in a fire. Yet rather would I die here than that to-morrow all the folk should have me for a gaping-stock."

On her brow she made the cross, and let herself slip down into the moat; and when she came to the bottom, her fair feet and fair hands, which had not recked how it might hurt them, were all bruised and broken, and the blood flowed from them freely in a dozen places: nevertheless, she felt neither pain nor grief, because of the great fear that she had. And if she was in trouble over getting in, she was in yet greater about getting out. She bethought herself that to remain there was no good, and she found a sharp stake which those within had thrown for defending the castle, and made steppings one above the other, and so climbed till by dint of great pains she reached the top.

Now the forest lay within two bow-shots, and covered a good thirty leagues in length and breadth; and in it were beasts, savage and serpentine. She was fearful that if she entered therein they would kill her: then again she thought that, if men found her there, they would bring her back into the town to burn.

Now one sings.

Nicolette, the bright of brow,
Up the fosse has mounted now,
And her sore distress to show
Unto Christ her prayer lets go:
"Father, King of Majesty,
Now know I no way to flee;
If I go to forest-bower,
Wolves will surely me devour,
Lions also, and wild-boars,—
Many a one there runts and roars.
If I wait till day be clear,
So that they can find me here,
Then the fires will lighted grow
Where my body burned must go.
But, by God's high Majesty,
Sooner would I have it be
That the wolves my body tore,
And the lion and wild boar,
Than into the city hie!
          That will not I!"

Now they tell and narrate and the tale goes on.

NICOLETTE bewailed her full bitterly, even as you have heard. She commended herself to God, and fared forth till she came into the forest She dared not go deep in it for fear of the wild beasts and the serpents; so she hid herself in a dense thicket, and sleep took her; and she slept till the full prime of the next day, when the herd-boys came forth from the town and drove their beasts between the wood and the river. And they betook themselves apart to a most beautiful spring which was on the edge of the forest, and spread a cloak, and on that put their bread. While they were eating, Nicolette was awakened by the cries of the birds and of the shepherds, and she hastened towards them.

"Fair children," said she, "the Lord God be your aid!"

"God bless you!" said the one who was more ready of tongue than the rest.

"Fair children," said she, "know you Aucassin, the son of the Count Garin of Beaucaire?"

"Yes, we know him well."

"So may God help you, fair children," said she; "tell him that there is a beast in this forest, and that he is to come and hunt it; and if he can take it, he would not part with one limb of it for a hundred gold marks, nay, not for five hundred, nor for any price."

And they looked at her and saw her so beautiful that they were all astonished.

"I tell him?" said he that was more ready of tongue than the rest. "Sorrow be his who shall ever speak of it, or who shall ever tell him! This is a phantom that you tell of, for there is no such costly beast in this forest, neither stag, nor lion, nor wild-boar, whereof a single limb were worth more than two pence or three at the most: and you speak of so big a price! Evil be to him who credits your tale, or who ever shall tell it him. You are a fay, and we have no care for your company; you keep your own path!"

"Ah, fair children!" said she; "you will do this! The beast holds such a medicine that Aucassin will be cured of his wound. And I have here five sous in my purse; take them and tell him! And within three days ought he to hunt; and if, in three days, he find it not, never will he be cured of his wound."

"By my faith!" said he, "we will take the money; and if he come hither we will tell him; but never will we go to look for him!"

"In God's name!" says she.

Then she takes leave of the herd-boys, and goes her way.

Now one sings.

Nicolette, with brow so sweet,
From the herd-boys turned her feet,
And, her path set forth upon,
Deep in leafy woods was gone,
Where the track grew faint and wan;
Till she came upon a place
Where the road by seven ways
Thence through all the country ran.
So to thinking she began
How her lover she might prove
By his word to be her love.
Stems of field-lilies she broke,
And the leafage of the oak,
And with other leaves as well
Shaped thereof a dainty cell;
Ne'er was seen so sweet before.
And by God's own Truth she swore,
Should Aucassin chance that way,
And for love of her not stay,

Nor to rest awhile agree,
Ne'er shall he her lover be,
    Nor his love she.

Now they tell and narrate and the tale goes on.

NICOLETTE had made the cell, even as you have heard and had it told, very fair and very fit, and had decked it well without and within with flowers and with leaves. And she laid herself down hard by the cell, in a close thicket, to know what Aucassin would do.

And the cry and the rumour went throughout the land and through all the country that Nicolette was lost. Some say that she is fled away, and some say that the Count Garin of Beaucaire has caused her to be slain. Whosoever had joy of it Aucassin was not glad. And the Count Garin, his father, had him taken out of prison; and he summoned the knights and the ladies of the land, and let make a mighty rich feast wherewith he thought to comfort Aucassin his son.

While the feast was at its height, Aucassin stood leaning upon a balcony, all sad and cheerless: whosoever felt joy, Aucassin had no mood for it, for naught saw he there of the thing he loved. A knight looked at him, and came up to him, and addressed him:

"Aucassin," said he, "from the same cause of sickness that you have, have I been sick. I will give you good counsel if you have the will to believe me."

"Sir," said Aucassin, ""Gramercy! Good counsel would I hold dear!"

"Get on a horse," says he, "and go along yonder forest to cheer you! and you will see the flowers and the herbs, and you will hear the small birds sing. Peradventure you will hear some word for which you will be the better."

"Sir," says Aucassin, "Gramercy! That will I do!"

He slips out of the hall and goes down the stair, and comes to where his horse was in stable. He bids put on the saddle and bridle, he sets foot to stirrup and mounts, and goes forth from the castle. And he wandered on till he came to the forest, and so rode till he came to the spring, and finds the herd-boys at the hour of None. And they had a cloak spread out on the grass, and were eating their bread and making very merry.

Now one sings.

Now the herd-boys come about,
Esmer's lad and Martin's lout,
Fruelin and little John,
Robin's son and Auberon,
Said the one, "Fair fellowship,
Aucassin, I pray God keep!
Faith! a pretty youth for show,

And the well-clad maid also,
She that had the blondy hair,
Open face and eyes of vair:
Nor did she her pence deny,
Out of which we cakes can buy,
Also knives in cases set,
Cornet, too, and flageolet,
Bagpipes, too, and shepherd's clubs.
God heal his rub!"

Now they tell and narrate and the tale goes on.

WHEN Aucassin heard the shepherds, he called to mind Nicolette, his most sweet friend, whom he so loved, and he bethought him that she had been there; and he set spurs to his horse, and came to the herd-boys.

"Fair children, God be your aid!"

"God bless you!" said he that was morc ready of tongue than the rest.

"Fair children," said he, "say again the song that you were saying just now !" "We will not say it!" said he that was more ready of tongue than the rest. "Sorrow be his now who shall sing it for you, fair sir!"

"Fair children," said Aucassin, "do you not know me?"

"Yes, we know well that you are Aucassin, our young lord; but we are not yours, we are the Count's."

"Fair children, you will do this, I pray you!"

"'Od's heart, hearken!" quoth he. "Why should I sing for you if it suit me not?—when there is no man so rich in this country, except the Count Garin in his own body, who if he found my oxen or my cows or my sheep in his fields or in his corn would be so hardy toward having his eyes scored out, as to dare drive them from it. And so why should I sing for you if it suit me not?"

"So may God be your aid, fair children, you will do so! And take ten sous which I have here in a purse!"

"Sir, the money will we take; but I will not sing to you, for I am sworn of it; but I will tell it you if you wish."

"In God's name!" said Aucassin. "I would rather have it told than nothing." "Sir, we were here just now, between Prime and Tierce, and were eating our bread by this spring, even as we do. now. And a maiden came here, the most beautiful thing in the world, so that we believed her to be a fairy, and this whole wood was bright with her. And she gave us of that she had so much that we made covenant with her, if you came here, to tell you that you should go hunting in this forest, where there is a beast which, if you could take it, you would not part with one of its limbs for five hundred marks of silver, nor for any price; for the beast holds such a medicine that if you can catch it you will be cured of your wound. And within three days were you to have caught it; and if you have not caught it never will you see it again. Now hunt it if you will, or, if you will, leave it, for I have quit myself well of it towards her."

"Fair children," said Aucassin, "enough have you told thereof, and God grant me to find it!"

Now one sings.

Aucassin the words heard say
Of his dear and dainty may;
Deep they entered to his heart,
From the herds he paced apart,
'To the deep woods went with speed;
Quick beneath him stepped his steed,
At a gallop bore him well.
Then spake he, three words to tell:
"Nicolette, of dainty shape,
I for you to woods escape;
Neither stag nor boar I chase,
'Tis for you the track I trace.
Your grey eyes, and dainty show,
Your bright laugh, and words so low,
My poor heart have brought to death.
But if so God wills me breath,
You once more my eyes shall meet,
    Friend, sister, sweet!"

Now they tell and narrate and the tale goes on.

AUCASSIN ranged through the forest from path to path, and his charger bore him on at a great pace. Think not that the briars and the thorns spared him! Never at all; but so did they tear his raiment that scarcely could one anywhere have joined it across; and the blood ran from his arms, and his sides, and his legs in forty places, or thirty, so that after the youth one might follow the traces of blood which fell upon the grass. But he thought so much on Nicolette, his sweet friend, that he felt neither pain nor grief; and he ranged all day through the forest by such ways that never did he get news of her. And when he saw that the evening approached, he began to weep because he found her not.

All down an old grass-grown path he was riding, when he looked before him in the mid-way and saw a youth of such sort as I will tell you. Big-grown was he, and a marvel, ugly and ill favoured. He had a great tuft-head blacker than charcoal, and more than a hand's breadth between his two eyes; and he had vast cheeks and a huge flat nose, and great splay nostrils, and thick lips redder than a broiled collop, and big teeth yellow and ugly. And he was shod in leggings and shoes of bull's hide bound with bark to above the knee; and he was clothed in a cape wrong on both sides, and was leaning on a great club.

Aucassin made haste towards him, and was greatly afraid when he took stock of him.

"Fair brother, God be thine aid!

"God bless you!" said he.

"So may God help thee, what art thou doing here?"

"What is that to you?" said he.

"Nothing," said Aucassin; "I ask you not but with good intent."

"But wherefore are you weeping?" said he, "and making such a grievous to-do? Surely, were I as rich a man as you are, all the world would not make me weep."

"Heh! but do you know me?" said Aucassin.

"Yes, I know well that you are Aucassin, the son of the Count; and if you tell me wherefore you are weeping, I will tell you what I am doing here."

"Certes," said Aucassin, "I will tell you full willingly. This morning I came to hunt in this forest, and I had a white greyhound, the most beautiful on earth, and I have lost it. For this am I weeping."

"To hear!" said he, "by the heart our Lord had in His body, that you wept for a stinking hound ! Ill grief befall him who shall ever again take account of you, when there is no man so rich in this land but, if your father asked of him ten or fifteen or twenty, he would have rendered them too willingly and been only too glad! But I ought to weep and make dole."

"And for what cause thou, brother?"

"Sir, I will tell you. I was hired to a rich farmer? and I drove his plough; four oxen there were to it. Now three days since there happened to me a great misadventure, whereby I lost the finest of my oxen, Roger, the best of my team. And him I go seeking, and have neither eaten nor drunk these three days past. And I dare not go to the town lest they should put me in prison, since I have not wherewith to pay for it. Of all the wealth of the world I have nothing of more worth than you see on my body. A meagre mother had I, and she had naught of worth above a poor mattress, and that they have taken from under her back, and she lies on the bare straw; and I am weighed down a deal more about that than about myself. For wealth comes and goes: if now I have lost, I shall gain another time, and shall pay for my ox when I can, nor ever for this will I be a-weeping. And you wept for a dirty dog! Ill grief befall him who shall ever again take count of you!"

"Certes, thou art of good comfort, fair brother; may thou be blessed! And how much was thine ox worth?"

"Sir, twenty sous are demanded of me for it; I cannot get abatement of a single mite."

"Now take," said Aucassin, "the twenty which I have here in my purse, and pay for thine ox."

"Sir," said he, " mighty thanks! And may God grant you find that which you seek!"

He parts from him, and Aucassin rides on. The night was fair and still, and he wandered on till he came hard by to where the seven ways branched, and saw before him the wattled lodge which Nicolette had made; and the cell was decked without and within, and above and before with flowers, and was so fair that more so it could not be.

When Aucassin perceived it, he stopped all at once; and the rays of the moon shone into it.

"Ah God! " cried Aucassin, "here was Nicolette, my sweet friend, and this made she with her beautiful hands. For the sweetness of her, and for the love, here will I alight now, and lay me there for the rest of this night."

He drew his foot out of the stirrup to light down, and the horse was great and high. He thought so much on Nicolette, his most sweet friend, that he fell against a stone so heavily that his shoulder flew out of joint. He knew himself sorely damaged, but he strove as best he was able, and with his other hand he fastened his horse to a thorn. And he turned himself on his side, so that he came backwards into the lodge. And he looked through the trellis of the cell and saw the stars in heaven; and he saw one of them there brighter than the rest, and he began to say:

Now one sings.

Little star, I yonder see,
    Stepping with the moon thro' air,
Nicolette is there with thee,
    My small love with locks so fair.
God, methinks, hath made her leave
Earth to be the star of eve.
Whatsoever fate might send,
    Would I were with thee so high!
Close I'd kiss thee without end;
    Though a king's own son were I,
Surely you for me were meet,
    Friend, sister sweet!

Now they tell and narrate and the tale goes on.

WHEN Nicolette heard Aucassin, she came to him, for she was not far off. She entered into the lodge, and threw her arms about his neck, and kissed and clasped him.

"Fair sweet friend, well found be you!"

"And you, fair sweet friend, be you, too, well found!"

468

They kissed each other and embraced, and their joy was beautiful.

"Ah! sweet friend," said Aucassin, "I was but now sorely wounded in my shoulder, and now I feel neither pain nor grief since I have you!"

She handled him and found that he had his shoulder out of joint. And she so managed and drew it to place with her white hands, that, as God willed who loveth lovers, it came back to its setting. And then she took flowers, and fresh grass, and green leaves, and bound them on with the hem of her smock, and he was all healed.

"Aucassin," said she, "fair sweet friend, take counsel what you will do. If your father tomorrow bids search this forest, and they find me, whatever may become of you, they will slay me."

"Certes, fair sweet friend, I should be sore grieved at that! But if I have power, they shall never get hold of you."

He mounted on his horse and took his friend up in front of him, kissing and embracing; and they fared forth toward the open plain.

Now one sings.

Aucassin, the fair, the bright,
The amorous, the gentle knight,
From the deep wood issuing out
Claspeth arms his love about:
Where on saddle-bow she lies,
Fast he kisses brow and eyes,
Kisses mouth and kisses chin.
She, the while, lets speech begin:
"Aucassin, my fair sweet friend,
To what land are we to wend?"
"Sweet and dear, what do I know ?
Naught to me is where we go;
Track or forest let us ride,
So but I with you may bide!"
On they fare by vale and down,
Pass by borough and by town,
Till at dawn the sea they scanned,
And there 'lighted where the land
        Became the strand.

Now they tell and narrate and the tale goes on.

AUCASSIN had lighted down, both he and his friend, as you have heard and had it told. He held his horse by the bridle and his friend by the hand, and they began to go along the seashore.

And Aucassin saw a ship that was sailing by, and could see that there were merchants upon it, for they were quite close to the shore. And he summoned them and they came to him; and he made such terms with them that they took him into their ship.

And when they were on the high sea a storm rose, mighty and marvellous, which bore them from land to land till they were come to a strange country, and entered the port of the Castle of Torelore.

Then they asked what land that was, and they were told that it was the land of the King of Torelore.

Then asked he what manner of man that was, and had he wars; and they told him:

"Yea, great!"

Then he took leave of the merchants, and they commended him to God. He mounts on his horse with his sword girt on, and his friend before him, and made on until he was come to the castle. He demanded where the king was, and they told him that he was lying in child-bed.

"And where, then, is his wife?"

And they told him that she was in the field, and had led thither the whole force of the country.

And Aucassin heard it, and it seemed to him a great marvel. And he came to the palace and lighted down, both he and his friend, and she held his horse, and he went up into the palace with his sword girt, and fared on till he came to the chamber where the king lay in child-bed.

Now one sings.

Courteous to the chamber sped
Aucassin, the gentle bred.
Straight he to the couch did win,
Where the king was lying-in.
There in front of him stopped he
Thus to speak—now hearken ye!"
Fool, what folly here gets done?"
Quoth the king, "I bear a son.
When my month is at an end,
And I'm well upon the mend,
Then to hear mass shall I go,
As my ancestors did so,
And my great wars to maintain,
March against my foes again,

Till none remain."

Now they tell and narrate and the tale goes on.

WHEN Aucassin heard the king talk in such fashion, he took all the bed-clothes which were upon him, and hurled them down the chamber. He saw at his back a cudgel; so, taking it, he turns him about, and beat and battered him till he was like to have killed him.

"Ah! fair sir," cried the king, "what do you want of me? Are you out of your senses that you beat me in my own house?"

"By God's heart!" quoth Aucassin, "you illgotten son of a good-for-nothing, I will kill you if you do not swear to me that never again shall a man in your country go lying in childbed!"

So he swore to him; and when he had sworn it:

"Sir," said Aucassin, "now take me to where your wife is in the field!"

"Sir, willingly!" said the king.

He mounts on a horse, and Aucassin mounts on his, and Nicolette stayed in the queen's chambers. And the king and Aucassin rode away till they came where the queen was; and they found that the battle was of roasted crab-apples and eggs, and fresh cheeses.

And Aucassin began to watch them, and thereon marvelled he full hard.

Now one sings.

Aucassin has stopped, and so,
Leaning on his saddle-bow,
He begins to see aright
All the pitch and toss of fight.
They had brought in warlike zest
Rounds of cheeses freshly pressed,
Wild wood-apples roasted soft,
Rank horse-mushrooms from the croft;
Who at fords most mud can stir
They proclaim the vanquisher.
Aucassin, the valiant knight,
Set to gaze on such a sight,
　　Laughed outright.

Now they tell and narrate and the tale goes on.

WHEN Aucassin beheld this marvel, he came to the king and spake to him.

"Sir," said Aucassin, " are these here your enemies?"

"Yes, sir," said the king.

"And would you that I should avenge you of them?"

"Yes," said he, "I would willingly."

And Aucassin sets hand to sword, and hurls himself among them, and begins to smite right and left, and kills many of them.

And when the king saw that he was killing them, he took him by the bridle, and said:

"Ah! fair sir, do not kill them in such fashion!"

"How?" said Aucassin, "do you grudge I should avenge you?"

"Sir," said the king, "too much have you done of it! It is not at all the custom for us to kill one another."

These turned to flight, and the king and Aucassin fare back to the Castle of Torelore.

And the people of the country tell the king to drive Aucassin out of his territory, and to keep Nicolette with his son, since she seemed indeed a lady of high lineage.

And Nicolette heard it, and was nowise glad thereat, and she began to say:

Now one sings.

"King, and lord of Torelore,"
Spake fair Nicolette at last,"
Fool your people take me for.
When my sweet friend holds me fast,
Clasps and finds me soft and round,
'Then to school am I so bound,
Paces, graces, dance-array,
Harps and viols making gay,
Jigs and mirth at nimpole play
　　　May all away!"

Now they tell and narrate and the tale goes on.

AUCASSIN dwelt at the Castle of Torelore, and Nicolette, his friend, in great ease and pleasantness, for he had with him Nicolette, his sweet friend, whom he so loved. Now while he was in such ease and in such pleasantness, a fleet of Saracens came by sea, and laid siege to the castle, and took it by main force. They took the booty, and carried away the men and women captives. They took Nicolette and Aucassin, and they bound Aucassin hand and foot, and cast him into one ship and Nicolette into another.

And on sea there arose a storm which separated them. The ship in which was Aucassin went drifting so far across sea that it came to the Castle of Beaucaire;

and the people of the country ran to the wreck and found Aucassin, and recognised him.

And when they of Beaucaire beheld their young lord they made great joy over him, for Aucassin had dwelt at the Castle of Torelore a good three years, and his father and his mother were dead. They brought him to the Castle of Beaucaire, and became all his men; and he held his land in peace.

Now one sings.

Thus was Aucassin set down
At Beaucaire, his native town;
Through that realm and countryside
Everywhere did rest abide.
By the Might of God he sware
That his heart had deeper care
For the fair-browed Nicolette,
Than for all his kin, though yet
They in life no more had share.
"Thee, sweet friend, so bright ot brow,
Where to seek I know not now!
Never realm hath God made be,
But by land or over sea,
If I thought to find thee there,
    I'd thither fare!"

Now they tell and narrate and the tale goes on.

NOW we will let go of Aucassin, , and will tell of Nicolette. The ship, in which Nicolette was, belonged to the king of Carthage; the same was her father, and she had twelve brothers, all princes or kings.

When they beheld Nicolette so beautiful, they offered her very great honour, and made a feast for her. And much they inquired of her who she might be, for indeed she seemed a right noble lady of high lineage. But she knew not how to tell them who she was, since as a small child she had been carried away.

They sailed on till they were come beneath the city of Carthage; and when she saw the walls of the castle, and the country, she recognised that it was there she had been nursed, and thence taken when a small child. But not so small a child was she that she did not know well how she had been daughter to the king of Carthage, and that she had been brought up in the city.

Now one sings.

Nicolette of wit and worth

Now is come to ends of earth;
Sees the buildings and the walls,
And the palaces and halls.
All whereof she makes lament.
"Woe is me, my high descent!
King's daughter of Carthage town,
Cousin to an Emir's crown!
Savage folk here hold me prize.
Aucassin, well-born and wise,
Fair lord, honourably placed,
Your sweet love so bids me haste,
Calls and gives me such great care;
God the Spirit grant my prayer—
Yet to hold in my embrace
You, and have you kiss my face,
Mouth and all around, above,
　　Fair lord, liege-love!"

Now they tell and narrate and the tale goes on.

WHEN the king of Carthage heard Nicolette speak thus, he threw his arms about her neck.

"Fair sweet friend," said he, " tell me who you are! Do not be afraid of me!"

"Sir," said she," I am daughter to the king of Carthage, and was carried away, a small child, full fifteen years ago."

When they heard her speak after this fashion, they knew well that she told the truth, and they made full great rejoicings over her, and led her into the palace in great honour as being the king's daughter. For lord they willed to give her a king of Paynim; but she had no heart to wed.

She was there full three days or four. And she bethought her by what device she would be able to go in quest of Aucassin. She purchased a viol and learned to play thereon, till they would have her one day be married to a king, a rich Paynim. And that night she stole forth, and came to the sea-port, and took shelter at the house of a poor woman upon the shore.

And she took a certain herb, and therewith smeared she her head and face, so that she was all dark and stained. And she let make coat and mantle and shirt and breeches, and fitted herself in the guise of a minstrel. And she took her viol, and went to a skipper, and made such terms with him that he took her on to his ship. They hoisted their sails and passed over the high seas until they were come to the land of Provence. And Nicolette set forth and took her viol, and went playing through the country till she came to the Castle of Beaucaire, where Aucassin then was.

Now one sings.

At Beaucaire, the tower below,
Aucassin did one day go;
There upon a terrace set,
Round him his bold barons met.
Grass and flowers he sees spring,
And he hears the small birds sing;
Whom he loves he calls to mind,
Nicolette, the maiden kind,
His dear love of many a day;
Then to sighs and tears gives way.
See, then, Nicolette below
Brings her viol, brings her bow,
And with speech her tale has told:
"Hark to me, ye barons bold,
Ye on ground and ye on height!
Would you hear a song recite,
Aucassin, the gentle knight,
Nicolette, the valiant fair,
How long time their love did wear?
How went search through forest shade,
How, at Torelore when stayed,
Ta'en one day by Paynim foe.
Naught of Aucassin we know;
But the valiant Nicolette
Is in Carthage Castle set,
Tended by her father's hand,
Who is lord of all that land.
Her in marriage would they bring
Felon lord, of pagans king.
Nicolette cares naught for none,
Lordling dear, she loves but one—
Aucassin the name he bears;
And by God's own name she swears,
Ne'er with baron will she plight,
If he be not her true knight
        And dear delight."

Now they tell and narrate and the tale goes on.

WHEN Aucassin heard Nicolette speak thus, he was most glad of heart; and he drew her on one side and asked her:

"Fair sweet friend," said

Aucassin, "know you nought of this Nicolette of whom you have just now sung?"

"Sir, yes ! I know of her as the most noble creature, and the most gentle and the most wise that ever was born. And she is daughter to the king of Carthage, who took her when Aucassin was taken, and brought her to the city of Carthage, whereafter he learned verily that she was his daughter, and made full great rejoicings thereat. And every day did they will to give her for lord one of the highest kings in all Spain. But she would rather let herself be hanged or burned than take any one of them, however rich he might be.

"Ah! fair sweet friend," said the Count Aucassin, "if you would go back to that land, and would tell her to come and speak to me, I would give you of my substance as much as you would dare to ask or take. And know that for the love of her I have no will to take a wife, let her be of never so high lineage, but will wait for her; nor will I ever have a wife if I have not her. And if I had known where to find her, I should not have now to be seeking her."

"Sir," said she, "if you would do this, I would go in quest of her for your sake, and for hers, whom I love much."

He pledges her his word and then he bids give her twenty pounds. She parts from him; and he weeps for the sweetness of Nicolette. And when she beholds him weeping:

"Sir," says she, "be not dismayed, since in a little while I shall have brought her to you into this town; so will you behold her."

And when Aucassin heard it, he was full glad of it, and she departs from him, and fares into the town to the house of the Viscountess; for the Viscount, her god-father, was dead. There she took shelter, and held speech with her until she had revealed to her her business. And the Viscountess knew her again, and learned for a truth that it was Nicolette, whom she had brought up.

And she let her be washed and bathed and lodged there a full eight days. And she took a certain herb which was called eye-wort, and anointed herself with it, and she was as beautiful as ever she had been at any day. And she clothed herself in rich silk-cloth, of which the lady had store, and she sat herself in the chamber on a silken quilt; and she called the lady and told her to go for Aucassin her friend. And she did so.

And when she came to the palace she found Aucassin, who was weeping and sorrowing after Nicolette, his beloved, for that she delayed so long. And the lady spake to him and said: "Aucassin, now bewail yourself no longer, but come you on with me, and I will show you the thing in the world that you love most, for it is Nicolette, your sweet friend, who from far-off lands is come seeking you."

And Aucassin was glad.

Now one sings.

Now when Aucassin heard say
That his dear and dainty may
Had in that land come to be,
Glad as ne'er before was he.
With the dame he wends his way
To the house, nor may he stay
Till they to the chamber get
Where within sat Nicolette.
When the sight of him she had
Never was her heart so glad;
Up she leapt and t'wards him ran.
And when sight had Aucassin,
Both his arms to her went out,
Soft embraced her all about,
While he kissed her eyes and face;
Thus they stayed the whole night's space.
And when morn made morrow there,
Aucassin did wed the fair
To be Lady of Beaucaire.
Then did they through many days
Lead a life of joyous ways;
Now has Aucassin his bliss,
Also Nicolette's is his.
Sung and said, the tale is o'er:
      I know no more.

SECTION 19

MYSTICAL LOVE
Excerpts from MECHTHILD VON MAGDEBURG
Flowing Light of the Godhead

Introduction by Albrecht Classen

Beginning with the thirteenth century, medieval Europe witnessed the rise of a religious movement called "mysticism." There had been mystics in previous centuries, but only now did this movement gain momentum. The mystic experiences visions, revelations, and dreams in which he or she encounters God, an angel, a martyr, a saint, or any other representative of the world beyond. Mystics begin a direct discourse with God and are thus privileged as his favorites. Mystical experiences give the visionaries peculiar authority over the institution of the Church, and thus these people have always been viewed with awe, suspicion, respect, fear, and admiration.

Mysticism is a phenomenon that cannot be explained in rational terms, it is a matter of belief or disbelief. Mysticism concerns medieval literary scholars, however, insofar as it provided thirteenth and fourteenth-century women with an unexpected access to literacy and religious authority. These women writers were devout Christians and closely obeyed the general rules of the Church, but their religious independence and their individual, if not personal approach to Christ gave them enough strength openly to attack the various shortcomings in the Church. The mystics often taught and preached large crowds, but they were not allowed, being women, to preach on doctrinal issues, to officiate at Mass or to give absolution. Because they claimed to have talked face to face with God, they were often considered spiritual leaders who offered alternatives to the corrupt clergy.

Female mysticism was best represented in Germany, but there were many mystics also in France, Italy, Spain, Sweden, and England. The greatest contributions by the medieval mystics were new concepts of female roles within the spiritual universe, a new understanding of human approaches to God, and new uses of language to talk about their experiences. In many respects, mysticism as a spiritual and "feminist" movement became the crucial key for medieval women to participate in the written culture and to claim their role as equal partners within a predominantly patriarchal society.

The mystical confessions, visions, and revelations were often copied by the women's confessors, then translated into Latin, and later retranslated into the vernacular. At times mystics wrote down their own experiences, and at other times they received help from other women mystics to compose their texts. The mystical accounts often represent a combination of autobiographies and spiritual prayers, hymns, exaltations, and even travelogues. Claiming that their writings reflected their personal experiences gave them a unique status within the medieval Church, and also within their society. Often these mystic writers were ridiculed and viciously attacked, particularly when their visions appeared to be a scam and contradicted the teachings of the Church. But many of the mystics gained a great reputation as mouthpieces of God and direct eyewitnesses.

Mechthild von Magdeburg was one of the major German women mystics from the thirteenth century. Her early life is not well known to us, but we can say that she was born near Magdeburg ca. 1208 into a wealthy, perhaps aristocratic family. She received a thorough education and appears to have been closely familiarized with contemporary vernacular literature. Very early in her life she left her family to lead a life of a beguine. A beguine follows the same ideals as a nun in a convent, but lives by herself or with other non-ordained women in a house, either outside, sometimes within cities. From ca. 1250 onwards Mechthild experienced many religious visions, but kept these to herself, although she wrote them down, as her confessor Heinrich von Halle urged her to do. In ca. 1270 she entered the convent of Helfta near Eisleben where she died in 1282, considered to be a saint. Helfta was, at that time, a famous center of female mysticism and housed such reputable mystics such as Gertrud von Hackeborn (died in 1291), Mechthild von Hackeborn (died in 1298), and Gertrud die Grobe (died in 1301/02). Mechthild von Magdeburg considerably increased through her visions and writing the convent's renown.

Mechthild's *Flowing Light of the Godhead* has come down to us in one Middle High German manuscript and a number of extracts in other manuscripts. Generically it is extremely difficult to define her visionary account because it contains visions, prayers, hymns, dialogues, narratives, autobiographical references, and didactic sermons. Mechthild experienced the peculiar *unio mystica*, a form of bridal mysticism in which her soul and God entered a form of spiritual wedding and join in the wedding bed. The original manuscript, written in Low German, is lost; the text is only extant in a High German manuscript copied around 1343/45 by a member of the Basel "Gottesfreunde" (friends of God). Later the *Flowing Light* was also translated into Latin which indicates the general level of acceptance of Mechthild's visions as coming directly from God and thus as being important for the Church.

BIBLIOGRAPHY

Valerie M. Lagorio, "The Medieval Continental Women Mystics: An Introduction," *An Introduction to the Medieval Mystics of Europe.* Ed. Paul E. Szarmach (Albany: State University of New York Press, 1984), 161–193.

Meister Eckhart and the Beguine Mystics. Hadewijch of Brabant, Mechthild of Magdeburg, and Marguerite Porete. Ed. Bernard McGinn (New York: Continuum, 1994).

Frank Tobin, *Mechthild von Magdeburg. A Medieval Mystic in Modern Eyes.* Literary Criticism in Perspective (Columbia, S.C.: Camden House, 1995).

Albrecht Classen, "Binary Oppositions of Self and God in Mechthild von Magdeburg," *Studies in Spirituality* 7 (1997): 79–98.

Elizabeth A. Andersen, *The Voices of Mechthild of Magdeburg* (Oxford, Bern, et. al.: Peter Lang, 2000)

Sara S. Poor, *Mechthild of Magdeburg and Her Book* (Philadelphia: University of Pennsylvania Press, 2004).

MINNE'S GREETING TO THE QUEEN, MECHTHILD'S SOUL, AND THE HUNT OF LOVE (CA. 1250–1270)

How Minne and the Soul spoke together:

Mechthild's Soul came to Minne and greeted her with deep meaning, saying, "God greet you Lady Minne."

Minne: God reward you, dear lady Queen.
Soul: Lady Minne, you are very welcome to me.
Minne: Lady Queen, I'm honored by your greeting.
Soul: Lady Minne, you struggled a long time with the high holy ghost, and you conquered him so that he gushed all at once into Mary's humble maidenhead.
Minne: Lady Queen, it was for your honor and delight.
Soul: Lady Minne, you have taken from me everything I ever won on earth.
Minne: Lady Queen, you've made a blissful exchange.
Soul: Lady Minne, you've taken my childhood from me.
Minne: Lady Queen, I've given you heavenly freedom for it.
Soul: Lady Minne, you've taken my whole youth.
Minne: Lady Queen, I've given you many holy virtues for it.
Soul: Lady Minne, you've taken my friends and kin.
Minne: Ah, Lady Queen, that's a worthless lament!

Soul:	Lady Minne, you've taken the world from me, worldly honor, and all worldly riches.
Minne:	Lady Queen, in an hour I'll recompense you on earth with all you desire of the Holy Ghost.
Soul:	Lady Minne, you have so harassed me that my body is seized by sundry ills.
Minne:	Lady Queen, I've given you much high wisdom.
Soul:	Lady Minne, you have squandered my flesh and my blood.
Minne:	Lady Queen, by that you've been enlightened and raised up with God.
Soul:	Lady Minne, you are a robber woman. Pay me back for that!
Minne:	Lady Queen, then take my very self!
Soul:	Lady Minne, now you have repaid me a hundredfold here on earth.
Minne:	Lady Queen, now have you claimed God and his whole kingdom! (Book I.i)

The Soul's handmaids and Minne's beatings:

The holy Christian virtues are the Soul's handmaids. The Soul in sweet sorrow cries out her anguish to Minne.

Mechthild's Soul speaks:
Ah, dearest Lady,
you've been my lady-in-waiting lurking so long,
now tell me what's to become of me?
You have hunted, seized, and tied me so fast
and wounded me so deeply
that I shall never be healed.
You have beaten me with a club.
Tell me whether I shall ever finally recover!
Shall I not be slain by your hand?
It would have been better for me if I had never
known you.

Lady Minne's reply:
I hunted you for my delight;
I seized you for my desire;
I bound you tightly for my joy;
When I wounded you, you became one with me.
When I beat you with a club, I became your strong
ravisher.
It was I who drove out the Almighty from
heaven's kingdom

and deprived him of his human life,
then gave him gloriously back to his father.
How could you, vile worm, think you could
 recover from me?

Mechthild's Soul:
Tell me, my Queen, I thought a small medicine
 from heaven
that God had often given me
might help me to escape you.

Lady Minne:
If a captive wants to escape death,
let her reach for water and bread.
The medicines that God has given you
are nothing more than days of grace in this life.
But when your Easter Day dawns
and your body then meets its death blow,
I shall be there, encircling you, piercing you,
and I shall steal your body
and give it to Love.

Mechthild's Soul:
Ah, Lady Minne,
I have written this letter dictated from your lips.
Now give me your great seal to affix to it.

Lady Minne:
She whom God has captured for himself
knows where the seal must be pressed.
It lies between the two of us.

Mechthild's Soul:
Be quiet, Minne, give me no more advice; I and all
 earthly creatures bow to you.
Oh my dearest lady,
tell my friend his couch is ready,
and I am lovesick for him.
If this letter is too long, I have plucked a few
 blossoms from its meadow.
This is its sweet lament:
Whoever dies of love shall be entombed in God.
 (Book I.iii)

THE SOUL COMES TO COURT

The courtly journey of the Soul to whom God shows himself:

When the poor soul comes to court, she is prudent and well-behaved. She joyfully gazes at her God. Ah, how lovingly she is welcomed there! She keeps quiet, but is extravagantly eager for his praise. And he shows her with great yearning his sacred heart. It is like red gold burning in a great coal fire. And God lays her in his glowing heart so that the high prince and the little maidservant embrace and are made one like water and wine. Then she is annihilated and takes leave of her senses so that she can do no more, and he is sick with love for her as he always was, for he neither grows nor diminishes. She says, "Lord, you are my solace, my desire, my flowing stream, my sun, and I am your mirror!" This is the journey to court for the enamored Soul, who cannot live without God. (Book I.iv)

How God comes to the Soul:

> I come to my love
> as a dew upon the blossom. (Book I.xiii)

How the Soul welcomes and praises God:

Ah joyful sight! Ah loving greeting! Ah minne-like embrace! Lord, the wonder of you has wounded me! Your favor has quelled me! O you lofty rock, you are so nobly cleft; none may nest in you but your dove and nightingale. (Book I.xiv)

How God receives the Soul:

Be welcome, darling dove; you have flown so fervently over earth's kingdom that your feathers rise strong to the kingdom of heaven. (Book I.xv)

How God compares the Soul to four things:

You taste of the grape, you smell of balsam, you glitter like the sun, you are the increase of my highest love. (Book I.xvi)

The soul praises God in five things:

> O you God, gushing forth with your gifts!
> O you God, flowing in your love!
> O you burning God in your desire!

O you melting God in the union of your love!
O you God resting on my breast, I cannot be without
    you! (Book I.xvii)

God compares the soul to five things:

O you fair rose in the thornbriar!
O you fluttering bee in the honey!
O you pure dove in your being!
O you lovely sun in your shining!
O you full moon in your sphere!
I can never turn away from you. (Book I.xviii)

God caresses the soul in six things:

You are my pillow, my minne-bed, my secret resting place, my deepest desire, my highest honor. You are a delight of my godhood, a solace of my manhood, a brook for my burning heat. (Book I.xix)

The Soul responds to God in six things:

You are my mirror—mountain peak of perfection—a feast for my eyes, a losing of myself, a storm of my heart, a ruin and scattering of my forces, and my highest safety! (Book I.xx)

THE CELESTIAL WEDDING OF MARY AND OF THE SOUL

The tidings to Mary; how the virtues follow one another and how the soul is a jubilus—a shout of joy—in the Trinity:

The sweet dew of the Trinity that has no beginning sprang from the eternal Godhead in the flower of the chosen Virgin, and the fruit of the flower is an immortal god, a mortal man and a living consolation of everlasting love.

Our Redeemer has become our Bridegroom! The Bride has become drunk with the sight of his noble face. In her greatest strength she takes leave of her senses; in her greatest blindness she sees most clearly, in her greatest clarity she is both dead and living. The longer she is dead, the more joyously she lives. The more joyously she lives, the more she journeys. The more she tastes Minne, the more she is flowing. The richer she grows, the poorer she becomes. The deeper she dwells, the wider she ranges. The more she offers herself, the deeper are her wounds. The more she storms, the more minne-like is God toward her. The higher she floats, the more beautifully she shines from the glance of the Godhead as she comes nearer to him. The more she labors, the more softly she rests. The more she grasps, the more quietly she falls silent.

484

The more loudly she cries out, the greater wonder she works with his power and her might. The more her desire grows, the greater the wedding feast, the more enclosed the minne-bed. The tighter the embrace, the sweeter the kisses of their mouths. The more lovingly they gaze at each other, the harder it is to part. The more he gives her, the more she squanders, the more she has. The more humbly she takes her leave, the sooner she comes back. The more ardent she is, the more she glows again. The more she burns, the more gloriously she shines. The more enveloping God's praise of her, the more avid is her longing for him.

This is how our sweet Bridegroom went in the shout of joy of the holy Trinity. Since God wished to be alone no longer, he made the soul and gave his own great love to her.

Therefore, O Soul, what are you made of that you soar so high above other creatures and, though you mingle with the Holy Trinity, yet you remain yourself?

Soul: You spoke about my origins, and now I will tell you the truth—I was created in the same state of Minne, and so nothing can solace or arise from my nobility except Minne alone. (Book I.xxii)

The Bridegroom's beauty, and how the Bride shall follow him:

Vide, mea sponsa! See, my Bride! How beautiful my eyes are, how fair is my mouth, how fiery is my heart, how gentle are my hands, how swift my feet—and follow me!

You shall be martyred with me, betrayed through envy, tracked to an ambush, seized in hatred, bound through hearsay, your eyes bandaged so that you won't recognize truth, beaten by the world's rage, dragged to judgment through confession, beaten with sticks, sent to Herod with mockery, stripped with banishment, scourged with poverty, crowned with temptation, spat upon with abuse. You shall carry your cross in the hatred of sin, be crucified in the denial of all things by your own will, nailed on the cross with the holy virtues, wounded with minne, die on the cross in holy steadfastness, your heart pierced with indwelling oneness, released from the cross in true victory over all your enemies, buried in paltriness, raised up from death to a blessed end, carried to heaven on a draught of God's breath. (Book I.xxix)

You shall be a lamb in your pain, a turtledove, a bride:

You are my lamb in your pain—
You are my turtledove in your moaning—
You are my bride in your abiding. (Book I.xxxiv)

God asks the Soul what she brings:

You hunt sorely for your love.
Tell me—what do you bring me, my Queen? (Book I.xxxix)

The Soul answers that it is better than four things:

Lord, I bring you my treasure:
It is greater than the mountains,
Wider than the world,
Deeper than the sea, higher than the sky,
More beautiful than the sun, more manifold than
    the stars,
And more weighty than earth's whole kingdom.
    (Book I.xl)

The seven ways to Minne, the bride's three gowns, and the dance:

God speaks: Ah, Soul filled with minne, do you wish to know
    where your path lies?
The Soul: Yes, dear Holy Ghost, teach it to me.
[*God speaks:*] You must overcome the sorrow of contrition, thepain of confession,
    and the labor of repentance, the love of the world, the temptation of the
    Devil, the luxuriance of the flesh, the destruction of your own will which so
    fiercely drags down many souls that they never can come back to true love.
    Then when you have beaten down most of your enemies, you are so tired
    that you cry out, "Beautiful youth, I'm longing for you—where shall I find
    you?" The young man will say:

"I hear a voice
that speaks a little of minne.
I have courted her many days
but her voice has never come to me.
Now I am stirred,
I must go to her.
She is the one who bears pain and minne together.
In the morning, in the dew, there is the sheltered
    rapture that first enters the soul."

Her chambermaids, the five senses, speak: Lady, you must gown yourself in many
    colors.
Soul: Love, where shall I go?
The senses:

We have heard it rumored
that the Prince is coming to you
in the dew and in the lovely song of birds.
Ah, lady, do not delay!

So the Soul dresses herself in a shift of gentle humility, so lowly that she can endure nothing under it. Over it goes a white gown of clear chastity, so pure that she can endure neither thoughts nor words nor sentiments that might sully it. Then she covers it with a mantel of holy reputation, which she has gilded with all the virtues.

Then she goes into the wood, which is the company of blessed folk. There the sweetest nightingales sing in harmonious union with God, both day and night, and she hears many sweet voices there of the birds of holy understanding. But the young man still does not come. He sends her messengers, for she wants to dance. He sends her Abraham's faith, the Prophets' yearnings, and the chaste humility of our lady St. Mary, all the holy virtues of Jesus Christ, and all the goodness of his chosen ones.

And so a lovely dance of praise will take place. Now the young man comes and speaks to her:

"Maiden, as gallantly as you follow the dance, now, my chosen partner, you will lead the dance!" But she says:

> I cannot dance, lord, unless you lead me.
> If you want me to leap ardently,
> you must yourself first dance and sing.
> Then I will leap into minne,
> from minne into understanding,
> from understanding to enjoyment,
> from enjoyment to far beyond all human sense.
> There shall I stay and whirl still dancing in a ring.
> (Book I.xliv)

THE HEAVENLY WINE CELLAR

Minne speaks:
> If you'll come with me to the wine cellar
> it will cost you a great deal.
> Even if you buy a thousand marks worth of wine,
> your money will be squandered in an hour.

If you want to drink wine straight, without water, you'll keep spending more than you have, and the tavernkeeper won't pour you the full amount. You'll be poor and naked, despised by all those people who'd rather seek pleasure in a pool of muddy water than waste their wealth in the lofty wine cellar.

> You'll also have to suffer
> when those people who go with you to the wine

cellar envy you.
How scornful they'll be of you
because they dare not risk the huge expense,
preferring to drink their wine diluted with water!
Darling lady bride, I'll go to the tavern,
and eagerly spend all that I have,
and let myself be dragged through hot coals of
    love,
and submit to being beaten with the fiery brands
    of love's slanderers,
so that I can go often to that blessed wine cellar!

Mechthild's Soul answers:

I choose eagerly to go there, since I can't do without Minne. While he torments and insults me—this one who pours out the tavernkeeper's wine for me—still, he has been drinking it too.

I've become so drunk with wine
that I am truly thrall to all creatures,
and it seems to me in my human disgrace
and my newfound wantonness
that no man ever treated me so badly before—
he can do any kind of sin with me, unblessed
    woman that I am.

And so I would not take vengeance on my enemies for my sorrow, even though I know they might break God's law.

Minne comforts the Soul:

Dearest playmate, when it happens that the wine cellar is locked, you must take to the street, hungry, poor and stripped bare, and so despised that nothing is left for you of the banquet of Christian living except your own faith; then you can still have Minne, for that is never spoiled.

Lady Bride, I have such hunger for the heavenly
    father
that I forget all sorrow.
And I have such thirst for his son
that it takes all earthly yearning from me.
And I have for both of them such a ghostly need
that it goes higher than all I can grasp
of the father's wisdom.
But I can endure all the work of the son,
and all the solace of the Holy Ghost
that befalls me.

Whoever is seized by this torment must always—however unworthy—hold fast to God's holiness. (Book III. iii)

22. CONCERNING THE MESSAGE TO MARY AND HOW ONE VIRTUE IS FOLLOWED BY ANOTHER, AND HOW THE SOUL BECAME A CRY OF JOY OF THE HOLY TRINITY, AND HOW MARY SUCKLED ALL THE SAINTS AND STILL DOES TODAY

The sweet dew of the infinite Trinity sprang forth from the well of the eternal Divinity in the flowers of the chosen maidens; the fruit of the flowers has become an immortal god, a mortal man, and a living comfort of eternal life; our salvation has become a Bridegroom. The Bride has become drunk at the sight of the noble countenance. She takes leave of herself in her moment of greatest strength, and she sees most clearly in her moment of severest blindness. In this moment of great clarity she is both dead and alive. The longer she lives, the more joyously she lives. The more joyously she lives, the more she experiences. The more she needs love, the more love flows to her. The more she fears.[6] The richer she becomes, the poorer she becomes. The more profound her experiences, the more extensive they are. The more obedient she is, the deeper her wounds. The more she raves, the more lovingly God is disposed towards her. The more highly she floats, the more beautifully she glows in the reflection of the Divinity as she approaches Him. The harder she labors, the more sweetly she rests. The more she is enveloped, the more quiet she becomes. The more loudly she cries, the greater the miracles He performs through her with His might. The more her pleasure grows, the greater her nuptial enjoyment becomes. The closer she embraces, the sweeter the kisses on her mouth taste. The more lovingly they gaze at each other, the more reluctantly they part from each other. The more He gives her, the more she consumes, the more she has. The more humbly she takes her leave, the sooner she returns. The more excited she remains, the sooner she is enkindled. The more feverish she is, the more she glows. The more ample God's praise becomes, the greater her longing remains.

This is how our graceful Bridegroom fared in the cry of joy of the Holy Trinity. Since God no longer wished to be by Himself, He created the souls and bestowed on them great love. "Of what are you made, soul, that you climb so far above other creatures, that you mingle with the Holy Trinity and yet remain in yourself?" "You have spoken of my beginning, and I honestly tell you: I was created in the same condition as Love. That is why I wish to console no creature, as would be my noble nature, nor do I wish to confide in anyone but Love."

"Holy Lady Mary, you are the mother of this wonder. When did this happen to you?"

"When our Father's exultation was grieved by Adam's fall, so that He had to be angry. Therefore, the eternal wisdom of the almighty Divinity received the wrath together with me. So the almighty Father chose me for a Bride, in order to have something to love, for His beloved Bride, the noble soul, was dead. And so the Son chose me for a Mother, and the Holy Ghost received me as a love. Then I alone became the Bride of the Holy Trinity and the Mother of orphans, and brought them before the eyes of God, so that they might not sink, though many of them did. I was, therefore, the Mother of many a noble child, and my breasts began to fill with the pure, unspoiled milk of true, tender mercy, and I suckled the prophets and sages, before God was born. Later on during my childhood, I suckled Jesus, and during my youth I suckled God's Bride, holy Christianity, at the cross, and I became emaciated and miserable at the thought that the sword which inflicts physical pain should cut Jesus spiritually in my soul."

There they were both opened, His wounds and her breasts. The wounds poured out and the breasts flowed, so that the soul quickened and was even cured. As he poured the bright red wine into her red mouth, she was born out of the open wounds and quickened; she was childlike and very young. In order to recuperate completely after her death and her birth, she needed the Mother of God as mother and nurse. God, it was and is right. God was her rightful father and she His rightful bride, and she is like Him in all her sufferings. "Lady, at your age you suckled the Holy Apostles with your maternal teachings and your fervent prayers, so that God's honor and will might work through them. Lady, you suckled then, and are still suckling to this day, martyrs with great faith in their hearts, confessors with holy protection over their ears, maidens with your chastity, widows with constancy, fools with kindness, sinners with intercession.

"Lady, now you must suckle us, for your breasts are still so full that you cannot suppress it. If you no longer wished to suckle, the milk would cause you much pain. For I have truly seen your breasts so full that seven streams poured out of them, especially from the breast above my body and my soul. Within one hour, you take from me a labor which no friend of God could suffer without heartbreak. So you must suckle us until the Day of Judgment: you must empty yourself until God's children, as well as yours, are weaned and fully grown in the eternal body. Ah, afterwards we must profess our faith and will see with boundless joy the milk and the very same breast which Jesus kissed so much."

23. YOU SHOULD PRAY THAT GOD MAY LOVE YOU MUCH, DEEPLY, AND FOR A LONG TIME, SO THAT YOU MAY ATTAIN PURITY, BEAUTY, AND LONGEVITY

Ah, Lord, love me much, and love me deeply and for a long time; for the more deeply you love me, the purer I shall become; the more you love me, the more beautiful I shall become; the longer you love me, the holier I shall become here on earth.

24. HOW GOD ANSWERS THE SOUL

Loving you ardently is my nature, for I myself am love, loving you much from My longing, for I long to be loved much in return. Loving you for a long time comes from My eternity, for I am infinite.

25. CONCERNING THE WAY TO ENJOY SUFFERING THROUGH GOD

God leads His chosen children on strange paths. It is a strange path, a noble path, and a holy path, which God Himself has walked, when a man suffered pain without sin and without fault. On this path the soul which cries for God rejoices, for she naturally rejoices in being with her Lord, who, through His benevolence, has suffered many pains. And her dear Lord, the Heavenly Father, gave His beloved Son to be tortured by pagans, martyred by the Jews without any fault of his own. And the time has come that some people who appear to be spiritual torture God's children physically and martyr their spirit, for He wants them to resemble His beloved Son, who suffered both physically and spiritually.

26. IT IS ALONG THIS PATH THAT THE SOUL DRAWS HER SENSIBILITIES AND IS FREE OF HEARTACHE

It is a rare and elevated path, on which the faithful soul strolls, leading the senses as one leads the blind. On this path the soul is free and lives without heartache, for she only wants to be like her Lord, who clearly makes all things right.

27. HOW TO BE WORTHY OF THIS PATH, KEEP IT, AND BE COMPLETE

Three things render one worthy of this path, so that one may recognize and enter it. The first is that man must force himself into submission to God utterly, keep the blessing, and bear it willingly, giving up everything which man might want. The second keeps man on the path, so that he may think of anything but sin. The third renders man complete on this path, when he does all things alike for the glory of God; since, before God, I will treat even my lowliest need as though I were in the highest state of contemplation which a human may attain; the reason is that if it is done out of love for God, it is all the same. If, however, I sin, then I am not on this path.

28. LOVE CAN KILL US, IF IT IS UNRESTRICTED AND CONTINUOUS; THAT IS THE FOLLY OF FOOLS

I delight in having to love Him who loves me, and I long to love Him until death, unrestricted and continuously; rejoice, my soul, for your life has ended through love! Love Him so much that you would want to die for the love of Him, and you will blaze more and more like a living spark in the great fire of the living majesty. You will be so filled with love's fire,

That you will be at home here.
You must no longer instruct me.
I cannot turn from love.
I must be her captive;
No other way shall I live.
Where she lives, there I shall stay

In life as well as death:
That is the folly of fools,
Who live without heartache.

29. CONCERNING THE BEAUTY OF THE BRIDEGROOM AND HOW THE BRIDE SHOULD FOLLOW HIM

See, My wife: see how beautiful My eyes are, how right My mouth is, how fiery My heart is, how agile My hands are, how quick My feet are, and follow Me. You shall be martyred with Me, betrayed by envy, sought out by falsehood, captured by hatred, bound by slander, blindfolded so that the truth may be withheld from you, slapped by the wrath of the world, brought before the court in confession, boxed on the ears with punishment, sent before Herod in scorn, undressed in wretchedness, flogged with poverty, crowned by temptation, looked down upon in degradation; you shall bear your cross despising sin, shall be crucified renouncing all that you desire, be nailed to the cross with holy virtues; wounded by love, you shall die on the cross with holy constancy, be pierced in your heart by constant union, removed from the cross in true victory over all your foes, buried in obscurity, and, finally, in a holy conclusion, you shall rise from the dead and ascend into heaven, drawn in by God's breath.

30. CONCERNING THE SEVEN OFFICES

Matins: Love's fullness, what sweet ruin!
Prime: Love's longing, what sweet pain!
Terce: Love's pleasure, what sweet thirst!
Sext: Love's feeling, what sweet refreshment!
Nones: Love's death, what sweet plight!
Vespers: Love's flowing, what sweet outpouring!
Complines: Love's repose, what sweet joy!

31. YOU SHOULD DISREGARD DEGRADATION

I was degraded much, says our Lord: do not be surprised; if this precious vessel here was disdained and looked down upon, what should happen to the vinegar container, which contains nothing good of its own?

32. YOU SHOULD DISREGARD THE PRAISE, PAIN, GOOD INTENTION, AND SADNESS OF SIN

When they praise you, you should be ashamed; when they hurt you, you should be glad; when they do you good, you should be afraid; when you act against Me, you should be saddened. If you are not saddened, see how much and for how long I was saddened by you.

33. CONCERNING SUSTENANCE, COMFORT, AND LOVE

My soul spoke thus to her love: Lord, Your kindness is the amazing sustenance of my body; Your clemency is the special comfort of my soul. Love is the repose of my eternal life.

34. IN YOUR PAIN, YOU SHOULD BE A LAMB, A TURTLEDOVE, AND A BRIDE

In your pain, you are My lamb.
In your sighs, you are My turtledove.
In your waiting, you are My Bride.

35. THE DESERT HAS TWELVE CHARACTERISTICS

You shall not love this;
You shall flee from that;
You shall stand alone;
And go to no one.
You shall be very industrious
And free from all things.
You shall free the captives
And restrain the free.
You shall refresh the sick
And still take nothing for yourself.
You shall drink the water of pain
And kindle the fire of love with the wood of virtue;
Then will you live in the true desert.

36. CONCERNING MALICE, GOODNESS, AND WONDERS

You shall be adorned with the malice of your foes.
You shall be glorified with the virtues of your heart.
You shall be crowned with your good deeds.
You shall be elevated by our mutual love.
You shall be sanctified by My joyous wonders.

37. THE SOUL ANSWERS GOD, SAYING THAT SHE MIGHT BE WORTHY OF THIS GRACE

O my dear, I rejoice in undeserved degradation; I long for heartfelt virtues;
Unfortunately I lack good deeds.
I shall spoil our mutual love;
I am really unworthy of this beautiful wonder.

38. GOD IS JUBILANT OVER THE SOUL'S VANQUISHING FOUR SINS

In Heaven, Our Lord is jubilant over the loving soul He has on earth and He says:

"Behold, how she, who has wounded Me, ascends!
She has thrown off the ape of the world.
She has vanquished the bear of unchastity.
She has tread on the lion of pride.
She has torn the belly of the wolf of greed.
And she comes running like an exhausted stag
To the well, which I am.
She soars like an eagle
Out of the depths to the heights."

39. GOD ASKS THE SOUL WHAT SHE IS BRINGING

You are very rushed in love;
Tell me, what do you bring Me, My queen?

40. SHE REPLIES THAT IT IS BETTER THAN FOUR THINGS

Lord, I bring you my gem:
It is taller than the mountains, wider than the world,
deeper than the sea,
Higher than the clouds, fairer than the sun, more
multitudinous than the stars,
Weightier than all the earth.

41. PRAISING HER, GOD ASKS THE NAME OF THE GEM

Your image of My Divinity, ennobled by My Humanity, adorned with My Holy Spirit, what is the name of your gem?

42. THE GEM IS CALLED PLEASURE OF THE HEART

Lord, it is called the pleasure of my heart, which I have removed from the world, retained for myself, and denied to all creatures; now I can carry it no further. Lord, where shall I place it?

43. PLACE YOUR PLEASURE IN THE HOLY TRINITY

You shall place the pleasure of your heart nowhere but in My divine heart and at My human breast. There alone will you be comforted and kissed by My spirit.

44. CONCERNING SEVEN WAYS OF LOVE, THE BRIDE'S THREE DRESSES, AND DANCING

God says: "Ah, loving soul, do you wish to know your way?" The soul: "Yes, dear Holy Spirit, teach me." "You vanquish the distress of repentance and the pain of confession, the hardship of atonement, love of worldly things, and the temptations of the Devil, the superfluousness of the flesh and the cursed will-fulness which tear apart many a soul so badly that she can never find her way to real love, and you have struck down most of your enemies. You are now weary and say: Fair youth, I long for you, where may I find you? The youth thus speaks:

"I hear a voice
Which partly sounds of love.
I wooed her many a day,
Now that the voice does not reach me
I am aroused,
I must go to see her.
It is she who bears both sorrow and love
In the morning dew—embracing tenderness—
Which first enters the soul."
Thus her chamberlains, her five senses, speak:
The senses: "Lady, you should dress yourself."
The soul: "Love, where am I to go?"
The senses: "We have well heard the rumor that the prince
will come to see you
In the dew and with the birds singing.
Ah, Lady, do not tarry."

So she dresses in the shirt of gentle humility, such humility that she cannot tolerate anything beneath her. Over that she wears a white dress of pure chastity, so pure that she cannot tolerate thoughts, words, or contacts that might soil her. She places around her shoulders a cloak of holy fragrance which she has repaid with all the virtues.

And she goes into the forest into the company of holy people. There the very sweetest nightingales sing of the tempered unity between God's day and night, and she hears many a sweet voice coming from the birds of holy recognition. Still the youth did not come. Now she sends out messengers, for she wants to dance, and sends for praise of Abraham and the longing of the prophets, for the chaste humility of Our Lady Mary and all the holy virtues of Jesus Christ, and for the piety of His chosen ones. And this became a beautiful dance of praise.

Then the youth came and said to her: "Maiden, you shall dance as well as my chosen ones have danced." To that she says:

"I cannot dance, Lord; You are distracting me.
If You wish me to leap,
Then You must lead me with Your singing.
Then I will leap into recognition,
From recognition into practice,
From practice over all human senses.
There will I stay and still crawl onward."

(How the bride sings): "And now the youth must sing through me into You and through You from my longing, from You of necessity.

Then the youth speaks: "Maiden, you did this dance of praise very well. You shall have your way with the Son of the Maiden, for you are now inwardly tired. Come at midday to the shade of the well into the bed of love; there you shall be refreshed with Him."

The maiden says:

"Oh, Lord, that is sublime;
She who is the companion of Your love,
She who has no love of her own,
She will forever be moved by You."

Then the soul says to the senses, who are her chamberlains: "Now I am tired of dancing for a while. Leave me; I must go and refresh myself."

The senses say to the soul: "Lady, to refresh you, the tears of the love of Holy Mary Magdalene should suffice for you."

The soul: "Silence, my lords; you all do not know what I mean.
Leave me in peace;
I wish to drink a little undiluted wine."
Senses: "Lady, great love is prepared
In the chastity of maidens."
Soul: "That may be so; it is not my best quality."
Senses: "The blood of the martyrs would refresh you much."
Soul: "I am martyred so often
That I cannot go there."
Senses: "Pure people like to seek the advice of confessors."
Soul: "I always want to follow advice,
Both in actions and omissions—
Only now I do not wish to go there."
Senses: "You will find great security in the wisdom
Of the apostles."
Soul: "I have that wisdom with me,
So that I might make the best decision."
Senses: "The angels possess clarity
And the beautiful color of love.
For refreshment, lift yourself up to them."
Soul: "The delight of the angels makes my love painful
If I cannot see their Lord and my Bridegroom."
Senses: "Then refresh yourself in the holy, harsh life
Which God gave to John the Baptist."
Soul: "I am prepared to accept that kind of life.
Still, the power of love is greater than hardship."
Senses: "Lady, if you refresh yourself in love,
Then lean over the lap of the Maiden
To the little child, and see and taste

How the joy of the angels suckled the exotic milk
From the eternal Maiden."
Soul: "That is a childlike love,
Suckling and rocking a child;
I am a fully grown Bride,
And I wish to go to my love."
Senses: "Lady, if you go there,
Then we will be blinded,
For the Divinity is fiery and hot;
You well know
About all the fire and the glow from the heavens and the holy people
And the burning that flows from His divine breath,
And about His human mouth
And the counsel of the Holy Spirit;
Who can remain there for even one hour?"
Soul: "Fish will not drown in water,
Birds will not sink in air,
Gold will not spoil in fire,
For it is there that it obtains its true and brilliant color.
God has given to all His creatures
The gift of making use of their talents.
How can I fight my nature?
I should forfeit all to go to God
Who is my Father by nature,
My brother by His Humanity,
My Bridegroom by Love,
And I am His since the beginning of time.
Do you not wish me to experience my nature?
He is capable of both powerful burning and soothing refreshment.
Now do not distress yourselves too much.
You shall yet instruct me
On my return.
I will require your teachings,
For the world has many snares."

So the dearest one goes to the fairest in the secret chambers of the innocent Divinity: there she finds love's bed and love's dress, prepared for God and man. Then our Lord says: "Stay, Lady Soul." "What do You command, Lord?" "You shall take leave of yourself." "Lord, what will become of me?" "Lady Soul, you are so much a part of My nature that nothing can be between you and Me. Never was an angel so magnificent that he was granted for even one hour that which is given to you for eternity. Therefore, you must shed both your fear and shame, as well as all outward virtues. Instead, you shall want to experience eternally those virtues which you bear within yourself by nature. That is your noble longing and your fathomless desire, which I shall fill eternally with My endless generosity."

> "Lord, now I am a naked soul,
> And You, in Yourself, a beautifully adorned God.
> Our communion
> Is eternal life without death."
> Then ensued a blessed quiet,
> According to both their wishes.
> He gives Himself to her and she to Him,
> And only she knows what happens to her at this moment,
> And that is good enough for me.
> Now things cannot remain like this for long.
> When two lovers meet in secret
> They must take leave of each other undivided.
> Dear friend in God, this path in love I have written for you.
> It is God Who must place it into your heart.
> Amen.

45. CONCERNING EIGHT DAYS ON WHICH THE LONGING OF THE PROPHETS IS ACCOMPLISHED

> There is a day of longing and blessed joys in the coming of Christ.
> There is a day of rest and incarnate delectation in the birth of Christ.
> There is a day of loyalty and blessed union, Maundy Thursday.
> There is a day of kindness and heartfelt love, Good Friday.
> There is a day of power and joyful happiness, the Resurrection.
> There is a day of faith and wretched misery, the day of the Ascension.
> There is a day of truth and flaming consolation, Pentecost. There is a day of justice and the hour of truth, Judgment Day.

This makes one week during which we shall practice constancy for seven days, and one of them—the Day of Judgment—Our Lord will spend with us all.

46. CONCERNING THE MANIFOLD BEAUTY OF THE BRIDE AND HOW SHE COMES TO THE BRIDEGROOM, HOW HER SERVANTS ARE NINEFOLD

The Bride is clothed in the sun, walks on moonshine, and is crowned with Unity. She has a curate, who is Fear, and who has a golden crozier in his hand, which is Wisdom. The curate is clothed in the blood of the Lamb. And Wisdom is clothed in goodness and crowned in honor. The Bride has four ladies-in-waiting. Love guides the Bride. Love is clothed in chastity and crowned in dignity. The second lady is Humility; she guards the Bride and is clothed in lack of recognition and crowned with exaltation. The third lady is Repentance; she is clothed with grapes and crowned with happiness. The fourth lady is Mercy; she is clothed with ointment and crowned with bliss. The two of them dress the Bride in her cloak, which is the Holy Scent. She has a bishop, who is Faith and who takes the Bride before the Bridegroom. The bishop is clothed in precious stones and crowned with the Holy Ghost. The bishop has two knights: one is Strength, who is clothed for battle and crowned with victory; the other is Courage, who is clothed in grace and crowned with beatitude. The Bride has a chamberlain, who is Caution, and who is clothed in constancy and crowned with steadfastness; he bears a light for the Bride and follows her on the carpet. The light is Judiciousness, which is clothed in modesty and crowned with kindness. The carpet is Holy Awareness, which is clothed in good will and crowned with God's approval. The Bride has a gift, which is Longing; it is clothed in desire and crowned with peace. She has a minstrel, who is Amiability. His harp is Tenderness; it is clothed in favor and crowned with support.

The Bride has five kingdoms. The first is the eyes, which are inhabited by tears and adorned with power. The second is thought, which is inhabited by conflict and adorned with advice. The third is speech, which is inhabited by necessity and adorned with loyalty. The fourth is hearing, which is inhabited by the word of God and adorned with consolation. The fifth is touch, which is inhabited by force and adorned with pure practices.

These five kingdoms have a guardian, who is Sin, clothed in discipline and crowned with patience. The Bride has a pack animal, which is the body; it is bridled with unworthiness; degradation is its fodder, and its stable file confessional. The burden which it bears is innocence. The Bride has a furbearer; it is Hope, who is clothed in truth and crowned with song. She holds a palm, which is victory over Sin; in the other hand she holds a box containing longing and love, which she wants to take to her loved one. She wears a hat with peacock feathers, which are good reputation on Earth and high honor in the Kingdom of Heaven. And so she goes on her way, which is Gentleness, covered by flowing honey and crowned with safety. And so she sings: "Chosen Love, I long for You. You take and give me much heartache. I also receive much senseless distress from You. When You, Lord, are master here, then I shall be delivered from myself."

He speaks:

"Sweet love, think of the hour
When you will fully comprehend your discovery,
And do not want for anything,
For at all times I shall be embracing you.

And so the Lord says to His chosen Bride: "Come, My chosen one, and be crowned." He gives her the crown of truth, which may be worn by no one but clerics. In the crown four virtues can be seen: wisdom and sorrow, longing and moderation. May God give us all this crown! Amen.

* * * *

How long will you be impatient?
When I wound you most of all,
I anoint you at the same time in the most loving way.
The greatness of My kingdom is yours alone
And you shall have power over Me Myself.
I am lovingly inclined to you.
If you have the weights, I have the gold.
For all that you have done, omitted and suffered for My sake
I will recompense you,
And I will forgive you eternally
For everything according to your will."
"Lord, I must ask You two things:
Instruct me in Your grace!
When my eyes mourn in misery
And my mouth is closed in simple-mindedness,
My tongue is bound with misery,
My senses ask me hourly
How I am; so it is with me, Lord,
All for longing for You.
My flesh atrophies, my blood dries up,
My bones grow cold, my veins convulse,
And my heart dissolves with love for You,
And my soul burns like the roar of a hungry lion.
How will I be, and where are You?
Dear love, tell me that."
"You are like a new bride
Whose only love has left her sleeping,
He to whom she had inclined herself with total trust.
From whom she cannot bear to part from him for even one hour.
When she awakens she can have him no more
Than her senses can bear,
And this causes her to begin her lamentations.
While the youth is not at home with her
She must be very much at one with him.
"I come to you at my pleasure whenever I wish;
If you are modest and still
And conceal your sorrow as best you can,
The power of love will grow in you.
Now I will tell you where I am.
I Myself am in all places and in all things
As I ever was without beginning,
And I await you in the orchard of love

And pick for you the flower of sweet reunion
And ready your bed there
With the pleasurable grass of holy knowledge,
And the bright sun of My eternal Divinity
Will shine on you with the concealed wonder of My delight,
Which you have bred in Me a little secretly.
And I lower the highest tree of My Holy Trinity
So that you can pick the green, white, and red apples of My gentle humanity;
And the shade of My Holy Spirit shall protect you
From all earthly sorrow,
So that you will forget your heartache.
As you embrace the tree I will teach you the song of the maidens,
The melody, the words and the sweet harmony—
Unintelligible to those
Who are imbued with lasciviousness.
And yet they shall have a sweet exchange.
My love, now begin to sing, and let Me hear how well you can do it."
"Ah, my beloved, I am hoarse in the throat of my chastity,
But the sweetness of Your kindness
Has cleared my throat so that I now can sing.
So, Lord, Your blood and mine are one, untainted;
Your voice and mine are one, undivided;
Your robe and mine are one, immaculate;
Your mouth and mine are one, unkissed.
These are the words to the song of the voice of love,
And the sweet sound of the heart must linger
Since it was not written by human hands."

26. ABOUT THIS BOOK AND ITS AUTHOR

I was warned about this book and was told by men
That it should not be preserved
But destroyed by fire.
Then I did what I have done since childhood,
And that is to pray when I am troubled.
I leaned toward my loved one and said:
"Alas, Lord, now I am very troubled.
For Your glory I must remain unconsoled away from You.
You have misled me
In making me write this book."
At that God immediately revealed Himself
To my sad soul, holding this book in His right hand,
And said: "My love, do not upset yourself too much;
The truth cannot be burned by anyone.

He who wants to take it from My hand
Must be stronger than I.
This book is threefold
And describes only Me.
The parchment which surrounds it
Describes My pure, white, and righteous humanity
Which suffered death for your sake.
The words which describe My marvelous Divinity
Flow hourly into your soul from My divine mouth.
The voice of the words describes My living spirit
And fulfills in itself the right truth.
Now see in all these words
How commendably they proclaim My omniscience;
So do not doubt yourself."
"Alas, Lord, were I a learned man
And You had worked this miracle in me
It would forever bring You glory.
But how can anyone believe
That You have built a golden house
In this filthy slough,
To live here with Your Mother
And all creatures
As well as Your heavenly servants?
Lord, I cannot find earthly wisdom in that."
"Daughter, many a wise man has lost his precious gold
Through carelessness on the big highway,
Hoping to come to higher learning;
Someone else will find it.
I have by nature done that many a day.
Whenever I bestowed a special grace
I always sought for the lowest,
The least, the best concealed place.
The highest mountain cannot receive
The revelation of My grace,
For the flood of My Holy Spirit
Flows by nature into the valley.
You find many a wise master, learned in the scripture
Who himself is a fool in My eyes.
And I will tell you more:
It is a great honor for Me
And strengthens Holy Christianity significantly
That the unlearned mouth teaches
The erudite tongues about My Holy Spirit."

"Alas, my Lord, I sigh, and I yearn
And I pray for Your scribe,
Who has written this book for me
That You may reward him, too, with the grace
Never granted to man.
For Lord, Your gift is a thousand times more
Than Your creatures can ever receive."
Our Lord said:
"They have written it with golden letters;
Thus all the words in this book
Shall be inscribed on their top cloaks
Eternally manifest in My Kingdom
With heavenly, shining gold,
Written above all their other adornments.
For free love must always be the highest of all human attributes."
As Our Lord was saying these words
I perceived the glorious truth
In eternal dignity:
"Alas, Lord, I ask You to preserve this book
From the eyes of falsehood,
For that has come to us from Hell;
It never came from the Heavenly Kingdom.
It is in Lucifer's heart
And is born in spiritual conceit,
Reared in hatred,
And grown in the mighty anger so great
That no virtue is its friend.
So God's children must go down
And be suppressed in degradation
If they want to receive the highest honor with Jesus.
We must wear at all times
The holy color
In order to shield ourselves against shortcomings.
Toward our fellow Christians we must act with love,
When they stray, we must faithfully warn them,
And so we can prevent many a useless chatter.
Amen."

SECTION **20**

THE ROMANCE OF THE ROSE

Guillaume de Lorris and Jean de Meun

The Romance of the Rose is one of the great monuments of medieval literature. Guillaume de Lorris began the poem around 1237 but left it incomplete at line 4058. An anonymous poet provided a seventy-eight-line conclusion, which proved to be of only temporary value, for Jean de Meun, around 1277, wrote a vast new amplification which reached its ending at line 21,780.

Thus *The Romance* stands today like some great French cathedral, conceived by its first architect in early Gothic, temporarily enclosed by a modest apprentice, and then extended on a grandiose plan and executed in an advanced and ornate style.

Like a Gothic cathedral, it includes both the grotesque and the sublime, the profane and the sacred. The uninitiated can enjoy its individual details; the sophisticated can appreciate its complex architectonics. For despite its varied workmanship, the whole is controlled by the Gothic instinct for the order which underlies diversity.

BIBLIOGRAPHY

Guillaume de Lorris and Jean de Meun, *The Romance of the Rose*. Trans. by Harry W. Robbins. Ed., and with an Introduction, by Charles W. Dunn (New York: Dutton, 1962).

Maxwell Luria, *A Reader's Guide to the Roman de la Rose* (Hamden, Conn.: Archon Books, 1982).

Heather Arden, *The Romance of the Rose*. Twayne's World Authors Series; TWAS 791 (Boston: Twayne Publishers, 1987).

Sylivia Jean Huot, *Rethinking The Romance of the Rose: Text, Image, Reception*. Middle Ages Series (Philadelphia: University of Philadelphia Press, 1992).

Kelly, Douglas, *Internal Difference and Meanings in the Roman de la Rose* (Madison: University of Wisconsin Press, 1995).

Albrecht Classen, "Guillaume de Lorris" (285–86) and "Jean de Meun" (345–47), *Encyclopedia of Medieval Literature*, ed. Jay Ruud (New York: Facts on File, 2006).

GUILLAUME DE LORRIS

I. The Poet dreams a dream
[Old French original, lines 1–128]

> Many a man holds dreams to be but lies.
> All fabulous; but there have been some dreams
> No whit deceptive, as was later found.
> Well might one cite Macrobius, who wrote
> The story of the Dream of Scipio,
> And was assured that dreams are ofttimes true.
> But, if someone should wish to say or think
> 'Tis fond and foolish to believe that dreams
> Foretell the future, he may call me fool.
> Now, as for me, I have full confidence
> That visions are significant to man
> Of good and evil. Many dream at night
> Obscure forecasts of imminent events.
> When I the age of twenty had attained—
> The age when Love controls a young man's heart—
> As I was wont, one night I went to bed
> And soundly slept. But then there came a dream
> Which much delighted me, it was so sweet.
> No single thing which in that dream appeared
> Has failed to find fulfillment in my life,
> With which the vision well may be compared.
> Now I'll recount this dream in verse, to make
> Your hearts more gay, as Love commands and wills;
> And if a man or maid shall ever ask
> By what name I would christen the romance
> Which now I start, I will this answer make:
> *"The Romance of the Rose* it is, and it enfolds
> Within its compass all the Art of Love."
> The subject is both good and new. God grant
> That she for whom I write with favor look
> Upon my work, for she so worthy is
> Of love that well may she be called the Rose.
>
> Five years or more have passed by now, I think,
> Since in that month of May I dreamed this dream—

In that month amorous, that time of joy,
When all things living seem to take delight,
When one sees leafless neither bush nor hedge,
But each new raiment dons, when forest trees
Achieve fresh verdure, though they dry have been
While winter yet endured, when prideful Earth,
Forgetting all her winter poverty
Now that again she bathes herself in dew,
Exults to have a new-spun, gorgeous dress;
A hundred well-matched hues its fabric shows
In new-green grass, and flowers blue and white
And many divers colors justly prized.
The birds, long silent while the cold remained—
While changeful weather brought on winter storms—
Are glad in May because of skies serene,
And they perforce express their joyful hearts
By utterance of fitting minstrelsy.
Then nightingales contend to fill the air
With sound of melody, and then the lark
And popinjay with songs amuse themselves.
The young folk then their whole attention give
To suit the season fair and sweet with love
And happiness. Hard heart has he, indeed,
Who cannot learn to love at such a time,
When he these plaintive chants hears in the trees.

In this delightful month, when Love excites
All things, one night I, sleeping, had this dream.
Methought that it was full daylight. I rose
In haste, put on my shoes and washed my hands,
Then took a silver needle from its case,
Dainty and neat, and threaded it with silk.
I yearned to wander far outside the town
To hear what songs the birds were singing there
In every bush, to welcome the new year.
Basting my sleeves in zigzags as I went,
I pleased myself, in spite of solitude,
Listening to the birds that took such pains
To chant among the new-bloom-laden boughs.

Jolly and gay and full of happiness,
I neared a rippling river which I loved;
For I no nicer thing than that stream knew.

From out a hillside close thereby it flowed.
Descending full and free and clear and cold
As water from a fountain or well.
Though it was somewhat lesser than the Seine,
More broad it spread; a fairer I ne'er saw.
Upon the bank I sat, the scene to scan.
And with the view delight myself, and lave
My face in the refreshing water there;
And, as I bent, I saw the river floor
All paved and covered with bright gravel stones.
The wide, fair mead reached to the water's edge.
Calm and serene and temperate and clear
The morning was. I rose; and through the grass
Coasting along the bank I followed down the stream.

2. The Dreamer comes to a garden wall [129–520]

When I'd advanced a space along the bank,
I saw a garden, large and fair, enclosed
With battlemented wall, sculptured without
With many a figure and inscription neat.
Because of all the painted images
I will recall the wall, and will describe
The appearance of these figures, and will tell
As much of them as I remember now.

Amid most there I saw malignant Hate,
Who quarrelsome prime mover seemed in all
Contentions, and fulfilled with wickedness.
She was not well arrayed, but rather seemed
A frenzied dame, with dark and frowning face
And upturned nose, hideous and black with dirt.
Wrapped in a filthy towel was her head.

Upon her left an equal figure stood
Close by; and, carved upon the stone above,
Her name I read. She was called Felony.

Just at her right was stationed Villainy,
Who was so like her fellowimage carved
That in no feature could I difference see;
And she as wicked seemed—spiteful and proud
And evil-spoken. Well he knew his trade

Who could devise and paint the image so
That it seemed foul and churlish as alive,
Filled with injurious thoughts, a woman wont
But seldom to perform what she should do.

Next her was painted greedy Covetousness,
Inciting men to take and never give,
But fill their money chests. The usurers
She tempts to lend to many, in desire
Of gaining and amassing property.
'Tis she impels to robbery the thieves
And harlots; and great pity 'tis, and sin,
For at the last the most of them are hanged.
'Tis she makes men purloin their neighbors' goods,
Deceive, miscount, embezzle, rob, and steal.
'Tis she makes all the tricksters and the scamps
Who, pleading by false technicality,
Too often strip of rightful heritage
Young men and maids. Knotty and bent her hands
Had grown, as was but right; for every day
Does Covetousness incite to larceny.
She cares for naught except within her net
To get her neighbors' wealth; this she holds dear.

Another image, Avarice, I saw
Sitting by the side of Covetousness;
And she was ugly, dirty, weak, and lean,
Wasted and greener than a garden leek.
Such her complexion was, she seemed diseased,
Or like one famine fated, only fed
On bread concocted with strong, caustic lye.
Her shrunken limbs in rags were scarcely clothed;
Her seemingly dog-bitten cloak was torn,
Worn out, and poor—with older fragments patched.
Hard by her mantle hung from shaky pin;
It was of brunet cloth, not lined with fur—
Rather with sheepskin, shaggy, coarse, and black.
Her robe was ten years old, at least, for she
Would be the last to rush to get new clothes;
It weighed most heavily upon her mind
If each new dress she failed to wear out quite.
Even a costume threadbare, out of date,
She'd not, unless hard pressed, replace with new.

Her purse she clutched and hid within her hand
So tightly tied that long delay she made
Before a penny she could take therefrom
In case there was no help for it; she meant
That it for gain should open, not dispense.

Beside her sad, unsmiling Envy stood,
Who never in her life a thing enjoys
Unless it be to hear or see some ill
Or some discomfiture on good men fall;
For nothing moves her like mischance or harm.
They please her well; her heart has most delight
When she beholds someone of lineage high
Descend to shameful depths.
When someone mounts
To honor by his prowess or his wit,
That sorely wounds her; when some good appears,
It well becomes her to be rancorous.
Envy displays so much of cruelty
That never she her loyalty will hold
To man or woman; and she has no kin,
How close soever, she will not desert.
She would not even wish her father well!
But you would know her malice dearly bought,
For in such torment great she always is,
And feels such woe when weal befalls a man,
Her felon heart seems breaking. Thus does God
Upon her sin a fitting vengeance take.
Envy will never let an hour go by
When all from her reproaches are secure.
I think, if Envy knew the very best
Of men who live near by or overseas,
She still would find some fault in him to blame;
And if he were so perfect in his wit
That she could never all his fame destroy,
Still would she try to lessen it at least
And by her words diminish his repute.
Now in that painting did I Envy note
To have an ugly look, a sidewise glance,
And never gaze direct, for face to face
She could not stare; but one eye in disdain
She closed. When anyone on whom she looked
Was loved or praised by others for good sense

Or gentleness or beauty, then with ire
She flamed, and seemed about to melt like wax.

Close beside Envy, painted on the wall,
Was Sorrow, showing by her jaundiced hue.
That heavy dolor weighed upon her heart.
Not even Avarice looked so pale and lean
As she; for woe, distress, chagrin, and care
From which she ever suffered, night and day,
Had yellowed and emaciated her.
Such martyrdom no person born has known,
Nor felt such sad effects of ire, as she
Seemed to have felt; and no man, I believe,
Could please her e'er by doing anything.
Nor did she wish, at any rate, herself
To comfort or relieve from all the woe
That her heart knew. For any human help
Too much depressed, too deeply grieved was she.
Most dolorous she seemed, and had not failed
To scratch her cheeks; and, as if filled with rage,
In many places had she torn her robe,
Considering it as naught. Her hair, unbound,
Lay all about her neck, torn by her hands
Because of her unbounded spleen and grief.
Now you should know it for a fact that she
Wept most profoundly ever. There's no man
So hard of heart that, seeing her distress,
Would not profoundly pity her estate;
For she would beat and tear her breast, and smite
Her fists together most relentlessly.
So woebegone a wretch was she that all
Her thought was on her pain; she never knew
The joy of being fondled or embraced.
For you should know, in truth, that one in woe
Has no desire for caroling or dance;
Nor can she school herself, who lives in grief,
To merriment. Joy is woe's opposite.

Old Age was painted next to Sorrow there,
Shrunken at least a foot from what her height
Had been in youth. She scarce could feed herself
For feebleness and years. Her beauty gone,
Ugly had she become. Her head was white

As if it had been floured. 'Twere no great loss
Were she to die, for shriveled were her limbs—
By time reduced almost to nothingness.
Much withered were her cheeks, that had been soft;
And wrinkled foul, that formerly were fair.
Her ears hung pendulous; her teeth were gone;
Years had so lamed her that she could not walk
Four fathoms' distance without aid of crutch.
Time is forever fleeting, night and day,
Without sojourn, and taking no repose;
But as he goes he steals away from us
So secretly that he appears to stand,
Although he never rests, nor stays his course;
So that no man can say that time is now.
Ask of some well-read clerk; ere he can think
Three times will Time already have passed by.
This never-lingering Time, who all day long
Is going on and never will return,
Resembles water that forever flows
But ne'er a drop comes back. There is no thing
So durable, not even iron itself,
That it can Time survive, who all devours
And wastes. He changes all—makes all things wax
With nourishment, and wane then in decay.
'Twas Time who made our fathers old, and kings
And emperors, and who will do as much
For you and me ere Death shall us demand.
This Time, who has the power to senescate
All things on earth, had so reduced Old Age,
It seemed to me that, willy-nilly, she
Had to her infancy again returned.
No power she had, and no more force or sense
Than yearling child, although she did appear
Like one who in her prime was sage and wise;
Henceforth she would be nothing but a sot.
Her body well protected was, and clothed
In furry mantle, warm against the cold
Which otherwise had wholly frozen her;
For all old folk feel chills habitually.

The image standing next was well portrayed
To be a hypocrite, but she was named
Pope Holy. She it is who secretly

Contrives to take us unaware, and then
She does not hesitate at any ill.
Outwardly she appears a saint demure,
With simple, humble, pious person's face;
But under heaven there's no evil scheme
That she has never pondered in her heart.
The figure well her character did show,
Though she was of a candid countenance.
Well shod and clothed like good convent nun,
She held a psalter in her hand, and took
Much pains to make her feigned prayers to God
And call upon all male and female saints.
She was not gay or jolly, but she seemed
Attentive always to perform good works.
She wore a haircloth shirt, and she was lean,
As though with fasting weary, pale, half dead.
To her and to her like will be refused
Entrance to Paradise. The Gospel says
Such folk emaciate their cheeks for praise
Among mankind, and for vainglory lose
Their chance to enter Heaven and see God.
Last painted was the form of Poverty,
Who could not buy a rope to hang herself,
For she had not a penny in her purse;
Nor could she sell her clothes, for she was bare
As any worm, clad only in a sack
That fitted tight and was most poorly patched.
It served her for a mantle and a cloak,
But nothing else she had for covering.
I think that, if the weather had been bad,
She would have died of cold; for she did quake,
Clinging and cowering in a little coign,
Far from the others, like a mangy bitch.
Poverty-stricken folk where'er they be
Are always shamed and spited. Curse the hour
When poor men are conceived, to be ill fed,
To be ill shod, to be ill clothed—alas,
To be unloved and never to be raised
Into a place of profit or esteem!

I scanned these images upon the wall
Full well, for as already I've explained
They stood out prominent in blue and gold.

High was the wall, and neatly built and squared.
Its bulk, in place of hedge, a garden fenced.
To which no low-born man had ever come,
For it was quite too fine a place for such.
Willingly would I have found a guide
Who, by means of ladder or of stile,
Might bring me therewithin; for so great joy
And such delight as in that place might be
Were seldom known to man, as I believe.
A generous and safe retreat for fowl
That garden was; ne'er was a place so rich
In trees bedight with songsters of all kinds;
For there were found three times as many birds
As there can be in all the rest of France.
The full accord of their most moving songs
Delicious was to hear. It would delight
The world; and, as for me, it brought such joy.
That when I heard it I had gladly paid
One hundred pounds to have had entry there
That I might the assembly (whom God save!)
Both see and hear. Warblers that were therein
Sang most enthusiastically their notes
In gracious, courteous, pleasing songs of love.
Most powerfully stirred by all their tunes,
I tried to think how I might entrance gain
Into the garden by some trick or scheme.
However, not a portal could I see,
Nor did I know what one might do to find
An opening or door into the place;
Nor was there anyone whom I might ask
To show the way, for I was all alone.
Distracted then, and anxious, I became
Until I finally bethought myself
That no fair garden ever was without
Some means of entry, either stile or gate.
Then hotfoot I set out to gird the wall
Of square-cut stone, and all the enclosure large.
A tiny wicket—narrow, fully barred—
At last I found; there was no other door.
For want of better, at this gate I promptly knocked.

3. The Dreamer enters the Garden of Mirth [521–776]

Full many a time I smote and struck the door

And listened for someone to let me in,
When finally the yoke-elm wicket gate
Was opened by a maiden mild and fair—
Yellow her hair as burnished brazen bowl—
Tender her flesh as that of new-hatched chick—
Radiant her forehead—gently arched
Her brows—as gray as falcon's her two eyes,
And spaced so well that flirts might envy her.
Her chin was dimpled. Mingled white and red
Was all her face—her breath sweet as perfume.
Of seemliest dimensions was her neck
In length and thickness—free from wen or spot;
A man might travel to Jerusalem
And find no maid with neck more fair and smooth
And soft to touch. Her throat was white as snow
Fresh fallen upon a branch. No one need seek
In any land a lady daintier,
With body better made or form more fair.
A graceful golden chaplet on her head
Was set than which no maiden ever had
One more becoming, chic, or better wrought.
Above the polished chaplet she had placed
A wreath of roses fresh from morning dew.
Her hair was tressed back most becomingly
With richest comb. Her hand a mirror bore
Her fair, tight sleeves most carefully were laced.
White gloves protected her white hands from tan.
She wore a coat of rich green cloth of Ghent
All sewed with silk. It seemed from her attire
That she was little used to business.
When she was combed, adorned, and well arrayed,
Her daily task was done. A joyful time—
A year-long, carefree month of May—was hers,
Untroubled but by thoughts of fitting dress.

When thus for me she had unlocked the gate,
Politely did I thank the radiant maid
And also asked her name and who she was.
She answered pleasantly, without disdain:
"All my companions call me Idleness;
A woman rich and powerful am I.
Especially I'm blessed in one respect:
I have no care except to tress and comb

My hair, amuse myself, and take mine ease.
My dearest friend is Mirth, a genteel beau,
Who owns this garden planted full of trees
That he had brought especially for him
From that fair land where live the Saracens;
And, when the trees grew tall, he ordered made
The wall that, as you see, surrounds the whole,
Together with the images outside,
Which are not beautiful nor yet genteel,
But dolorous and sad, as you've observed.
To find diversion, Mirth oft seeks these shades
With all his company, who live in joy
And pleasure. Certainly he's now within,
Listening to the songs of nightingale,
Of wind thrush, and of many another bird.
Here with his friends he joy and solace finds,
For never could he want more pleasant place
Or one where he could more divert himself.
The fairest folk that you'll find anywhere
Are Mirth's companions, whom he keeps with him."

When Idleness had told and I had heard
Her tale most willingly, I said to her:
"Dame Idleness, believe me when I say THE DREAMER
That since Sir Mirth, a generous gentleman,
Is now within this garden with his friends,
I hope the assembly may not so prevent
Me that I may not see them all today.
I feel that I must meet them, for I think
The company is courteous and well taught
As well as fair." Without another word
The gate by Idleness was opened wide;
I entered then upon that garden fair.

When once I was inside, my joyful heart
Was filled with happiness and sweet content.
You may right well believe I thought the place
Was truly a terrestrial paradise,
For so delightful was the scenery
That it looked heavenly; it seemed to me
A better place than Eden for delight.
So much the orchard did my senses please.
The singing birds throughout the garden thronged:

Here were the nightingales, and there the larks;
Here were the starlings, and the jays were there;
Here were the turtledoves, and there the wrens;
Here were the goldfinches, and there the doves;
Here were the thrushes, and the tomtits there.
New flocks from every side came constantly
As others of the singing seemed to tire.
The merle and mavis to surpass them all
Seemed striving; elsewhere, in each tree and bush
Where were their nests, parrots and other birds
Delighted in the song. A service meet,
As I have told you, all these birds performed;
For such a song they sang as angels sing,
And sang it, truly, to my great delight.
No mortal man e'er heard a fairer tune.
So soft and sweetly pealed their melody
That, if a man comparison should seek,
It seemed no hymn of birds, but mermaids' song,
Who for their voices clear, serene, and pure
Are Sirens called. These birds were not unskilled
Apprentices but tuneful journeymen,
And to their craft they gave their greatest care.
You may well know that, when I heard these tunes
And saw the verdant place, I was most gay.
Never so merry I—so glad of heart—
Until the day I knew that garden's charms!
Then I perceived most plainly and well knew
That Idleness had excellently served
In placing me in midst of such delight.
Well I resolved to be her faithful friend
Because she oped for me the wooden gate.

Henceforth, if I know how, I'll tell the tale
Of what befell; and, first, what did Sir Mirth,
And what the company he had, in brief
I will recount; the garden then describe.
No man could list the whole in little space;
But I will versify so orderly
That none may have a chance to criticize.

The birds kept on performing all their rites;
Sweetly and pleasantly they sang of love
And chanted sonnets courteously and well.

In part songs joining, one sang high, one low.
Their singing was beyond reproach; their notes
With sweetness and contentment filled my heart.

When I had listened for a little while
Unto the birds, I could no more refrain
From going straight to see Sir Mirth himself.
I much desired to know the state he kept
And his entourage. Turning to the right
And following a little path, with mint
And fennel fringed, into a small retreat,
Straightway I found Sir Mirth taking his ease.
With him he had so fair a company
That when I saw them I was quite amazed
To think whence such fine people could have come;
For, truly, winged angels they did seem.
No earth-born man had ever seen such folk.
This noble company of which I speak
Had ordered for themselves a caroling.
A dame named Gladness led them in the tune;
Most pleasantly and sweetly rang her voice.
No one could more becomingly or well
Produce such notes; she was just made for song.
She had a voice that was both clear and pure
About her there was nothing rude, for she
Knew well the dance steps, and could keep good time
The while she voiced her song. Ever the first
Was she, by custom, to begin the tune;
For music was the trade that she knew best
Ever to practice most agreeably.
Now see the carol go! Each man and maid
Most daintily steps out with many a turn
And farandole upon the tender grass.
See there the flutists and the minstrel men,
Performers on the viol! Now they sing
A rondolet, a tune from old Lorraine;
For it has better songs than other lands.
A troop of skillful jugglers thereabout
Well played their parts, and girls with tambourines
Danced jollily, and, finishing each tune,
Threw high their instruments, and as these fell
Caught each on finger tip, and never failed.
Two graceful demoiselles in sheerest clothes,

Their hair in coifferings alike arrayed,
Most coyly tempted Mirth to join the dance.
Unutterably quaint their motions were:
Insinuatingly each one approached
The other, till, almost together clasped,
Each one her partner's darting lips just grazed
So that it seemed their kisses were exchanged.
I can't describe for you each lithesome glide
Their bodies made—but they knew how to dance!
Forever would I gladly have remained
So long as I could see these joyful folk
In caroling and dancing thus excel themselves.

4. The Dreamer meets the companions of Sir Mirth [777–1278]

A while I scanned the scene in all details
Until a winsome lady me espied;
Her name was Courtesy. May God forbid
She ever be but gallant, debonair!
She called to me, "Fair friend, why stand you still?
Come here and take a partner for this set,
If dancing with us may afford you joy."
With neither hesitation nor delay
I joined the throng; I was no whit abashed.
You may believe that when fair Courtesy
Asked me to join the dance and caroling
Most pleasing 'twas to me, who scarce had dared,
Though much I envied them, and greatly longed,
To join the band. But now, one of the crowd,
I covertly endeavored to observe
The faces and the forms of those who danced,
And also watched their fashions, manners, styles.
So now those who were there I will describe.

Sir Mirth was fair and straight, of stature tall.
In no group could you find a finer man.
His face was white and rosy—apple-like—
Genteel and elegant his well-shaped mouth,
His gray-blue eyes, his finely chiseled nose,
His curling yellow hair. His shoulders broad,
His narrow waist, his nobly gracious form,
Compact in all its members, made one think
Of some great artist's portrait masterpiece.
Polite and agile and adroit was he;

You never saw one lighter on his feet.
He wore no beard or mustache, for the hair
Upon his face was still but tender down;
A youthful gentleman was he as yet.
Now he was clothed richly in samite cloak
Embroidered with the figures of fair birds
And ornamented all with beaten gold.
His coat was particolored and well slashed
And pinked in curious guise. His feet were shod
With shoes both slashed and laced most artfully.
For pleasure and for love a rosy wreath
His lady fair hail set upon his head;
Most fitting and divine this crown appeared.

Now do you know who his sweet mistress was—
The lady that did hate him least of all?
Her name was Gladness, she a singer gay
Who since she was but seven summers old
Had given him all her love. Now in the dance
Mirth held her by a finger; she held his.
Well did they suit each other—she a belle
And he a beau. Color of new-blown rose
Glowed in her flesh so tender smallest briar
Might scratch it, seemingly. Her forehead white
Was smooth and flawless over arching brows
Of brown that shaded joyous, smiling eyes
Seeming in constant contest with her mouth
Which should laugh first, and always they did win.
I know not what to say about her nose;
An artist could no daintier make of wax.
Her little lips were always pursed to kiss.
Her head was shining gold. But why should I
Go on to tell you any more of her?
That she'd a perfect form you may well guess.
Her hair was bound in finest gilded lace.
She wore a quite new orfray coronal.
Of chaplets twenty-nine at least I've seen
But never one more finely worked in silk.
Her body was adorned and richly clad
In gilded samite gown that matched the coat
Her lover wore, of which she was most proud.

Upon the other side of Gladness stood

The God of Love, who at his own sweet will
Distributes amity. He lovers rules;
'Tis he abates the pride of men; 'tis he
Makes thralls of lords, puts ladies in their place
Whene'er he finds them puffed up with conceit.
Not knavish in his manner was the god,
And in his beauty there was much to praise.
I hesitate to tell you of his clothes,
For 'twas no silken robe he wore, but one
Made all of flowers worked with amorous art.
In lozenges and 'scutcheons, lions, birds,
Leopards were portrayed, and other beasts,
In every part. Of colors most diverse
Were flowers worked, blossoms in many a guise
Placed cunningly: the periwinkle blue,
The yellow flowers of broom, and violets.
No bloom exists that was not woven there
In indigo or yellow or in white.
The rose leaves that were interlaced with them
Were long and broad. He wore a rosy crown
Upon his head. A flock of nightingales
That flew above the crown would barely skim
The leaves. Now there were various birds about:
Besides the nightingales were popinjays
And orioles and larks. The God of Love
An angel seemed, descended from the sky
Love had with him Sweet Looks, a bachelor
Who customary fellow was to him;
And, gazing on the carolers, he held
Two Turkish bows belonging to the god.
One bow was made of bitter-fruited tree;
Knotted and gnarled it was at either end
And blacker than a wall. The other bow
Was made of slender, graceful, pliant stem,
Well shaped and polished smooth, and painted o'er,
For ornament, with maids and bachelors,
Glad faced and frolicsome, on every side.
With these two bows Sweet Looks, who seemed no knave,
Held for his master, five in either hand,
Ten arrows. Darts well feathered and well notched,
Cutting and hard and sharp enough to pierce,
Though golden pointed, did his right hand hold.
They were not nude of iron or of steel,

But save for shafts and feathers were all gold.
The ends were tipped with hook-like golden barbs.
Sharpest and swiftest of these arrows five—
The one best leathered and the one most fair—
Was Beauty called; Simplicity was one
That sorer wounds, in my opinion;
Another one was Independence named,
Feathered with valor and with courtesy;
The fourth, which bore the heaviest barb, and so
If shot from far could little damage do
But aimed from near at hand was dangerous,
Was called Companionship; the fifth and last,
Fair Seeming named, least grievous was of all,
But made the deepest wound, though him it hit
Could hope for speedy cure, for sovereign power
Its venom has to heal the wound it makes.
Five other arrows of quite different guise
He also held. They were of ugly iron;
Blacker than fiends in Hell, also, were they.
Pride was the first; the second, of like force,
Was Villainy, envenomed and made black
With felony; the third was christened Shame;
Despair and Faithlessness were fourth and fifth.
These arrows had a close relationship
And similarity; the hideous bow,
Crooked and knobby, fitly suited them,
And well enough it could such arrows shoot.
Opposing virtues had these arrows five
Against the others, but I will not tell
At present all their force and all their power.
However, ere my story finds an end,
I'll not forget their meaning to explain
And all the truth of what they signified.

Now will I turn again unto my tale
And all the faces and the forms describe
Of those most noble folk there in the dance.
The God of Love seemed most attached to one
Of all the noble dames, and danced with her;
Her name was Beauty, like the arrow fair,
And she possessed the finest qualities.
She was not dark or brown, but rather bright,
And as the moon makes all the stars appear

Like feeble candles, so she dimmed the rest
Of that fair company. Her flesh was white
As fleur-de-lis, translucent as the dew.
She was as modest as a blushing bride;
She had no need to use an ogling glance.
Her form was straight and slender, and her face
Was clear and delicate. She sought no aid
From primping and adorning, powder, paint.
Her yellow hair—so long it touched her heels—
Her well-formed mouth and nose and cheeks and eyes—
With sweetness filled my heart. So help me God,
When I remember all her grace of limb,
It seems there's no such other in the world.
To summarize, she was both fair and young,
Neither too thin nor stout, neat and genteel,
Agreeable and pleasant, frank yet wise.

Standing by Beauty's side I next saw Wealth,
A lady of great haughtiness and pride—
A stately dame. He who in word or deed
Should dare offend against herself or hers
Would hardy be and bold; for she can aid
Or hinder. Not today or yesterday
Was it first known that rich folk have great might
To bring to joy or grief. So high and low
To Wealth gave mighty honor; her to serve
Was all the care of those who sought her grace.
"My lady" was she called by each of them,
For all on earth are well within her power
And fear her. Many a traitor thronged her court,
And many an envier and flatterer.
These are the ones most careful to dispraise
And even blame those worthiest of love.
The flatterer, first to his victim's face,
In his deceit, will praise him, and beguile
The world with well-oiled tongue; but afterward,
Behind his back, his praises to the bone
He picks, that he may honored men debase
And dissipate the righteous one's repute.
With lying many flatterers have flayed
Full many a worthy man who would have been
In confidence at court, but by their wiles
Have banished been. May evil overtake

All envious flatterers; for honest men,
Such as we are, love not their way of life.

Dame Wealth had on a robe of purple grain;
Consider it no deceit when now I say
That in this world none with it can compare
For beauty, richness, and becomingness;
With golden orfrays was the purple edged,
Each bearing portraiture of duke or king
Renowned in story; and about her neck
Most richly edged and collared was the gown
With band of gold, enameled and annealed.
And you should know that she had precious stones
More than enough, which brilliantly did flash.
About her purple robe Wealth proudly wore
A gorgeous girdle buckled with a clasp
That bore a magic stone; for whosoe'er
Should wear this stone need fear no poisoning.
She could not die from any venom's power.
Well might such stone be prized; it would be worth
More than the treasures that are found at Rome
To any wealthy man. Another stone
The pendant of the precious buckle formed;
It could the toothache cure, and any man
Who, fasting, on it gazed would be assured
Of perfect sight all day, such was its power.
Upon the golden tissue there were studs
Of purest gold, each one of size and weight
That would be worth a besant at the least.
Dame Wealth upon her yellow tresses wore
A golden circlet; never was there seen,
As I believe, more fair. Set in the gold
Were precious stones, and he would be more skilled
Than I who could describe and estimate
The gems that in that sterling gold were set.
Rubies there were, sapphires and garnets fine,
And two-ounce emeralds; but in the front,
Set with skilled workmanship within a round,
There was a carbuncle so clear and bright
That, when the evening fell, a man at need
Might light his way by it at least a league.
Such brilliance had the stone that all the place
Shone with the glow about her face and head.

Holding him by the hand, Wealth led a youth
Most beautiful, who was her paramour.
He was a man who studied to maintain
An open house for hospitality.
Well dressed was he and shod; his stables good
Held many a priceless horse; and rather he
Had been accused of murder or of theft
Than that his stable should have housed a nag.
With Lady Wealth and her benevolence
To be acquainted he was therefore glad;
For ever in his mind was one thought fixed:
How he might sojourn most luxuriously;
And she would furnish him the wherewithal
For his expenditures as if she drew
Her money from a chest big as a barn.

Next Lady Largesse followed in the dance;
Well nurtured was she and well taught to spend
And to do honor. Alexander's kin
Was she, and never knew such joy as when
She could to someone say, "The thing is thine."
The wretched Avarice is not more quick
To take than Lady Largesse is to give;
God grants her such increase in all her goods
That she's ne'er able to bestow so much
That she has not more left. Much laud and praise
Has she, and fools and sages 'neath her sway
She holds by means of her unbounded gifts.
If any should her hate, I think that she
By serving them would make them all her friends;
Therefore she has the love of rich and poor.
Most foolish of all men is stingy lord;
No sin degrades the great like avarice.
No miser seignory or lands should win;
For he will have no friends to do his will.
Who wishes to be loved must not too dear
Hold his own treasure, but good will acquire
By generous gifts. Just as the magnet draws
The stubborn iron subtly to itself,
So gold and silver draw the hearts of men.
Largesse had on a new-made purple gown—
Sarcenet it was—and at the neck

The collar was unfastened; for this dame
Had just bestowed her brooch upon a friend.
However, this loose style became her well;
For now below her fair and well-formed face
Her neck was well displayed, and through the silk
Her skin showed white and clear and delicate.

Dame Largesse, who so worthy was and wise,
For partner had a knight from overseas;
And Arthur, King of Britain, was his kin.
'Twas he that bore the brilliant gonfanon,
Insignium of glory. Great renown
Was his; of him do minstrels stories tell
Before both lords and kings. This knight had come
Late from a tournament where he maintained,
In many a joust and many a massed assault,
The honor of his lady. He had pierced
Fully many a buckled shield, and many a helm
Had he unseated, many a knight unhorsed,
By virtue of his valor and his strength.

After all these did Franchise dancing come;
She was not a brunette, nor dull of hue,
But rather white as snow; her genteel nose
Was longer than the nose of Orléans.
Her gray eyes laughed; her eyebrows arched above;
Her yellow hair was long. Like turtledove's
Was her simplicity; her tender heart
Was debonair; she dared not say or do
To anyone a thing that was not meet.
If any man were dying for her love,
On him she would take pity, probably;
For such a rueful, pious, loving heart
She had that, lest he do a desperate deed.
She'd aid a man who suffered for her sake.
She wore a gabardine of finest wool—
A richer one in Arras you'd not find—
That was so finely sewed in every part
That at each point it was a perfect fit.
Franchise was very nicely dressed. No robe
So well becomes a maid as gabardine;
A woman more coquettish seems, and quaint,
In it than when she wears a common coat.

The gabardine, which was of white, proclaimed
That she who wore it was both pure and good.

Side by side with her there danced a youth
Whose name I did not learn, but one who seemed
Genteel as if the son of Windsor's lord.

Next her came Courtesy, much praised by all;
For she had neither folly nor conceit.
God bless her, she my invitation gave
To join the dance when first I reached the place!
She was not overnice or overbold,
But reasonable and wise; no insolence
E'er hindered her fair words and fairer deeds.
None misbespoken ever was by her;
She held no rancor against anyone.
A clear brunette was she, with shining face.
No lady of more pleasant grace I know;
Her form seemed that of empress or of queen.

Holding her in the dance a young knight came,
Worthy and fair of speech, upon all men
Conferring honor. Fair and fine was he,
Well skilled feats of arms, well loved by her.

Fair Idleness came afterward, and I
Secured her as a partner in the dance.
Already I've described her form and dress;
I'll say no more of them. She was the one
Who did me such a kindness at the gate
When, through the wicket, she admitted me
To see this flowering garden—these fine folk.

The last that I remember of the band
Was Youth, who in her clear and laughing face
Scarce showed the passage of twelve winter's time.
She seemed still innocent—had yet no thought
Of evil or deceit—and gaiety
And joy were all her care; for well you know
That youthful creatures think but of delight.

Her sweetheart was so intimate with her
That they would kiss as often as they pleased,

And all the world might see their open love.
They were no whit ashamed lest some might speak
Of them insinuating words; they let
All see them kissing like two turtledoves.
The boy was like the girl—both young and fair;
Well matched were they in age, as they were matched in heart.

5. The God of Love pursues the Dreamer [1279–1438]

Thus danced those I have named and many more
Who of their consort were; all folk well taught,
Frank, and genteel they uniformly were.
When I had scanned the countenances fair
Of those who led the dance, I had the whim
To search the garden farther and explore
The place, to examine all the trees found there:
The laurels, hazels, cedars, and the pines.

Just then the dance was ended; for the most
Departed with their sweethearts to make love,
Shaded beneath the secret-keeping boughs.
Foolish were he who envied not such life
As there they led! It lusty was, God knows!
He who might have a chance to live that way
Might well deprive himself of other boons;
For there's no better paradise on earth
Than any place where lover finds a maid
Responding freely to his heart's desire.
Straightway I wandered from the scene of love,
Amusing myself alone among the trees;
When suddenly the God of Love did call
To him Sweet Looks, who bore his weapons two.
No longer idle was the golden bow.
He was required to string it, and he did
Without delay; then with the arrows five,
Shining and strong and ready to be shot,
He handed it unto the God of Love,
Who, bow in hand, pursued me distantly.
Meant he to go so far as shoot at me?
Would God might guard me from a mortal wound!
Enjoying all the orchard, fancy free,
Unheedingly I went upon my way;
But still he followed, for in no one spot
Unto the garden's end did I make pause.

The enclosure was a perfect measured square
As long as it was broad. Except some trees
That would have been too ugly for the place,
There is no fruitful one that was not there
In numbers, or at least in ones and twos.
Among the trees that I remember well
There were pomegranates, grateful to the sick.
And many fig trees, date palms, almond trees.
The nut trees were most plentiful of all,
Such as are in their seasons fully charged
With nutmegs not insipid nor yet sharp.
A man could find whatever tree he wished:
Licorice and gillyflower cloves,
A malagueta pepper tree, whose fruit
Is given the name of Grains of Paradise,
With many another most delightful spice,
Zodary, anis seed, and cinnamon,
That makes good eating when a meal is done.
With all these foreign trees familiar grew
Those that bore loads of quinces, peaches, pears,
Chestnuts and other nuts, and medlars brown,
Apples, and plums that were both white and black,
Fresh vermilion cherries, hazel nuts,
Berries of beam tree, sorbs, and many more.
With lofty laurels and high pines the place
Was stocked, with cypress and with olive trees
That are so scarce as to be notable,
And great wide-branching elms, and hazels straight,
Hornbeams, beeches, aspens, and the ash,
Maple, and oak, red spruce. Why mention more?
There were so many trees of divers sorts
That should I try to name them all I'd find
The task a tiresome one. But you should know
That all these trees were spaced as was most fit,
Each from its neighbor distant fathoms five
Or six, and yet the branches were so long
And high that for defense against the heat
They knit together at the tops and kept
The sun from shining through upon the ground
And injuring the tender, growing grass.

Roebuck and deer rambled about the lawns,

And many a squirrel climbed from tree to tree;
From out their burrows rabbits freely ran,
Of which there were not less than thirty kinds
That tourneyed on the dewy, verdant grass.
In places there were clear, refreshing springs,
Quite void of frogs and newts, and shaded cool,
From which by conduits almost numberless
Mirth had conveyed the water to small brooks
That made a swift and pleasant murmuring sound.
About the streamlets and the fountain brinks,
Beside the waters bright and frolicsome,
The grass was short and thick, where one might lie
Beside his sweetheart as upon a couch;
For, from the earth made soft and moist by springs,
Luxuriant grew the turf as one might wish.
The excellence of climate there produced,
Winter and summer, great supply of flowers
Embellishing the whole environment.
Most fair the violets, and fresh and new
The periwinkles bloomed, and other flowers
Were marvelously yellow, white, and red.
Exceeding quaint appeared the grassy mead,
As if enameled in a thousand hues
Or painted with the blooms, whose odors sweet
Perfumed the air. But I'll not bore you more
With long account of this delightful place.
'Tis better now that I should make an end;
For not all the beauty I recall,
Nor all the garden's sweet delightfulness.

Well, on I went, turning first right then left,
Till I had searched out and beheld each sight—
Experienced each charm the place possessed.
The God of Love followed me everywhere,
Spying continually, like hunter skilled
Who waits the time when he his quarry finds
In the best place to take the deadly stroke.
At last I reached the fairest spot of all
Where flowed a spring beneath a spreading pine.
Not since King Pepin's time or Charlemagne's
Has such a tree been seen; so high its crown
It towered o'er all others in the place.
Nature with cunning craftsmanship had set

The fountain that was underneath the tree
Within a marble verge, and on the stone
About the border, in small letters carved:
"Here t'was that Fair Narcissus wept himself to death."

6. The Poet tells the story of Narcissus [1439–1614]

Narcissus was a youth whom Love once caught
Within his snare and caused such dole and woe
That in his grief he rendered up his ghost.
Now Echo, a fine lady, loved him more
Than any creature born, and was for him
So lovesick that she said she needs must die
If she had not his love. But of his own
Beauty he was so proud that hers he scorned,
And neither for her weeping nor her prayers
Would satisfy her passion. When she knew
Herself refused, she suffered so much pain
And anger, and she took it in such despite,
That hopelessly she pined away and died.
But just before the end she prayed to God,
And this was her request: that whom she'd found
Disloyal to her love, Narcissus' self
In his hard heart should someday tortured be
And burn with such a love that he would find
No joy in any thing; thus he might know
And comprehend what woe a loyal maid
Had felt when she so vilely was refused.
The prayer was reasonable, and therefore God
Ordained that she this recompense should have;
And so Narcissus, as one day by chance,
Returning from the hunt, tired with the chase
That up and down the hills had led him far,
He came upon that fountain clear and pure,
Beneath the shadow of the pine, and stopped
To quench the thirst that, with excessive heat
And great fatigue, had robbed him of his breath.
He gazed upon the fountain which the tree
Encircled with its reins and, kneeling down,
Prepared himself to drink a pleasant draft.
But in the limpid waters he perceived
Reflected nose and mouth and cheeks and eyes.
The sight dismayed him, and he found himself
By his own loveliness betrayed; for there

He saw the image of a comely youth.
Love knew how best to avenge the stubbornness
And pride Narcissus had displayed to him.
Well was he then requited, for the youth,
Enraptured, gazed upon the crystal spring
Until he fell in love with his own face;
And at the last he died for very woe.
That was the end of that; for when he knew
Such passion must go e'er unsatisfied,
Although he was entangled in Love's snare,
And that he never could sure comfort find
In any fashion or by any means,
He lost his reason in but little space,
For very ire, and died. And so he got
The just reward that he had merited
For his refusal of a maiden's love.
You ladies, who refuse to satisfy
Your lovers, this one's case should take to heart;
For, if you let your loyal sweethearts die,
God will know how to give you recompense.

When this inscription had assured me well
That it was certainly the very spring
Of fair Narcissus, I withdrew a bit
Lest I like him might in its waters gaze;
For cowardly I felt when I recalled
The misadventure that occurred to him.
But then I thought that I assuredly
Might, without fear, into the waters look
Of that ill-omened spring; for my dismay
Had been but foolishness. I then approached
And kneeled before the fountain to observe
How coursed the water o'er the pebbled floor
That bright as silver fine appeared to me.
'Twas the last word in fountains! None more fair
In all the world is found; for fresh and new
The water ever bubbled up in waves
In height and depth at least two fingers' breadth.
About it all the tender grass grew fine
And thick and lush, nourished by the spring;
And, since the source did not in winter fail,
The grass lived all the year and could not die.

Two crystal stones within the fountain's depths
Attentively I noted. You will say
'Twas marvelous when I shall tell you why:
Whene'er the searching sun lets fall its rays
Into the fountain, and its depths they reach,
Then in the crystal stones do there appear
More than a hundred hues; for they become
Yellow and red and blue. So wonderful
Are they that by their power is all the place—
Flowers and trees, whate'er the garden holds—
Transfigured, as it seems. It is like this:
Just as a mirror will reflect each thing
That near is placed, and one therein can see
Both form and color without variance,
So do these crystals undistorted show
The garden's each detail to anyone
Who looks into the waters of the spring.
For, from whichever side one chance to look,
He sees one half the garden; if he turn
And from the other gaze, he sees the rest.
So there is nothing in the place so small
Or so enclosed and hid but that it shows
As if portrayed upon the crystal stones.
The Mirror Perilous it is, where proud
Narcissus saw his face and his gray eyes,
Because of which he soon lay on his bier.
There is no charm nor remedy for this;
Whatever thing appears before one's eyes,
While at these stones he looks, he straightway loves.
Many a valiant man has perished thence;
The wisest, worthiest, most experienced
Have there been trapped and taken unawares.
There a new furor falls to some men's lot;
There others see their resolution change;
There neither sense nor moderation holds
The mastery; there will to love is all;
There no man can take counsel for himself.
'Tis Cupid, Venus' son, there sows the seed
Which taints the fountain, and 'tis there he sets
His nets and snares to capture man and maid;
For Cupid hunts no other sort of bird.
By reason of the seed sown thereabout
This fountain has been called the Well of Love,

Of which full many an author tells in books
Of old romance; but never will you hear
Better explained the truth about the place
Than when I have exposed its mystery.
Long time it pleased me to remain to view
The fountain and the crystals that displayed
A hundred thousand things which there appeared.
But I remember it as sorry hour.
Alas, how often therefore have I sighed!
The mirrors me deceived. Had I but known
Their power and their force, I had not then
So close approached. I fell within the snare.
That sorely has betrayed and caught full many a man.

7. The Dreamer falls in love with the Rose [1615–1680]

Among the thousand things reflected there
I chose a full-charged rosebush in a plot
Encinctured with a hedge; and such desire
Then seized me that I had not failed to seek
The place where that rose heap was on display
Though Pavia or Paris had tempted me.
When I was thus o'ertaken by this rage,
Which many another better man has crazed,
Straightway I hurried toward the red rosebush;
And I can tell you that, when I approached
The blooms, the sweetness of their pleasant smell
Did so transfuse my being that as naught
Compared to it the perfume would have been
Within my entrails, had I been embalmed.
Had I not feared to be assailed or scorned,
One rose, at least, to handle and to smell,
I would have plucked; but I had heavy fear
Lest it might irk the owner of the place,
Who might thereafter cause me to repent.
What pile of ruddy roses was there seen,
More beautiful than any others known
Beneath the sky! Some only tiny buds
Still tightly closed—others more open were;
Yet others that belonged to later crop
Would follow in their season, all prepared
To open wide their petals. Who could hate
Such folded buds! For roses spreading wide
Within one day will surely all be gone;

But fresh the buds will still remain at least
Two days or three; so they allured me most.
Never in any place grew they more fair.
Most happy he who might succeed to pluck
A single one! Could I a chaplet have
Of such, I'd highly prize no other wealth.

One of these buds I chose, so beautiful
That in comparison none of its mates
I prized at all; and I was well advised,
For such a color did illumine it—
So fine was its vermilion—that it seemed
That in it Nature had outdone herself;
For surely she could not more beauty give.
Four pairs of leaves had she in order set
About the bud with cunning workmanship.
The stalk was straight and upright as a cane,
And thereupon the bud was seated firm,
Not bending or inclined. Its odor spread,
The sweetness burdening the air about.
Now when I smelled the perfume so exhaled
I had no wish to go, but drew more near,
Intending to secure the tempting bud
If I dared stretch my hand; but briars sharp
And piercing kept me far away from it.
Pointed and scratching thistles, nettles, thorns
With hook-like barbs, prevented my advance
And made me fear to feel a doleful injury.

8. The God of Love makes the Lover his man [1681–2010]

The god of love, who, ever with bent bow
Had taken care to watch and follow me,
Beneath a fig tree lastly took his stand;
And when he saw that I had fixed my choice
Upon the bud that pleased me most of all
He quickly chose an arrow; nocking it,
He pulled the cord back to his ear. The bow
Was marvelously strong, and good his aim,
And when he shot at me the arrow pierced
My very heart, though entering by my eye.
Then such a chill seized me that since that day
I oft, remembering it, have quaked again
Beneath a doublet warm. Down to the ground

I fell supine; thus struck, my heart stopped dead;
It failed me, and I fainted quite away.
Long time I lay recovering from my swoon,
And when I gained my senses and my wits
I still was feeble, and supposed I'd lost
Great store of blood, but was surprised to find
The dart that pierced me drew no drop of gore;
The wound was dry. With both my hands I tried
To draw the arrow, though it made me groan.
And finally the feathered shaft came out.
But still the golden barb named Beauty stayed.
Fixed in my heart, never to be removed.
I feel it yet, although I do not bleed.
Anxious and greatly troubled then was I
Because of double peril; I knew not
What I could say or do to ease my wound
Or find a doctor who with herb or root
Could offer unexpected remedy.
My heart still bade me strive to reach the bud—
Would have naught else. It seemed as if my life
Depended on possession of the Rose,
For certainly my pain was much relieved
But by its sight and smell and nothing more.
As I commenced to drag myself again
Toward the bud that did such sweet exhale,
The God of Love another arrow seized,
Headed with gold, and named Simplicity.
This is the second dart that many a man
And many a woman, too, has brought to Love.
When he perceived my close approach, he shot.
Without a warning, through my eye and heart,
This arrow, which was neither steel nor iron,
But one no man or woman born could draw;
For though with little effort I removed
The shaft, the arrowhead remains within.
Now know it for a truth that if I had
Great wish before to gain the crimson bud
Then was my longing doubled; for the more
My wound gave pain, the more desire increased
More closely to approach the little flower
That sweeter smelled than any violet.
Better for me had been a swift retreat,
But I could not deny my heart's command;

Where'er it led me I, perforce, must go.
But still the archer took the utmost pains
And strove to stop me. I could not escape
Without more woe. To overcome me quite
He sent another arrow to my heart.
This was named Courtesy; the wound it made
Was wide and deep; it stretched me in a faint
Beneath a branching olive tree near by.
Long time without a motion there I lay,
And when I stirred at last, my first attempt
Was to remove the arrow from my side.
Again the shaft came out and left the head,
Which wouldn't budge for all that I could do.

Anxious and sad in mind I took a seat.
Greatly the wounds tormented me, and urged
That to the bud, toward which so forcefully
I was attracted, I should drag myself;
Though ever anew the archer menaced me,
And scalded child should e'er hot water dread.
However, sheer necessity is strong.
Though thick as hail I'd seen a shower fall
Of square-cut rocks and stones pell-mell, yet Love,
Who all things else surpasses, gave to me
Such hardihood and such courageous heart
That willingly his bidding I'd obeyed.
Feeble as dying man, I raised myself
Upon my feet and forced my legs to walk.
Not for the archer would I quit the task
Of reaching the fair flower that drew my heart.
But there so many briars and thistles were,
And bramble bushes, that I failed to pass
The barrier and to the rose attain.
The best that I could do was close to stand
Beside the hedge of piercing thorns that hemmed
The rosary about. But of one thing
I got much joy: I was so near the bud
That I could smell the marvelous perfume
That it suffused—its beauty freely see.
And such reward I had of that delight
That in my joy my ills were half forgot.
My wounds seemed largely remedied and eased;
For never could I other pleasure find

Like to sojourning there, and night and day
Remaining near the place. When I had stayed
But little time, the God of Love, whose care
Was now to rack my heart, began anew
His dire assault. My mischief to increase,
He aimed another arrow at my side,
Which, entering below my breast, produced
Another wound. 'Twas called Companionship,
Than which there's nothing that more quickly quells
The scruples of a lady or a maid.
Now all the dolor of my wounds returned;
Three times successively I swooned away.

Upon reviving, I complained and sighed
Because my pain increased and grew the worse
So that I had no hope of cure or help
And rather would have died than lived; for sure
It seemed that Love would lastly martyr me.
Yet, notwithstanding, I could not depart.
Meanwhile the god another arrow seized,
Fair Seeming named, most prized, and, as I think,
Most powerful of all to circumvent
Intended drawing back from Love's employ
By any lover who's afraid of pain.
Sharp is its point for piercing, and its edge
As cutting as a blade of razor steel;
But Love had with a precious unguent smeared
The point, lest too severely it should wound;
For he willed not that I should die, but wished
That I might some alleviation have
By means of grateful salve that brought relief.
With his own hands he had the ointment made
To comfort loyal lovers and dispel
Their woes the better. Wounded was my heart
With this last arrow that he shot at me,
But through the wound the remedy soon spread
And so restored my all-but-ebbing pulse.
I would have been in evil case and died
But for that balm. Then I withdrew the shaft,
Though, as before, the head remained within,
Anointed with the antidote for pain.
Thus were there buried well within my breast
Five arrowheads that could not be removed.

Although the ointment gave me much relief,
Nevertheless my wounds so sorely ached
That I was pale. This arrow had strange power
To mingle weal with woe; for well I knew
That it both hurt and healed. If agony
Was in the point, assuaging was the balm;
If one part stung me, yet the other soothed.
Thus while it helped, it at the same time harmed.

Straightway with rapid step the God of Love
Approached me, and the while he came he cried:
                    THE GOD OF LOVE
"Vassal, you now are seized; there's nothing here
To aid you in defense or toward escape.
In giving yourself up make no delay;
For the more willingly you abdicate
That much more quickly will you mercy gain.
He is a fool who with refusal thwarts
The one whom he should coax and supplicate.
Against my power no striving will avail.
Be well advised by me that foolish pride
Will gain you nothing; cede yourself as thrall
Calmly and with good grace, as I desire."
I answered simply, "Sire, to you I give   THE LOVER
Myself most willingly; nor will I strive
To make resistance to your will. Please God
That I rebellious thoughts may never have
Against your rule. 'Twere neither just nor right.
Do what you please with me: or hang or slay.
My life is in your hands. I cannot swerve.
I cannot live a day against your will.
By you to weal and welfare I might mount
That by no other could I gain. Your hand,
Which thus has wounded me, must give me cure;
Make me your prisoner. I'll feel no ire
So long as I am saved from your disdain.
Of you so much that's good I've heard men say
That 'tis my wish to yield myself to you.
Completely in your service then to be,
Body and soul. If I perform your will,
Nothing can give me grief. But, furthermore,
I hope that at some time I may have grace
To gain that which I now so much desire.

538

I yield myself upon this covenant."

At this I wished to kiss his foot, but he,
Taking me by the hand, thus made reply:
"Much do I love you, and I praise the speech THE GOD OF LOVE
That you have made; never could such response
Come from a villainous, untutored man.
So largely have you gained by it that now,
For your advantage, it is my desire
That you should pay me homage, press my lips
Which no infamous man has ever touched.
No churl or villain did I ever kiss;
Rather he must be courteous and frank
That I thus make my man; though, without fail,
He must sore burdens bear in serving me.
But I the greatest honor do to you,
And you should most appreciative be
That you so good a master have, and lord
Of high renown; for Love the banner bears
And gonfanon of courtesy. So kind,
So frank, so gentle, and so mannerly
Is he that those who serve and honor him
Shall find that in their hearts cannot remain
Injustice, villainy, or base desire."

At that, with clasped hands I became his man.
Most proud was I when his lips touched my mouth;
That was the act which gave me greatest joy.
Then he demanded hostages of me.
                THE GOD OF LOVE
"From one and from another, friend," said he,
"I have received full many homages
In which I found myself deceived; with guile
False felons often have their oaths betrayed.
But they shall know how much it weighs with me;
If ever again I get them in my power,
Most dearly will I make them pay for it.
Now, since I love you, it is my desire
To be so very certain of your love
And so to league you to me that you ne'er
Will do that which you should not, or deny
Your covenant and promises to me.
'Twould be too bad if you should trick me—you

Who seem so honest."
           Then I made reply,
"Sire, I know not why you ask of me   THE LOVER
Security and pledge; for you, in truth,
Must know that you have stolen my heart away
And seized it so that even if it wished
It could not act for me against your will.
This heart is yours; it is no longer mine;
For good or ill it does as you command.
No one can dispossess you of my heart;

The Lover learns the Commandments of Love [2011–2264]

Thus I did all he wished, and when past doubt
My loyalty was placed I said to him:
"My lord, to do your will is my desire;   THE LOVER
I pray you take my service graciously.
To me you owe it to maintain good faith.
'Tis not because of dastardy I speak.
For by no means do I your service fear;
But vain is servant's toil to do his best
If, when he offers him his services,
His master looks on him disdainfully."
             THE GOD OF LOVE

Love answered, "Now be not at all dismayed;
Since you have placed yourself among my train,
With favor I'll your services receive
And raise you to a high degree, unless
Misconduct forfeits you that place; but hope
For no great good within a little space.
Pain and delay you must a while endure.
Support and suffer the distress which now
Racks you with pain, for well I know the drug
That shall effect your cure; but hold yourself
In loyalty and I'll provide such balm
As shall your wounds make well. Yes, by my head!
Your cure I'll soon complete if you'll but serve
With willing heart, and follow night and day
All the commandments I true lovers give."

"Sire." answered I, "before you leave this place, THE LOVER
For God's sake, your commandments give to me.

'Tis my intention to preserve them all;
But, if I'm ignorant of them, I fear
I soon should wander from the proper path.
The more desirous am I now to learn,
Because I would misunderstand no point."

THE GOD OF LOVE

Said Love, "You've spoken very well. Now hear
And learn my rules. Schoolmasters lose their toil
When pupils, listening, give not their hearts
To treasuring up the counsels they receive."

The God of Love then gave to me the charge
Which you are now to learn, and word by word
The ordinances he set forth of love.
Well are these points explained in my romance.
Whoso desires to love, let him attend;
For, from now on, my story will improve.
Most profitable 'twere to listen close,
For he who tells this tale his business knows.
The end of all this dream is very fine;
The substance of it is a novelty.
He who shall hear the story through and through
Quite well will understand the game of love,
Provided that he will the patience have
The dream's signification to await,
Which I expound in language of romance.
When you have heard my exposition through,
The meaning of the dream, which now is hid,
Shall be quite plain to you. I do not lie.

"Beware of Villainy, above all things;   THE GOD OF LOVE
I'll have no backsliding in this respect
Unless you wish to be a renegade,"
Said Love. "All those who Villainy admire
Shall excommunicate and cursed be.
Why should I love her? Villainy breeds churls.
Villains are cruel and unpitying,
Unserviceable, and without friendliness.

"Then guard yourself from telling. what your hear
That better were untold; 'tis not the part
Of worthy men to gossip scandalously.
Notorious and hated was Sir Kay,

The Seneschal, just for his mockery;
While Sir Gawain for courtesy was praised.
As much of blame Sir Kay, the insolent.
Received because he cruel was and fell
And scandalous above all other knights.

"Be reasonable to men both high and low—
Companionable, courteous, moderate—
And when you walk along the street take care
To be the first with customary bow;
Or, if another greets you first, be quick
To render back his greeting, nor be mute.

"Then guard yourself against all ribaldry
And dirty speech; let not your lips unclose
To name a vulgar thing; no courteous man
I hold him who indulges in foul talk.

"In ladies' service labor and take pains;
Honor and champion them; and if you hear
Calumnious or spiteful talk of them
Reprove the speaker; bid him hold his tongue.
Do what you can damsels and dames to please.
Let them hear you narrate most noble tales.
You'll gain a worthy reputation thus.

"Then guard yourself from pride. If you judge well,
You'll find that it is but a foolish sin.
One stained with vanity can not apply
His heart to service or humility.
Pride nullifies the aim of lover's art.

"The one who in Love's service would succeed
Genteelly should conduct himself and act.
Attainment of the ultimate in love
Is quite impossible in any case
For one who has no amiability.
But elegance in manners is not pride;
He who is mannerly will realize,
Unless he is a mere presumptuous fool,
That one's most valued who most lacks conceit.

"Maintain yourself well as your purse can bear

In clothing and in haberdashery;
Good dress and well-selected ornaments
Improve a man immensely. Trust your clothes
Only to one who knows his business well,
Who can with skillfulness the sleeves adjust—
Make every seam produce a perfect fit.
Laced boots and shoes buy often, fresh and new,
Fitting so well that churls will marvel oft
How into them and out of them you get.
Your gloves, your belt, your purse should be of silk.
If you have not the means, restrain your taste;
But give yourself the best you can afford.
A coronet of blares costs but a bit,
And roses at the time of Pentecost
Require no great outlay; such each may have.
Let no filth soil your body; wash your hands;
Scour well your teeth; and if there should appear
The slightest line of black beneath your nails
Never permit the blemish to remain.
Lace your sleeves and comb your hair, but try
No paint or other artificial aid—
Unsuitable e'en for a female's use.
Unless she be of ill repute, or such
As through misfortune must seek spurious love.

"Then after this you must remember well
Forever to maintain your cheerfulness.
Dispose yourself to gladness and delight,
For Love cares nothing for a mournful man.
Love brings a very jolly malady
In midst of which one laughs and jokes and plays.
Lovers by turns feel torments first, then joys.
Lovesickness is a changeable disease:
One hour it bitter is, the next as sweet;
One hour the lover weeps, the next he sings;
Now he is glad, distracted next he groans.
If you know how to play a cheerful game,
With which you may amuse the company,
'Tis my command that you make use of it;
For everyone should do in every place.
That which he knows will advantageous be,
Because by this he gets thanks, grace, and praise.

"If you know that you're quick and lithe of limb,
Avoid no contests of agility;
If you look well on horseback, up and down
You ought to spur your steed; and if you know
How well to break a lance, you'll gain great praise;
You'll be much loved if you're expert in arms.
If you've a voice that's sweet and pure and clear,
Seek no excusal when you're asked to sing;
For well-sung song will furnish much delight.
'Tis advantageous that a bachelor
Should be expert in playing flute or viol;
By this and dancing he'll advance his cause.

"Let no one think that you are miserly,
For such a reputation causes grief;
It is most fitting that a lover wise
Should give more freely from his treasury
Than any common simpleton or sot.
Naught of the lore of love the miser knows,
Whom giving does not please. From avarice
The one who wishes to progress in love
Must guard himself full well; for any swain
Who for a pleasant glance or winsome smile
Has given his heart entirely away
Ought well, after so rich a gift, his goods
Willingly to offer and bestow.

"Now shortly I'll review what I have said,
For best remembered are things briefly told:
Whoever wishes to make Love his lord
Must courteous be and wholly void of pride,
Gracious and merry, and in giving free.

"Next I enjoin as penance, night and day,
Without repentance, that you think on Love,
Forever keeping ceaselessly in mind
The happy hour which has such joy in store.
That you may be a lover tried and true,
My wish and will are that your heart be fixed
In one sole place whence it can not depart
But whole and undivided there remain;
For no halfhearted service pleases me.
He who in many a place bestows his heart

Has but a little part to leave in each;
But of that man I never have a doubt
Who his whole heart deposits in one place.
When you have given your heart, then lend it not;
To lend what one has given is scandalous.
Unconditionally one should make
His gift, and thus a greater merit gain.
The bounty of a thing that's merely lent
Is paid for with a mere return of thanks;
But great should be the guerdon of free gift.
Give, then, not only freely but with grace;
For debonairly given gift is best.
Things given grudgingly are nothing worth at all."

10. The Lover learns the Pains of Love [2265–2580]

"When, as my sermoning advises you,   THE GOD OF LOVE
Your heart you have bestowed, there will befall
Adventures hard and heavy for Love's thane.
Often, when you're reminded of your love,
You'll find it necessary to depart
From company, lest they perceive your wound.
Then in your loneliness will come to you.
Sighs and complaints, tremors and other ills.
Tormented will you be in many ways:
One hour you will be hot, another cold;
One hour you will be flushed, another pale;
No quartan fever that you ever had—
Nor quotidian either—could be worse.
The Pains of Love you will experience
Ere you recover thence; for times will come
When you will half forget yourself, bemused,
And long time stand like graven image mute
Which never budges, stirs, or even moves
Its foot, its hand, its finger, or its lips.
At last you will recover, with a start,
Your memory, reviving in a fright.
Like craven coward, from your heart you'll sigh;
For you should know all lovers act that way
When they have felt the woes that you will feel.

"Then time 'twill be for you to recollect
The sweetheart that too long you've left alone,

And you'll exclaim, 'My God, how hard my lot   THE LOVER
That where my heart has gone I may not go!
Why did I send to her my heart alone?
Never I see, but always think, of her
Powerless to send my eyes to guide my heart,
I prize not what they see apart from it.
Ought they to linger here? No, let them go
To visit her for whom my spirit yearns.
Slothful am I far from my heart to stay.
God help me; I am nothing but a fool!
I'll go straightway; no longer will I wait.
Until I see her face, I'll ne'er have ease.'
You'll start upon your way in such a case   THE GOD OF LOVE
That often you will fail of your design
And waste your steps in vain; you will not find
Her whom you seek. Then naught there is to do
Except, mournful and pensive, to return.

"Then will you be anew in sad estate.
To you will come cold shiverings and sighs,
And pains that prick more sharp than hedgehog's quills.
(Who doubts this fact, let him ask lovers true.)
But nothing will appease your soul. Again
You make assay to see, perchance, the one
On whose account you suffer so much care,
Hoping you may succeed by utmost pains.
Great diligence you'll willingly exert
To feast and satisfy your hungry eyes.
Her beauty with great joy will fill your soul;
But sight of her your heart will broil and fry.
The glowing coals of love will burst ablaze.
The more you gaze upon her whom you love,
The hotter will the fire engage your heart.
Sight is the grease that swells the amorous flame.
Each lover customarily pursues
The burning conflagration. Although scorched,
He hugs it closer; for its nature's such
As makes him contemplate his lady love
Although at sight of her he suffers pain.
The closer that he gets, the more he loves.
Sages and fools in this, at least, agree
That he who's next the fire will burn the most.
"The more you see of her, the less you wish

Ever to leave her; but, when you must part,
Remembrance of her stays the livelong day
And the impression that you've been a fool
Not to have had the hardihood to speak,
But rather to have boobied by her side,
Awkward and dumb, and let the chance escape.
Well will you think that you have been remiss
Not to address the fair one ere you left.
Disadvantageous it will seem to you,
For if you had but gained a greeting fair
You would have valued it a hundred marks.
Bewailing then your fate you'll seek new chance
To wander in the street where you have seen
The lady whom you dared not interview.
Gladly, if possible, you'll seek her home;
All your meanderings and wanderings
Inevitably lead you to that place.
But from all men your purpose you'll conceal,
Seeking excuses other than the one
That makes you stroll near the attractive spot.
In such equivocation you are wise.

"If it should happen that you meet the fair
Where you can greet and have a word with her,
Then you will feel your color change; a chill
Will run through all your veins; and, when you try
To hold converse, your thoughts and words will fail.
Or, if you do succeed to start a speech,
Of every three words you'll say scarcely two,
So shameful your embarrassment will be.
No man so prudent lives that in such case
He'll not forget himself, unless he be
Pretended lover who but acts a part.
False lovers can their self-assurance keep
And undismayed say all that they desire.
Strong flatterers are they and traitors vile—
Felons who one thing think, another speak.

"When to an end your conversation comes,
Though you have not one word missaid, you'll think
You have been duped into forgetfulness
Of something special that you planned to say;
Then will your martyrdom begin again.

This is the struggle, this the sorry strife,
This is the battle that forever lasts.
Lovers will never gain all that they seek;
Always it fails them; never have they peace;
No consummation of the war there'll be
Until it is my will to call a truce.

"A thousand more annoyances at night
You'll have, and in your bed but small repose;
For, when you wish to sleep, there will commence
Tremblings, agitations, shivers, chills.
From one side to the other you will toss—
Lie on your stomach first, then on your back—
Like one with toothache seeking ease in vain.
Then will return the memory of her
Whose shape and semblance never had a peer.
I'll state a miracle that may occur:
Sometimes you'll dream that your beloved one,
Fair-eyed and naked quite, lies in your arms,
And yields herself companion to your love.
Then castles in the land of Spain you'll build,
And naught will please you but to fool yourself
With pleasant thoughts whose basis is a lie.
But e'en this fiction will not long remain,
And then you'll weep and thus make your complaint:
'Ye gods, have I but dreamed? What is this, then?   THE LOVER
Where do I lie? Whence came this thought to me?
Would it might come again—ten, twenty times
A day! It fed and filled my soul with joy
And happiness; but its departure kills.
Might I again experience that bliss
And be where I then thought I was, I vow
That willingly I would give my life.
Death could not grieve me should his summons come
While I lay clasped within my sweetheart's arms.
But I, tormented thus and grieved by love,
Constant complaint and loud lament must make.
However, if the God of Love would grant
That I might utterly enjoy my love,
Well purchased were my woe at such a price!
Alas! I ask too much. I am not wise
Such an outrageous bargain to demand.
A fool's request deserves a sharp rebuff;

Therefore I know not what I dare to say.
Many a greater and more worthy one
Than I has had in love less recompense
And thought himself well favored, nonetheless.
But, if a single kiss and nothing more
The fair one would allot to ease my pain,
Most rich reward I'd have for all my woe.
But now for me the future darkly looms;
Well may I hold myself a fool who dare
To set my heart upon so high a prize
That neither joy nor profit may I gain.
Yes, I'm a silly churl so to prefer
A look from her above another one's
Complete surrender. Should the gods me aid
To get, this instant, longed-for sight of her,
How soon should I be cured! Oh, help me, God!
Why does the dawn so long delay? I lie
Too long lamenting on this lonely couch
Where I no ease can have without my love.
Naught but annoyance 'tis to lie abed
When one can have no comfort or repose.
I'm troubled now, when I would fain arise,
Because the night has lingered all too long
And day breaks all too slowly in the east.
O Sun, for God's sake, haste; make no delay—
Speed the departure of the night obscure
Which, with its cares, has worn its welcome out!'

"If I know aught of the distress of love, THE GOD OF LOVE
I know that thus you'll waste away the night
And get but little rest. And when at length
You can no longer bear to lie awake,
You'll rise and dress yourself, put on your shoes,
And make your toilet ere you see the dawn.
Then furtively you'll seek, in rain or snow,
By shortest path, the mansion of your love,
Who, soundly sleeping still, scarce thinks of you.
By postern gate an hour you'll wait alone,
Hoping that perchance it may unclose;
But there you'll cool your heels in wind and sleet.
Then the front door you'll try, or elsewhere seek
Some unbarred window—any opening—
Where you may listen for some sound within

That may betoken who's asleep, who wakes.
And if by chance your sweetheart is the one
Who only is awake, I counsel you
To let her hear your groans and your complaints
That she may know that, troubled by her love,
You in your bed could find no more repose.
Unless her heart is hard, she should be touched
With pity for the one who bears such pain.

"For love of that high sanctuary, then,
Because of which you're robbed of all your rest,
At your departure kiss the blessed door;
And that no man may see you in the street
Before the house, take care to go away
While twilight lingers—ere the dawn is clear.
Such comings and such goings in the night,
Such wakings and such watchings, such complaints,
Make lovers' bodies thin beneath their clothes.
Of this yourself will an example be:
Love leaves true lovers neither flesh nor blood.
This fact helps one identify false churls
Who, wishing to betray ingenuous maids,
Attempting to deceive them, say they've lost
Completely their desire for meat and drink;
Yet ne'er an abby prior's more fat than they!

"With one thing more I charge you, and command
That you your reputation make secure
For generosity, by many gifts
Bestowed upon the lady's serving maid,
That she may name you as a worthy man.
Hold dear and honor all your lady's friends;
Advantage may well come through them to you.
When those who have her confidence recount
How they have found you courteous, true, and kind,
Your love will prize you half as much again.
Depart not from your sweetheart's native land;
Or, if you must, by dire necessity,
Be sure to leave your heart as hostage there,
And plan a quick return; make absence brief.
Let her well know how long the hours seem
When you're away from her who guards your heart.
Now I have told you how and in what guise

Lovers should do my bidding; do it, then,
If you would lastly gain your pleasure with your love."

II. The Lover learns the Remedies for the Pains of Love [258–2764]

When love had thus commanded me, I said:
"Sir, how and by what means may I endure   THE LOVER
The evils you have just detailed to me?
They overwhelm my mind with grievous fear;
For how can any man live and support,
In every place and time, such sighs and griefs,
Such tears and cares, such burnings and such pains,
And so severe a strain? So help me God,
I marvel much that anyone could live,
Were he not made of steel, in such a hell.

The God of Love, explaining, thus replied:
THE GOD OF LOVE
"No man has good unless he purchase it.
Fair friend, I swear this by my father's soul:
Things dearest paid for are the dearest prized,
And good seems best when it is bought with ill.
It's true that naught with lovers' woes compares.
No more than man can pump the ocean dry
Can story or romance love's griefs exhaust.
Yet lovers live as long as e'er they can;
To flee from Death each has a right good will!
The wretch immured in filthy dungeon dark,
Annoyed by vermin, eating barley bread
Or only oaten cake, dies not for that;
Hope gives him comfort, and he's confident
Some chance will offer freedom to him yet.
Like aspiration have the thralls of Love;
Though held in prison, they expect relief.
Hope so consoles them that with willing heart
They give themselves up thus to martyrdom.
Hope makes them bear such ills as none can tell
For sake of joys a hundred times more great.
It's Hope revives them, making them forget
Adversities they've suffered. Blest be Hope,
Who does the cause of lovers so advance!
Most courteous is Hope; she never lags
Six feet behind the valiant, till their end,
In spite of mischief or of peril dire.

Even the thief who feels the hangman's rope
By Hope is made still to expect reprieve.
This will I warrant: Hope will not depart
But ever succor you in your most need;
And with this Hope I give you three more gifts
That solace those who're caught within my net.

"Sweet Thought, who e'er recalls what Hope accords,
Is first of those who comfort all my thralls.
Whene'er a lover weeps and sighs and groans
And is in torment, then Sweet Thought will come,
Within short space, to drive away his gloom,
Reminding him of all the joy that Hope
Has promised him, setting before his view
His sweetheart's laughing eyes, her saucy nose
Neither too small nor large—her rose-red lips
Exhaling sweet perfume, and all her parts
The memory of which can pleasure give.
Then, doubling all his joy, a tender look
Or welcome kind or smile he will recall
Which his dear fair one has sometime bestowed.
Sweet Thought thus often calms the rage of love.
I willingly bestow on you this boon
As well as others, which if you refuse
You'll be ungrateful, for they're not less sweet.

"The second gift is called Sweet Speech, who lends
To many a man and maid great comforting;
For lovers always long to talk of love.
Because of this a dame made up a song,
About her love, which I remember well:
Whatever they may say, I joy to hear
Men talk to me about my lover dear.
Well did she know what power in Sweet Speech lies;
For she had tested it in many a way.
I counsel you, therefore, to seek a friend,
Secret and sage, to whom you may reveal
     Whate'er you wish, discovering your heart.
     A great advantage you will gain by this;
For, when your malady gives you most pain,
You'll go to him for comfort, and converse,
You two alone, of her who has your heart—
Of her appearance, her sweet countenance,

Her beauty. Then you will recount the state
Of all your being, asking his advice—
What you may do, and how, to please your love.
If he who is your friend has set his mind
Upon some sweetheart, then his confidence
Is of most worth; for he of course will tell
His lady's name and what her station is,
And whether she's a widow or a maid.
So you will not suspect him of designs
Upon your lady, or have any fear
Of treachery; for you with him and he
With you will then have made an interchange
Of utmost trust. You'll know how sweet it is
To have a friend with whom your thoughts are safe.
When you have tested him, you'll feel well paid
To get such comforting as he can give.

"My third gift is Sweet Sight, child of Regard,
Who stays away from those far from their loves,
So take my counsel and remain near yours.
Delicious to the taste of those who love,
The solace is that Sweet Sight offers them.
Delightful meetings have the eyes at morn
To which God shows the sanctuary blest
For sight of which they are most envious.
Nothing will seem mischance to them that day!
They fear no dust or rain or other grief.
And when the well-taught eyes gain such delight
They are too courteous to hide their joy
But rather wish with it to please the heart
And calm its woes; for such good messengers
Are lovers' eyes that to the heart straightway
They send the news of whatsoe'er they see,
And then in joy the heart forgets its grief
And all the gloom that troubled it before.
Just as the rising sun puts shades to rout,
So does Sweet Sight drive darkness from the heart
Which night and day lay languishing for love.
Heart nothing doubts when eyes have longed-for sight.

"Now I've explained away your fears, I think;
For truthfully I've told you all the means
By which lovers are cased and kept from death,

And for your comfort now you know you have
At least Sweet Thought, Sweet Speech, Sweet Sight, and Hope.
It is my will that these shall be your guard
Till better aids you gain, for these, indeed,
Are but an earnest of the more that is to come.

JEAN DE MEUN

THE ROMANCE OF THE ROSE, PART II, CONCLUSION

The Lover makes his way into the Ivory Tower [21346–21694]

A hundred thousand thanks I offered him
And promptly, like a pilgrim most devout,
Precipitate, but fervent and sincere,
After that sweet permission, made my way
Like loyal lover toward the loophole fair,
The end of all my pilgrimage to achieve.

With greatest effort I conveyed with me
My scrip and pilgrim staff so stiff and stout
That it no ferrule needed to assure
That it would hold the path and never slip.
The scrip was of a supple leather made
Most skillfully, without a single seam;
Nor was it empty. As it seemed to me,
Since none had opened it, Nature had placed
Most diligently, with the greatest care,
The hammers therewithin together laid.
When she had subtly manufactured it.
Excelling Daedalus in craftsmanship,
She lent the scrip to me. I think 'twas done
Because she thought that I might have to shoe
My palfreys when I felt their footsteps slip.
So should I do, if I but felt the need.
Most certainly; for, thanks be unto God!
I well know how to do such smithy work.
Truly I tell you that I better love
My scrip and hammers than my lute and harp.
When such equipment Nature furnished me,
Much was I honored; and I learned its use
Till I became a craftsman wise and good,

It was she, too, who furnished me my staff—
Another gift—and ere I went to school,
To polish it would have me set to work;
But for a ferrule she cared not a straw.
Nor valued less the staff for want of it.
Since I received it, I have always kept
The staff with me. I've never lost it yet;
Nor shall I lose it if I can prevent
Its loss; and not for fifty million pounds
Would I e'er part with it. Dame Nature made,
When she presented it, a lovely gift;
And therefore I must ever guard it well.
When I upon it gaze, I'm always glad
And thank her for the present. When I feel
Its sturdiness, I'm overjoyed and gay.
Much comfort has it given me many a time,
And well it's served me in full many a place.
Where I have put it. Know you how it serves?
When I am journeying and chance upon
A hidden place obscure, I thrust my staff
Into the ditches bottomless to sight,
Or test with it the depths of dubious fords.
Now I can boast that I've so well assayed
Such depths that I have often saved myself
From perishing therein. By springs and streams
I make my way in perfect confidence.
If e'er I find the bed too deep—the banks
Too steep—I much prefer to coast the flood
And make my way two leagues along the shore.
I suffer less fatigue than I should feel
In risking water that is perilous,
As I know well by sore experience;
Though in such waters I have ne'er been drowned.
Soon as I test the depths that I would ford
And find no bottom with my staff or oar,
I go around, and, keeping near the banks,
Find my way out, at least eventually.
To find an exit I could ne'er be sure
Had I not the equipment Nature gave.

Now let us leave these dangerous, slippery trails
To those who willingly would travel them,
And hold our way, not by the wagon roads

But by delightful footpaths, pretty lanes
Which lead the happy man to fond delights.
There's more productive gain in trodden roads
Than in new-broken paths; and there men find
Fair properties that livings will provide.
It is by Juvenal himself affirmed
That one who'd quickly come to great estate
Can find no shorter road—no better way—
Than to invest in some old, moneyed dame;
For if she finds his service to her taste
She soon will raise him to a high degree.
Ovid repeats a maxim proved and true
That whoso will a wealthy widow take
Soonest attains the greatest recompense.
Great riches are acquired most rapidly
By sending goods to market by such roads.

But he who'd steal an older woman's love,
Or even purchase it most lawfully
When Cupid catches him within his net,
Should take good care that naught he says or does
Resembles subterfuge or trickery;
For tough old pallid dames, who've left their youth,
Having of yore been flattered, duped and tricked,
When they're deceived again, more readily
Perceive the subtlety of flatterers
Than do the tender maids who doubt no ruse
When they give ear to their deceivers' talk
And think all guileful lies the gospel truth,
Since they have not been scorched. But wrinkled dames,
Malicious and hard baked, are in the art
Of fraud so well instructed that they know
The science well by old experience.
When they are thus approached by flatterers
Who hope to capture them with fairy tales,
And play upon their ears, and labor long
To gain their grace by humbleness and sighs
And begging mercy with hands joined in prayer,
With bowed heads kneeling, weeping lavish tears,
And torturing themselves that they may gain
Better belief, making reigned promises
Of heart and body, services and wealth,
Calling to witness all the holy saints

That are, have been, or ever more shall be,
And thus with windy words attempt deceit
As does the fowler hidden in the woods,
Who with his whistled notes decoys the birds
To come within the nets where they'll be caught,
And is abroached by all the foolish fowl
Who don't know how to meet his sophistries
But are deceived as by a metaphor,
As are the silly quail who hear the sound
The fowler makes to win them to his trap
And hover round, and then beneath the net.
Which he has stretched upon the springtime grass
So thick and fresh, they flutter and are lost,
Unless some older quail refuse the snare
Because she has been singed and almost caught,
Having seen other netting likewise spread,
From which she has escaped by miracle—
So older women who have once been lured,
And by their suitors tricked by flatteries,
Hearing the words that they have heard before
And seeing the attitudes that they have seen,
The more they've been deceived, the more they're sly
To recognize, far off' the trick again.
If suitors seriously make their vows
To gain their just deserts from Cupid's game,
Like those in fact entangled in the net,
Whose torture is so pleasant, and whose toil
Is so delightful that there's nothing else
Half so agreeable to them as hope
Which grieves them more than it encourages,
Then do they fear to swallow hook with bait,
And listen close and try to figure out
Whether it's truth or fable they are told.
They weigh each word, so much they fear deceit
Because they have experienced it before
And of it have a lively memory.
All try to please her, thinks each aged dame.

You, if you wish, may turn your hearts to these,
The sooner to enrich yourselves; or you
Who study your delight, and pleasure find
In them, may jog along such well-worn roads
As will provide most solace and most joy.

You others who prefer the younger girls
(That you may never be by me deceived,
Whate'er my masters may command—and good
Are all behests that they have given me)
Again I tell you for the very truth—
Believe it he who will—that one does well
To try them all that he may better know
How to regale himself with what is best.
'Tis thus that gourmands do who of all food
Are connoisseurs, and many viands taste—
Roasted, and boiled, and fried, in gelatin,
In batter, or in souse—when they inspect
Their kitchens. and know well what should be praised
Or blamed, and what should be or sweet or sour;
For many a time they've tasted all the foods.
Know well, and have no doubt of it, that he
Who never tastes the bad can hardly know
How good things ought to taste; who knows not shame
Will scarcely recognize what honor means;
Who learns not first what real discomfort is
Will scarcely know what things are comfortable;
And he who's never suffered any pain.
Will scarcely realize when he's at ease.
No one should offer solace to a man
Who has not learned its worth through suffering.
'Tis thus with all such opposites: the one
Explains the other. He who would define
A thing must have in mind its opposite
Or else no definition can he frame;
For he who knows not both cannot conceive
The difference between them. This unknown,
No proper definition can there be.

The sacred relics of the ivory tower
I hoped to touch with all my equipage
If I so close approach might win for it
And get it through the little opening.
So after all my wanderings and toil—
Like pilgrim agile still and vigorous—
I knelt at last, and without more delay,
Between the two fair pillars I've described,
With staff unshod; for very fain was I,
With heart devout and full of piety,

To worship in that sanctuary sweet,
Which to be highly honored well deserved
Though now it lay flat fallen on the ground.
None of the structure had escaped the fire
Which toppled down all that was not destroyed.
A little then I pushed aside the shroud
That curtained the fair relics, and approached
The image that I knew was close within.
Devotedly I kissed the sacred place.
Safely to sheathe my staff within the shrine,
I thrust it through the loophole, while the scrip
Dangled behind it. Carefully I tried
To thrust it in; it bounded back again
Once more I thrust it in without avail;
Always it back recoiled. Try as I might,
Nothing could force the staff to enter there.
Then I perceived a little barricade,
Which though I well could feel I could not see,
Quite near the border of the opening,
Which from the inside fortified the shrine,
Having been placed there when it first was made,
And still remaining fast and quite secure.
More vigorously then I made assault;
But often as I thrust, so oft I failed.

If you had seen me there thus tourneying,
You would have been much taken with the sight
And would have thought of Hercules the Great
And, to dismember Cacus, how he strove.
Three times he assailed the gate, and thrice he failed;
Three times he struck, and thrice, exhausted, fell;
Three times he sat, hard-breathing, in the glen,
Such labor and such pain he had endured.
So I, when I had struggled there so long
That I perspired in very agony
Because the palisade would not give way,
Was just as tired, I think, as Hercules,
Or even more. However, at the last,
My battery availed to this extent
That I perceived a narrow passageway
By which I thought to gain admission there,
Though I must quite destroy the palisade.
Pushing within this little, narrow path

By which I entrance sought, as I have said.
I broke down the obstruction with my staff.
Then through the passageway that I had made,
Though 'twas too narrow and too small for me,
I got inside—or, rather, half inside.
Sorely I grieved no farther to get in,
But could not do what was beyond my power,
Though not for anything would I relax
My efforts till the staff was quite inside.
At last I got it in, but still the scrip
Remained outside, its hammers knocking there
For entrance; and so narrow was the path
That therein I was placed in great distress.
The passage would have been by far too small
For me to traverse it, and well I knew
By this that none had ever passed that way.
I was the first of men to tread that road;
The place was not accustomed to receive
The tributes pilgrims well might bring to it.
I know not whether it has offered since
Of its advantages to more than me;
But I assure you, even if it had,
I love it so that I would not believe
The truth, for no one readily mistrusts
That which he loves, no matter how defamed.
I'd be the last to credit evil tales.
However, at the least, I know that then
It never had been pierced or battered down.
I myself entered there because I ne'er
Without such entrance could have plucked the bud.
Imagine how I acted when I found
That quite at my disposal was my Rose!
Listen while I describe the deed itself,
So if you, too, should have a chance to go,
When spring's sweet season shall have come again,
To pluck a full-blown flower or tight-closed bud,
You then so wisely may conduct yourself
That you may never fail to gain your end.
Unless a better method you have learned,
Employ that one you hear me now explain.
If you can make the passage more at ease,
Or better, or with greater subtlety,
And not too much exert or tire yourself,

Use your own system when you've heard my plan.
At least this much advantage you will have,
That I will teach you, without asking pay,
My method. Listen to me, therefore, willingly.

100. The Lover wins his Rose [21695–21780]

Tormented by my labors, I approached
So near the rose tree that I could at will
Lay hands upon her limbs to pluck the bud.
Fair Welcome begged me, for the love of God,
That no outrageous act I should perform,
And to his frequent prayers I gave assent
And made a covenant with him that I
Would nothing do beyond what he might wish.

I seized the tree by her tender limbs
That are more lithe than any willow bough,
And pulled her close to me with my two hands.
Most gently, that I might avoid the thorns,
I set myself to loosen that sweet bud
That scarcely without shaking could be plucked.
I did this all by sheer necessity.
Trembling and soft vibration shook her limbs;
But they were quite uninjured, for I strove
To make no wound, though I could not avoid
Breaking a trifling fissure in the skin,
Since otherwise I could have found no way
To gain the favor I so much desired.

This much more I'll tell you: at the end,
When I dislodged the bud, a little seed
I spilled just in the center, as I spread
The petals to admire their loveliness,
Searching the calyx to its inmost depths,
As it seemed good to me. It there remained
And scarcely could unmingle from the bud.
The consequence of all this play of mine
Was that the bud expanded and enlarged.
But I'd not misbehaved more than I've told;
Rather, I'd done so well in my attempt
That never did the sweet bud turn from me
Or think it any harm, but e'er complied.
And let me do whatever she supposed

I ought to do most to delight myself.

Of course she did remind me of my pledge
And say I was outrageous in demands,
And that I'd done what I should not have done;
But ne'ertheless she never did forbid
That I should seize and strip and quite deflower
Both trunk and limbs of every leaf and bloom.

When I perceived that I had such success
That my affair no longer was in doubt
And that I nobly had achieved my end,
I felt most thankful and recognizant,
As any honest debtor ought to feel,
Toward all the friends who had so aided me.
I felt myself beholden much to them,
Since by their aid I had become so rich
That, to affirm the truth, not Wealth herself
Was half so wealthy. First unto the God
Of Love and Venus, who had helped me most,
And then to all the barons in his train,
Then to Fair Welcome and that other Friend
Who proved himself to be a friend indeed,
Whom I pray God that He will ne'er restrain
From aiding loyal lovers, I gave thanks
With savory kisses, ten or twenty times.
But Reason I forgot, whose hortatives
Had make me waste so many pangs in vain.
As well as Wealth, that ancient villainess
Who had no thought of pity when she warned
Me from the footpath where she kept her ward.
Thank God she did not guard that passageway
By which I made my entrance secretly,
Little by little, notwithstanding all
The efforts of my mortal enemies
Who held me back so much, especially
The guardian Jealousy, with her sad wreath
Of care, who keeps true lovers from the Rose.
Much good their guardianship is doing now!
Ere I remove from that delightful place
Where 'tis my hope I ever can remain,
With greatest happiness I'll pluck the blooms
From off the rosebush, fair in flower and leaf.

This, then, is how I won my vermeil Rose.
Then morning Came, and from my dream at last I woke.

SECTION **21**

Selections from GERMAN POETRY FROM THE BEGINNINGS TO 1750

Oswald von Wolkenstein

Selection, Translation, and Introduction by Albrecht Classen

Just as in the case of many medieval poets, Oswald's work was entirely unknown to modern scholarship until 1800 when his first manuscript was rediscovered in Vienna. His songs appeared to be an oddity, though, and did not conform with the traditional Middle High German *Minnesang*. For a long time only few people concerned themselves with Oswald's oeuvre, despite Beda Weber's literary biography (1850) and Arthur von Wolkenstein-Rodenegg's first thoroughly scholarly treatise on his medieval forefather. When Norbert Mayr published the first modern article, and in 1961 the first modern monograph on Oswald von Wolkenstein, he opened the floodgates for entirely new perspectives on this poet, as a stream of new investigations of his life and work, and scores of critical examinations of his songs have appeared since then, indicating that from now on Oswald was acclaimed as one of the major medieval German poets. Until recently philologists tended to label him "the last minnesinger" for lack of any other term for his highly idiosyncratic poetry, although this term could be applied only in a very limited sense of the word. This South-Tyrolean composer and musical performer was not yet influenced by the Italian Renaissance, but many aspects in his texts and melodies catapult him beyond his own time. Both his contemporaries and even modern scholarship for a long time failed to understand the unique characteristics of his work, whereas today Oswald is considered to be one of the best Middle High German poets.

Oswald belonged to the landed gentry of Southern Tyrol, but he was only the second son in his family and thus had to struggle most of his life to secure a financially and economically safe position within society. Maybe for that reason he was enormously self-centered and made many attempts to establish himself as the leading politician of his region. The other problem was that the Duke of Tyrol, Frederick, strove to centralize his government and to subdue the noble families under his rule. Oswald sought to align himself with the German Emperor Sigismund and served him for a couple of years as translator diplomat, messenger, entertainer, and negotiator in Italy, France, Spain, and Germany. Twice, however, he was imprisoned by his enemies and the duke for personal and political reasons; he was even tortured and then forced to pay an enormous amount of money to his lord to gain his freedom again (1421, 1427). After Frederick's death in 1439, however, the Tyrolean nobles could breath more freely for a while, until, beginning in the second half of the fifteenth century, the move to centralize the government gained the upper hand again, finally crushing the landed gentry, and with them the Wolkenstein family.

For a while Oswald also entered the service of the Bishop of Brixen but eventually, at the end of his life, succeeded in laying the foundation for a more or less independent position in Tyrol. His political and legal advice was highly appreciated by his fellow aristocrats, by the Emperor, and by other ducal dignitaries in Germany.

There is hardly any other medieval poet we know so much about as Oswald because his life is reflected in more than thousand political, legal, religious, and other types of documents. In addition, Oswald wrote detailed autobiographical, though highly stylized poems in which he discusses his wedding and marital life, his political and military struggles, and his many travels all over Europe and partly the Near East. Most of these references have been confirmed with the help of chronicles, letters, and other source material referring to him.

Oswald had his more than 130 songs collected in two luxurious manuscripts during his life time. After his death his family had the songs copied a third time. Only few of his poems gained, however, wider popularity, even though a handful of his more traditional texts were also included in some fifteenth and sixteenth-century song books. One of the unique features of Oswald's personal manuscripts is that surprisingly realistic portraits of him were included as frontispieces. One of them might have been painted by the Italian Renaissance artist Antonio Pisanello or one of his students.

In addition, Oswald's songs are, to a large extent, accompanied by musical notations, many of them contrafacta (copies) from religious songs performed in Northern Italy, Flanders, the Netherlands, and Northern France. At the same time a number of his songs show clear signs of influence from the Middle High German poets Walther von der Vogelweide (ca. 1200–ca. 1220) and Neidhart (ca. 1220–ca. 1240) with his peasant satires. The Mönch von Salzburg (ca. 1365–1395) also left his mark on Oswald's oeuvre. It is very likely that he learned much from his Italian contemporaries, the so-called *poeti minori* or *poeti realistici* with their realistic themes of city life, travel accounts, eroticism, and political issues.

Both the musical style of his songs and their content mark Oswald as a highly innovative and self-conscious poet fully aware both of the literary tradition of the German Middle Ages and contemporary late-medieval poetry all over Europe. Oswald cannot yet be defined as a German Renaissance poet, but his work is beginning to shed the vestiges of the past and shows the way into the future. Apart from his travel songs and political satires, Oswald composed famous marital love songs, *pastourellas*, and other types of erotic songs.

BIBLIOGRAPHY

George Fenwick Jones, *Oswald von Wolkenstein*. Twayne's World Authors Series; TWAS 236 (Boston: Twaine, 1973).

Alan T. Robertshaw, *Oswald von Wolkenstein: The Myth and the Man*. Göppinger Arbeiten zur Germanistik, 178 (Göppingen: Kümmerle, 1977).

Die Lieder Oswalds von Wolkenstein. Ed. Karl Kurt Klein. 3rd newly revised and expanded ed. by Hans Moser, Norbert Richard Wolf and Notburga Wolf. Altdeutsche Textbibliothek, 55 (Tübingen: Niemeyer, 1987).

Albrecht Classen, *Die autobiographische Lyrik des europäischen Spätmittelalters*. Amsterdamer Publikationen zur Sprache und Literatur, 91 (Amsterdam-Athens/GA: Editions Rodopi, 1991).

Albrecht Classen, "Oswald von Wolkenstein," *German Writers of the Renaissance and Reformation 1280–1580*, Dictionary of Literary Biographies, 179, ed. James Hardin and Max Reinhart (Detroit-Washington, D.C.-London: Gale Research, 1997), 198–205.

Albrecht Classen, *The Poems of Oswald von Wolkenstein: An English Translation of the Complete Works (1376/77–1445)*. The New Middle Ages (New York: Palgrave Macmillan, 2008).

The 15th Century

OSWALD VON WOLKENSTEIN (1376/77–1445)

Kl (ein) 77 O MARGIE, MARGE, DEAR MARGARET

"O Margie, Marge, dear Margaret,
for whom I yearn and would caress,
may thy good name thou ever keep."
"Whate'er the charge, Os, my pet,
from thee I'll learn true faithfulness
and ever aim thy praise to reap,"
"I greet these words and shall engrave
them in the bottom of my heart
as from thy rosy lips they part."
"My sweet, this too is what I crave,
and I'll never waiver."
"I'll think of thy favor."
"Think, dearest Ossie, just of me,
thy Marge will bring delight to thee."

"Thou canst not give, nor I desire
more joy than when thou hast my form

held fast, as one locked in a cell."
"For thee I'll live and shall not tire
of holding then; I'll keep thee warm
with pleasure, and shall do it well."
"My dear, I owe thee gratitude
and I shall ne'er forget thy love;
thou'rt always she I'm dreaming of."
"No fear that I'll be mean or rude
needst thou have, my treasure."
"My thanks can have no measure."
"O, dearest man, I feel so good
when I embrace thee as I would."

"I cannot know more joy than this:
thy love and wondrous body, too,
which lustfully to mine is pressed."
"I overflow with keenest bliss
and thrill with passion through and through
whene'er thy hands caress my breast."
"My bride, the best of sugarbread,
whose sweetness flows through all thy limbs,
is that thy lovelight never dims."

"Abide, and trust what I have said,
Os, with faith unbending."
"Be thy love unending!"
"Let fortune never separate
us two, nor harm a love so great!"

J. W. Thomas

Kl(ein) 1

Stanza 2:

She was such a beauty,
with whom I spent so much time,
thirteen years or more,
always loyal in her service
however she liked it.
There was never a person in the world more dear to me.
In many lands have I ridden,
where I never forgot the good woman.
I have suffered much
because of her, with longing hate.
Her red lips have seduced my heart.
Because of her I have seen much in the world,

free of the very dear little hands.
Joyfully she has lent me many a night
her bare arms.
Sadly enough, this has come to an end,
since I am shackled on my arms and legs.

Stanza 3:

Before her I lie securely bound
by iron and by rope.
Through many a heavy burden
she has withdrawn from me my happiness.
O Lord, you can surely be the judge:
the time has come for you to purify me.
Out of love
we have often not been able to keep us safe from pain
and I never could free myself completely from love
since I am lying here, tightly
bound by her rope,
now my sickly life could be easily destroyed.
With hair and skin
God has brought me down heavily because of her
as a result of my grave sins,
which burden me heavily.
She [my lady] gives me penance and longing pain,
so much that I am not able to sing about half of it.

Stanza 5:

Love is a word,
a treasure above all is he who perfects love in a pleasant way.
Love overcomes all things;
love even forces the Lord God
to dispel the sinner's troubles
and to give him joy's consolation.
Love, sweet hoard,
how have you bared me so unlovingly
that I never repaid with love him
who carried out his death
for me and many a cold sinner.
This I await here on great sorrow's pyre.
Had I only used halfway
for God in a useful fashion my love
which I brought so tenderly to the woman
who treats me so badly,
then I would pass on without any sin.

568

Oh worthy love, how heavy is your bond.

I am deeply sorry
that I have so wantonly angered him

Kl 33

The dark color in the West
frightens me and fills me with yearning
because I am missing her and am all alone
here in this night without any cover.
She who can embrace me so lovingly
with her white arms and hands,
she is far away; so far that I cannot help it
but must begin to sing out of desperation.
All my limbs are sighing when I stretch,
when I sigh for my beloved,
she, who alone arouses all my desires,
which is an ancient-old natural feeling.
I roll back and forth
in the night without catching sleep.
Desirous thoughts approach me
like irresistible weapons, coming from the distance.
When I do not find my beloved on her bed,
whenever I try to touch her,
then there is, in addition to my other pain, fire in the roof
as if hoar-frost were burning me.
She fetters me all over without any ropes
when the day breaks.
Constantly her lips awaken
in me the desire to sing.
In this way, dear Gret, I spend
the night until the early morning.
The image of your sweet body pierces my heart,
I sing quite openly about it.
Come, dear honey! A rat[1] is frightening me so badly
that I awake very often.
Beloved, you who never grants me rest, neither in
the morning nor in the evening, help me
let us make the bed creak!
Then I would sing out loud for joy,
when I imagine in my heart

---

1. Oswald seems to use the 'rat' as a metaphor for the penis.

how my beautiful beloved
embraces me at dawn so tenderly and softly.

Kl 53

Wake up happily, gently, gracefully, beamingly,
       delightfully, softly, and calmly
in a pleasant, sweet, pure, quiet manner,
you attractive beautiful woman.
Stretch and rise, show your noble and graceful body;
open your bright and shining eyes!
Notice secretly
how the stars are disappearing
in the shining brightness of the clear sun.
Let's go to the dance
let's make a wreath
from yellow, brown, blue and grey,
yellow, red and white,
violet flowers.

Your full red mouth
should speak
with whispering, singing, chatting and deft words
which will enflame my heart
and tenderly
wakens me up from my sleep
when I notice such a dear, red, narrow slit
formed into a smile
with white shining teeth,
smiling, softly roundish, pink colored lips,
really bright
like a painting.

If she wanted, she should, and would come,
       and would take from my heart
this bitter heart-felt pain.
Then she would place her breast on it.
Look, my sadness would be swept away.
No other graceful and attractive girl
could lift up my heart with more joy
without instilling it with pain
in such a delightful, loving pure lust.
Mouth kisses mouth,
tongue to tongue, breast onto chest,
tummy to tummy, hair to hair

really fast
always push hard.

Kl 56

"You treasure full of consolation,
          who gives me consolation now?
Dearly beloved, how long will I have to wait for you?
Your absence gives me pain
and saddens me; I beg you,
please listen to me, give me advice and help
as soon as possible.

Friend, you are happiness, joy, glory and benediction.
Day and night time is passing filled with longing.
Many heavy sighs
hurt my heart badly, but it does not sway,
really not,
it is always loyal.

Your budding little mouth gives me joy,
your little teeth impress me; he who is successful
he can truly sing easily.
My heart does not want and cannot become healthy again
without you; it wants to please you.
Therefore I have chosen you,
beloved lady, to submit myself to you.

My heart notices often and well
how a strange glance causes a pleasant excitement
when one is caught in the traps of love.
Lady, your ropes and nets
have caught me entirely.
Nobody but you with your wonderful and pure body
can rescue me.

Kl 61

Good fortune and well-being galore
do I wish you, wife, for the new year,
(and) loyalty to be sure,
(that) I never fail in my service to you;
please take note of that.
This is caused by your dear little red mouth,

a pair with your red cheeks,
shone on by bright, clear eyes;
Your ears so small, your hair above

in crimped, twisted locks,
curly gold, speckled with yellow.

Nose, teeth, chin, throat, the neck downwards
falls in full
right to the place of the little white breasts.
The recess there elicits loud acclaim:
every member well proportioned.
Arms and fingers long, two small hands,
the shiny tummy so slippery,
and hair[2] of perfection as well.
Amply backed up by a rounded fanny,
richly endowed with a hard mass.
And the little feet, swinging.

No sorrow on her tender body,
excluded by propriety, pure virtue;
young, noble, the appearance of nobility.
Her gait joins in
with probity masterful.
She is without reproach and fine.
My beloved dear, do not forget me.
And since I am indeed called yours,
so let your dear heart be wooed again
by what I have beseeched so long
and what tempts me passionately.

Kl 70

"Sir Innkeeper, we are very thirsty:
Bring the wine, bring the wine, bring the wine,
may God turn suffering into joy.
Bring the wine, bring the wine, bring the wine,
May your health prosper.
Pour in, pour in, pour in."

"Gretel, would you want to be my mistress?
Say it, say it, say it!"
"Yes, if you buy me a little purse
then I would be willing, then I would be willing, willing,
but do not tear my little skin,[3]
just poke, just poke, just poke, just poke!"

---

2. Apparently a reference to her pubic hair.
3. Obviously a reference to the hymen.

"Now, dear John, do you want to dance with me?
Then come, then come, then come!
We want to jump around like the geese!
John, do not stumble, John, do not stumble, John, do not stumble
and be careful with my slit[4]
Push nicely, push further, push! Push John, push!"

"Now play, little Heinz, Philip, beloved!
Rush, be happy and wild, rush, be happy and wild, rush,
         be happy and wild
Form couples, move around, hit the drums!
Hans and Lucy, Cunz and Cathy, Benz and Claire,
jump like calves! Chase around, little Jack!
Juchei, hei! Juchei, hei! Juchei, hei!"

"The dance is beginning! The fresh wine must bubble!
Give it to me! give it to me! give it to me!
Hep, Henry, still another little Giustiniani.[5]
Move, friend, move, friend, move friend!
Metz and Diemut, eat the delicacies!
Go, go, go, go, go, go, go, go!"

"Now hurry, they are eating in the village.
Do not linger, do not linger, do not linger!
Follow them, Conrad, lazy shuffler,
you idiot, you idiot, you idiot!
You stare like a carp!
Run, my boy, run, my boy, run, my boy!

Kl 76

A hay collecting girl in the cool dew
walks with her white, naked and slender feet through the meadow.
Her appearance makes me happy.
The reason is her brown hairy scythe[6]
when I helped her, to move the gate
and to press it against the fence,
to move the wooden peg and to push it in,
very tightly, so that the girl
did not have to worry any further to loose the geese.

---

4. This can either mean the fold of the dress, or simply the vagina.
5. The term is used for a well-known lyrical genre developed by the Venetian composer and musician Leonardo Giustiniani.
6. The scythe is here a metaphor for the vagina.

When I saw the beauty approach me while building the fence,
I became extremely excited
until I could remove all hindrance for her
between two fence poles.
I had already whetted
my little hatchet, ready for service,
it was sharp and wet. I helped her,
as well as I could to rake the grass.
"Do not jerk, my honey! " "But no, dear John!"

After I had mowed the clover
and closed all the gaps in her fence,
she wanted, in addition,
that I should mow once more in the lower meadow.
She would give me as reward
a little wreath made from roses.
"Comb the flax, raise it up!
Put a fence around it, if you like, to make sure it grows!"
"Dearly loved goose, your beak looks so good in your face!"

Kl 107

"Come, dearest man!
I gladly give myself
to you all the time!
Come, dear friend,
and happily pull away from misfortune!
Come, my beloved, escape
all the traps of the devious spies!
Come quickly, take away my the pain from my heart
and give me poor woman some consolation!
Your masculinity enlivens my soul and spirit
more than anything else in the world."

"Your words and gestures
ease my worries;
Lady, the news make me even happier
that a noble, young, and honorable woman desires for me
who makes my heart happy again
without any pain
with the help of diverse entertainment.
Your graceful and beautiful body
does not allow me to grow old, because I am refreshed
and showered through bright eyes."

"The departure throws me into misery,
your departure means death for me.
You eyes, you are turning red.
I am lost,
deprived of reason.
My female virtue, this highest goal
loses all the power through the desire.
If you do not write to me soon
and if you stay away for long,
if you do all that,
I am afraid
never to see you again."

SECTION 22

THE DAWN OF THE RENAISSANCE
Selections from A BOOK OF FACETIAE

Poggio Bracciolini

Introduction by Albrecht Classen

The *Facetiae* by Poggio Bracciolini were highly popular reading material throughout the fifteenth and still the sixteenth centuries, as we can tell from the thirty four editions in the fifteenth century alone. But soon these erotic tales were labelled as pornographic and quickly disappeared from the stacks in the libraries because many sixteenth-century moralists and theologians lambasted Poggio for his "outrageously immoral" work which allegedly lacked, as they saw it, any form of decency and embarrassed the readers. The Council of Trent (1545-63) even placed it on the *Index Expurgatoris* (issued in 1564).

Perhaps contrary to our expectations, Poggio was a highly learned and outstanding scholar and member of early Florentine humanism. He possessed remarkable skills as a Latinist and was a passionate researcher in manuscripts from classical antiquity. Some of his teachers were the humanists Coluccio Salutatis and Immanuel Chrysoloras. From 1403 he was employed as a scriptor, or secretary, at the papal court in Rome, first under Pope Boniface IX, then under the antipope John XXIII, dethroned in 1414. In this function he travelled with the court to the international Council of Constance (1414–1418) where representatives of the Church and of all major European countries discussed the conditions and fate of the Papacy and the Church as an institution. Poggio travelled during his free time to the abbeys of Fulda, Germany, Cluny (France), and St. Gallen (Switzerland) where he discovered many manuscripts of unknown speeches of Cicero, the missing parts of Quintilian *Institutio oratoria*, Lucretius' *De reru natura*, the *Argonauticon libri* by Valerio Flaccho, several comedies by Plautus, and the *Silvae* of Statius.

After a short period of exile in England, Poggio returned to the papal court where he was employed from 1423–1452. During that time he composed many facetious, but also critical and satirical dialogues such as *On Avarice* (1428), *On the Unhappiness of Princes* (1440), *On Nobility* (ca. 1440), *On the Vicissitudes of Fortune* (ca. 1448), and *Against Hypocrites* (1449). Scholars have characterized his style as a combination of Petrarch's literary classicism with Boccaccio's skill as story teller. In particular, Poggio attacked the corruption and moral decline of the late medieval Church, which was a common theme of his time all over Europe. In particular, this criticism is most vehemently, but also most satirically expressed in his *Liber facetiorum*, composed from 1433 until 1452 when it was rearranged for publication.

In his entertaining but didactic table talks and dialogues, first published in 1510, he argued, for instance, for the Latin origin of the Romance languages. After his retirement from the papal court he returned to Florence where he was appointed Chancellor in 1453. His last work was a history of his hometown, *Historia florentina* from 1476, which circulated widely throughout the next two hundred years. Poggio was highly acclaimed for his highly learned and also elegant style in his many letters and his treatises, all of which he composed in the Latin of classical antiquity.

Although the *Book of Facetiae* could appear, at first sight, to be pornographic in nature, it is rather a collection of humorous tales in the vein of Boccaccio's *Decameron*. The allusions to eroticism and love are to be understood as vehicles to teach the readers a lesson and to illustrate certain points of morality and ethics. In the fifteenth century people thought differently about the body and experienced a much lower shame level than in the subsequent centuries. Poggio's frank and uninhibited description of sexual material does not serve as erotic entertainment, but functions as a means to satirize and ridicule stupid behavior, corruption, greed, and other foibles and failures of human beings.

BIBLIOGRAPHY

Bernard J. Hurwood, Poggio Bracciolini: The Facetiae (New York: Award Books, 1968).

Two Renaissance Book Hunters: the Letters of Poggius Bracciolini to Nicolaus de Niccolis, trans. from the Latin and annotated by Phyllis Walter Goodhart Gordan (New York: Columbia University Press, 1991).

LET NOT THE ENVIOUS CARP AT THIS BOOK OF FACETIAE ON ACCOUNT OF ITS UNADORNED STYLE

I am sure there will be many who will first censure these confabulations of mine as insubstantial things, unworthy of a serious man, and who will then demand for them a more polished mode of expression and greater eloquence. I think I shall have sufficiently redeemed myself in the eyes of these critics if I respond that our ancestors, as I have read, who were very prudent and learned and who delighted in witticisms, jests, and stories, deserved not censure but praise. For why should I think it disgraceful on my part to follow their example in this matter (since I cannot do so in other things), and spend that same time in the trouble of writing which other men waste in tale-telling at gatherings and groups of their fellows, especially as my labor is not dishonorable, and can provide readers with some merriment? It is a proper and almost necessary thing, indeed commended by the wise, that our minds, oppressed with various concerns and troubles, be relieved on occasion from cares and be diverted towards mirth and relaxation by sort of amusement. But to require eloquence in trivial things, or in those instances where witticisms must be expressed word for word, or in relating the remarks of other persons, seems the sign of a cavilling critic. Indeed, there are some things which cannot be expressed more ornately, for they have to be recounted just as they were told by those who brought them forward in our confabulations.

Some critics will perhaps think that this apology of mine is a cover for my lack of talent—I agree with them. Let them narrate this same material more ornately and with more polish themselves. I urge them to do so, in order that the Latin tongue may be enriched in our day even in light compositions. The practice of writing things will promote both learning and eloquence. Indeed, I myself wanted to find out whether many things which are deemed difficult of expression in Latin could be written without absurdity. Since nothing ornate nor any amplitude of language can be employed in such things, it will be satisfaction enough for my wit if I seem to have related them in ways not completely devoid of eloquence.

Moreover, let those who set themselves up as overly stern censurers or bitter critics refrain from reading these confabulations (for thus do I wish them to be called). I wish to be read by witty and humane men, as Lucilius was by the Consentines and Tarentines. But if some of my readers should be somewhat uncultivated, I do not refuse them the right to think what they will, as long as they do not reproach the writer, who has written these facetiae to life the spirit and exercise his skill.

A WIDOW WHO WAS SEIZED WITH LUST FOR A MENDICANT

The race of hypocrites is the worst of all alive. Once at a gathering at which I was present conversation arose concerning them. It was said that although they have everything in abundance, and burn with ambition for possessions and dignities, by dissembling and feigning they act so as to make it seem as if they pursue these honors not by their own choice, but unwillingly and at the command of others. Then someone who was present said that they were like a certain Blessed Paolo who dwelt at Pisa, one of those who are commonly called Apostles, and whose custom is to sit at the doorway of a house, asking nothing.

When we asked him to tell us who the fellow was, he said "Paolo, who because of the sanctity of his life was commonly surnamed 'Blessed,' sat sometimes at the doorway of a certain widow, who offered him food in charity. This woman often took notice of Paolo (he was a handsome fellow) and developed a passion for him. Once when she had given him food, she requested him to return the next day, saying that she would see to it that he dined well. After Paolo had frequently approached the woman's house, she finally invited him to come inside to take his meal. He agreed, and when he had abundantly stuffed his belly with food and drink, the lust-driven woman embraced Paolo, kissed him, and said that he would not depart thence without having carnal knowledge of her. Pretending to be reluctant, he denied any interest in the woman's fervent desire. But when she plied him even more obscenely he finally yielded to the widow's insistence, saying 'If you want to commit so great a sin, as God is my witness you'll have to do it yourself.' Then he went on: 'Take this damned flesh' (his cock was already hard) 'and use it as you will—I won't touch it at all today.' And so under the guise of unwillingness he screwed the woman, although on account of pretended continence he would not touch his own flesh, and attributed all the sin to the woman."

A YOUNG WOMAN WHO ACCUSED HER HUSBAND OF HAVING A SMALL PRICK

A young nobleman of outstanding handsomeness took to wife the daughter of the Florentine knight Nereo de' Pazzi, among others of his time an eminent and outstanding man. After a few days, as was customary, the young girl returned to visit her father, not animated and cheerful as other brides usually are, but sad, and with a long face, gazing on the ground. Calling her secretly into a bedchamber, her mother asked "Is everything all right?" "As you wish," the weeping girl replied, "for you have not married me to a man, but to one who lacks manhood; he has nothing or little of that bodily part on account of which marriages are made." Deeply grieving her daughter's fortune, the mother communicated the matter to her husband [Nereo]. As soon as the thing became known among the relatives and wives who were present at the feast, the whole house was filled with grieving and sorrow. All said that a girl of outstanding beauty had not been married, but immolated. A short time afterwards the girl's husband arrived, for whose sake the feast was prepared. When he saw everyone with a sad and despondent face he was surprised at the strange sight, and asked what had happened. There was no one who dared reveal the reason for the sorrow, but finally someone a little bolder than the rest told him that the girl had said he was lacking in manhood. Then the spirited youth said "By no means shall this be a pretext to upset us or to spoil our feast. The charge will be disposed of quickly. When all were seated at the table, men as well as women, and the meal was nearly done, the youth rose up and said "Fathers, I understand that I have been accused of something. I want you to be witnesses as to whether it is true or not." Thereupon he took out his extremely large prick (short garments were used in those days), and having placed it on the table, he directed everyone's attention to its exceptionality and magnitude, asking if it ought to be faulted or scorned. The greater part of the women who were present wished that their husbands were as abundantly endowed, and a great many of the men knew that they were more than matched by a man with such a tool. Everyone turned to the young girl, and severely reproached her foolishness, each person upbraiding her individually. Then she replied "Why are you blaming me? Why am I being rebuked? Our jackass, which I recently saw in the countryside, is a beast, and he has a member this long" (here she held out her arm). "This husband of mine, who is a man, does not have half that length." The simple-minded girl believed that the sexual organ ought to be longer in men than in beasts.

A PREACHER WHO PREFERRED TEN VIRGINS TO ONE MARRIED WOMAN

An insufficiently circumspect friar was preaching to the people at Tivoli, fulminating and inveighing at great length against adultery. And among other things, he said adultery was so grave a sin that he would rather have carnal knowledge of ten virgins than one married woman. Many who were present would have made the same choice.

A WOMAN'S WITTY RESPONSE

A woman was once asked by her husband why it was that although both male and female were equal participants in the pleasure of intercourse, nevertheless men were more apt to solicit and pursue women rather than the other way around. She replied, "There is a very good reason why this is so, that we should be asked by men. The fact is that we are always prepared and ready for intercourse, whereas you are not. So it would be useless for us to solicit men, when they are unprepared." A knowledgeable and witty response.

GUGLIEMO, WHO HAD A LOVELY PRIAPEAN TOOL

In our town of Terranuova there was a man named Gugliemo, a carpenter, who was well-endowed with a Priapean tool. His wife divulged this information to her female neighbors. When she died, the carpenter took as a new wife a simple young girl named Antonia, who during her betrothal had found out from those neighbors about the man's huge weapon. And so, on the night when she first slept with her husband, the trembling girl was unwilling to come close to him or submit to intercourse. Finally the carpenter understood what the girl was afraid of, and he reassured her, saying that what she had heard was true, but that he had two pricks, a small one and a larger one. "Therefore, so as not to hurt you," he said, "tonight I will use the small one, which will give you only a very little pain. Later on I'll use the bigger one, if you see fit." The girl consented and yielded to her husband, without any cry or pain. But after a month, having become somewhat freer and bolder, while caressing her husband at night the girl said "Husband, if you like, you may use the bigger one this time." The man laughed at his wife's good appetite, since in this respect he was built half as big as a jackass. Afterwards I heard him tell the story at a gathering of other fellows.

A RESPECTABLE WOMAN'S REMARK UPON SEEING AN ADULTERESS'S GARMENTS IN THE WINDOWS

One morning an adulteress had spread out at her windows the various garments given to her by her lover. A respectable woman, passing by the house and seeing all the clothing, said "Just as the spider weaves her webs, so too does this woman make her wardrobe with her ass, displaying to everyone the handiwork of her private parts."

A PERUGIAN'S REMARK TO HIS WIFE

The Perugians are considered witty and sophisticated men. A wife by the name of Petruccia, who was planning to go to a festival the next day, asked her husband to buy her a new pair of shoes. The man agreed, and at the same time ordered her to cook a chicken for his dinner before she left home in the morning. When she had prepared the meal the wife exited the front doorway, but just at that moment she saw a youth of whom she was deeply enamored. She returned into the house, and signalled the youth to follow her inside, since her husband was away. And lest there should be any further delay, the wife ascended the stairs and lay down on the floor, in such a way that she could be seen from the doorway. With the youth on top of her, she embraced his buttocks with her feet and calves, and set to work fulfilling her desire. Meanwhile her husband, thinking that she had already started for the festival and would return later, asked a friend to dinner, saying that his wife would not be at the meal. When they arrived at the house the husband entered first, and saw his wife at the top of the stairs, shaking her feet over the youth. "Hey Petruccia!" he exclaimed, "By God's ass" (for such is their customary oath). "If that's your way of walking, you'll never wear out those shoes."

A FRIAR TO WHOM A WIDOW MADE CONFESSION

At Florence a friar, one of those of the Order of Observants, was hearing a lovely widow confess her sins. During their talk the woman drew close to the man, and when she brought her face nearer to his so as to speak more intimately, her fresh young breath made his temperature increase. Finally a head which had previously been lying down began to rise up, so much so that the friar was somewhat discomfited. Sighing and fidgeting from this fleshly annoyance, he asked the woman to leave, but she requested that he enjoin a penance upon her. The friar replied "Penance! You've imposed one on me."